Grade 8

Addison-Wesley Mathematics

Robert E. Eicholz
Sharon L. Young

Phares G. O'Daffer
Carne S. Barnett

Randall I. Charles
Charles R. Fleenor

Stanley R. Clemens
Freddie L. Renfro
Joan E. Westley

Gloria F. Gilmer
Mary M. Thompson

Andy Reeves
Carol A. Thornton

▲▼ Addison-Wesley Publishing Company

Menlo Park, California ▪ Reading, Massachusetts ▪ New York
Don Mills, Ontario ▪ Wokingham, England ▪ Amsterdam ▪ Bonn
Sydney ▪ Singapore ▪ Tokyo ▪ Madrid ▪ San Juan ▪ Paris
Seoul, Korea ▪ Milan ▪ Mexico City ▪ Taipei, Taiwan

PROGRAM ADVISORS

John A. Dossey Professor of Mathematics
Illinois State University, Normal, Illinois

Bonnie Armbruster Associate Professor, Center for the Study of Reading
University of Illinois, Champaign, Illinois

Karen L. Ostlund Associate Professor of Science Education
Southwest Texas State University, San Marcos, Texas

Betty C. Lee Assistant Principal
Ferry Elementary School, Detroit, Michigan

William J. Driscoll Chairman, Department of Mathematical Sciences
Central Connecticut State University, New Britain, Connecticut

David C. Brummett Educational Consultant
Palo Alto, California

MULTICULTURAL ADVISORS

Bill Bray   Moyra Contreras   Barbara Fong   Jeanette Haseyama
James Hopkins   Carol Artiga MacKenzie   Gloria Maldonado   Mattie McCloud
Marsha Muhammad   Margarita Perez

CONTRIBUTING WRITERS

Betsy Franco   Mary Heinrich   Penny Holland   Marilyn Jacobson
Ann Muench   Gini Shimabukuro   Marny Sorgen   Connie Thorpe
Sandra Ward   Judith K. Wells

EXECUTIVE EDITOR

Diane H. Fernández

Contents

2

DATA ANALYSIS AND STATISTICS

3

AREA AND VOLUME

4

EQUATIONS IN ALGEBRA

5

INTEGERS AND INTEGER EQUATIONS

8

RATIO AND PROPORTION

9

PERCENT

10

APPLICATIONS OF PERCENT

11

DISCRETE MATH: COUNTING PROBLEMS

12

PROBABILITY

13

GEOMETRY

14

SQUARE ROOTS AND SPECIAL TRIANGLES

RESOURCE BANK AND APPENDIX

Dear Student:

This is the year you join the big leagues! You will be introduced to new ideas and new approaches to problem-solving.

You are going to discover how data analysis and statistics are useful tools to better understand your world. You will see how probability and logical reasoning can help you make better decisions, whether it's buying a new car or planning a budget. You will also explore area and volume, algebraic equations, applications of percent, real numbers and special triangles, motion geometry, and much more.

This year will be exciting, and you already have all the groundwork you need to be a real math whiz. Your book is designed to make math interesting just for you. As you read through the chapters, you will find lessons that apply math problems to many real-life situations.

You will have opportunities to work with partners and in groups. Plus, there's a helpful Resource Bank in the back of the book, which includes a Data Bank, a Skills Review Bank, a Calculator Bank, a Computer Bank, a Table of Measures, Mathematical Symbols, and more. These resources were specifically designed to help make math more meaningful for you.

This is your year to shine in mathematics! Good luck. We know you will enjoy this book.

From your friends at Addison-Wesley.

1

MATH AND LANGUAGE ARTS

DATA BANK

Use the Langauge Arts Data Bank on page 505 to answer the questions.

1 If you play the first version of Lewis Carroll's alphabet game with four complete alphabets, how many consonants will be left in the bag?

OPERATIONS, PROPERTIES AND PROBLEM SOLVING

THEME: LITERATURE

2 If Carroll had 4,288 letters in his Common Room register, how many letters were in his registers all together?

3 If you were building a cage for your new pet ostrich, how tall would the door have to be in order for you to be certain the ostrich could fit?

4 **Using Critical Thinking** Based on the excerpt from Symbolic Logic, decide which of the following is true: All birds ab are c; All birds ac are e; All birds d are a.

Writer Lewis Carroll was also a mathematical lecturer at Oxford University from 1855 to 1881.

Numbers and Place Value

EXPLORE **Study the Table**

The population of the United States has always grown, but some groups decline from time to time, while others grow rapidly. Would you say the change from 1980 to 2000 is generally a decline or an increase? By 2010 about one-third of the 18-year-olds will be African-American or Hispanic compared to one-fifth in 1985. Is that a decline or an increase?

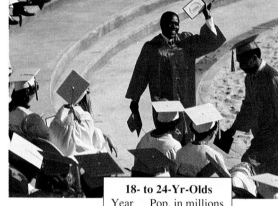

18- to 24-Yr-Olds	
Year	Pop. in millions
1980	30.2
1985	28.8
1990	25.5
1995	23.6
2000	24.1
2010	27.0

U.S. Census Bureau

TALK ABOUT IT

1. Which year shows the largest population of 18- to 24-yr-olds?

2. Does 25.5 mean "twenty-five and five tenths"? Explain.

3. What would a line graph of the data in the chart look like?

All numbers have a largest place value period name. This fact can be used to write the number 75,600,000,000 in terms of its largest place value period name—billions.

Billions		Millions			Thousands			Units		
7	5	6	0	0	0	0	0	0	0	0

75 billion   600 million
or
0.6 billion

75,600,000,000
is the same as
75.6 billion.

Write each number in standard notation.

1. 25.4 thousands   2. 106 billions   3. 298.25 millions

Write each number in terms of its largest place value period name.

4. 345,600,000   5. 28,400,000,000   6. 13,500,000,000,000

PRACTICE

Write each number in standard notation.

1. 326 thousand
2. 129 million
3. 13.4 million
4. 45.5 billion
5. 2.8 billion
6. 947.6 thousand

Write each number in terms of its largest place value period name.

7. 53,900,000
8. 29,500,000,000
9. 62,000,000,000
10. 68,300,000
11. 1,800,000
12. 34,100,000,000

APPLY

MATH REASONING

13. Arrange these numbers in order from smallest to largest.

45.6 million   324.5 thousand   345 thousand   1.8 billion

PROBLEM SOLVING

Use the graph at the right to answer these questions.

14. In standard notation, how much did CBS pay to telecast the Olympic Games in 1960?
15. How much more did ABC pay in 1976 than they did in 1968?
16. Between which two Olympic years was the increase in cost the greatest?
17. **Data Hunt** Find data in a newspaper or magazine reported in terms of its largest place value period. Write the numbers using standard notation.

Cost of Broadcast Rights for the Summer Games

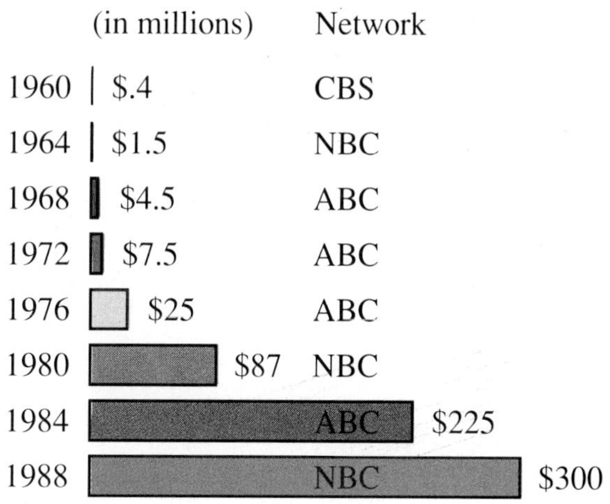

(in millions)
Network
1960
$.4
CBS
1964
$1.5
NBC
1968
$4.5
ABC
1972
$7.5
ABC
1976
$25
ABC
1980
$87
NBC
1984
ABC
$225
1988
NBC
$300

ESTIMATION

18. The population of the United States in 1970 was 203.3 million. In 1980 it was 226.5 million. Estimate what the population of the United States might be in 2000.

More Practice, page 522, set A

Numerical Expressions

EXPLORE **Compare the Expressions**

A **numerical expression** is a name for a number. The numerical expression 35 + 18 is a name for 53. The expression (15 + 7) · 9 is a name for 198. Notice that in this book we use a dot (·) to indicate multiplication.

Basic properties for addition and multiplication show how to change one numerical expression into another equivalent numerical expression.

Property	Examples
Commutative Property	$a \cdot b = b \cdot a \quad a + b = b + a$
Associative Property	$(a + b) + c = a + (b + c)$
	$(a \cdot b) \cdot c = a \cdot (b \cdot c)$
Identity for Multiplication	$a \cdot 1 = a$
Identity for Addition	$a + 0 = a$
Distributive Property	$a \cdot (b + c) = (a \cdot b) + (a \cdot c)$
Zero Product Property	$a \cdot 0 = 0$

TALK ABOUT IT

1. Which property tells us that we can add or multiply in any order?

2. Is the distributive property true if the operation of subtraction replaces addition?

When you **evaluate** a numerical expression, you find the number it represents.

Examples Use the basic properties to evaluate each numerical expression.

A $(5674 \cdot 345) \cdot 0 = $ ▓ The zero property tells us the product will be 0.

B $82 + (18 + 29) = $ ▓ The associative property allows us to write (82 + 18) + 29. Using mental math, 82 + 18 = 100, 100 + 29 = 129.

Use the basic properties to evaluate each numerical expression.

1. $\frac{4}{3} \cdot 1 = $ ▓

2. $(68 + 25) + 75 = $ ▓

3. $(12 \cdot 2) + (8 \cdot 2) = $ ▓

Use the basic properties to evaluate each numerical expression.
Name the property you used.

1. $12 + 0 = $ ▥

2. $238 \cdot 1 = $ ▥

3. $5{,}294 + $ ▥ $= 5{,}294$

4. $56 \cdot 65 = 3{,}640$
$65 \cdot 56 = $ ▥

5. $84 + (12 + 58) = 154$
$(84 + 12) + 58 = $ ▥

6. $(12 \cdot 13) \cdot 14 = 2{,}184$
$12 \cdot (13 \cdot 14) = $ ▥

7. $8 \cdot (2 + 4) = 48$
$(8 \cdot 2) + (8 \cdot 4) = $ ▥

8. $(12 \cdot 36) + (12 \cdot 31) = 804$
$12 \cdot (36 + 31) = $ ▥

9. $28 \cdot $ ▥ $= 28$

10. $302 \cdot 12 = 12 \cdot $ ▥

11. $(3 + 57) + $ ▥ $= 3 + (57 + 2)$

12. $(3 \cdot 15) + (3 \cdot 62) = 3 \cdot ($ ▥ $+ 62)$

13. ▥ $\cdot (3 \cdot 6) = (4 \cdot 3) \cdot 6$

14. $7 \cdot (12 + 37) = (7 \cdot 12) + ($ ▥ $\cdot$ ▥ $)$

MATH REASONING Fill in the operations to make each statement true.

15. $(8 + 4) \cdot 3 = (8$ ▥ $3) + (4$ ▥ $3)$

16. 12 ▥ $1 = 12$

17. 64 ▥ $0 = 64$

18. $(15$ ▥ $6)$ ▥ $43 = 15$ ▥ $(6$ ▥ $43)$

PROBLEM SOLVING

19. The expression $(2 \cdot \$12.50) + \$1.50$ gives the cost of two CDs including tax. What is the total cost?

20. The expression $(5 \cdot \$7.00) - \$3.50 + \$1.89$ is the cost of 5 cassette tapes with a discount coupon, including tax. What is the total cost?

▶ **ALGEBRA**

Find the number for n using mental math and the basic properties.

21. $741 \cdot n = 741$

22. $36 + n = 73 + 36$

23. $84 \cdot n = 84$

24. $7 \cdot (8 + n) = (7 \cdot 8) + (7 \cdot 2)$

25. $(16 + n) + 47 = 16 + (53 + 47)$

Reviewing Mental Math

LEARN ABOUT IT

EXPLORE **Analyze the Expressions**

Two mental math techniques that are probably familiar to you are **counting on** and **compatible numbers.**

Consider how you would do each problem using mental math.

TALK ABOUT IT

BULLETIN BOARD

A: 125 + 532 + 275
B: 568 + 200
C: 49 + 24 + 151 + 26

1. For which expression would you begin with one addend and count by 100's?

2. For which expressions would you group numbers that are easy to add? What numbers would you group?

3. Which technique is called counting on and which one is called compatible numbers?

Here are two more mental math techniques.

Break apart Use place value and the distributive property to break apart numbers to make easier calculations.

Example: 4×52 $\qquad$ $52 = (50 + 2)$, so
$$4 \times (50 + 2) = 4 \times 50 + 4 \times 2 = 200 + 8$$
$$4 \times 52 = 208$$

Compensation Change a problem to one that you can solve using mental math. Then adjust the answer to compensate for the change.

Example: 58×4 $\qquad$ Adjust to $60 \times 4 = 240$.
60 fours is 2 more fours than 58 fours.
Subtract 2 fours or 8. $240 - 8 = 232$.
$$58 \times 4 = 232$$

TRY IT OUT

Use mental math to evaluate each expression. Name the technique you used.

1. $72 - 3$ $\qquad$ **2.** $2 \times 34 \times 5$ $\qquad$ **3.** $18 + 21 + 22 + 19 + 20$

4. $1.46 + 1.55 + 1.54$ $\qquad$ **5.** $4.6 + 3.0$ $\qquad$ **6.** $25 + 18 + 25 + 12$

Use counting on or compatible numbers to evaluate each expression.

1. 32 + 4
2. 30 + 47
3. 132 + 18 + 27

4. 157 + 10
5. 4.2 + 3.8 + 1.2
6. 26 + 24 + 15

Break apart numbers or use compensation to evaluate each expression.

7. 31 × 4
8. 73 × 5
9. 49 × 3

10. 99 × 7
11. 28 × 6
12. 62 × 2

Evaluate using mental math. Name the technique you used.

13. 3.7 + 1.3 + 1.5
14. 22 × 4
15. 68 + 40 − 4

16. 39 × 2
17. 85 − 30 + 2
18. 78 × 3

APPLY

MATH REASONING

19. Use mental math to find the amount of change you would receive from $20.00 if you purchased a music poster.

PROBLEM SOLVING

20. A concert was attended by 20,000 people. The price of a ticket was $22. How much money was taken in for tickets?

21. An average of 400 people attended each basketball game at Lincoln Jr. High. Tickets were $2 each. If there were 20 games, how much money was taken in altogether?

MIXED REVIEW

Write each number in standard notation.

22. 24 thousand
23. 7.1 million
24. 52.3 billion
25. 314.2 million

Find the missing value. Name the property used.

26. ▓ × 724 = 724
27. 8 + 4 = 4 + ▓
28. 4.87 × 0 = ▓

Find the answers.

29.   2.48
     + 8.01

30.   1004
     − 876

31.   120
     − 79,04

32.   356
     × 1.7

More Practice, page 522, set C

Reviewing Estimation Techniques

EXPLORE **Study the Procedures**

Rounding is the estimation technique you are using when you reason $34 \times 298 \approx 30 \times 300 = 9,000$. You are using **substituting compatible numbers** when you replace the numbers in the original problem with compatible numbers to make a simpler problem.

TALK ABOUT IT

1. You could estimate $815 \div 26$ by computing with which compatible numbers: a) $810 \div 30$,   b) $800 \div 20$,   or   c) $750 \div 25$?

2. What compatible numbers might you use to estimate $917 \div 37$?

3. If you use $600 \div 15 = 40$ to estimate $685 \div 16$, is it correct to say you are using *rounding*? Explain.

Here are two additional estimation techniques.

Front-End Estimation

Estimate $726 + 185 + 223 + 115 + 329$

$726 + 185 + 223 + 115 + 329 \approx 1,400$	add front end digits
$85 + 15 = 100 \quad 26 + 23 + 29 \approx 75$	look for compatible numbers
$1,400 + 100 + 75 = 1,575$	adjust the sum
$726 + 185 + 223 + 115 + 329 \approx 1,575$	

Clustering

Estimate $491 + 485 + 515 + 506 + 497$

$491 + 485 + 515 + 506 + 497$ the addends cluster around 500
$5 \times 500 = 2500$
$491 + 485 + 515 + 506 + 497 \approx 2,500$

Estimate. Name the technique you used.

1. $325 + 276 + 550 + 461$
2. $706 \div 35$
3. $1251 + 8795$
4. $46 + 51 + 53 + 50 + 46 + 48$
5. 67×812
6. $586 \div 59$

Estimate. Use rounding or substitute compatible numbers.

1. 27 × 134

2. 478 + 43

3. 304 × 49

4. 285 − 32

5. 389 × 42

6. 972 ÷ 89

Estimate. Use front-end estimation or clustering.

7. 278 + 312 + 294 + 331

8. 132 + 482 + 926 + 578 + 272

9. 572 + 389 + 120 + 437 + 834

10. 712 + 689 + 739 + 672

Estimate. Name the technique you used.

11. 439 + 632 + 329 + 876

12. 987 × 65

13. 729 ÷ 68

14. 577 + 672 + 621 + 598

15. 381 ÷ 23

16. 27 × 482

17. 574 + 647 + 328 + 463

18. 782 + 810 + 763 + 829

APPLY

MATH REASONING

19. Write a number in the blank to complete 278 × ▓ ≈ 18,000 in two different ways.

PROBLEM SOLVING

20. Airplane landings at a large airport were recently restricted from 94 per hour to 82 per hour. If this rate were to exist for 24 hours, about how many planes would land in one day?

21. A round-trip airline ticket from San Francisco to New York might cost $745. About how much would it cost a family of four (each buying a ticket) to fly to New York and back?

▶ **USING CRITICAL THINKING   Justify Your Answer**

22. Use the following problem to show why front-end estimation might be better to use in some cases than rounding.   327 + 143 + 476 + 531

Introduction to Problem Solving

UNDERSTAND
ANALYZE DATA
PLAN
ESTIMATE
SOLVE
EXAMINE

LEARN ABOUT IT

This checklist can help you solve problems. **Multiple-step** problems require more than one operation or equation to solve.

Understand the Situation
You want to find the difference in the profit from 500 books.

Analyze the Data
Planned price: 6 shillings
Changed price: $7\frac{1}{2}$ shillings
Number of books sold: 500

Plan What to Do
First find the difference in the price of one book. Multiply that by the total number of books.

Estimate the Answer
$1 \times 500 = 500$; $2 \times 500 = 1,000$ shillings. The answer should be between 500 and 1,000.

Solve the Problem
$7\frac{1}{2}$ shillings $-$ 6 shillings $= 1\frac{1}{2}$ shillings

$1\frac{1}{2}$ shillings $\times 500 = 750$ shillings
750 shillings more profit would be made on 500 copies at the higher price.

Examine the Answer
750 shillings is between 500 and 1,000, so the answer is reasonable.

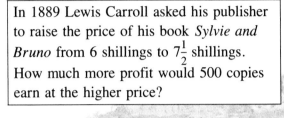

In 1889 Lewis Carroll asked his publisher to raise the price of his book *Sylvie and Bruno* from 6 shillings to $7\frac{1}{2}$ shillings. How much more profit would 500 copies earn at the higher price?

TRY IT OUT

Solve. Use any problem solving strategy.

1. Suppose the price of *Sylvie and Bruno* was changed to 8 shillings. How much more profit would be made on 500 copies at this price than at 6 shillings?

2. The price of a set of Carroll's *Alice in Wonderland* and *Through the Looking Glass* was 12 shillings. How much would it cost to buy 2 sets?

Solve. Use any problem solving strategy.

1. Jose's school is having a book sale. All used paperback books are $0.50. All hardcover books are $1.25. How much will it cost Jose to buy 2 hardcover books and 4 paperbacks?

2. Fiona has 4 books overdue at the library. One book is 2 days overdue, and the other 3 are 4 days overdue. There is a fine of 5¢ per day. How much money does Fiona owe the library?

3. Franklin has decided to put his baseball cards in photo albums to protect them. He has found that he can fit 6 baseball cards on a page. The photo albums he is planning to purchase have 50 pages. How many photo albums does he need to buy if he has 534 baseball cards?

4. When Lewis Carroll's aunt asked him to recommend an album for pictures, he wrote that he found one which held 120 pictures. Four pictures fit on each page. How many pages would this album have?

5. Carroll helped support his cousin by sending her £30 (thirty pounds) a year, plus another £30 for each year her son, Willie, was in college. How much money did he send her all together for 5 years, 2 of which Willie was in college?

6. In 1877 Lewis Carroll was helping plan a musical based on *Alice in Wonderland*. A musician said he would set the 8 songs in the book to music for 30 guineas each. Carroll figured he would pay him another 160 guineas for other songs and incidental music. How many guineas would Carroll pay the musician all together?

7. Once the printer of *Through the Looking Glass* did a poor job on a press run, and Carroll wrote to complain that, "Of the 50 pictures, 26 are over-printed, 8 of them being so much so as to be quite spoiled." How many pictures did Carroll not complain about?

8. **Language Arts Data Bank** Write a true statement about mince pies, based on the excerpt from *Symbolic Logic*. **DATA BANK**

9. **Understanding the Operations** Which operation would you use to solve the following problem. Why?

   How much money does Angelo need to save if he wants to purchase a copy of *The Hunting of the Snark* for *x* if he only has $\boxed{y}$?

Using Critical Thinking

"I can prove that 13 × 7 is 28," said Cathy. "That will be pretty hard to do," Juan responded as he estimated the product." "But I'll look at your weird proof and tell you where you went wrong." "Maybe so," said Cathy." "But this one is not easy to explain!"

Cathy's "Proof" that 13 × 7 = 28

$$
\begin{array}{r}
13 \\
13 \\
13 \\
13 \\
13 \\
13 \\
+\ 13 \\
\hline
28
\end{array}
\qquad
\begin{array}{r}
13 \\
\times\ 7 \\
\hline
21 \\
7 \\
\hline
28
\end{array}
\qquad
\begin{array}{r}
13 \\
7\overline{)28} \\
7 \\
\hline
21 \\
21 \\
\hline
0
\end{array}
$$

3, 6, 9, 12, 15, 18, 21,
22, 23, 24, 25, 26, 27, 28
The sum is 28.

Check it by
Multiplying.
3 × 7 = 21
1 × 7 = 7
21 + 7 = 28

Or check by dividing.
7 into 8 is 1.
Subtract the 7, leaving 21.
7 into 21 is 3.
The quotient is 13.

TALK ABOUT IT

1. How do you think Juan knew without working it out that Cathy's product was incorrect?

2. Explain Cathy's methods for addition, multiplication, and division. Explain why each is incorrect.

3. What important idea of mathematics has been ignored in the methods above?

1. Here is the way one student did column addition. Make up three more problems and use this method to find the sums. Do you think the method works for any column addition?

A.
$$
\begin{array}{r}
6 \\
7 \\
8 \\
9 \\
+\ 4 \\
\end{array}
\qquad
\begin{array}{r}
6 \\
7_3 \\
8 \\
9_1 \\
4_0 \\
\hline
34
\end{array}
$$

B.
$$
\begin{array}{r}
5^13 \\
3 \\
-\ 27 \\
\hline
26
\end{array}
$$
Add 10 to both numbers

2. Do some other subtraction problems like B. Will this method always work? Why?

POWER PRACTICE/QUIZ

Write each number in standard notation.

1. 427 million

2. 2.5 billion

3. 1.327 thousand

Write each number in terms of its largest place value period.

4. 32,500,000,000

5. 274,300

6. 4,300,000

Use the basic properties to help you find the missing numbers.

7. $16 \cdot \text{\rlap{||||}} = 0$

8. $12 \cdot \text{\rlap{||||}} = 12$

9. $4 \cdot (17 + 22) = (4 \cdot 17) + (4 \cdot \text{\rlap{||||}})$

10. $23 \cdot 5 = \text{\rlap{||||}} \cdot 23$

11. $19 + \text{\rlap{||||}} = 19$

12. $2 + (3 + 4) = 2 + (\text{\rlap{||||}} + 4)$

Use mental math and the basic properties to help you evaluate each expression.

13. 41×5

14. $543 + 30$

15. 99×8

16. $24 + 49 + 26$

17. $751 \times 25 \times 4$

18. $(20 + 3) \times 15$

Estimate.

19. $6,523 \div 660$

20. 489×28

21. $248 + 316 + 294 + 327$

22. $5,275 + 1,927 + 3,044$

23. $7,623 \div 25$

24. $14 + 18 + 16 + 13 + 15 + 16$

PROBLEM SOLVING

25. How much could you save by subscribing to *TV Weekly* rather than buying 52 single issues in 1 year?

26. Jane has a subscription to Junior Scholastic. How much is she paying per issue?

Prices of Popular Magazines

Magazine	1-Year subscription	Single copy
TV Weekly	$20.00 (52 issues)	$0.50
Seventeen	$13.95 (12 issues)	$1.50
Boys' Life	$13.00 (12 issues)	$1.50
Junior Scholastic	$15.00 (18 issues)	not available

27. The Clays have subscriptions to *Boys' Life* and *Seventeen*. During the year the Greens purchased 9 single issues of each of those same magazines. Which family paid more money for their magazines?

28. In one year *TV Weekly* sells about 8.5 million copies to subscribers, and about 8.8 million copies at newsstands. About how many copies of *TV Weekly* must be printed each week?

29. Mai has $35 to spend on magazine subscriptions. She wishes to subscribe to *Seventeen* and *Junior Scholastic*. Does she have enough money to do this?

15

Order of Operations

EXPLORE **Analyze the Situation**

Carrie and Kim each used a calculator to find the total cost of 3 rolls of film. Each roll of film cost $4 and shipping and handling was $2.

Kim's Plan:
1st-Add 4 and 2
2nd-Multiply the sum by 3

Carrie's Plan:
1st-Multiply 3 and 4
2nd-Add 2 to the product

TALK ABOUT IT

1. What operation did Kim do first? second?

2. What operation did Carrie do first? second?

3. Which order for doing the operations do you think gives the correct answer? Why?

The situation above shows that the **order of the operations** can make a difference. To be sure that each expression has one value, we agree to follow this order of operations.

Order of Operations
1. Compute inside parentheses.
2. Do all multiplication and division next, from left to right.
3. Do all addition and subtraction last, from left to right.

Example

Find the value of $3 \cdot (16 - 5) + 8$

$$3 \cdot (16 - 5) + 8 = 3 \cdot 11 + 8 \quad \text{Compute inside parentheses first.}$$
$$= 33 + 8 \quad \text{Do multiplication next.}$$
$$= 41 \quad \text{Do addition last.}$$

Find the value of each expression. Use the order of operations.

1. $8 \cdot 5 - 12$

2. $45 + 9 \div 3$

3. $12 \cdot 5 + 18 \div 2$

4. $7 \cdot (34 - 18)$

5. $(34 + 6) \div 2 \cdot 10$

6. $(24 - 13) + (24 \cdot 2)$

Find the value of each expression. Use the order of operations.

1. $17 - 8 + 3$ **2.** $17 - (8 + 3)$ **3.** $20 - 12 \div 2$

4. $3 \cdot 7 - 3$ **5.** $3 \cdot (7 - 3)$ **6.** $(20 - 12) \div 2$

7. $2 \cdot 5 + 2 \cdot 3$ **8.** $2 \cdot (5 + 3)$ **9.** $20 \div 4 \cdot 4$

10. $32 \cdot 2 + (11 - 7) \cdot 6$ **11.** $3 \cdot (14 - 7) - 18$

12. $74 - (8 + 7) \cdot 4$ **13.** $(18 \div 6) + (3 \cdot 9) - 20$

APPLY

MATH REASONING Use each of the numbers 1, 3, 5, 7 and 9 exactly once, with any operation signs and grouping symbols you wish.

14. Write an expression for the smallest whole number possible.

15. Write an expression for the largest whole number possible.

PROBLEM SOLVING

Find the total cost of each of the following orders. There is a $6 shipping charge for each order regardless of the size of the order.

16. 2 tires

17. 2 inner tubes and 1 package of reflectors

Bicycle Supplies	
▪ tires	**$24** each
▪ reflectors	**$6** a package
▪ inner tubes	**$10** each

▶ **CALCULATOR**

Some calculators are programmed to follow the order of operations. With others you must think about the order of operations and enter numbers and operations in the order in which they must be performed. Test your calculator by entering:

12 ÷ 4 + 5 × 2 =

Does your calculator follow the order of operations?

Use your calculator to evaluate each expression.

18. $26 + 11 \cdot 12$ **19.** $2 \cdot 7 + 3$ **20.** $20 - (12 \div 6) - 2$

21. $48 \div 6 + 6$ **22.** $48 \div (6 + 6)$ **23.** $(20 - 12) \div (6 - 2)$

More Practice, page 522, Set E

Relating the Operations

Benjamin Banneker

Black Heritage USA 15c

EXPLORE

Two Benjamins, Benjamin Franklin
and Benjamin Banneker were early
Americans with many related interests.

Benjamin Franklin
■ first published *Poor Richard's Almanac* in 1732
■ wrote poetry and proverbs
■ invented a lightning rod and stove
■ was president of the Pennsylvania Society for the Abolition of Slavery

Benjamin Banneker
■ first published *Benjamin Banneker's Almanac* in 1792
■ wrote poetry and mathematical puzzles
■ invented a striking clock
■ was a mathematician, astronomer, and surveyor

TALK ABOUT IT

1. What are some of the ways these men were related? What
   are some ways mathematical ideas are related?

2. After farming all day, Banneker worked late to calculate the
   planets' positions for his almanac. He often worked 12 hours
   a day, 6 days a week. Give some mathematical expressions
   to represent relationships between the hours he worked in a
   day and in a week.

Addition, subtraction, multiplication, and division are related.
Here are some ways to think about these relationships.

Division as repeated subtraction:
$$24 \div 6 = 24 - 6 - 6 - 6 - 6$$

Multiplication as repeated addition:
$$6 \times 4 = 6 + 6 + 6 + 6$$

TRY IT OUT

1. Write a pair of related addition and
   subtraction equations.

2. Write two equations that are related to
   8×4.

3. How is subtracting 8 from 32 four times
   related to $32 \div 8$?

4. What division equation is related to
   $30 - 5 - 5 - 5 - 5 - 5 - 5$?

18

1. Write an addition and a division equation that are related to 7×12.

2. Use the numbers 5, 8, and 40 to write related addition, subtraction, multiplication, and division equations.

3. Give an example to show how subtraction is related to division.

4. Write two related subtraction equations.

Write two related equations for each of the following.

5. 24 groups of 200

6. How many 54's are in 324?

7. 29 rows with 15 in a row

8. What number added to 26 is 71?

9. 96 inches is how many feet?

10. 12 years with 365 days per year

APPLY

MATH REASONING

11. Suppose $a + 54 = 131$. Write a subtraction problem you can solve to find the value for a. You can check with your calculator.

PROBLEM SOLVING

DATA BANK

12. In one of his almanacs, Franklin counts the number of ancestors we descend from. For example, if you count your parents, their parents and grandparents, you get 14 ancestors in 3 generations. How many ancestors would make up 10 generations?

13. **Language Arts Data Bank**
Write two word problems that can be solved using related equations. Use the information about the lives and accomplishments of Benjamin Franklin and Benjamin Banneker.

   MIXED REVIEW

Find the answers.

14. $24\overline{)3792}$

15. $18\overline{)9108}$

16. $36\overline{)75.6}$

17. $0.12\overline{)6.492}$

Evaluate each expression.

18. $24 - 2 \cdot 8$

19. $(24 - 2) \cdot 8$

20. $18 + 16 \div 4$

21. $7 \cdot (13 - 4) - 19$

Problem Solving
Developing a Plan

UNDERSTAND
ANALYZE DATA
PLAN
ESTIMATE
SOLVE
EXAMINE

When you have a problem to solve, you
need to answer two questions as you
develop a plan for solving it.

- *Do I need an exact answer or an estimate?*
- *Which calculation method (paper and
  pencil, mental math, or a calculator)
  should I use?*

Deciding When to Estimate

Example Decide whether you need an exact answer or an estimate.

Marguerite works at an animal shelter on weekends. She
earns $4.10 an hour. Last weekend she worked 7.5 hours.

A How much did she earn last weekend?

*Good business means that you get paid exactly what you
earned. Marguerite needs an exact answer.*

B Suppose she is saving money for a jacket costing $105.
How many hours does she need to work at the animal
shelter (at $4.10/hr) to earn this amount of money?

*You do not need to know the exact number of hours. An
estimate is all that is needed in this situation.*

Choosing a Calculation Method

Don't assume you should always use a calculator to solve a
computation problem. First try mental math. If mental math is
not appropriate, choose between paper and pencil and a calculator.

Decide whether you need an exact answer or an estimate. Select
the appropriate calculation method if you need an exact answer.

1. You want to purchase 3 new science
   fiction novels costing $3.75, $4.55, and
   $5.25. You have $15.00. Is that enough?

2. How much change should you get from
   $20 if you purchase a record costing
   $11.89, and tax is 5%?

Decide if you need an exact answer or an estimate, determine
the best calculation method, and solve the problem.

1. Hai has $5.00 he is planning to spend on baseball cards. If each pack of cards costs $0.40, does he have enough money to purchase 10 packs of cards?

2. Ariel bought a poster for $12.95 at the museum. He gave the cashier $20.00. How much change did he get back?

3. The marching band is selling grapefruits and oranges to raise money to pay for their trip to the Rose Bowl Parade. There are 120 members in the band, and the total cost of the trip is going to be $2,880.00. If they make $4.00 in profit on each case of fruit that is sold, how many cases must each band member sell to pay for the trip?

4. Jaime's boy scout troop was packing to go on a camping trip. Jaime was in charge of packing the cans of food. He found that they had 35 cans to pack. If he could fit 16 cans in a box, how many boxes did he need?

5. Lupe wishes to purchase 3 boxes of popcorn before the parade starts. She has $4.00. If each box costs $0.75, does she have enough money for the popcorn?

6. Tammy is saving money to buy a new bicycle. The bicycle she wants is $238. If she saves $12 a week, how many weeks will it take her to save enough money?

7. The Union High School basketball team has decided they want new court shoes to match their uniforms. There are 20 people on the team. The shoes cost $48.95 a pair plus 6% tax. How much money must the basketball team raise in order to purchase the shoes?

8. **Determining Reasonable Answers** A student used a calculator to find the exact answer to the problem below. Decide whether the answer shown is reasonable. If it's not, tell why.

Problem: How much change should you get from a $50 bill if you buy two $13.95 sweaters, including 6.5% tax?

More Practice, page 544, set A

Exploring Algebra
Variables and Algebraic Expressions

EXPLORE **Solve to Understand**

A **variable** is a letter, such as n or x, that reserves a place for a number. Expressions containing variables, such as $n - 23$, or $2x$, are called **algebraic expressions.** All the properties that are true for numerical expressions are also true for algebraic expressions.

Math Point

Multiplication can be indicated by writing numbers and expressions next to one another. For example, $2x$ means 2 times x, $3(x + 2)$ means 3 times $(x + 2)$, and $3mn$ means 3 times m times n.

Geometric figure (a) at right is a model for the algebraic expression $x + 2$, where x represents the unknown length of that piece.

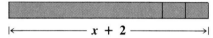

Write algebraic expressions for these geometric figures.

(b)

(c)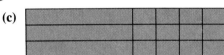

TALK ABOUT IT

1. Suppose the piece of length x were drawn longer or shorter than shown in figure (a). Would the algebraic expression still be $x + 2$?

2. Write another algebraic expression for figures (b) and (c).

To evaluate an algebraic expression, replace the variable with a number and evaluate the numerical expression that results.

Examples

A Evaluate $y - 23$ for $y = 52$
$$52 - 23 = 29$$

B Evaluate $2m - n$ for $m = 12$ and $n = 5$
$$(2 \cdot 12) - 5$$
$$24 - 5 = 19$$

Evaluate each algebraic expression.

1. $t + 19$ for $t = 37$ **2.** $(t \div 8) + 6$ for $t = 72$ **3.** $t + 5k$ for $k = 15$ and $t = 4$

PRACTICE

Evaluate each algebraic expression.

1. $m - 54$ for $m = 128$ **2.** $82 + n$ for $n = 65$ **3.** $87 - x$ for $x = 34$

4. $2b$ for $b = 12$ **5.** $3k - 2$ for $k = 3$ **6.** $4 + 2n$ for $n = 6$

7. $25 - 3x$ for $x = 5$ **8.** $m \div 7$ for $m = 84$ **9.** $3r + 41$ for $r = 12$

10. $pq + 3$ for $p = 4$ and $q = 5$

11. $(5h) + (3k)$ for $h = 6$ and $k = 7$

12. $4(b + 11) - c$ for $b = 3$ and $c = 10$

13. $r + (rp)$ for $r = 25$ and $p = 0$

14. $a(b + 6)$ for $a = 8$ and $b = 24$

APPLY

MATH REASONING

15. Draw a geometric figure as in the Explore activity that shows $5y + 5$.

16. Draw a figure that shows that $3(m + 1) = (3m) + (3 \cdot 1)$

PROBLEM SOLVING

17. The equation $A = lw$ gives the area A of a rectangle in terms of the length l and the width w. Find the area of a rectangle with $l = 12$ cm and $w = 15$ cm.

18. The equation $C = p + (ip)$ gives the total cost C of an item including tax where i is the tax rate and p is the cost of the item before tax is included. Find the total cost of an item which costs $20 without tax and with a tax rate of $0.05.

▶ MENTAL MATH

Evaluate each algebraic expression using mental math.

19. $52m$ for $m = 3$ **20.** $5y$ for $y = 69$

21. $t + r + 40$ for $t = 28$ and $r = 30$ **22.** $360 + g + h$ for $g = 154$ and $h = 140$

23. $164 - g$ for $g = 20$ **24.** $k + i$ for $k = 724$ and $i = 235$

25. $5d + 30$ for $d = 25$ **26.** $(a + b) - c$ for $a = 75$, $b = 65$, and $c = 45$

Data Collection and Analysis

UNDERSTAND
ANALYZE DATA
PLAN
ESTIMATE
SOLVE
EXAMINE

Group Skills
Listen to Others
Encourage and Respect Others
Explain and Summarize
Check for Understanding
Disagree in an Agreeable Way

Learning to work cooperatively with other students takes effort on the part of each group member. In this book you will often be asked to work together and make group decisions. The skills in the chart are some of the ways you can help each other work as a group.

When someone in your group doesn't understand a problem or an idea it is helpful to explain or summarize. Work with your group to make a list of at least five things that are helpful in making a clear explanation. Keep these ideas in mind when you do the activity below.

Cooperative Activity

This is called a Latin Square. It is a 4 × 4 arrangement of 4 red, 4 blue, 4 yellow, and 4 purple squares. In a Latin Square, no color can appear twice in the same row or column. The pattern on this Latin Square is made by marking the diagonals of any squares of the same color that touch corners. When a series of squares touch corners, draw the diagonal from the middle of the first square to the middle of the last square.

Your job is to find as many ways as you can to make Latin Square patterns. Draw the patterns on graph paper and mark the diagonals.

See if you can find more than 5 patterns. If one pattern can be rotated to match another pattern, the patterns are not considered to be different.

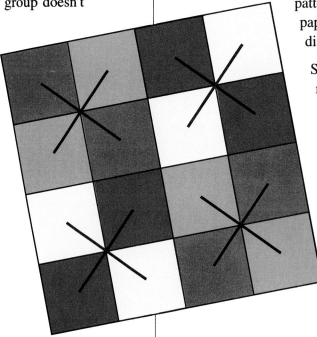

24

1. How many different patterns did you find to make a Latin Square?

2. How many patterns do you think are possible?

3. Did you find any "tricks" for making a new Latin Square from one you already made? Explain.

4. Was there any confusion about the direction for making Latin Squares? Were any helpful explanations given in your group?

1. Tell what your group could do to improve the way explanations are given.

WRAP UP

Math Sentence Completion

Use a mathematical term or phrase from this chapter to complete each sentence.

1. The estimation technique of _____ is used when you reason $11 \times 498 \approx 10 \times 500$ or $5{,}000$.

2. The number 4.52 million written in _____ is 4,520,000.

3. If you add 47 and 53 first to find $47 + 28 + 53$, you are using _____ numbers.

4. You should compute inside parentheses before adding, subtracting, multiplying or dividing according to the _____.

Sometimes, Always, Never

Which of these words should go in the blank: *sometimes*, *always*, or *never*? Explain your choice.

5. A number written in standard notation will __?__ have the same value as the number written in terms of its largest place value period.

6. When you use the counting on technique, you __?__ begin with one addend and count on by hundreds.

7. When adding three-digit numbers, front-end estimation __?__ requires adding the digits in the ones place.

8. Mental math is __?__ the best way to solve a problem.

Project

Bring some supermarket newspaper ads to class. Pick out five different items. Note the prices. Estimate the total cost of the items using mental math. Tell which technique you used. Calculate the exact cost of the items with your calculator.

POWER PRACTICE/TEST

Part 1   Understanding

1. Which equation is an example of the commutative property?

   A $3 + 7 = 7 + 3$

   B $(3 + 7) + 4 = 3 + (7 + 4)$

   C $3 + 0 = 3$

   D $3 + 7 = 10$

2. Which equation is an example of the identity property for multiplication?

   A $4 \cdot 3 = 3 \cdot 4$

   B $(4 \cdot 3) \cdot 2 = 4 \cdot (3 \cdot 2)$

   C $4 \cdot 1 = 4$

   D $(4 \cdot 3) \cdot 2 = (4 \cdot 2) + (3 \cdot 2)$

3. $395 + 406 + 382 + 397 + 410 + 409 \approx 6 \times 400$ is an example of estimating using the technique of _____.

4. Write an addition equation related to $3 \times 5 = $ ▓.

5. Finding the sum $275 + 360 + 125$ by first adding 275 and 125 is an example of the mental math technique _____.

Part 3   Skills

6. Write 40.03 million in standard notation.

7. Write 503,010,000,000 in terms of its largest place value period name.

Estimate.

8. $4,352 \div 64$

9. $61,324 - 15,805$

10. $325 + 756 + 275 + 144$

Find the value of each expression.

11. $8 - 3 \times 2$

12. $10 + 15 \div 3$

13. $2(x + 12)$ for $x = 1$

Part 3   Applications

14. The equation $P = 6l + 4s$ gives the number of people (P) that can be seated in a restaurant with large (l) and small (s) tables. How many people can be seated at 8 large and 20 small tables?

15. John is building a bookshelf. Lumber will cost $8.35, paint will cost $2.00, and hardware will cost $2.05. He has $12.00. Can he afford the materials for the bookshelf?

16. **Challenge** At Big Hits, tapes cost $7 and CDs cost $11. You have saved $35 and would like to spend it at Big Hits. However, there is also a concert you would like to go to next week. Tickets for the concert are $15. Write a question based on this information. Then find the answer.

27

ENRICHMENT
Napier's Bones

Scottish mathematician John Napier (1550–1617) invented a simple calculator that could be used to multiply any number by a 1-digit number. The calculator was probably given the name Napier's Bones because some versions of it were made of bone. Napier's Bones consisted of nine strips labeled 1 through 9 plus an index also labeled 1 through 9.

Here is the way to use Napier's Bones to find 475 × 7.

Place the strips headed 4, 7, and 5 side by side. Place the index beside the three strips. Use the numbers that are opposite 7 on the index. Start at the right and add diagonally to find the product.

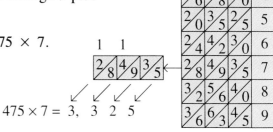

$$475 \times 7 = 3,\ 3\ 2\ 5$$

Make a copy of the ten strips of Napier's Bones. Use them to find these products.

1. 87 × 5

2. 635 × 8

3. 128 × 9

4. 2,675 × 6

Did you notice that there is a certain type of number that cannot be multiplied using Napier's Bones?

You can make the calculator work for numbers containing zeroes by adding a zero strip that can be used as a place holder. For example, to multiply 402 × 5, you would use the strips 4, 0, and 2 and the index.

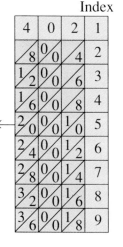

$$402 \times 5 = 2,\ 0\ 1\ 0$$

Use Napier's Bones to find these products.

5. 305 × 8

6. 2,084 × 5

CUMULATIVE REVIEW

1. Add.

43,926 + 1,732 + 680,157

- **A** 1,292,617
- **B** 725,815
- **C** 735,815
- **D** 635,815

2. Multiply.

468 × 509

- **A** 238,212
- **B** 27,612
- **C** 238,232
- **D** 6,552

3. Divide.

47)28,567

- **A** 67 R 38
- **B** 607 R 38
- **C** 670 R 38
- **D** 678 R 38

Use the figure at the right for problems 4–6.

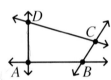

4. Name two perpendicular lines.

- **A** $\overleftrightarrow{AD}$ and $\overleftrightarrow{CD}$
- **B** $\overleftrightarrow{AD}$ and $\overleftrightarrow{DA}$
- **C** $\overleftrightarrow{AD}$ and $\overleftrightarrow{AB}$
- **D** $\overleftrightarrow{AD}$ and $\overleftrightarrow{BC}$

5. Name a ray.

- **A** $\overleftrightarrow{BD}$
- **B** $\overrightarrow{B}$
- **C** $\overline{BC}$
- **D** $\overrightarrow{BC}$

6. Name an obtuse angle.

- **A** $\angle DAR$
- **B** $\angle ADC$
- **C** $\angle ABC$
- **D** $\angle CBD$

7. What is the standard notation for 36.8 billion?

- **A** 36,800,000,000
- **B** 36,800,000
- **C** 368,000,000,000
- **D** 368,000,000

8. Which property is shown by the equation $3 \cdot (2 \cdot 7) = (3 \cdot 2) \cdot 7$?

- **A** Distributive Property
- **B** Identity for Multiplication
- **C** Commutative Property
- **D** Associative Property

9. Which property should be used to solve the equation $34 + \text{▐▐▐▐} = 34$?

- **A** Zero Product Property
- **B** Commutative Property
- **C** Identity for Addition
- **D** Distributive Property

10. Use the order of operations to find the value of $(6 \cdot 4) + 8 \div 2$.

- **A** 36
- **B** 9
- **C** 40
- **D** 28

11. Last year 63 sporting events were held at Central Stadium. The total attendance for the year was 3,734,479. Estimate the average attendance at each event.

- **A** 5,000
- **B** 50,000
- **C** 60,000
- **D** 600,000

12. The equation $P = 2(l + w)$ gives the perimeter (P) of a rectangle of length (l) and width (w). Find the perimeter of a room with $l = 12$ ft and $w = 10$ ft.

- **A** 34 ft
- **B** 44 ft
- **C** 24 ft
- **D** 20 ft

2

DATA
ANALYSIS
AND
STATISTICS

THEME: ENVIRONMENTAL ISSUES

MATH AND SCIENCE

DATA BANK

Use the Science Data Bank on page 494 to answer the questions.

1 Is the population growth greater in developing or developed countries?

2 Is the number of species in the tropical rain forest areas of the world greater or less than half of the total number of species in the world?

3 If you were going to construct a number line to show the numbers of extinct species of plants, in what units would you mark the number line?

4 **Using Critical Thinking** Describe the relationship between population growth and species extinction. Give some reasons to explain this relationship.

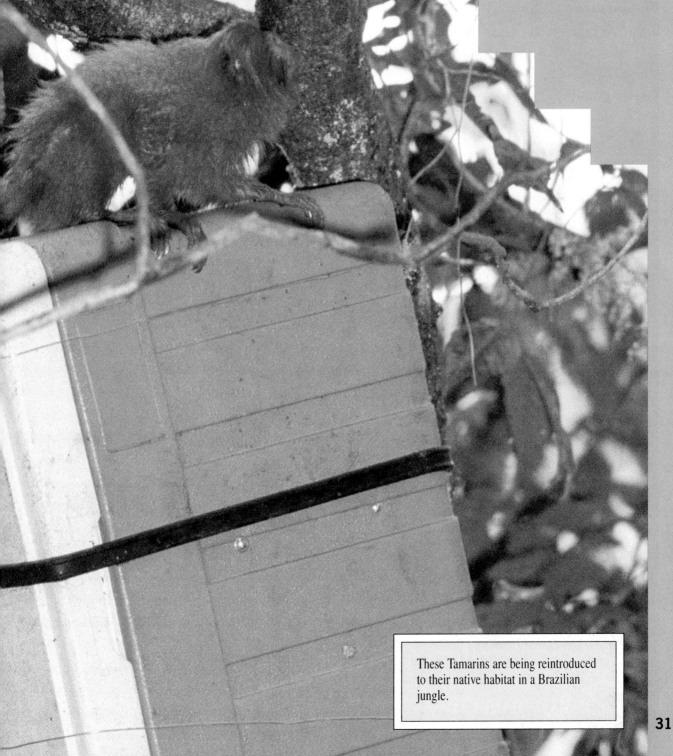

These Tamarins are being reintroduced to their native habitat in a Brazilian jungle.

31

Divided Bar Graphs

EXPLORE Complete the Graph

Work in groups. Use this table of data to draw a bar graph like the one that has been started at the right.

Each bar represents the estimated U.S. water withdrawal in billions of gallons per day. Each bar is divided to show the breakdown for irrigation, power-cooling, industrial, and municipal use.

Water Usage	1954	1980	2000
irrigation	176	167	184
power-cooling	74	259	429
industrial	33	104	233
municipal	17	29	42

TALK ABOUT IT

1. How will you complete the vertical scale?

2. When you stack the power-cooling bar on top of the irrigation bar, where on the vertical scale will the top of the power-cooling bar for 1980 be?

3. What title would you give the graph?

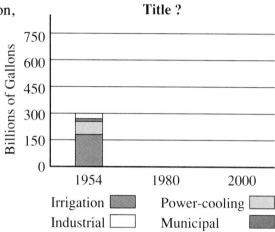

To draw a divided bar graph follow these steps:

- Draw and label each axis. Select an appropriate vertical scale.
- Choose a color for each division of the bars. Indicate the meaning of each color.
- Add the appropriate data together to determine the different section of each bar. Draw the bars.
- Give the graph a title.

TRY IT OUT

Use the graph to answer the questions.

1. How many people rode the ferris wheel?

2. If 1,000 adults and 3,000 children rode the roller coaster, where on the vertical scale will the top of the third bar be?

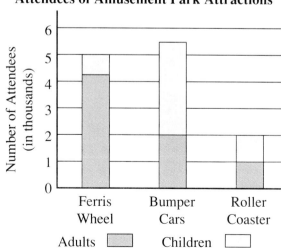

Use the Television Viewing divided bar graph to answer questions 1–5.

1. Which program category attracts the largest audience?

2. Which program category attracts the smallest children's audience?

3. If you wanted to advertise suntan lotion to teenagers, which type of program would you sponsor?

4. About how many a) adults, b) teens, and c) children view drama programs?

5. Of all comedy viewers, about how many are a) adults, b) teens, c) children?

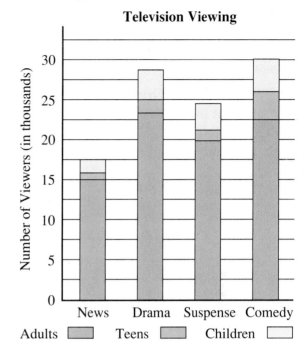

Television Viewing

Adults □ Teens ▨ Children ▢

MATH REASONING

6. Using the divided bar graph above, Estelle estimated the total number of people in the Television Viewing audience to be about 100,000 people. Sarah disagreed. She didn't think it was reasonable to draw any conclusions about the size of the viewing audience. Do you agree with Estelle or Sarah? Why?

PROBLEM SOLVING

7. Construct a divided bar graph using the information in this table.

How Water is Used			
	Public	Industry	Irrigation
Canada	18%	70%	11%
U.S.	10%	49%	41%
Mexico	5%	7%	88%
India	3%	4%	93%

8. **Science Data Bank** Consider the data in the table in exercise 7. Mexico and India are developing nations. Canada and the United States are developed nations. Compare how water is used in developing versus developed nations.

DATA BANK

▶ **ALGEBRA**

9. Use these equations to find the value of bars A, B, and C.

$B + C = 10$ $B - C = 6$
$B + C + 2 = A$

A	B	C

Circle Graphs

LEARN ABOUT IT

EXPLORE Study the Graph

A group of joggers were asked: "How many miles do you jog each day?" The circle graph at the right shows their answers.

TALK ABOUT IT

Daily Jogging Distance

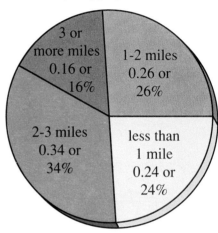

1. What fraction of the joggers run 1–2 miles every day?

2. What is the sum of all the percents in the circle graph?

3. If you polled 100 joggers at random, about how many do you think would say they jog 2–3 miles per day?

You can use the following percents to estimate the size of circle graph regions.

$$10\% = \frac{1}{10} \qquad 20\% = \frac{1}{5} \qquad 25\% = \frac{1}{4} \qquad 33\% = \frac{1}{3} \qquad 50\% = \frac{1}{2}$$

Examples Use the circle graph above to estimate each answer.

A If you polled 720 joggers, approximately how many would jog 1–2 miles daily?

26% is approximately $\frac{1}{4}$, and $\frac{1}{4}$ of 720 = 180

About 180 out of 720 joggers jog 1–2 miles per day.

B Do more joggers jog less than 1 mile or 1–2 miles?

More joggers jog 1–2 miles. 26% > 24%

TRY IT OUT

Use the circle graph above to answer each question.

1. Do more joggers jog 1–2 miles or 2–3 miles?

2. If 150 joggers were surveyed, about how many would say they jog less than 1 mile?

In a recent survey teenagers were asked, "How late are you allowed to stay out on a school night?" Their responses are summarized in the circle graph at the right.

1. What percent of the teenagers surveyed must be home by 11:00 p.m. or before?

2. What percent of the teenagers surveyed must be home by 10:00 p.m. or before?

3. If 500 teenagers were surveyed, about how many must be home before 9:00 p.m.?

4. If 500 teenagers were surveyed, about how many are not allowed out on school nights?

5. If 150 of the teenagers surveyed are chosen at random, about how many are allowed to stay out past 10:00 p.m.?

School Night Curfew

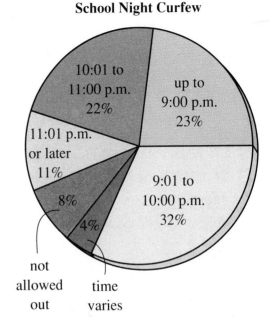

MATH REASONING Use the circle graph at the right for exercises 6–10.

6. If there are 50 drivers in the under 20 category, approximately how many drivers are in the 20 to 34 age group?

Ages of American Drivers

PROBLEM SOLVING

7. If 30,000 drivers were included in the survey, about how many more drivers are in the 35 to 49 age group compared to the 50 to 64 age group?

8. **Unfinished Problem** Write a problem that can be answered using the following information. A driver under age 20 pays about $1\frac{1}{2}$ times as much for car insurance as the average driver. The average adult pays $420 per year for insurance.

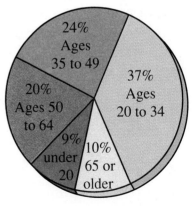

▶ **ESTIMATION**

Suppose the population of a city is about 25,348. Estimate to answer each question.

9. How many drivers are age 65 or older?   10. How many drivers are 50 to 64 years old?

Choosing Graphs

Three types of graphs are circle graphs, bar graphs, and line graphs. It is important to choose the best type of graph for displaying a set of data.

EXPLORE **Examine the Data** Work in groups. Try to make a bar graph, a circle graph, and a line graph using the data in this table.

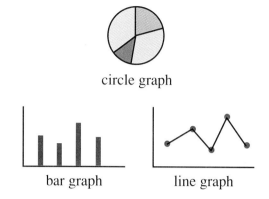

circle graph

bar graph   line graph

TALK ABOUT IT

1. Which type of graph works best? Why?

2. Which type of graph is not appropriate for the given data? Explain why.

3. Can you always draw a circle graph to represent data stated in percents? Why or why not?

Percent of rain forest that will be lost by 2000 A.D. at current rate of deforestation.	
Brazil	33%
Mexico/Columbia/Guatemala	33%
Ecuador/Nicaragua/Honduras	50%
Costa Rica	80%
Philippines	20%

- **Circle graphs** are used to show the parts of a whole. Often the parts are expressed as percents. The sum of all the percents in a circle graph is 100%. Thus, the data in the table above cannot be displayed using a circle graph.
- **Bar graphs** are used to compare amounts.
- **Line graphs** are often used to show trends that change over time.

TRY IT OUT

Which type of graph would you use to represent the data in each table?

1.
Sandwich Prices	
Deli A	$1.95
Deli B	$2.50
Deli C	$2.98
Deli D	$2.25
Deli E	$1.99

2.
Types of Phone Calls	
Business	48%
Information	9%
Friends	23%
Relatives	15%
Other	5%

3.
Money in Circulation (per person)	
1985	$691.74
1980	$558.28
1975	$380.08
1970	$265.39
1965	$204.14

Which types of graphs are appropriate for each set of data? Explain your answers.

1.

Airline Costs	
Flight Crew	11%
Fuel Oil	28%
Passenger Service	10%
Aircraft Service	16%
Promotion	15%
Maintenance	10%
Other	10%

2.

Types of Video Games Teenagers Said They Buy	
Target Games	78%
Adventure Games	46%
Educational Games	35%
Trivia Games	16%

3.

Electric Energy used in Manufacturing Industries (in billions of kilowatt-hours)	
1960	362.0
1970	584.1
1980	716.9

APPLY

MATH REASONING **4.** Amelia wanted to budget $1,000 a month for her expenses. She estimated that she would spend $650 on rent, $200 on food, $80 on gas, and $70 on entertainment. Could Amelia draw a circle graph to represent her new budget? Why or why not?

PROBLEM SOLVING

Decide whether a circle graph, a bar graph, or a line graph is most appropriate for each set of data. Then, draw the graphs.

5. *Consumer Reports* stated that grocery shoppers fit into the following categories. Those that shop:

Usually at one store	41%
At several stores	21%
Always at one store	38%

6. Science Data Bank Use data on world distribution of species and extinction of species to make (a) a circle graph, (b) a bar graph, and (c) a line graph.

USING CRITICAL THINKING **Make a Prediction**

7. Estimate the life expectancy of a man who is 45.

8. Estimate the life expectancy of a woman who is 70.

9. Predict the difference in life expectancy for a man who is 70 compared to a woman who is 70.

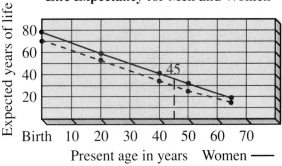

Life Expectancy for Men and Women

Expected years of life

Present age in years   Women ——   Men — —

Problem Solving
Using the Strategies

| UNDERSTAND |
| ANALYZE DATA |
| PLAN |
| ESTIMATE |
| SOLVE |
| EXAMINE |

LEARN ABOUT IT

Many problems can be solved in more than
one way. Julie selected the strategy **Use Objects**.
Greg selected the strategy **Draw a Picture.**

Keith's father took Keith and his sister on a camping trip.
To cross a stream they used a small canoe that could only
hold 1 adult or 2 children. How many trips across the stream
did they make to get Keith, his father, and his sister across?

Julie's Solution

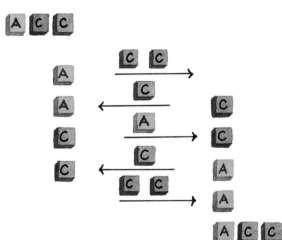

Greg's Solution

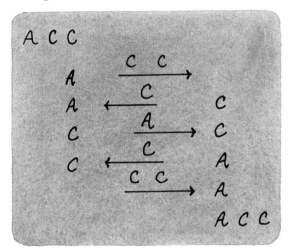

They made 5 trips across the stream.

TRY IT OUT

Solve. Use Objects or Draw a Picture.

1. Keith, his sister, and his father went on a
   second camping trip. Keith's mother
   came along. To cross a stream they still
   had to use the canoe that could only hold
   1 adult or 2 children. How many trips
   across the stream did they make to get
   the family to the other side?

2. Jenny decided to paddle a canoe 8 miles
   upstream. She could paddle 3 miles in an
   hour but then she had to rest for 30
   minutes. While she rested, the canoe
   drifted 1 mile downstream. At this rate
   how long will it take Jenny to paddle 8
   miles?

Solve. Use any problem solving strategy.

Some Strategies	
Act Out	Solve a Simpler Problem
Use Objects	Make an Organized List
Choose an Operation	Work Backward
Draw a Picture	Look for a Pattern
Guess and Check	Use Logical Reasoning
Make a Table	Write an Equation

1. Eva bought 5 pounds of trail mix for her camping trip. If the trail mix cost $2.19 per pound, how much did she pay?

2. Tom has a loaf of french bread. He wants to cut it into 10 equal slices. How many cuts will he have to make?

3. An annual pass to Alpine Lake costs $25. The fee for one day is $2.50. If you plan to go to the lake for 3 days, would it be worthwhile to buy an annual pass? What about 10 days? 15 days?

4. The forest rangers at Sequoia Camp are building a low fence to enclose a display of native plants. The area they are going to enclose is a rectangle 15 feet long and 12 feet wide. If they put a post at each corner and a post every 3 feet in between the corner posts, how many posts will they use?

5. The editors of *Camping Today* surveyed their readers to find out how many times a year they go camping. If 1,200 readers responded to the survey, use the graph at the right to predict how many go camping more than 10 times a year.

6. Perry is trying to climb up a very steep hill that has a gravel surface. In 10 minutes he can climb 5 feet, but he also slides back 2 feet. At this rate, how long will it take Perry to climb 16 feet?

7. Victor is headed south on a 10-day hiking trip. He plans to spend each night at a different camp. Lake Camp is 23 miles north of Sky Camp and 8 miles south of Hill Camp. Victor hiked 5 miles to Hill Camp the first day. He stayed at Lake Camp the second day. He reached Sky Camp on the fifth day. How far did he hike in 5 days?

8. Use the graph below to predict how many campers in a group of 450 go camping 5 or fewer times a year.

Number of Camping Trips per Year

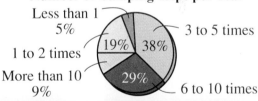

Less than 1
5%

1 to 2 times

More than 10
9%

3 to 5 times

19% 38%

29%

6 to 10 times

Stem and Leaf Plots

Before data can be shown in a graph, it must be organized.
One way is to construct a **stem and leaf plot.**

EXPLORE Examine the Data

The heights of eighth grade students in a class were measured
in centimeters and recorded as follows: 163, 161, 172, 165,
170, 165, 166, 159, 158, 169, 172, 162, 172, 181, 180, 166,
157, 158, 177, 161, 158, 156, 163, and 168.

TALK ABOUT IT

1. Are there any data in the 140s? Are there any in the 150s?

2. Can you tell at a glance whether there are more students
with heights in the 160s or in the 170s?

Question 2 can easily be answered after you make a stem and
leaf plot to organize the data. Follow these steps.

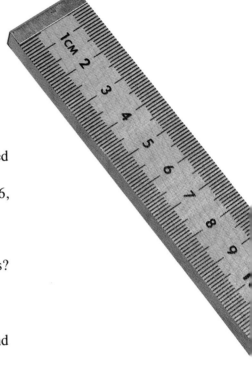

- Draw a two column table as shown and enter
  the labels "Stem" and "Leaf."

- Write in the stem column 15, 16, 17, and 18 to
  represent the 150s to the 180s.

- Consider each height one at a time. Record the
  last digit of each height in the leaf column after
  the appropriate stem. For example, the height of 163 has a leaf
  of 3 which is recorded in the row at the right of the stem, 16.
  Each item of the data contributes one digit to the leaf column. The
  completed stem and leaf plot for the data above is shown.

stem	leaf
15	9, 8, 7, 8, 8, 6
16	3, 1, 5, 5, 6, 9, 2, 6, 1, 3, 8
17	2, 0, 2, 2, 7
18	1, 0

TRY IT OUT

Use the stem and leaf plot shown above to answer these questions.

1. How many leaves does the stem 16
have?

2. How many times does the height 158
appear?

3. How many times does the height 165
appear?

4. Which height occurs more frequently,
165 or 172?

40

In science class, Mike and Cora recorded the daily water intake
of several white mice.

Day	1	2	3	4	5	6	7	8	9	10	11	12	13	14	15
Water in Milliliters	25	31	35	28	40	37	41	26	36	38	19	44	28	18	41

1. Make a stem and leaf plot for the data above.

2. Use the stem and leaf plot to name two
   values that are repeated.

3. Are there more values with a stem of 2
   or a stem of 3?

4. Did the white mice consume less than or
   more than 30 milliliters of water on
   most days? How can you answer this
   question without counting the data?

5. On how many days did the mice
   consume less than 20 milliliters of
   water? How can you answer this
   question without counting the data?

MATH REASONING

6. Use the stem and leaf plot you made in
   exercise 1 above to estimate the average
   water intake of the mice.

PROBLEM SOLVING

7. Make a stem and leaf plot for this set of
   data. Were there more weights in the 130s
   or the 140s? Which weight occurs 3 times
   in the set of data? Explain the method you
   used to answer these questions.

Weights of Team Members
122, 143, 156, 162, 134, 119,
136, 148, 160, 146, 154, 143,
129, 154, 127, 120, 156, 128,
135, 143, 139, 121, 163, 157,
138, 129, and 143.

MIXED REVIEW

Write each in standard notation.

8. 214 thousand   9. 8.3 million   10. 813.2 thousand   11. 4.1 trillion

Find the missing value. Name the property used.

12. $14 \cdot \text{▓} = 14$ 13. $7 \cdot (3 + 2) = (7 \cdot 3) + (\text{▓} \cdot 2)$ 14. $129 \cdot 0 = \text{▓}$

Frequency Tables and Histograms

A **frequency table** shows the number of times an item occurs in a set of data. A **histogram** is a bar graph of the data in a frequency table.

EXPLORE **Examine the Table**

The table at the right lists the last 40 sales at a sporting goods store.

TALK ABOUT IT

1. Make a stem and leaf plot that represents the 40 sales. Use the number of dollars as the stems and the number of cents as leaves.

2. Use your stem and leaf plot to complete the frequency table. Notice that the frequency intervals have a width of $5.00.

3. Explain how the histogram shows the data in the frequency table.

The bars of a histogram touch because there are no gaps between the grouping intervals.

Amount of Sales				
$3.85	$3.59	$13.45	$9.18	$6.55
$2.42	$2.45	$8.69	$14.28	$6.78
$10.39	$3.95	$5.20	$11.28	$6.39
$5.47	$7.47	$1.65	$15.95	$5.39
$7.71	$4.37	$6.10	$5.19	$2.45
$4.49	$6.45	$3.78	$7.18	$16.39
$3.95	$8.53	$6.45	$7.47	$10.25
$4.55	$11.72	$12.39	$4.49	$9.46

Frequency Table	
Groupings Intervals	Frequency
0 to $4.99	13
$5.00 to $9.99	
$10.00 to $14.99	
$15.00 or more	

Histogram for Sales

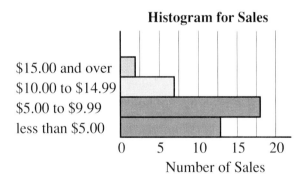

TRY IT OUT

1. The heights of 24 eighth graders were recorded in centimeters. Make a frequency table and histogram with frequency intervals that have widths of 10 cm.

Heights of Eighth Graders					
170	163	158	181	157	158
161	165	169	180	158	156
172	166	172	166	177	163
165	159	172	162	161	168

The table at the right lists the purchases at Health Food Haven at lunch time.

Luncheon Sales at Health Food Haven				
$2.25	$12.52	$3.67	$10.88	$9.10
$3.03	$14.00	$4.98	$12.22	$10.25
$11.41	$3.39	$4.33	$4.60	$6.72
$7.85	$7.99	$13.21	$5.44	$9.10
$4.12	$6.57	$8.42	$10.91	$8.77
$6.40	$5.78	$5.83	$7.99	$5.83
$4.73	$7.50	$4.80	$9.20	$11.35
$2.88	$4.60	$10.70	$9.11	$13.80
$3.70	$13.21	$8.25	$11.99	$4.97
$4.80	$12.97	$5.84		

1. Make a stem and leaf plot that represents the luncheon sales. Use the number of dollars as the stems and the number of cents as the leaves.

2. Use the stem and leaf plot you made in exercise 1 to make a frequency table for this data with interval widths of $3.00.

3. Use the frequency table you made in exercise 2 to make a histogram for this data using $3.00 intervals.

4. Make a frequency table for this data using $4.00 intervals.

5. Use the frequency table you made in exercise 4 to make a histogram for this data using $4.00 intervals.

APPLY

MATH REASONING In the histogram at the right estimate the quantity represented by:

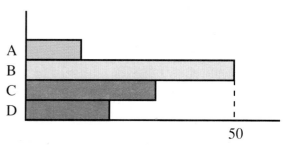

6. Bar A   7. Bar C   8. Bar D

PROBLEM SOLVING

An employee recorded the time it took customers at the Quik-Food Counter to be served. She recorded the data in a frequency table with 30 second intervals.

9. Make a histogram of the Serving Time Frequencies.

10. Make a frequency table and a histogram of the serving time data using 60 second intervals.

Serving Time Frequencies

Serving Time in Seconds	Tally	Frequency
0–30	‖	2
31–60	⊞ ⊞	10
61–90	⊞ ‖‖	8
91–120	⊞ ⊞ ⊞	15
121–150	⊞ ⊞ ⊞ ⊞ ⊞ ‖	27
151–180	⊞ ⊞ ⊞ ‖‖‖‖	19
181–210	⊞ ⊞ ⊞ ‖	17
211–240	⊞ ⊞ ‖	12

▶ **CALCULATOR**

Find a decimal to the nearest tenth for the variable x that gives the best approximation. Use your calculator and the strategy Guess and Check.

11. $x \cdot x \approx 20$

12. $x \cdot x \approx 30$

Using Critical Thinking

Mr. P. R. Smooth was describing the Prestigious Corporation.

"Our beginning salaries are very competitive," he said. "The average salary of the last 5 new employees was $20,000. Also, a recent sample showed that our average wage for hourly employees is $10.50. And on top of that, our profits are soaring!"

Mr. Smooth gave the information below to support his claims.

Prestigious Corp.

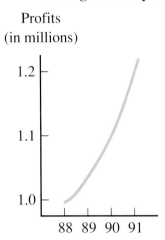

Last 5 New Employee Salaries	
Person A	$10,000
Person B	$10,000
Person C	$10,000
Person D	$10,000
Person E	$60,000
Average:	$20,000

Hourly Wage Sample	
Person A	Made $40 @ $4/hr
Person B	Made $40 @ $8/hr
Person C	Made $40 @ $10/hr
Person D	Made $40 @ $20/hr
Average hourly wage:	
($4 + $8 + $10 + $20) ÷ 4 = $10.50	

TALK ABOUT IT

1. What claims did Mr. Smooth make about Prestigious Corp.?

2. Do you think Mr. Smooth's claims about yearly salary, hourly wages, and profits are misleading? Why or why not?

3. What have you learned from this situation?

TRY IT OUT

1. Are the yearly salary data realistic? Explain.

2. How many hours did each person in the hourly wage sample work? What was the total number of hours worked? What were the total wages made? What is the average wage per hour using this data? Why is this different from Mr. Smooth's claim?

3. How could you change the scale and labeling so that it would look like the profits for the Prestigious Corporation weren't growing very fast?

44

POWER PRACTICE/QUIZ

The chart shows data from last year's T-shirt sales at Metro Junior High. The divided bar graph shows September sales. Copy and complete the divided bar graph.

	Sep.	Oct.	Nov.	Dec.
small	55	30	10	25
medium	75	50	25	85
large	20	15	15	50

1. Where on the vertical scale is the top of the medium bar for October?

2. For which of the months would you order the most T-shirts this year?

3. How do the divisions showing the mediums sold each month compare to the divisions for small and large?

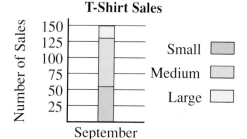

Tell which type of graph could be used to display the data in order to answer each question.

4. What is the trend in total sales over the four months?

5. What are the trends in sizes purchased over the months?

6. What percent of the total November sales were small T-shirts? medium T-shirts? large T-shirts?

Make a stem and leaf plot of the data at the right. Then answer each question.

Donations Pledged to Eighth Graders							
37	17	44	25	30	18	26	15
24	28	35	24	36	12	32	30
17	14	41	21	26	38	42	33
40	36	23	33	41	37	24	18

7. How many students got more than 40 pledges?

8. How many students got less than 20 pledges?

9. Use your stem and leaf plot to make a frequency table. Have the first interval be ''under 15 pledges.'' Show grouping intervals with a width of 5 pledges.

10. Use your frequency table to make a histogram.

PROBLEM SOLVING

11. Anita built a fence around a 21 ft by 18 ft rectangular garden. She put a post at each corner and a post every 3 ft between corners. How many posts did she use?

12. Dan wants to cut a strip of wood into 6 equal parts. How many cuts must he make?

45

Mean, Median, and Mode

There are three types of measures that describe the "average" of a list of numbers. These measures of central tendency are called the **mean,** the **median,** and the **mode.**

EXPLORE **Study the Information**

Manuel made a frequency table to help him determine which size of toothpaste customers selected most often.

TALK ABOUT IT

Toothpaste Selections	
Size	How Frequently Selected
3 ounces	5
4.1 ounces	8
4.6 ounces	5
5.3 ounces	11
6.5 ounces	7

1. If each customer bought one tube of toothpaste, how many customers were surveyed?

2. Write the set of data that is represented by this table.

To Find the Mean

Find the sum of the values and divide by the number of values.

When the data is from a frequency table, the sum can be found by multiplying each item by its frequency and finding the sum of these products.

Use your calculator to help you compute the mean.

$$\text{mean} = \frac{3(5) + 4.1(8) + 4.6(5) + 5.3(11) + 6.5(7)}{5 + 8 + 5 + 11 + 7}$$

$$= \frac{15 + 32.8 + 23 + 58.3 + 45.5}{36} = \frac{174.6}{36} = 4.85$$

To Find the Median

Arrange the numbers in order from smallest to largest. Find the middle number if possible or add the two middle numbers and divide by 2.

3, 3, 3, 3, 3, 4.1, 4.1, 4.1, 4.1, 4.1, 4.1, 4.1, 4.1, 4.6. 4.6, 4.6, 4.6, **4.6, 5.3,** 5.3, 5.3, 5.3, 5.3, 5.3, 5.3, 5.3, 5.3, 5.3, 6.5, 6.5, 6.5, 6.5, 6.5, 6.5, 6.5

$$\text{median} = \frac{4.6 + 5.3}{2} = 4.95$$

To Find the Mode

Look for the value that occurs the most times.

mode = 5.3

Include the following new data in the frequency table above: The 7-ounce size was selected 5 times.

1. Find the new mean. 2. Find the new median. 3. Find the new mode.

A survey was taken in which parents, teachers, and teenagers were asked, "How much should a teenager spend out of the $20.00 he or she earns each day?"

Survey Results

Amount	Frequency of Response		
	Parents	Teachers	Teenagers
$5	3	1	0
$6	3	1	1
$8	5	0	1
$10	3	4	8
$12	1	3	3
$15	2	4	3

1. Copy and complete the table below by finding the mean, median, and mode of the amount of money chosen by each group.

2. Did parents, teachers, or teens have the highest mean?

3. Was the median for teachers' responses higher or lower than the mean for teachers' responses?

4. What is the mode for parents? Is it close to the mean for parents? Close to the median?

5. There are two modes for teachers' responses. Are they close to the mean?

	Mean	Median	Mode
Parents			
Teachers			
Teenagers			

6. How did teachers respond differently from parents?

7. How did teenagers respond differently from parents?

MATH REASONING Create a set of data for each statement that shows it is true.

8. The mode of a set of data can be the largest number of the set.

9. The mean of a set of data can be larger than the median.

10. The median of a set of data can be larger than the mean.

PROBLEM SOLVING

11. **Determine a Reasonable Answer** Without solving the problem, tell which of the answers seems reasonable. The mean of Nancy's earnings for 4 weeks was $89. Which amounts show how much she earned each week?

   A $95, $86, $82, $93
   B $85, $86, $87, $88
   C $88, $89, $92, $95
   D $89, $89, $89, $93

▶ **MENTAL MATH**

To find the mean of 34, 36, and 35, think: Take 1 from 36 and give it to 34. Then, all three amounts equal 35. Use this method to find the mean for each set of data.

12. 44, 46, 42   13. 75, 85, 80, 90, 70   14. 58, 64, 58, 61, 59

Box and Whisker Graphs

Graphic images help us interpret data. A **box and whisker graph** is one way to provide a picture of the central tendency of data.

EXPLORE **Study the Table**

You can draw a box and whisker graph to display the data given in the stem and leaf plot at the right.

TALK ABOUT IT

1. How many items of data are listed in the stem and leaf plot?

2. List the data in order. Which item has the highest value? Which item has the lowest value?

3. What is the median of the data?

To complete a box and whisker graph of the above data follow the steps below.

- Find the median of the upper half of the data and label it Q_U to represent the **upper quartile.**
- Find the median of the lower half of the data and label it Q_L to represent the **lower quartile.**
- Mark an appropriate vertical scale and draw a box that connects the upper quartile to the lower quartile. A line across the box indicates the median. Label the median "MD." For this data, MD = 82.
- Draw lines, "whiskers," from the box to the **highest** (H) and **lowest** (L) data items.

stem	leaf
18	5
16	8
12	8, 3
8	7, 3, 1
6	4, 4
4	8
3	6, 3

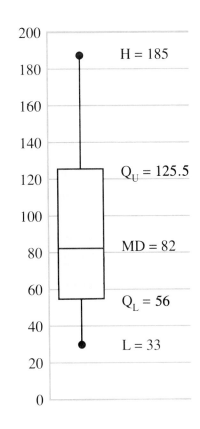

TRY IT OUT

Draw a box and whisker graph for each of these sets of data.

1. 12, 23, 24, 24, 28, 37, 49, 51, 53, 54, 54, 63, 65, 67, 92, 98

2. 23, 45, 46, 46, 49, 25, 72, 48, 63, 18, 29, 53

Draw a box and whisker graph for each set of data.

1. 1.2, 3.1, 3.5, 4.8, 5.3, 5.8, 6.2, 6.3, 6.9, 7.2, 7.7, 9.2

2. 38, 42, 17, 98, 77, 54, 29, 41

3. 9.8, 4.2, 5.1, 3.8, 4.5, 1.7, 1.9, 6.4

4. 12, 23, 21, 38, 19, 26, 75, 37, 82, 54, 29, 41

Questions 5–8 refer to the three sets of data shown as box and whisker graphs.

5. Which set of data has the greatest difference between its highest and lowest value?

6. Which set of data has the smallest difference between its upper quartile and lower quartile?

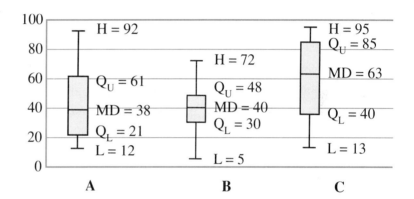

MATH REASONING

7. For which set of data is the mean most nearly equal to the median? Why?

8. For which set of data is the mean probably greater than the median? Why?

PROBLEM SOLVING

9. Suppose that the top 12 hitters on a girls' softball team have the following batting averages: 0.429, 0.408, 0.388, 0.385, 0.360, 0.358, 0.340, 0.338, 0.330, 0.258, 0.200, and 0.115. Does the box and whisker graph of this data look most like graph A, B, or C?

10. If you were the coach of a softball team, would you prefer your team's batting averages to look like graph B or C? Why?

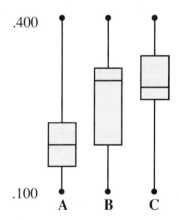

▶ **USING CRITICAL THINKING Justify Your Answer**

11. Is it possible for the mean of a set of data to fall outside the box portion of a box and whisker graph of the data? Illustrate with an example.

More Practice, page 524, set B

Significant Digits and The Mean

EXPLORE Study the Table

In 1989, about 89 percent of all U.S. Hispanics lived in only 9 states. The table at the right shows some data for these states. What would you say was the average Hispanic population for these nine states?

TALK ABOUT IT

1. What was California's Hispanic population in 1989?

2. Do you believe that there were exactly 549,000 Hispanics in New Mexico?

STATES WITH LARGEST HISPANIC POPULATIONS, 1989

State	Hispanic population (thousands)	Percent of U.S. Hispanics	Percent of state's population
California	6,762	33.7	24.3
Texas	4,313	21.5	25.8
New York	1,982	9.9	11.2
Florida	1,586	7.9	12.7
Illinois	855	4.3	7.5
Arizona	725	3.6	20.8
New Jersey	638	3.2	8.4
New Mexico	549	2.7	36.7
Colorado	421	2.1	13.0

Note: 89% of all U.S. Hispanics live in only nine states.
Source: U.S. Bureau of the Census, *The Hispanic Population of the U.S. March 1989* (1990)

The numbers in the table are approximate; they have been rounded to the nearest thousand. The nonzero digits in each number are called **significant digits.** For example, the number for California, 6,762,000 has four significant digits; the number for Colorado has three significant digits.

If you find the mean of the numbers in the table with a calculator, you get 1,981,222.2. But since the numbers in the table are accurate only to the nearest thousand, your answer should also be recorded to the nearest thousand—1,981,000.

TRY IT OUT

The data are accurate to the nearest person (ones).

1. Find the average population for 1990.

2. Find the average projected population for 2000.

3. How many significant digits are in the number for the 1990 Chinese population?

PROJECTION OF THE ASIAN-AMERICAN POPULATION, 1990–2000

Ethnic group	1990	2000
Filipino	1,405,146	2,070,571
Chinese	1,259,038	1,683,537
Vietnamese	859,638	1,574,385
Korean	814,495	1,320,759
Japanese	804,535	856,619
Asian Indian	684,339	1,006,305
Other Asian	706,470	1,338,188

Source: Population Reference Bureau (Washington D.C.)

Data are accurate to the nearest hundreds place.

1. Find the average sale price for the five cities for 1989.

2. Find the average sale price for the five cities for 1990.

3. Find the average sale price for Chicago over three years.

Data are accurate to the nearest ones place.

4. What is the average number of immigrants from each region annually from 1820–1989?

5. What is the average number of people from all countries for 1989:

Median Sales Price of Existing Single-Family Homes (in thousands of dollars)

City	1988	1989	1990
Boston	$181.2	$181.9	$177.3
Chicago	$98.9	$107.0	$112.3
Detroit	$73.1	$73.7	$75.5
Phoenix	$80.0	$78.8	$82.3
St. Louis	$78.1	$76.9	$77.0

Number of Immigrants by Region of Last Residence

Region	1820–1989	1989
Europe	36,977,034	94,338
Asia	5,697,301	296,420
Caribbean	2,590,542	87,597
South America	1,163,482	59,812
Africa	301,348	22,485

APPLY

MATH REASONING

6. The following numbers tell how many children were born to families in a certain neighborhood during the last 10 years.
2, 1, 1, 3, 4, 3, 1, 1, 2, 2, 2, 1, 1, 1, 1, 2, 2, 5, 4, 3, 3, 2, 2, 2, 1
How would you report the average number of children born per family? Can the average be reported in more than one way?

PROBLEM SOLVING

7. The 8th grade basketball team averaged 35.7 points in their last 3 games. The team scored 46 and 28 points in two of the games. How many points did they score in the third game?

▶ ESTIMATION

8. Estimate the mean and median of both sets of data.
Set A: 20, 22.4, 21.45, 22.213, and 20.714
Set B: 20, 22.4, 21.45, 22.213, 20.714, 100, and 21.111
Are the means and medians for the two sets of data the same? Explain your answer.

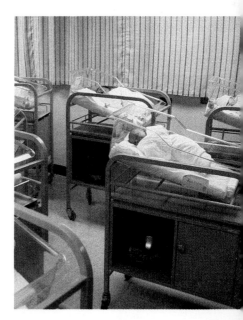

Problem Solving
Understanding the Question

UNDERSTAND
ANALYZE DATA
PLAN
ESTIMATE
SOLVE
EXAMINE

LEARN ABOUT IT

An important first step in solving a problem
is to understand the question. Sometimes it
helps to ask the question in a different way.

America's first space station was Skylab, launched in 1973.
During 1973 and 1974, Skylab was manned for 3 different
time periods, 28 days, 59 days, and 84 days. For how many
days was Skylab manned?

Begin by reading the question. → For how many days was Skylab manned?

Then, ask the question in a → What is the total number of days that Skylab was
different way.   manned?

TRY IT OUT

Read each problem. Select the question that is another version
of the question asked in the problem.

1. Skylab was 3 stories high and had a
usable volume of 9,300 cubic feet. The
NASA international space station will
have a usable volume of 30,611 cubic
feet. How much greater is the volume of
the space station than Skylab?

   a) How many times larger is the space
   station?
   b) How many fewer cubic feet did
   Skylab have?

2. Viking 1 landed on Mars on July 20,
1976. It was expected to function for 3
months, but continued to operate for $6\frac{1}{2}$
years. How many times longer did
Viking 1 operate than expected?

   a) How many times shorter was its
   expected life than its actual time of
   operation?
   b) How much longer did it operate than
   expected?

Write a question to complete each problem.

3. In 1966, Surveyor 1 sent almost 10,400
pictures of the moon. In 1968, Surveyor
2 sent 3,343 pictures.

4. Soviet astronaut Yuri Romanenko holds
the world record for time in space. His
first 2 missions totaled over 105 days.
His third mission lasted 326.5 days.

Solve. Use any problem solving strategy.

1. Astronaut John Young has had more space flights than any other astronaut. His 6 flights totaled about 34.8 hours. Find the average length of each flight.

2. Soviet astronaut Yuri Gagarin was the first man in space. His flight lasted 1 hour 48 minutes. Alan Shepard was the first American in space. His flight was 15 minutes. How much longer was Gagarin's flight?

3. The earth's surface is mostly water. Only about $\frac{1}{4}$ of the surface is land. Use the table below to find the approximate number of square miles of land on the Earth.

Earth	
Diameter	7,927 miles
Circumference	24,902.4 miles
Surface Area	196,949,970 square miles

4. Jupiter has 1 more moon than Uranus. Uranus has 6 fewer moons than Saturn. Jupiter has 8 times as many moons as Mars. Uranus has 15 moons. How many moons does Mars have?

5. The closest distance the moon is from the earth is 221,463 miles. The farthest distance the moon is from the earth is 252,710 miles. What is the mean distance from the moon to the earth?

6. Mir is a permanently manned Soviet space station that was launched in 1986. Its length is about 3.1 times its diameter. Its diameter is 13.7 feet. Find its length.

7. Jill knows that 6 of the planets take longer than the Earth does to revolve around the sun, but she can't remember their order. Neptune takes almost twice as long as Uranus, but not as long as Pluto. Saturn takes less than half as long as Uranus, but longer than Jupiter. The time it takes Mars to revolve around the sun is between the Earth's time and Jupiter's time. Arrange the 6 planets in order from the longest period of revolution to the shortest.

8. **Suppose** Darin has $15 to spend. He decides to buy 2 posters, one with pictures of astronauts and the other with pictures of spacecraft. Each poster cost $4.25. How much did Darin spend for posters? Tell which of the following would change the solution to the above problem.

   a) Darin bought 3 posters.
   b) Darin had $20 to spend.
   c) Darin also bought a book about space travel.

Exploring Algebra
Evaluating Expressions

LEARN ABOUT IT

The algebraic expression $360p$ can be used when drawing circle graphs.

EXPLORE **Study the Information**

The results of a National Science Foundation Survey are listed in the table at the right. Recall that $96\% = 0.96$ and $25\% = 0.25$.

TALK ABOUT IT

1. Does 0.41 or 0.59 represent female teachers who teach grades 7–9?

2. For which grade levels are over half the teachers female?

3. Which group of teachers is represented by the decimal 0.26?

Mathematics, Science, & Social Studies Teachers		
Grade Level	Female	Male
K–3	96%	4%
4–6	75%	25%
7–9	41%	59%
10–12	26%	74%

To draw a circle graph you need to know the angle sizes for each sector. Since there are 360 degrees in a circle, you can use the expression $360p$ to find each angle size.

For example, to draw the circle graph for grades 10–12, evaluate $360p$ for $p = 0.26$.

$$360 \cdot 0.26 = 93.6$$

Therefore, to construct the sector that represent female teachers that teach grades 10–12, you need to use an angle of 93.6°.

Grades 10-12

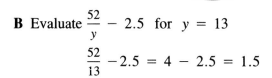

Male 74%

Female 26%

Examples

A Evaluate $360p$ for $p = 0.25$
$360 \cdot 0.25 = 90$

B Evaluate $\dfrac{52}{y} - 2.5$ for $y = 13$

$$\frac{52}{13} - 2.5 = 4 - 2.5 = 1.5$$

TRY IT OUT

Evaluate each expression.

1. $360p$ for $p = 0.59$

2. $3.7 + 4.2t$ for $t = 20$

3. $\dfrac{150}{k}$ for $k = 30$

4. $4y + 52$ for $y = 15$

Evaluate these expressions.

1. $2x + 5$ for $x = 23$ **2.** $\dfrac{y}{6} - 4$ for $y = 180$ **3.** $3a - 15$ for $a = 37$

4. $\dfrac{c}{9} - 3$ for $c = 189$ **5.** $6a + 7.2$ for $a = 7$ **6.** $x - 9.1$ for $x = 12.3$

7. $a + 15.8$ for $a = 6.7$ **8.** $\dfrac{x}{3} + 10$ for $x = 33$ **9.** $2c - 3$ for $c = 17$

When the expression $\dfrac{9}{5}C + 32$ is evaluated for C = 20°
Celsius it describes the number of degrees F (Fahrenheit). Find
°F for each of these cases.

10. C = 30°   **11.** C = 10°   **12.** C = 40°   **13.** C = 37°

MATH REASONING

14. Water freezes at 0°C and 32°F. Complete the pattern in this table.

°C	0	5	10	15	20	25	30	35
°F	32	41	50					

15. Complete this generalization that describes the relationship
between °C and °F. Beginning at 0°C and counting by 5s
compares to beginning at 32°F and counting by ___s.

PROBLEM SOLVING

16. Of the teachers that teach grades 7–9, 41% are female. What
is the angle measure of each sector of the circle graph?

Grades 7-9

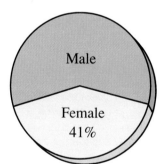

Write each in terms of its largest place value period.

17. 24,900,000   **18.** 421,100,000   **19.** 8,711,000   **20.** 19,000

Estimate. Name the technique you used.

21. $32 + 26 + 73$ **22.** $42 \cdot 830$ **23.** $97 \cdot 87$

Find the value of each expression. Use the basic properties and mental math.

24. $13.4 \cdot 0 \cdot 8.6$ **25.** $(13 + 7) \cdot (7 + 13)$ **26.** $1.2 \cdot 10 + 6$

Data Collection and Analysis
Group Decision Making

UNDERSTAND
ANALYZE DATA
PLAN
ESTIMATE
SOLVE
EXAMINE

Doing a Survey

Group Skill:
Check for Understanding

Your school newspaper is researching an article on environmental concerns. Your group is in charge of taking a survey of people in your area to find what issues concern them.

Collecting Data

1. Make a list of environmental concerns such as energy conservation, destruction of rain forests, and toxic waste.

2. Decide upon the four issues your group feels are most important.

3. Ask at least 20 adults and 20 teenagers to select the environmental concern from your list that they feel is most important. Record the responses in a table.

Organizing Data

4. Make a double bar graph using the data from your table.

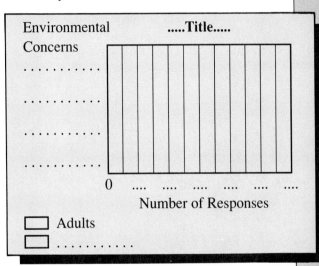

5. Did you title and label all the parts of your graph?

56

6. Write a summary of your findings. Did adults and teenagers have similar concerns about the environment? If their opinions differ, can you think of some reasons why this might be?

WRAP UP

Statistics Word Match

Match each phrase on the left with one or more letters on the right.

1. Sum of values divided by the number of values
2. Often used to represents parts of a whole
3. Middle number in a set of data
4. Difference between two numbers on a scale
5. Special kind of bar graph
6. Tells how many times each data value occurs
7. Way of organizing data
8. Value that occurs the most times

a. circle graph
b. histogram
c. mean
d. mode
e. interval width
f. median
g. stem and leaf plot
h. frequency table

Sometimes, Always, Never

Which of these words should go in the blank: *sometimes*, *always*, or *never*? Explain your choice.

9. A line graph is __?__ the best way to show data.
10. The mean, median, and mode for a set of data are __?__ the same number.
11. The median is __?__ the smallest value in a set of data.

Project

Find two different kinds of graphs in a magazine or newspaper. Write a paragraph explaining what they are supposed to show, and why they are good or bad graphs.

POWER PRACTICE/TEST

Part 1 Understanding

1. Sarah surveyed students to find out what they earned on afterschool jobs. Which graphs would best show her results?

   A circle graph or bar graph   B line graph or circle graph

   C bar graph or line graph   D line graph, circle graph or bar graph

2. In which stem in the stem and leaf plot at right are there more values?

   A 100s   B 200s   C 300s

Stem	Leaf
1	15, 24, 11, 37, 47, 12
2	13, 57, 13, 59
3	72, 43, 12, 26, 45

Part 2 Skills

3. Evaluate $2x - 3.1$ for $x = 2.2$

4. Construct a frequency table and histogram for the set of data
   2, 4, 10, 2, 2, 16, 2, 10, 16, 2, 10, 2.

5. Construct a box and whisker graph for the set of data: 11, 12, 21, 27, 39, 40, 44, 52, 59, 63, 75, 80.

6. Find the mean, median, and mode for the set of data
   1, 4, 5, 6, 3, 8, 6, 5, 7, 6, 9, 1.

7. Find the mean to the correct number of significant digits for the set of data
   3.2, 4.8, 5.7, 1.9, 0.3.

8. Construct a divided bar graph using the information in the table below.

   Favorite Yogurt Flavors

	Adults	Children
vanilla	275	150
chocolate	325	260
strawberry	115	130

9. What percent of the students surveyed said they prefer English or history?

Part 3 Application

10. Bart wants a $150 bike. Each week he earns $30 and spends $10. How soon will he save enough for the bike?

11. **Challenge** Make a frequency table and histogram for the data listed at the right. Use an interval width of $1.00.

Bookstore Sales

$0.59	$2.12	$0.75	$1.16
$0.25	$0.90	$1.52	$0.75
$2.00	$0.30	$0.85	$1.00
$1.25	$0.95	$1.25	$0.50

59

ENRICHMENT
Finding a Sample Mean

Imagine that you have been hired by a school to choose books for students. One of the ways you evaluate a book's level of reading difficulty is by the length of the words. How can you find the mean number of letters per word in a particular selection?

Instead of counting the number of letters in every word, you can take a 10-word random sample. Then you can compute the mean number of letters per word in the sample.

In the selection at right (A), the first 100 words have been numbered. B is a computer-generated list of random numbers. You can take a random sample by finding the words in the selection that correspond to the numbers in the first row of the computer-generated list (C).

1. What is the mean number of words in the 10-word sample?

2. Choose another row in the table and take a 10-word sample. What is the mean number of words in this sample?

3. What do you estimate the mean number of letters per word to be for the entire selection?

4. Suppose that you did not have a computer-generated list of random numbers. How else might you choose a random sample of words from the article?

5. Suppose that you had a much longer selection and wanted to find the mean number of words per sentence. How might you go about doing this?

A.

1 2   3 4 5 6 7   8   9 10   11 12
A twelve-year-old boy of one hundred years ago might be

13   14   15 16 17 18   19   20   21 22 23 24 25
shaken awake at four in the morning. He would get up in the

26   27   28   29 30 31 32   33 34 35 36 37   38
dark, dash cold water on his face, stuff a roll in his pocket,

39 40 41 42 43 44 45   46 47 48 49 50 51   52 53
and set off to walk the three miles or so to the factory or the

54 55 56 57   58   59   60   61 62 63 64   65 66
mill or the mine. Before dawn, he would be at work. In the

67 68 69 70 71 72   73   74 75 76 77 78 79 80
middle of the day, he would have half an hour to eat his roll.

81 82   83   84   85 86 87   88   89 90   91
When he finished his work, it would already be dark. He

92   93   94   95   96   97   98 99   100
would work every day except Christmas. He might earn . . .

B. **Computer-Generated Random Numbers 1 to 100**

23	77	30	9	11	78	40	29	96	85
56	75	75	51	72	45	76	87	61	74
18	57	49	8	76	20	41	32	66	80
4	59	11	17	99	60	26	31	10	81
38	94	22	35	27	62	34	77	18	57
70	21	81	23	93	62	27	4	69	45
43	74	93	29	67	99	21	62	42	15
92	47	30	4	60	97	81	35	5	69
40	38	68	62	33	71	32	50	70	10
66	28	35	2	61	3	74	72	66	81

C. **Random Numbers**

Random number	Word	Number of letters
23	up	2
77	to	2
30	on	2
9	years	5
11	might	5
78	eat	3
40	set	3
29	water	5
96	except	6
85	work	4
		Total 37

CUMULATIVE REVIEW

1. Subtract.
   837,416 − 72,549

   A 764,867   B 15,877

   C 909,975   D 764,875

2. Divide.
   28,531 ÷ 342

   A 90 R251   B 80 R171

   C 83 R145   D 92 R91

3. Name a radius.

   A $\overline{AB}$

   B $\overline{OA}$

   C $\overline{CD}$

   D $\overline{EF}$

4. Express 23,500,000 in terms of its largest place value period name.

   A 235 million   B 235 thousand

   C 23.5 million   D 23.5 billion

5. Which property is shown by the equation $3 \cdot (4 + 8) = (3 \cdot 4) + (3 \cdot 8)$?

   A Associative Property

   B Identity for Addition

   C Identity for Multiplication

   D Distributive Property

6. Burgers cost 89¢ each. What mental math technique would be best to use to determine the cost of 5 burgers?

   A Breaking apart

   B Compensation

   C Compatible numbers

   D Counting on

7. Use the order of operations to find the value of $7 \cdot (3 − 1) + 2$.

   A 22   B 16

   C 18   D 28

8. For which item is an estimate acceptable?

   A Amount of tax owed

   B Amount earned per week

   C Average of student's test scores during a grading period

   D Miles per hour during a 2-day trip

9. Which type of graph would be most appropriate to show the change in rainfall amounts during the past 10 summers?

   A Bar graph   B Divided bar graph

   C Line graph   D Circle graph

10. Find the median of the data given in this frequency table.

Value	Frequency
3	4
5	2
7	1
9	5

    A 7   B 9

    C 5   D 6

11. During this week, Joe consumed the following numbers of calories each day: 2,560, 2,400, 2,320, 2,510, 2,500, 2,290, and 2,650. Find the mean of this data to the correct number of significant digits.

    A 2460   B 2461.4

    C 2461   D 2500

3

AREA AND VOLUME

THEME: LOST CITIES

MATH AND
SOCIAL STUDIES

DATA BANK

Use the Social Studies Data Bank on page 496 to answer the questions.

1 How old is the Pyramid of the Sun?

What is the area of the base of the Pyramid of the Sun?

 What is the total length of the Great Ball Court at Chichén Itzá, Mexico?

Using Critical Thinking
Draw the side view of the Pyramid of the Sun.

The Pyramid of the Sun was a center of ceremonies in the ancient city of Teotihuacan.

63

Area

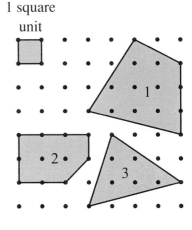

1 square
unit

LEARN ABOUT IT

EXPLORE Use Dot Paper

Work in groups. Draw these three polygons on
dot paper. See how many ways you can divide
regions **1** and **2** into rectangles and triangles.

TALK ABOUT IT

1. Which region can be divided into 5 square units
and 1 triangle?

2. Which region can be divided into three triangles and one
2×2 square?

3. Show that region 3 can be described as 1 large rectangle
minus 3 triangles.

Some triangles are exactly half of a
rectangle. The area of triangle (a) is 2
square units. The area of triangle (b)
is $4\frac{1}{2}$ square units.

To find the area of an irregularly
shaped region, divide the region into
triangles and rectangles, if possible.
Find the areas of the triangles and
rectangles, then add them together.

(a)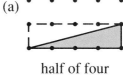

half of four
square units

(b)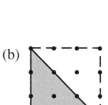

half of nine square units

(c)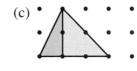

Area = 1 + 2
= 3 square units

(d)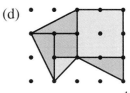

Area = $4 + 4 \cdot 1 + \frac{1}{2}$
= $8\frac{1}{2}$ square units

TRY IT OUT

Draw each region on dot paper and divide it into rectangles and
triangles. Find the area of each region.

1.

2.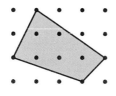

3.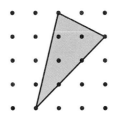

4.

Draw each region on dot paper. Find the area of each region.

1.   **2.** 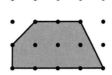 **3.** 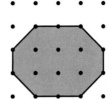 **4.**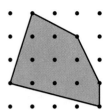

5. 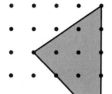 **6.** 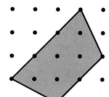 **7.** 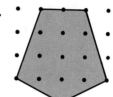 **8.**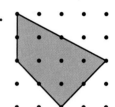

APPLY

MATH REASONING Estimate which region of the pair has the greater area.

9. (a) (b) 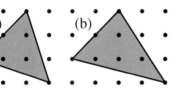 **10.** (a) (b)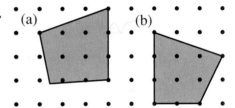

PROBLEM SOLVING

11. Suppose you are asked to estimate the area of this lake. Draw a polygon that approximates the boundary of the lake and find the area of the polygon.

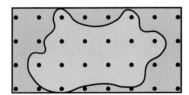

12. Be a Problem Finder Write two problems that you can solve using this figure.

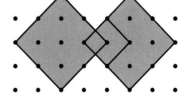

▶ **ESTIMATION**

13. Use estimation to order these regions from smallest to largest.

(a) (b) (c)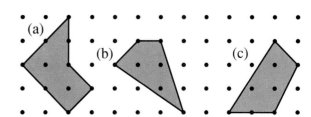

More Practice, page 524, set D

Area of Polygons

LEARN ABOUT IT

EXPLORE **Study the Situation**

Archaeologists excavate for ruins from previous cultures. Working on a site, or dig, is slow and expensive, so surveyors try to outline the site to be excavated as precisely as possible.

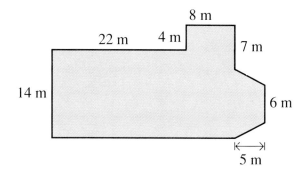

TALK ABOUT IT

1. How can you divide the dig into 2 rectangles and a trapezoid?

2. How long is the longer base of the trapezoid shaped region?

3. What is the area, in square meters, of each rectangular region?

The figures below show how the formulas for the area of a parallelogram, a triangle and a trapezoid are developed.

The area (A) of a parallelogram is equal to the area of the associated rectangle.	The area (A) of a triangle is half the area of the associated parallelogram.	The area (A) of a trapezoid is half the area of the associated parallelogram.

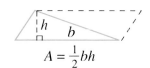

$A = bh$ $A = \frac{1}{2}bh$ $A = \frac{1}{2}(b_1 + b_2)h$

To find the area of the dig, first find the area of the trapezoid.
$A = \frac{1}{2}(6 + 11) \cdot 5 = 42.5$ Add the areas of the rectangles and the trapezoid. $A = (4 \cdot 8) + (14 \cdot 30) + 42.5$
$= 32 + 420 + 42.5 = 494.5$. The area of the dig is 494.5 m².

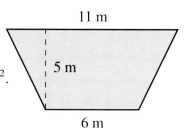

TRY IT OUT

Find the area of each polygon.

1.

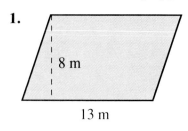

8 m

13 m

2.

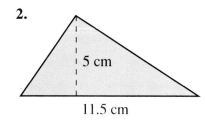

5 cm

11.5 cm

3.

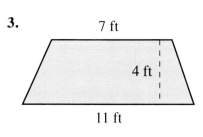

7 ft

4 ft

11 ft

Find the area of each polygon.

1. 3 cm   2 cm

2. 3.5 ft   7.1 ft

3. 4.5 in.   6.5 in.

4. 5 cm   11 cm

5. 5 m   4 m   8 m

6. 15.5 in.   7 in.

7. 7.1 ft   12 ft   18 ft

8. 5 cm   3 cm   7 cm   12 cm

MATH REASONING

9. Estimate the area of a trapezoidal shaped field with bases 277.64 m and 319.71 m and height 197.8 m by rounding each length to the nearest 10 m.

PROBLEM SOLVING

10. When archaeologists have outlined a site, they set up a grid system to help chart the location of structures and artifacts. This diagram shows the aerial view of a dig. Each square on the grid has an area of 5 m². What is the area of the dig?

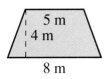

11. Social Studies Data Bank Many Mayan sites include courts for playing a ball game. What is the area of the ceremonial court in Chichén Itzá?

DATA BANK

12. Arrange the numbers in order from smallest to largest.

21.4 thousand   8.1 million   81.32 thousand   4.01 billion

Find the missing value. Name the property used.

13. ▦ × 2.1 = 2.1   **14.** ▦ × 0 = 0   **15.** 9 · (8 + 2) = (▦ · 8) + (▦ · 2)

Evaluate. Use mental math when possible.

16. 2.8 + 3.1n for n = 20   **17.** 24.6 − t + t for t = 18.25

Area of Circles

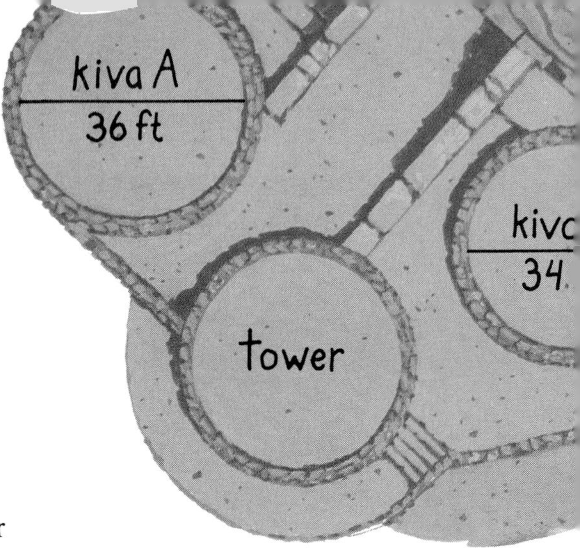

kiva A
_____
36 ft

kiva
___
34

tower

EXPLORE Study the Situation

At Mesa Verde in Colorado, Pueblo Indians
built the Cliff Palace, a multi-storied building
with about 200 rooms. It includes a tower and circular
underground rooms called kivas. Could it be that the Pueblos
discussed that the ratio $\frac{C}{d}$ is constant? What is this numerical value?

TALK ABOUT IT

1. What are the radius and diameter of
kiva A?

2. Use the formula $C = \pi d$ to find the
circumference of kiva B. Use 3.14 for π.

Here is why $A = \pi r^2$ is a reasonable formula for the area of a circle.

**A circle is divided
into equal parts.**

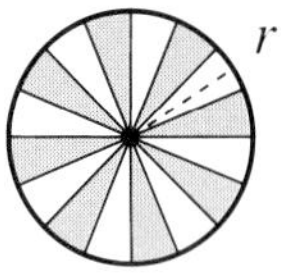

The parts fit together to form a shape like a parallelogram.

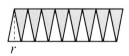

This figure has the same area as the circle.
The base is equal to half the circumference $\left(\frac{1}{2}\pi d = \pi r\right)$
and the height is equal to the radius (r).

The area of the figure above is approximately equal to the base
times the height. $A = \pi r \cdot r = \pi r^2$.

What are the areas of kiva A and kiva B?

Area of kiva A
$A = \pi \cdot 18^2 = \pi \cdot 324$
$\approx 3.14 \cdot 324 = 1{,}017.36$

Area of kiva B
$A = \pi \cdot 17^2 = \pi \cdot 289$
$\approx 3.14 \cdot 289 = 907.46$

The area of kiva A is about 1,017.36 ft^2 and of kiva B is about
907.46 ft^2.

What is the floor area of each of these kivas? Use 3.14 for π.

1. $r = 15$ ft **2.** $d = 6$ m **3.** $r = 2$ m **4.** $d = 20$ ft

68

Find the area of each circle. Use 3.14 for π. Round answers to the nearest hundredth. You may want to use your calculator.

1. $r = 3$ cm   2. $r = 22$ m   3. $d = 18$ km   4. $d = 34$ in.

5. $r = 10$ cm   6. $r = 0.1$ m   7. $d = 6.4$ ft   8. $d = 10$ cm

9. $r = 0.6$ m   10. $d = 23.4$ ft   11. $r = 3.6$ in.   12. $d = 7.2$ cm

13. $r = 13.5$ ft   14. $d = 204.6$ m   15. $d = 34.68$ m   16. $r = 19$ in.

17. $d = 21.7$ cm   18. $d = 4.8$ m   19. $r = .7$ ft   20. $r = 2.2$ km

21. Find the area of a circle with a diameter of 12 m.

22. Find the area of a circle with a diameter of 2.7 in.

MATH REASONING Find the area and circumference of each circle using mental math. Give your answers in terms of π.

23. $d = 4$ m   24. $r = 3$ in.   25. $d = 8$ cm

PROBLEM SOLVING

26. One of the smallest circular kivas at Pueblo Bonito is 8 feet across. One of the largest is 47 feet across. What is the difference in the floor area between the two kivas?

27. **Extra Data** At Chichén Itzá, Mexico, there is an astronomical observatory built by Mayans. It has a round tower 41 feet high and 37 feet in diameter. What is the area of the base?

28. **Social Studies Data Bank** What would the diameter of a circle be if the area of the circle was equal to the area of the base of the Pyramid of the Sun?

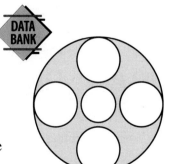

▶ **CALCULATOR**

29. This disc has a 30 cm diameter. The circular cutout at the center has a diameter of 8 cm, and the four other cutouts each have a diameter of 10 cm. Use a calculator to find the area of the shaded region.

Exploring Algebra
Variables in Geometry

EXPLORE **Study the Information**

This lesson combines formulas you already know to find the area and perimeter of more complex figures. The area of a frame can be obtained by finding the difference of the areas of the outer and inner rectangles.

TALK ABOUT IT

1. Which expression gives the area of the frame: LW, lw, or $LW - lw$?

2. What is the area of the outer rectangle if $L = 35$ cm and $W = 20$ cm?

3. What is the area of the inner rectangle if $l = 30$ cm and $w = 15$ cm?

4. Find the area of the outer rectangle minus the area of the inner rectangle.

Known formulas are often combined to write expressions for the perimeter and area of other figures. Sometimes a calculator may help.

Example Find the perimeter of the track shown. Evaluate for $l = 125$ yards and $w = 60$ yards.

$l + \dfrac{1}{2}\pi w + l + \dfrac{1}{2}\pi w$ gives the perimeter

$125 + \dfrac{1}{2}\pi \cdot 60 + 125 + \dfrac{1}{2}\pi \cdot 60$

$= 125 \boxed{+} 0.5 \boxed{\times} \pi \boxed{\times} 60 \boxed{+} 125 \boxed{+} 0.5 \boxed{\times} \pi \boxed{\times} 60$

≈ 438.4 The perimeter of the track is about 438.4 yards.

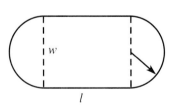

1. Write an expression for the area of the square picture frame with a circular opening.

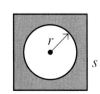

2. Find the area of the picture frame if $s = 10$ in. and $r = 4$ in. Use 3.14 for π.

Choose the expression for the area of the shaded region in each figure. Curves are circles or half-circles.

1.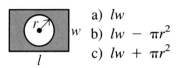
    a) lw
    b) $lw - \pi r^2$
    c) $lw + \pi r^2$

2.
    a) s^2
    b) πs^2
    c) $\pi r^2 - s^2$

Find the perimeter of each figure to the nearest hundredth. Curves are circles or half circles. Use 3.14 for π.

3.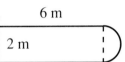

4.

5.

6.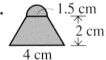

Find the area of the shaded region of each figure to the nearest hundredth. Curves are circles or half circles. Use 3.14 for π.

7.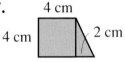

8.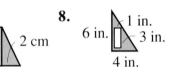

9.

10.

MATH REASONING

11. The expression lw represents the area of a rectangle. Does this expression sometimes, always, or never represent an odd number?

PROBLEM SOLVING

12. A record has a radius R that is 15 cm to the outer edge. The radius r to the point where the grooves begin is 7 cm. Write an expression for the area of the grooved part of the record.

▶ **MENTAL MATH**

Find the area of the shaded region of each figure.

13.

14.

Problem Solving
Using the Strategies

UNDERSTAND
ANALYZE DATA
PLAN
ESTIMATE
SOLVE
EXAMINE

This problem can be solved in more than one way. Rob used **Guess and Check.** Margo used the strategy **Draw a Picture.**

> Some eighth grade students and teachers went to the Architectural History Museum to see an exhibit on famous structures. Student tickets were $3 and adult tickets were $4. They spent $39 for 12 tickets. How many students went to the exhibit?

Rob's solution:

Try 5 students and 7 adults	$5 \cdot 3 + 7 \cdot 4$ $15 + 28 = 43$	too much.
Try 10 students and 2 adults	$10 \cdot 3 + 2 \cdot 4$ $30 + 8 = 38$	not enough.
Try 9 students and 3 adults	$9 \cdot 3 + 3 \cdot 4$ $27 + 12 = 39$	

Margo's solution:

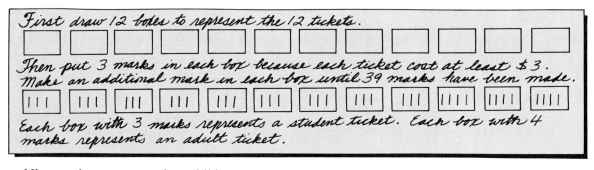

First draw 12 boxes to represent the 12 tickets.

Then put 3 marks in each box because each ticket cost at least $3. Make an additional mark in each box until 39 marks have been made.

Each box with 3 marks represents a student ticket. Each box with 4 marks represents an adult ticket.

Nine students went to the exhibit.

TRY IT OUT

Solve. Use Guess and Check or Draw a Picture.

1. A group of 54 students from Franklin Junior High went to see the World Trade Center. They rode in 10 vehicles. The cars could take 5 students each and the station wagons 7 students each. How many station wagons did they use?

2. At the Architectural History Museum, the students were given some blocks to build a model of a pyramid. Each wall of the model has 66 blocks and was a triangle with 1 less block in each row than in the row below it. How many blocks should they put in the bottom row?

Solve. Use any problem solving strategy.

Some Strategies	
Act Out	Solve a Simpler Problem
Use Objects	Make an Organized List
Choose an Operation	Work Backward
Draw a Picture	Look for a Pattern
Guess and Check	Use Logical Reasoning
Make a Table	Write an Equation

1. The largest pyramid ever built is Quetzalcoatl, 63 miles southeast of Mexico City. Its total volume is estimated at 4.3 million cubic yards. The volume of the Pyramid of Cheops in Egypt is 3.36 million cubic yards. How much greater is the volume of Quetzalcoatl?

2. The Pyramid of Cheops contains over 2 million blocks. The average weight of each block is 2.5 tons. If it takes 11 adults to move 1 ton, about how many adults will it take to move one of the blocks?

755 ft   755 ft   450 ft

3. Use the diagram of the pyramid to find the area of its square base.

4. Lamar is reading a book about the great pyramids. The book is 87 pages long. He finished the book in 6 days. He read 3 more pages each day than the day before. How many pages did Lamar read the first day?

5. The museum has large square tables that will seat 3 people on each side. They put them together to make one long table for 36 students. How many tables did they use?

6. The area of a rectangle is 2,100 m^2. Its width is 8 m less than its length. Find the dimensions of the rectangle.

7. Mrs. Ardito bought 42 cans of juice for a field trip to the Alamo. Apple-raspberry juice comes in 4-packs. Pineapple-orange comes in 6-packs. How many cans of each kind of juice did she purchase?

8. It is believed that the Great Wall of China was originally over 6,200 miles long. Much of it has been destroyed. Today the main wall is 2,150 miles long with additional branches of 1,780 miles. How much has been destroyed?

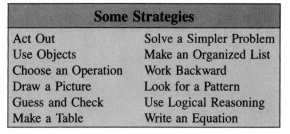

73

Using Critical Thinking

Joe's math teacher posted this description on the bulletin board and challenged the class to put regular polygons together to make regular polyhedra. "You can see," she said as she put 3 equilateral triangles together, "to make a polyhedron, you first have to be able to fit regular polygons together at a corner to make what I call a 3-dimensional roof."

"I've made a regular polyhedron by putting two roofs together," Joe said.

"I'm working on a polyhedron with a roof made from 3 regular hexagons," said Francisco. "It could be pretty large!"

"I hate to tell you this," Aretha said with a smile, "but you guys are both out of it!"

A **regular polyhedron** is a closed space figure made of regular polygons that are arranged the same at each vertex.

TALK ABOUT IT

1. Can you give an example of a regular polyhedron?

2. Do you think the figure Joe is making is really a regular polyhedron? Use your models to explain.

3. Do you think Francisco can make a regular polyhedron as he has described? Explain your thinking.

TRY IT OUT

Use models to help answer the following.

Which of the following can be made into 3-dimensional roofs?

1. 3 equilateral triangles? 4? 5? 6?

2. 3 squares? 4? more than 4?

3. 3 regular pentagons? more than 3?

4. 3 regular hexagons? more than 3?

5. When can a 3-dimensional roof be made from a certain regular polygon?

6. Describe some regular polyhedra that can be made using the roofs you found in Exercises 1–4.

POWER PRACTICE/QUIZ

Draw each region on dot paper. Divide the region into triangles and rectangles and find the area of the region.

1.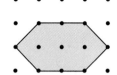

2.

3.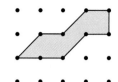

Find the area of each polygon.

4.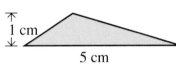
2 in.
4 in.

5. 1 cm
5 cm

6. 2.5 ft
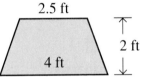
4 ft
2 ft

Find the area and circumference of each circle. Use 3.14 for π.

7. $r = 10$ m   **8.** $d = 2.3$ in.   **9.** $d = 5$ cm   **10.** $r = 14$ ft

Find the area of the shaded region to the nearest hundredth. Use 3.14 for π.

11.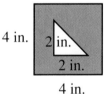
4 in.   2 in.
2 in.
4 in.

12.
6 m

13.
3 ft   5 ft
4 ft

Find the perimeter of each figure to the nearest hundredth. Use 3.14 for π.

14.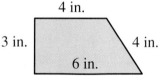
4 in.
3 in.   4 in.
6 in.

15.
2 ft
2 ft

16.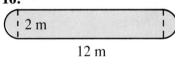
2 m
12 m

PROBLEM SOLVING

17. A circular pool has a diameter of 10 m. It is surrounded by a wooden deck that is 20 m long and 15 m wide. What is the area of the deck?

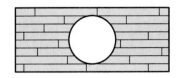

18. A circle with a diameter of 8 cm can be placed inside a trapezoid as shown. What is the area of the trapezoid?

6 cm
10 cm   10 cm
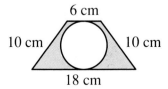
18 cm

75

Surface Area

LEARN ABOUT IT

EXPLORE **Analyze the Situation**

Eileen Monaghan is a designer of cereal boxes which are made by folding a single piece of cardboard. She needs to decide what size rectangle is needed to make one box. What size piece would you order?

TALK ABOUT IT

1. What is the area of the front of the box?

2. Can the box be made from a 21 in. × 12 in. piece of cardboard?

3. What is the total area of all six pieces of the box?

The total area of the cut apart box is called the **surface area** of the box. In a similar way we define the surface area of any **space figure** or **solid** such as a prism, a cylinder and a pyramid. Imagine cutting each apart and laying it flat. This process is demonstrated for the cylinder.

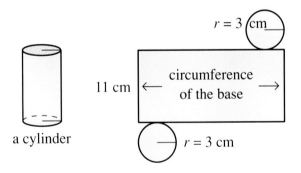

a cylinder

Area of each circle $= \pi \cdot 3^2 \approx 28.26 \text{ cm}^2$
Area of the rectangle $= 2\pi \cdot 3 \cdot 11$
$\approx 207.24 \text{ cm}^2$
Surface Area $\approx 2 \cdot 28.26 + 207.24$
$= 263.76 \text{ cm}^2$

TRY IT OUT

1. Find the area of the front face of this rectangular prism.

2. Find the area of the top face of the prism.

3. Find the surface area of the prism.

4. Find the surface area of a cylinder with a base radius 4 cm and a height of 5 cm.

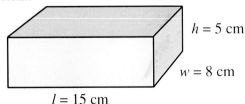

$h = 5$ cm

$w = 8$ cm

$l = 15$ cm

1. Which is the pattern for this prism?

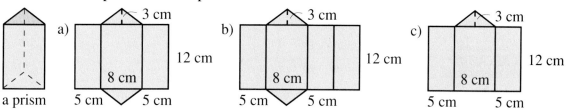

a prism

2. Find the surface area of the prism above.

Find the surface area of each rectangular prism.

3.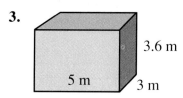

4.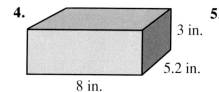

5.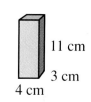

Find the surface area of each cylinder. Use 3.14 for π.

6.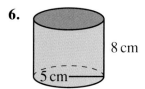

7.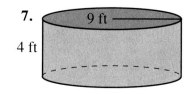

8.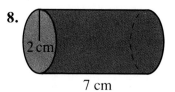

MATH REASONING

9. Compare a cube and a pyramid with identical square bases and the same height. Estimate which one has the greater surface area.

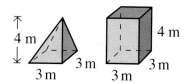

PROBLEM SOLVING

10. Steel barrels with a base radius of 2 ft and a height of 3 ft are to be painted on the outside. If one gallon of paint covers 200 ft^2, how many barrels can be painted with one gallon of paint?

▶ **ALGEBRA**

11. A rectangular prism has length l, width w, and height h. Which formula can be used to find the surface area S of a rectangular prism?

a) $S = lwh$ b) $S = 2wl + 2hw + 2hl$ c) $S = l + w + h$

More Practice, page 525, set C

Comparing Surface Area and Volume

EXPLORE **Study the Information**

Some questions about a container relate to the amount of surface on the container and other questions relate to the amount the container will hold. That's the distinction between **surface area** and **volume.**

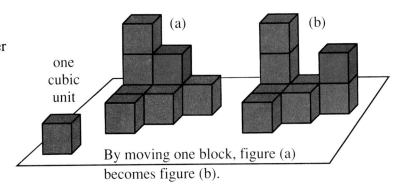

one cubic unit

By moving one block, figure (a) becomes figure (b).

TALK ABOUT IT

1. How does the volume of figure (a) compare with the volume of figure (b)?

2. Moving the shaded cube from one position to another changes the surface area by how many square units?

3. Estimate which building has the greater surface area.

The surface area is the number of square units on the surface of a solid. The volume of a solid is the number of cubic units needed to make the solid. A cubic unit is a cube with edges one unit in length. To find the volume of some solids, you can count the number of cubic units in the solid.

To find the volume, count

To find the surface area, count

The volume is 5 cubic units

The surface area is 22 square units

TRY IT OUT

Find the volume and the surface area of each of these solids.

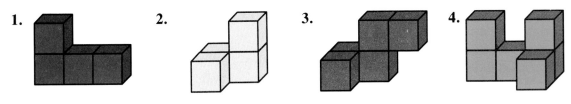

1.   2.   3.   4.

Find the volume and surface area of each of these figures.

1.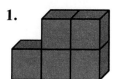

2.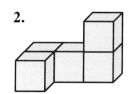

3.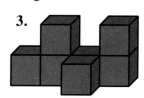

4.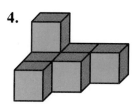

Find the volume of each of these figures.

5.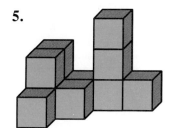

6.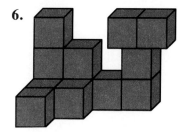

7.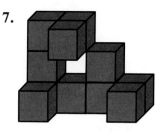

8.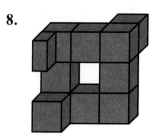

9.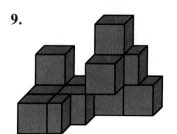

10.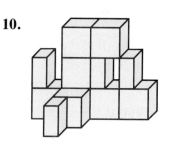

MATH REASONING

11. Order these figures at right from smallest to largest in volume and then in surface area.

(a)

PROBLEM SOLVING

12. How can you change the position of one cube in figure (b) and reduce the surface area by 4 square units?

(b) (c)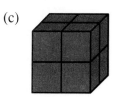

▶ **USING CRITICAL THINKING   Discover a Pattern**

13. Given twelve cubes, draw the figure with the smallest surface area. What is the surface area of the figure?

More Practice, page 525, set D

Volume of Prisms and Cylinders

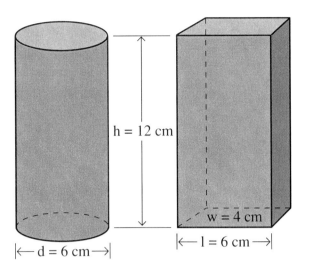

LEARN ABOUT IT

EXPLORE Analyze the Situation

A manufacturer needs to decide whether to use a **cylinder** or a **rectangular prism** for a fruit juice container. Suppose the two containers have the same height and the length of the box equals the diameter of the can. Estimate which container holds more.

TALK ABOUT IT

1. Which is greater, the base area of the cylinder or the base area of the prism?

2. Do you still believe your estimate?

You can find the volume of many containers using the formula *V = Bh,* where *B* is the area of the base and *h* is the height of the container.

Examples

A For a box or rectangular prism, $B = lw$ so
$V = lwh.$
$V = 6 \cdot 4 \cdot 12 = 288$
The volume of the box, or rectangular prism, is 288 cm³.

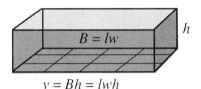

$v = Bh = lwh$

B For a can or cylinder $B = \pi r^2$ so $V = \pi r^2 h.$
$V = \pi \cdot 3^2 \cdot 12 = 108\,\pi$
$V \approx 3.14 \cdot 108 \approx 339.12$ Use 3.14 for π.
The volume of the can, or cylinder, is 339.12 cm³.

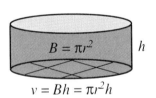

$v = Bh = \pi r^2 h$

TRY IT OUT

Find the volume of each of these space figures. Use 3.14 for π.

1.  $h = 5$ cm
$l = 15$ cm $w = 7$ cm

2. 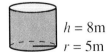 $h = 8m$
$r = 5m$

3. 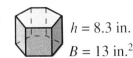 $h = 8.3$ in.
$B = 13$ in.²

4. Find the volume of a rectangular prism with $l = 5.5$ cm, $w = 3.2$ cm, and $h = 9$ cm.

Find the volume of each prism or cylinder. Use 3.14 for π.

1. 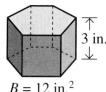 3 in.

$B = 12$ in.^{2}

2.   18 mm

5 mm

3 mm

3. 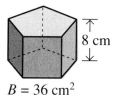 8 cm

$B = 36$ cm^2

4. 2.0 ft

$\longleftarrow$ 18.4 ft $\longrightarrow$

Find the volume of each rectangular prism.

5. $l = 18$ cm
$w = 5$ cm
$h = 2$ cm

6. $l = 3$ m
$w = 2$ m
$h = 14$ m

7. $l = 21.4$ in.
$w = 2.8$ in.
$h = 4.5$ in.

Find the volume of each cylinder to the nearest hundredth.
Use 3.14 for π.

8. $r = 6$ ft
$h = 3$ ft

9. $r = 3$ in.
$h = 12$ in.

10. $r = 2.4$ cm
$h = 23.7$ cm

APPLY

MATH REASONING

11. A square based prism and a cylinder have the same
volume. The radius of the base of the cylinder is equal to
the length of the prism. Which is taller?

PROBLEM SOLVING

12. What is the volume of concrete needed
to make a sidewalk 20 m long, 1.5 m
wide, and 0.15 m thick?

13. The circumference of a cylindrical
water tank is 25 ft and its height is 30
ft. What is the volume of the tank to
the nearest cubic foot?

 MIXED REVIEW

Evaluate. Use mental math when possible.

14. $180 \div 3.2\,a$ for $a = 6$

15. $4b \div 3 - 1$ for $b = 9$

16. $\dfrac{96}{k} - 4.7$ for $k = 3$

17. Find the mean for the scores.

18. Find the median for the scores.

19. Find the mode for the scores.

Quiz Score	Frequency
10	3
9	8
8	10
7	5
4	4

More Practice, page 526, set A

Volume of Pyramids and Cones

EXPLORE **Use Plastic Space Figures**
Work in groups. Compare a cone and
cylinder with the same radius and height.
Fill the cone with water, then pour the water
into the cylinder. Do this until the cylinder
is full.

TALK ABOUT IT

1. How many cones full of water does it take
   to fill the cylinder?

The volume of a cylinder with base area B and height h is $V = Bh$.
A cone with the same base and height has the volume $V = \frac{1}{3}Bh$.

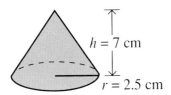
$h = 7$ cm
$r = 2.5$ cm

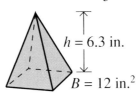
$h = 6.3$ in.
$B = 12$ in.^{2}

Find the volumes of the cone and pyramid above.

$V = \frac{1}{3}\pi r^2 h$

$V = \frac{1}{3}\pi \cdot 2.5^2 \cdot 7$

$V \approx \frac{1}{3} \cdot 3.14 \cdot 6.25 \cdot 7$

$V \approx 45.79$ cm^3

$V = \frac{1}{3}Bh$

$V = \frac{1}{3} \cdot 12 \cdot 6.3$

$V = 25.2$ in.^{3}

TRY IT OUT

Find the volume of each space figure to the nearest hundredth.
Use 3.14 for π.

1.

9 cm
4 cm

2.

8.2 m
$B = 90$ m^2

3.
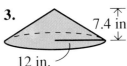
7.4 in.
12 in.

4.
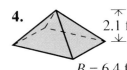
2.1 ft
$B = 6.4$ ft^2

82

Find the volume of each space figure to the nearest hundredth.
Use 3.14 for π. You may want to use your calculator.

1. 6 cm 2 cm

2. 10 in. $B = 8 \text{ in.}^2$

3. 3.1 ft 2 ft

4. 3.8 m $B = 7 \text{ m}^2$

5. 5.6 ft $B = 27.1 \text{ ft}^2$

6. 9.8 m 4.4 m

7. 5.6 in. 10.2 in.

8. 5.5 cm $B = 30.4 \text{ cm}^2$

9. Find the volume of a cone with a radius of 8 cm and a height of 5.1 cm.

MATH REASONING

10. A cone and a cylinder have the same base. If the cone's height is 6 times the height of the cylinder, how much greater is the volume of the cone?

PROBLEM SOLVING

11. The Apollo spacecraft which took N. Armstrong, E. Aldrin, and M. Collins to the moon and back is cone shaped. It is 13 ft in diameter and about 8.9 ft high. About how much space was there per crew member, to the nearest cubic foot?

8.9 ft

13 ft

12. The Great Pyramid in Egypt was originally approximately 137 m high and 220 m on each side of its square base. What was the volume of this pyramid?

▶ **USE CRITICAL THINKING**   **Discover the Pattern**

13. Spheres are stacked up in successively larger pyramids. Count the number of spheres in each stack. Find the pattern and give the next 3 numbers.

More Practice, page 526, set B

Problem Solving
Estimating the Answer

| UNDERSTAND |
| ANALYZE DATA |
| PLAN |
| ESTIMATE |
| SOLVE |
| EXAMINE |

LEARN ABOUT IT

Before solving a problem, it is important to decide what would
be a reasonable answer. You can do this by estimating the answer.

> Paula is painting the walls and the
> ceiling in her bedroom. She needs to
> know the total area to decide how much
> paint to buy. Use the diagram to find the
> area.

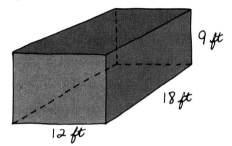

9 ft
18 ft
12 ft

Before solving the problem, estimate the answer.
Begin by rounding each of the dimensions.

12 ft	⟶	10 ft
18 ft	⟶	20 ft
9 ft	⟶	10 ft

Then use the numbers to get an estimate for the total area.

ceiling	$10 \cdot 20 = 200$	200
side walls	$(10 \cdot 20) \cdot 2 = 400$	400
front and back walls	$(10 \cdot 10) \cdot 2 = 200$	+200
The answer should be about 800 ft²		800

Now solve the problem.

ceiling	$12 \cdot 18 = 216$	216
side walls	$(9 \cdot 18) \cdot 2 = 324$	324
front and back walls	$(9 \cdot 12) \cdot 2 = 216$	+216
The answer is 756 ft²		756

756 ft² is a reasonable answer because it is close to 800 ft².

TRY IT OUT

Before solving each problem, estimate the answer. Then solve
the problem and decide if your answer is reasonable. Use 3.14 for π.

1. A cylindrical planter is 18 in. high. The
   radius of its base is 10 in. How many
   cubic inches of dirt will the planter hold?

2. Neil is painting the walls and ceiling in
   the family room. The room is 14 ft wide,
   17 ft long and 8 ft high. Find the total area.

Solve. Use any problem solving strategy.

1. Find the volume of a tropical fish tank that is 6 ft long, $1\frac{1}{2}$ ft wide, and $1\frac{3}{4}$ ft high.

$1\frac{3}{4}$ ft

6 ft

$1\frac{1}{2}$

2. Carmen is planning to purchase fish for her new fish tank. The fish she wants need $1\frac{1}{2}$ ft³ of water each. If her fish tank is 5 ft long, 2 ft wide and $1\frac{1}{2}$ ft high, how many fish can she put in the tank?

3. A rectangular box is twice as long as it is wide. Its height and width are the same. If the volume of the box is 128 in.³, find its dimensions.

4. Jennifer wants to cover an oatmeal box and its lid with fabric. Use the picture to find how many square inches of fabric she will need.

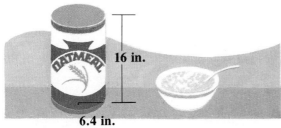

16 in.

6.4 in.

5. Odra has a block of cheese that is 4 in. wide, 6 in. long, and 4 in. high. He wants to cut it into 1-inch cubes. What is the least number of cuts he can make?

6. The Gulf Tower in Houston is 725 ft tall and has 52 stories. About how high is each story?

7. A cylindrical drinking glass is 4 in. high and 2 in. across. If an ounce of juice is about 1.8 in.³, find how many ounces of juice the glass will hold.

JUICE

8. Hung bought 5 rolls of wallpaper. Each roll cost $14.75 including tax. How much did he spend?

9. **Extra Data** This problem has extra data. Tell what data is necessary to solve this problem. Julie bought 2 gallons of paint for $8.95 each and a roller and pan for $6.50. She gave the clerk $30.00. How much did Julie spend?

More Practice, page 544, set C

Applied Problem Solving
Group Decision Making

UNDERSTAND
ANALYZE DATA
PLAN
ESTIMATE
SOLVE
EXAMINE

Group Skill:
Listen to Others

You just brought home a friendly black and white rabbit from the animal shelter. You want to make a pen for your rabbit to protect him.

Facts to Consider

1. The pen will run along one side of a shed, so that side of the pen will not use any fence.

2. The pen will need to be enclosed with with wire fencing on three sides and the top.

3. Your parents will give you 45 feet of fencing to use for the pen. The fencing is 48 inches wide.

4. Your pen should have plenty of room for your rabbit to roam around and a space for a 24″ by 20″ rabbit food box.

Some Questions to Answer

1. If you build a rectangular pen that is 8 feet long and 9 feet wide, would you have enough fencing to build the top of the pen?

2. Suppose you build a pen that is a semi-circle 14 feet in diameter. Would you have enough fencing to build the top of the pen?

3. Would the rectangular pen or the semi-circular pen have the greatest ground area?

4. Besides the area, what other things might you want to consider before building your pen?

What Is Your Decision?

Based on the information you have, draw a picture of the pen your group would build and give its dimensions. Tell how much fencing your pen will use and give the ground area of the pen.

WRAP UP

Formula Language

What does the specified variable represent in each formula?

1. the letter B in the formula $V = \frac{1}{3}Bh$.

2. the letter h in the formula $V = \pi r^2 h$.

3. the letter w when using the formula $A = lw$.

4. the letter r in the formula $A = \pi r^2$.

5. the letter C in the formula $C = 2\pi r$.

6. the letter d in the formula $C = \pi d$.

7. the letter A in the formula $A = bh$.

8. the letter l in the formula $B = lw$.

9. the letter V in the formula $V = \pi r^2 h$.

10. the letter b_1 in the formula $A = \frac{1}{2}(b_1 + b_2)h$.

Sometimes, Always, Never

Which of these words should go in the blank: *sometimes*, *always*, or *never*? Explain your choice.

11. Area is __?__ measured in square units.

12. For a circle, the ratio $\frac{C}{d}$ is __?__ a constant.

13. If a pyramid and a prism have the same height and the same base area, then they will __?__ have the same volume.

Project

Devise a strategy for finding out how many basketballs would fit into your classroom.

POWER PRACTICE/TEST

Part 1   Understanding

1. Choose the expression for the area of the shaded region.

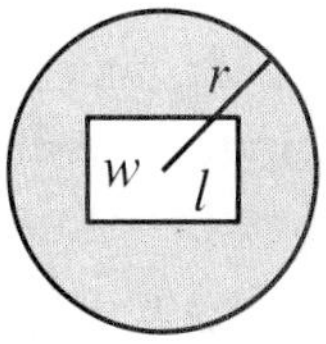

   A πr^2 **B** lw **C** $lw - \pi r^2$ **D** $\pi r^2 - lw$

2. Cube A will be moved and placed on top of cube B. What measure of the solid will change?

   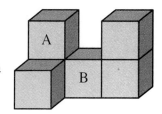

   A volume   **B** surface area

   C volume and surface area   **D** neither volume nor surface area

Part 2   Skills

Find the area of each polygon.

3.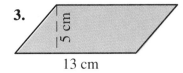

4.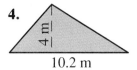

5.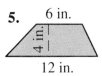

6. Find the area of a circle with a diameter of 10 cm. Use 3.14 for π.

7. Find the area of this region.

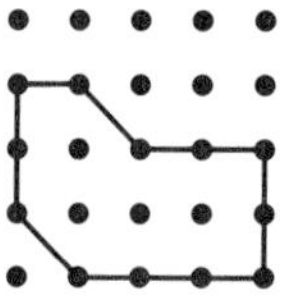

8. Find the volume of this cone.

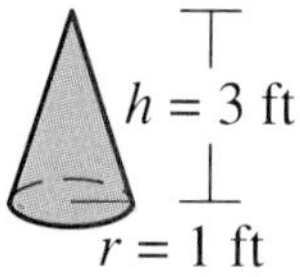

Find the surface area and volume of each figure. Use 3.14 for π.

9.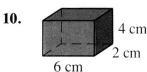

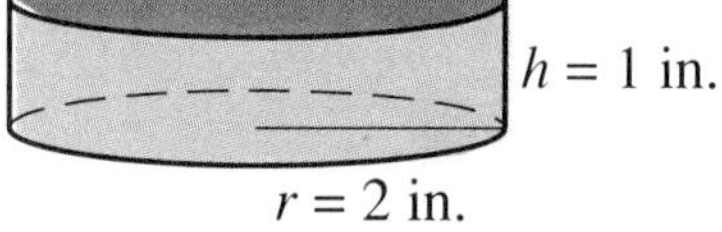

10.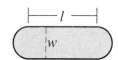

Part 3   Applications

11. The base of a triangle is 2 in. greater than its height. Its area is 24 in². Find the dimensions of the triangle.

12. A cylindrical tank 23 ft high with a 12 ft radius needs paint. A gallon of paint covers 400 ft². How many gallons of paint are needed?

13. **Challenge** The figure at the right shows a pool with half circles at each end. Write an expression for the area of the pool. Find the area if l = 15 ft and w = 18 ft.

89

ENRICHMENT
Front, Top, and End Views

Construction workers, machine operators, architects, and others must often be able to visualize space figures from blueprints or drawings. The drawings frequently show views of the figure from the front, top, and end of the figure.

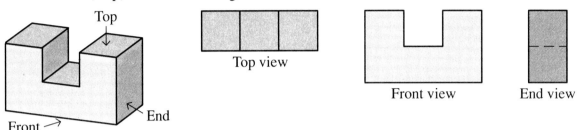

The three views of this U-shaped block show all the features of the block. Dashed lines show edges that exist, but are hidden from the viewer.

Draw front, top, and end views for each of these space figures.

1.   **2.**   **3.**

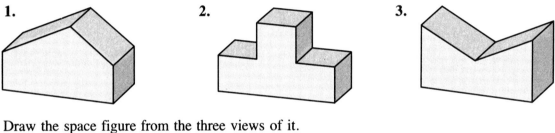

Draw the space figure from the three views of it.

4.

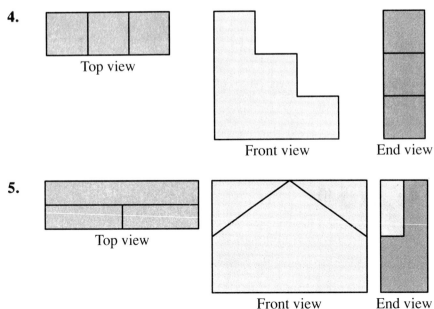

5.

CUMULATIVE REVIEW

1. Add.
$25.03 + $146.28 + $3.46 + $0.82

  A $175.86   **B** $202.59

  C $256.77   **D** $175.59

2. Subtract.
$2,306.00 − $15.84

  A $7.22   **B** $2290.16

  C $38.90   **D** $2311.84

3. Divide.
$40,007 \div 68$

  A 588 R 23   **B** 58 R 53

  C 591 R 19   **D** 556 R 1

4. The equation $d = rt$ gives the distance (d) traveled in terms of rate of speed (r) and time (t). Find the distance traveled if $r = 50$ mph and $t = 7$ h.

  A 300 mi   **B** 57 mi

  C 507 mi   **D** 350 mi

5. Which equation is related to
$8 - 2 - 2 - 2 - 2 = $ ▨?

  A $8 - 2 = $ ▨   **B** $8 \div 2 = $ ▨

  C $8 + 8 = $ ▨   **D** $8 \times 2 = $ ▨

6. What value appears most often in this stem and leaf table?

Stem	Leaf
21	11, 42, 21, 42, 21
42	12, 21, 53, 56, 99
56	38, 47, 38, 25, 38

  A 21   **B** 42

  C 5,638   **D** 2,121

7. Find the area of this triangle.

  A 12 cm^2 **B** 7 cm^2

  C 6 cm^2 **D** 8 cm^2

8. What is the surface area of this figure when the face of each cube is 1 unit^2?

  A 19 units^2 **B** 34 units^2

  C 32 units^2 **D** 38 units^2

Use the prism shown at the right for problems 9 and 10.

9. Find the surface area.

  A 31 in.^{2} **B** 30 in.^{2}

  C 50 in.^{2} **D** 62 in.^{2}

10. Find the volume.

  A 10 in.^{3} **B** 62 in.^{3}

  C 30 in.^{3} **D** 20 in.^{3}

11. Mr. McDonald is fencing his circular garden area. The diameter of this area is 5 m. How much fence does he need? Use 3.14 for π.

  A 7.85 m   **B** 15.7 m

  C 19.6 m   **D** 10 m

12. Tawana is making a pyramid-shaped paperweight that she will fill with sand. Its base is 9 in.^{2} and its height is 5 in. What is its volume?

  A 45 in.^{3} **B** 22.5 in.^{3}

  C 135 in.^{3} **D** 15 in.^{3}

4

MATH AND
LANGUAGE ARTS

DATA BANK

Use the Language Arts
Data Bank on page 504 to
answer the questions.

1 How old was Benjamin
Franklin when he stopped
publishing his almanac?

EQUATIONS
IN ALGEBRA

THEME: EARLY AMERICANS

African-American Benjamin Banneker
helped design the layout of our nation's
capital.

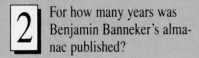

2 For how many years was Benjamin Banneker's almanac published?

3 For how many years did the publication of the two almanacs overlap?

4 **Using Critical Thinking** What season is being depicted in the sample page from Benjamin Banneker's almanac? How can you tell?

Introduction to Equations

EXPLORE **Read the Information**

Balanced scales can help you understand equations. The scale at the right is balanced. The variable c represents the weight of a can. Each marble weighs 1 gram. Since the scale is balanced, the left side is equal to the right side. We write the equation $2c + 4 = 4c + 2$.

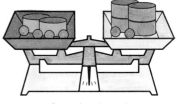

$2c + 4 = 4c + 2$

TALK ABOUT IT

1. If you add 10 marbles to each pan, what happens to the scale?

2. What equation represents removing 2 marbles from each pan?

3. If you remove half of thc objccts on each pan, what equation results?

An equation is like a balanced scale. Both sides of an equation remain equal if you add, subtract, multiply, or divide by the same number on each side. Also, if two quantities are equal you can **substitute** one for the other.

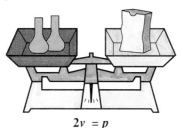

$2v = p$

This scale is balanced.

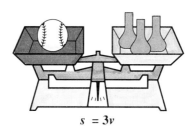

$s = 3v$

This scale is balanced.

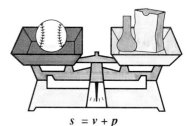

$s = v + p$

This scale is also balanced. The paper bag (p) was substituted for 2 vases ($2v$).

TRY IT OUT

Use the examples above to decide whether these scales are balanced or not.

1.

2.
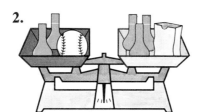

3.
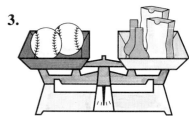

94

These scales are balanced.

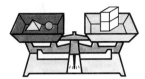 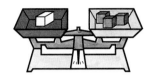 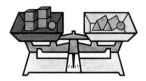

Decide if each scale balances or not. For balanced scales, write an equation.

1. 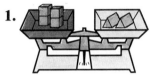 **2.** 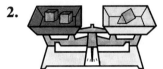 **3.**

4.  **5.**  **6.**

7.  **8.**  **9.**

MATH REASONING

10. Scales that are unbalanced represent **inequalities** rather than equations. Use the balanced scales on this page to decide which side of this scale is heavier. Assign a variable name to each type of block and write an inequality that represents this scale by using > (greater than) or < (less than).

PROBLEM SOLVING

11. Mario was packing a box with 20 bags of nuts of equal weight. The box and 5 bags weighed 22 ounces. After adding 2 more bags, the box weighed 26 ounces. If the box is packed with all the bags, how much will it weigh?

▶ **WRITING TO LEARN**

12. Write a paragraph that explains why this scale is balanced. Use the fact that the scales at the top of the page are balanced.

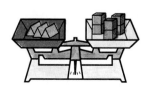

More Practice, page 526, set C

Solving Equations Using Mental Math

LEARN ABOUT IT

The equation $x + 5 = 8$ is true only when x represents 3. We say that the **solution** to $x + 5 = 8$ is $x = 3$.

EXPLORE **Read the Information**
When Anna saw her brother's homework she said, "I can solve those equations without paper and pencil if I think carefully." Which of these equations can you solve using mental math?

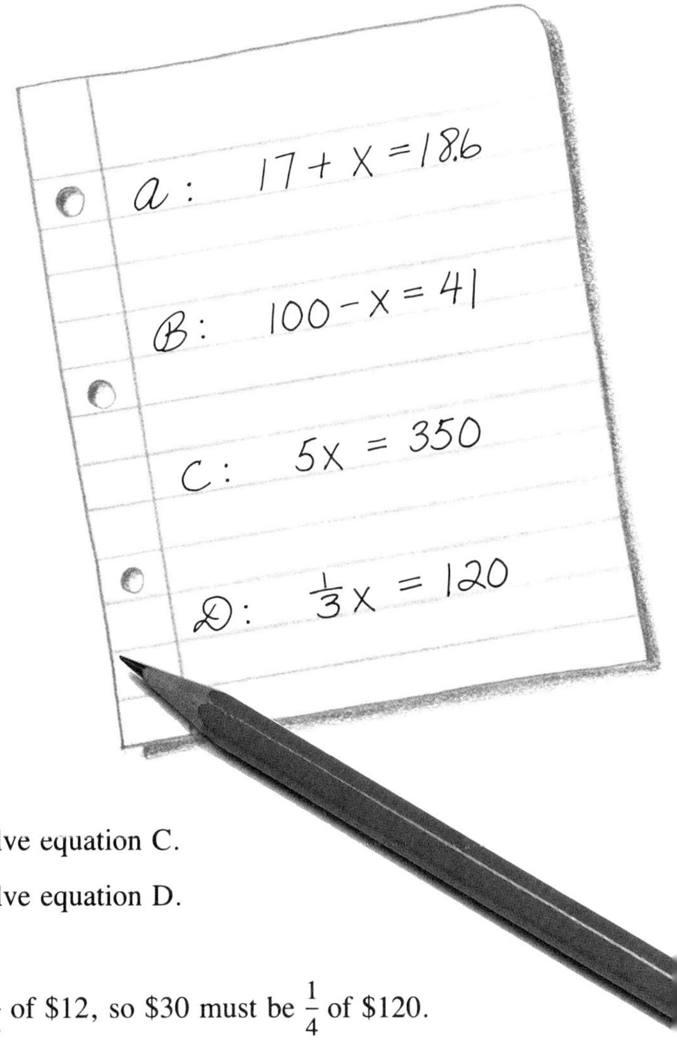

TALK ABOUT IT

1. For equation A is it correct to reason "17 plus 1 is 18, so I need to add 1.6 to 17 to get 18.6"?

2. For equation B is it correct to reason "100 minus 60 equals 40—I'll subtract 1 less to get 41, so x must be 59"?

Handwritten note:

$a: \quad 17 + X = 18.6$

$\mathcal{B}: \quad 100 - X = 41$

$C: \quad 5X = 350$

$\mathcal{D}: \quad \frac{1}{3}X = 120$

3. Explain the reasoning you would use to solve equation C.

4. Explain the reasoning you would use to solve equation D.

Examples Solve using mental math.

A $\frac{1}{4}z = \$30$ Think: \$3 is $\frac{1}{4}$ of \$12, so \$30 must be $\frac{1}{4}$ of \$120.

  $z = \$120$

B $400 = h - 21.5$ Think: After 21.5 is subtracted from the number h the result
  $h = 421.5$ is 400. So, h must be 21.5 more than 400 or 421.5.

TRY IT OUT

Solve using mental math.

1. $16 + x = 31$ **2.** $\frac{1}{3}x = 50$ **3.** $3x = 240$

4. $20.1 - x = 15$ **5.** $2x = 180$ **6.** $60 - x = 42$

Solve these equations using mental math.

1. $20 + t = 39$

2. $100 - h = 89$

3. $\frac{1}{5}x = 20$

4. $150 = 5w$

5. $4s = 480$

6. $36 = 10y$

7. $98 + z = 152.7$

8. $\frac{1}{100}n = 2$

9. $38 = \frac{1}{2}b$

10. $32 + v = 100$

11. $n - 199 = 501$

12. $\frac{2}{3}m = 50$

13. $\frac{3}{5}l = 15$

14. $r - 35 = 75$

15. $121 = x - 39$

Write an equation for each scale below. Solve the resulting equation using mental math.

16.

17.

18.

19.

APPLY

MATH REASONING

20. The scales below are balanced. Find the weight of a small cube using mental math.

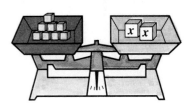

PROBLEM SOLVING

21. The equation $D = 60t$ represents the distance (D) a car would travel going 60 miles per hour. At this rate, how long (t) would it take to travel 420 miles?

▶ **ESTIMATION**

Find the whole number that is an estimate of the solution to each equation.

22. $3x = 16$

23. $4x = 25$

24. $5y = 61$

25. $5y = 46$

More Practice, page 526, set D

Problem Solving
Using the Strategies

| UNDERSTAND |
| ANALYZE DATA |
| PLAN |
| ESTIMATE |
| SOLVE |
| EXAMINE |

This problem can be solved in at least 2 different ways. Tanya used **Guess and Check.** Val used the strategy **Make an Organized List.**

Lamont spent $36 at Books Revisited. He bought 13 books. Some were hardback and some were paperback. He didn't buy any magazines. How many paperbacks did Lamont buy?

Tanya's solution:

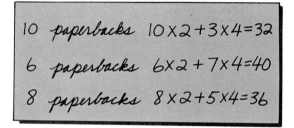

10 paperbacks $10 \times 2 + 3 \times 4 = 32$

6 paperbacks $6 \times 2 + 7 \times 4 = 40$

8 paperbacks $8 \times 2 + 5 \times 4 = 36$

Val's solution:

Paperbacks	Hardbacks	Total
13	0	$26
12	1	28
11	2	30
10	3	32
9	4	34
8	5	36
7	6	38

Lamont bought 8 paperbacks.

Hardbacks $4.00

Paperbacks $2.00

Magazines $1.00

TRY IT OUT

Solve. Use Guess and Check or Make an Organized List.

1. Brenda spent $46 on 15 items at Books Revisited. She bought some hardbacks and twice as many paperbacks as magazines. How many of each did she buy?

2. Otis spent $4.10. He got 5 coins totalling $0.90 in change. What coins did Otis get?

Solve. Use any problem solving strategy.

Some Strategies

Act Out	Solve a Simpler Problem
Use Objects	Make an Organized List
Choose an Operation	Work Backward
Draw a Picture	Look for a Pattern
Guess and Check	Use Logical Reasoning
Make a Table	Write an Equation

1. Mr. Allen had 78 books in his room at the beginning of the year. Since then students have donated some additional books. Now he has 105 books. How many books did his students donate?

2. Lew read 3 consecutive pages in a poetry book. He noticed that the pages totalled 57. What 3 pages did Lew read?

3. Books Revisited made this chart to show sales for the month of October. How many paperbacks and hardbacks did they sell during the month?

October Sales				
	1st week	2nd week	3rd week	4th week
Hardbacks	108	127	150	131
Paperbacks	185	143	206	224
Magazines	53	61	28	45

4. Books Revisited made $3,767 in sales during October. Use the prices on the left page to find how much was collected just for paperbacks.

5. Two classes are working together on research projects. There are 59 students and they are working in groups of 4 and 5. There are 14 groups. How many are groups of 5?

6. Myra is reading *Roll of Thunder, Hear My Cry* by Mildred Taylor. The book has 237 pages. She started the book on Friday, read 3 times as many pages on Saturday as on Friday, and then read 12 more pages on Sunday than on Saturday. She still has 183 pages left to read. How many pages did Myra read each day?

7. Ryan is reading a 517 page book. He has already read 125 pages. If he reads 28 pages each day, how many weeks will it take him to complete the book?

Inverse Operations

LEARN ABOUT IT

EXPLORE

An old African proverb states that "One falsehood spoils a thousand truths." You could think of falsehood as undoing truth. In mathematics, an inverse operation is the operation that undoes another operation.

Mohandas Gandhi, who led India to independence through non-violent protest, said, "Non-cooperation with evil is as much a duty as is cooperation with good."

TALK ABOUT IT

1. What are some other words that undo each other?

2. What operation is the inverse of division?

3. A cassette tape that used to cost $14 now costs $16, but if you mention your favorite radio station at the checkout you get a $2 discount. Which operation has undone another one?

You can use inverse operations to simplify expressions.

Examples

A y Begin with the variable y.

$8y$ The variable y is multiplied by 8.

$\frac{8y}{8}$ Divide the expression by 8 to undo the multiplication.

y The result is y.

B x Begin with the variable x.

$\frac{x}{5}$ The variable x is divided by 5.

$\frac{x}{5} \cdot 5$ Multiply the expression by 5 to undo the division.

x The result is x.

TRY IT OUT

Show the inverse operation that gets the variable alone.

1. $y - 20$

2. $15x$

3. $\frac{a}{7}$

4. $g + 36.4$

Show the inverse operation that gets the variable alone.

1. $x - 7$ **2.** $n + 20$ **3.** $4h$ **4.** $a + 6.2$

5. $k \div 29$ **6.** $w - 10$ **7.** $75p$ **8.** $g - 43$

9. $\dfrac{m}{8.3}$ **10.** $16.7y$ **11.** $9.6a$ **12.** $\dfrac{y}{10}$

13. $3.75b$ **14.** $g \div 45$ **15.** $\dfrac{a}{62}$ **16.** $32.4c$

APPLY

MATH REASONING

17. Jennie Wong picked a number. She multiplied the number by 6, added 16 to the result, subtracted 20, and last she divided by 2. Her final result was 10. What was the original number she picked?

PROBLEM SOLVING

18. Sara had b dollars in her savings account when she began taking care of her neighbor's puppy. She earned $3.50 per day for two weeks and put half her earnings into a savings account. Write an expression to represent Sara's new balance at the end of two weeks. What operation would get the variable b alone?

19. Language Arts Data Bank Benjamin Franklin wrote many famous proverbs that are still used today. Write two word problems using the data about Benjamin Franklin that can be solved using inverse operations.

MIXED REVIEW

Find the surface area of each prism. Find the volume of each prism.

20.

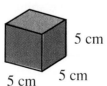

5 cm
5 cm   5 cm

21.

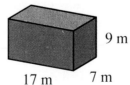

9 m
17 m   7 m

22.

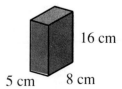

16 cm
5 cm   8 cm

One-Step Equations

EXPLORE **Examine the Picture**

Consider the two-pan scale at the right. It represents the equation $x + 3 = 6$. To solve this equation you need to find all the replacements for x that make the equation true.

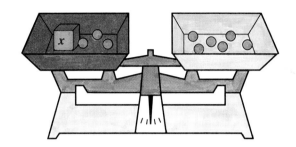

TALK ABOUT IT

1. Suppose two marbles are taken from the left pan. How many marbles must be taken from the right pan for the scale to balance?

2. How many marbles should be taken from each pan to get x by itself?

These **properties of equality** will help you to solve equations.

For all numbers a, b, and c	
1. If $a = b$, then $a + c = b + c$	**3.** If $a = b$, then $ac = bc$
2. If $a = b$, then $a - c = b - c$	**4.** If $a = b$ and $c \neq 0$, then $\dfrac{a}{c} = \dfrac{b}{c}$

Examples Solve and check these equations.

A
$$x + 3 = 115$$
$$x + 3 - 3 = 115 - 3$$
$$x = 112$$

You need to get the variable alone.
To undo adding 3, subtract 3 from both sides.

Check $112 + 3 \stackrel{?}{=} 115$
$115 = 115$

Replace x with 112 in $x + 3 = 115$.

B
$$\frac{y}{7} = 1.5$$
$$\frac{y}{7} \cdot 7 = 1.5 \cdot 7$$
$$y = 10.5$$

To undo dividing by 7, multiply both sides by 7.
How can you check to make sure the solution to B is correct?

Solve and check these equations.

1. $x - 5 = 121$ **2.** $y + 15 = 23.7$ **3.** $\dfrac{x}{5} = 13$

Solve and check these equations.

1. $x + 22 = 49$

2. $y - 17 = 105$

3. $\frac{w}{3} = 36$

4. $5a = 115$

5. $\frac{c}{20} = 8$

6. $7.2\,b = 21.6$

7. $w - 20.2 = 100$

8. $\frac{z}{5} = 11$

9. $y - 12 = 87$

10. $x + \frac{2}{7} = \frac{6}{7}$

11. $6y = 36.6$

12. $26 = \frac{n}{5}$

13. $17 = a - 2.9$

14. $a - 2\frac{2}{3} = 5\frac{1}{3}$

15. $17.25 = 16.2 + x$

Write and solve equations to find the value of the variable.

16.

area = 3.45, b, 1.5

17.
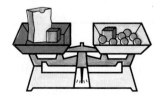

18.
x 15

48

MATH REASONING Is the solution to each equation a whole number
or a decimal? Do not solve the equation.

19. $x + 2.5 = 7$

20. $x - 3.5 = 7.5$

21. $2x = 8.4$

PROBLEM SOLVING

22. The equation $\frac{b}{3} = n$ represents the
nonwater portion (n) of your body
weight (b). How much do you weigh if
the nonwater portion of your body
weighs 40 pounds?

23. The distance (d) from the moon to the
earth increases 4 feet each year (y). The
increased distance is represented by
$d = 4y$. In how many years will the
moon be one mile further away?

▶ **USING CRITICAL THINKING**   **Use Logical Reasoning**

24. Solve this puzzle.

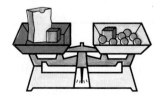

This scale balances.

This scale balances.

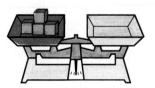

How many marbles does it
take to balance this scale?

Problem Solving
Data From a Table

| UNDERSTAND |
| ANALYZE DATA |
| PLAN |
| ESTIMATE |
| SOLVE |
| EXAMINE |

To solve some problems you need data from a table, a graph, or some other source outside the problem. To solve this problem you need data from a table of postage rates.

Look in the weight column to find the line that has the weight of the first package.

Over 7 oz, but not over 8 oz.

Read the rate for that line.

$1.90

Do the same thing for the second package.

Over 5 oz, but not over 6 oz.
$1.44

Add the two rates to find the total postage.

$1.90 + $1.44 = $3.34

Madeline spent $3.34 for postage.

Madeline sent 2 packages to her cousins. One of the packages weighed 8 oz and the other weighed $5\frac{1}{2}$ oz. How much did Madeline spend for postage?

First Class Postage Rates

Weight	Rates
First oz.	$0.29
over 1 oz. but not over 2	0.52
over 2 oz. but not over 3	0.75
over 3 oz. but not over 4	0.98
over 4 oz. but not over 5	1.21
over 5 oz. but not over 6	1.44
over 6 oz. but not over 7	1.67
over 7 oz. but not over 8	1.90
over 8 oz. but not over 9	2.13
over 9 oz. but not over 10	2.36
over 10 oz. but not over 11	2.59
over 11 oz. but not over 12	2.82

TRY IT OUT

Solve. Use data from the table above.

1. Rodrigo mailed a letter that weighed $3\frac{1}{4}$ oz. He gave the postal clerk $1. How much change did Rodrigo get back?

2. Ricardo sent a $1\frac{1}{2}$ oz letter and a $10\frac{3}{4}$ oz package. How much did he spend for postage?

3. Erica sent a special delivery letter. The fee was $7.65 in addition to the first class postage. The letter weighed 3 oz. How much did it cost her?

4. The fee for certified mail is $1.00 in addition to the first class rate. How much does it cost to send a certified letter that weighs less than 1 oz?

Solve. Use any problem solving strategy. Use data from the postage rates table.

1. Express Mail service is available for articles that weigh up to 70 lb. The rate for a 1 oz letter is $9.95. Avelino sent three 1 oz letters Express Mail. How much did this cost?

2. Each person in the United States sends an average of 589 letters a year. The population of Kansas City is 161,148. About how many letters are sent from Kansas City every year?

3. The rate for a postcard is $0.10 less than the rate for a 1 oz letter. Christie wrote to 12 friends and spent $2.98 on postage. How many letters and how many postcards did she write?

4. Mrs. Kim sent a pair of earrings to her mother. The earrings cost $68 so she sent them insured mail. The package weighed $6\frac{3}{4}$ oz. Use the table to find how much she spent for postage and insurance.

5. Mabel bought a book of 29¢ stamps for $5.80 and some 15¢ stamps for $3.60. How many 15¢ stamps did Mabel buy?

Insured Mail. Fees, in addition to postage, for coverage against loss or damage:	
Value	Fees
$ .01 to $50	$ 0.75
$ 50.01 to $100	1.60
$ 100.01 to $200	2.40
$ 200.01 to $300	3.50

6. Luisa used eight stamps to mail a package to her cousin in Nicaragua. Some were 50¢ stamps and some were 29¢ stamps. How many of each did she use if the total postage was $3.37?

7. Heidi sent 3 letters to pen pals in France. Each letter weighed $2\frac{1}{2}$ oz and cost $2.12 to mail. How much less would it have cost her to mail the same 3 letters to friends in the United States?

8. **Understanding the Operations**
Name the operation you would use to solve this problem. Nagia spent $11 at the post office. She spent $4 for stamps and the rest to mail a package. How much did it cost to mail the package?

More Practice, page 546, set E

Using Critical Thinking

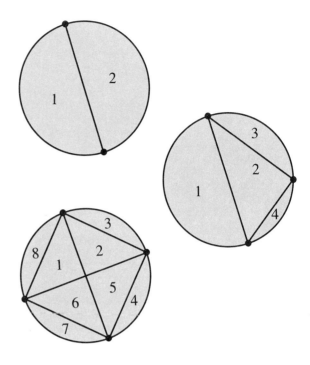

LEARN ABOUT IT

Some of Mike's friends were joking about finding crazy ways to cut up a pizza. "Let's start by making two marks on a round piece of cardboard, and connecting them," said Tom. "Then we'll make a third mark and connect it to the other two." Maria said, "I'll make a table to show the results"

"We don't need to go any further in the table," said Maria. "It is clear that the number of pieces doubles each time." "Wait a minute," said Helen. "I've tried it for 5 and 6 marks, and I'm not sure you are right!"

TALK ABOUT IT

1. What is Maria's group trying to do?

2. Do you agree with Maria? How could you convince someone that her conclusion is correct or incorrect?

3. Draw pictures to show the cases for 5 and 6 marks. What is your conclusion?

4. What have you learned from this situation?

marks	pieces
2	2
3	4
4	8
5	
6	

TRY IT OUT

If you make 0 straight cuts in a circular pizza, it divides the pizza into **1** piece. One cut divides it into **2** pieces, and **2** cuts divide it into **4** pieces. Verify this, then predict how many pieces you will get with 3 cuts. Check your prediction.

POWER PRACTICE/QUIZ

This scale balances.

Decide if the other scales balance.

1.    2. 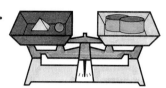   3.

Solve these equations. Use mental math.

4. $3 \cdot w = 270$

5. $1.8 = \frac{1}{2}x$

6. $a + 20 = 102.4$ **7.** $50 \div z = 0.5$

8. $320 = t - 8.4$ **9.** $0.5 + r = 1.5$ **10.** $y \div 6 = 60$ **11.** $b - 1.6 = 8.4$

Solve these equations.

12. $x + 1.5 = 2.4$ **13.** $\frac{x}{3} = 26.4$ **14.** $2.5x = 1$ **15.** $x - 15.52 = 16.93$

Write and solve an equation to find the value of the variable.

16.    **17.**    **18.**

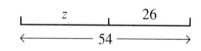

PROBLEM SOLVING

19. Delia needs 3 different flyers printed. She wants 30 copies of the first flyer, 300 copies of the second flyer, and 750 copies of the third flyer. What is the total cost?

20. Lori ordered 100 copies of her holiday form letter. How much less would it cost to order 10 more?

Copy Service Rates
(prices for copies from one original)
25 copies cost 6¢ each, or $1.50.
50 copies cost 5.5¢ each, or $2.75

number of copies	price per copy
1 → 25	6¢
26 → 50	5.5¢
51 → 100	5¢
101 → 500	4.5¢
501 → 1,000	4¢
over 1,000	3¢

Two-Step Expressions

You can use inverse operations to get the variable alone in two-step expressions.

EXPLORE Read the Information

Mark stores his cassette tapes in a box that weighs 1.2 pounds. The box and 15 tapes weighs 4.2 pounds.

TALK ABOUT IT

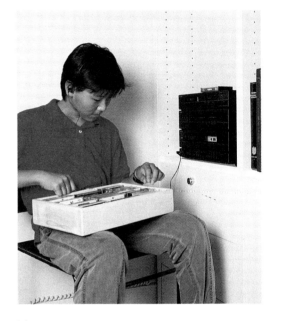

1. If w represents the weight of one tape, does $15w + 1.2$ represent a) the weight of 15 tapes, b) the weight of the box, or c) the weight of the tapes and the box?

2. To get the variable w alone in the expression $(15w + 1.2)$ would you first a) subtract 1.2 or b) subtract $15w$?

3. What would you do in the second step to get the variable w alone?

Two-step algebraic expressions are built by starting with a variable and performing two operations. You get the variable alone by using inverse operations.

Example Write the steps that show how you build and undo the expression $2x + 5$.

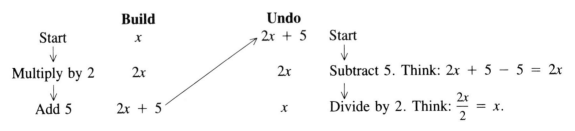

	Build	**Undo**	
Start	x	$2x + 5$	Start
↓ Multiply by 2	$2x$	$2x$	Subtract 5. Think: $2x + 5 - 5 = 2x$
↓ Add 5	$2x + 5$	x	Divide by 2. Think: $\frac{2x}{2} = x$.

Write the steps that show how you build and undo these expressions.

1. $3x - 7$ 　　　　 2. $2y + 17$ 　　　　 3. $\frac{z}{5} + 8$ 　　　　 4. $14x - 27$

Write the steps that show how you build and undo these expressions.

1. $4w - 69$ **2.** $3b + 18$ **3.** $9x - 4$ **4.** $\dfrac{k}{5} - 15.3$

5. $3n + \dfrac{2}{3}$ **6.** $\dfrac{m}{3} + 14$ **7.** $\dfrac{x}{5} - 103.2$ **8.** $10c + 19.35$

9. $\dfrac{y}{4} + 81$ **10.** $4.65f - \dfrac{2}{5}$ **11.** $13z - 5.8$ **12.** $21y + 7.3$

Replace each ? with an expression that represents the pictured situation.
Write the steps you would use to get the variable alone.

13.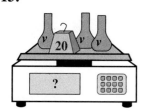

14.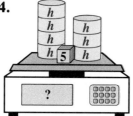

15.

perimeter = ?

MATH REASONING Use mental math to answer these questions.

16. Is $x = 1$, $x = 2$, or $x = 3$ the solution to $2x + 3 = 7$?

17. Is $x = 1$, $x = 2$, or $x = 3$ the solution to $3x - 1.5 = 7.5$?

18. Is $x = 5$, $x = 10$, or $x = 15$ the solution to $2.5x - 1.5 = 23.5$?

PROBLEM SOLVING

19. Write 3 expressions that tell how much it costs to leave a dog at the kennel for d days. There is a daily cost plus a 1-time per visit "flea dipping fee."

Size	Flea Dip	Cost/Day
large	$3.50	$6.00
medium	2.50	5.75
small	2.00	4.50

20. Write Your Own Problem Write a problem that can be answered using this data. The tallest cut Christmas tree on record was a 221-foot Douglas fir. A 6-foot tree is the size most often purchased.

▶ **CALCULATOR**

Write an equation that represents each situation. Then find the weight of each of the six boxes that are equal in weight.

21.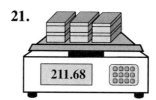

22.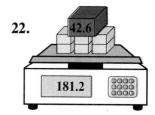

Two-Step Equations

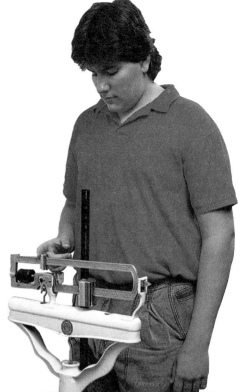

EXPLORE Study the Information

Jon's height is 175 centimeters. Assuming that Jon is an average person, we can find his approximate weight in kilograms by solving the equation $175 = \frac{w}{0.98} + 102$.

TALK ABOUT IT

1. To get the variable alone in the expression $\frac{w}{0.98} + 102$, what would you do first?

2. To solve the equation $175 = \frac{w}{0.98} + 102$ what do you think you would do first? What do you think your second step would be?

To solve a two-step equation, decide on the two inverse operations needed to get the variable alone. Use the properties of equality.

$$\text{height} = \frac{w}{0.98} + 102$$

Examples Solve these equations.

A
$$2p + 25 = 125$$
$$2p + 25 - \mathbf{25} = 125 - \mathbf{25} \quad \text{Subtract 25 from both sides to undo adding 25.}$$
$$2p = 100$$
$$\frac{2p}{2} = \frac{100}{2} \quad \text{Divide both sides by 2 to undo multiplying by 2.}$$
$$p = 50$$

B
$$\frac{x}{6} - 4 = 12$$
$$\frac{x}{6} - 4 + \mathbf{4} = 12 + \mathbf{4} \quad \text{Add 4 to both sides to undo subtracting 4.}$$
$$\frac{x}{6} = 16$$
$$\frac{x}{6} \cdot 6 = 16 \cdot 6 \quad \text{Multiply both sides by 6 to undo dividing by 6.}$$
$$x = 96$$

Solve and check each equation.

1. $2x - 18 = 28$ **2.** $\frac{x}{7} - 2 = 15.1$ **3.** $5y + 12 = 33$ **4.** $\frac{a}{3} - 5 = 2.3$

Solve and check each equation.

1. $2x + 15 = 27$ **2.** $3y - 18 = 54$ **3.** $\dfrac{x}{2} - 5 = 21$

4. $\dfrac{a}{7} + 10 = 24$ **5.** $2a - 9 = 31$ **6.** $9c - 8 = 19$

7. $\dfrac{x}{3} - 4 = 8.2$ **8.** $\dfrac{y}{2} - 12 = 2.4$ **9.** $\dfrac{d}{5} - 1 = 0.5$

10. $21c + 8 = 29$ **11.** $10a + 13 = 17$ **12.** $6b + 20 = 23.6$

Write and solve the equation represented by each figure.

13. 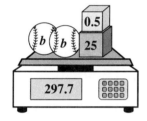   **14.**

MATH REASONING Solve using mental math.

15. $4x + 13 = 113$ **16.** $10x - 50 = 90$ **17.** $10x - 11 = 989$

PROBLEM SOLVING

18. A pizza is cut into eight slices. Three slices cost $2.86 with 16¢ tax. What does the whole pizza cost, without tax?

MIXED REVIEW

Find the area of each circle with the given radius. Use 3.14 for π.

19. $r = 10$ m   **20.** $r = 2.1$ in.   **21.** $r = 8$ cm

Find the volume of each figure.

22. 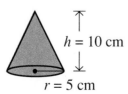   **23.** 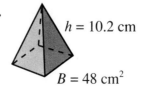   **24.**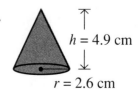

More Practice, page 527, set D

111

Inequality Relations

Equations are statements of equality. Often statements of inequality are needed to describe mathematical situations.

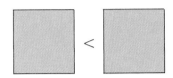

Select numbers
from the set
1, 2, 3, 4.

EXPLORE **Make a Table**

Work in groups. The symbol $<$ is read as "is less than." Make a table that shows all the ways to write true statements by selecting numbers from the set 1, 2, 3, 4 to fill the boxes.

TALK ABOUT IT **See teaching notes.**

1. How many inequalities are in your table?

2. The symbol $\leq$ means "is less than or equal to." If $<$ is changed to $\leq$, how many more inequalities are there when the boxes are filled in?

3. If $>$ means "is greater than," what do you think $\geq$ means?

Examples Using the symbols $<$, $\leq$, $>$, or $\geq$, find all the ways to fill each ⬚ to make a true statement.

A 3 ⬚ 5
   3 $<$ 5 and 3 $\leq$ 5

B 7 ⬚ 5
   7 $>$ 5 and 7 $\geq$ 5

C 4 ⬚ 4
   4 $\leq$ 4 and 4 $\geq$ 4

Find all the solutions to each inequality selected from the set 1, 2, 3, 4, 5, 6.

D $x \geq 4$
   $x = 4, 5,$ or 6

E $x < 6$
   $x = 1, 2, 3, 4,$ or 5

F $x \leq 3$
   $x = 1, 2,$ or 3

Fill in each ⬚ with $\geq$ or $\leq$ to make the statement true.

1. 5 ⬚ 3

2. 5 ⬚ 3 + 4

3. 8 ⬚ 8

Find all the solutions to each inequality selected from the set 1, 2, 3, 4, 5, 6, 7, 8.

4. $x \geq 3$

5. $x < 7$

6. $x > 1$

Using the symbols $<$, $\leq$, $>$, or $\geq$ find all the ways to fill each ▓
to make a true statement.

1. 9 ▓ 11   **2.** 8 ▓ 3   **3.** 12 ▓ 12   **4.** 6 ▓ 1

5. 3 + 4 ▓ 2 + 3   **6.** 6 − 2 ▓ 7 − 3   **7.** 8 − 2 ▓ 3 · 4   **8.** $\dfrac{12}{3}$ ▓ $\dfrac{15}{3}$

Find all the solutions to each inequality selected from the set
1, 2, 3, 4, 5, 6, 7.

9. $x > 6$ **10.** $y > 4$ **11.** $d \leq 2$ **12.** $5 > c$

13. $a \leq 7$ **14.** $g + 4 \leq 7$ **15.** $x + 3 \geq 5$ **16.** $a - 4 \geq 2$

APPLY

MATH REASONING

17. List all the possible ways to make a true statement by
filling the boxes with numbers selected from the set
1, 2, 3, 4.

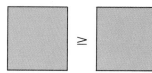

In each problem, the arrows → represent either $<$, $\leq$, $>$, or $\geq$.
Decide which type of inequality is represented by each arrow diagram.

18. 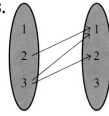   **19.** 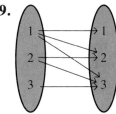   **20.** 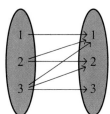   **21.**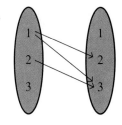

PROBLEM SOLVING

22. Concert tickets cost $8 each for main
floor seats and $5.50 each for balcony
seats. How many tickets can Sarah buy
with $21.75?

23. Write Your Own Problem Juan
received a profit of $0.12 for each
paper he sold. A radio controlled car
cost $98.95 and an adventure game cost
$46.95.

▶ **USING CRITICAL THINKING**

24. Suppose all the statements below are true.
$$a < b \qquad b < c \qquad c = d$$

Which of the statements in the box must also be true?

$b > a$	$a < c$
$b < d$	$c = a$

More Practice, page 527, set E

Functions

Many physical situations
that generate number pairs
are examples of **functions.**

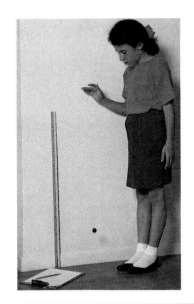

EXPLORE Complete the Table

Megan had a "super ball"
that bounced to 0.8 of the
height from which she
dropped it.

Drop height	200 cm	150 cm	100 cm	75 cm
Bounce height	160 cm	120 cm	?	?

TALK ABOUT IT

1. Which of these rules did you use to complete the table: a)
   subtract 0.8 from the drop height, b) multiply the drop
   height by 0.8, or c) divide the drop height by 0.8?

2. For a specific drop height are there several possible bounce
   heights or only one bounce height?

The rule that describes the relationship between bounce height
(b) and drop height (d) can be expressed as

bounce height = $0.8 \cdot$ (drop height), or
$$b = 0.8d$$

When $b = 0.8d$ is evaluated for $d = 500$, the result is
$b = (0.8)(500) = 400$. Since for every value of d there is
a unique value for b, the expression $b = 0.8d$ is a **function.**

TRY IT OUT

1. The equation $f = 5d$ describes the force f of a spring that is
   compressed a distance of d units. Complete this table.

Distance (d)	2	4	6	?	?	?
Force (f)	10	20	30			

2. With a partner, use a tape measure and another kind of ball
   to make a function table and equation like the one above.

Use the equation distance = speed · time ($d = st$) to complete each table of values.

1. If a car is traveling 35 miles per hour, the distance it travels can be expressed as the function equation $d = 35t$. Complete the table below to find the distance the car travels over a 1–5 hour span of time.

Time (t)	1	2	3	4	5
$d = 35t$	35	?	?	?	?

2. A jet plane flies 620 miles per hour. The distance it travels can be expressed as the function equation $d = 620t$. Complete the table below to find the distance the jet travels over a 1–5 hour span of time.

Time (t)	1	2	3	4	5
Distance (d)	620	?	?	?	?

Complete each of these tables of values for the given function.

3.

Time (t)	1	2	3	4	5
$d = 48t$	48	?	?	?	?

4.

Time (t)	1	2	3	4	5
$d = 8t + 3$	11	?	?	?	?

5. The function rule $r = 350t$ describes the total r for t months for an apartment that rents for $350 per month. Complete a table of values that shows the total rent paid after 1 month, 2 months—up to 12 months.

6. The function rule $f = 50d$ describes the force of a spring that has been compressed d units. Complete a table of values for the first 5 units of d.

MATH REASONING

7. A ball is dropped from 3 meters and bounces 1.5 meters. Write an equation using b (bounce height) and d (drop height) that describes this ball.

PROBLEM SOLVING

8. A train travels 350 miles in 5 hours. How far will it travel in t hours?

CALCULATOR

9. Use a calculator with an x^2 key to complete this table of values.

x	12	24	36	48	60
x^2	?	?	?	?	?

Function Tables

EXPLORE Complete the Table

When people make a television show, they shoot many more hours of film than are used in the final edited version. The table shows how one company estimates how long a film will be after editing.

TALK ABOUT IT

1. Suppose you shot 7.5 hours of film. How many hours of film would you expect to have left after editing?

2. Describe how the length of the film before editing and after editing are related.

Before Editing	After Editing
2.5 hours	0.5 hours
7.5 hours	1.5 hours
10.0 hours	2.0 hours
12.5 hours	___ hours
15.0 hours	___ hours

In the table above, the length before editing is the **input** value and the length after editing is the **output.** We can use a variable such as n to represent the input value of a function and $f(n)$, read "f of n" to represent the output value.

Examples Use $n = 1, 2, 3, 4$ to make a function table for each rule.

A function rule: $n + 2$

n	$f(n)$
1	$1 + 2 = 3$
2	$2 + 2 = 4$
3	$3 + 2 = 5$
4	$4 + 2 = 6$

B function rule: $2n + 1$

n	$f(n)$
1	$2(1) + 1 = 3$
2	$2(2) + 1 = 5$
3	$2(3) + 1 = 7$
4	$2(4) + 1 = 9$

C function rule: $\dfrac{n + 3}{2}$

n	$f(n)$
1	$\dfrac{1 + 3}{2} = 2$
2	2.5
3	3
4	3.5

TRY IT OUT

For each function rule, make a table like the ones above.

1. function rule: $3n - 1$ **2.** function rule: $2(n + 3)$ **3.** function rule: $\dfrac{n + 2}{2}$

Complete each table of input-output pairs $(n, f(n))$ for these function rules.

1. function rule: $7 - n$

n	$f(n)$
1	6
2	
3	
4	
5	

2. function rule: $5n - 3$

n	$f(n)$
1	2
2	7
3	
4	
5	

3. function rule: $12 - 2n$

n	$f(n)$
1	10
2	8
3	
4	
5	

4. function rule: $\dfrac{n + 1}{4}$

n	$f(n)$
1	
2	
3	
4	
5	

5. function rule: $3(n + 2)$

n	$f(n)$
1	
2	
3	
4	
5	

6. function rule: $\dfrac{4x - 2}{3}$

n	$f(n)$
1	
2	
3	
4	
5	

MATH REASONING Use n to write a function rule for each function table.

7. function rule?

n	1	2	3	4	5
$f(n)$	2	3	4	5	6

8. function rule?

n	1	2	3	4	5
$f(n)$	4	5	6	7	8

9. function rule?

n	1	2	3	4	5
$f(n)$	7	6	5	4	3

PROBLEM SOLVING

10. A spring stretches n cm when a $75n$ gram weight is attached to it. Suppose you attach a weight that stretches the spring 4 cm. How many grams is the weight you attached?

11. Language Arts Data Bank The symbol ⊙ represents the sun in Benjamin Banneker's table of predictions. On June 1, 1647, the sun rose at 4:43 a.m. and set at 7:17 p.m. How many hours of sunlight did Banneker predict for June 7, 1647?

▶ **CALCULATOR**

12. Use a calculator that has a square root $\left(\sqrt{}\right)$ key. Select any five whole numbers n and calculate the corresponding "output" number $\sqrt{n}$.

n	
$\sqrt{n}$	

More Practice, page 528, set A

Graphing Functions

input		output
0.25	$y = 2x + 1$	1.5
x	function rule	y

Input-output values are frequently written using x for input and y for output.

$2 \boxed{\times} 0.25 \boxed{+} 1 \boxed{=} \boxed{ 1.5}$

EXPLORE Use a Calculator

Work in groups. Consider the function at the right. Use the function rule and the values for x to complete the table.

TALK ABOUT IT

1. When the input value is $x = 0.33$, how many output values did you get?

x	0.25	0.33	0.5	1	2	3	4
y	1.5						

2. For each input value, how many output values do you get?

Each input value x and its corresponding value y make up an ordered pair (x, y). These ordered pairs are solutions to the function and can be plotted on a grid.

Example Graph the function $y = \dfrac{1}{x}$

First, complete a table of input-output values.

x	0.25	0.33	0.5	1	2	3	4
y	4	3	2	1	0.5	0.33	0.25

Then graph these ordered pairs on the x-y grid. For example, when x is 0.25 and y is 4, the ordered pair is (0.25, 4). To plot (0.25, 4) begin at (0, 0), move right 0.25 units, and then up 4 units. Place a dot on the grid.

Last, connect the points with a continuous line.

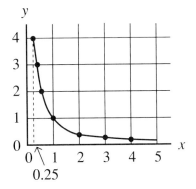

Construct a table of input-output values for each function. Then graph the solutions.

1. $y = \dfrac{2}{x}$　　　　2. $y = x + 2$　　　　3. $y = 6 - x$　　　　4. $y = \dfrac{1}{2x}$

Complete this table of input-output values for each function.
You may want to use your calculator.

1. $y = 5 - x$ **2.** $y = x + 1$

3. $y = \dfrac{0.5}{x}$ **4.** $y = \dfrac{3}{2x}$

x	0.25	0.33	0.5	1	2	3	4
y							

For each of the following functions, make an x-y grid such as
the one on the previous page. Use the process illustrated in the
example to graph each function.

5. $y = 5 - x$ **6.** $y = x + 1$ **7.** $y = \dfrac{0.5}{x}$ **8.** $y = \dfrac{3}{2x}$

MATH REASONING

9. Suppose the graphs of $y = 5 - x$ and $y = 3 - 0.5x$
represent ski slopes. Which one represents the steepest
slope?

PROBLEM SOLVING

10. Mary was growing mold for her science project. At the end
of the first day, the mold was growing as a circular spot
with a radius of $\frac{1}{4}$ cm. Over a period of days, the radius
doubled each day. If x represents days and y represents
radius in cm, graph the daily growth curve over 6 days.

▶ **USING CRITICAL THINKING   Find a Relationship**

11. These graphs show a relationship between the quantities x
and y. Match each phrase with one graph: a) as x increases
y decreases, b) as x increases y increases, c) as x decreases
y increases and d) as x decreases y decreases

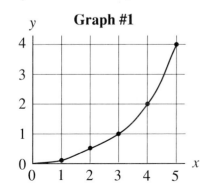

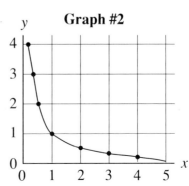

Exponential Notation

Special symbols and notation are often used when writing mathematical expressions. Exponents are used as a short form for writing repeated factors.

EXPLORE Study the Table

The repeated factor is called the **base.** The **exponent** shows the number of times the factor is repeated.

$4 \cdot 4 \cdot 4 = 4^3 \leftarrow$ **exponent**
$\qquad\qquad\quad \uparrow$ **base**

Repeated Factors	Short Form	Read As
$2 \cdot 2 \cdot 2 \cdot 2$	2^4	"2 to the fourth power"
$5 \cdot 5 \cdot 5 \cdot 5 \cdot 5 \cdot 5$	5^6	"5 to the sixth power"
$8 \cdot 8$	8^2	"8 to the second power or 8 squared"
$(0.1)(0.1)(0.1)$	$(0.1)^3$	"(0.1) to the third power or (0.1) cubed"

TALK ABOUT IT

1. What is the base in the expression 17^4? What is the exponent?

2. What is the exponential notation for $7 \cdot 7 \cdot 7 \cdot 7 \cdot 7$?

3. How would you write 2^3 as a standard numeral?

To multiply two expressions with the same base, *add* the exponents.

$$4^3 \cdot 4^2 = (4 \cdot 4 \cdot 4)(4 \cdot 4) = 4^{3+2} = 4^5 = 1{,}024$$

4 is a factor $3 + 2$ times.

To divide two expressions with the same base, *subtract* the exponents.

$$\frac{2^5}{2^3} = \frac{2 \cdot 2 \cdot 2 \cdot 2 \cdot 2}{2 \cdot 2 \cdot 2} = 2^{5-3} = 2^2 = 4$$

Each group equals 1.

The exponents 0 and 1 have special meanings.
A base to the zero power equals one. $b^0 = 1$ when $b \neq 0$

A base to the first power equals the base itself. $b^1 = b$

For each expression, identify the base and the exponent. Then write each in standard notation.

1. 5^3　　　2. 3^2　　　3. 2^5　　　4. 6^0　　　5. 7^1　　　6. 3^4

Write each of these expressions as in standard notation.

1. 3^4 **2.** 4^0 **3.** 5^2 **4.** 2^6

5. 5^1 **6.** 3^3 **7.** 4^2 **8.** 6^0

Write each of these expressions in exponential notation.

9. $6 \cdot 6 \cdot 6 \cdot 6$ **10.** $(2 \cdot 2)(2 \cdot 2 \cdot 2)$ **11.** $3 \cdot 3 \cdot 3 \cdot 3$ **12.** $6 \cdot 6 \cdot 6$

13. $(4 \cdot 4 \cdot 4)(4 \cdot 4)$ **14.** $5 \cdot 5 \cdot 5$ **15.** $7 \cdot 7$ **16.** $9 \cdot 9 \cdot 9 \cdot 9 \cdot 9$

First, write the exponent for each. Then write each in standard notation.

17. $3^2 \cdot 3^7 = 3^?$ **18.** $4^2 \cdot 4^2 = 4^?$ **19.** $2^3 \cdot 2^5 = 2^?$ **20.** $6^2 \cdot 6^1 = 6^?$

21. $\dfrac{5^3}{5^3} = 5^?$ **22.** $\dfrac{4^5}{4^4} = 4^?$ **23.** $\dfrac{3^8}{3^4} = 3^?$ **24.** $\dfrac{6^4}{6^2} = 6^?$

MATH REASONING   Solve using mental math.

25. $2^n = 8$ **26.** $2^n = 32$ **27.** $2^n = 64$

28. $3^n = 9$ **29.** $3^n = 27$ **30.** $2^n = 128$

PROBLEM SOLVING

31. Suppose you place a single penny on the first square of a checkerboard, two pennies on the second square, four pennies on the third square, etc. Express in exponential notation the number of pennies stacked on the 64th square.

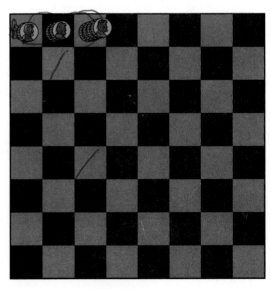

32. Estimate the height of the stack of pennies on the 64th square in problem 31. Will it be a) about 10 feet tall, b) about as tall as a 4 story building, c) about as tall as a skyscraper, or d) will it reach beyond the moon?

▶ **ESTIMATION**

Decide which number is larger without calculating an exact answer.

33. 2^5 or 2^7 **34.** 3^6 or 3^5 **35.** 2^8 or 4^2

Data Collection and Analysis
Group Decision Making

UNDERSTAND
ANALYZE DATA
PLAN
ESTIMATE
SOLVE
EXAMINE

Doing a Questionnaire

Group Skill:
Explain and Summarize

You are giving advice to the student council at your school and you want to know what other students think are the most important issues for the council to work on. You can make a questionnaire to find out. A **questionnaire** is a written or printed list of questions used to gather information.

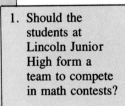
Collecting Data

1. Make a list of issues which might be of concern to the students at your school. Think about school rules, assemblies, sports, or fund raisers.

2. Make a questionnaire with at least four questions. Ask students to rate each question. This is an example of the type of question you could write.

   How important do you think each of these issues is for the student council to discuss in their meetings? Rate each one.

3. Your **sample,** the group of students you give the questionnaire to, should consist of at least 20 students in your school. Discuss with other members of your group how to select an **unbiased** or fair sample. Will you want an equal number of boys and girls? Is it important to have students from different grade levels?

4. Test your questionnaire on a few classmates. Change unclear questions.

5. Make and distribute the questionnaires to the students in your sample.

1. Should the students at Lincoln Junior High form a team to compete in math contests?	not important				very important
	1	2	3	4	5

Organizing Data

6. Compute the average rating for each question on your questionnaire. Make a bar graph to show the averages.

Presenting Your Analysis

7. Prepare a presentation for the student council. Be ready to tell them how you selected your sample, decided which questions to ask, and give your results.

WRAP UP

Algebra Unknowns

Use the clues below. Choose a word from the box to complete
the sentence.

base	two-step	inverse
relation	exponent	solution
inequality	equality	function

1. Input-output pairs form a _____.

2. Properties of _____ help you solve equations.

3. In a _____, every input value has one and only one output value.

4. The repeated factor in an exponential expression is called the _____.

5. Multiplication and division are _____ operations.

6. In an exponential expression, the _____ shows the number
   of times a factor is repeated.

7. The symbols $<$ and $>$ are used to write statements of _____.

8. A _____ makes an equation true.

Sometimes, Always, Never

Which of these words should go in the blank: *sometimes*,
always, or *never*? Explain your choice.

9. If $a > c$ and $b = a$, then __?__, $b > c$.

10. If a number is multiplied by another number, then divided
    by that same number, the result will __?__ be a number
    twice as large as the original number.

11. Any number except 0 raised to the zero power is __?__
    equal to one.

Project

Write three different one-step equations that have the same
solution. Then write three different two-step equations that have
the same solution as before. Graph these on a coordinate plane.

POWER PRACTICE/TEST

Part 1   Understanding

1. Division is the inverse of

   A Addition   **B** Evaluation

   C Multiplication   **D** Subtraction

2. To get the variable c in $c - 25$ alone,

   A add c **B** add 25

   C subtract c **D** subtract 25

3. Write the steps needed to get the variable in $2n + 5$ alone.

4. True or false? $3 > 0.05$, so $3 \geq 0.05$.

5. True or false? $10^0 = 0$.

6. Is this table a function table? Why?

7. A scale that is out of balance is like an

   A equation.   **B** inequality.

s	1	2	3	1	2	3
t	1	2	3	4	5	6

Part 2   Skills

Solve. Use mental math when possible.

8. $v + 27 = 70$ 9. $\frac{c}{5} = 39$ 10. $\frac{b}{4} + 3 = 5.2$ 11. $6h - 4 = 26$

For each inequality below, find the solutions from the set 1, 2, 3, 4, 5, 6.

12. $x > 2$

13. $m + 3 \leq 5$

14. Write a function rule for this function table.

x	1	2	3	4
$f(x)$	9	8	7	6

15. Make a table of input-output values for the function $y = \frac{3x}{2}$. Graph the function on an x-y grid.

16. Write $6 \cdot 6 \cdot 6 \cdot 6$ in exponential notation.

17. Write $3^2 \cdot 3^4$ in standard notation.

Part 3   Applications

18. In a food drive Juan got 4 fewer cans than Sally. Kai got half as much as Sally. In all they collected 286 cans. How many cans did each person get?

19. Use the table to write an algebraic expression for the cost of a cab ride of d miles.

20. **Challenge** A cab ride cost $9.75. How many miles long was the ride?

> **Cab Fare**
> $1.00, plus $1.25 per mile

ENRICHMENT
Computer Numbers

We probably use base ten (decimal) numbers because we have ten fingers. People who work on computer and data transmission equipment often need to use other systems: the most common are the base 2 and base 16 systems.

Normally we use ten digits: 0, 1, 2, . . ., 9. However, for **binary** numbering, we use only two digits, 0 and 1. 0 means zero and 1 means one, but $10_{\text{base }2}$ means one group of 2 and 0 groups of 1. Stop and think about it for a minute.

What do you think that $101_{\text{base }2}$ means? Use place value to help. It means 1 group of four (2 times 2), zero groups of 2, and one group of 1, or five in the base 10 system.

Decide what the following base 2 numbers mean:

1. $11_{\text{base }2}$ **2.** $100_{\text{base }2}$ **3.** $111_{\text{base }2}$ **4.** $1000_{\text{base }2}$

Try to write these base 10 numbers in base 2.

5. 9   **6.** 12   **7.** 13   **8.** 16

The number $1000000_{\text{base }2}$ looks large, but it is only sixty-four in the decimal system. People find it difficult to handle numbers written with only ones and zeros, so another system with sixteen digits is used. The digits are 0, 1, 2, 3, 4, 5, 6, 7, 8, 9, A, B, C, D, E, F. The six letters of the alphabet are used for digits for the numbers we normally call ten, eleven, twelve, thirteen, fourteen, and fifteen. $2B_{\text{base }16}$ is a **hexidecimal** ("hex") number. It means two groups of sixteen and B (eleven) groups of one. That is the same as forty-three in base ten. Decide what the following base 16 numbers mean:

9. $10_{\text{base }16}$ **10.** $100_{\text{base }16}$ **11.** $FF_{\text{base }16}$ **12.** $ABC_{\text{base }16}$

Try to write these base 10 numbers in base 16.

13. 9   **14.** 12   **15.** 13   **16.** 16

17. Make a three column table. List the numbers from 0 through 32 base 10 in the first column, the same numbers base 2 in the second column, and the same numbers again in base 16. Look for patterns. Can you discover how to change numbers between base 2 and base 16.

CUMULATIVE REVIEW

1. Which is the same as 4.8 million?

   A 480,000,000   **B** 48,000,000

   C 4,800,000   **D** 408,000,000

2. Which shows the commutative property?

   A $1 + 3 = 2 + 2$ **B** $21 = 2 \cdot 10 + 1$

   C $2 \cdot \pi = \pi \cdot 2$ **D** $4 = 4 \cdot 1$

3. Which shows the mental math technique breaking apart to find $7 \cdot 53$?

   A $7 \cdot 50$ **B** $7 \cdot 50 + 3$

   C $75 + 3$ **D** $7 \cdot 50 + 7 \cdot 3$

4. What does this graph imply?

   A Boys spent 25% of their money on clothes.

   B Girls spent less than boys on clothes.

   C Girls spent about 50% more on clothes than boys.

   D Girls had more money than boys.

   Boys Girls

   Clothes ☐
   Other ☐

5. Which graph is good for showing how percentages of a budget are spent on various items?

   A bar graph   **B** divided bar graph

   C line graph   **D** circle graph

6. Find the mean of the soccer scores in this frequency table.

   A 2.3   **B** 2.5

   C 10   **D** 23

No. of Games	Final Score
2	1
4	2
3	3
1	4

7. What is true about this box and whisker graph?

   80
   70   H = 71
   60   $Q_U = 58$
   50   MD = 49
   40
   30
   20   $Q_L = 25$
   10   L = 15
   0

   A The mode is 49.

   B Most values fell below 25.

   C The upper and lower quartiles contain the same number of scores.

   D The mean and median are equal.

8. "Toya earned $12 on Monday and $15 on Tuesday. What is the difference in her earnings for these two days?" Which of the following is another way to ask the question in the problem?

   A What did Toya earn in all?

   B Which day did Toya earn more?

   C What did Toya earn per hour?

   D How much more did Toya earn on Tuesday than Monday?

9. Which expression defines the area of the shaded region?

   A $s^2 - \frac{1}{2}\pi r^2$

   B $s^2 - \pi r^2$

   C $s^2 + \pi r^2$

   D $\pi r^2 - s^2$

10. Jo's times for the 100 m dash were 12.78 s, 13.52 s, and 11.76 s. Find her mean time to the correct number of significant digits.

    A 12.7 s   **B** 12.687 s

    C 12.69 s   **D** 12.686 s

127

5

INTEGERS AND INTEGER EQUATIONS

MATH AND HEALTH AND FITNESS

DATA BANK

Use the Health and Fitness Data Bank on page 490 to answer the questions.

1 A diver dives to a depth of 160 ft and stays there for 30 minutes. How many stops does the diver have to make during his ascent? What is the tota ascent time?

THEME: SCUBA DIVING

2 The pressure underwater is measured in **atmospheres.** Use $x = (y + 33) \div 33$, where x is the pressure in atmospheres and y is the depth underwater, to find the absolute pressure in atmospheres for each depth in the Air Decompression Table.

3 An "empty" scuba tank at sea level contains air at 1 atmosphere of pressure. The **absolute atmospheric** pressure (A) of a tank equals its gauge pressure (g) plus atmospheric pressure. Find the gauge pressures for the absolute pressures you found in question 2.

4 **Using Critical Thinking** Some dives require no decompression time. In the table "No Decompression" Limits, find a pattern in the relationship between depth and bottom time for the depths listed from 60 to 90 feet.

This scuba diver must allow plenty of time to reach the surface before her air supply runs out.

Integers and Absolute Value

EXPLORE **Study the Information**

The Celsius temperature scale was designed so that the freezing point of water would be zero. Warmer temperatures are represented by positive numbers, and colder temperatures are represented by negative numbers.

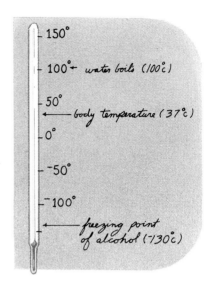

TALK ABOUT IT

1. What temperature would you call the *opposite* of $^+50°$? The *opposite* of $^-200°$?

2. Is 25° higher or lower on the scale than 57°?

3. How far away from zero is $^-150°$? How far away from 0 is $^+150°$?

Each integer has an **opposite** integer.
The **opposite** of $^+4$ is $^-4$.
The **opposite** of $^-15$ is $^+15$.
The **opposite** of 0 is 0.

Opposites Property
The sum of any integer and its opposite is 0. $^+7 + ^-7 = 0 \qquad ^-23 + ^+23 = 0$ $^+n + ^-n = 0$

Integers **increase** going **from left to right** on a number line.

$^-2$ **is less than** $^+7$	$^-14$ **is greater than** $^-39$	0 **is greater than** $^-5$
Write $^-2 < ^+7$	Write $^-14 > ^-39$	Write $0 > ^-5$

The **absolute value** of an integer is its distance from 0 on the number line.

The absolute value of $^-7$ is 7.
It is 7 units from 0 to $^-7$.
Write $|^-7| = 7$.

The absolute value of 4 is 4.
It is 4 units from 0 to 4.
Write $|4| = 4$.

TRY IT OUT

Use > or < to show which is larger.

1. $^-17$ ▥ 0

2. $^-250$ ▥ $^-260$

3. $^+24$ ▥ $^-30$

Complete each statement.

4. $^-5 + 5 = $ ▥

5. $|^+95| = $ ▥

6. $|48| = $ ▥

Write the opposite of each integer.

1. $^+35$ **2.** $^-29$ **3.** $^+52$ **4.** $^-129$

Use > or < to show which is larger.

5. 75 ▓ 32   **6.** 35 ▓ 27   **7.** $^-60$ ▓ 95   **8.** 12 ▓ $^-63$

9. 32 ▓ 46   **10.** $^-34$ ▓ $^-18$ **11.** $^-28$ ▓ $^-95$ **12.** 35 ▓ $^-35$

Find the absolute value of each number.

13. $|45|$ **14.** $|^-86|$ **15.** $|6.7|$ **16.** $|^-375|$ **17.** $|^-12.3|$ **18.** $|^-12.96|$

Complete each statement. Use the opposites property.

19. $4 + {}^-4 = $ ▓   **20.** $2 + $ ▓ $= 0$ **21.** $^-5 + $ ▓ $= 0$ **22.** ▓ $+ {}^-7 = 0$

23. $^-4.5 + $ ▓ $= 0$ **24.** $^-2.7 + $ ▓ $= 0$ **25.** $12.75 + $ ▓ $= 0$ **26.** $0.75 + $ ▓ $= 0$

MATH REASONING Picture a number line in your mind. Think *less than* means *to the left of* and *greater than* means *to the right of*. Find the integer which is:

27. 1 less than $^-85$ **28.** 5 less than $^-4$ **29.** 10 less than $^+8$

PROBLEM SOLVING

30. Death Valley, the lowest point in North America, is 282 ft below sea level. Longs Peak in Colorado has an elevation of 14,256 ft. Would you say that Death Valley has an elevation of $^+282$ ft or $^-282$ ft?

31. If you said that Death Valley has an elevation of $^+282$ ft, then would Longs Peak have an elevation of $^+14{,}256$ ft or $^-14{,}256$ ft?

▶ **ALGEBRA**

32. Which of these equations always results in a true statement when you substitute any integer for x?

    a) $x + 3 = 3 + x$ b) $x + 2 = 5$ c) $|x| = x$

More Practice, page 528, set D

Addition of Integers

EXPLORE **Use Counting Chips**

Let each white chip represent 1 and each red chip represent ⁻1. Since 1 + ⁻1 = 0, you can think of 1 and ⁻1 as "cancelling each other." Now you can see that the chips in the box represent 3.

Work with a partner. One person takes some white chips and the other takes some red chips. Record the integers those chips represent. Combine sets of chips and record the integer they represent. Repeat the activity several times using different numbers of chips.

"ZAP!"

TALK ABOUT IT

1. When you combine red and white chips, how do you decide what integer they represent?

2. What happens if you choose the same number of red and white chips?

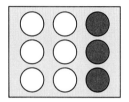

⁻4 + ⁻2   means   →   so ⁻4 + ⁻2 = ⁻6

5 + ⁻2   means   →   so 5 + ⁻2 = 3

The examples above illustrate the following rules:

- To add integers with *like signs*, add the absolute values of the integers and use the common sign.

- To add integers with *unlike signs*, subtract the smaller absolute value from the larger absolute value. Use the sign of the larger.

TRY IT OUT   Use counting chips to model each sum.

1. 42 + ⁻11   **2.** ⁻736 + ⁻40   **3.** ⁻66 + 12   **4.** 40 + ⁻3

132

Find the sum.

1. 5 + ⁻2   **2.** 8 + ⁻3   **3.** ⁻3 + 7   **4.** 3 + ⁻7

5. 2 + ⁻8   **6.** 9 + ⁻6   **7.** ⁻8 + ⁻5   **8.** ⁻4 + ⁻1

9. 6 + ⁻6   **10.** 5 + ⁻6   **11.** 12 + ⁻4   **12.** 10 + ⁻57

Find the sum.

13. 4 + ⁻5 + 8   **14.** 3 + ⁻8 + ⁻1   **15.** ⁻9 + 4 + 5   **16.** ⁻7 + ⁻3 + ⁻2

17. ⁻6 + 10 + ⁻5   **18.** ⁻5 + ⁻3 + 9   **19.** 2 + 7 + ⁻5   **20.** ⁻6 + 12 + ⁻9

21. 6 + ⁻3 + 4   **22.** 11 + ⁻7 + ⁻8   **23.** ⁻4 + 9 + 4   **24.** 3 + ⁻7 + ⁻1

APPLY

MATH REASONING Addition of integers can be represented as moves on a number line. Positive arrows point to the right. Negative arrows point to the left. The number line below shows ⁻4 + 5 = 1.

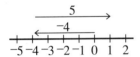

Draw a number line and show each equation.

25. ⁻5 + 4 = x   **26.** 3 + ⁻7 = y   **27.** ⁻4 + ⁻2 = z

PROBLEM SOLVING

28. Sarah owed her parents $7. She earned $18 baby sitting, bought a $12 tape and gave the rest to her parents toward her debt. How much does she owe now?

29. Stan is holding $12, an I.O.U. to his sister for $7.40, and a bill for $3.00 for club dues. How much does he have left for his brother's birthday gift?

▶ **MENTAL MATH**

Find these sums using mental math.

30. the integers from ⁻2 to ⁺5

31. the integers from ⁻10 to ⁺10

32. the integers from ⁻10 to ⁺12

33. the integers from ⁻21 to ⁺19

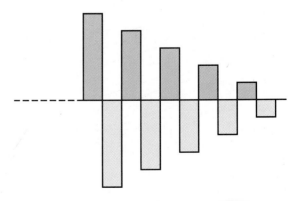

More Practice, page 528, set E

Subtraction of Integers

LEARN ABOUT IT

EXPLORE Use Counting Chips

Work in groups. Suppose you use counting chips to represent an integer. The diagram shows you can add pairs of positive and negative chips to that integer and not change its value.

Use chips to model the subtraction problems below. Write and complete the equations.

a) $^-4 - {}^-3 = p$ Start with $^-4$. Take away $^-3$.

b) $4 - {}^-3 = q$ Start with 4. Take away $^-3$.

c) $1 - {}^-4 = r$ Start with 1. Take away $^-4$.

d) $^-2 - {}^-4 = s$ Start with $^-2$. Take away $^-4$.

This shows 5

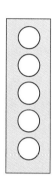

This also shows 5

TALK ABOUT IT

1. For which of the problems did you have to add some positive-negative pairs?

2. Which problem above has the same answer as $4 + 3$?

You can show the following relationships with counting chips.

$5 - 2 = 3$ and $5 + {}^-2 = 3$ $^-6 - {}^-2 = {}^-4$ and $^-6 + {}^+2 = {}^-4$

$3 - {}^-4 = 7$ and $3 + 4 = 7$ $^-1 - {}^-5 = 4$ and $^-1 + 5 = 4$

These examples show that **subtracting an integer is the same as adding the opposite.**

Other Examples

$6 - 3 = 6 + {}^-3 = 3$ (Subtracting positive 3 is the same as adding negative 3.)

$^-21 - {}^-30 = {}^-21 + {}^+30 = 9$ (Subtracting negative 30 is the same as adding positive 30.)

TRY IT OUT   Use chips to model each difference.

1. $8 - {}^-5$ **2.** $^-7 - {}^-2$ **3.** $3 - 8$ **4.** $^-3 - 5$ **5.** $7 - 9$ **6.** $4 - {}^-9$

Subtract.

1. ⁻3 − 4   **2.** 11 − ⁻8   **3.** 3 − 7   **4.** ⁻6 − ⁻4

5. ⁻8 − 2   **6.** ⁻10 − ⁻11   **7.** ⁻9 − ⁻6   **8.** 4 − 11

9. ⁻9 − ⁻5   **10.** ⁻4 − ⁻7   **11.** 2 − ⁻2   **12.** ⁻2 − 2

13. ⁻4 − 0   **14.** ⁻5 − ⁻5   **15.** 17 − 37   **16.** 1 − 45

17. 38 − ⁻2   **18.** 4 − 17   **19.** 0 − ⁻5   **20.** ⁻16 − ⁻8

21. ⁻81 − ⁻81   **22.** 55 − 86   **23.** 23 − ⁻12   **24.** ⁻16 − ⁻50

Perform the operations inside the parentheses first.

25. ⁻7 + (3 − ⁻8)   **26.** (3 − ⁻4) − 2   **27.** (3 − ⁻5) + ⁻1

MATH REASONING

28. Suppose Anita's parents pay her for yard work by giving her $5 cash and canceling her $2 debt. Do you interpret this transaction as a) 5 − 2, b) 5 − ⁻2, or c) ⁻5 − ⁻2?

PROBLEM SOLVING

29. The Dead Sea is 397 m below sea level. Mount Everest is 8,848 m above sea level. How much higher is Mount Everest than the Dead Sea?

30. The top of the highest submerged mountain is 366 m below sea level. Its base is 9,053 m below sea level. How high is this submarine mountain?

31. An elevator went up 2 floors and then went down 5 floors. What do you know about the floor that it began on?

▶ **ESTIMATION**

Use clustering to estimate the values of these expressions.

32. 23 + 26 + ⁻14 + 25 + ⁻15 + ⁻16

33. 122 + ⁻25 + 126 + ⁻24 + ⁻26

34. 28 + (3 − 5) + (6 − 9) + 27

More Practice, page 529, set A

Multiplication and Division of Integers

EXPLORE Study the Situation

The number of students eating in the school cafeteria has been decreasing over the past at an average rate of 20 per year. Assume this change continues at the rate of ⁻20 students per year. What will be the decrease over the next 3 years?

3	⁻20	⁻60
Years from now (+)	Decrease in rate (−)	Decrease in students (−)

TALK ABOUT IT

1. Is the situation *three years ago* described by a) ⁻3 · ⁻20 or b) ⁻3 · 20?

2. Should the situation three years ago be described by a) 60 or b) ⁻60?

3. Why do your answers to question 1 and question 2 explain that the product of two negative integers should be positive?

Your answers should make these rules seem reasonable.

> The product or quotient of **two positive** or **two negative** integers is **positive.** The product or quotient of a **positive and a negative** integer is **negative.**

Examples Find each product or quotient.

A 8 · 12 = 96	two positive integers	48 ÷ 12 = 4
B ⁻15 · ⁻10 = 150	two negative integers	⁻88 ÷ ⁻11 = 8
C 7 · ⁻11 = ⁻77	one positive and one negative	45 ÷ ⁻9 = ⁻5
D ⁻25 · 6 = ⁻150	one negative and one positive	⁻100 ÷ 5 = ⁻20

TRY IT OUT

Compute.

1. 45 · ⁻5 **2.** ⁻12 · ⁻7 **3.** 99 ÷ ⁻11 **4.** ⁻80 ÷ ⁻5 **5.** 0 · ⁻312

Compute.

1. ‾13 · 3 **2.** 4 · ‾18 **3.** ‾18 ÷ ‾9 **4.** 10 · 8

5. ‾12 · 0 **6.** 32 ÷ ‾2 **7.** ‾18 · ‾9 **8.** ‾19 · ‾3

9. 25 ÷ ‾5 **10.** ‾51 ÷ ‾3 **11.** 11 · ‾3 **12.** ‾17 · 0

13. ‾81 ÷ 9 **14.** ‾7 · ‾22 **15.** 13 · 3 **16.** 100 ÷ ‾25

17. (4 · ‾6) · ‾9 **18.** ‾6 · (7 · ‾12) **19.** (42 ÷ ‾7) · 2 **20.** ‾6 · (16 ÷ ‾4)

Compute. Remember the order of operations.

21. 5 · (2 + ‾4) **22.** ‾12 · (5 + ‾7) **23.** (‾4 · 3) + ‾24 **24.** (5 + ‾3) · ‾4

25. 16 · (‾13 + 12) **26.** 2 · (‾81 − ‾79) **27.** 12 ÷ 2 − ‾3 **28.** (‾1 ÷ 4) − 10

MATH REASONING

29. The product of an *even number* of negative integers is __?__.

30. The product of an *odd number* of negative integers is __?__.

PROBLEM SOLVING

31. Yi owed his brother $9. Three days this week he borrowed $0.85 from his brother for lunch. How much does he owe his brother now?

32. **Unfinished Problem** Write and solve a problem from these facts. The record depth for a breath-held dive is 344 ft (Jacques Mayol, 1983). Mayol descended in 104 seconds on a sled, and ascended in 94 seconds.

MIXED REVIEW

Solve these equations.

33. $2x = 6.4$ **34.** $2p + 15 = 25$ **35.** $\frac{x}{7} + 6 = 10$

Find the circumference of each circle. Use 3.14 for π.

36. $r = 7$ m **37.** $r = 10$ cm **38.** $r = 0.2$ cm **39.** $r = 22$ in.

More Practice, page 529, set B

Using Critical Thinking

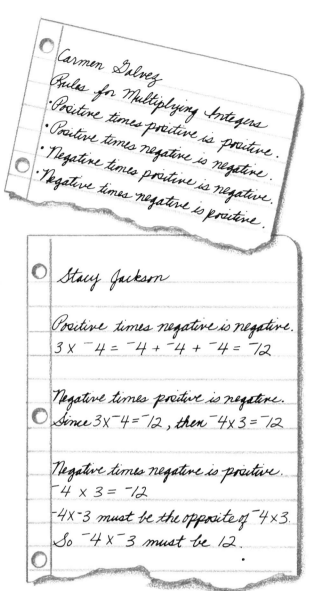

Carmen Galvez
Rules for Multiplying Integers
• Positive times positive is positive.
• Positive times negative is negative.
• Negative times positive is negative.
• Negative times negative is positive.

LEARN ABOUT IT

"These negative numbers are strange," Carmen said. "I can see that a positive times a positive is positive, but how could you ever *prove* the others, especially that a negative times a negative is a positive?"

"I can prove the rules using patterns," said Eric. "For example:

$$3 \cdot 2 = 6$$
$$3 \cdot 1 = 3$$
$$3 \cdot 0 = 0$$
$$\text{so } 3 \cdot {}^-1 = {}^-3.\text{"}$$

"Patterns are okay," Tanya agreed, "but you can't always be sure just by looking at a pattern."

"I think I've found a way to prove the last 3 rules," said Stacy as she wrote some equations on her paper.

Stacy Jackson

Positive times negative is negative.
$3 \times {}^-4 = {}^-4 + {}^-4 + {}^-4 = {}^-12$

Negative times positive is negative.
Since $3 \times {}^-4 = {}^-12$, then ${}^-4 \times 3 = {}^-12$

Negative times negative is positive.
${}^-4 \times 3 = {}^-12$
${}^-4 \times {}^-3$ must be the opposite of ${}^-4 \times 3$.
So ${}^-4 \times {}^-3$ must be 12.

TALK ABOUT IT

1. What were the students trying to do?

2. Why did Tanya discourage the use of patterns?

3. Explain Stacy's proof of the last 3 rules. Can you give reasons why each of her statements are true?

4. Do you think Stacy has proved the rules? Why or why not?

TRY IT OUT

Use Stacy's method or other methods, to convince someone that the following are true.

1. $3 \cdot {}^-2 = {}^-6$ **2.** ${}^-2 \cdot 3 = {}^-6$ **3.** ${}^-2 \cdot {}^-3 = 6$

POWER PRACTICE/QUIZ

Write the number that is the opposite of each.

1. 0   **2.** $^+3$ **3.** $^-3$

Write the number that is the absolute value of each.

4. $|0|$ **5.** $|^+3|$ **6.** $|^-3|$

Use < or > to compare the integers.

7. $^+5$ ▥ $^-5$ **8.** $^-2$ ▥ $^+1$ **9.** 0 ▥ $^-10$

Complete each of the following.

10. $^-5 + {^+5} =$ ▥   **11.** $|^+2| =$ ▥   **12.** $^-4 +$ ▥ $= 0$

Add or subtract. Perform operations inside parentheses first.

13. $^-7 + {^-5}$ **14.** $7 + {^-8}$ **15.** $10 + {^-1}$

16. $6 - {^-7}$ **17.** $3 - {^-4} + {^-5}$ **18.** $^-8 + {^-7} + {^-6}$

19. $(^-8 + {^-4}) + 8$ **20.** $(^-1 - 5) - {^-6}$ **21.** $(^-3 - {^-2}) + 5$

Multiply or divide. Perform operations inside parentheses first.

22. $^-7 \cdot {^-70}$ **23.** $27 \div {^-3}$ **24.** $40 \cdot {^-3}$

25. $^-36 \div {^-9}$ **26.** $156 \div {^-3}$ **27.** $^-8 \cdot {^-70}$

28. $(^-4 \cdot {^-6}) \div {^-2}$ **29.** $(^-6 \div 3) + 2$ **30.** $(^-30 \div 5) - 6$

PROBLEM SOLVING

31. In an experiment, the temperature rose 7°, dropped 10°, and then rose another 4°. If the beginning temperature was $^-3°$, what was the final temperature?

32. In another experiment, the temperature dropped 3° every minute for 5 minutes. If the beginning temperature was 10°, what was the final temperature?

33. During a 10-minute period, the experimental temperature rose 20° to reach 0°. What was the beginning temperature?

Solving Equations Using Mental Math

EXPLORE **Study the Situation**

Solutions to equations can be positive or negative numbers. The solution to the "world record" temperature rise problem on the board can be found by solving the equation $t + 49 = 45$. Can you solve this equation using mental math?

> *The temperature rose 49° F in only 2 minutes at Spearfish South Dakota in 1943. The rise ended at 7:32 a.m. at 45°. What was the temperature at 7:30 a.m.?*

TALK ABOUT IT

1. Does t have to be a positive integer, or a negative integer? How can you tell?

2. What can you add to 49 to reduce it to 45?

3. Write an equation that checks that your answer is the correct solution to the equation.

Simple equations can sometimes be solved by asking *what number must replace the variable to result in a true statement.* When possible, solve an equation using mental math.

Examples Solve using mental math.

A $3x = {}^-15$
  $x = {}^-5$
  Check: $3 \cdot {}^-5 = {}^-15$

Think: 3 times 5 is 15, so x must be ⁻5.

B $x + 5 = {}^-20$
  $x = {}^-25$
  Check: ${}^-25 + 5 = {}^-20$

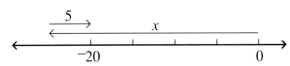

Think: x has to be 5 less than –20, –25 is 5 less than –20.

Solve using mental math.

1. $4n = 100$
2. $54 + m = {}^-10$
3. $x + {}^-5 = 45$
4. $3y = {}^-24$
5. $5 = x + {}^-3$
6. ${}^-2x = 18$
7. $m - 5 = {}^-12$
8. $y - {}^-2 = 11$

Solve these equations using mental math.

1. $^-5x = 150$ **2.** $m + {}^-3 = 2$ **3.** $12n = {}^-24$ **4.** $x + {}^-9 = 23$

5. $125 + {}^-n = 115$ **6.** $234m = 0$ **7.** $^-12 + {}^-x = 9$ **8.** $^-x + 32 = {}^-8$

9. $47 + x = 30$ **10.** $6n = 120$ **11.** $^-7x = 14$ **12.** $^-6 + m = 120$

13. $^-3x = 144$ **14.** $^-2 + n = 78$ **15.** $\dfrac{n}{2} = {}^-5$ **16.** $^-m + 34 = 21$

17. $\dfrac{x}{^-4} = 9$ **18.** $8m = {}^-48$ **19.** $125 + m = {}^-125$ **20.** $36x = {}^-36$

MATH REASONING Solve these equations using mental math.

21. $2x + 1 = 5$ **22.** $3x + {}^-1 = 11$ **23.** $4n + 2 = 10$

PROBLEM SOLVING

24. The record temperature drop for one day is 100°F (Browning, Mt., 1916). The day started at $^+44$°F. What was the temperature 24 hours later?

25. Luke's watch may look strange, but it loses only 1 second per day. He set it at the time shown on New Year's Day, and then left it alone the entire year. What time was it really when the watch showed this same time the following New Year's Day?

▶ **CALCULATOR**

Guess and Check can be used to find a solution to an equation. Use a calculator to find the best guess for the solution to the given equation.

26. $x - {}^-48 = 196$

　　a) $x = 240$ b) $x = 244$ c) $x = 148$

27. $3n + {}^-34 = 29$

　　a) $n = 20$ b) $n = 21$ c) $n = 24$

Solve these equations using Guess and Check.

28. $3n = {}^-492$ **29.** $x + {}^-28 = 333$ **30.** $2x - 8 = {}^-112$

Solving One-Step Equations

LEARN ABOUT IT

EXPLORE **Solve to Understand**

Write an expression that describes the
operation you would perform on both sides
of the equation to isolate the variable x in
each of these equations.

A. $x + {}^-23 = 7$
B. $^-2x = 9$
C. $x - {}^-17 = 35$

TALK ABOUT IT

1. Subtracting 23 from both sides is the same as adding what number?

2. Adding $^-14$ to both sides is the same as subtracting what number?

3. Subtracting $^-7$ from both sides is the same as adding what number?

Examples Solve each equation by isolating the variable.

A

$$x + {}^-4 = {}^-52$$
$$x + {}^-4 + 4 = {}^-52 + 4 \qquad \text{Add the inverse of } {}^-4 \text{ to each side of the equation.}$$
$$x = {}^-(52 - 4) \qquad \text{Apply the rule for adding } {}^+ \text{ and } {}^- \text{ numbers.}$$
$$x = {}^-48 \qquad \text{Compute.}$$
$$\text{Check: } {}^-48 + {}^-4 = {}^-52$$

B

$$\frac{k}{3} = {}^-2$$
$$\frac{k}{3} \cdot 3 = {}^-2 \cdot 3 \qquad \text{Multiply each side of the equation by 3.}$$
$$k = {}^-(2 \cdot 3) \qquad \text{Apply rule for multiplying } {}^+ \text{ and } {}^- \text{ numbers.}$$
$$k = {}^-6 \qquad \text{Compute.}$$
$$\text{Check: } \frac{{}^-6}{3} = {}^-2$$

TRY IT OUT

Solve.

1. $12x = {}^-84$ **2.** $x - 46 = {}^-83$ **3.** $^-5x = 125$ **4.** $x + 5 = {}^-34$

Solve these equations.

1. $x + {}^-7 = 28$ **2.** $14x = {}^-56$ **3.** $y - {}^-37 = 41$ **4.** ${}^-21k = {}^-126$

5. $n \div 17 = {}^-5$ **6.** $m + 32 = 48$ **7.** ${}^-13z = 65$ **8.** $c - 8 = {}^-23$

9. $\dfrac{h}{31} = {}^-7$ **10.** $26j = 78$ **11.** $\dfrac{p}{{}^-14} = 3$ **12.** $b \div {}^-16 = {}^-4$

13. $3s = {}^-231$ **14.** ${}^-11x = {}^-165$ **15.** $y - {}^-89 = {}^-93$ **16.** $f - 43 = {}^-32$

17. $n - 22 = {}^-25$ **18.** $b - {}^-30 = 25$

MATH REASONING   Use mental math to solve the equations.

19. $2w = {}^-50$ **20.** ${}^-4h = {}^-200$ **21.** $n + {}^-60 = {}^-100$

22. $k - 25 = 100$ **23.** $x + 300 = 0$ **24.** ${}^-11s = {}^-88$

PROBLEM SOLVING

25. After heavy rains, the Mississippi River almost flooded. Three days later the river had dropped 12 ft to reach the ${}^-15$ ft mark. How high did the river get?

26. **Data Hunt** Look up the highest and lowest points in your state; compare them to each other.

27. The deepest lake in the world is Lake Baykal in the USSR. It is 6,365 ft deep. The surface of the lake is 1,493 ft above sea level. How far below sea level is the deepest point?

▶ **USING CRITICAL THINKING**   Draw a Conclusion

If the minute hand on a clock turns clockwise, we say it rotates at 360° per hour.

28. If it starts at 12:00 and rotates 726°, what time is it?

29. Marc's watch was running fast when it said 6:00. He rotated the minute hand ${}^-30°$ to correct it. What time was it?

Solving Two Step Equations

LEARN ABOUT IT

EXPLORE   Solve to Understand

The speed of an arrow is about 50 meters per second when released. If shot straight up, its speed (s) in meters per second after t seconds is approximately

$$s = {}^{-}10t + 50.$$

TALK ABOUT IT

1. What is its upward speed 1 second after release? 3 seconds after?

2. At the instant it stops heading up and begins falling, what is its speed?

To solve two-step equations: Add the necessary opposite integer to both sides of the equation. Multiply or divide both sides of the resulting equation as appropriate.

Examples   Solve.

A
$$0 = {}^{-}10t + 50$$
$$0 + {}^{-}50 = {}^{-}10t + 50 + {}^{-}50 \qquad \text{Add } {}^{-}50 \text{ to both sides of the equation.}$$
$$^{-}50 = {}^{-}10t \qquad \text{Compute.}$$
$$^{-}50 \div {}^{-}10 = {}^{-}10t \div {}^{-}10 \qquad \text{Divide both sides of the equation by } {}^{-}10.$$
$$5 = t \qquad \text{Compute.}$$
Check: $^{-}10 \cdot 5 + 50 = 0$

B
$$\frac{x}{^{-}5} - {}^{-}9 = {}^{-}11$$
$$\frac{x}{^{-}5} - {}^{-}9 + {}^{-}9 = {}^{-}11 + {}^{-}9 \qquad \text{Add } {}^{-}9 \text{ to both sides of the equation.}$$
$$^{-}5 \cdot \frac{x}{^{-}5} = {}^{-}5 \cdot {}^{-}20 \qquad \text{Multiply both sides of the equation by } {}^{-}5.$$
$$x = 100 \qquad \text{Compute.}$$
Check: $\dfrac{100}{^{-}5} - {}^{-}9 = {}^{-}20 - {}^{-}9 = {}^{-}11$

TRY IT OUT

Solve these equations.

1. $3x + {}^{-}7 = {}^{-}97$ 2. $4y - {}^{-}8 = {}^{-}12$ 3. $23 = {}^{-}7n + {}^{-}5$ 4. $2x - 5 = 9$

144

Solve these equations.

1. $2x + 5 = 27$ **2.** $5x - {}^-3 = {}^-12$ **3.** ${}^-3n + 7 = 4$

4. $4y - 4 = 24$ **5.** $2 = 5m - {}^-2$ **6.** $12t - 4 = {}^-100$

7. $6n + 5 = 47$ **8.** $15b - 30 = 15$ **9.** $6 = 6j + 6$

10. $14 + 4c = 26$ **11.** ${}^-10 = 3x - {}^-23$ **12.** $15y + 5 = {}^-55$

13. $\dfrac{h}{3} + {}^-2 = 14$ **14.** $4 + \dfrac{{}^-t}{10} = {}^-26$ **15.** $\dfrac{s}{{}^-2} + {}^-15 = 12$

APPLY

MATH REASONING If helium balloons are taped to a scale they provide an upward force giving the scale a negative reading. Write and solve an equation for each scale.

16.

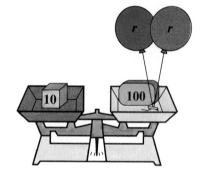

17.

PROBLEM SOLVING

18. Brian owed his older sister $3.50. He started borrowing $0.50 a day from friends to buy a snack after school. He stopped borrowing money when he owed a total of $10.00 How many days did he borrow money from his friends?

19. Talk about your solution Write and solve an equation for this problem. Compare it to a friend's. Are your solutions the same?
A city with 100,000 people has been growing at the rate of 1,500 per year. How long ago was the population 70,000?

▶ **MENTAL MATH**

Break apart a factor to complete these using mental math.

20. ${}^-23 \cdot 8$ **21.** $41 \cdot {}^-9$ **22.** $11 \cdot {}^-32$ **23.** ${}^-15 \cdot 9$

24. $1025 \div {}^-5$ **25.** $625 \div {}^-25$ **26.** ${}^-125 \cdot 6$ **27.** $18 \cdot 40$

Problem Solving
Using the Strategies

UNDERSTAND
ANALYZE DATA
PLAN
ESTIMATE
SOLVE
EXAMINE

LEARN ABOUT IT

Sometimes translating a verbal statement to an equation is the key to solving a problem. Read the verbal statement carefully, thinking about the meaning of each phrase.

Sarah's paycheck from Water World for $48 is $4 more than twice what she earned last week. How much did she earn last week?

Rosanna used the strategy **Write an Equation** to solve this problem.

First Rosanna wrote the data from the problem in simpler terms.

4 more than twice last week's is 48

She then represented the missing information with a variable.

x = amount earned last week

Using the variable, she translated the simplified verbal statement into an equation.

2x   +   4   =   48
twice last week   four more than   is   48

Finally, she solved the equation, and checked her answer.

$$2x + 4 = 48$$
$$2x + 4 - 4 = 48 - 4$$
$$2x = 44$$
$$\frac{2x}{2} = \frac{44}{2}$$
$$x = 22$$

check
$$2(22) + 4 \stackrel{?}{=} 48$$
$$44 + 4 = 48 \checkmark$$

TRY IT OUT

Solve. Use the strategy Write an Equation.

1. A number is divided by 4, resulting in 20. What is the number?

2. Water temperature increases by 5.7° to 48.3°. What was the original temperature?

146

Solve. Use any problem solving strategy.

1. The water temperature in the pool dropped 9° overnight. In the morning, the temperature was 62°. What had the temperature been in the pool the day before?

2. Sandy's $28 paycheck from the aquarium was $3 less than twice Lucas' paycheck. How much did Lucas earn?

3. April took $30.59 out of her savings account to buy a bathing suit, leaving $513.69 in the account. What was the original balance?

4. Caesar was scuba diving. He descended 20 ft from a depth of 110 ft. What was the final depth of his dive?

5. The largest Atlantic bigeye tuna caught with a rod and reel weighed 375.5 lb. The largest yellowfin tuna caught with a rod and reel weighed 388.75 lb. How much more did the yellowfin tuna weigh?

6. The Gulf of Mexico is 582,100 mi². The Gulf of California is 59,100 mi². How much larger is the Gulf of Mexico than the Gulf of California?

7. Jack, Bobby, and Tom went on a fishing trip. Each of them caught a fish. They caught a trout weighing 2 lb, a bass weighing 3 lb, and a catfish weighing 5 lb. None of them caught a fish that starts with the same letter as their name. Jack didn't catch the biggest fish. Bobby caught a bigger fish than Tom. Who caught which fish?

8. Suneal, Michael, Sam, Shyra, Elizabeth, and Akira were going swimming. They had learned in swim class that you should swim with a partner. How many different swim pairs are possible?

Graphing with Integers

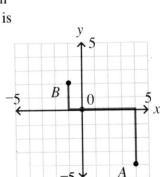

The map on the right shows:

Great N.E. Channel
Olinda Entrance

7

2nd 3-Mile Opening
1st 3-Mile Opening
Cook's Passage
Lark's Passage
2

Flora Passage

−5   0   5   10

Magnetic Passage
Flinders Passage

−5

Queensland,
Australia

Swain Reef

Saumarez
Reef

−10

Capricorn Channel
Curtis Channel

LEARN ABOUT IT

EXPLORE Study the Map

The Great Barrier Reef, the longest reef in the world, is 1,250 miles long. It has many passages and channels. Glenn and Susan were planning to go scuba diving at the reef. They marked some of the many openings on their map to help guide them. They also drew a grid over the map to assist them in estimating distances. They chose the Flora Passage as the origin (0, 0) because they were familiar with that area of the reef.

TALK ABOUT IT

1. The ordered pair for Magnetic Passage is (2, ⁻3). Describe how to find the Magnetic Passage on the map above.

2. What ordered pairs describe the locations of the Great N.E. Channel and Capricorn Channel?

On the **coordinate plane** above, the horizontal line through (0, 0) is called the **x-axis.** The vertical line through (0, 0) is called the **y-axis.**

Examples Draw a coordinate plane and plot the points for these locations.

A Flinders Passage: (4, ⁻4)
Start at (0, 0). Go 4 units right, then down 4 units.

B Lark's Passage: (⁻1, 2)
Start at (0, 0). Go 1 unit left, then up 2 units.

y
5

B   0

−5   5   x

−5   A

TRY IT OUT

1. Give the coordinates for Swain Reefs and the Capricorn Channel.

2. Which passage is located at (⁻4, 4)?

3. What is located at (⁻2, 3)?

148

Give coordinates for each point.

1. *A*　　　　2. *R*　　　　3. *N*

4. *E*　　　　5. *J*　　　　6. *C*

7. *K*　　　　8. *O*　　　　9. *F*

10. *I*　　　　11. *B*　　　　12. *P*

13. *M*　　　　14. *D*　　　　15. *G*

16. *Q*　　　　17. *L*　　　　18. *H*

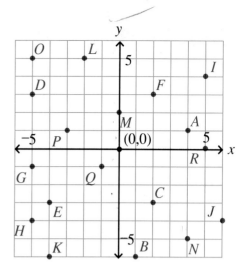

Use graph paper and make a coordinate plane. Plot these points.

19. *S* (5, 8)　　　20. *T* (1, ⁻10)　　　21. *U* (⁻12, 10)　　　22. *V* (⁻7, ⁻4)

23. *W* (6, ⁻2)　　　24. *X* (0, 7)　　　25. *Y* (⁻3, ⁻7)　　　26. *Z* (⁻5, 0)

On a coordinate plane, draw line segments to connect these pairs of points.

27. (⁻8, 0) to (10, 0)　　　28. (⁻6, ⁻4) to (8, ⁻4)　　　29. (1, 12) to (1, 2)

30. (⁻6, 2) to (1, 12)　　　31. (10, 0) to (8, ⁻4)　　　32. (8, 2) to (1, 12)

33. (1, 2) to (1,0)　　　34. (8, 2) to (⁻6, 2)　　　35. (⁻6, ⁻4) to (⁻8, 0)

MATH REASONING

36. Estimate the coordinates of Curtis Channel on the map on the previous page.

PROBLEM SOLVING

37. **Health and Fitness Data Bank** In the "No Decompression" Limits chart, let *x* be the depth in feet and *y* be the bottom time limit. For depths between 60 ft and 90 ft, plot the points (*x, y*). What do you notice about the points you have plotted? Is this true for all depths in the chart?

▶ **USING CRITICAL THINKING　Use Symmetry**

38. Use the symmetry of this figure to find the coordinates of the points *A, B, C, D, E, F, G,* and *H.*

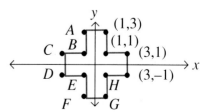

More Practice, page 529, Set F

149

Ordered Pairs that Solve Equations

LEARN ABOUT IT

EXPLORE **Study the Situation**

When you substitute 2 for x and 5 for y in the equation $y = 2x + 1$, you obtain a true statement. The ordered pair $(2, 5)$ is a solution to the equation.

The pressure in a diving tank is measured in pounds per square inch (psi) at 70°F. When the temperature changes, the pressure changes. The formula $y = 5x$, where x is the change in temperature, can be used to find the change in pressure (y).

TALK ABOUT IT

1. For no change in temperature, what is the change in pressure?

2. What five ordered pair solutions do you find when you substitute 1, 2, 3, 4, and 5 for x?

To complete a table of input–output values for a function substitute a value for x, and compute the corresponding value for y.

Example Complete the table of input–output values for the function $y = 2x - 1$ by letting $x = {}^-2, {}^-1, 0, 1, 2,$ or 3.

x	3	2	1	0	-1	-2
$2x - 1$	$2 \cdot 3 - 1$	$2 \cdot 2 - 1$	$2 \cdot 1 - 1$	$2 \cdot 0 - 1$	$2 \cdot {}^-1 - 1$	$2 \cdot {}^-2 - 1$
y	5	3	1	$^-1$	$^-3$	$^-5$
(x, y)	$(3, 5)$	$(2, 3)$	$(1, 1)$	$(0, {}^-1)$	$({}^-1, {}^-3)$	$({}^-2, {}^-5)$

These pairs $(3, 5), (2, 3), (1, 1), (0, {}^-1), ({}^-1, {}^-3), ({}^-2, {}^-5)$ are **solutions** to the equation $y = 2x - 1$. There are many others.

TRY IT OUT

Construct a table of input–output values for each of these functions. Use input values $x = {}^-2, {}^-1, 0, 1, 2, 3$.

1. $y = x + 3$ 2. $y = 2x + 5$ 3. $y = 5x - 10$ 4. $y = 3x - {}^-2$

150

Use $x = {}^-2, {}^-1, 0, 1, 2$ to complete a table of input–output values.

1. $y = 3x + 7$ **2.** $y = {}^-2x - 9$ **3.** $y = 4x - 5$

4. $y = 15 - x$ **5.** $y = 2x$ **6.** $y = 2 - 3x$

7. $y = 3x + 5$ **8.** $y = x + 7$ **9.** $y = 5x + 3$

APPLY

MATH REASONING Each balloon has a ''negative'' weight of x.
Each container has a ''positive'' weight of y. Write an equation
for each scale. Find 2 input–output pairs for each.

10. 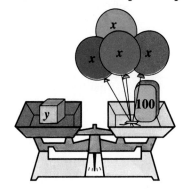   **11.**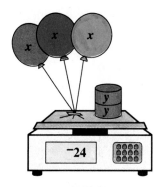

PROBLEM SOLVING

12. Air pressure of 3,000 psi in a diving tank at 70°F is common.
What would be the air pressure in the tank at 140°F?

13. **Health and Fitness Data Bank** The formula
$P = 14.7 + 0.45f$ gives the pressure (P) in pounds per
square inch a diver experiences at a depth of f feet
underwater. Use a calculator to find the pressure on a diver
at the depths given in the ''No Decompression'' Limits Table.

MIXED REVIEW

Write in exponential notation.

14. $6 \cdot 6 \cdot 6 \cdot 6 \cdot 6$ **15.** $7 \cdot 7 \cdot 7$ **16.** $2 \cdot 2 \cdot 2 \cdot 2 \cdot 2$

Write the exponent for each.

17. $4^2 \cdot 4^6 = 4^?$ **18.** $8^3 \cdot 8^7 = 8^?$ **19.** $7^2 \cdot 7^3 = 7^?$

More Practice, page 530, set A

Graphing Linear Functions

EXPLORE Make a Graph

Mai is allowed to watch a total of 10 hours of TV during the school week. Some shows are a half hour long and some are an hour long. You can let x represent the number of half-hour shows and y represent the number of hour shows Mai will watch. The equation $\frac{1}{2}x + y = 10$ describes Mai's situation.

Copy the table above the graph and use the equation to complete it.

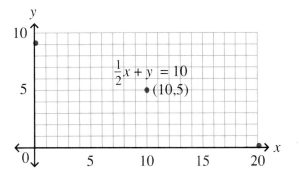

half hour	x	0	2	10	20
hour	y	?	9	?	?

TALK ABOUT IT

1. Why is x multiplied by $\frac{1}{2}$? Why is $\frac{1}{2}x + y$ equal to 10?

2. Suppose Mai watches 10 half-hour shows. How many hour shows could she watch? Suppose she watches no (0) half-hour shows, then how many hour shows could she watch?

3. Find the three points graphed above. Which ordered-pair solutions to the equation do those points represent?

The functions in this lesson have graphs that form straight lines. They are called **linear functions.**

Example Graph $y = 2x - 5$.

- Make a table:

x	0	1	2	5
y	⁻5	⁻3	⁻1	5

- Plot the points $(0, {}^-5)$, $(1, {}^-3)$, $(2, {}^-1)$, and $(5, 5)$.

- Draw a line through the points.

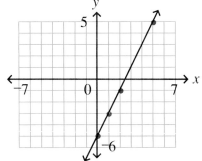

Make a table of input-output values for each function, and graph it. You may want to use your calculator.

1. $y = 2x - 1$ 2. $y = 3x + 1$ 3. $y = x - 6$ 4. $y = 2x - 6$

152

Complete a table of input–output values and graph each linear equation.

1. $y = x + 4$

2. $y = 12 - x$

3. $y = 3x$

4. $y = {}^-2x + 6$

5. $y = 4x - 5$

6. $y = {}^-2x + 1$

7. $y = x - 8$

8. $y = {}^-x$

9. $y = 9 - x$

10. $y = x - 5$

11. $y = 2x - 1$

12. $y = x + 2$

13. $y = 12 - 2x$

14. $y = 5x + {}^-10$

15. $y = 3x - 12$

MATH REASONING

16. Match each equation with one line that has been graphed.

(a) $y = 7 - x$

(b) $y = {}^-\dfrac{1}{2}x - 2$

(c) $y = 2x$

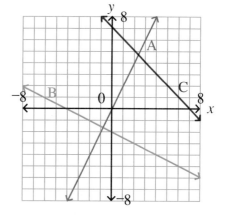

PROBLEM SOLVING

17. Mai's parents allow her to watch 12 hours of TV each week during vacations. Find 3 solutions to her new equation $y = 12 - \dfrac{1}{2}x$.

18. The higher above sea level, the easier it is to boil water. The Celsius boiling point of water can be approximated by the formula

$$t° = 100° - 5°m$$

where m is the altitude in miles. At what temperature does water boil in Denver, the "mile high" city? At what temperature does water boil at a mountain camp 3 miles above sea level?

▶ **MENTAL MATH**

19. Halley's comet is visible from earth about every 76 years. It was last visible in 1986. How old were you then? How old will you be when it is visible again?

Problem Solving
Using the Strategies

UNDERSTAND
ANALYZE DATA
PLAN
ESTIMATE
SOLVE
EXAMINE

LEARN ABOUT IT

Two different strategies can often be used to solve the same problem. Drew used **Draw A Picture** to solve this problem. Anna used **Make an Organized List**.

> The P.E. classes at McKinley Jr. High will be taking track, baseball, volleyball and soccer next semester. How many different arrangements of these 4 activities are possible?

Drew's solution

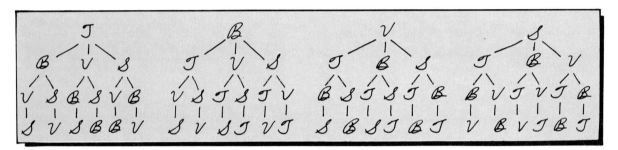

Anna's solution

T B V S	B T V S	V T B S	S T B V
T B S V	B T S V	V T S B	S T V B
T V B S	B V T S	V B T S	S B T V
T V S B	B V S T	V B S T	S B V T
T S V B	B S T V	V S T B	S V T B
T S B V	B S V T	V S B T	S V B T

There are 24 different arrangements possible.

TRY IT OUT

Solve. Use **Make an Organized List** or **Draw a Picture.**

1. For P.E., David has 5 shirts, 3 pairs of shorts and 2 pairs of shoes. How many different outfits can he wear?

2. The members of a basketball team wear jerseys with 2-digit numbers on the back. They use the digits 1, 2, 3, 4, and 5. How many 2-digit numbers are possible?

Solve. Use any problem solving strategy.

Some Strategies	
Act Out	Solve a Simpler Problem
Use Objects	Make an Organized List
Choose an Operation	Work Backward
Draw a Picture	Look for a Pattern
Guess and Check	Use Logical Reasoning
Make a Table	Write an Equation

1. Ein Bokek, on the shores of the Dead Sea is 1,299 ft below sea level. La Paz in Bolivia is 11,916 ft above sea level. Find the difference in elevation between the 2 towns.

2. The Pacific Ocean is 28,635 ft deep at the Mariana Trench. The top of Mount Everest is 29,028 ft above sea level. What is the difference in elevation between the highest and lowest points on the Earth?

3. Flo, Ben, Jackie, and Carl are members of a relay team. If Ben does not run first, how many different running orders are possible?

4. Ming scored a total of 29 points in soccer games this season. He played in 14 games. About how many points did he score per game?

5. Beth, Maria, Malcolm, Jerome, and Juanita competed in a race. Maria finished 3 ft ahead of Beth. Malcolm came in 10 ft behind the winner. Juanita beat Jerome by a foot and won the race. Maria finished 2 ft ahead of Malcolm. By how many feet did Juanita beat Maria?

6. Raul was in charge of deciding on the colors of the uniforms for his baseball team. He could choose any 2 of the following colors: red, white, green, gold, blue, and black. How many different combinations does he have to choose from?

7. Doug and Odra are playing a game of darts. Each threw 3 darts. Use the dart board to find the scores that are possible with 3 darts.

8. At the end of the 1987–88 basketball season, Kareem Abdul-Jabbar's average was about 25.3 points per game. He had played 1,486 games. How many points had he scored?

More Practice, page 545, set A

Applied Problem Solving
Group Decision Making

UNDERSTAND
ANALYZE DATA
PLAN
ESTIMATE
SOLVE
EXAMINE

Group Skill:
Disagree in an Agreeable Way

Your class plans to have a car wash to raise money for a field trip. Your group is in charge of deciding how much to charge to wash each car.

Facts to Consider

1. You want to have a profit of at least $150 to pay for the trip.

2. You conducted a survey to find out how much people would pay to have their car washed. The results are reported in this table.

What is the most you would pay to have your car washed?

Amount	Number of people
$2.00	6
$2.50	8
$3.00	15
$3.50	8
$4.00	7
$4.50	6

3. You plan to have enough students to wash 5–7 cars per hour.

4. Everything you need to wash the cars will be donated.

156

1. If you charge $3.50 a car, how many people would be willing to pay that amount?

2. Write an equation to show that the amount charged per car, times the number of cars per hour, times the number of hours worked, equals the total amount earned. Tell what each letter in your equation represents.

3. Use your equation to find out how much you will make in 1 hour if you charge $3.50 a car and wash 7 cars.

4. What is the greatest number of cars you can wash in 7 hours?

5. If you charge $3.00 a car, and work 7 hours at full capacity, how much money will you make?

6. If you charge $5.00 a car, how many cars will you have to wash to make $150?

What Is Your Decision?

How much will you charge to wash each car? How many cars will you have to wash to make $150 at that rate? Will enough people be willing to pay the price you charge?

WRAP UP

Math Match

Match each phrase on the left with a letter on the right.

1. The absolute value of ⁻3
2. The sum of 5 and ⁻19
3. The difference between ⁻2 and 10
4. Two more than the absolute value of ⁻12
5. The origin of a coordinate system
6. An ordered pair with different x and y values
7. A number to the right of 21 on the number line
8. A number to the left of ⁻44 on the number line
9. A number greater than 14 but less than 18
10. The opposite of 7

a. ⁻7
b. (0, 0)
c. 14
d. 37
e. ⁻50
f. 12
g. 17
h. ⁻14
i. 3
j. (2, 6)

Sometimes, Always, Never

Which word should go in the blank, sometimes, always, or never? Explain your choice.

11. A number raised to the third power will __?__ be negative.

12. The product of 15 negative numbers will __?__ be negative.

13. A number that is larger than another number __?__ will be to the right of that number on a number line.

14. The absolute value of a number is __?__ equal to that number.

Project

Use a calculator to find the sum of the integers from 1 to 5 including 1 and 5. Then do the same for 1 to 10, 1 to 15, 1 to 20, 1 to 25, and 1 to 30, inclusive. What do all of your answers have in common? Can you explain why this happens?

POWER PRACTICE/TEST

Part 1   Understanding

1. Which statement is true? Why?

   A The absolute value of any non-zero number can be positive or negative.

   B The absolute value of any non-zero number is always positive.

   C The absolute value of any non-zero number is always negative.

2. To subtract an integer, add _____. Use an example to show this is true.

3. The product of two negative integers is _____. Use an example to show this is true.

4. Solve $\frac{y}{3} = {}^-5$ using mental math. Explain your reasoning.

Part 2   Skills

Compute.

5. $^-49 + 12$

6. $(^-5 + {}^-7) + 4$

7. $7 - 10$

8. $^-4 \cdot 8$

9. $^-56 \div {}^-8$

10. $(^-6 \cdot {}^-8) \div {}^-12$

Solve.

11. $^-12x = {}^-96$

12. $b + 15 = {}^-4$

13. $\frac{x}{5} = 10$

14. $^-5m - {}^-7 = {}^-3$

15. $\frac{s}{^-4} + 6 = 9$

16. $3n + 4 = {}^-14$

Give coordinates for each point.

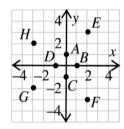

17. H

18. E

19. G

20. A

21. Make a table of input-output values and graph the linear equation $y = {}^-2x - 1$.

Part 3   Applications

22. Anchorage, Alaska, is located at 61° N latitude. Perth, Australia, is 93° farther south than Anchorage. At what latitude is Perth?

23. **Challenge** Ms. Ortega is buying a sofa. Write an equation that indicates that her monthly payment (p) equals $\frac{1}{6}$ of the cost (c) of the sofa, less the $75 deposit.

ENRICHMENT
Understanding Compound Statements

Compound statements are two or more statements connected by words such as **and, or,** or **if-then.** You must think carefully to decide whether a compound statement is true or false.

A **conjunction** is formed using the connective **and.**
Example: 7 is an odd number **and** 4 is an even number.

A **disjunction** is formed using the connective **or.**
Example: 46 is divisible by 2 **or** 59 is divisible by 3.

An **implication** is formed using the connectives **if** and **then.**
Example: If 64 is divisible by 16, **then** 128 is divisible by 16.

Tell which kind of compound statement is given. Then tell whether it is true or false.

1. If 3 times a number is ⁻12, then the number is 4.

2. 27 is a multiple of 3 and 21 is a multiple of 9.

3. 169 is a square number or 169 is a prime number.

4. If a number is less than 80, then that number is less than 100.

5. If $xy = 0$, then x is equal to 0.

6. If $x + y = 0$, then x and y are opposites of each other.

Each Venn diagram suggests an implication. Write the implication using if-then connectives.

Example

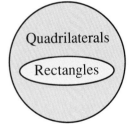

Implication: If a figure is a rectangle, then the figure is a quadrilateral.

7.

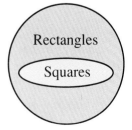

8.

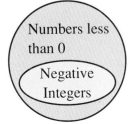

CUMULATIVE REVIEW

1. Which types of graphs would be most appropriate to show how many students preferred three different lunch menus?

   A bar graph and circle graph

   B divided bar graph and circle graph

   C line graph and bar graph

   D line graph and divided bar graph

2. This stem and leaf table shows the points scored by a football team during each game of the season. Which statement is true?

Stem	Leaf
1	2, 2
2	7, 6, 1
3	5, 9
4	2

   A Their median score was 12 points.

   B They played 4 games.

   C During most games, they scored more than 25 points.

   D Their mean score was 26.5 points.

3. Find the area of this trapezoid.

   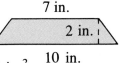

   A 17 in.^{2} B 34 in.^{2}

   C 140 in.^{2} D 19 in.^{2}

4. Find the volume of this solid if the face of each cube is 1 in^2.

   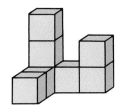

   A 33 in.^{3} B 18 in.^{3}

   C 8 in.^{3} D 7 in.^{3}

5. What operation should be used to simplify $h \div 10$ so the variable is alone?

   A subtract 10   B divide by 10

   C multiply by 10   D add 10

6. Solve $7c = 42.7$.

   A $c = 298.9$ B $c = 6.1$

   C $c = 35.7$ D $c = 49.7$

7. Which statement is true?

   A $5 \geq 5$ B $3 > 4$

   C $4 \leq 3$ D $7 < 6$

8. A car was travelling 45 mph. What values would complete this table describing the distance the car travelled over 5 hours?

Time (t)	1	2	3	4	5
$d = 45t$	45	?	?	?	?

   A 50, 55, 60, 65   B 90, 180, 360, 720

   C 46, 47, 48, 49   D 90, 135, 180, 225

9. What is the standard notation for 6^3?

   A 18   B 729   C 9   D 216

10. Grain is stored in a cone-shaped building. The diameter of the base is 30 ft and the height is 20 ft. What is the volume of this building? Use 3.14 for π.

    A $18,840$ ft^3 B $4,710$ ft^3

    C $56,520$ ft^3 D $14,130$ ft^3

6

NUMBER THEORY

THEME: URBAN OPEN SPACES

MATH AND
SOCIAL STUDIES

DATA BANK

Use the Social Studies Data Bank on page 498 to answer the questions.

1 How many bricks would you order to build an 8-inch thick wall 4 feet high and 8 feet long?

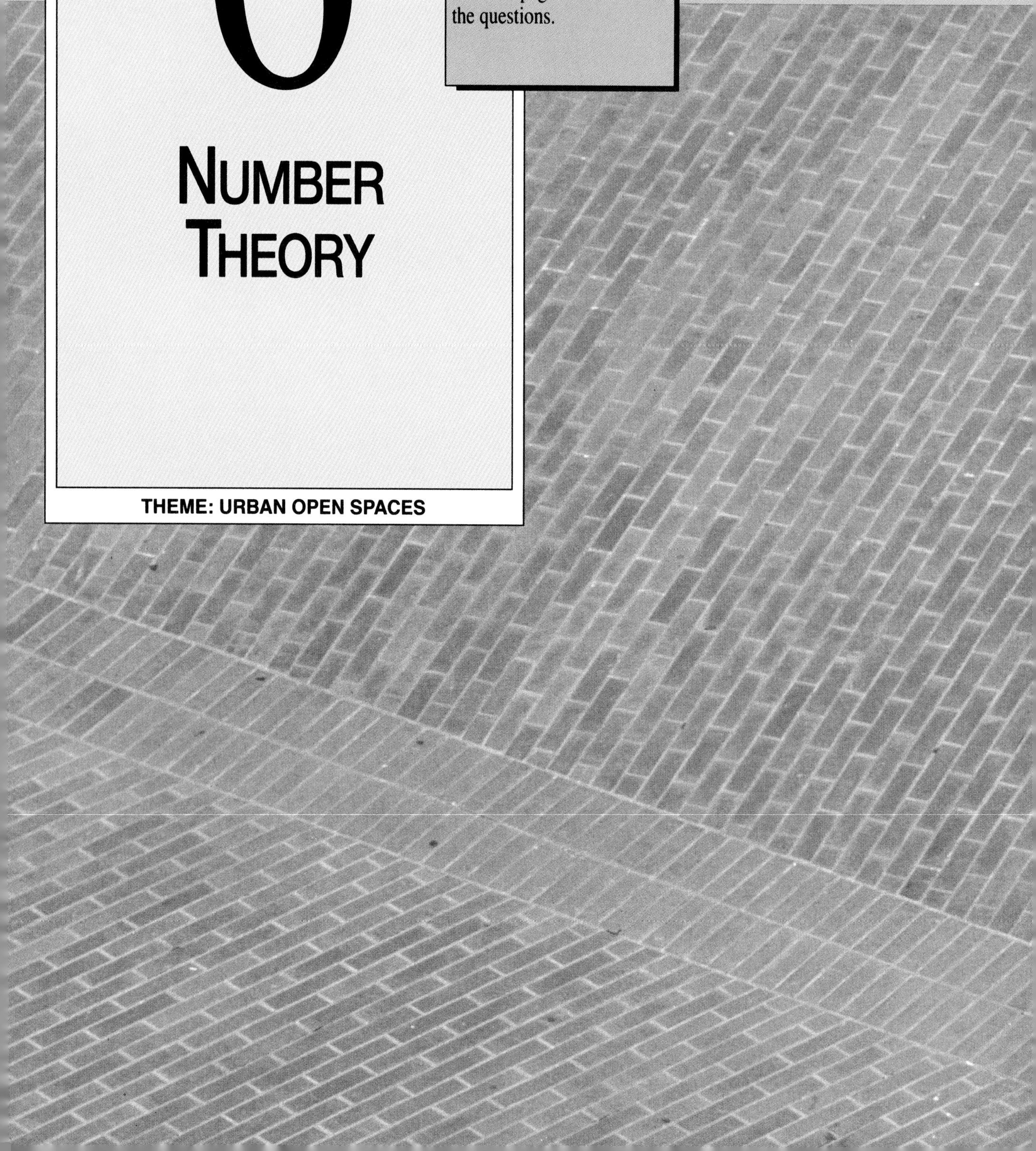

2 How many bricks would you order to build a patio measuring 12 feet by 20 feet?

3 What is the nominal size of a standard English brick?

4 **Using Critical Thinking** For the nominal sizes of standard English and U.S. bricks, how do the dimensions' length, width and height relate to each other? What advantages can you see to these dimensions?

Many communities have open spaces where people can meet, hear a concert, or even skateboard.

163

Factors and Multiples

EXPLORE Use Grid Paper

Vietta has 24 square tiles. Draw all the
ways she could make a rectangular patio
using all the tiles.

TALK ABOUT IT

Each tile represents 1 square unit

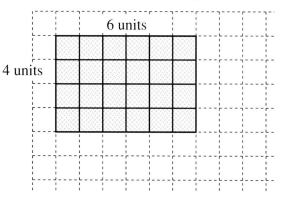

6 units

4 units

1. How many different rectangles
   can be formed with the 24 tiles?

2. List all the numbers that are side lengths
   of the different rectangles.

When two or more whole numbers are multiplied to form a
product, each is called a **factor** of the product. The product of
two whole numbers is a **multiple** of each of the numbers.

factor   factor   multiple of each factor

↓   ↓   ↓
1 · 24 =   24   The numbers 1, 2, 3, 4, 6, 8, 12 and 24 are the factors
2 · 12 =   24   of 24.
3 · 8 =   24   When 24 is divided by one of its factors, the remainder
4 · 6 =   24   is zero.

Examples

A Tell whether 7 is a factor of 84.

$84 \div 7 = 12$
Since the remainder is zero, 7 is a factor
of 84.

B List the first seven nonzero multiples of 6.

6, 12, 18, 24, 30, 36, 42
Multiply 6 by 1, 2, 3, 4, 5, 6, and 7.

C Find the factors of 12.

Since 1 · 12, 2 · 6, and 3 · 4 are all equal to 12,
the factors of 12 are 1, 2, 3, 4, 6, and 12.

List the factors and the first four nonzero multiples of each number.

1. 9   **2.** 16   **3.** 25   **4.** 20   **5.** 30   **6.** 42

164

State if the first number is a factor of the second. Explain why or why not.

1. 6, 36 **2.** 4, 14 **3.** 7, 28 **4.** 5, 65 **5.** 6, 40

6. 8, 73 **7.** 9, 29 **8.** 10, 60 **9.** 11, 121 **10.** 3, 276

List all the factors of each number.

11. 18 **12.** 21 **13.** 36 **14.** 27 **15.** 48

16. 50 **17.** 64 **18.** 72 **19.** 88 **20.** 100

List the first five nonzero multiples of each number.

21. 7 **22.** 8 **23.** 10 **24.** 12 **25.** 18

26. 11 **27.** 13 **28.** 20 **29.** 24 **30.** 32

APPLY

MATH REASONING Determine whether each statement is true or false. If false, give a counterexample.

31. If 12 is a multiple of x, then 24 is a multiple of x.

32. If x is a factor of 36, then 36 is a multiple of x.

33. If 3 is a factor of both x and 12, then x is a multiple of 12.

PROBLEM SOLVING

34. If Vietta had 12 more square tiles, she would have a total of 36. How many different rectangular patios could she build with these 36 tiles?

35. Social Studies Data Bank You want to build a patio measuring 24 ft × 8 ft × 4 in. without cutting any bricks. Which pattern would you select? *Use U.S. bricks.*

▶ **CALCULATOR**

You can use a calculator with a memory to find the factors of a whole number. Follow the steps at the right. Find the factors of each number.

36. 76 **37.** 94 **38.** 165 **39.** 154

Enter the number, push (M+) to record it in the memory. Then perform this sequence, each time changing your trial divisor from 2, 3, 4, 5 ... in order.

This key displays   trial divisor
the number
in memory. → (MR) (÷) 2 (=)

When the final display is a whole number, the trial divisor and the display number are factors of the number in the memory.

Divisibility

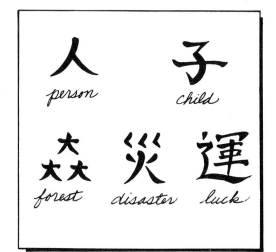

人 person
子 child
森 forest
災 disaster
運 luck

LEARN ABOUT IT

EXPLORE **Read the Information**

Even though Ross has learned to read and write hundreds of Japanese kanjii characters, he will be reading at a third grade level when he goes to Japan as an exchange student.

TALK ABOUT IT

1. If Ross has learned 5 kanjii characters a day, which of these numbers of characters could he have already learned? Explain your answer.   a) 87   b) 105   c) 124   d) 910   e) 264

2. If Ross has learned 3 kanjii characters a day, which of these numbers of characters could he have already learned? a) 87   b) 105   c) 124   d) 910   e) 264

If a is a factor of b, then b is **divisible by** a. For example, since 5 is a factor of 30, 30 is divisible by 5.

A **divisibility rule** is a *shortcut* for determining when one number is divisible by another.

Rules for Divisibility by 2, 3, and 5
■ A number is **divisible by 2** if its ones digit is even (0, 2, 4, 6, 8).
■ A number is **divisible by 3** if the sum of its digits is divisible by 3.
■ A number is **divisible by 5** if the ones digit is 0 or 5.

Examples

A Is 105 divisible by 3 or 5?
Since $1 + 0 + 5$ is 6 and 6 is divisible by 3, the number 105 is divisible by 3. Since its ones digit is 5, the number 105 is also divisible by 5.

B Is 234 divisible by 2 or 3?
Since its ones digit is even, the number 234 is divisible by 2. Since $2 + 3 + 4$ is 9, and 9 is divisible by 3, the number 234 is also divisible by 3.

TRY IT OUT

State whether each number is divisible by 2, 3, or 5.

1. 513   **2.** 1358   **3.** 2100   **4.** 4332   **5.** 5472   **6.** 18,648

State whether each number is divisible by 2 or 5.

1. 122   **2.** 235   **3.** 446   **4.** 1,238   **5.** 1,557

6. 3,690   **7.** 6,782   **8.** 17,455   **9.** 26,704   **10.** 40,820

State whether each number is divisible by 3.

11. 331   **12.** 645   **13.** 702   **14.** 566   **15.** 813

A number is divisible by 6 if it is divisible by both 2 and 3.
State whether each number is divisible by 6.

16. 236   **17.** 484   **18.** 735   **19.** 2,688   **20.** 4,128

A number is divisible by 4 if the number formed by its last two digits
is divisible by 4. State whether each number is divisible by 4.

21. 144   **22.** 374   **23.** 260   **24.** 3,048   **25.** 4,243

APPLY

MATH REASONING Study this example to determine a rule for divisibility by 11.

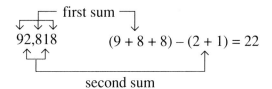

$(9 + 8 + 8) - (2 + 1) = 22$

Since 22 is divisible by 11, the number
92,818 is also divisible by 11.
If the result is 0, the original number is
divisible by 11.

Determine whether these numbers are divisible by 11.

26. 814   **27.** 9163   **28.** 57,642   **29.** 22,583   **30.** 725,043

PROBLEM SOLVING

31. Mike practiced his piano lessons the same number of hours
per week. He practiced 312 hours in all. He practices less than
13 h a week. What is the greatest number of hours he could have
practiced each week?

▶ **MENTAL MATH**

A number that is *not* divisible by 2 or 3 or 5 is not divisible by any of
their products. Use mental math to determine which of these numbers
is *not* divisible by any of the numbers 2, 3, 4, 5, 6, 8, 9, 10, or 12.

32. 77   **33.** 777   **34.** 91   **35.** 1771   **36.** 441

More Practice, page 530, set D

Primes and Composites

EXPLORE **Discover a Pattern**

Work in groups. Copy the table at the right.

- Circle 2 and cross out all other multiples of 2.
- Circle the next number that has not been crossed out and cross out all of its multiples.
- Continue this process until all numbers except 1 are either circled or crossed out.

1	2	3	4	5	6	7	8	9	10
11	12	13	14	15	16	17	18	19	20
21	22	23	24	25	26	27	28	29	30
31	32	33	34	35	36	37	38	39	40
41	42	43	44	45	46	47	48	49	50
51	52	53	54	55	56	57	58	59	60
61	62	63	64	65	66	67	68	69	70
71	72	73	74	75	76	77	78	79	80
81	82	83	84	85	86	87	88	89	90
91	92	93	94	95	96	97	98	99	100

TALK ABOUT IT

1. How many circled numbers have a 2, 4, 6, 8, or 0 for their ones digit?

2. Select several circled numbers at random. What are the factors of these numbers?

A prime number is a whole number greater than 1 that has exactly two factors, 1 and the number itself.

Factors of 17: 1, 17
The number 17 is prime.

Factors of 79: 1, 79
The number 79 is prime.

A composite number is a number greater than 1 that has more than two factors.

Factors of 121: 1, 11, 121
The number 121 is composite.

Factors of 30: 1, 2, 3, 5, 6, 10, 15, 30
The number 30 is composite.

The numbers 1 and 0 are neither prime nor composite. The number 1 has only one factor, itself. How many factors does the number 0 have?

List all the factors of each number. Then, state whether each number is prime or composite.

1. 33 **2.** 43 **3.** 57 **4.** 71 **5.** 82 **6.** 93

List all the factors of each number. Then, state whether it is prime or composite.

1. 48   **2.** 67   **3.** 31   **4.** 69

5. 45   **6.** 34   **7.** 41   **8.** 53

9. 37   **10.** 51   **11.** 64   **12.** 59

13. 146   **14.** 177   **15.** 159   **16.** 147

17. What is the smallest prime number?

18. How many even prime numbers are there?

APPLY

MATH REASONING

19. The numbers 41 and 43 are both prime. Since their difference is only 2, they are called **twin primes.** Find two other pairs of twin primes.

20. The number $1,001 = 7 \cdot 11 \cdot 13$. The factors 7, 11, and 13 are three **consecutive primes.** The number 2,431 is also the product of three consecutive prime factors. What are the factors of 2,431?

PROBLEM SOLVING

21. Jane was using her calculator to determine whether 2,137 is prime. She checked 2,137 ÷ 4, which gave the result 534.25 and concluded that 4 is not a factor. Sarah said, "There is no point in checking 4. You can tell from the divisibility test for 2 that 2 is not a factor. If 2 is not a factor, then 4 cannot be a factor." Do you agree with Sarah? Why?

22. If there are whole numbers a and b such that $ab = 64$ and if a is less than 8, then b is greater than 8. Why does this mean you only need to determine whether any of the primes 2, 3, 5, and 7 are factors of 64 before you conclude that 64 is a prime?

▶ **ALGEBRA**

23. A problem posted on the math club bulletin board stated: Is the result of $n^2 - n + 11$ where n represents a whole number always a prime?

Find a value for n that shows that this is not true.

Using Critical Thinking

Nicole decided to find the smallest positive number in the world. She entered the number 1 into her calculator and divided it by 2. She continued, dividing by 2 over and over again. She got the result 0.0000001. When she divided that by 2, Nicole got the message "ERROR". "Look at that," she said. "You can't divide 0.0000001 by 2."

Kieko said, "That can't be right." She did the same things on her calculator, and said, "When I divide 0.0000001 by 2, I get zero."

"My calculator shows 5.-08," exclaimed Carlos.

Archie was listening. He said, "Maybe your calculators can't divide those numbers, but I can. I can keep dividing each result by 2 as often as I please and get a good answer."

TALK ABOUT IT

1. What were the students doing on their calculators?

2. Do you think Carlos' calculator divided 0.0000001 by 2? Explain.

3. Do you think Carlos can continue dividing by 2 on his calculator?

4. Do you really think Archie can divide by 2 as often as he pleases? Explain.

TRY IT OUT

1. Use your calculator. Enter 1. Multiply it by 2. Continue multiplying by 2 until the calculator gives a strange answer. Explain what is happening.

2. Add 1 and 2 on your calculator. Divide the result by 2. Add 1 to the result, and divide by 2. Again, add 1 to the result and divide by 2. Repeat this over and over, until something interesting happens. Describe what happens.

State if the first number is a factor of the second.

1. 3, 12   **2.** 5, 72   **3.** 14, 7

List all the factors of each number.

4. 12   **5.** 48   **6.** 16

7. 17   **8.** 81   **9.** 120

List the first five nonzero multiples of each number.

10. 3   **11.** 11   **12.** 8

13. 15   **14.** 10   **15.** 21

State whether each number is divisible by 2 or 4.

16. 100   **17.** 225   **18.** 262

State whether each number is divisible by 3 or 5.

19. 840   **20.** 123   **21.** 483

List all the factors of each number. Then state whether each number is prime or composite.

22. 41   **23.** 25   **24.** 51

State whether each number is prime or composite.

25. 73   **26.** 98   **27.** 121

PROBLEM SOLVING

28. Maria's soccer practices last 3 hours each. Could she have practiced a total of 57 hours this month?

29. Admission to the aquarium is $4 for adults and $3 for children. Matt collected a total of $20 ‖‖‖ for 60 tickets on Tuesday. Find the last digit for the amount that Matt collected.

30. Karen has been studying Spanish. She is trying to learn 4 new words each day. So far, she has learned between 250 and 275 words. What are all the possible numbers of words that she could have learned so far?

Prime Factorization

EXPLORE Study the Information

A standard concrete block measures 16 in. × 8 in. × 8 in. Half blocks measure 8 in. × 8 in. × 8 in. In a section of a masonry yard, there were 30 concrete half blocks.

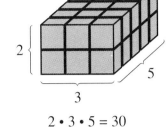

$2 \cdot 3 \cdot 5 = 30$
One way to arrange 30 half blocks.

TALK ABOUT IT

1. How many different ways could you arrange the 30 half blocks into a rectangular prism?

Every composite number can be expressed as the product of prime numbers. You can construct a factor tree to find the **prime factors** of 84.

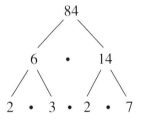

Start with any two factors of 84.

Continue to find factors until all factors are prime.

$2^2 \cdot 3 \cdot 7$ is the **prime factorization** of 84.

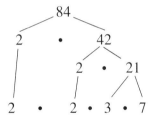

Examples Use repeated division by primes to find the prime factorization of each number.

A 60

$2\overline{)60}$
$2\overline{)30}$
$3\overline{)15}$
  5

$60 = 2^2 \cdot 3 \cdot 5$

B 231

$3\overline{)231}$
$7\overline{)77}$
  11

$231 = 3 \cdot 7 \cdot 11$

C 286

$2\overline{)286}$
$11\overline{)143}$
  13

$286 = 2 \cdot 11 \cdot 13$

TRY IT OUT

Find the prime factorization of each number.

1. 45 **2.** 63 **3.** 38 **4.** 32

5. 16 **6.** 81 **7.** 28 **8.** 99

Use factor trees to find the prime factorization of each number.

1. 24   **2.** 44   **3.** 36   **4.** 42   **5.** 75

6. 120   **7.** 105   **8.** 153   **9.** 80   **10.** 198

Use repeated division to find the prime factorization of each number.

11. 64   **12.** 72   **13.** 87   **14.** 102   **15.** 216

16. 180   **17.** 432   **18.** 363   **19.** 600   **20.** 315

Solve each equation to find the number whose prime factorization is given.

21. $n = 2^3 \cdot 3$ **22.** $n = 7 \cdot 2^2$ **23.** $n = 3^4$ **24.** $n = 7 \cdot 5^2$

25. $n = 3^2 \cdot 11$ **26.** $n = 2^5$ **27.** $n = 5^4$ **28.** $n = 5^2 \cdot 2^3$

MATH REASONING Use repeated division on your calculator to answer each question below.

29. The number 101 is prime. Is 1,001?   **30.** The number 109 is prime. Is 1,009?

PROBLEM SOLVING

31. A stack of 720 concrete half blocks forms a rectangular prism that is 10 feet wide by 8 feet long. How many blocks high is it?

32. **Social Studies Data Bank** If you ordered a ton of U.S. bricks you would have about 500. What are the approximate dimensions of some of the rectangular prisms that could be formed using these 500 bricks?

Add or subtract.

33. $^+7 - {^+10}$ **34.** $^+8 + {^-4}$ **35.** $^-5 - {^-2}$ **36.** $^-6 + {^-3}$

37. $^-8 + {^+10}$ **38.** $^+16 - {^-8}$ **39.** $^+10 - {^-15}$ **40.** $^-10 - {^+7}$

Evaluate each expression for $a = 2.5$, $b = 1.7$, $c = 0.02$.

41. $a(b + c)$ **42.** $ab + ac$ **43.** $(ab) \cdot c$ **44.** $a \cdot (bc)$

More Practice, page 531, set B

Problem Solving
Using the Strategies

UNDERSTAND
ANALYZE DATA
PLAN
ESTIMATE
SOLVE
EXAMINE

LEARN ABOUT IT

To solve some problems you may find it helpful to use more than one strategy. To solve this problem, you can **Use Objects, Solve a Simpler Problem, Make a Table,** and **Look for a Pattern.**

Begin with a Simpler Problem, then Use Objects to make a model.

Paul is building a monument at the entrance to a Civil War battlefield. The monument includes a pyramid made out of cannonballs. He wants to put 8 cannonballs on each side of the bottom layer. How many cannonballs will he need to complete the monument?

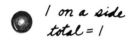 1 on a side total = 1   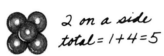 2 on a side total = 1 + 4 = 5    3 on a side total 1 + 4 + 9 = 14

Then Make a Table to show the number of cannonballs on a side and the total number of cannonballs. Then Look for a Pattern.

Number on a side	1	2	3	4	5	6	7	8
Number in the bottom layer	1	4	9	16	25	36	49	64
Total	1	5	14	30	55	91	140	204

Paul needs 204 cannonballs.

TRY IT OUT

Solve. Use any problem solving strategy.

1. Another monument is also a pyramid but its base is a triangle. If there are 8 cannonballs on each side of the bottom layer, how many cannonballs are in the monument?

2. Erin is building a 2-ft high wall by putting T-shaped blocks end-to-end. She used 20 blocks. Find the perimeter of her wall.

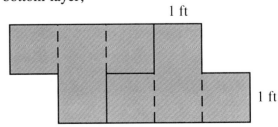

1 ft

1 ft

174

Solve. Use any problem solving strategies.

1. Brian was the first person to arrive at the theater to see *Gone With the Wind*. Each group that arrived after Brian had 2 more people than the previous group. After the sixteenth group arrived, how many people were in the theater?

2. Pietro has 4 boxes that weigh a total of 45 lb. If he adds 2 lb to the first box, subtracts 2 lb from the second box, multiplies the weight of the third box by 2, and divides the weight of the fourth box by 2, the boxes will all weigh the same. Find the original weight of each box.

3. The Statue of Liberty weighs 450,000 lb and is 152 ft tall. The average eighth grader weighs about 112 lb. About how many eighth graders would it take to equal the weight of the Statue of Liberty?

Some Strategies	
Act Out	Solve a Simpler Problem
Use Objects	Make an Organized List
Choose an Operation	Work Backward
Draw a Picture	Look for a Pattern
Guess and Check	Use Logical Reasoning
Make a Table	Write an Equation

4. There were 2,213,363 people who fought in the Civil War. Of those, 2,128,948 were in the army. The rest were in the navy. How many were in the navy?

5. The Jackson's had a new patio installed. It took the contractor and his apprentice 21 hours to complete the job. They used 96 stone tiles and 2 sacks of mortar. Use the price list to find the total cost of the patio.

Tiles		Labor	
Concrete	$0.49 each	Contractor	$28./hr
Stone	$0.85 each	Apprentice	$11./hr
Ceramic	$1.10 each		
Mortar	$2.50/sack		

6. A large pizza is cut into pieces using 6 straight cuts. All the pieces are the same size. If the pieces cannot be stacked for cutting, what is the greatest number of pieces you can get?

7. Scott's history book has 16 chapters. He is just beginning chapter 5. The chapters average 36 pages each. How many pages are in the book?

8. Jessica added 8 odd numbers and got 20 for the answer. She used some of the numbers more than once. How many different ways could she get 20 using 8 odd numbers?

More Practice, page 545, set B

Greatest Common Factor

EXPLORE **Use a Venn Diagram**
- Draw circles and label them *A* and *B*.
- List all the factors of 12 in circle *A* and all the factors of 30 in circle *B*.
- No factor of 12 and 30 should be written more than once. So, the numbers that are factors of both 12 and 30 should be written in the section where circles *A* and *B* overlap.

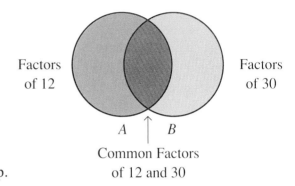

Factors of 12   Factors of 30

A ↑ *B*

Common Factors of 12 and 30

TALK ABOUT IT

1. What numbers are factors common to both 12 and 30?

2. Which number is the greatest factor common to both 12 and 30?

Another way to find the **Greatest Common Factor** or **GCF** is to list all the factors of each number.

Numbers	Factors
18	**1, 2, 3, 6,** 9, 18
24	**1, 2, 3,** 4, **6,** 8, 12, 24

Numbers	Factors
12	**1, 2, 3,** 4, 6, 12
30	**1, 2, 3,** 5, 6, 10, 15, 30
45	**1, 3,** 5, 9, 15, 45

The common factors of 18 and 24 are **1, 2, 3, 6.** The GCF of 18 and 24 is 6.

The common factors of 12, 30, and 45 are **1** and **3.** The GCF of 12, 30, and 45 is 3.

You can also use prime factorization to find the GCF of several numbers.

$18 = 2 \cdot 3 \cdot 3$
$24 = 2 \cdot 2 \cdot 2 \cdot 3$
$GCF = 2 \cdot 3 = 6$

Write the prime factorization for each number. The GCF is the product of all the common prime factors.

$21 = 3 \cdot 7$
$110 = 2 \cdot 5 \cdot 11$
$GCF = 1$

Since there are no common prime factors, 1 is the GCF. The numbers 21 and 110 are **relatively prime.**

Find the GCF of each pair of numbers.

1. 8, 12   **2.** 18, 27   **3.** 16, 32   **4.** 12, 15   **5.** 24, 30

List the factors to find the GCF of each set of numbers.

1. 8, 24 **2.** 36, 48 **3.** 18, 45 **4.** 28, 35 **5.** 75, 100

6. 9, 16 **7.** 32, 56, 72 **8.** 30, 45, 60 **9.** 24, 28, 40 **10.** 12, 16, 44

List prime factorizations to find the GCF of each set of numbers.

11. 20, 70 **12.** 28, 44 **13.** 70, 14 **14.** 19, 57 **15.** 16, 56

16. 27, 36, 81 **17.** 30, 48, 120 **18.** 16, 28, 40 **19.** 18, 36, 72 **20.** 35, 45, 63

21. Show that 25 and 72 are relatively prime.

22. Show that 15 and 28 are relatively prime.

APPLY

MATH REASONING Which of these statements is true? If the statement is false, give a counterexample.

23. Two prime numbers are always relatively prime.

24. Two even numbers are never relatively prime.

25. If two numbers are relatively prime, one of the numbers must be a prime.

PROBLEM SOLVING

26. Ken does 36 laps around the track every day in his wheelchair. Joe runs 28 laps around the track each day. Each does a certain number of complete miles each day. At most, how many times around the track makes a mile?

▶ **USING CRITICAL THINKING** Find a Pattern

27. Copy and complete the graph below to find the GCF of 4 and each whole number from 5 to 15. Describe the pattern you see.

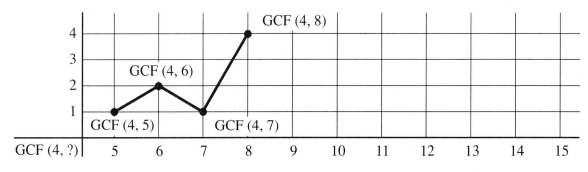

More Practice, page 531, set C

Least Common Multiple

EXPLORE **Analyze the Situation**

Work in groups. Carlos wanted to make a floor with square patterns using 8 in. × 12. in. tiles.

TALK ABOUT IT

1. Can Carlos design a square 32 in. × 32 in. with 8 in. × 12 in. tiles?

2. Can Carlos design a square 36 in. × 36 in.?

3. What is the smallest square Carlos can design with his tiles?

The **Least Common Multiple (LCM)** of two or more numbers is the smallest *nonzero* number that is a multiple of all the numbers.

Multiples of 4: **0**, 4, 8, **12**, 16, 20, **24**, 28 . . .   Multiples of 8: **0**, 8, 16, **24**, 32, 40 . . .
Multiples of 6: **0**, 6, **12**, 18, **24**, 30 . . .   Multiples of 12: **0**, 12, **24**, 36, . . .
Common multiples: **0, 12, 24,** . . .   Common multiples: **0, 24,** . . .
The LCM is 12.   The LCM is 24.

You can also use prime factorizations to find the LCM.

$12 = 2 \cdot 2 \cdot 3$ Select one prime for $16 = 2 \cdot 2 \cdot 2 \cdot 2$
each column shown.
$18 = 2 \cdot \quad 3 \cdot 3$ $9 = \qquad\qquad 3 \cdot 3$

$30 = 2 \cdot \quad 3 \cdot \quad 5$ Find the product of the primes. $15 = \qquad\qquad 3 \cdot \quad 5$

$LCM = 2 \cdot 2 \cdot 3 \cdot 3 \cdot 5 = 180$ $LCM = 2 \cdot 2 \cdot 2 \cdot 2 \cdot 3 \cdot 3 \cdot 5 = 720$

List the multiples to find the LCM of each pair.

1. 3 and 4   **2.** 10 and 12   **3.** 9 and 12   **4.** 15 and 25   **5.** 18 and 24

Use prime factorizations to find the LCM of each set of numbers.

6. 12 and 20   **7.** 18 and 20   **8.** 30 and 40   **9.** 6, 8, and 12   **10.** 2, 12 and 16

List the multiples to find the LCM of each pair.

1. 6 and 10   **2.** 4 and 14   **3.** 8 and 20   **4.** 10 and 15

5. 15 and 18   **6.** 12 and 16   **7.** 4 and 10   **8.** 18 and 32

Use prime factorizations to find the LCM of each pair.

9. 9 and 12   **10.** 20 and 25   **11.** 8 and 18   **12.** 6 and 14

13. 14 and 21   **14.** 22 and 33   **15.** 13 and 65   **16.** 15 and 75

17. 27 and 36   **18.** 21 and 28   **19.** 18 and 32   **20.** 30 and 70

Find the LCM of each set of numbers.

21. 4, 8, 12   **22.** 8, 16, 20   **23.** 3, 5, 7   **24.** 9, 12, 15

25. 8, 10, 12   **26.** 4, 6, 15   **27.** 7, 21, 84   **28.** 6, 15, 9

APPLY

MATH REASONING The LCM of a set of numbers is either a) the
largest number in the set, b) the product of the numbers, or c)
between the largest number and the product. Use mental math
to determine which choice is correct for each group of numbers.

29. 12, 24   **30.** 5, 45   **31.** 3, 5, 7   **32.** 7, 14, 35

PROBLEM SOLVING

33. Eva spent the same amount of money to
purchase cassette tapes and compact
discs. If a cassette tape costs $12 and a
compact disc costs $15, how much did
she spend on each?

34. Doug dove down a multiple of 15 m
holding his breath. Jerome dove down a
multiple of 20 m with scuba equipment.
They both dove down to the same depth.
They dove down less than 100 m. How
deep could they have gone?

MIXED REVIEW

Solve these equations.
35. $3x = {}^-15$ **36.** $4 + y = 10$ **37.** $3c + {}^-8 = 13$ **38.** ${}^-4x + 7 = 15$

Find the area of each circle with the given radius. Use 3.14 for π.

39. $r = 6$ cm   **40.** $r = 20$ mm   **41.** $r = 0.3$ cm   **42.** $r = 2.1$ m

Exploring Algebra
Functions with Exponents

LEARN ABOUT IT

EXPLORE **Complete the Table**

The distance (d) an object falls is related to the time (t) of the
fall by $d = 9.8t^2$, with d in meters and t in seconds. Copy and
complete the chart at the right.

To find the value of t^2 using your calculator,
first enter the value of t. Then, press the $\boxed{y^x}$
key and enter the exponent 2. Last, press
the equal sign key for the result.

t	t^2	$d = 9.8\,t^2$
1.2	1.44	
2.3		
3.4		
4.1		
5.4		

value of t	raised to the second power	equals	result
↓	↓	↓	↓
1.2	$\boxed{y^x}$ 2	$\boxed{=}$	1.44

TALK ABOUT IT

1. If you know the value of t^2, how do you
   find d using your calculator?

2. Do you fall faster or slower as
   time increases? How can you
   tell from the chart?

Example Use your calculator to complete the following table of values.

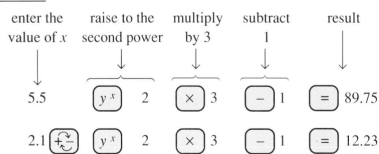

x	$y = 3x^2 - 1$
5.5	89.75
⁻2.1	12.23

The change sign key changes 2.1 to ⁻2.1.

TRY IT OUT

Use your calculator to evaluate $y = 3x^2 + 2$ for each value.

1. $x = {}^-2$ **2.** $x = 4.3$ **3.** $x = {}^-5.2$ **4.** $x = 8.4$

Complete each table by using your calculator to evaluate each expression.

1.

x	$y = 5x^2 + 5$
$^-2$	
$^-1.2$	
0	
3.3	
4.5	

2.

x	$y = 2x^2 - 4$
$^-1.5$	
2.3	
3.1	
4.2	
6	

3.

x	$y = x^3$
$^-2$	
$^-1.6$	
1.2	
4	

4.

x	$y = {}^-3x^2 + 1$
0	
2	
3.4	
5	

APPLY

MATH REASONING For each expression find a value of x for which y is negative or state that y is always positive.

5. $y = 3x^2 + 7$ **6.** $y = x^2 - 2$ **7.** $y = x^3 + 1$ **8.** $y = x + 8$

PROBLEM SOLVING

9. A window washer on the Sears Tower, the tallest office building in the U.S., dropped his sponge. A pedestrian saw the accident and counted 4.5 seconds until the sponge hit the ground. How many meters above the ground was the window washer?

10. The weight in pounds of a cube of ice is given by $0.033e^3$ where e is the edge length in inches. What is the weight of a block of ice if it is 10 inches on each edge?

▶ **ESTIMATION**

In a function such as $y = x^2 - x + 5$, you can estimate the value of y for large values of x by ignoring all terms except the term to the highest power. For example, for $x = 67$, the value of y is approximately 67^2 or 4,489.

Find an estimated evaluation of $y = x^2 - x + 5$ for each value.

11. $x = 79$ **12.** $x = 110$ **13.** $x = 132$ **14.** $x = 250$

Problem Solving
Extra Data

UNDERSTAND
ANALYZE DATA
PLAN
ESTIMATE
SOLVE
EXAMINE

LEARN ABOUT IT

Sometimes a problem has Extra Data. This data is not needed to solve the problem.

First, find the data needed to solve the problem.

In January 1989, the toll on the Golden Gate Bridge in San Francisco increased from $1 to $2. For the first 6 months, you could buy a book of 16 tickets for $20. How much did each ticket cost?

> *You could buy a book of 16 tickets for $20.*

The other data is extra.

> *The information that the toll increased from $1 to $2 and that you could buy the book for 6 months is not needed.*

Solve the problem using only the needed data.

> $20 \div 16 = 1.25$

Each ticket cost $1.25.

TRY IT OUT

Solve. Tell which data is extra.

1. Lori buys a book of tickets every 3 weeks. Starting in July 1989, a $20 book of tickets had 12 tickets instead of 16. Now how much does each ticket cost?

2. Ken commutes 35 mi to work each day. Last year he had to pay the toll on the Golden Gate Bridge 252 times. How many books of 12 tickets did Ken have to buy?

182

Solve. Use any problem solving strategy.

1. The graph shows the number of miles of toll roads, bridges, and tunnels in 6 states. Find the total number of miles for the highest 3 states.

2. Use the graph to find how many more miles of toll roads, bridges and tunnels New York has than Oklahoma.

3. Ned and Rita spend the same amount on tolls each month. Ned commutes 15 miles a day. Rita commutes 42 miles and spends $10 a week on tolls. How much do they each spend in one month?

4. A crew is installing new lights on both sides of a 1,600 ft bridge. They put a tall high intensity light every 100 ft including both ends. Between each pair of tall lights they are installing 3 road level lights. How many of each kind of light did they need?

5. The Golden Gate Bridge is the third longest suspension bridge. Its main span is 4,200 ft. Humber Bridge in Great Britain is the longest at 4,626 ft. The Verrazano-Narrows Bridge in New York is 4,260 ft long. How much shorter is the Golden Gate Bridge than the Humber Bridge?

6. In 1991 the Transbay Ferry Company raised its fare from $6.00 to $8.00 per car. What is the percent of increase?

7. The Angostura suspension bridge in Venezuela is 5,507 ft long. Its main span is 2,336 ft long. What percent of the Angostura's total length is the main span?

Toll Miles

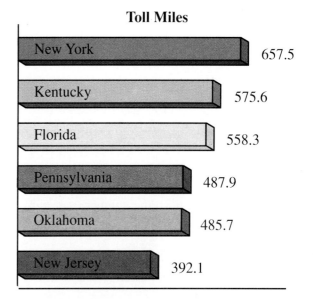

State	Toll Miles
New York	657.5
Kentucky	575.6
Florida	558.3
Pennsylvania	487.9
Oklahoma	485.7
New Jersey	392.1

Penang Bridge in Malaysia's busiest seaport, Penang.

8. **Talk About Your Solution** The Lincoln Tunnel in New York is about twice as long as the Baytown Tunnel in Texas. Together they are about 12,300 feet long. About how long is each bridge? Compare solutions with your classmates. Do you think some solutions are better than others? Explain.

More Practice, page 547, set C

183

Data Collection and Analysis
Group Decision Making

UNDERSTAND
ANALYZE DATA
PLAN
ESTIMATE
SOLVE
EXAMINE

Doing a Simulation

Group Skill:
Encourage and Respect Others

To win a car on the Spin-To-Win quiz show just spin the wheel and pick a key. If the key fits the car shown on the spinner, you win the car!

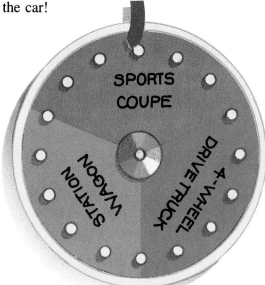

Predict how often a contestant will win a car. One out of two contestants? One out of three contestants? Since you want to find out what is likely to happen, you can use a **simulation** where you act out the quiz show contest.

Collecting Data

1. Make a spinner and three paper keys for your group. Write the names of three cars on the spinner and on the back of each key.

2. Have members of your group take turns being "contestants". Each contestant picks a key and then spins the spinner. If the car shown on the spinner matches the car shown on the back of the key, the contestant wins the car. Record how many contestants must spin before a car is won. Keep a record of 25 trials.

Trial	Number of contestants before a prize is won.
1	5
2	10
3	8
4	9
5	7
—	—
—	—

3. Look at the data you collected. How many times did just one contestant spin before a prize was won? two contestants? three contestants? Record these numbers in order under **frequency** in a table like the one below. To find the decimal part of the total number of trials, divide each frequency by the total number of trials (25). Record your answer to the nearest hundredth.

Number of contestants before a prize is won	frequency	Decimal part of the total number of trials
1	0	0.00
2	1	0.04
3	0	0.00
4	2	0.08
—	—	—
—	—	—

Presenting Your Analysis

4. What is the most common number of contestants it takes to get a winner? the next most common?

5. Were your predictions close or were you surprised? Do you think you would get similar results if you tried this simulation again? Why or why not?

185

WRAP UP

Number Theory Fill-In

Write the phrase from the box that correctly completes each statement.

Prime number	consecutive	primes	factors
composite number	multiples	greatest common factor	
Prime factorization	divisible	least common multiple	

1. The _____ of 9 and 6 is 18.

2. The numbers 59 and 61 are twin _____.

3. A _____ of both 8 and 20 is 40.

4. The numbers 3 and 7 are _____ of 21.

5. The number 10 is _____ by 2 and 5.

6. A number greater than 1 that has only itself and 1 as factors is a _____.

7. A number greater than 0 that has more than two factors is a _____.

8. The numbers 7, 11, and 13 are _____ primes.

9. $2 \times 3 \times 7$ is the _____ of 42.

10. The _____ of 20 and 30 is 10.

Sometimes, Always, Never

Decide if each of these statements is sometimes true, always true, or never true.

11. A number __?__ is divisible by 3 if the sum of its digits is equal to 3.

12. The greatest common factor of two numbers is __?__ equal to one of the numbers.

13. The number 10 can __?__ be a prime factor of a number.

14. The least common multiple of three numbers is __?__ the product of all of the numbers.

Project

Devise a strategy for finding all the prime numbers between 1 and 100. Use this information to find all the prime numbers between 100 and 200.

POWER PRACTICE/TEST

Part 1   Understanding

1. Is 7 a factor of 37? Why or why not?

2. Is 12,315 divisible by 2, 3, or 5?

3. Is 1,332 divisible by 4 or 6?

State whether each number is prime or composite.

4. 47

5. 12

6. 91

7. Name two relatively prime numbers. Show why they are considered relatively prime.

8. Which statement is true?

   A The GCF of two numbers may be one of the numbers.

   B The GCF of two numbers is always greater than one number and less than the other.

   C The GCF of two numbers may be greater than both numbers.

   D The GCF is always greater than the LCM.

Part 2   Skills

9. List all the factors of 90.

10. Find the prime factorization of 12,375.

11. List the first five nonzero multiples of 6.

12. Use a factor tree to find the prime factorization of 48.

13. Solve $n = 2^3 \cdot 5^2$ to find the number whose prime factorization is given.

Find the GCF of each set of numbers.

14. 18, 54

15. 12, 64

16. 12, 30, 60

Find the LCM of each set of numbers.

17. 18, 24

18. 8, 14

19. 10, 12, 24

Part 3   Applications

20. A clerk needs to arrange 144 cereal boxes in a display with the same number of boxes in each row. Determine which of the following represent the number of rows she could make: 2, 3, 4, 5, 6.

21. **Challenge** A family has narrowed its choice for floor tiles to three. One is 6 in. by 8 in., one 4 in. by 4 in., and the third is 3 in. by 5 in. The floor is 8 ft by 10 ft. 8 in. Which of the tile choices will fit, without cutting any of the tiles?

187

ENRICHMENT
Finding Large Primes

Mathematicians have long been fascinated with the identification of prime numbers, particularly large primes. In 1640, French mathematician Pierre de Fermat asserted that all numbers of the general formula $2^{2^n} + 1$ are prime. Unfortunately, Fermat's theory proved to be wrong. Only the first 4 Fermat numbers ($n = 1, 2, 3, 4$) are prime.

1. Use a calculator to find the values of the second, third, and fourth Fermat numbers. The first Fermat number is done for you.

   a. $2^{2^1} + 1 = 5$

   b. $2^{2^2} + 1 =$

   c. $2^{2^3} + 1 =$

   d. $2^{2^4} + 1 =$

2. Find the fifth Fermat number. Prove that it is composite by dividing it by 641.

In 1644, another French mathematician, Father Marin Mersenne, discovered prime numbers of the form $2^n - 1$. Mersenne asserted that the numbers were prime for values of $n = 1, 2, 3, 5, 7, 13, 17, 19, 31, 67, 127$, and 257.

As it turned out, Mersenne missed three primes, the primes for the numbers 61, 89, and 107—and was wrong about two—$2^{67} - 1$ and $2^{257} - 1$ are composite. With the aid of computers, mathematicians have proven that $2^{21,701} - 1$ and $2^{44,497} - 1$ are also prime.

3. Use a calculator to find the value of the following Mersenne prime numbers.

   a. $n = 3$

   b. $n = 19$

   c. $n = 17$

   d. $n = 15$

CUMULATIVE REVIEW

1. Find the area of this polygon.

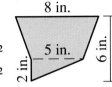

A 36 in.²   B 44 in.²

C 49 in.²   D 31 in.²

Use the figure at the right for problems 2 and 3.

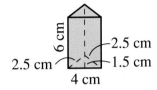

2. Find the surface area.

A 78 cm²   B 84 cm²

C 60 cm²   D 36 cm²

3. Find the volume.

A 18 cm³   B 84 cm³

C 78 cm³   D 36 cm³

4. Write $(3 \cdot 3)(3 \cdot 3 \cdot 3 \cdot 3)$ in exponential notation.

A 3^8 B 3^6 C 6^3 D 3^4

5. Name the opposite of 12.

A 21   B $-\dfrac{1}{12}$ C $^-12$ D $\dfrac{1}{12}$

6. Subtract. $4 - {}^-4$

A $^-8$ B 0   C 4   D 8

7. Solve $\dfrac{t}{4} = 36.8$.

A $t = 147.2$ B $t = 32.8$

C $t = 40.8$ D $t = 9.2$

8. What steps are needed to undo $3b - 14$?

A first division, then addition

B first addition, then division

C first subtraction, then multiplication

D first subtraction, then division

9. Solve $v + 37 = {}^-42$.

A $v = {}^-79$ B $v = {}^-5$

C $v = 79$ D $v = 5$

10. Which function rule will result in the input-output pairs given in this function table?

function rule?					
n	1	2	3	4	5
$f(n)$	1	3	5	7	9

A $n + 1$ B $\dfrac{n + 1}{2}$

C $2(n - 1)$ D $2n - 1$

11. Which ordered pair is a solution to $y = {}^-3 + x$?

A $(^-2, 1)$ B $(1, {}^-2)$

C $(^-1, 2)$ D $(^-2, {}^-1)$

12. On a coordinate plane, where would you find the point $(^-6, 0)$?

A 6 units below the origin

B 6 units above the origin

C 6 units left of the origin

D 6 units right of the origin

13. Before the storm, the rainfall for the year was 2 in. below normal. It rained 4 in. during the storm. Use an integer to represent the rainfall for the year after the storm as compared to the normal.

A 4   B $^-2$ C $^-4$ D 2

14. Joe owed $58 for the jacket he put on layaway. Each week for the last 3 weeks he paid $15 toward the jacket. How much does he still owe?

A $13   B $43   C $45   D $40

7

RATIONAL NUMBERS

THEME: SUBATOMIC PHYSICS

MATH AND SCIENCE

DATA BANK

Use the Science Data Bank on page 492 to answer the questions.

---

1 Quarks and leptons are sub atomic particles. For every subatomic particle there is an antiparticle with an electrical charge that is the opposite. What i the charge of an anti-electron?

2 On a number line, would the charge of a muon neutrino be shown to the left or the right of the charge of a muon?

3 The basic unit of energy used to measure the energy content of subatomic particles is the "electron volt." How many times greater than a kiloelectron volt is one million electron volts?

4 **Using Critical Thinking** Physicists use flavor and color to describe quarks. Quarks and antiquarks come in red, blue, and green. There is a red up quark, an anti-red anti-up quark, and so forth. How many kinds of quarks and antiquarks are there?

Physicists learn about subatomic particles through observation and mathematical reasoning.

x

Fractions

LEARN ABOUT IT

EXPLORE Look for a Pattern

An interior decorator is experimenting with several designs for a restaurant wall. She is considering several different sizes of shaded mirrors.

TALK ABOUT IT

1. Match one of these fractions $\frac{4}{6}$, $\frac{12}{18}$, or $\frac{2}{3}$ with each design.

2. How would you draw a figure that represents $\frac{21}{18}$?

Equivalent fractions are fractions that represent the same quantity. Multiplying or dividing both **numerator** and **denominator** by the same number results in an equivalent fraction. Use **cross multiplication** to decide if two fractions are equivalent.

Examples Write = or ≠ for each ⫴.

A $\begin{array}{c} \frac{4}{6} \Join \frac{6}{9} \end{array}$
$9 \cdot 4 = 36$
$6 \cdot 6 = 36$
$\frac{4}{6} = \frac{6}{9}$ equivalent fractions

B $\begin{array}{c} \frac{5}{8} \Join \frac{6}{10} \end{array}$
$5 \cdot 10 = 50$
$8 \cdot 6 = 48$
$\frac{5}{8} \neq \frac{6}{10}$ not equivalent fractions

Find the **lowest terms fractions** by dividing numerator and denominator by the GCF. An **improper fraction** is one with the numerator greater than or equal to the denominator. Any improper fraction can be written as a **mixed number** or whole number.

Examples Write each fraction in lowest terms or as a mixed number.

C $\frac{15}{35} = \frac{15 \div 5}{35 \div 5} = \frac{3}{7}$ **D** $\frac{40}{36} = \frac{40 \div 4}{36 \div 4} = \frac{10}{9} = 1\frac{1}{9}$ **E** $\frac{11}{15}$ GCF is 1

TRY IT OUT

Write = or ≠ for each ⫴.

1. $\frac{8}{12}$ ⫴ $\frac{4}{6}$

2. $\frac{6}{14}$ ⫴ $\frac{9}{21}$

Express each as a mixed number or fraction in lowest terms.

3. $\frac{11}{88}$ **4.** $\frac{21}{35}$ **5.** $\frac{15}{33}$ **6.** $\frac{35}{14}$

Write = or ≠ for each ⫿.

1. $\frac{3}{7}$ ⫿ $\frac{21}{49}$ **2.** $\frac{5}{19}$ ⫿ $\frac{4}{17}$ **3.** $\frac{7}{13}$ ⫿ $\frac{23}{35}$ **4.** $\frac{8}{18}$ ⫿ $\frac{20}{45}$

Express each improper fraction as a mixed number or fraction in lowest terms.

5. $\frac{17}{8}$ **6.** $\frac{9}{81}$ **7.** $\frac{14}{3}$ **8.** $\frac{20}{7}$

9. $\frac{42}{6}$ **10.** $\frac{18}{27}$ **11.** $\frac{60}{11}$ **12.** $\frac{19}{4}$

13. $\frac{63}{90}$ **14.** $\frac{25}{5}$ **15.** $\frac{53}{12}$ **16.** $\frac{21}{42}$

17. Give two fractions that are equivalent to $\frac{28}{49}$.

18. The fraction $\frac{19}{7}$ is between what two whole numbers?

MATH REASONING

19. Find how many ways the digits 1, 2, 3, 4, and 7 can be placed in the boxes to make a true statement. Numbers may be repeated more than once. The fraction part of the mixed number should be a proper fraction.

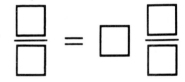

PROBLEM SOLVING

20. A steak house advertised $\frac{1}{2}$ pound portions on their ground beef platter. An inspector discovered the portions weighed 7 ounces and fined the owners for false advertising. Why?

21. At Harley's Pizza shop each pizza that is baked is cut into eight slices and sold by the slice. If 38 students each order one slice of pizza, how many pizzas need to be baked?

▶ **ALGEBRA**

Suppose that a, b, and c represent distinct nonzero whole numbers. Algebraic expressions in the form of a fraction can be expressed in lowest terms by canceling all factors that are common to the numerator and denominator. For example, the fraction $\frac{5ab}{25b}$ in lowest terms is $\frac{a}{5}$.

Express these fractions in lowest terms.

22. $\frac{15ab}{16b}$ **23.** $\frac{15a}{35a}$ **24.** $\frac{abc}{2bc}$

More Practice, page 531, set E

Rational Numbers and the Number Line

A number that can be expressed in the fractional form $\frac{a}{b}$, where
a and b are integers and $b \neq 0$, is called a **rational number.**
Each rational number represents one point on the number line.
Equivalent fractions represent the same rational number.

EXPLORE **Examine the Number Line**

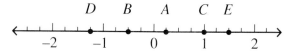

Rational numbers can be represented in
different forms. For example, the point E in
this figure represents the rational number one and one-half which can be
written as a mixed number $1\frac{1}{2}$, an improper fraction $\frac{3}{2}$, or a decimal 1.5.

TALK ABOUT IT

1. What rational number corresponds to point C? point B? point A?

2. Write the rational number that corresponds to point D as a
   mixed number, an improper fraction, and a decimal.

Each rational number has an opposite rational number.

The **opposite** of $\frac{1}{2}$ is $\frac{-1}{2}$.

The **opposite** of $-\frac{8}{5}$ is $\frac{8}{5}$.

The **opposite** of $1\frac{3}{4}$ is $-1\frac{3}{4}$.

Opposites Property
The sum of any rational number and its opposite is 0.
$-\frac{3}{2} + \frac{3}{2} = 0 \qquad -\frac{1}{2} + \frac{1}{2} = 0$

There are three ways to show a negative rational number. For
example, $-\frac{1}{2}$, $\frac{-1}{2}$, and $\frac{1}{-2}$ all represent the opposite of $\frac{1}{2}$.

Write a fraction or mixed number and a decimal that correspond
to the given point.

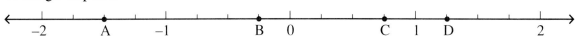

1. Point A **2.** Point B **3.** Point C **4.** Point D

5. Write in three different ways the opposite of the number that
   corresponds to point C.

Write in both fraction and decimal form a rational number that corresponds to the given point. If appropriate, write the fraction as a mixed number.

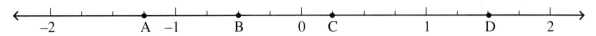

1. Point A **2.** Point $\dot{B}$ **3.** Point C **4.** Point D

5. Write in three different ways the opposite of the number that corresponds to point C.

Write the opposite of each in three different ways.

6. $\dfrac{5}{6}$ **7.** $\dfrac{1}{2}$ **8.** $\dfrac{4}{3}$ **9.** $\dfrac{5}{2}$

10. $\dfrac{1}{10}$ **11.** $\dfrac{3}{8}$ **12.** $\dfrac{8}{3}$ **13.** $\dfrac{7}{2}$

Write the opposite of each of these rational numbers.

14. $\dfrac{-2}{3}$ **15.** $\dfrac{6}{-7}$ **16.** $\dfrac{-5}{3}$ **17.** $-\dfrac{1}{6}$

18. 6.5 **19.** 2^3 **20.** -0.01 **21.** $-5\dfrac{1}{5}$

MATH REASONING Write the missing numbers. Use the opposites property.

22. $\dfrac{^-3}{4} + \text{▦} = 0$ **23.** $\text{▦} + \dfrac{4}{5} = 0.$ **24.** $-3\dfrac{1}{2} + 3\dfrac{1}{2} = \text{▦}$ **25.** $0 = \dfrac{7}{-10} + \text{▦}$

PROBLEM SOLVING

26. If a river rises 6 inches, its water level changes $+\dfrac{1}{2}$ feet. If the level changes $-1\dfrac{1}{2}$ feet, has the river risen or fallen?

27. During a drought the water level of a river changes $-\dfrac{1}{4}$ feet each week. After six weeks of drought, how much must the water level change to return to its original level?

▶ **ESTIMATION**

Write a rational number that is an estimate for the rational number that corresponds to the given point.

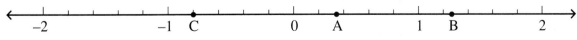

28. Point A **29.** Point B **30.** Point C

Comparing and Ordering Rational Numbers

EXPLORE **Study the Information**

Quarks are particles that are building blocks for all other particles. Triplets of quarks make up leptons, which in turn make up atoms. Quarks have a fractional electric charge. Leptons have electric charges of 0 or -1.

TALK ABOUT IT

1. Which particles have a positive charge? a negative charge?

2. Which particle has the largest charge?

Comparing Fractions Which is less, $\frac{5}{9}$ or $\frac{3}{5}$?

$\frac{5}{9} = \frac{25}{45}$ and $\frac{3}{5} = \frac{27}{45}$. $25 < 27$. So $\frac{5}{9} < \frac{3}{5}$.

1. Rename using a common denominator.
2. Compare numerators.

Mixed Numbers Which is less, $3\frac{4}{5}$ or $4\frac{1}{5}$? $4\frac{1}{5}$ or $4\frac{1}{6}$?

$3 < 4$, so $3\frac{4}{5} < 4\frac{1}{5}$. And $\frac{1}{5} > \frac{1}{6}$, so $4\frac{1}{5} > 4\frac{1}{6}$.

1. Compare whole number parts.
2. Compare fractional parts.

Decimals Which is greater, 6.327 or 6.35?

6.327 ⦀ 6.35 $5 > 2$, so $6.35 > 6.327$.

1. Compare digits in the first decimal place they differ.
2. The numbers compare the same as those digits.

Since $6.327 < 6.35$ it follows that $-6.35 < -6.327$. In general, if $a < b$ then $-b < -a$.

To compare three or more numbers, use repeated inequality symbols.

$-1\frac{1}{2} < \frac{-7}{8} < \frac{1}{4}$ means $-1\frac{1}{2} < \frac{-7}{8}$ and $\frac{-7}{8} < \frac{1}{4}$.

Compare. Use $<$ or $>$.

1. $\frac{3}{7}$ ⦀ $\frac{4}{9}$ 2. $3\frac{2}{7}$ ⦀ $3\frac{2}{5}$ 3. 5.23 ⦀ 5.216 4. -2.157 ⦀ -8.72

Compare. Use $<$ or $>$.

1. $\dfrac{2}{5}$ ||| $\dfrac{3}{7}$

2. -7 ||| $^-3$

3. $4\dfrac{1}{2}$ ||| $3\dfrac{3}{4}$

4. $\dfrac{1}{12}$ ||| $-5\dfrac{3}{12}$

5. 3.863 ||| 3.9

6. 7.025 ||| 7.18

7. -3.1 ||| -2.8

8. -5.7 ||| -5.3

9. 0.1 ||| -0.01

10. $-\dfrac{4}{5}$ ||| $-\dfrac{2}{3}$

11. $\dfrac{5}{3}$ ||| $\dfrac{3}{5}$

12. -7.6 ||| -6.7

13. $-2\dfrac{1}{3}$ ||| $-2\dfrac{1}{4}$

14. 9.99 ||| -10

15. $\dfrac{6}{7}$ ||| $\dfrac{8}{9}$

16. -5.9 ||| -6.1

Use repeated inequalities to order these numbers.

17. $-2, 3, -6$

18. $-4, -1, -8$

19. $-4, -1, \dfrac{1}{2}$

20. $\dfrac{-2}{3}, \dfrac{1}{3}, \dfrac{-5}{3}$

21. $-1, -1.1, -1.11$

22. $-\dfrac{3}{8}, \dfrac{1}{4}, -\dfrac{1}{2}$

MATH REASONING Place the digits 3, 4, 5, and 6 in these boxes to make true statements.

23. $0 < \dfrac{\square}{\square} < 1$

24. $\dfrac{\square}{\square} < \dfrac{\square}{\square}$

25. $3 < \square\dfrac{\square}{\square} < 5$

PROBLEM SOLVING

26. **Science Data Bank** The electrical charge of a hadron is equal to the sum of the charges of the quarks it contains. A proton is made up of 2 up quarks and 1 down quark. A neutron is made up of 1 up quark and 2 down quarks. Is the charge of a neutron greater than the charge of a proton?

DATA BANK

▶ **CALCULATOR**

To find the decimal form of $\dfrac{71}{8}$ calculate $71 \div 8$. Use a calculator to find the decimal form for each of these rational numbers and decide which one is greater.

27. $\dfrac{23}{98}, \dfrac{12}{49}$

28. $\dfrac{13}{78}, \dfrac{7}{40}$

29. $\dfrac{8}{19}, \dfrac{17}{39}$

30. $\dfrac{19}{41}, \dfrac{6}{13}$

31. One approximation of the number π is $\dfrac{22}{7}$. Is that greater than or less than 3.14? Is it greater than or less than the value for π on your calculator? Can you find any other fractions that are very close to π?

More Practice, page 532, set B

Rational Numbers as Decimals

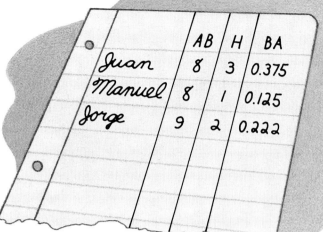

LEARN ABOUT IT

EXPLORE Read the Table

Juan, Manuel, and Jorge were on a Pony League team. The box score shows the number of At Bats (AB), Hits (H), and their Batting Average (BA) for a double header.

TALK ABOUT IT

1. Whose BA is calculated by 1.000 ÷ 8? by 2.000 ÷ 9? Do these divisions end with remainders of zero?

A **terminating decimal** ends with repeating zeros. A decimal which has a group of digits that repeat endlessly is a **repeating decimal.**

Examples Find a decimal for the fraction $\frac{7}{11}$.

A
```
      .6363
  11)7.0000
     66
     ──
     40
     33
     ──
     70
     66
     ──
     40
     33
     ──
      7
```
remainder
of 7
repeats
the original problem.

B 7 ÷ 11 = [0.6363636]

   or

7 / 11 [F D] [0.6363636]

$\frac{7}{11} = 0.6363636$ is a

repeating decimal

A bar over a digit or group of digits indicates they repeat. $\frac{7}{11} = 0.\overline{63}$

Other Examples Find a decimal for each fraction.

C $\frac{7}{8} = 0.875$ **D** $-\frac{1}{6} = {}^-0.1\overline{6}$ **E** $\frac{19}{12} = 1.58\overline{3}$

TRY IT OUT

Find a decimal for each fraction. Use a bar to show a repeating decimal.

1. $\frac{2}{3}$ 2. $\frac{4}{5}$ 3. $-\frac{3}{8}$ 4. $-\frac{4}{11}$ 5. $\frac{17}{12}$

Find a decimal for each fraction. Use a bar to show a repeating decimal.

1. $\frac{3}{5}$ 2. $\frac{1}{15}$ 3. $\frac{16}{25}$ 4. $\frac{3}{20}$ 5. $\frac{5}{11}$

6. $\frac{2}{3}$ 7. $\frac{3}{8}$ 8. $-\frac{7}{20}$ 9. $\frac{1}{11}$ 10. $\frac{5}{16}$

11. $-\frac{2}{9}$ 12. $\frac{12}{25}$ 13. $\frac{7}{8}$ 14. $-\frac{5}{6}$ 15. $\frac{8}{11}$

16. $\frac{9}{40}$ 17. $-\frac{11}{50}$ 18. $\frac{11}{12}$ 19. $\frac{13}{99}$ 20. $\frac{5}{9}$

21. $\frac{14}{12}$ 22. $\frac{25}{11}$ 23. $\frac{31}{11}$ 24. $-\frac{13}{12}$ 25. $\frac{83}{10}$

26. Find the decimal representations for $\frac{1}{7}, \frac{2}{7}, \frac{3}{7}, \frac{4}{7}, \frac{5}{7}, \frac{6}{7}$. What pattern do you see?

MATH REASONING Arrange each list of numbers in order from smallest to largest.

27. $0.4, \frac{3}{8}, 0.37$

28. $\frac{1}{16}, 0.16, \frac{1}{6}$

29. $\frac{1}{11}, 0.09, -0.9$

30. $\frac{-7}{8}, -0.8, -0.87$

31. $0.371, 0.317, 0.3173$

32. $\frac{1}{20}, 0.0\overline{5}, 0.\overline{05}$

PROBLEM SOLVING

33. In 1987 Don Mattingly of the New York Yankees had 186 hits in 569 at bats. What was his batting average? (Round to the nearest thousandths.)

34. In 1987 the New York Mets as a team had 1,499 hits in 5,601 at bats and the Cincinnati Reds at 1,478 hits in 5,560 at bats. Which team had the higher batting average?

▶ **USING CRITICAL THINKING   Use Logic**

35. Yolanda divided 1 by 17. Her calculator showed 0.0588235. She concluded that $\frac{1}{17} = 0.0588235$. Explain why she is not correct.

More Practice, page 532, set C

Adding and Subtracting Rational Numbers

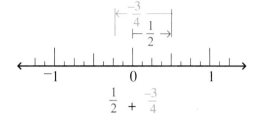

Figure A

LEARN ABOUT IT

As with integers, to subtract rational numbers, add the opposite. For example, $\frac{1}{2} - \frac{3}{4} = \frac{1}{2} + \frac{-3}{4}$.

EXPLORE Draw a Number Line

Draw a number line. Then draw arrows as shown above to find a) $\frac{3}{4} + \frac{-7}{8}$ and b) $\frac{-1}{4} - \frac{1}{2}$.

TALK ABOUT IT

1. Is the rational number in Figure A positive or negative?

2. Is $\frac{-1}{4} - \frac{1}{2}$ equal to $\frac{-1}{4} + \frac{-1}{2}$ or $\frac{-1}{4} - \frac{-1}{2}$?

3. Is $\frac{-1}{4} - \frac{1}{2}$ positive or negative?

To add or subtract fractions with like denominators, add or subtract the numerators. Write this result over the denominator.

> For all integers, a, b, and c, where $c \neq 0$,
>
> $$\frac{a}{c} + \frac{b}{c} = \frac{a+b}{c} \qquad \frac{a}{c} - \frac{b}{c} = \frac{a-b}{c}$$

When the fractions have unlike denominators, change them to equivalent fractions with the same denominator.

Examples Find the sum or difference.

A $\frac{-3}{4} + \frac{1}{2} = \frac{-3}{4} + \frac{2}{4} = \frac{(-3+2)}{4} = \frac{-1}{4}$ **B** $\frac{-7}{8} - \frac{3}{8} = \frac{(-7 + -3)}{8} = \frac{-10}{8} = \frac{-5}{4} = -1\frac{1}{4}$

C $\frac{-1}{5} - \frac{2}{5} = \frac{(-1-2)}{5} = -\frac{3}{5}$ **D** $\frac{5}{6} + \frac{3}{4} = \frac{10}{12} + \frac{9}{12} = \frac{19}{12} = 1\frac{7}{12}$

TRY IT OUT

Find the sum or difference. Express the answer in lowest terms.

1. $\frac{-2}{5} + \frac{4}{5}$ **2.** $\frac{1}{6} - \frac{5}{6}$ **3.** $\frac{-1}{8} - \frac{3}{4}$ **4.** $\frac{1}{3} + \frac{-2}{5}$

5. $\frac{3}{8} - \frac{1}{4}$ **6.** $\frac{7}{8} + \frac{3}{4}$ **7.** $\frac{1}{8} - \frac{7}{16}$ **8.** $-\frac{5}{8} + \frac{1}{3}$

Find the sum or difference. Express the answer as a mixed number or fraction in lowest terms.

1. $\dfrac{-1}{4} + \dfrac{7}{8}$

2. $\dfrac{3}{5} + \dfrac{3}{4}$

3. $\dfrac{7}{8} - \dfrac{1}{4}$

4. $\dfrac{5}{7} - \dfrac{-1}{3}$

5. $\dfrac{-1}{2} + \dfrac{1}{5}$

6. $-\dfrac{7}{16} + \dfrac{3}{4}$

7. $\dfrac{5}{18} - \dfrac{-5}{6}$

8. $\dfrac{-7}{8} + \dfrac{5}{6}$

9. $\dfrac{-7}{8} + \dfrac{1}{2}$

10. $\dfrac{4}{5} - \dfrac{-2}{3}$

11. $\dfrac{1}{8} - \dfrac{7}{8}$

12. $\dfrac{-1}{4} - \dfrac{7}{8}$

13. $\dfrac{3}{4} + \dfrac{1}{2} + \dfrac{7}{8}$

14. $\dfrac{1}{3} + \dfrac{1}{6} + \dfrac{1}{2}$

15. $\left(\dfrac{-1}{2} + \dfrac{7}{8}\right) - \dfrac{3}{4}$

16. $\dfrac{1}{5} + \dfrac{2}{3} + \dfrac{11}{15}$

Solve.

17. $x - \dfrac{1}{2} = \dfrac{3}{4}$

18. $x - \dfrac{7}{8} = \dfrac{-1}{4}$

19. $x + \dfrac{1}{4} = \dfrac{5}{8}$

MATH REASONING Estimate.

20. $\dfrac{-3}{8} + \dfrac{3}{7}$

21. $\dfrac{1}{4} - \dfrac{1}{3}$

22. $\dfrac{7}{8} - \dfrac{-4}{5}$

23. $\dfrac{5}{8} + \dfrac{-7}{8}$

PROBLEM SOLVING

24. The Central School Band marched in a parade that went north $\dfrac{5}{8}$ mile, east $\dfrac{1}{2}$ mile, south $\dfrac{1}{4}$ mile, east $\dfrac{1}{4}$ mile, and then north $\dfrac{7}{16}$ mile. How far north of its beginning point did the parade end?

MIXED REVIEW

State whether each number is prime or composite, and list all factors.

25. 35

26. 21

27. 19

28. 32

29. 77

Find the Greatest Common Factor for each set of numbers.

30. 30, 40

31. 6, 16

32. 21, 14

33. 12, 16

Find the answers.

34. $-10 + 11$

35. $-8 \cdot -7$

36. $16 \div -8$

37. $-20 - 3$

Adding and Subtracting Mixed Numbers

LEARN ABOUT IT

EXPLORE Study the Information

Designers and craftsmen often need to add and subtract mixed numbers to calculate lengths.

TALK ABOUT IT

1. Distance A is the sum of what two mixed numbers?

2. Estimate. Is length A less than 17 or greater than 17?

3. To find length B subtract $7\frac{5}{8}$ from what length?

To add or subtract mixed numbers with unlike denominators:

- Rename fractions with a common denominator.
- Add or subtract the fraction parts. Rename if necessary.
- Add or subtract the whole number parts.

Add, then rename

$$12\frac{3}{4} = 12\frac{6}{8}$$
$$+ \ \ 4\frac{5}{8} = \ \ 4\frac{5}{8}$$
$$\overline{\qquad 16\frac{11}{8} = 17\frac{3}{8}}$$

Rename, then subtract

$$17\frac{3}{8} = 16\frac{11}{8}$$
$$- \ \ 7\frac{5}{8} = \ \ 7\frac{5}{8}$$
$$\overline{\qquad 9\frac{6}{8} = 9\frac{3}{4}}$$

Examples

A
$$5\frac{1}{3} = 5\frac{4}{12} = 4\frac{16}{12}$$
$$- 2\frac{3}{4} = 2\frac{9}{12} = 2\frac{9}{12}$$
$$\overline{\qquad\qquad\qquad 2\frac{7}{12}}$$

B
$$-1\frac{2}{3} + 3\frac{2}{5} = \frac{-5}{3} + \frac{17}{5}$$
$$= \frac{-25}{15} + \frac{51}{15} = \frac{26}{15} = 1\frac{11}{15}$$

TRY IT OUT

Add or subtract. Express your answer in lowest terms.

1. $3\frac{2}{7} + \frac{4}{7}$
2. $4\frac{1}{3} - 3\frac{5}{6}$
3. $2\frac{7}{8} - 1\frac{1}{4}$
4. $2\frac{2}{3} + 3\frac{4}{5}$

Find the sum or difference. Express your answer as a mixed number or fraction in lowest terms.

1. $3\frac{1}{4}$
    $+\ 7\frac{1}{2}$
    _____

2. $12\frac{1}{3}$
    $+\ 3\frac{1}{4}$
    _____

3. $8\frac{3}{4}$
    $-\ 5\frac{1}{2}$
    _____

4. $12\frac{7}{8}$
    $-\ 9\frac{3}{4}$
    _____

5. $\frac{-1}{4} + 2\frac{1}{8}$

6. $1\frac{3}{5} - \frac{3}{4}$

7. $5\frac{5}{16} - \frac{1}{4}$

8. $3\frac{5}{7} - 1\frac{1}{3}$

9. $19\frac{7}{8} + 4\frac{1}{4}$

10. $6\frac{2}{5} + 4\frac{1}{3}$

11. $12\frac{1}{8} - 5\frac{3}{4}$

12. $15\frac{1}{5} - 8\frac{2}{3}$

13. $1\frac{1}{4} + 2\frac{1}{2} + \frac{5}{8}$

14. $2\frac{1}{4} + \frac{5}{6} + 3\frac{1}{2}$

15. $\left(3\frac{1}{2} + 1\frac{3}{4}\right) - \frac{5}{8}$

16. $3\frac{1}{5} - \left(9\frac{2}{3} + 5\frac{4}{15}\right)$

17. $\frac{-1}{4} + 2\frac{1}{8} - 1\frac{3}{4}$

18. $10\frac{3}{4} + \left(5\frac{1}{3} - 1\frac{1}{2}\right)$

19. $9 - \left(4\frac{4}{9} - 2\frac{1}{2}\right)$

20. $\left(10 - 6\frac{5}{12}\right) + 2\frac{1}{4}$

21. $\left(12 + 3\frac{7}{8}\right) - 3\frac{1}{6}$

MATH REASONING Use *breaking apart* to add $2\frac{1}{2} + 3\frac{7}{8}$ using mental math.

Think: $\frac{7}{8} = \frac{4}{8} + \frac{3}{8}$ so $2\frac{1}{2} + 3\frac{7}{8} = (2 + 3) + \left(\frac{1}{2} + \frac{1}{2}\right) + \frac{3}{8} = 6\frac{3}{8}$

Find the sum using mental math.

22. $2\frac{1}{2} + 3\frac{5}{6}$

23. $5\frac{1}{4} - \frac{3}{4}$

24. $3\frac{7}{8} + 1\frac{1}{4}$

25. $3\frac{5}{8} + 8\frac{1}{4}$

PROBLEM SOLVING

26. If length B $= 8\frac{5}{8}$ and length A $= 5\frac{1}{4}$, find length C.

27. If length D $= 7\frac{1}{8}$ and length F $= 3\frac{1}{4}$, find length E.

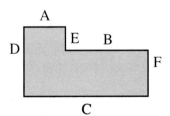

▶ **ESTIMATION**

Use clustering to estimate each of these sums or differences.

28. $12\frac{1}{8} + 11\frac{3}{4} + 12\frac{1}{16}$

29. $4\frac{2}{3} + 5\frac{1}{3} + 4\frac{7}{8} + 4\frac{15}{16}$

30. $3\frac{9}{11} + 4\frac{1}{9}$

31. $\left(5\frac{1}{3} - 2\frac{7}{8}\right) + \left(9\frac{1}{7} - 6\frac{1}{6}\right)$

Using Critical Thinking

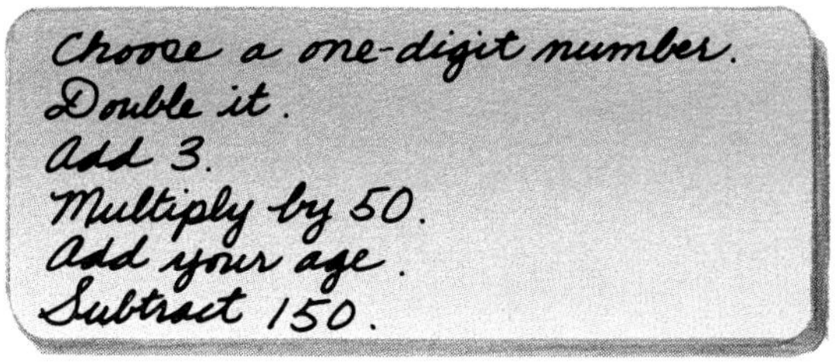

"Think of any number," said Theresa, "and follow the directions on the card I gave you."

"Well, what do you know about that!" exclaimed Greg when he had finished. "I think I'll try again to see if it works for a different number."

"Isn't it a neat trick?" said Theresa, after Greg had checked some more numbers.

"I wouldn't call it a trick," Greg responded as he began to write these equations on his paper. "In math there is always a way to explain why something works."

Choose a one-digit number.
Double it.
Add 3.
Multiply by 50.
Add your age.
Subtract 150.

$$n$$
$$2n$$
$$2n + 3$$
$$100n + 150$$

TALK ABOUT IT

1. What did Theresa ask Greg to do?

2. Try the "trick" with different numbers. What do you discover?

3. Why did Greg write the expressions shown? What other expressions do you think Greg wrote?

4. How could you use the expressions to explain why the "trick" works?

1. A student claimed he could find a situation where the above "trick" would not work. Do you agree? Why or why not?

2. How could you change the "trick" so the final number would show a person's birthdate followed by his or her age?

3. Make up and try a similar "trick" that uses different numbers.

POWER PRACTICE/QUIZ

Write = or ≠ to show if the pairs of fractions are equivalent.

1. $\frac{6}{9}$ ⫴ $\frac{8}{12}$ **2.** $\frac{12}{20}$ ⫴ $\frac{18}{30}$ **3.** $\frac{2}{3}$ ⫴ $\frac{4}{9}$ **4.** $\frac{3}{16}$ ⫴ $\frac{4}{18}$

Write each improper fraction as a mixed number and each
mixed number as an improper fraction in lowest terms.

5. $1\frac{6}{8}$ **6.** $\frac{18}{10}$ **7.** $\frac{27}{6}$ **8.** $8\frac{5}{3}$ **9.** $6\frac{3}{7}$

Write a lowest terms fraction and a decimal that corresponds to each point.

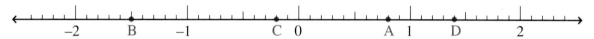

10. point **A**   **11.** point **B**   **12.** opposite of point **C**   **13.** opposite of point **D**

Order the numbers from least to greatest.

14. $\frac{5}{12}, \frac{3}{10}, \frac{4}{9}$ **15.** $-1, -1\frac{5}{8}, -1\frac{2}{3}$ **16.** $-3.4, -3.45, -3.04$

Write each fraction as a decimal. Use a bar to show repeating decimals.

17. $\frac{9}{8}$ **18.** $\frac{8}{9}$ **19.** $\frac{7}{12}$ **20.** $\frac{5}{6}$ **21.** $\frac{3}{11}$

Add or subtract. Write answers in lowest terms.

22. $\frac{-5}{8} + \frac{-1}{2}$ **23.** $\frac{-5}{6} + \frac{8}{9}$ **24.** $\frac{-4}{5} - \frac{2}{3}$

25. $3\frac{1}{5} + -3\frac{1}{4}$ **26.** $-1\frac{1}{9} + -2\frac{1}{6}$ **27.** $\left(1\frac{1}{3} - 2\frac{1}{8}\right) - 3\frac{5}{6}$

PROBLEM SOLVING

28. Ryan wants to cut a 40-inch board into three lengths: $12\frac{3}{8}$ in., $16\frac{3}{4}$ in., and $7\frac{5}{16}$ in. If each cut wastes $\frac{1}{8}$ in., what is the length of the left over piece?

29. Mel jogs the outer track while Larry jogs the inner track of the park. How much farther does Mel jog in one lap than Larry jogs?

30. In the last hour, the temperature has dropped $2\frac{3}{4}°$ to reach $-5\frac{5}{8}°$. What was the temperature an hour ago?

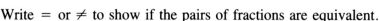

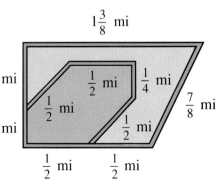

Multiplying Rational Numbers

EXPLORE **Examine the Diagram**

Suppose that the floor of a room is being tiled with rectangular tiles. If $\frac{3}{5}$ of the length and $\frac{3}{4}$ of the width are covered, what fraction of the floor is covered?

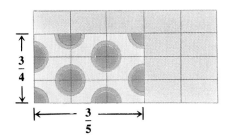

TALK ABOUT IT

1. Does this question ask about the length, area, or perimeter of this room?

2. How many of the 20 rectangular regions are covered with tile?

3. What fraction of the floor is covered?

> For all rational numbers $\frac{a}{b}$ and $\frac{c}{d}$, with $b \neq 0$, and $d \neq 0$, $\frac{a}{b} \cdot \frac{c}{d} = \frac{ac}{bd}$

Since multiplication of rational numbers involves multiplication of integers, the rules for integers must also hold for rational numbers.

> Positive times positive is positive
> Negative times negative is positive
> Positive times negative is negative

Examples Multiply.

long method—multiply the numerators then the denominators. Express the answer in lowest terms.

A $\dfrac{^-4}{5} \cdot \dfrac{^-7}{16} = \dfrac{^-4 \cdot ^-7}{5 \cdot 16} = \dfrac{28}{80} = \dfrac{7}{20}$

B $-2\dfrac{1}{7} \cdot 1\dfrac{2}{3} = \dfrac{^-15}{7} \cdot \dfrac{5}{3} = \dfrac{^-75}{21} = -3\dfrac{4}{7}$

shortcut—divide the numerator and denominator by a common factor, then multiply.

$\dfrac{^-4}{5} \cdot \dfrac{^-7}{16} = \dfrac{\overset{-1}{\cancel{^-4}} \cdot ^-7}{5 \cdot \underset{4}{\cancel{16}}} = \dfrac{7}{20}$

$-2\dfrac{1}{7} \cdot 1\dfrac{2}{3} = \dfrac{\overset{-5}{\cancel{^-15}} \cdot 5}{7 \cdot \underset{1}{\cancel{3}}} = \dfrac{^-25}{7} = -3\dfrac{4}{7}$

Find the products.

1. $\dfrac{^-5}{6} \cdot \dfrac{3}{5}$

2. $\dfrac{^-3}{8} \cdot \dfrac{^-5}{6}$

3. $2\dfrac{7}{10} \cdot 1\dfrac{5}{6}$

4. $-3\dfrac{1}{4} \cdot -2\dfrac{2}{5}$

Find these products. Express the answer as a mixed number or fraction in lowest terms.

1. $\dfrac{5}{8} \cdot \dfrac{7}{10}$

2. $\dfrac{^-9}{16} \cdot \dfrac{4}{5}$

3. $\dfrac{^-5}{6} \cdot \dfrac{^-4}{5}$

4. $\dfrac{2}{3} \cdot \dfrac{^-8}{9}$

5. $4\dfrac{3}{8} \cdot 2\dfrac{1}{5}$

6. $3\dfrac{3}{4} \cdot \dfrac{^-5}{12}$

7. $\dfrac{^-3}{4} \cdot 4\dfrac{2}{9}$

8. $3\dfrac{3}{10} \cdot \dfrac{7}{11}$

9. $^-1\dfrac{1}{7} \cdot ^-4\dfrac{1}{2}$

10. $\dfrac{5}{6} \cdot ^-9$

11. $^-4\dfrac{1}{6} \cdot ^-2\dfrac{2}{5}$

12. $\dfrac{^-7}{20} \cdot \dfrac{5}{8}$

13. $\dfrac{^-5}{16} \cdot 3\dfrac{1}{5}$

14. $^-2\dfrac{2}{3} \cdot 1\dfrac{3}{16}$

15. $6 \cdot 3\dfrac{2}{3}$

16. $^-4\dfrac{2}{7} \cdot ^-5\dfrac{1}{4}$

17. $4\dfrac{1}{12} \cdot ^-3\dfrac{6}{7}$

18. $^-2\dfrac{3}{4} \cdot 1\dfrac{1}{10}$

19. $\dfrac{^-3}{8} \cdot 2\dfrac{2}{3}$

20. $^-6\dfrac{2}{3} \cdot 4\dfrac{3}{8}$

MATH REASONING Multiply. Express the answer as a mixed number or fraction in lowest terms.

21. $\dfrac{2}{3} \cdot \dfrac{^-5}{6} \cdot \dfrac{3}{5}$

22. $\dfrac{^-3}{8} \cdot 2\dfrac{2}{3} \cdot 2\dfrac{1}{2}$

23. $-6\dfrac{2}{3} \cdot 4\dfrac{3}{8} \cdot -\dfrac{9}{10}$

24. $4\dfrac{2}{3} \cdot 1\dfrac{9}{19} \cdot -3\dfrac{1}{6}$

PROBLEM SOLVING

25. It takes Jack about $1\dfrac{1}{2}$ work days to install a tile floor in an average size kitchen. How many days would it take him to install floors for 5 kitchens?

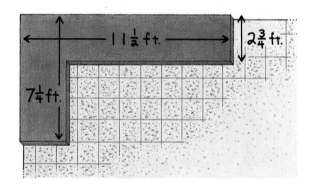

26. Some kitchen cabinets have been arranged as shown. How much would it cost to put a counter top on these cabinets if it costs $15 per square foot?

▶ **MENTAL MATH**

Use the *breaking apart* method to multiply $3\dfrac{1}{3} \times 4$ using mental math.

Think: $3\dfrac{1}{3} = \left(3 + \dfrac{1}{3}\right)$ so $3\dfrac{1}{3} \cdot 4 = \left(3 + \dfrac{1}{3}\right) \cdot 4 = 3 \cdot 4 + \dfrac{4}{3} = 12 + 1\dfrac{1}{3} = 13\dfrac{1}{3}$.

Use mental math to find these products.

27. $5\dfrac{2}{3} \cdot 3$

28. $7 \cdot 3\dfrac{1}{7}$

29. $2\dfrac{1}{5} \cdot ^-3$

30. $2\dfrac{3}{8} \cdot 4$

More Practice, page 533, set A

Exploring Algebra
Reciprocals and Negative Exponents

EXPLORE **Study the Information**

If the product of two numbers is 1, each of the numbers is the **reciprocal** of the other. For example, 3 and $\frac{1}{3}$ are reciprocals; $\frac{7}{8}$ and $\frac{8}{7}$ are reciprocals. Copy these numbers. Draw lines connecting the reciprocals.

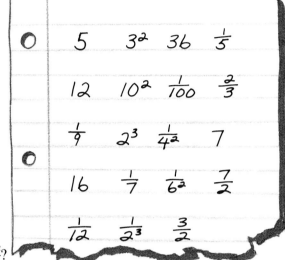

TALK ABOUT IT

1. What is the reciprocal of the integer n? of $\frac{1}{n}$?

2. What is the reciprocal of the rational number $\frac{a}{b}$?

3. What number is the reciprocal of $3\frac{1}{4}$?

Study the pattern in this table to see why a reciprocal can be represented by a **negative exponent.**

$3 \cdot 3 \cdot 3$	$3 \cdot 3$	3	1	$\frac{1}{3}$	$\frac{1}{3 \cdot 3}$	$\frac{1}{3 \cdot 3 \cdot 3}$
3^3	3^2	3^1	3^0	3^{-1}	3^{-2}	3^{-3}

To multiply two powers of the same base add the exponents.

Examples Simplify. Write the expression with positive exponents

A $\dfrac{3^7}{3^4} = \dfrac{3 \cdot 3 \cdot 3 \cdot 3 \cdot 3 \cdot 3 \cdot 3}{3 \cdot 3 \cdot 3 \cdot 3} = 3^3$ 　　　 **B** $\dfrac{10^2}{10^7} = 10^2 \cdot 10^{-7} = 10^{(2-7)} = 10^{-5} = \dfrac{1}{10^5}$

$3^7 \cdot 3^{-4} = 3^{(7-4)} = 3^3$

C $\dfrac{2^3 \cdot 5^4}{2^2 \cdot 5^6} = 2^3 \cdot 5^4 \cdot 2^{-2} \cdot 5^{-6} = 2^{(3-2)} \cdot 5^{(4-6)} = 2 \cdot 5^{-2} = \dfrac{2}{5^2}$

Simplify. Write the expression with positive exponents.

1. $\dfrac{5^4}{5^2}$ 　　　　　 2. $10^{12} \cdot 10^{-15}$ 　　　 3. $\dfrac{3^2 \cdot 5^3}{3^5 \cdot 5}$ 　　　　 4. $\dfrac{x^7}{x^3}$

Write the reciprocal of each number.

1. $\frac{1}{7}$
2. $\frac{2}{3}$
3. 4
4. $2\frac{3}{5}$

5. 2^2
6. 10^5
7. 6^3
8. 10^{-3}

Simplify. Write the expression with positive exponents.

9. $\frac{3^4}{3^2}$
10. $\frac{10^7}{10^4}$
11. $\frac{5^3}{5^8}$
12. $\frac{2^3 \cdot 2^4}{2^8}$

13. $\frac{3^9}{3^2 \cdot 3^4}$
14. $(-3)^2 (-3)^5$
15. $2^7 \cdot 2^{-3}$
16. $10^{-7} \cdot 10^5$

17. $\frac{3^{-2}}{3^{-4}}$
18. $\frac{2^{-3} \cdot 2^4}{2^3}$
19. $\frac{x^6}{x^4}$
20. $\frac{y^3}{y^{-6}}$

MATH REASONING Use Guess and Check to find an integer n that solves each of these equations.

21. $2^n = 4$
22. $3^n = 27$
23. $10^n = \frac{1}{10}$
24. $2^n = \frac{1}{2}$

PROBLEM SOLVING

25. One byte (pronounced bite) is the amount of computer memory needed to store a single letter of the alphabet. One Kilobyte (K) = 1024 bytes. The number 1024 is what power of two?

▶ **ALGEBRA**

Solve $\frac{2}{3}x = 8$ by multiplying by a reciprocal.

Solution $\left(\frac{3}{2} \cdot \frac{2}{3}\right)x = \frac{3}{2} \cdot 8$ or $x = 3 \cdot 4 = 12$.

Solve.

26. $\frac{2}{5}x = 10$
27. $\frac{2}{3}x = \frac{8}{9}$
28. $\frac{4}{5}x = -20$
29. $\frac{3}{8}x = \frac{-5}{8}$

30. $\frac{9}{2}x = 18$
31. $\frac{3}{11}x = \frac{3}{11}$
32. $\frac{16}{81}x = \frac{40}{27}$
33. $\frac{13}{29}x = \frac{3}{17}$

Dividing Rational Numbers

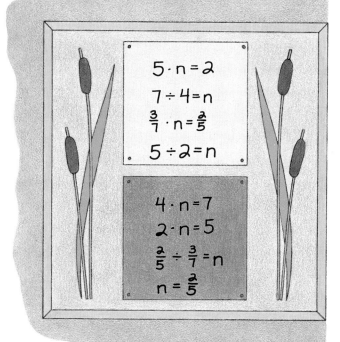

LEARN ABOUT IT

6 ÷ 2 is the number *n* such that 2 · **n** is 6.

EXPLORE **Examine the Equations**

Match each division equation on this bulletin board with a multiplication equation that means the same thing.

TALK ABOUT IT

1. Is there a match for each equation?

2. Does $\frac{2}{3} \div \frac{5}{6} = n$ mean the same thing as

$\frac{5}{6} \cdot n = \frac{2}{3}$ or $\frac{2}{3} \cdot n = \frac{5}{6}$?

Question 2 suggests this division method.

Look at the divisor.	Find the reciprocal of the divisor.	Multiply the dividend by the reciprocal of the divisor.
$\frac{2}{3} \div \frac{5}{6}$	$\frac{6}{5}$	$\frac{2}{3} \cdot \frac{6}{5} = \frac{4}{5}$

Here is why this method works.

$$\frac{2}{3} \div \frac{5}{6} = \frac{\frac{2}{3}}{\frac{5}{6}} = \frac{\frac{2}{3} \cdot \frac{6}{5}}{\frac{5}{6} \cdot \frac{6}{5}} = \frac{\frac{2}{3} \cdot \frac{6}{5}}{1} = \frac{4}{5}, \text{ so } \frac{2}{3} \div \frac{5}{6} = \frac{2}{3} \cdot \frac{6}{5}$$

Examples Find each quotient. Express as a mixed number in lowest terms.

A $3\frac{1}{5} \div 4 = \frac{16}{5} \cdot \frac{1}{4} = \frac{4}{5}$

B $^-5 \div ^-2\frac{3}{4} = \frac{-5}{1} \div \frac{-11}{4} = \frac{5}{1} \cdot \frac{4}{11}$

$= \frac{20}{11} = 1\frac{9}{11}$

TRY IT OUT

Find these quotients. Express in lowest terms.

1. $\frac{3}{8} \div \frac{3}{4}$

2. $\frac{-1}{5} \div \frac{3}{10}$

3. $1\frac{7}{8} \div 1\frac{2}{3}$

4. $\frac{-5}{6} \div \frac{-7}{12}$

Find these quotients. Express as a fraction or mixed number in lowest terms.

1. $\frac{2}{3} \div \frac{5}{8}$ **2.** $\frac{8}{15} \div \frac{4}{5}$ **3.** $\frac{5}{9} \div \frac{1}{15}$ **4.** $\frac{3}{8} \div \frac{11}{24}$

5. $3\frac{2}{3} \div \frac{8}{9}$ **6.** $2\frac{9}{11} \div \frac{2}{11}$ **7.** $1\frac{4}{5} \div 1\frac{3}{10}$ **8.** $\frac{9}{10} \div \frac{1}{5}$

9. $2 \div 1\frac{1}{5}$ **10.** $\frac{2}{3} \div 2\frac{1}{2}$ **11.** $6\frac{1}{2} \div 1\frac{2}{3}$ **12.** $5\frac{1}{4} \div 2\frac{2}{3}$

13. $4\frac{1}{4} \div 4$ **14.** $1\frac{2}{7} \div 3\frac{3}{14}$ **15.** $\frac{1}{7} \div 5$ **16.** $1\frac{1}{11} \div 1\frac{1}{32}$

Perform these operations.

17. $\left(2\frac{1}{3} + 1\frac{5}{8}\right) \div \frac{3}{4}$ **18.** $\left(\frac{5}{8} \div \frac{3}{10}\right) \div 3\frac{3}{4}$ **19.** $\left(6\frac{1}{3} - 1\frac{5}{6}\right) \div 2\frac{1}{4}$

MATH REASONING Solve.

20. $\frac{1}{2} \cdot n = \frac{1}{4}$ **21.** $\frac{2}{3} \cdot n = \frac{4}{9}$ **22.** $\frac{1}{3} \cdot n = \frac{1}{2}$

PROBLEM SOLVING

23. A piece of lumber that is $9\frac{7}{8}$ in. wide is cut into three pieces equal in width. How wide is each piece?

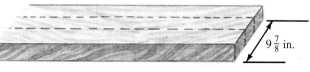

24. Floor boards $3\frac{1}{2}$ in. wide are to be laid to repair an opening that is $12\frac{1}{4}$ in. wide. How many boards are needed?

Find the prime factorization of each number.

25. 46   **26.** 165   **27.** 72   **28.** 210

Find the Least Common Multiple for each set of numbers.

29. 4, 8   **30.** 6, 8   **31.** 2, 3, 5   **32.** 14, 6, 21

Evaluate $y = 5x^2 - 4$ for each value of x.

33. $x = 0$ **34.** $x = 1$ **35.** $x = -1$ **36.** $x = 7$

More Practice, page 533, set B

Problem Solving
Using the Strategies

UNDERSTAND
ANALYZE DATA
PLAN
ESTIMATE
SOLVE
EXAMINE

LEARN ABOUT IT

For some problems it is helpful to use several strategies. To solve this problem, you can use **Solve a Simpler Problem, Make an Organized List, Make a Table,** and **Look for a Pattern.**

The physics department at Redwood High School bought 12 new computers. They want to divide the computers among 4 classrooms so that each gets at least one new computer. In how many ways can they do this?

You can begin with Simpler Problems and Make an Organized List.

4 computers	5 computers	6 computers	7 computers
1111	1112, 1121	1113, 1131, 1311, 3111	1114, 1141, 1411, 4111, 1123, 1321, 3121, 1132,
	1211, 2111	1122, 1212, 2112,	1312, 3112, 1213, 1231, 3211, 2113, 2131,
		1221, 2121, 2211	2311, 1222, 2122, 2212, 2221,

Then you can Make a Table.

number of computers	4	5	6	7	8	9	10	11	12
Number of ways	1	4	10	20	35	56	84	120	165
first difference		3	6	10	15	21	28	36	45
second difference			3	4	5	6	7	8	9

Now, you can Look for a Pattern.

Increase each second difference by 1. Use each second difference to find the next first difference. Use each first difference to find the next "number of ways".

The physics department can divide the 12 computers among the 4 classrooms in 165 ways.

TRY IT OUT

Solve. Use any problem solving strategies.

1. Ms. Lopez gave each pair of students in her class 20 toothpicks for an experiment. If she gave at least 2 to each student, in how many ways could she give each pair 20 toothpicks?

2. Mr. Genetti bought 15 physical science lab kits. He wants to divide them among 3 classrooms so that each gets at least 1 kit. In how many ways can he do this?

Some Strategies	
Act Out	Solve a Simpler Problem
Use Objects	Make an Organized List
Choose an Operation	Work Backward
Draw a Picture	Look for a Pattern
Guess and Check	Use Logical Reasoning
Make a Table	Write an Equation

Solve. Use any problem solving strategy.

1. Kevin spent 8 hours on homework last week. He spent $2\frac{3}{4}$ hours working on a science project. His history report took $\frac{2}{3}$ hour more than his science project. How long did his history report take?

2. The computer club has 18 members and 9 computers. If the members work in pairs, how many different pairs are possible.

3. An elementary school in Oregon has 468 students. Use the table to find about how many computers the school has.

States with fewest students per computer in public schools	
Wyoming	16.5
Alaska	18.1
Minnesota	20.3
Washington, D.C.	22.0
New York	23.9
Nevada	23.9
South Dakota	24.8
Oregon	25.7

4. If you add the numerator and the denominator of a fraction, the sum is 8. If you subtract the numerator and the denominator, the difference is 1 more than a perfect square. If you multiply them, the product is 1 less than a perfect square. Find the fraction.

5. Of the 76,900 computers in the public schools, $\frac{3}{5}$ were in elementary schools and $\frac{1}{5}$ were in high schools. How many more computers were in elementary schools than in high schools?

6. Tanya is using a computer to help her learn vocabulary words. She learned 2 words the first day. Each day after that she learned 2 more words than the previous day. How many words had she learned after 20 days.

7. In the school year 1987–1988, there were 76,900 computers being used as teaching tools in 80,000 public schools. About $\frac{4}{25}$ of them were in junior high schools. How many computers were there in junior high schools?

8. Regina and her brother are sharing a bookshelf that is 12 ft long. Regina started at the left end and filled $\frac{1}{3}$ of the shelf. Her brother started at the right end and filled $1\frac{1}{2}$ times as much. How many feet are still empty?

More Practice, page 546, set C

Scientific Notation

EXPLORE Study the Information

A human blood cell can be seen through a microscope and is as small as 0.0003 in. in diameter. In contrast, the planet Mercury can be seen with a telescope and is about 36,000,000 miles from the sun.

TALK ABOUT IT

1. How far is Mercury from the Sun?

2. Write the number 10^7 in standard form.

3. Multiply the value you got for 10^7 by 3.6. What do you think this value represents?

Scientific notation is a method for writing numbers using powers of 10.

36,000,000	=	3.6	$\times$	10^7
Standard numeral		**A number greater than or equal to 1 but less than 10**		**A power of 10**

0.0003	=	3	$\times$	10^{-4}
Standard numeral		**A number greater than or equal to 1 but less than 10**		**A power of 10**

Examples

A $8,900,000,000 = 8.9 \times 10^9$

B $0.0008\,9 = 8.9 \times 10^{-4}$

C $4.23 \times 10^5 = 423,000$

D $1.835 \times 10^{-5} = 0.00001835$

TRY IT OUT

Write in standard form.

1. 5.2×10^5 **2.** 3.9×10^7 **3.** 4.8×10^{-4} **4.** 8.5×10^{-7}

Write in scientific notation.

5. 23,500 **6.** 140,000,000 **7.** 0.00045 **8.** 0.000000589

Write in standard form.

1. 3.7×10^4
2. 7.9×10^{-8}
3. 1.2×10^8
4. 4.6×10^3

5. 5.01×10^{-9}
6. 3.102×10^7
7. 4.5×10^{-3}
8. 9.9×10^9

9. 3.91×10^{-4}
10. 6.108×10^{-5}
11. 4.002×10^4
12. 5.8009×10^7

Write in scientific notation.

13. 2,340,000
14. 800,000,000
15. 4,701,000
16. 0.0000004

17. 0.00001002
18. 5,600,000,000
19. 0.000908
20. 0.005006

MATH REASONING Complete these generalizations. Fill in each
blank with either the phrase "large number" or "small
number". Illustrate your answer using scientific notation.

21. a small number $\times$ a small number = _____.

22. a small number $\div$ a small number = _____.

23. a small number $\div$ a large number = _____.

PROBLEM SOLVING

24. The mass of a subatomic particle can be described in terms
of its energy. The mass of an electron is 510,000 electron
volts. The mass of a proton is 938.3×10^6 electron volts.
How much greater than the mass of an electron is the mass
of a proton?

25. **Science Data Bank** The mass of a neutron is 939,600,000
electron volts. Write the mass of a neutron using each
electron volt unit (KeV, MeV, GeV, TeV).

▶ **CALCULATOR**

When you multiply $123,456 \times 6,789$ on some calculators, the
display reads $\boxed{8.3814 \quad 08}$. What does that mean?

Use your calculator to complete these products or quotients.

26. $(5.24 \times 10^8)(4.89 \times 10^{17})$
27. $(8.2 \times 10^{12})(3.68 \times 10^7)$

28. $(4.6 \times 10^8)(7.3 \times 10^{-15})$
29. $(4.3 \times 10^{-8})(3.5 \times 10^{-3})$

More Practice, page 533, set C

Problem Solving
Finding Related Problems

UNDERSTAND
ANALYZE DATA
PLAN
ESTIMATE
SOLVE
EXAMINE

LEARN ABOUT IT

When you have a problem to solve, thinking of **related problems** may help.

Japanese-American street fair.

At a street fair, La Keisha and La Jon are buying two pieces of jewelry together to get one free. How many combinations of three pieces can they choose from the following?

African bead earrings   Navajo ring
Moroccan necklace   Thai silver bracelet
Jamaican ankle bracelet

Pete and Armand are sharing two chicken dishes and one rice dish from the food booths. How many different combinations could they choose from?

Chicken	*Rice*
Barbequed	Mexican rice
Teriaki	Red beans and rice
Enchilada	Fried rice

Making an organized list can help you solve both of these problems since both deal with combinations.

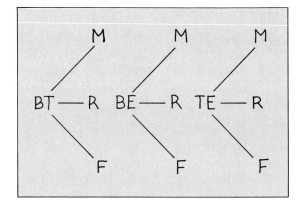

I'll start with combinations that have African bead earrings.
AMT, AMJ, AMN, ATJ,
ATN, AJN
Then I'll look for other combinations.
JMT, JMN, JTN, NMT

La Keisha and La Jon could choose from 10 different combinations.

Pete and Armand could choose from 9 different combinations.

TRY IT OUT

Solve. Tell how you think the problems are related.

1. The Hunan beef dinner has 70 calories fewer than a beef burrito. Together they have 990 calories. How many calories does each meal have?

2. The street fair has 40 food and crafts booths. There are 8 more food booths than crafts booths. How many of each are there?

216

Solve. Use any problem solving strategy.

1. Ruth has $7\frac{1}{2}$ cups of cooked rice. She wants each serving to be $\frac{3}{4}$ cup. How many servings does she have?

2. A restaurant can seat 102 people. Some of the tables can seat 4 people, and some can seat 6 people. How many 4-person tables does the restaurant have?

3. A can of chicken broth costs $1.29 and contains $14\frac{1}{2}$ ounces. Julia used $1\frac{3}{4}$ cups of chicken broth to make soup. How many ounces were left? (1 c = 8 oz)

4. At a food booth, Jung and Alain bought two burritos for $1.50 each, two tamales for $0.99 each, and two orders of sopapillas for $1.25 each. They paid for their food with two $5.00-bills and divided the change evenly. How much change did each get?

5. A cup of plain popcorn has 0.3 g of fat and 0.8 g of protein. With butter added, 1 c of popcorn has 1.92 g of fat and 0.9 g of protein. Suki ate 4 cups of popcorn with butter and Terry ate 4 cups without butter. How many more grams of fat did Suki consume than Terry?

6. La Keisha and La Jon met three friends for lunch at the Chinese food booth. There were 15 different foods to choose from, so the girls agreed that each person would choose a different food. How many combinations of five foods are possible?

7. The American Heart Association recommends that less than $\frac{3}{10}$ of your daily intake of calories come from fat. An eighth grade girl needs about 2,150 calories each day. About how many of those calories should come from fat?

8. **Develop a Plan** Mei attended a Japanese banquet. On the tables he saw a dish of rice for every 2 guests, a dish of steamed vegetables for every 3 guests, and a dish of meat for every 5 guests. He counted 62 dishes altogether. If the number of dishes and guests comes out evenly, how many people attended the banquet?
   a. List 2 or more strategies you think might help you solve this problem.
   b. Solve the problem.
   c. Look back at your solution. What strategies did you use? Do you think that was the best way to solve the problem? Why or why not?

Applied Problem Solving
Group Decision Making

UNDERSTAND
ANALYZE DATA
PLAN
ESTIMATE
SOLVE
EXAMINE

Group Skill:
Listen to Others

Your class is sponsoring a school dance and your group must decide if you will have a live band or a disc jockey. Your group is also in charge of deciding how much admission to charge for the dance.

Facts to Consider

1. You gave a survey to a sample of 50 students and had the following results:

> *What is the most you would pay for admission to a dance with a live band?*
>
> | $1.00 | $2.00 | $3.00 | $4.00 | $5.00 |
> |---|---|---|---|---|
> | 0 student | 2 students | 9 students | 38 students | 1 student |
>
> *What is the most you would pay for admission to hear a disc jockey?*
>
> | $1.00 | $2.00 | $3.00 | $4.00 | $5.00 |
> |---|---|---|---|---|
> | 4 student | 10 students | 29 students | 7 students | 0 students |

2. You expect from 150 to 175 students to attend the dance.

3. The less you charge for admission, the more likely students are to attend the dance.

4. The Bees will cost $250 plus $\frac{1}{4}$ of the amount taken in by the admission charge. They play three sets for a total of 3 hours.

5. The disc jockey will charge a flat rate of $60 per hour with a 3-hour minimum. That rate includes bringing in and setting up a professional stereo system and supplying an extensive collection of music.

6. You would like to have a minimum of $100 left after paying for the band or disc jockey.

1. If you hire the disc jockey for 3 hours what will the total charge be?

2. If you hire the disc jockey and 150 students come to the dance, what is the least you could charge and still have $100 left over?

3. How much would you pay the Bees if 125 students came to the dance and paid $3.00 admission each?

4. Suppose you hire the Bees and 150 students come to the dance. If you charge $3.00 per student, how much would be left after paying the band?

5. If you hire the Bees and only 150 students come to the dance, what is the least you could charge per student and still have $100 left over?

What Is Your Decision?

Would your group choose the live band or the disc jockey? Support your decision with a chart showing how you computed your projected costs and profits.

WRAP UP

Rational Language

Match each phrase on the left with the term on the right it best describes.

1. way of expressing very large or very small numbers
2. gives product of 1 when multiplied by the number
3. quantity expressed as a whole number and a fraction
4. fractions that represent the same quantity
5. GCF of the numerator and denominator is 1
6. numerator of fraction is smaller than the denominator
7. another way to write $\dfrac{1}{x}$
8. top number in a fraction
9. a decimal with a finite number of digits
10. numerator of fraction is larger than the denominator

a. equivalent fractions
b. proper fraction
c. terminating decimal
d. numerator
e. improper fraction
f. reciprocal of a number
g. scientific notation
h. negative exponent
i. fraction in lowest terms
j. mixed number

Sometimes, Always, Never

Decide if each of these statements is sometimes true, always true, or never true.

11. A repeating decimal is a rational number.

12. The numbers $12\frac{1}{2}$, 12.5, and $\dfrac{25}{2}$ all have the same value.

13. If the numerator of a fraction is divided by the denominator, the division creates a repeating decimal.

Project

Use reference books to find the distances from earth to 10 different stars. Express the distances in scientific notation. Then order the stars according to distance from earth, beginning with the closest star.

POWER PRACTICE/TEST

Part 1   Understanding

1. Are $\frac{6}{10}$ and $\frac{9}{15}$ equivalent fractions? Why or why not?

Use the number line below to answer questions 2 and 3.

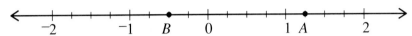

2. Express the rational number corresponding to point A in 2 different ways.

3. Express the rational number opposite point B in 2 different ways.

4. Use exponents to express the reciprocal of 2^5 in two ways.

Part 2   Skills

Compare. Use $<$ or $>$.

5. $-1\frac{2}{5}$ ▒ $-\frac{11}{10}$

6. $-\frac{4}{9}$ ▒ $-\frac{13}{14}$

7. 0.1 ▒ 0.11

Find a decimal for each fraction. Indicate repeating decimals.

8. $\frac{-11}{40}$

9. $\frac{7}{6}$

10. $\frac{18}{6}$

11. Write the reciprocal of $^-2\frac{3}{4}$.

12. Simplify $\frac{3^2 \cdot 3^4}{3^8}$.

Compute. Express your answer as a mixed number or fraction in lowest terms.

13. $\frac{^-1}{2} - \frac{^-1}{6}$

14. $^-1\frac{1}{2} + 1\frac{1}{6}$

15. $(8 + 5\frac{3}{4}) - 6\frac{3}{5}$

16. $^-2\frac{3}{4} \cdot 1\frac{1}{3}$

17. $\frac{^-2}{3} \cdot 2\frac{1}{4} \cdot \frac{^-4}{5}$

18. $2\frac{5}{8} \div 2\frac{3}{4}$

19. Write 2.7×10^6 in standard notation.

20. Write 0.00417 in scientific notation.

Part 3   Applications

21. Ron got 21 of 25 right on a math test, 11 of 12 on an English test, and 26 of 30 on a history test. On which test did Ron do best?

22. Challenge The shelves of this bookcase are evenly spaced. The short shelf is two-thirds as long as others. What is the least whole number of linear feet of lumber needed to make the bookcase?

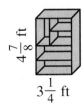

$4\frac{7}{8}$ ft

$3\frac{1}{4}$ ft

221

ENRICHMENT
Buffon's Needle

As you know, π is the ratio of the circumference of a circle to the diameter of a circle.

An approximate value for π to 20 decimal places is 3.14159265358979323846.

A French naturalist, Comte de Buffon (1707–1788), claimed that the following method, based on probability, can be used to give an approximate value for π.

To try it, follow the steps below.

1. Draw several parallel lines that are a needle's length apart. (Use a toothpick for a needle.)

2. Drop the needle on the paper from a height of 30 cm. Record whether the needle hits or misses a line. Do this at least 100 times. Use tally marks to record your results in a chart like this.

Hits	Misses

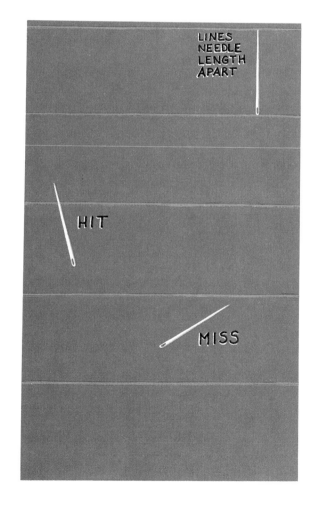

3. Follow these steps.

   A. Count the number of times you dropped the needle.

   B. Multiply that number by 2.

   C. Divide by the number of "hits" you made.

   D. Compare the quotient you got with the value of π.

4. How close did you come to the value of π?

222

CUMULATIVE REVIEW

1. In which pair of numbers is one number a factor of the other number?

   A 2, 17   B 4, 34

   C 7, 16   D 6, 42

2. Which statement is true?

   A A number is divisible by 2 if it contains the digit 2.

   B A number is divisible by 3 if its ones digit is divisible by 3.

   C A number is divisible by 4 if its last two digits are divisible by 4.

   D A number is divisible by 5 only if its ones digit is 5.

3. Which number is prime?

   A 53   B 0

   C 39   D 119

4. Find the prime factorization of 36.

   A $2^2 \cdot 9$ B $2^2 \cdot 3^2$

   C $2^2 \cdot 3^3$ D $2 \cdot 2 \cdot 9$

5. Find the GCF of 24 and 40.

   A 120   B 4

   C 40   D 8

6. Find the LCM of 5, 9, and 18.

   A 810   B 45

   C 90   D 18

7. Write $5^3 \cdot 5^0$ in standard notation.

   A 15   B 625

   C 125   D 0

8. Which statement is true?

   A $-35 < {}^-42$ B $35 < -42$

   C $-35 > 42$ D ${}^-35 > {}^-42$

9. Solve $\frac{m}{6} + 5 = 7$.

   A $m = 12$ B $m = 2$

   C $m = 72$ D $m = 8$

10. Solve $\frac{d}{4} - 6 = -8$.

    A $d = -3\frac{1}{2}$ B $d = -8$

    C $d = 56$ D $d = 8$

11. Find three solutions for the equation $y = -3x + 2$.

    A $(-1, 5), (0, 2), (2, -4)$

    B $(-4, 2), (2, 0), (5, -1)$

    C $(-1, -1), (0, 2), (2, 8)$

    D $(-1, -5), (0, 2), (2, -4)$

12. The temperature went from 10° above zero to 2° below zero in 3 hours. Find the average temperature change each hour.

    A 3   B -4

    C -2 D 4

13. The formula for finding the volume (V) of a rectangular prism with a square base is $V = s^2 \cdot h$, where s is the length of one side of the base and h is the height. Find the volume of a box where $s = 3$ m and $h = 5$ m.

    A 45 m^3 B 30 m^3

    C 25 m^3 D 15 m^3

8

RATIO AND PROPORTION

THEME: FILM EDITING

MATH AND
FINE ARTS

DATA BANK

Use the Fine Arts Data Bank on page 500 to answer the question.

1 What fraction of the width of a 70mm film format is the width of each film format shown in the Scale Drawing of Film Formats?

2 Measure the 65mm film format in the scale drawing to the nearest centimeter. Compare the measurements you make of the drawing to the actual dimensions indicated on the drawing.

3 The shutter angle of a camera determines how much light reaches the film. Which shutter angle in the table on Motion Picture Camera Exposure Times equals the sum of the angles of a triangle?

4 **Using Critical Thinking** Look for a pattern in the series of exposure times for each shutter angle listed in the table on Motion Picture Camera Exposure Times. Write expressions for the first five numbers in the series that will work for each pattern.

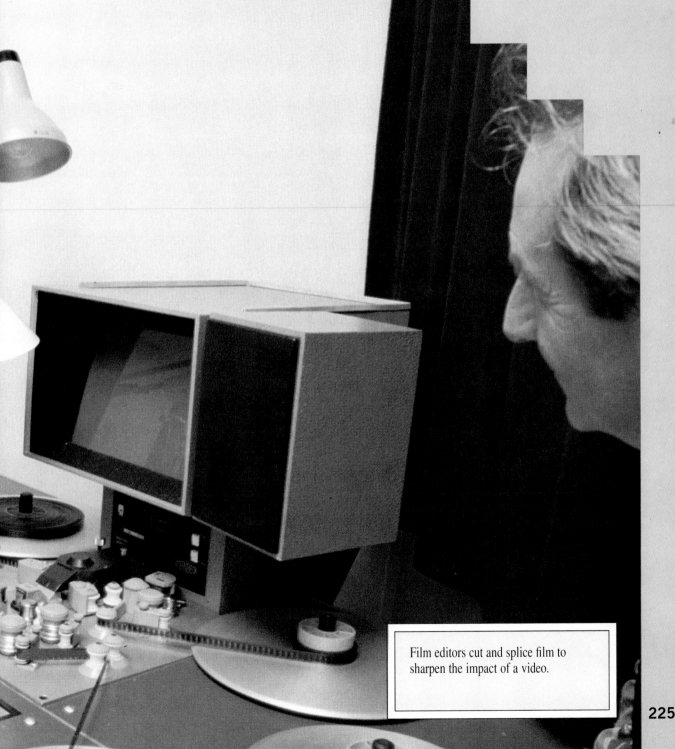

Film editors cut and splice film to sharpen the impact of a video.

Ratio and Proportion

A **ratio** is a comparison of one number to another.

EXPLORE **Study the Situation**

Betsy and her brother run a gardening business during the summer. The fuel for their mowers is a mixture of oil and gasoline. Some mowers use a mixture of one part oil to 16 parts gasoline.

This ratio of oil to gasoline can be written in three ways: 1 to 16, 1 : 16, or $\frac{1}{16}$.

TALK ABOUT IT

1. What is the ratio of gasoline to oil?

2. How much oil is added to 32 ounces of gasoline?

Ratio of 1 to 16

1	parts of oil	2	3	4	5	6
16	parts of gasoline	32	48	?	?	?

×2
×3

3. How many ounces of gasoline are needed for 4 ounces of oil?

A statement that two ratios are equal is called a **proportion**.

$\frac{1}{16}$ and $\frac{3}{48}$ are equal ratios. $\frac{1}{16} = \frac{3}{48}$ is a proportion.

Example

Paint is mixed in the ratio of 1 part of blue pigment to 12 parts of base. Some proportions are:

$\frac{1}{12} = \frac{2}{24}$ and $\frac{2}{24} = \frac{3}{36}$

Ratio of 1 to 12

1	parts of pigment	2	3	4	5	6
12	parts of base	24	36	?	?	?

×2
×3

Write each ratio in two other ways.

1. 5 to 7   **2.** $\frac{1}{7}$ **3.** 3 : 4   **4.** 1 to 11

5. Kim mixes punch with 1 part grape juice and 3 parts apple juice. Make a table for this ratio and write three proportions from it.

Write each ratio in two other ways.

1. 3 to 5   **2.** $\frac{1}{8}$ **3.** 5 : 9   **4.** $\frac{35}{9}$

5. 2 : 7   **6.** 4 to 1   **7.** $\frac{5}{18}$ **8.** 8 to 3

9. Materials A and B are mixed in a ratio of 1 to 4. Complete this ratio table and write four proportions from it.

ratio of 1 to 4	parts of A	2	3	4	5
	parts of B	?	?	?	?

Complete ratio tables and write three proportions for each.

10. Ratio of 1 to 7.   **11.** Ratio of 1 to 13.   **12.** Ratio of 1 to 22.

13. Ratio of 2 to 5.   **14.** Ratio of 3 to 4.   **15.** Ratio of 6 to 1.

MATH REASONING The ratio of 1 to 5 is less than the ratio of 3 to 8 since $\frac{1}{5} < \frac{3}{8}$.

Compare these ratios. Use < or >.

16. 1 to 4 and 2 to 9   **17.** 3 to 5 and 4 to 7   **18.** 5 to 11 and 7 to 13

PROBLEM SOLVING

This table appears on a container of oil for use with mower engines.

19. For a ratio of 24:1 how many ounces of oil should be mixed with 3 gallons of gasoline?

20. One gallon equals 128 fluid ounces. Which entries in this table represent an exact ratio and which are approximations?

GASOLINE TO OIL RATIO						
Gallons of Gasoline	16:1	20:1	24:1	32:1	40:1	50:1
	Ounces of Oil To Be Added					
1	8	6	5	4	3	3
2	16	13	11	8	6	5
3	24	19	16	12	10	8
4	32	26	21	16	13	10

▶ **MENTAL MATH**

The ratio 8 to 2 is a **whole number ratio** because $\frac{8}{2} = \frac{4}{1}$, and $\frac{4}{1}$ equals a whole number. Show that each of these is a whole number ratio.

21. 48 to 6   **22.** 60 to 5   **23.** 15 to 3   **24.** 51 to 3

More Practice, page 533, set D

Rate

A **rate** is a ratio comparing two different units. Frequently used rates are miles per hour, meters per second, and dollars per hour.

EXPLORE Study the Situation

The rate a movie camera or projector runs is measured in frames per second (fps). Standard projection rate is 24 fps. When the camera rate is higher than the projection rate, slow motion is created. Fast motion occurs when the camera rate is lower than the projection rate.

TALK ABOUT IT

1. What is the normal rate of filming and projection?

2. Old silent movies were filmed at 16 fps. What happens when they are projected at standard rate?

3. What type of motion would a camera rate of 96 fps produce?

4. At standard rate, how many frames would you film in 1 minute?

Example   If a projector shows 780 frames in 12 seconds, what is its rate?

Write the ratio $\frac{780}{12}$. Find a ratio with denominator 1. Divide or use a table.

$\frac{780 \text{ frames}}{12 \text{ seconds}} = 780 \div 12 = 65 \text{ fps}$

frames	780	390	195	65
seconds	12	6	3	1

Other Examples Simplify each rate.

A $\frac{\$48}{8 \text{ hr}} = \$6/\text{hr}$

B $\frac{400 \text{ m}}{12.5 \text{ sec}} = 32 \text{ m/sec}$

C $\frac{310 \text{ miles}}{5 \text{ hours}} = 62 \text{ mph}$

Simplify each rate.

1. $\frac{\$72}{8 \text{ hr}}$

2. $\frac{275 \text{ words}}{5 \text{ minutes}}$

3. $\frac{324 \text{ students}}{12 \text{ teachers}}$

4. $\frac{861 \text{ miles}}{14 \text{ hours}}$

Simplify each rate. Either complete a table or do the division in one step.

1. $\dfrac{80 \text{ km}}{8 \text{ hr}}$

2. $\dfrac{125 \text{ liters}}{50 \text{ min}}$

3. $\dfrac{1,200 \text{ words}}{6 \text{ min}}$

4. $\dfrac{51 \text{ teams}}{17 \text{ schools}}$

5. $\dfrac{28 \text{ days}}{4 \text{ weeks}}$

6. $\dfrac{45 \text{ people}}{15 \text{ cars}}$

7. $\dfrac{480 \text{ pupils}}{16 \text{ teachers}}$

8. $\dfrac{5,000 \text{ people}}{100 \text{ square miles}}$

9. $\dfrac{\$63}{12 \text{ meals}}$

10. $\dfrac{275 \text{ min}}{5 \text{ classes}}$

11. $\dfrac{\$40}{5 \text{ hr}}$

12. $\dfrac{135 \text{ revolutions}}{3 \text{ min}}$

13. A plane flies at 650 miles per hour. How far does it travel in 3 hours?

14. Joe's car consumed 15 gallons of gasoline on a 537 mile trip. How many miles per gallon did he average?

MATH REASONING Estimate each of these rates to the nearest whole number.

15. $6.26 for 3 hours of parking. What is the hourly rate?

16. 82 km in 2.5 hours. What is the rate of travel?

PROBLEM SOLVING

17. For George Lucas' film *The Empire Strikes Back,* a camera that could run up to 96 fps was built to film special effects. How many more frames could this camera film in 5 minutes than one at a normal rate of 24 fps?

18. **Fine Arts Data Bank** The formula for exposure time in seconds is exposure time $= \dfrac{\text{shutter angle}}{360 \cdot \text{frames per second}}$.

    Use this formula to determine which times given in the Motion Picture Camera Exposure Times table are exact and which are approximations.

▶ **USING CRITICAL THINKING   Do Some Comparing**

19. The ratio $\dfrac{\text{distance}}{\text{time}}$ is the rate called speed.
    One mile is 5,280 feet. Is 40 mi/h faster than 44 ft/sec?

More Practice, page 533, set E

Unit Pricing

LEARN ABOUT IT

A rate that compares an item's cost per unit is called the **unit price.** Unit pricing allows consumers to make price comparisons and find the best buy.

EXPLORE Compare the Data
Grocery stores usually post both the item price and the unit price for each product. Compare the item price and the unit price for two different sizes of breakfast cereal.

TALK ABOUT IT

1. Which size box has the higher item price?

2. Which size box has the lower unit price?

3. Would you expect the larger quantity to have the lower or higher unit price?

Examples Find the unit price. You may want to use your calculator.

A 11 oz box of cereal for $2.33.
To find the unit price of an item follow three steps.

$$\frac{\$2.33}{11 \text{ oz}}$$ Write a ratio of price to number of units.

$2.33 $\boxed{\div}$ 11 $\boxed{=}$ $0.2118182 Divide the price by the number of units.

$0.21 per ounce Round the unit price to the nearest cent.

B Ground Beef: 5 lbs for $6.95

Unit Price $= \dfrac{\$6.95}{5} = \$1.39/\text{lb}$

C Oranges: 4 lb bag for $3.28

Unit Price $= \dfrac{\$3.28}{4} = \$0.82/\text{lb}$

TRY IT OUT

Find the unit price. Round the answer to the nearest cent.

1. 8 oz of soap for $1.45

2. 200 sheets of paper for $1.98

3. 1 dozen bagels for $2.50

4. 10 gallons of gasoline for $12

Find the unit price. Round the answer to the nearest cent.

1. Apples: 3 lb bag for $1.89

2. Frozen juice: 16 oz can for $1.59

3. Ribbon: 6 yd for $2.25

4. Beef: 5 lb roast for $11.28

5. Bread: 24 oz for $1.68

6. Grapefruit: 4 for 95¢

7. Soup: 10.5 oz for $0.70

8. Eggs: 1 dozen for $1.49

Which is the better buy?

9. Cereal: 8 oz for $1.39 or 12 oz for $2.10?

10. Frozen corn: 1 lb bag for $1.89 or 10 oz box for $1.29

11. Milk: 1 gal for $1.89 or $\frac{1}{2}$ gal for $0.99?

12. Cottage cheese: 0.45 kg for $1.55 or 0.6 kg for $2.05.

MATH REASONING Why are the two unit prices not comparable?

13. Apples: 3 lb bag for $2.49 or 1 dozen for $3.35.

PROBLEM SOLVING

14. Bananas cost $0.35/lb. Manuel bought $0.77 worth. How many pounds of bananas did he buy?

15. One brand of potatoes costs $5.95 for a 5 kg bag. A 10 lb bag of another brand costs $5.25. If 1 kg ≈ 2.2 lb, which is the better buy?

16. **Data Hunt** Visit a grocery store and compare applesauce prices. By comparing various brands and sizes, determine the best buy.

Compute. Express the answers as a mixed number or fraction in lowest terms.

17. $\frac{2}{3} + \frac{1}{6}$

18. $4\frac{3}{4} - 2\frac{5}{8}$

19. $18 - {-2}$

20. $-\frac{1}{7} + -\frac{1}{7}$

21. $\frac{3}{5} \cdot \frac{1}{2}$

22. $-2\frac{1}{3} \cdot -4\frac{1}{8}$

23. $-\frac{3}{8} \div \frac{2}{3}$

24. $-4\frac{1}{2} \div 3\frac{2}{5}$

Evaluate $y = 4x^2 - 7$ for

25. $x = 1$

26. $x = 2$

27. $x = 0$

28. $x = -2$

More Practice, page 534, set A

Solving Proportions

$$\begin{array}{l} \dfrac{2}{32} \bowtie \dfrac{3}{48} \rightarrow 32 \times 3 = 96 \\ \rightarrow 2 \times 48 = 96 \end{array}$$

EXPLORE Find a Relationship

Two equal ratios are said to be **proportional.** One way to verify that ratios are proportional is by using cross multiplication. For example, the ratio 2 to 32 is proportional to the ratio 3 to 48.

Select pairs of ratios from this bulletin board that are proportional. Use cross products to verify the proportion.

WHICH RATIOS ARE PROPORTIONAL ?

15 to 36 $\dfrac{14}{21}$ 26:39 $\dfrac{6}{15}$

$\dfrac{18}{45}$ 3 to 7 $\dfrac{20}{48}$ 12:28

TALK ABOUT IT

1. What is the fraction form of 15 to 36?

2. What ratio is proportional to $\dfrac{6}{15}$?

3. What is the solution to the proportion $\dfrac{x}{6} = \dfrac{2}{3}$?

Solving a proportion is like solving an equation involving two fractions.

Examples Solve these proportions.

A $\quad \dfrac{x}{48} = \dfrac{3}{4}$

$\quad\quad 4x = 144 \quad\quad$ Find the cross products.

$\quad \left(\dfrac{1}{4}\right) 4x = \left(\dfrac{1}{4}\right) 144 \quad$ Multiply both sides by the reciprocal of 4.

$\quad\quad\quad x = 36 \quad\quad$ Simplify.

B $\dfrac{x}{52} = \dfrac{5}{4}$

$4x = 260$

$x = 65$

C $\dfrac{s}{10} = \dfrac{1}{4}$

$4s = 10$

$s = 2.5$

D $\dfrac{8}{22} = \dfrac{12}{t}$

$8t = 264$

$t = 33$

TRY IT OUT

Solve these proportions.

1. $\dfrac{x}{30} = \dfrac{5}{6}$ 　　　 **2.** $\dfrac{9}{12} = \dfrac{3}{x}$ 　　　 **3.** $\dfrac{8}{n} = \dfrac{4}{7}$ 　　　 **4.** $\dfrac{2}{5} = \dfrac{x}{35}$

State the equation you would solve to find the missing number.

1. $\dfrac{d}{2} = \dfrac{27}{18}$ **2.** $\dfrac{33}{11} = \dfrac{3}{x}$ **3.** $\dfrac{8}{12} = \dfrac{t}{3}$ **4.** $\dfrac{5}{y} = \dfrac{100}{25}$

Solve these proportions.

5. $\dfrac{x}{15} = \dfrac{8}{10}$ **6.** $\dfrac{2}{3} = \dfrac{y}{18}$ **7.** $\dfrac{13}{a} = \dfrac{1}{6}$ **8.** $\dfrac{7}{3} = \dfrac{t}{18}$

9. $\dfrac{3}{2} = \dfrac{15}{n}$ **10.** $\dfrac{12}{t} = \dfrac{3}{5}$ **11.** $\dfrac{x}{60} = \dfrac{2}{5}$ **12.** $\dfrac{10}{s} = \dfrac{4}{9}$

13. $\dfrac{1}{6} = \dfrac{w}{500}$ **14.** $\dfrac{4}{1} = \dfrac{15}{y}$ **15.** $\dfrac{7}{3} = \dfrac{n}{3}$ **16.** $\dfrac{m}{3,500} = \dfrac{3}{1,000}$

17. Sometimes proportions are written in the form 2:3 = 4:6. Solve the proportion 3:5 = x:12.

MATH REASONING Find the whole number that is nearest the solution to each proportion. You may want to use your calculator.

18. $\dfrac{x}{17} = \dfrac{12}{5}$ **19.** $\dfrac{y}{11} = \dfrac{2}{5}$ **20.** $\dfrac{44}{9} = \dfrac{7}{x}$ **21.** $\dfrac{u}{8} = \dfrac{2}{9}$

PROBLEM SOLVING

22. A fruit punch is made with 2 parts of fruit juice and 3 parts of soda water. How much soda water should be mixed with 5 liters of fruit juice?

23. A certain medicine is mixed in the ratio of 25 parts of medicine to 400 parts of saline solution. How many milliliters of medicine should be added to 10 milliliters of saline solution?

▶ **ESTIMATION**

Without making an exact calculation, choose the best estimate.

24. $\dfrac{x}{5} = \dfrac{4}{9}$ a) $x = 1.8$ b) $x = 2.1$ c) $x = 2.5$

25. $\dfrac{x}{10} = \dfrac{10}{31}$ a) $x = 3.1$ b) $x = 3.9$ c) $x = 4.2$

Scale and Proportion

LEARN ABOUT IT

A model of the ancient Library of Alexandria in Egypt was built for the TV series *Cosmos* from a scale drawing. The scale is the ratio of any length on the drawing and its counterpart in the model.

EXPLORE Use a Ruler

Work in groups. This scale drawing shows the floor plan of the model library's Great Hall. Measure distances on this drawing to the nearest cm.

TALK ABOUT IT

1. Is the actual distance from *A* to *B* on the model less than or greater than 1 meter?

Follow these steps to find the actual length *AB* in the Great Hall model.

Measure the length *AB* in the drawing. Let L equal the actual length on the model.

$$\frac{\text{measured length } AB \text{ in centimeters}}{\text{actual length } L \text{ in meters}} = \frac{6}{L}$$

Set the ratio $\dfrac{\text{measured length } AB}{\text{actual length } L}$ equal to the scale ratio $\dfrac{5 \text{ centimeters}}{1 \text{ meter}}$.

Solve the proportion $\dfrac{6}{L} = \dfrac{5}{1}$.

$$5L = 6$$

$$L = \frac{6}{5} = 1.2$$

The length of *AB* in the Great Hall model is 1.2 meters.

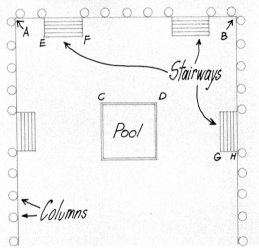

Floor Plan: Great Hall of the Library
Scale: 5cm = 1m

TRY IT OUT

From these drawing measurements find the equivalent model lengths.

1. *EF* = 1 cm   **2.** *CD* = 1.5 cm   **3.** *GH* = 0.5 cm   **4.** *AC* = 3 cm

Measure each distance to the nearest cm.
Write a proportion to solve each problem.

1. Find the height *JK* of the Great Hall
   model back wall.

2. Find the distance *LM* between murals.

3. Find the mural's dimensions *LN* and *NP*.

4. The photograph at the right shows an
   amoeba enlarged 100 times under a
   microscope. What is the actual width of
   the amoeba if the enlarged width is 25 mm?

5. A photograph of a bacteria that has been enlarged
   50,000 times has a diameter of 5 cm. What
   is the actual diameter of the bacteria?

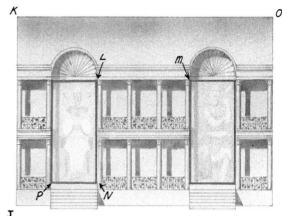

Back Wall Plan of the Great Hall
Scale : 5cm=1m

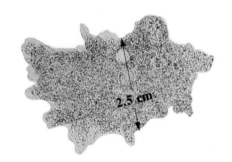

2.5 cm

MATH REASONING

6. The 290 mile distance from St. Louis to Chicago measures
   5 cm on a map. Estimate the scale of the map.

PROBLEM SOLVING

7. The model of the Great Hall described above is 1.5 meters
   long, 1.3 meters wide, and 1 meter high. It was built on a
   scale of 24:1 to the actual dimensions. What were the actual
   dimensions of the Great Hall?

8. **Fine Arts Data Bank**   Determine the scale used for the
   Scale Drawing of Film Formats by measuring the distances
   to the nearest cm. What measurement would you use to add
   a 70 mm film format to the scale drawings? An 8 mm film
   format?

DATA
BANK

▶ **COMMUNICATION   Writing to Learn**

9. On an $8\frac{1}{2}$ in. × 11 in. sheet of paper, make a scale drawing
   of your classroom. Describe the scale you used in order for
   your drawing to fit the page.

Using Critical Thinking

b

LEARN ABOUT IT

"That's strange" exclaimed Jerome, as he measured lengths to the nearest mm and calculated the ratio of *a* to *b* in each picture. "I wonder why this happens. Is it just by chance?"

Liz thought a while and responded "I don't think so—it just happens too often!"

"Wait a minute" said Francisco. "I disagree. You've just picked some special lengths that work. I'll bet you could do that for any number."

a

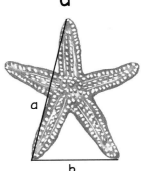

b

TALK ABOUT IT

1. What was Jerome doing?

2. Try Jerome's activity. What do you think he discovered?

3. Do you agree with Liz or Francisco? Support your conclusion.

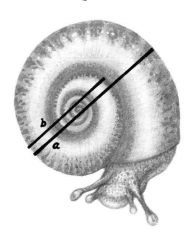

TRY IT OUT

1. The early Greeks constructed a Golden Rectangle like this, and called the ratio of its length to its width the Golden Ratio. Construct a Golden Rectangle, measure and give an approximation for the Golden Ratio.

   ■ Draw a unit square *ABCD*.
   ■ Put a compass on midpoint *M* and draw an arc *CF*.
   ■ Extend sides and draw rectangle *ABEF*.

2. How do the ratios you found in the pictures above compare with the Golden Ratio?

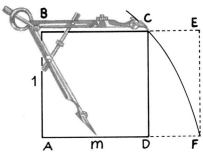

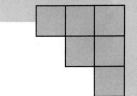

POWER PRACTICE/QUIZ

Science club members are in the ratio 3 seventh graders to 5 eighth graders.

1. Write the ratio of seventh graders to eighth graders in 3 ways.

2. What is the ratio of eighth graders to seventh graders?

3. Complete the table and write three proportions from the table.

seventh graders	6	?	12	15
eighth graders	?	15	?	?

For each animal, write a ratio for

a. the number of heart beats per minute and
b. the number of heart beats per second.

cat	30 beats in 15 seconds
dog	15 beats in 10 seconds
mouse	267 beats in 30 seconds

4. cat   **5.** dog   **6.** mouse

Find the unit price to the nearest cent for each box of food.

7. crackers:
8 oz for $1.73

8. cereal:
12 oz for $1.43

9. oatmeal:
42 oz for $2.79

10. Which is the better buy: an 18-oz jar of peanut butter for $1.53 or a 2-lb jar of the same brand for $2.75?

Solve these proportions.

11. $\dfrac{x}{9} = \dfrac{4}{6}$

12. $\dfrac{7}{35} = \dfrac{x}{70}$

13. $\dfrac{6}{x} = \dfrac{4}{9}$

14. $\dfrac{16}{20} = \dfrac{12}{x}$

PROBLEM SOLVING

Three models of a room will be made from this scale drawing. Fill in the chart to show the actual length and width of each model.

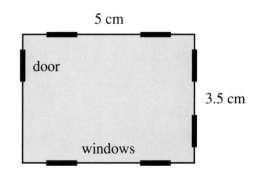

	model	scale	length	width
15.	A	1 cm:1 m		
16.	B	4 cm:1 m		
17.	C	2 cm:3 m		

18. How much greater in floor area is the largest model than the smallest model?

19. A math class is in the ratio 5 girls to 4 boys. Can there be 20 students in the class? What is the largest class size with fewer than 40 students?

237

Similar Triangles

LEARN ABOUT IT

EXPLORE Use Grid Paper

Copy triangles A and B onto grid paper.
Then draw a triangle (A') the same shape as
A but with sides twice as long. Draw
another triangle (B') the same shape as B
but with sides $\frac{4}{3}$ as long.

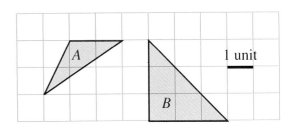

TALK ABOUT IT

1. How long are the shortest sides of triangles A and A'?

2. How long are the shortest sides of triangles B and B'?

3. Find the ratios of the lengths of the shortest sides of the
   triangles.

Triangles are **similar** if the measures of their corresponding
angles are equal and the lengths of their sides are proportional.

$\triangle ABC$ is similar to $\triangle DEF$.
Write $\triangle ABC \sim \triangle DEF$.

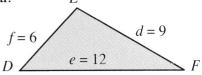

$m\angle A = m\angle D$	$m\angle B = m\angle E$	$m\angle C = m\angle F$
$\dfrac{a}{d} = \dfrac{3}{9} = \dfrac{1}{3}$	$\dfrac{b}{e} = \dfrac{4}{12} = \dfrac{1}{3}$	$\dfrac{c}{f} = \dfrac{2}{6} = \dfrac{1}{3}$

Example $\triangle HIJ \sim \triangle KLM$. Find length k.

$\dfrac{k}{11} = \dfrac{10}{6}$ Set up a proportion.

$6k = 110$ Cross multiply.

$k = \dfrac{110}{6} = \dfrac{55}{3} = 18\dfrac{1}{3}$ Solve for k.

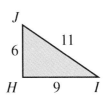
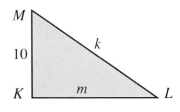

TRY IT OUT
---

1. Find length x in $\triangle XYZ$.

2. Find length z in $\triangle XYZ$.

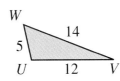
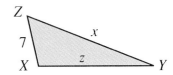

238

Each pair of triangles is similar. Find length x for each pair.

1.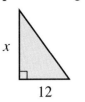

2.

3.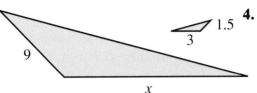

4.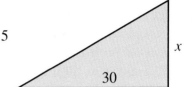

5.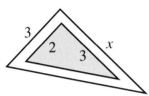

6.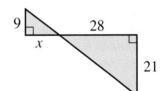

MATH REASONING

7. Two rectangles are **similar** if the ratio of length to width for one rectangle is equal to the ratio of length to width for the other rectangle. Steve said, "All rectangles are similar." Decide whether or not Steve is correct by drawing rectangles on grid paper.

PROBLEM SOLVING

8. A surveyor wants to find the distance AB across the pond. He constructs $\triangle CDE$ similar to $\triangle CAB$ and measures the distances as shown on this figure. Find AB.

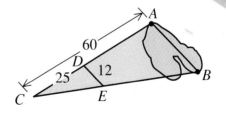

▶ **ALGEBRA**

$\triangle ABC \sim \triangle DEF$. Write and solve a proportion to find each unknown length.

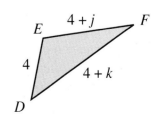

9. Find length EF. **10.** Find length DF.

More Practice, page 534, set C

Problem Solving
Using the Strategies

UNDERSTAND
ANALYZE DATA
PLAN
ESTIMATE
SOLVE
EXAMINE

To solve some problems you first need to understand the relationships among the data and then use that information to draw conclusions. For this problem, it helps to make a **table** and then use **Logical Reasoning** to fill it out.

Since they each prefer different books, there will be exactly one "yes" in each column and in each row. Rhonda's brother likes to read adventure stories, so Carol and Rhonda do not. Carol does not like science fiction.

> Wayne, Carol, Dave, and Rhonda each like different kinds of books. Rhonda's brother reads adventure stories. Carol doesn't like science fiction. Dave used to read animal books, but now he is always involved in a mystery. Which kind of book does each prefer to read?

	Wayne	Carol	Dave	Rhonda
Adventure		no		no
Sci-Fiction		no		
Animal				
Mystery				

Dave reads mysteries; therefore no one else likes mysteries, and Dave likes nothing else.

	Wayne	Carol	Dave	Rhonda
Adventure		no	no	no
Sci-Fiction		no	no	
Animal			no	
Mystery	no	no	yes	no

Wayne must prefer adventure books, and Carol must like animal books. That leaves science fiction for Rhonda.

Wayne prefers adventure books, Carol animal stories, Dave mysteries, and Rhonda science fiction.

	Wayne	Carol	Dave	Rhonda
Adventure	yes	no	no	no
Sci-Fiction	no	no	no	yes
Animal	no	yes	no	no
Mystery	no	no	yes	no

Solve. Use any problem solving strategy.

1. Fay, Scott, Ella, and Nick each play a different instrument—piano, flute, violin and guitar. Ella carries her instrument to her lesson each week. Scott broke a string while he was playing. Nick's mouth gets tired when he practices too much. Ella uses a bow when she plays. Which instrument does each play?

2. Molly, Stan, Jose, and Darcy have different classes first period—math, art, P.E., and English. Stan was almost late to second period because he had to clean some brushes. Molly doesn't have to solve equations until after lunch. Jose is reading a play first period. Which class does each have first period?

Solve. Use any problem solving strategy.

<table>
<tr><td colspan="2">Some Strategies</td></tr>
<tr><td>Act Out</td><td>Solve a Simpler Problem</td></tr>
<tr><td>Use Objects</td><td>Make an Organized List</td></tr>
<tr><td>Choose an Operation</td><td>Work Backward</td></tr>
<tr><td>Draw a Picture</td><td>Look for a Pattern</td></tr>
<tr><td>Guess and Check</td><td>Use Logical Reasoning</td></tr>
<tr><td>Make a Table</td><td>Write an Equation</td></tr>
</table>

1. A $5\frac{1}{2}$ foot fence post casts a 7 foot shadow. If a lighthouse casts a 140 foot shadow, how tall is the lighthouse?

2. Melanie helped put numbers on new lockers at school. The numbers started at 51 and continued on consecutively. She applied the numbers one digit at a time. When finished, she had used 413 digits. How many new lockers were there?

3. Tomatoes cost $0.68 a pound, and lettuce $0.59 a head. Kuan spent $3.65 for a head of lettuce and some tomatoes. How many pounds of tomatoes did he buy?

4. Chan, Thompson, Stein, and Markov are presidents of four different school clubs. Thompson doesn't know the ski club president, but has heard of him. Chan used to belong to the bike club, but now she is president of a different club. The president of the chess club and his sister also belong to the photography club. Stein just became president of her club. Who is president of which club?

5. A river is 23 km long. Use the diagram to find the width of the river.

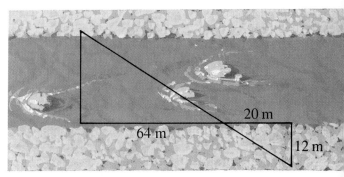

6. A backpacker wants to walk across a 50 mile wide desert. He can walk 20 miles a day. His food and water are packaged in one day amounts; and he can carry enough for two days. How many days will it take him to cross the desert?

7. Kuan checked out 3 books at the library for 2 weeks. The first book is 260 pages long, and he wants to finish it by Sunday night. He read the first 65 pages in 2 hours. At this rate, how long will it take him to finish the book?

More Practice, page 547, set D

Tangent Ratio

In this lesson you will learn about the **tangent ratio** for acute angles of right triangles.

$$\tan A = \frac{\text{length of opposite side}}{\text{length of adjacent side}}$$

$$\mathbf{\tan A = \frac{a}{b}}$$

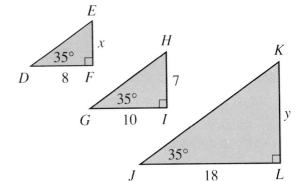

EXPLORE Compare the Triangles

These three right triangles are similar. In fact, all right triangles with a 35° angle are similar:

$$\tan G = \frac{7}{10}$$

TALK ABOUT IT

1. Is the ratio $\frac{5.6}{8}$ equal to the ratio $\frac{7}{10}$?

2. Is the ratio $\frac{12.6}{18}$ equal to the ratio $\frac{7}{10}$?

3. If you drew several more right triangles with a 35° angle, what would be the ratio of the opposite side to the adjacent side?

In any right triangle with a 35° angle, the tangent of that angle always equals the same number. So tan 35° = 0.7 to the nearest thousandth.

Examples Find tan A to the nearest thousandth.

A

$$\tan 27° = \frac{6}{12} = 0.5$$

B

$$\tan 23° = \frac{4}{9} = 0.444$$

C

$$\tan 63° = \frac{9}{4.5} = 2$$

Find tan A to the nearest thousandth.

1.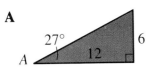

2.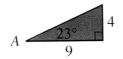

3.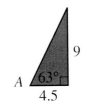

Find tan A to the nearest hundredth.

1.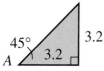

2.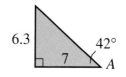

3.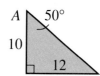

4.

5.

6.

7.

8.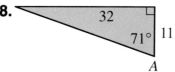

9.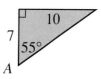

10. Find tan A and tan B. Show that (tan A) · (tan B) = 1.

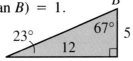

MATH REASONING

11. tan A is approximately ___?___ .
a) 0.1   b) 1   c) 10

PROBLEM SOLVING

12. Many house roofs have a $\frac{4}{12}$ pitch. This means that with every horizontal change of 12 units there is a vertical change of 4 units.

What is the tangent of the angle A formed by a $\frac{4}{12}$ pitched roof?

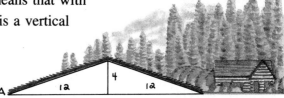

MIXED REVIEW

Compute. Express as a mixed number or fraction in lowest terms.

13. $33\frac{4}{5} - 17\frac{2}{3}$

14. $-3\frac{1}{6} \cdot -4\frac{1}{2}$

15. $-6\frac{2}{3} \div 2\frac{1}{3}$

16. $7\frac{1}{9} \div -4$

Find a decimal for each fraction.

17. $\frac{1}{4}$

18. $\frac{2}{3}$

19. $\frac{5}{8}$

20. $\frac{3}{5}$

21. $\frac{4}{9}$

More Practice, page 534, set D

Exploring Algebra
Indirect Measurement

LEARN ABOUT IT

EXPLORE **Think About the Situation**

Suppose that 100 feet from the base of a tall building you measure angle A formed by the top and bottom of the building and find it to be 48°. Then $\tan 48° = \dfrac{h}{100}$.

TALK ABOUT IT

1. Is the equation $\tan 48° = \dfrac{h}{100}$ equivalent to $h = 100 \cdot \tan 48°$ or $h = \dfrac{100}{\tan 48°}$?

2. If you know tan 48°, then you can solve for what unknown?

Some calculators are programmed so that you can find the tangent ratio of any angle.

To find tan 48°,

enter	press	display
48	tan	1.1106125

You can also use this table to find tan 48° rounded to the nearest thousandth.

To find the height (h) of the building substitute the value of tan 48° and solve.

$h = 100 \tan 48°$
$ = 100\,(1.111)$
$ = 111.1$ The building is 111.1 ft high.

angle	tangent	angle	tangent	angle	tangent
20°	0.364	35°	0.700	50°	1.192
21°	0.384	36°	0.727	51°	1.235
22°	0.404	37°	0.754	52°	1.280
23°	0.424	38°	0.781	53°	1.327
24°	0.445	39°	0.810	54°	1.376
25°	0.466	40°	0.839	55°	1.428
26°	0.488	41°	0.869	56°	1.483
27°	0.510	42°	0.900	57°	1.540
28°	0.532	43°	0.933	58°	1.600
29°	0.554	44°	0.966	59°	1.664
30°	0.577	45°	1.000	60°	1.732
31°	0.601	46°	1.036	61°	1.804
32°	0.625	47°	1.072	62°	1.881
33°	0.649	48°	1.111	63°	1.963
34°	0.675	49°	1.150	64°	2.050

TRY IT OUT

Use the table or a calculator to find each tangent to the nearest thousandth.

1. tan 23°   **2.** tan 35°   **3.** tan 52°   **4.** tan 61°

5. Find the height of a building if the angle determined by the top and bottom of the building 300 feet away is 48°.

Use a calculator or the table to find each tangent to the nearest thousandth.

1. tan 38°   **2.** tan 45°   **3.** tan 20°   **4.** tan 61°

5. tan 33°   **6.** tan 64°   **7.** tan 42°   **8.** tan 53°

Write and solve an equation using a tangent ratio to find the missing length to the nearest hundredth.

9.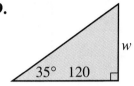

10.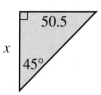

11.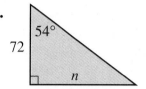

12.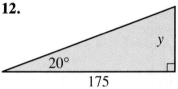

13.

14.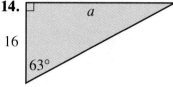

APPLY

MATH REASONING Use the table of tangent ratios to find the measure of angle A to the nearest degree.

15. tan A = 0.364   **16.** tan A = 1.600

PROBLEM SOLVING

17. Find the height (h) of the building shown in this figure.

18. Several floors were added to the building, making it 85 meters tall. What is the new measure of angle A to the nearest degree?

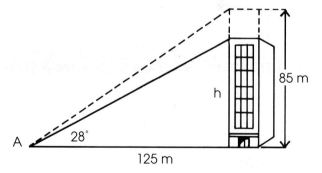

CALCULATOR

Use a calculator to decide whether these equations are true or false.

19. tan 45° = 1   **20.** tan 32° · tan 58° = 1   **21.** tan 25° + tan 10° = tan 35°

245

Problem Solving
Data From a Map

UNDERSTAND
ANALYZE DATA
PLAN
ESTIMATE
SOLVE
EXAMINE

LEARN ABOUT IT

To solve some problems you need data from a table, graph, or a source outside the problem. For this problem, you need data from the map.

> Tyrone lives in Canada. One day he drove from Calgary to Edmonton. How many kilometers did he drive?

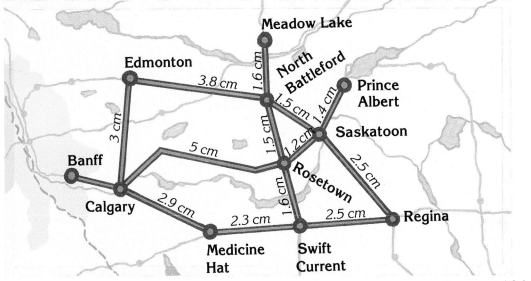

1 cm = 100 km

To find the actual distance, begin by measuring the distance on the map. Use the scale given on the map to set up a proportion.

Let d = the actual distance in kilometers.

The map distance is 3 centimeters.

Tyrone drove 300 kilometers.

$$\frac{3}{1} = \frac{d}{100}$$

$$1d = 300$$

$$d = 300$$

TRY IT OUT

Solve. Use any problem solving strategy.

1. Anaya drove from Medicine Hat to Swift Current. How many kilometers did she drive?

2. Anthony drove from Rosetown to Regina with a stop in Swift Current. Dawn went from Rosetown to Regina by way of Saskatoon. How much shorter was Dawn's trip than Anthony's?

Solve. Use any problem solving strategy.

1. Allison's family spent two weeks at Banff National Park. Food and lodging cost $118 a day. Lodging was $79 and the rest was food. How much did they spend for food?

2. Canada has 10,015,952 square kilometers of land. In 1989, the population was about 26,308,000. About how many people were there per square kilometer?

3. Larkin commutes between Rosetown and Saskatoon 5 days a week. Use the map of Canada to find how many kilometers she drives each week.

4. Some boys were playing a game. They put 8 markers in a circle—7 red and 1 white. Each player started by picking up a marker and then every 8th marker after that, going clockwise around the circle until all the markers were gone. The winner was the first boy to pick up the white marker last. Which marker did the winner pick up first?

5. Marco gave the cashier a $20 bill to pay for gasoline. Use the price list to find how much he spent for 12.9 gallons of unleaded gasoline.

REGULAR	$0.99 /gal.
UNLEADED	$1.09 /gal.
SUPER UNLEADED	$1.29 /gal.

6. Ann, Steve, Quincy, and Becky live in four different provinces—Alberta, British Columbia, Quebec, and Saskatchewan. None of them live in a province that starts with the same letter as his or her name. Becky used to live in Saskatchewan, but has never been to Alberta. Steve has always lived in British Columbia. Who lives in which province?

7. It took Zach $2\frac{1}{4}$ hours to drive from Saskatoon to Meadow Lake. Use the map of Canada to find how many kilometers per hour he averaged.

8. **Missing Data** Trisha's car gets 31.6 miles per gallon on the highway. One week she drove 474 miles on the highway. Make up some data to find how much she spent for gas.

More Practice, page 545, set C

Data Collection and Analysis
Group Decision Making

UNDERSTAND
ANALYZE DATA
PLAN
ESTIMATE
SOLVE
EXAMINE

Doing an Investigation

Group Skill:
Explain and Summarize

Suppose you study a list of 20 unrelated words. How many can you memorize after studying 30 seconds, 60 seconds, or 120 seconds? Do you think the number you can memorize increases steadily as you have more time to study?

Collecting Data

1. Have each person in your group make a list of 20 nouns such as horse, storm, television, and so on. Don't look at any one else's list! The nouns should not be in any particular order or be related to any particular thing.

2. Work with a partner from your group. One person is the timekeeper and the other is the memorizer. Study the words on your partner's list for 30 seconds. Then write down all the words you can remember. Study for another 30 seconds and make a new list of the words you remember. Repeat this activity four more times, each time adding 30 more seconds of study. Write down the number of seconds you studied each list. Switch roles with your partner.

Organizing Data

3. Make a line graph to show how many words you and your partner were able to remember after 30 seconds of study, 60 seconds of study, 90 seconds of study, and so on.

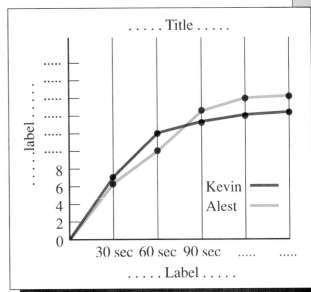

4. Check to see if you labeled and titled all parts of your graph.

5. Write a summary of the results of your memory investigation.

How were your results similar to those of your partner?
How were they different:
Did the number of words you remembered increase steadily?

6. Use your line graph to predict how many words you could memorize if you had 30 seconds more study time.

7. Did the lines on your line graph cross at some point? What does that mean if they did?

8. Do you think that your results would be different if you chose a different sample of words to memorize? For example, what if the words you selected were all animals? Would you be able to memorize them more quickly?

WRAP UP

Horatio's Ratios

Horatio's dog ripped his homework. See if you can help
Horatio put the subjects and predicates together correctly.

1. A rate

2. A unit price

3. Indirect measure

4. Scale

5. The Golden Ratio

6. Tangent ratio of an angle in a right triangle

7. A proportion

A. is formed by two equal ratios.

B. is a ratio formed by comparing values with different units.

C. is a ratio formed by comparing the length and width of a special rectangle.

D. is a rate that gives an item's cost per unit.

E. is a ratio between dimensions in a drawing and dimensions of the thing drawn.

F. is a ratio of the lengths of the leg opposite the angle and the leg adjacent to the angle.

G. is made possible by using the tangent ratio.

Sometimes, Always, Never

Which of these words should go in the blank: *sometimes*,
always, or *never*? Explain your choice.

8. As the size of a triangle increases, the tangent ratio _____ increases.

9. Indirect measurement is _____ the best way to measure an object.

10. If an improper fraction is changed to a percent, the percent will _____ be greater than 100.

11. The decimal equivalent of a fraction can _____ be both terminating and repeating.

Project

Choose one of these topics. Find three interesting facts about
each. Suggestions are:

- the Golden Ratio in art and nature
- unit pricing at the grocery store or gas pump
- indirect measurement in surveying

POWER PRACTICE/TEST

Part 1   Understanding

1. There are three trucks to every five cars on the expressway. Write the ratio of trucks to cars in three different ways.

2. Which equation would be useful in finding the missing length in the diagram?

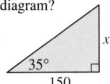

A $x = \dfrac{150}{\tan 35°}$ B $x = \dfrac{\tan 35°}{150}$

C $x = 150 \tan 35°$ D $150\, x = \tan 35°$

3. Which rate is equal to $\dfrac{\$35}{5\,\text{h}}$?

A $\dfrac{\$175}{\text{h}}$ B $\dfrac{\$7}{\text{h}}$

C $\dfrac{\$30}{\text{h}}$ D $\dfrac{\$40}{\text{h}}$

Part 2   Skills

4. Find the unit price of 32 oz of juice for $2.00. Round to the nearest cent.

5. Which is the better buy: 1 lb of cheese for $2.19 or 6 oz of cheese for $1.10?

Solve these proportions.

6. $\dfrac{c}{8} = \dfrac{18}{48}$

7. $\dfrac{5}{t} = \dfrac{20}{28}$

8. $\dfrac{1}{2} = \dfrac{5}{x}$

9. These triangles are similar. Find x.

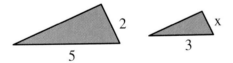

10. Find tan A to the nearest hundredth.

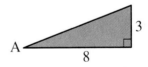

11. The scale of this drawing is 1 in. = 5 ft. Find the actual length of n.

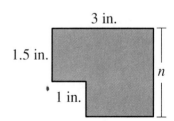

Part 3   Application

12. A car used 9.2 gallons of gas on a 264-mile trip. Estimate the rate of gas consumption.

13. **Challenge** The school principal is 1.6 m tall and casts a shadow 48 m long. The flagpole casts a shadow 300 m longer. How tall is the flagpole?

ENRICHMENT
Map Scales

The **scale** of a map or drawing is the ratio $\frac{\text{map distance}}{\text{actual distance}}$.

The scale of this map of part of Florida is $\frac{3 \text{ cm}}{85 \text{ km}}$.

To find the distance, d, between Fort Myers and Naples, use a ruler to find the map distance is 2.1 cm. Then set up the proportion.

$$\begin{array}{l} \text{map distance} \rightarrow \\ \text{actual distance} \rightarrow \end{array} \quad \frac{3}{85} = \frac{2.1}{d}.$$

Solve for d.

$$\begin{aligned} 3d &= 178.5 \\ d &= 59.5 \end{aligned}$$

The distance between Fort Myers and Naples is about 59.5 km.

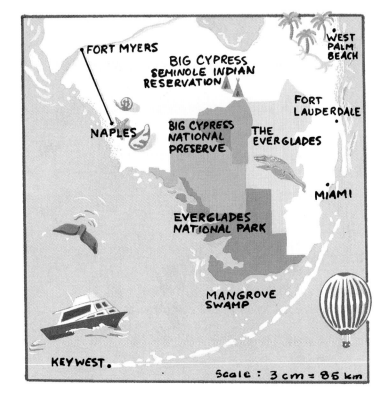

Find the straight line distance between each pair of cities.

1. Key West and Miami

2. Fort Lauderdale and Fort Myers

3. West Palm Beach and Key West

4. Naples and Miami

5. How much farther is it from Key West to West Palm Beach than it is from Fort Myers to Miami?

6. About how long would it take to drive from Fort Lauderdale to Miami at 62 kilometers per hour?

7. The driving distance from Key West to Miami is 251 km. How much more is this distance than the straight line distance?

8. It took Charlie 4 h 15 min to drive the 251 km from Key West to Miami. The speed limit was 88 km per hour. How much under the speed limit was Charlie's speed?

CUMULATIVE REVIEW

1. Solve. $-3x = 156$

   A 52   B -52

   C -432 D 432

2. Solve. $-7x - 9 = 12$

   A 3   B $\frac{3}{7}$ C $-\frac{3}{7}$ D -3

3. Which set of numbers are multiples of 36?

   A 72, 108, 144   B 36, 68, 104

   C 4, 9, 12   D 18, 36, 54

4. Which number is divisible by 6 and 9?

   A 4,128   B 5,472

   C 732   D 2,058

5. Which number is prime?

   A 81   B 147

   C 151   D 177

6. Which is correct?

   A $\frac{17}{34} \neq \frac{14}{28}$ B $\frac{12}{16} = \frac{24}{32}$

   C $\frac{10}{16} = \frac{26}{40}$ D $\frac{12}{44} \neq \frac{15}{55}$

7. Which is not the opposite of $\frac{8}{5}$?

   A $\frac{5}{8}$ B $\frac{-8}{5}$ C $-\frac{8}{5}$ D $\frac{8}{-5}$

8. Which is correct?

   A $-3 < -5 < -4$ B $-1\frac{1}{5} > \frac{2}{3}$

   C $-3 > -3.3 > -1.3$ D $2 > -3$

9. Which is the decimal for $\frac{17}{6}$?

   A $2.8\overline{3}$ B 2.8

   C $0.2\overline{83}$ D $2\frac{5}{6}$

10. Add. $\frac{-1}{2} + \frac{2}{3}$

    A $-\frac{1}{6}$ B $1\frac{1}{6}$ C $\frac{1}{6}$ D $\frac{1}{3}$

11. Subtract. $28\frac{5}{6} - 12\frac{7}{16}$

    A $16\frac{1}{5}$ B $16\frac{1}{8}$

    C $16\frac{1}{2}$ D $16\frac{19}{48}$

12. Multiply. $-2\frac{1}{5} \cdot 1\frac{1}{2}$

    A $\frac{15}{22}$ B $-3\frac{3}{10}$

    C $3\frac{3}{10}$ D $\frac{-15}{22}$

13. Anne, Seth, Eric, and Carole are to sit one behind the other. Seth and Eric are not to sit in front of or behind each other. How many different ways can they be seated?

    A 8   B 18   C 12   D 24

14. Which is the extra data in the problem? Five steel beams that are 8 m long and 0.65 m wide are used in a building. Each beam weighs 712.8 kg. What is the total weight of the beams?

    A number of beams

    B length and width

    C weight of each beam

    D total weight

9

PERCENT

THEME: SOUND RECORDINGS

MATH AND
FINE ARTS

DATA BANK

Use the Fine Arts Data Bank on page 502 to answer the questions.

1. If the cost of making a music video is $20,000 and a standard 50-50 formula is used, how much of the video production cost will come out of the record's royalties?

2 A music video's production cost has been paid off and the video's net income is $4,726. How much will the artist receive?

3 What is the standard packaging deduction for a record with a list price of $9.98?

4 **Using Critical Thinking** The cost of producing cassette tapes was high when they were introduced, but dropped to less than the cost of records. The same thing is happening with CDs. Do standard packaging deductions reflect past or present costs? How?

Recording engineers use an automated sound mixing console to balance voices and instruments.

Percent

EXPLORE Study the Grid

On this 10 × 10 grid, 21 unit squares are shaded. The shaded part can be described in terms of the whole grid in several ways.

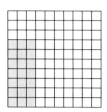

TALK ABOUT IT

1. What is the ratio of the number of shaded squares to the total number of squares?

2. What fraction of the squares are shaded?

3. What decimal represents the fraction of the squares that are shaded.

There are 37 shaded squares on the 10 × 10 grid below. We have considered three ways to describe the shaded part of the grid:

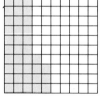

Ratio: 37 out of 100 squares are shaded.

Fraction: $\frac{37}{100}$ of the squares are shaded.

Decimal: 0.37 of the squares are shaded.

A fourth way to describe the shaded part is with a percent. **Percent** means **per hundred.** The symbol for percent is %.

37% means 37 per 100, or $\frac{37}{100}$, or 0.37.

Other Examples

A ratio can be described as a fraction, a decimal, or a percent.

A Fraction: $\frac{11}{100}$
Decimal: 0.11
Percent: 11%

B Fraction: $\frac{57}{100}$
Decimal: 0.57
Percent: 57%

C Fraction $\frac{31}{100}$
Decimal: 0.31
Percent: 31%

Describe each ratio as a fraction, a decimal, and a percent.

1. 19 out of 100

2. 77:100

3. 49 parts to 100 parts

Write a fraction, decimal, and percent for the shaded part of each region.

1.   **2.**   **3.**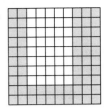

Express each ratio as a fraction, a decimal, and a percent.

4. 37 out of 100   **5.** 82:100   **6.** 47 parts to 100 parts

7. 88.5:100   **8.** 44 to 50   **9.** 3:25

Write each percent as a fraction with denominator 100. Express in lowest terms.

10. 48%   **11.** 23%   **12.** 75%   **13.** 60%

14. 16%   **15.** 88%   **16.** 30%   **17.** 28%

18. 5%   **19.** 12.5%   **20.** 87.5%   **21.** 37.5%

APPLY

MATH REASONING Compete each table of equivalent ratios to find
the ratio as a percent.

22.

ratio of 13 to 25	13	?	?		
	25	50	100		____%

23.

ratio of 11 to 20	11	?	?	?		
	20	40	60	80	100	____%

PROBLEM SOLVING

24. Of the 20 girls on the volleyball team, 12 played regularly. What percent played regularly?

25. Of 100 students who tried out for the cheerleading squad, twelve were selected. What percent was not selected?

▶ **MENTAL MATH**

Express each of these fractions as a percent.

26. $\frac{1}{2}$ **27.** $\frac{1}{4}$ **28.** $\frac{5}{20}$ **29.** $\frac{2}{5}$

Fractions and Percents

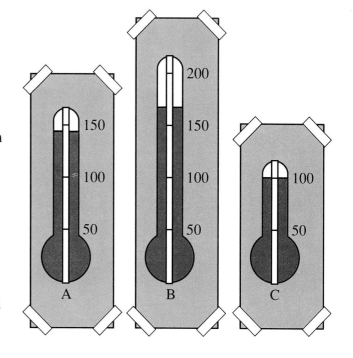

LEARN ABOUT IT

EXPLORE Compare the Data

Thermometers in front of the three eighth grade homerooms show that they set different goals for their class fundraiser.

- Room 101 reached $\frac{3}{4}$ of their goal.

- Room 102 reached $\frac{4}{5}$ of their goal.

- Room 103 reached $\frac{7}{8}$ of their goal.

Use a ruler or grid paper to decide which thermometer belongs to which room.

TALK ABOUT IT

1. Which room reached approximately 80% of its goal?

2. Which room reached the largest percent of their goal? Explain.

Here are three methods you can use to write a fraction as a percent.

Solve a Proportion

$$\frac{7}{8} = \frac{x}{100}$$

$$7 \cdot 100 = 8x$$

$$\frac{700}{8} = x$$

$$x = 87.5$$

$$\frac{7}{8} = \frac{87.5}{100}$$

$$= 87.5\% \text{ or } 87\frac{1}{2}\%$$

Find a Decimal

$$\frac{1}{3} = 1 \div 3 \text{ or } 3\overline{)1.000} \quad (0.333\ldots)$$

$$\frac{1}{3} = 33.\overline{3}\% \text{ or } 33\frac{1}{3}\%$$

Use a calculator

$$\frac{13}{16} = 13 \div 16$$

13 ÷ 16 = 0.8125

$$\frac{13}{16} = 81.25\% \text{ or } 81\frac{1}{4}\%$$

TRY IT OUT

Write a percent for each fraction.

1. $\frac{7}{10}$ **2.** $\frac{7}{20}$ **3.** $\frac{1}{8}$ **4.** $\frac{5}{12}$ **5.** $\frac{1}{6}$

Write a percent for each fraction.

1. $\frac{1}{4}$ **2.** $\frac{3}{4}$ **3.** $\frac{3}{10}$ **4.** $\frac{9}{10}$

5. $\frac{7}{100}$ **6.** $\frac{9}{20}$ **7.** $\frac{11}{50}$ **8.** $\frac{7}{12}$

9. $\frac{11}{16}$ **10.** $\frac{5}{6}$ **11.** $\frac{3}{40}$ **12.** $\frac{3}{8}$

Write each percent as a fraction with a denominator of 100.
Then write the fraction in lowest terms.

13. $33\frac{1}{3}\%$ **14.** $12\frac{1}{2}\%$ **15.** $11\frac{1}{9}\%$

APPLY

MATH REASONING List from smallest to largest.

16. $\frac{3}{8}$, 35%, 0.30   **17.** 42%, $\frac{2}{5}$, 4.0

18. 0.7, 68%, $\frac{85}{99}$ **19.** 3.5%, 0.07, $\frac{5}{20}$

PROBLEM SOLVING

20. Kim got 17 out of 20 questions correct on her math test. What percent did she get correct?

21. Irene had to get 85% correct on her midterm to get an A for the term. What fraction of the questions on the midterm did she need to answer correctly?

22. Jeff missed 4 questions on a 15 question quiz. What percent did he get correct?

23. Juan got 15 questions correct on the test for a 75%. How many questions were on the quiz?

24. On one test Jim got 80%, or 16 right. On a second test he got 50%, or 16 right. How many questions were on both tests?

▶ **ESTIMATION**

Choose the percent that is the best estimate for each fraction.

25. $\frac{14}{29}$ a) 40%   b) 50%   c) 60%

26. $\frac{17}{80}$ a) 24%   b) 29%   c) 35%

More Practice, page 535, set A

Large and Small Percents

EXPLORE Use Grid Paper

Work in groups. Draw a 10×10 square on a sheet of grid paper like the one shown at the right.

- If the 10×10 square represents 100%, shade a region that represents 120%.
- Shade a region that represents 5%.
- Shade a region that represents 0.5%.

TALK ABOUT IT

1. Is the 120% region larger or smaller than the 10×10 square? How much larger or smaller?

2. What fraction of a 1×1 square is the 0.5% region?

3. Complete this generalization: A percent greater than 100% is a number _____ 1. (greater than, less than, equal to)

4. Complete this generalization: A percent less than 1% is a number _____ 0.01. (greater than, less than, equal to)

Large and small percents can be changed to a decimal in the usual way.

$$112\% = \frac{112}{100} = 1.12 \qquad\qquad 0.5\% = \frac{0.5}{100} = 0.005$$

Such percents can also be changed to fractions in the usual ways.

$$137.5\% = \frac{137.5}{100} = \frac{1,375}{1,000} = 1\frac{3}{8} \qquad\qquad \frac{1}{2}\% = \frac{\frac{1}{2}}{100} = \frac{1}{2} \cdot \frac{1}{100} = \frac{1}{200}$$

Express each percent as a decimal.

1. 325%   **2.** 178%   **3.** 0.7%   **4.** 0.12%

Express each as a fraction or mixed number in lowest terms.

5. 275%   **6.** 0.6%   **7.** 156%   **8.** 0.375%

260

Express each percent as a decimal.

1. 225%   **2.** 150%   **3.** 800%   **4.** 439.5%

5. $\frac{1}{4}$%   **6.** 0.3%   **7.** $2\frac{1}{2}$%   **8.** 1.4%

Express each decimal as a percent.

9. 1.67   **10.** 14   **11.** 0.007   **12.** 1.003

Express each percent as a fraction or mixed number in lowest terms.

13. 350%   **14.** $5\frac{1}{2}$%   **15.** 18.5%   **16.** 140%

17. 0.75%   **18.** $\frac{1}{6}$%   **19.** $12\frac{1}{2}$%   **20.** 20%

Express each fraction as a percent.

21. $\frac{1}{32}$ **22.** $\frac{5}{3}$ **23.** $\frac{1}{12}$ **24.** $\frac{8}{5}$

APPLY

MATH REASONING Which two are equal?

25. A) 1.75   B) 1.75%   C) 17.5%   D) 0.0175

PROBLEM SOLVING

26. Stacy earns $150 a month part time. She will increase her hours next month by 100%. How much will she earn?

27. The amount Stacy earns next month is what percent of the amount she earns this month?

MIXED REVIEW

Find the unit price.

28. 1.5 L for $1.19   **29.** 12 oz for $0.68   **30.** 6 cans for $1.59

Solve.

31. $7n - 8 = 22$ **32.** $3x + 17 = 2$ **33.** $\frac{x}{6} + 25 = 30$

List all the factors of each number.

34. 25   **35.** 32   **36.** 46   **37.** 68   **38.** 12   **39.** 50

Using Percents
Finding a Percent of a Number

LEARN ABOUT IT

EXPLORE Study the Problem

Professional musicians get royalties, a percent of the amount of each CD or tape sold. A starting musician may get 7%, and a star 15% or more.

Assume this 10×10 grid represents the price of a CD. The blue portion represents a star's royalties. What percent is that?

TALK ABOUT IT

1. What is the ratio of the number of shaded squares to the total number of squares?

2. What fraction of the squares are shaded?

You can use proportions or equations to find a percent of a number.

Examples Find the percent of each number.

A 15% of 40

Solve a Proportion
Let $n = 15\%$ of 40
$$\frac{\text{part}}{\text{whole}} \frac{15}{100} = \frac{n}{40} \frac{\text{part}}{\text{whole}}$$
$$100n = 600$$
$$n = 6$$

Solve an Equation
Let $n = 15\%$ of 40
$$n = 0.15 \cdot 40$$
$$n = 6$$

15% of 40 is 6

B $66\frac{2}{3}\%$ of 36
$$\frac{2}{3} \cdot 36 = 24$$
$66\frac{2}{3}$ of 36 is 24

C $6\frac{1}{2}\%$ of 80
$$0.065 \cdot 80 = 5.2$$
$6\frac{1}{2}\%$ of 80 is 5.2

D 150% of 90
$$\frac{150}{100} = \frac{n}{90}$$
150% of 90 is 135

TRY IT OUT

Find the percent of each number.

1. 12% of 125
2. 7.8% of 21
3. $33\frac{1}{3}\%$ of 500
4. 270% of 45

262

Find the percent of each number.

1. 45% of 1,000

2. 140% of 80

3. 112% of 500

4. 25% of 48

5. 10% of 230

6. 75% of 36

7. 18% of 65

8. 14% of 36

9. 65% of 500

10. 35% of 92

11. 7% of 180

12. 270% of 45

13. 23.5% of 18

14. 15.5% of 30

15. 20% of 55

16. 90% of 30

17. 30% of 90

18. 15% of 105

19. 16.3% of 37

20. 64.3% of 200

21. 2% of 650

22. 400% of 28

23. 260% of 75

24. 325% of 90

25. What is 28% of 34?

26. Find $66\frac{2}{3}$% of 54.

27. What is 112% of 300?

28. Find $12\frac{1}{2}$% of 32

29. What is 9.4% of 50?

30. What is 1% of 250?

MATH REASONING Solve using mental math by expressing the percent as a fraction.

31. 75% of 360

32. $66\frac{2}{3}$% of 150

33. $33\frac{1}{3}$% of 393

PROBLEM SOLVING

34. How much would a musician with a 9% royalty get from one CD selling for $9.36?

35. A trio gets a 12% royalty. How much would each member get on tape sales of $3,672?

36. **Fine Arts Data Bank** A musician's royalties are typically based on price minus packaging deductions. Given that, how much would a 10% royalty be for a $14.98 CD?

▶ USING CRITICAL THINKING

Decide if each of these statements is true or false.

37. $31\% + 48\% = \frac{31}{100} + \frac{48}{100} = \frac{79}{100} = 79\%$

38. Kendra's family paid 31% of her $26 doctor bill from her first injury and 48% of the $78 doctor bill for her second injury. Her family paid 31% + 48% = 79% of the total bill of $104.

39. 25% of one number plus 37% of another number is 62% of the sum.

More Practice, page 535, set A

Using Percents
Finding What Percent One Number Is of Another

EXPLORE **Examine the Tables**

On Teacher Day, teachers took turns at the dunk tank. The students threw soft balls at a lever to try to dunk them. The table below the photo records the results.

TALK ABOUT IT

1. Who do you think is the most accurate thrower? Why?

2. Why is it clear that Marie is more accurate than Roger?

3. How many do you think Jamie will hit in 100 throws? Explain your thinking.

This table of equivalent ratios for Bev shows that her ratio of hits to attempts is equivalent to *n* hits per **100** attempts. That is,

$$\frac{8}{40} = \frac{n}{100} = n\%$$

Proportions or equations can be used to find what percent 15 is of 25.

Student	Accurate Hits	Attempts
Odus	2	5
Marie	16	20
Bev	8	40
Doc	24	60
Roger	13	20
Jamie	12	25

Bev's Record				
accurate hits	8	4	2	*n*
attempts	40	20	10	100

Solve a Proportion

$$\frac{15}{25} = \frac{n}{100}$$

$$25n = 1,500$$

$$n = 60$$

15 is 60% of 25

Solve an Equation

$$n \cdot 25 = 15$$

$$n = \frac{15}{25}$$

$$n = 0.60 = 60\%$$

15 is 60% of 25

1. What percent of 24 is 18?

2. 2 is what percent of 360?

3. 15 out of 60 is what percent?

4. What percent of 50 is 100?

Find the percent. Use mental math when possible.

1. What percent of 80 is 15?

2. What percent of 65 is 13?

3. What percent is 650 out of 325?

4. What percent is 21 out of 30?

5. 1 is what percent of 40?

6. 4 is what percent of 25?

7. 48 is what percent of 32?

8. 52 is what percent of 65?

9. What percent is 6 out of 48?

10. What percent of 86 is 215?

11. What percent is 6 out of 80?

12. 18 is what percent of 360?

13. 7 out of 21 is what percent?

14. 34 is what percent of 80?

15. 99 is what percent of 120?

16. What percent of 32 is 4?

17. 5 is what percent of 30?

18. What percent of 1,600 is 8?

19. 315 out of 6,000 is what percent?

20. 7 is what percent of 700?

21. 20 out of 60 is what percent?

22. 20 out of 80 is what percent?

23. 20 is what percent of 10?

24. 20 out of 200 is what percent?

APPLY

MATH REASONING Copy and complete:

25. If 9 is 15% of 60, then
    18 is ____% of 60
    27 is ____% of 60
    36 is ____% of 60

26. If b is a% of c, then
    $2b$ is ____% of c
    $3b$ is ____% of c
    $4b$ is ____% of c

PROBLEM SOLVING

27. On Teacher Day, there was a bulletin board of teachers' baby pictures. Gil won the prize by guessing 30 out of 36. What percent did he guess correctly?

28. 2,790 votes were cast for Teacher of the Year. Mr. Harn got 155 fewer votes than Ms. Blue. Ms. Blue got half as many votes as Ms. Ramirez, who won with 1,240 votes. What percent of the vote did Mr. Harn get?

▶ **CALCULATOR**

29. When the ÷ key on Julie's calculator broke, she combined a guess and check method and the multiplication key to find what percent of 110 the number 60.5 is. Explain how she might have done it.

More Practice, page 535, set C

265

Using Critical Thinking

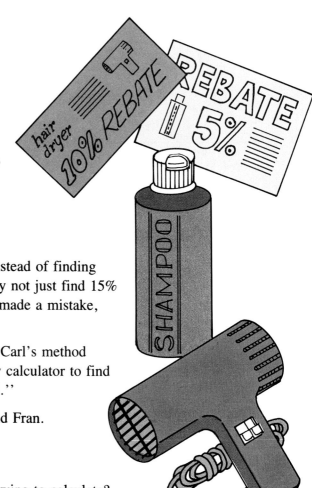

"I bought a hair dryer for $20.00. It came with a 10% rebate offer," said Fran. "I also bought shampoo for $4.50 that came with a 5% rebate offer. For the dryer, I get $2.00 back, and for the shampoo I get $0.23. That's a total of $2.23 in rebates."

"You sure made it difficult," said Carl. "Instead of finding 10% of $20.00 and adding 5% of $4.50, why not just find 15% of $24.50? And by the way, you must have made a mistake, because 15% of $24.50 is $3.68."

"Wait a minute," Beth said. "I don't think Carl's method works. I averaged 10% and 5% and used my calculator to find 7.5% of $24.50. The rebate should be $1.84."

"There's something odd going on here," said Fran. I'll need a little while to figure this out."

TALK ABOUT IT

1. What is a rebate? What are the students trying to calculate?

2. Is Carl's method correct? Why or why not?

TRY IT OUT

Which of these situations do you think show using percent correctly? Complete the calculations to support your decision.

1. State sales tax is 4%. City tax is 2%. Jan purchased an item for $25. She calculated her total tax by finding 6% of $25.

2. Bill received a 5% rebate on a purchase. He spent $13.00 for a book, and $3.50 for a magazine. He calculated his total rebate by finding 5% of $16.50.

3. Sam paid 6% tax on an $18 purchase. He paid 4% on a $24 purchase in another state. He calculated his total tax by finding 10% of $42.

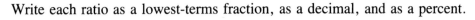

POWER PRACTICE/QUIZ

Write each ratio as a lowest-terms fraction, as a decimal, and as a percent.

1. 12 out of 100

2. 48:100

3. 75 parts to 100 parts

4. 15 out of 30

5. 8:12 $\frac{2}{3}$,

6. 60 parts to 72 parts

Write each percent as a decimal and as a lowest-terms fraction.

7. 64%

8. 20%

9. 132%

10. 500%

11. $37\frac{1}{2}\%$

12. $8\frac{1}{3}\%$

13. 2.5%

14. 0.25%

Write each fraction as a decimal and as a percent.

15. $\frac{9}{8}$

16. $\frac{25}{16}$

17. $\frac{7}{500}$

18. $\frac{17}{2500}$

Write the percent or the percent of a number.

19. Find 250% of 12.

20. What is $66\frac{2}{3}\%$ of 480?

21. What percent is 5 out of 6?

22. What percent of 18 is 24?

23. 96% of 75 is what number?

24. Find $287\frac{1}{2}\%$ of 24

25. 25 is what percent of 10?

26. 10 is what percent of 25?

27. 8 out of 5 is what percent?

28. $\frac{1}{4}\%$ of 50 is what number?

29. What is 12.5% of 728?

30. What percent of 600 is 12?

PROBLEM SOLVING

The charity auction began at noon. The committee's goal was to raise $125,000 by 6 p.m. They wanted to reach $\frac{1}{3}$ of their goal by 2 p.m. and 75% of their goal by 4 p.m.

31. What percent of their goal had they raised by 2 p.m.?

32. When did they reach 75%?

33. By 6 p.m., what percent of their goal had they reached?

34. Next year, the committee plans to raise 125% of what they raised this year. Describe the difference between next year's goal and this year's goal.

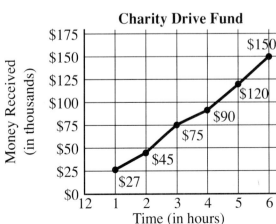

267

Problem Solving
Using the Strategies

UNDERSTAND
ANALYZE DATA
PLAN
ESTIMATE
SOLVE
EXAMINE

LEARN ABOUT IT

This problem can be solved using different strategies. Heather used **Guess and Check.** Roberto used the strategy **Work Backward.**

> Jamal saved some money to buy CDs and a CD changer. He spent $420 for a 6 disc player and $9 each for 5 CDs. After he received a $40 rebate on the player, he had $65 left. How much money had Jamal saved?

Heather's solution:

Try $500	500 − 420 = 80	80 − 5·9 = 35	35 + 40 = $75 too much
Try $475	475 − 420 = 55	55 − 5·9 = 10	10 + 40 = $50 not enough
Try $490	490 − 420 = 70	70 − 5·9 = 25	25 + 40 = $65 correct!

Roberto's solution:

Money Saved
? — −420 → ◯ — −5·9 → ◯ — +40 → $65

$490 ← +420 — (70) ← +5·9 — (25) ← −40 — $65

Jamal had saved $490.

TRY IT OUT

1. Nicole is giving away some old records. She gave half of them to her brother. Then she gave half of the remaining records to a friend. Her cousin took the last 5 records. How many records did Nicole give away?

2. Andy, Clara, and Mike sold tickets for a band concert. Clara sold half of the tickets. Andy sold $\frac{1}{3}$ as many tickets as Clara. Mike sold twice as many as Andy. If Mike sold 36 tickets, how many tickets did Andy, Clara, and Mike sell altogether?

268

Solve. Use any problem solving strategy.

1. Over a period of 15 years, the cost of the best tickets to the San Francisco Symphony increased by 320%. If tickets cost $10 in 1974, how much did they cost in 1989?

2. A theater has 5 different shows scheduled for next year—*Cats, The Tempest, Annie, The Wiz,* and *Guys and Dolls.* If *Cats* can only be scheduled last, and *Annie* must be either first or second, how many different schedules are possible?

3. Use the table to find how many more cassettes were sold than records and CDs.

4. A symphony hall has 2,675 seats on 3 levels. They sold season tickets for 56% of the seats. How many seats are taken by season ticket holders?

5. Juanita's uncle gave her some free tickets to a concert. She gave 2 to her sister and 4 to each of 3 friends. She still had 5 tickets left. How many free tickets did her uncle give her?

6. Compact discs were first introduced in 1983. Use the table below to find what percent CD sales were of the total sales 5 years later.

Sales	Jan–June 1988
CDs	70.4 million
Records	43.5 million
Cassettes	208.0 million

7. Ari was playing a game with pennies. He put some pennies in a pile. Then he doubled the number of pennies and took 24 away. He doubled the number of pennies and took 24 away two more times and had no pennies left in the pile. How many pennies were in the pile when Ari started?

8. Rod, Keith, Carrie, and Lyn each have tickets to different performances—ballet, symphony, opera, and theater. Keith's sister has the opera ticket and is married to the person who has a ballet ticket. The person who has tickets to the theater doesn't have any brothers or sisters. Both Lyn and the person who has symphony tickets are single. Who has tickets to which performance?

Using Percents
Finding a Number When a Percent of It Is Known

EXPLORE **Read the Information**

A backup singer in a band just received her first royalty check. The check was for $46. Her royalties are 1%. What was the sales amount her check was based on?

TALK ABOUT IT

1. If you know what 1% is, how can you find 100%?

2. Can you calculate the sales amount using mental math?

3. The lead singer gets 3% royalty. How would you find the amount of her check?

The table shows the **1% method.** This 1% method is convenient for estimation or mental calculations.

Amount of check	$46	$92	. . .	?
% of total	1%	2%	. . .	100%

Here are two other methods for finding a number when you know a percent of it.

Example 75% of what number is 60?

Solve a Proportion

$$\frac{75}{100} = \frac{60}{n}$$
$$75n = 6{,}000$$
$$n = 80$$

Solve an Equation

$$60 = 0.75n$$
$$\frac{60}{0.75} = n$$
$$n = 80$$

75% of 80 is 60

TRY IT OUT

Find the number.

1. 30% of what number is 15?

2. 120 is $66\frac{2}{3}\%$ of what number?

3. 147 is 350% of what number?

4. 150 is $7\frac{1}{2}\%$ of what number?

Find the number.

1. 26% of what number is 39?

2. 7% of what number is 84?

3. 55% of what number is 11?

4. 75% of what number is 60?

5. 30% of what number is 4.5?

6. 160% of what number is 80?

7. 125% of what number is 110?

8. 300% of what number is 258?

9. $33\frac{1}{3}$% of what number is 527?

10. $12\frac{1}{2}$% of what number is 50.4?

11. $66\frac{2}{3}$% of what number is 110?

12. $8\frac{1}{2}$% of what number is 12.75?

APPLY

MATH REASONING Use the 1% method to complete these problems using mental math.

13. 5% of what number is 25?

14. 6% of what number is 18?

15. 12% of what number is 48?

16. 15% of what number is 30?

PROBLEM SOLVING

17. A solo guitarist's royalty is 9%. What sales amount is a royalty check of $4,653 based on?

18. A band gets a total royalty of 8.75%. What would the band's cash amount of royalty be for a CD that earns a total of $5,520,000?

19. Fine Arts Data Bank The packaging deduction of a cassette tape is $1.796. What is the list price of the tape?

 MIXED REVIEW

Find the answers. Express in lowest terms.

20. $21\frac{4}{5} - 11\frac{6}{7}$

21. $-1\frac{1}{4} \cdot -4\frac{1}{3}$

22. $6\frac{2}{5} \div -2\frac{1}{3}$

23. $20 \div 1\frac{1}{2}$

State whether each number is prime or composite, and give all of its factors.

24. 17

25. 14

26. 18

27. 31

Evaluate $y = 4x^2 - 1$ for each value of x.

28. 0

29. 1

30. −1

31. 2

32. −2

33. 10

More Practice, page 535, set D

Exploring Algebra
Order of Operations

EXPLORE Study the Formula

Mr. Parker disguised familiar formulas. Study
his formula for converting temperatures
from Fahrenheit to Celsius. Can you change
the given temperatures to Celsius? Are your
answers reasonable?

$$C = \frac{5(F - 2^5)}{2 \cdot 2 + 5}$$

Evaluate for F = 212°
and F = 32°

TALK ABOUT IT

What are the two kinds of grouping symbols used in the
formula. What do they mean?

To evaluate an algebraic expression for a particular value, first
substitute the value for the variable in the expression, then:

Step 1: Compute within all grouping symbols, using MDAS
(first MULTIPLY and DIVIDE, then ADD and SUBTRACT).

Step 2: Compute above and below division bars, using MDAS.

Step 3: Apply MDAS in order, from left to right.

Example Evaluate $\dfrac{5(F - 2^5)}{2 \cdot 2 + 5} - 7$ for F = 59.

$$\frac{5(59 - 2^5)}{2 \cdot 2 + 5} - 7 \qquad \text{Substitute 59 for } F.$$

Step 1 $\dfrac{5(59 - 32)}{2 \cdot 2 + 5} - 7 \qquad$ Work in parentheses first.

$= \dfrac{5 \cdot 27}{2 \cdot 2 + 5} - 7 \qquad$ Work above and below division bar.

Step 2 $= \dfrac{135}{9} - 7 \qquad$ MDAS

Step 3 $= 15 - 7 = 8$

Evaluate.

1. $\dfrac{(4 - 2)^2}{1 + 2}$

2. $\dfrac{3^2(20 - 10)}{10 - (3 + 1)} - 7$

3. $1 + \dfrac{h(7 - 4)}{5^2 - 5}$ for $h = 40$

Evaluate.

1. $\dfrac{4(9-7)}{1+3}$

2. $5(3)-(9+2)$

3. $\dfrac{3(265-9)}{15-3}$

4. $\dfrac{5(2^2+1)}{20+5}$

5. $\dfrac{(3^2-1^2)}{5(3+1)}$

6. $\dfrac{3^2(5-2^2)}{4(2^3+1)}$

7. $\dfrac{4^2(30-10)}{15-(4+1)}$

8. $\dfrac{2^3(18-3^2)}{5(15\div3)}$

9. $3x+(5-2)$ for $x=4$ 10. $16\div(y^2-7)$ for $y=3$ 11. $12n^3-(3-7)$ for $n=2$

12. $\dfrac{4h-5}{h+5}$ for $h=20$

13. $\dfrac{h^2(3+5)}{5\cdot10}$ for $h=10$

14. $25-\dfrac{p(7-3)}{2+5\cdot2}$ for $p=6$

Evaluate. You may want to use your calculator.

15. $2\cdot5+9\div3$

16. $5\cdot9-8\div4$

17. $6+15\div3+2$

18. $7-18\div9\cdot4$

19. $15\div3+2\cdot6$

20. $2-3\cdot5-10$

MATH REASONING Sometimes you will find grouping symbols *inside* grouping symbols. Work from the inner grouping outward in evaluating these expressions.

21. $10-[4-(3-1)]$

22. $3b+\{15-(3\cdot2)\}$ for $b=6$

23. $[5\cdot(6-2)]^2$

24. $18+[5-(2-1)]$

25. $6c\div\{(c+1)-4\}$ for $c=5$

26. $\{2^2(42-8\cdot5)\}^2$

PROBLEM SOLVING

27. An active person uses about 30 fewer calories each day for each 1°C rise in temperature. If your body burns 3,200 calories at 0°C, what will you need at 35°C?

28. **Suppose** Which of these factors would change your answer to problem 27? a) the temperature going from 3°C to 38°C b) your body using 60 fewer calories for each 2°C rise c) the temperature dropping from 35°C to 0°C.

▶ **USING CRITICAL THINKING Create Your Own Formula**

29. Rewrite $F=\dfrac{9}{5}C+32$ the way Mr. Parker might have done.

(Hint: $9=3^2$; $5^2=25$; $5=2^2+1$.)
See if $C=0$ and $C=100$ give $F=32$ and $F=212$.

Problem Solving
Determining Reasonable Answers

UNDERSTAND
ANALYZE DATA
PLAN
ESTIMATE
SOLVE
EXAMINE

An important part of evaluating an answer to a problem is to check your work. This chart shows some ways you can do this.

Check Your Work

- Is the arithmetic correct?
- Did you use the strategies correctly?
- Is the answer reasonable?

Example

Do not solve the problem. Decide if the answer given is reasonable. If it is not reasonable, explain why.

Problem: The graph shows the percentage increase in house prices from 1987 to 1988 in 7 states. Kaki paid $209,500 for a home in Hawaii in 1987. By how much had the price increased in 1988?

Answer: The price had increased by $3,016.80.

To check if the answer is reasonable, round 14.4% down to 14%. Then round $209,500 down to $200,000.

Multiply 200,000 by 14%.

The correct answer should be a little more than $28,000 because the numbers were rounded down.

$3,016.80 is not a reasonable answer.

Increase in Home Prices from 1987 to 1988.

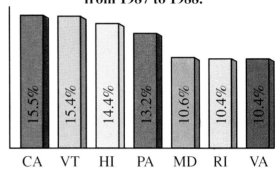

| CA | VT | HI | PA | MD | RI | VA |

15.5% 15.4% 14.4% 13.2% 10.6% 10.4% 10.4%

$14.4\% \longrightarrow 14\%$

$\$209,500 \rightarrow \$200,000$

$\$200,000 \cdot 0.14 = \$28,000$

| TRY IT OUT |

Do not solve the problem. Decide if the answer given is reasonable. If it is not reasonable, explain why.

1. Alan bought a home in Maryland in 1987. He paid $87,950. By how much had the price increased in 1988? Answer: The price had increased by $6,322.

2. In 1987, the median price of a home in Houston was $62,830. By 1988, it had dropped 9.6%. How much had it dropped? Answer: the median price dropped $6,031.68.

Solve. Use any problem strategy.

1. Use the table to find how many more homes were built before 1920 than in the 1940's.

2. Use the table to find about what percent of homes in the USA were built in the 1960's or later.

3. The median home has 5.2 rooms including 2.5 bedrooms. Use the table and the circle graph to find how many of the homes built in the 1970's have 5 rooms.

4. Daryl's family spends $536.52 a month on house payments, including taxes and insurance. Their payment is 24.3% of their monthly income. What is their monthly income?

5. There are 6,478 homes in a small town. Use the graph to predict how many of them have 7 or more rooms.

Number of Rooms in Homes

| USA Homes When They Were Built ||
Years	Number (in millions)
Up to 1919	11.1
1920–29	6.1
1930–39	6.8
1940–49	8.9
1950–59	14.0
1960–69	16.5
1970–79	26.4
1980–89	10.2
	100.4

6. A new home project has just been completed. One quarter of the homes have 2 bedrooms. One third of the remaining homes have 3 bedrooms. That leaves 14 homes with 4 or more bedrooms. How many homes are in the project?

7. If the interest rate on a home loan is $10\frac{3}{4}\%$, then the monthly payment will be $9.34 for each $1,000 borrowed. Peg borrowed $76,500. How much was her monthly payment?

8. **Think about your solution** Five friends live on different floors in the same apartment building. Carlos lives on the floor below Wayne. Melanie lives on a lower floor than any of her friends. There is one floor between Ben and Melanie. Ben has to go up 7 floors to visit Sandy. Carlos lives on the 8th floor and is 5 floors above Melanie. On what floors do the 5 friends live?
   a. Write your answer in a complete sentence.
   b. Write a description of how you solved the problem.
   c. Name the strategy or strategies you used to solve the problem.

More Practice, page 546, set A

Applied Problem Solving
Group Decision Making

UNDERSTAND
ANALYZE DATA
PLAN
ESTIMATE
SOLVE
EXAMINE

Group Skill:
Explain and Summarize

Your family is planning a camping trip. You figure your family will take about 144 photos in all, and you were told that it is less expensive to buy your film before you go. Should you buy rolls with 24 shots on each or with 36 shots on each? Should you buy slide film or print film? How much will it cost you in all?

Facts to Consider

- You'll want prints of at least $\frac{1}{4}$ of the photos to put in an album.

- You'll want about 15 more prints to give to grandparents and other relatives.

- You have a slide projector.

- Cost of film:

	24 photos per roll	36 photos per roll
Print film	$4.21	$5.37
Slide film	$5.46	$7.51

- Cost to develop film:

Print Film

Number of shots per roll	1 print of each shot	2 prints of each shot
24	$6.45	$ 8.85
36	$8.45	$12.05
Additional prints ordered later	$0.75 per print	

Slide Film

Number of shots per roll	Cost
24	$3.95
36	$5.50
Making prints from slides	$0.50 per print

Some Questions to Answer

1. Is it better to purchase print film in 24 or 36 shot rolls? What is the better buy for slide film?

2. Suppose you used print film in 36 print rolls.
   a) How many rolls would you need?

   b) How much would the film cost?

   c) How much would it cost to develop 2 prints of each?

d) Is there a way to buy the extra prints you need without getting 2 prints of each?

e) If so, show which is the best way for you to purchase extra prints.

3. How much would your costs be if you bought and developed slide film?

What Is Your Decision?

It's the day before the trip. What have you decided? Tell why you chose 24 or 36-shot rolls of film. Explain why you chose print or slide film. Tell how much the total cost will be.

WRAP UP

What Percent of These Can You Match?

4%	40%	$\frac{3}{4}$ $\frac{7}{5}$	0.3	%
n% of 16 is 4		300% of n		20% of 70 is n
75% of n is 30		per hundred		0.3% of n

Match each with the best example from the box.

1. finding a percent of a number

2. a small percent of a number

3. a large percent of a number

4. a fraction equal to 75%

5. finding a number when its percent of another number is known

6. meaning of percent

7. a percent equal to 0.4

8. a decimal equal to 30%

9. symbol for percent

10. finding what percent one number is of another

Sometimes, Always, Never

Which of these words should go in the blank: *sometimes*, *always*, or *never*? Explain your choice.

11. A percent of a number is __?__ less than the number.

12. 100% of a number is __?__ 100.

13. 100% of a number is __?__ 1.

Project

Look through newspapers and magazines to find examples of each of the following.

- finding a percent of a number
- finding a number when its percent of another number is given
- finding what percent one number is of another.

Include examples with large and small percents if you can. Which was the most difficult to find?

POWER PRACTICE/TEST

Part 1   Understanding

1. There are 27 tenors in the school choir of 100 members.

   Express this ratio as a fraction, a decimal, and a percent.

2. Which of the following is true about 150% of 50?

   A It is greater than 50, but less than 100.   B It is greater than 100.

   C It is equal to 50.   D It is less than 50.

3. Which statement is true?

   A Solving the proportion $\frac{18}{30} = \frac{n}{100}$ would tell what 18% of 30 is.   B Solving the proportion $\frac{18}{30} = \frac{n}{100}$ would tell what percent 18 is of 30.

   C Solving the proportion $\frac{18}{30} = \frac{n}{100}$ would tell 18% of what number is 30.   D Solving the proportion $\frac{18}{30} = \frac{n}{100}$ would tell what 30% of 18 is.

Part 2   Skills

4. Write a percent for $\frac{5}{8}$.

5. What percent of 600 is 3?

6. Express 925% as a decimal.

7. 240 is what percent of 75?

8. Find 21% of 72.

9. 63 is 175% of what number?

10. Express 0.875 as a fraction in lowest terms.

11. $33\frac{1}{3}\%$ of what number is 20?

Evaluate.

12. $\dfrac{3^2 + 12}{4 + 6 \div 3}$

13. $\dfrac{r(7 - 2^2)}{6 - r}$ for $r = 3$

Part 3   Applications

14. Mr. Paige noticed that $\frac{1}{3}$ of his books are fiction. Of those remaining, $\frac{1}{2}$ are history. Of the rest, $\frac{3}{4}$ are reference books. The last 5 are poetry. How many books does Mr. Paige have in his library?

15. **Challenge** A bank pays 8.6% interest quarterly. Jasmine calculated that $4,300 interest would be earned on a deposit of $5,000 at the end of a quarter. What is wrong with Jasmine's calculation? How much interest would be earned at the end of the quarter, on a deposit of $5,000?

279

ENRICHMENT
The Königsberg Bridge Problem

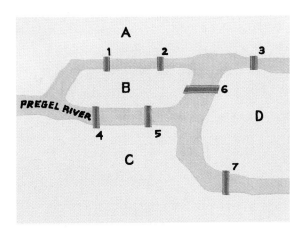

In the old Prussian City of Königsberg, there were 7 bridges across the Pregel River connecting 4 land areas marked A, B, C, and D on the map. This pattern of bridges suggested this problem to the residents of Königsberg:

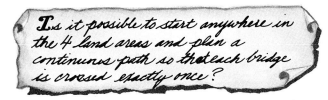

Is it possible to start anywhere in the 4 land areas and plan a continuous path so that each bridge is crossed exactly once?

Try the bridge problem. Can you do it?

No one knew the answer to this problem until the great Swiss mathematician Euler gave a solution to the problem in 1736. Euler said the problem could be solved by "a complete enumeration of all walks possible; then we would know if one of them fulfills the condition or none. This method, however, is, because of the great number of combinations, too difficult and cumbersome." Euler then gave a different way to solve the problem.

The Königsberg bridge problem involves a branch of mathematics that is now known as **topology**. Euler is considered to be one of the founders of topology.

1. Do you think Euler proved that it is possible to cross each of the 7 bridges of Königsberg exactly once or proved that it is impossible to do so?

2. Show where you would put an 8th bridge across the river so that all 8 bridges could be crossed exactly once.

CUMULATIVE REVIEW

1. Which is the GCF of 18, 30, 270?

   A 3 B 9

   C 6 D 18

2. Which is the LCM of 7, 63, 105?

   A 105 B 525

   C 315 D 441

3. What is $\frac{75}{120}$ in lowest terms?

   A $\frac{3}{25}$ B $\frac{15}{25}$

   C $\frac{5}{8}$ D $\frac{8}{15}$

4. Subtract.

   $$\frac{-7}{10} - \frac{-5}{6}$$

   A $-\frac{2}{15}$ B $1\frac{8}{15}$

   C $-1\frac{8}{15}$ D $\frac{2}{15}$

5. Which is the positive exponent simplification for $\frac{4^3 \cdot 5^3}{4^6 \cdot 5}$?

   A $\frac{5^2}{4^3}$ B $\frac{4^{-3}}{5^2}$

   C $\frac{4^3}{5^{-2}}$ D $\frac{4^{-3}}{5^{-2}}$

6. Which ratio represents the situation? The salad dressing recipe uses 1 part water to 3 parts oil.

   A $\frac{2}{3}$ B 1 of 3

   C 1:3 D 3:6

7. Simplify the rate: 85 km in 5h.

   A $\frac{17 \text{ km}}{5 \text{ h}}$ B 42.5 km/3 h

   C 17 km/h D $\frac{85 \text{ km}}{5 \text{ h}}$

8. Which is the unit price if 36 cans cost $12.00?

   A $0.33/can B $0.03/can

   C $0.30/can D $3.00/can

9. Solve.

   $$\frac{4}{10} = \frac{14}{x}$$

   A 5.6 B 35

   C 3.5 D 56

10. Use a proportion to find d.

    A $d = 0.64$ m B $d = 4.6$ m

    C $d = 6.4$ m D $d = 4$ m

11. Which symbol means "is similar to"?

    A $\cong$ B $\geq$ C $\sim$ D $=$

12. Find tan A.

    A 28 B 30

    C $\frac{14}{15}$ D $\frac{15}{14}$

13. Ravi bowled 6 games. Her scores were 138, 142, 150, 136, 148, and 144. What was her mean score?

    A 144 B 143

    C 150 D 136

14. Beresa made a string design in art class. The design had 12 pins equally spaced around a circle. Each pin was connected to each of the other pins with a string. How many pieces of string were used?

    A 12 B 132

    C 38 D 66

281

10

APPLICATIONS OF PERCENT

THEME: PHYSICAL FITNESS

MATH AND
HEALTH AND FITNESS

DATA BANK

Use the Health and Fitness Data Bank on page 491 to answer the questions.

1. Health Center A offers a family special on its one year membership that is 80% of the usual fee. What is the cost for a family of 4?

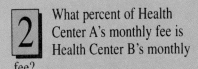

2 What percent of Health Center A's monthly fee is Health Center B's monthly fee?

3 What is the weight of a male distance runner who with 12 pounds of body fat is at the maximum of the usual range of percent body fat for his sport?

4 **Using Critical Thinking**
Lynn Cox was able to swim the frigid Bering Strait because her percent body fat was about 33%. Compare her with the average swimmer, and consider why she could swim in waters cold enough to kill most persons.

Exercise strengthens muscles and lowers the percentage of fat in our bodies.

Commission

EXPLORE **Solve to Understand**

One summer, Deb tried selling greeting cards. She was paid 12% of her total sales. She sold $24.50 worth in one month. How much did she earn?

TALK ABOUT IT

1. What data do you need to solve this problem?

2. What are you being asked to do?

3. Do you think Deb made more or less than $2?

When you are paid **on commission,** you are paid a percent of the sales you make. This percent is called your **rate of commission.**

To find the commission, multiply the rate times the total sales.

commission rate × total sales = commission

12 % × 24.50 = | 2.94 | Calculator display

Deb's commission is $2.94.

In some jobs, you might be paid a commission plus a regular monthly salary. Suppose Deb's commission rate is 2.5%, and that in addition she receives a salary of $20 per month.

Total monthly pay is commission plus monthly salary.

commission + salary = total pay

2.5 % × 24.50 = | 0.6125 | First find her commission.

+ 20 = | 20.6125 | Add the salary. Round to the nearest cent.

Deb earned $20.61 that month.

TRY IT OUT

Use a calculator to find the total monthly pay.

1. total sales: $75.25, commission rate: 35%, monthly salary: $30

2. total sales: $10,160, commission rate: 25%, monthly salary: $265.

284

Find the commission using a calculator. Round to the nearest cent.

1. total sales $46.75
   commission rate: 3.5%

2. total sales: $525
   commission rate: 6%

3. total sales $12,079
   commission rate: 10.5%

4. total sales: $98,000
   commission rate: $2\frac{1}{4}$%

5. total sales: $287.50
   commission rate: 21%

6. total sales: $1,752.30
   commission rate: 30.4%

Find the total pay using a calculator. Round to the nearest cent.

7. total sales: $462.35
   rate of commission: 12%
   monthly salary: $175.50

8. total sales: $14,670
   commission rate: 4.5%
   monthly salary: $2,200

9. total sales: $3,827.62
   commission rate: $35\frac{1}{2}$%
   monthly salary: $750.00

10. What is the commission on $46,578 worth of sales at 8.5% commission?

11. How much commission would you earn on $325.25 of sales at a commission rate of 4.1%?

MATH REASONING In each part find the commissions. Then write out a generalization from your results, and tell why it's true for any pairs of numbers.

12. a) Total sales: $39, commission rate: 25%
    b) Total sales: $25, commission rate: 39%

13. a) Total Sales: $14, commission rate: 89%
    b) Total Sales: $89, commission rate: 14%

PROBLEM SOLVING

14. After school, Dave makes chess pieces out of beach stones, and a craft store sells them for $17.95 a set. If Dave gets a 40% commission on any sales, how much does he make if two sets are sold?

▶ **USING CRITICAL THINKING Look for a pattern**

15. You have your choice of being paid in 2 different ways for selling tapes at a music store: A) $50 a month salary and a 2% commission on sales or B) 14% commission on sales. The first month you choose plan A, and you sell $250 worth of tapes. If your sales get higher and higher, at what point would you want to switch over to plan B?

More Practice, page 535, set E

Percent of Increase and Decrease

EXPLORE **Study the Graphs**

Kristin started a weight training program in January. One of these graphs shows that the amount she could bench press was 50% more in April than in January.

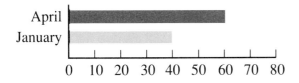
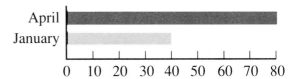

TALK ABOUT IT

1. What do you think 50% more means? 50% of what?

2. What is another way to describe the situation above?

3. Which graph shows 50% more weight in April? Explain.

To find the percent of increase or decrease, express the ratio of the increase or decrease to the original amount as a percent.

Examples Find the percent of increase or decrease.

A The amount Kristin could bench press increased from 44 lb to 55 lb.

Increase: $55 - 44 = 11$ Ratio: $\dfrac{11}{44} = 0.25 = 25\%$

$55\ \boxminus\ 44\ \boxminus\ \boxed{11}\ \boxdot\ 44\ \boxed{\%}\ \boxminus\ \boxed{25}$

The percent of increase from 44 to 55 is 25%.

B Kristin's body fat decreased from 32 lb to 28 lb.

Decrease: $32 - 28 = 4$ Ratio: $\dfrac{4}{32} = 0.125 = 12.5\%$

$32\ \boxminus\ 28\ \boxminus\ \boxed{4}\ \boxdot\ 32\ \boxed{\%}\ \boxminus\ \boxed{12.5}$

The percent of decrease from 32 to 28 is 12.5%.

TRY IT OUT

Find the percent increase or decrease. Round to the nearest tenth.

1. 150 to 132   **2.** 60 to 88   **3.** 460 to 450

Find percent increase or decrease. Round to the nearest tenth when needed.

1. 500 to 640

2. 200 to 188

3. 48 to 54

4. 150 to 120

5. 720 to 648

6. 96 to 168

7. 15 to 123

8. 8.8 to 11

9. 62.5 to 22.5

10. 15 to 4.5

11. 350 to 273

12. 800 to 716

13. 1,480 to 2,405

14. $12.18 to $16.24

15. 450 to 4,950

16. 0.42 to 0.25

17. $0.83 to $0.99

18. 88.8 to 90.3

19. What is the percent of change from 192 to 312?

APPLY

MATH REASONING Use mental math to find the percent increase or decrease.

20. 30 to 60

21. 20 to 25

22. 90 to 120

23. 40 to 70

PROBLEM SOLVING

24. Find the percent increase in weight between the second and third sets.

25. Find the percent decrease between the third and fourth sets.

26. Health and Fitness Data Bank A male athlete weighs 150 lb, of which 18 lb is body fat. He loses 11 lb of body fat and gains 3 lb of lean body mass through weight training. What is his percent decrease in weight? in pounds of body fat? If the athlete were originally over the ideal body fat percent for his sport and is now within the ideal for that sport, what might his sport be?

DATA BANK

> **Injury Rehabilitation Strengthening Program**
> (based on RM* of 12 lb.)
>
> 1st set: 10 repetitions at 6 lb.
> 2nd set: 10 repetitions at 9 lb.
> 3rd set: 10 repetitions at 12 lb.
> 4th set: 20 repetitions at 3 lb.
>
> *RM is the amount of weight the person can lift properly 10 times in a row.

▶ **USING CRITICAL THINKING Justify Your Answer**

27. Maureen's body fat was 26% in January. Between January and June, she reduced her body fat by 25%. In the next six months, her body fat increased 25%. Was her body fat back to 26%? Explain why or why not.

More Practice, page 536, set A

Estimating with Percent

LEARN ABOUT IT

It is often possible to use a simple fraction as an estimate of a percent.

EXPLORE Make a Table

Work in groups. Complete a reference card titled **Percent↔Simple Fraction** like the one started here. You can use it to do problems in this lesson.

TALK ABOUT IT

Percent ⟷ Simple Fraction

$50\% = \frac{1}{2}$	$20\% = \frac{1}{5}$
$33\frac{1}{3}\% =$	$40\% =$
$66\frac{2}{3}\% =$	$12\frac{1}{2}\% =$
$25\% =$	$16\frac{2}{3}\% =$
$75\% =$	$10\% =$

1. Which fraction does not appear in the table that you completed, $\frac{1}{5}$, $\frac{1}{6}$, $\frac{1}{7}$, or $\frac{1}{8}$?

2. Which of these simple fractions is nearest 17%?

3. Claire used the fraction $\frac{1}{5}$ instead of 23% to make an estimate of 23% of 500 million. Is this the best choice? What fraction would you have chosen?

You can often estimate an answer by using compatible numbers.

Examples

A Estimate 12.8% of 482.
12.8% is about $12\frac{1}{2}\%$
$12\frac{1}{2}\%$ is equivalent to $\frac{1}{8}$
482 is about 480
$\frac{1}{8} \cdot 480 = 60$
12.8% of 478 is about 60.

B 19 out of 62 is about what percent?
19 is about 20
62 is about 60
$\frac{20}{60} = \frac{1}{3} = 33\frac{1}{3}\%$
19 out of 62 is about $33\frac{1}{3}\%$.

C Estimate 18.9% of 149.
18.9% is about 20%
149 is about 150
20% of 150
$= 0.20 \cdot 150 = 30$
18.9% of 149 is about 30.

TRY IT OUT

Estimate the percent of the number.

4. 88% of 40
5. $26\frac{1}{3}\%$ of 42
6. 76% of 19
7. 13% of 80

Estimate a percent for each ratio.

8. 1 out of 79
9. 38 out of 120
10. 10 out of 79
11. 21 out of 62

Estimate the percent of the number.

1. 32% of 66   **2.** 17% of 60   **3.** 22% of 80   **4.** 68% of 151

5. 73.2% of 137   **6.** 9.3% of 72   **7.** 13% of 25   **8.** 58% of 198

Estimate the percent of the ratio.

9. 38 out of 51   **10.** 11 out of 68   **11.** 29 out of 115   **12.** 119 out of 161

13. 6 out of 35   **14.** 59 out of 241   **15.** 302 out of 389   **16.** 190 out of 310

17. 16 out of 162 is about what percent?   **18.** About how much is 74% of $200?

APPLY

MATH REASONING Use compatible numbers to estimate if the percent increase is closest to 25%, 50%, 75%, 100%.

19. 81 to 161   **20.** 121 to 182   **21.** 39 to 66   **22.** 83 to 104

PROBLEM SOLVING

23. 120 students were asked, ''What would you do with a lot of money?'' Estimate the number of students who made each response:

Buy a house	16%	Buy clothes	12%
Give to the poor	2%	Buy a car	31%
Travel around the world	6%	Other	6%
Save	27%		

MIXED REVIEW

Each pair of triangles is similar. Find length x.

24.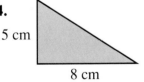
5 cm, 8 cm, x, 2 cm

25.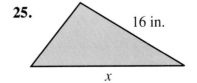
16 in., x

4 in., 5 in.

Find the prime factorization of each number.

26. 14   **27.** 20   **28.** 60   **29.** 24   **30.** 56

More Practice, page 536, set B

Using Critical Thinking

Andrea saw a description of these different types of propaganda that are used in advertisements to convince us about something.

"Okay, Fran," she said. "See if you can decide, just from the titles, which type of propaganda is used in the ads below."

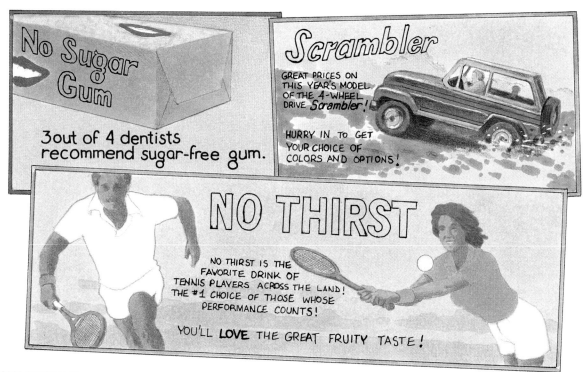

TALK ABOUT IT

1. What did Andrea ask Fran to do?

2. How would you match the propaganda types with the ads? Why?

3. How do you think advertisers come up with the information for their ads? What type of questions do you think were asked of dentists to get the results in the first ad?

TRY IT OUT

1. Write an ad that uses the propaganda technique called "something for nothing."

2. Write an ad that uses the propaganda technique called "transferring the feeling."

POWER PRACTICE/QUIZ

Find the commission to the nearest cent.

1. sales: $350
commission rate: 7%

2. sales: $75
commission rate: 8.4%

3. sales: $22,865.04
commission rate: $3\frac{1}{3}$% -

Find the total pay to the nearest cent.

4. sales: $52.80
commission rate: 25%
monthly salary: $15

5. sales: $2,564
commission rate: 5.5%
monthly salary: $500

6. sales: $97,800
commission rate: $8\frac{1}{8}$%
monthly salary: $1,375

Find the percent of increase or decrease. Round to the nearest tenth.

7. membership from $25 to $30

8. weight: from 200g to 150g

9. miles per gallon: from 20.5 to 28

10. hours per week: from 32 to 40

11. height: from 48 in. to 56 in.

12. distance: from 500 m to 575 m

13. rent: from $575 to $500

14. heart beats: from 175 to 100

Estimate the percent of a number.

15. 26% of 35   **16.** 62% of 54   **17.** 16% of 125   **18.** $32\frac{1}{2}$% of 335   **19.** 13% of 70

Estimate each ratio as a percent.

20. 432 out of 870   **21.** 49 out of 295   **22.** 27 out of 268   **23.** 19 out of 150

PROBLEM SOLVING

24. Of 50 students surveyed before a school election, 37 said they were voting for Ed. The final count was 182 votes for Ed and 125 votes for Dave. Were the results of the survey close to the results of the election?

25. Use percent of increase to compare the child's gain in height and weight during its first three years. Write a statement describing what you find.

	birth	1 yr	2 yr	3 yr
height (cm)	50	75	87	96
weight (kg)	3.4	10	12.5	14.5

26. Make a table showing the amount earned under each plan. Begin with sales of $1,000, $2,000, and so on. When is plan A better than plan B?

Plan A: 17% commission on all sales
Plan B: 3% commission on all sales + $500 salary

291

Problem Solving
Using the Strategies

| UNDERSTAND |
| ANALYZE DATA |
| PLAN |
| ESTIMATE |
| SOLVE |
| EXAMINE |

LEARN ABOUT IT

To solve some problems it may help to use more than one strategy. To solve this problem, you can **Draw a Picture, Solve a Simpler Problem, Make a Table, and Look for a Pattern**.

There are 12 teams playing in a volleyball tournament. Each team will play every other team once to determine first place. How many games have to be played?

You can begin with a Simpler Problem and Draw a Picture.

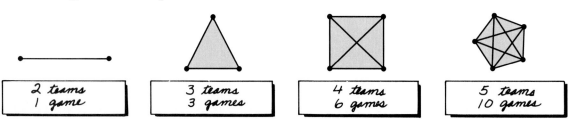

Then you can Make a Table showing teams and games and Look for a Pattern.

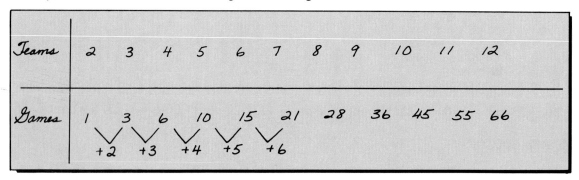

66 games have to be played.

TRY IT OUT

Solve. Use any problem solving strategy.

1. Jody made a display using juice cans for the snack bar. She put 1 less can in each row than in the row below it. The top row had 1 can. If Jody put 15 cans in the bottom row, how many cans did she use in her display?

2. A softball team has 9 players. How many different batting orders are possible with all 9 players?

292

Solve. Use any problem solving strategies.

Some Strategies	
Act Out	Solve a Simpler Problem
Use Objects	Make an Organized List
Choose an Operation	Work Backward
Draw a Picture	Look for a Pattern
Guess and Check	Use Logical Reasoning
Make a Table	Write an Equation

1. In the 1988 summer Olympic games, 242 gold medals were awarded. The United States won 36 of them. What percent of the gold medals did the U.S. win?

2. A square chessboard is divided into 64 smaller squares. How many different squares can you count on the chessboard, if you include all possible sizes?

3. On May 12, 1987, a set of 32 bronze chess playing pieces sold for a record $40,000. The pieces range in height from $2\frac{3}{4}$in. to 5 in. Find the average price per piece.

4. Jeff has 2 glasses, one that holds 4 oz and one that holds 9 oz. Neither glass has any markings to show smaller quantities. How can Jeff measure out exactly 6 oz of water using the 2 glasses?

5. Andrea's father works in a sporting goods store. He earns $960 a month plus 7.5% commission on all sales over $5,000. Last month his sales were $8,430. How much did he earn last month?

6. George, Linda, and Erica sold school sweatshirts. Linda sold 6 fewer than George. Erica sold half as many as George. Together they sold 74 sweatshirts. How many did each sell?

7. In 1974, season tickets to 49er's games cost $85. Fifteen years later, they cost $250. By what percent did the cost of the tickets increase?

8. The sporting goods store sells towels with local sports team emblems on them. The towels come in 2 sizes and 4 colors. There are 5 different emblems available. How many different towels are there to choose from?

More Practice, page 546, set B

Discounts and Sale Prices

EXPLORE **Consider the Situation**

At a local health center, you get 8% off the monthly fee if you are part of a school athletic group of 10 or more. Normally, 10 people would pay $399.90. What would they pay with a group discount?

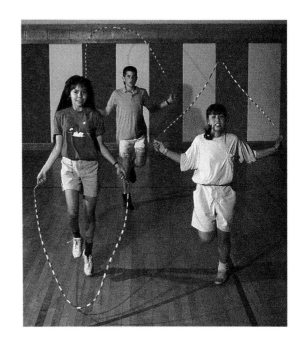

TALK ABOUT IT

1. What data will you need to solve this problem?

2. Do you estimate the price with the discount will be closer to $300 or $350? Why?

The **discount**(*d*) is the amount that the regular price is reduced.
The **sale price** is the regular price minus the discount.

Examples

A For an 8% reduction on $64.80 find the discount and the sale price.

Discount = discount percent × regular price
$$d = 8\% \cdot \$64.80 = 0.08 \cdot \$64.80$$
$$= \$5.184 \text{ or } \$5.18 \qquad \text{The discount is } \$5.18$$

Sale price = Regular price − Discount
$$= \$64.80 - \$5.18 = \$59.62 \qquad \text{The sale price is } \$59.62$$

B Mentally find the sale price if there is 25% off a regular price of $48.

Think: $\frac{1}{4} \cdot 48 = 12$, $48 - 12 = 36$

The sale price is $36.

C Use a calculator to find the sale price if there is $12\frac{1}{2}\%$ off the regular price of $64.89.

64.89 $\boxed{\times}$ 12.5 $\boxed{\%}$ $\boxed{=}$ $\boxed{\text{8.11125}}$

$\boxed{+/-}$ $\boxed{+}$ 64.89 $\boxed{=}$ $\boxed{\text{56.77875}}$

The sale price is $56.78.

Find the discount and the sale price. Round to nearest cent.

1. regular price: $1,638.95
   discount: 8.5%

2. regular price: $84
   discount: 50%

3. regular price: $245
   discount: 45%

Find the discount and the sale price. Round to the nearest cent.

1. regular price: $32
   discount percent: 75%

2. regular price: $250
   discount percent: 30%

3. regular price: $25.50
   discount percent: 12%

4. regular price: $1,234
   discount percent: 5%

5. regular price: $5,440
   discount percent: 12.5%

6. regular price: $125.90
   discount percent: 3%

7. regular price: $87.50
   discount percent: 33.3%

8. regular price: $140
   discount percent: 15%

9. regular price: $349.99
   discount percent: 20%

10. regular price: $9.99
    discount percent: 33.3%

11. regular price: $49.50
    discount percent: 45%

12. regular price: $298.95
    discount percent: 31%

APPLY

MATH REASONING Use mental math to decide which of the two given discounts will have the lower sale price.

13. 10% off of $93 or
    15% off of $105

14. 15% off of $80 or
    20% off of $90

15. 20% off of $130 or
    5% off of $120

16. 5% off of $55
    10% off of $102

17. 10% off of $245
    25% off of $300

18. 15% off of $410
    20% off of $500

PROBLEM SOLVING

19. A 1-year membership at the health center costs $269. If purchased during the month of January, it is on special for $249. How much is the percent discount?

20. **Health and Fitness Data Bank** For each health center in the Comparison of Health Center Fees, find the monthly, 1-year and 2-year rates with a student discount of 7% and a senior discount of 12%.

USING CRITICAL THINKING   Give a Counterexample

Write true or false. If false, give a counterexample.

21. An item that is reduced by 20% is followed in two weeks by a 10% decrease in the sale price. It costs the same as it would if it had been reduced by 30% initially.

22. A car has a 10% price increase when the new model comes out and a 10% price reduction 10 months later. Is its price the same as it was before the increase?

More Practice, page 536, set C

Exploring Algebra
A Formula for Simple Interest

LEARN ABOUT IT

Amount of interest at a 9% rate

EXPLORE Make a Table

Work in groups. Suppose you borrow money at 9% interest per year. You pay $9 to use $100 for one year and $18 for two years. Complete this table.

Amount	$50	$100	$150	$200
one year	$4.50	$9		
two years		$18		
three years				

TALK ABOUT IT

1. What would the table entries be in a $300 column?

2. What would the table entries be for four years?

In a savings account the bank pays you for the use of your money. With a loan, you pay the bank for the use of their money. You can find the interest (I), and the total amount (A) to be repaid by using formulas.

$I = PRT$ and $A = P + I$.

Principal (P): amount loaned or saved
Rate (R): percent per year
Time (T): Number of years the money is used.

Examples Find the interest (I) and the total amount (A) in each problem.

A $P = \$150, R = 4\%, T = 2$ years
$I = 150 \cdot 0.04 \cdot 2$
$I = 12$ The interest is $12.

$A = P + I$
$A = 150 + 12$ The amount is $162.

B A principal of $5,000 is borrowed for 4 years at 11%.

$I = 5{,}000 \times 0.11 \times 4$
$\quad = 2{,}200$
$A = 5{,}000 + 2{,}200 = 7{,}200$

The interest is $2,200 and the amount to be repaid is $7,200.

C Suppose you earned $270 last year in an account that pays 6% interest. What was your principal at the beginning of the year?

$I = PRT$ or $P = \dfrac{I}{RT}$

$P = \dfrac{270}{0.06} = 4{,}500$
The principal was $4,500.

TRY IT OUT

Find the interest (I) and the total amount (A) in each of these problems.

1. $P = \$1{,}200$
   $R = 8\%$
   $T = 2$ years

2. $P = \$5{,}500$
   $R = 7\%$
   $T = 6$ months

3. $P = \$3{,}500$
   $R = 12.5\%$
   $T = 36$ months

Find the interest (*I*) and the amount (*A*).

1. *P* = $140
   R = 5%
   T = 1 yr

2. *P* = $6,500
   R = 8%
   T = 3 yr

3. *P* = $670
   R = 9.5%
   T = 2 yr

4. *P* = $1,300
   R = 15.5%
   T = 4 yr

5. *P* = $5,000
   R = 4.8%
   T = 6 yr

6. *P* = $1
   R = 12%
   T = 20 yr

7. *P* = $850
   R = 6%
   T = 3 months

8. *P* = $2,500
   R = 13%
   T = 6 months

9. *P* = $1,500, *R* = 7%, and *I* = $420.
   Find *T*

10. *P* = $4,500, *I* = $90 and *T* = 2
   months. Find *R*

MATH REASONING Use mental math to answer these questions.

11. 5% simple interest for 2 years earns
   the same as 10% simple interest for
   __?__ years?

12. 12% simple interest for 4 years earns
   the same as 6% simple interest for
   __?__ years.

PROBLEM SOLVING

13. Twins go to a bank where one borrows
   $350 at 14% interest for 2 years and the
   other deposits $350 at 6.5% for 2 years.
   How much does the bank earn from
   these twins over the two years?

14. You discover a savings account that
   was opened $50\frac{1}{2}$ years ago. The account
   has earned $631.25 at a simple interest
   rate of 5% per year. How much was the
   original deposit?

▶ **CALCULATOR**

Suppose you now make $21,500 a year. You are offered a
14.5% raise, but will not get another for four years. Or you
can have a 5% raise each year for four years. Which is the
better offer?

Making Circle Graphs

You will find a percent of 360 when you construct a circle graph.

LEARN ABOUT IT

EXPLORE Study the Graph

A survey asked teenagers, "How many hours a week do you work?" Their responses are given below:

Less than 6 hours	12%
6 hours to 9 hours	33%
9 hours to 12 hours	42%
12 hours to 15 hours	12%
More than 15 hours	1%

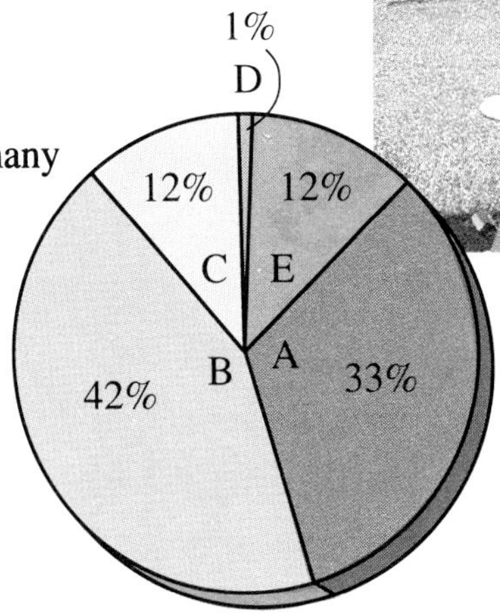

TALK ABOUT IT

1. What is the sum of the angles A, B, C, D, and E?

2. Why might you estimate the measure of angle A to be 120°?

3. Why do you know that the measure of angle D is exactly 3.6°?

Here's how to make a circle graph:

- Draw a circle and put a point at the center.
- Use a calculator as shown at the right to compute the number of degrees for each central angle of the graph.
- The sum of all these angles must be 360°, which represents the whole, or 100%.
- Use a protractor to draw each sector.
- Label each part and title the graph.

Number of Degrees in Each Angle

A: 360 $\times$ 33 % = **118.8** about 119°

B: 360 $\times$ 42 % = **151.2** about 151°

C: 360 $\times$ 12 % = 43.2 about 43°

D: 360 $\times$ 1 % = 3.6 about 4°

E: 360 $\times$ 12 % = 43.2 about 43°

TRY IT OUT

1. Find the number of degrees in each central angle. Draw the circle graph.

   Survey question: How much does lunch cost at school?

Less than $0.75	3%
$0.76 to $1.50	30%
$1.51 to $2.25	54%
$2.26 to $3.00	5%
More than $3.01	8%

Use your calculator to find the measure of the central angles.

1. Survey questions: How long are each of your classes?

less than 40 min	18%
41 min to 45 min	42%
46 min to 50 min	22%
more than 50 min	18%

2. Survey question: How much time do you spend studying each night?

less than 30 min	19%
31 min to 60 min	48%
61 min to 90 min	21%
more than 90 min	12%

Use a calculator to find the measure of each central angle.
Draw the circle graph to display the data.

3. Survey question: What do you do on your summer vacations?

go to camp	12%
work	41%
go on a family trip	11%
go to summer school	15%
other	21%

4. Survey question: What is your favorite subject?

English	14%	P.E.	11%
History	18%	Music	8%
Science	21%	Other	13%
Math	15%		

MATH REASONING You can estimate to check a circle graph.
Estimate the central angle for each of these percents.

5. For a percent close to 25%, you will draw an angle close to __?__°.

6. For a percent close to $33\frac{1}{3}$%, you will draw an angle close to __?__.°

7. For a percent close to 50%, you will draw an angle close to __?__.°

8. For a percent close to 20%, you will draw an angle close to __?__.°

Find the unit price to the nearest cent.

9. 1.8 L for $1.29 **10.** 16 oz for $0.99 **11.** 12 cans for $4.59

12. Find the mean, median and mode for these test scores.
97, 95, 76, 87, 57, 72, 65, 77, 87, 73, 72, 72, 75, 76

Problem Solving
Problems Without Solutions

| UNDERSTAND |
| ANALYZE DATA |
| PLAN |
| ESTIMATE |
| SOLVE |
| EXAMINE |

LEARN ABOUT IT

For some problems, no solution is possible. In this problem, you can use the strategy Make an Organized List to show that there is no solution.

> Darcy bought some cheese snacks at the grocery store. The total for her purchase was $2.46. She gave the clerk $3.00 and received 7 coins for change. What coins did the clerk give Darcy?

To get $0.54, Darcy had to have 4 pennies. Make an organized list of all the possibilities for the other 3 coins.

Q	3	2	2	1	1	1	0	0	0	0
D	0	1	0	2	1	0	3	2	1	0
N	0	0	1	0	1	2	0	1	2	3
P	4	4	4	4	4	4	4	4	4	4
Total	79¢	64¢	59¢	49¢	44¢	39¢	34¢	29¢	24¢	19¢

The list shows that Darcy could not have received $0.54 in change.

TRY IT OUT

Solve. If there is no solution, explain why.

1. The grocery store sells Cranapple juice in 4-packs and guava juice in 6-packs. Jean bought 45 cans of juice. How many packs of each kind did she buy?

2. Emily bought 4 pounds of fruit. She gave the clerk a $5.00 bill and received $1.75 in change. What did Emily buy?

3. Peter found some bran muffin recipes in a cookbook. The recipes were on 4 consecutive pages. He noticed that the page numbers totalled 97. On what page did the recipes begin?

Bananas 50¢ lb   Apples 75¢ lb   Grapes $1.25 lb

Solve. Use any problem solving strategy.

1. A single roll of paper towels costs $0.79. If you buy a case of 24 rolls, the price per roll is 12% less. About how much do you save per roll?

2. During a 5 year period, the price of coffee beans increased from $4.50 a pound to $6.30 a pound. Find the percent of increase.

3. Geraldo is cutting small circular pizzas into 12 pie-shaped pieces for a sample tray. He has 15 pizzas to cut. What is the least number of cuts he can make?

4. Tillamook cheese regularly sells for $2.85 a pound. This week it is on special for 20% off. How much will 3 pounds of cheese cost?

5. The graph shows sales in the meat and fish department for 1 week. They sold 775 separate items. Use the graph to find how many of the items were either fish or poultry.

6. Mrs. Nakagiri kept her weekly grocery receipts for one month. She spent $92.56 the first week, $107.21 the second week, $89.78 the third week, and $103.09 the fourth week. What was her average weekly grocery bill?

7. A box of cereal that regularly sells for $2.50 is on special for $1.90. What percent discount is that?

8. **Talking About Your Solution** The grocery store sells new potatoes in 3-lb bags and russet potatoes in 5-lb bags. Dennis bought 45 lbs of potatoes in 10 bags. How many bags of russet potatoes did he buy?

   Explain your solution to a classmate. Compare your solutions. Which solution do you think is better? Why?

Data Collection and Analysis
Group Decision Making

UNDERSTAND
ANALYZE DATA
PLAN
ESTIMATE
SOLVE
EXAMINE

Doing a Questionnaire

Group Skill:
Disagree in an Agreeable Way

Is there someone in your group that you think has a similar personality to yours? Is there someone that you think has a totally opposite personality from yours? Make a questionnaire to help you find out how well your personalities match, or **correlate.**

Collecting Data

1. Your group will design a questionnaire about personality. List at least 10 aspects of personality that you could use on the questionnaire. For example, you might want to know if a person has a temper, is shy, or likes to be alone.

2. Decide which personality traits to use for your questionnaire. The questionnaire will include at least 10 rating questions. The questions will be rated on a scale from 1 to 20.

3. Test the questionnaire to see if there are any parts that are unclear. Revise if necessary. Then make a copy of the questionnaire for each person in your group and for anyone else that you want to compare personalities with.

4. Have each person in the group fill out the questionnaire privately.

Questionnaire

Rate each question using a number from 1 to 20.   Rating

1. How shy are you?
   1 = very shy   20 = not shy at all   _____

2. Are you easy going?
   1 = very easy going   20 = not easy going   _____

3. Are you hot tempered?
   1 = very hot tempered   20 = not hot tempered _____

5. Work with a partner to make a scattergraph using the data in your questionnaires. Write your name and your partner's name along the scales of the scattergraph. Plot a point for each question on the questionnaire. Each point will represent an ordered pair showing how you rated the question and how your partner rated the question.

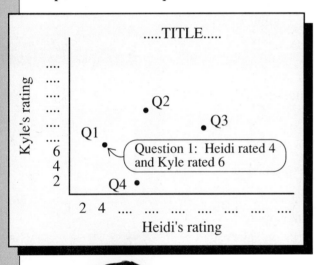

6. Choose different partners and make another scattergraph.

7. Look at the scattergraphs made in your group. How are they alike? How are they different? What would a scattergraph look like if you and your partner agreed exactly on every question?

8. Be prepared to discuss these questions with the rest of the class. Which graphs in your group look alike? Which show almost no agreement at all? How would the graph look if there are only one or two things you disagree about?

WRAP UP

Express Yourself

Give a mathematical expression for each of the following. Use decimals or fractions.

1. fifteen percent of sixty

2. five percent of some number

3. twelve percent of two hundred

4. twenty percent of forty-eight

5. twelve percent commission on two hundred dollars worth of sales

6. the number that is twenty percent of eighty.

7. the percent of increase if the number of auto thefts rose from 50 to 55

8. the percent represented by seven out of twenty-eight

9. the number that is thirty percent of ninety

10. a discount of eight percent on a twenty-dollar item

Sometimes, Always, Never

Decide if each of these statements is sometimes true, always true, or never true. Explain your choices.

11. The percent of a number is __?__ less than that number.

12. A change in the price of an item can __?__ be expressed as a percent of increase or a percent of decrease.

13. A person who works on commission __?__ makes more money at the same job than a person who works on salary.

Project

In your local newspaper find 5 items on sale. Calculate the percent of decrease for each item.

POWER PRACTICE/TEST

Part 1   Understanding

1. During last season, Mark averaged 8 points per game. This season he increased his average 50%. What does this mean?

A His average per game doubled.

B This season he averaged 5 points per game.

C This season he averaged 4 points per game.

D This season he averaged 12 points per game.

2. A landlord raised the rent 5% in January. She raised it another 5% in August. Is this the same as raising the rent 10% in August, and not raising it at all in January?

3. Choose the percent that is the best estimate for $\frac{15}{57}$.

A 20%   B 30%   C 25%   D 35%

Part 2   Skills

4. Find the total monthly pay.
total sales: $8,000
commission: 5%
monthly salary: $400

5. Find the measure of the central angles for a circle graph for the data below.

What grade did you earn in history?

A 10%   B 25%

C 40%   D 15%

Find the percent of increase or decrease.

6. 30 to 40   **7.** 70 to 35   **8.** 24 to 30

9. Estimate 38.7% of 248.   **10.** Estimate what percent 404 is of 599.

Use the information at the right for problems 11 and 12.

regular price: $40.00
discount percent: 25%

11. Find the discount.   **12.** Find the sale price.

Part 3   Applications

13. T & T will pay you a monthly salary of $600 plus 5% commission. R & R will pay you only a 15% commission. You estimate that your sales will be $8,000 a month. At which store will you earn more?

14. Challenge Ace Store deposited $5,200 in the bank at 7% interest. It borrowed $6,500 from the bank at 14%. How much will the bank earn from Ace this year? How much would Ace need to deposit so the bank and store would come out even?

ENRICHMENT
Compound Interest

If you had $500 in a savings account and earned 6% interest per year you could use the **simple interest** formula to find the interest you would earn in 2 years.

$$I = Prt \quad P = \$500, \quad r = 0.06, \, t = 2.$$
$$I = \$500 \cdot 0.06 \cdot 2 = \$60.00$$

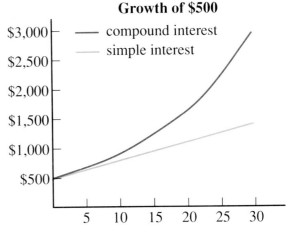

Growth of $500
— compound interest
— simple interest

Most banks and other financial institutions use **compound interest** instead of simple interest. The interest earned for each period is added on to the principal and interest is then calculated on the new amount. Money grows much more rapidly using compound interest.

The formula for computing the amount using compound interest is.

$$A = P(1 + r)^n$$
$A =$ amount, $P =$ principal, $r =$ interest rate per period
$n =$ number of periods.

Example: What would principal of $500 amount to in 2 years at an interest rate of 6% per year compounded 4 times a year?

Solution: $P = 500$, $n = 8$ (4 · 2 year), $r = 0.015$ (0.06 ÷ 4)

Use a calculator to find A.

Display

1 $\boxed{+}$ 0.015 $\boxed{=}$ $\boxed{y^x}$ $\boxed{8}$ $\boxed{=}$ $\boxed{\times}$ 500 $\boxed{=}$ 563.24629
$A = \$563.25$.

Find the total amount using the compound interest formula.

1. Savings account:
   $P = 800 \, I = 6\%$ per year
   Compounding quarterly.
   Time = 4 years ($n = 16$)
   $r = 0.015$

2. Money Market Fund
   $P = \$1500, \, I = 9\%$ per year
   Compounding monthly.
   Time = 1 year ($n = 12$)
   $r = 0.0075$

3. Suppose you put $1,000 in one account that earns 9% per year simple interest. Then you put $1,000 in another account earning 9% interest per year, compounded quarterly. About how long would it take each account to double to an amount of $2,000?

306

CUMULATIVE REVIEW

1. Divide.

$$-2 \div \frac{3}{4}$$

   A $2\frac{2}{3}$ **B** $\frac{3}{8}$

   C $-2\frac{2}{3}$ **D** $-1\frac{1}{2}$

2. Which is standard notation for 2.8×10^{-5}?

   A 28,000   **B** 280,000

   C 0.000028   **D** 0.00028

3. Which proportion is correct?

   A $\frac{14}{5} = \frac{28}{10}$ **B** $\frac{7}{8} = \frac{12}{15}$

   C $\frac{3}{8} = \frac{4}{10}$ **D** $\frac{3}{48} = \frac{5}{76}$

4. Simplify the rate $56 in 8h.

   A $\frac{\$7}{h}$ **B** $\frac{\$8}{h}$

   C $448   **D** $\frac{\$42}{6h}$

5. Which is the better buy for tomato sauce?

   A 3 cans for $0.70

   B 5 cans for $1.00

   C 6 cans for $1.25

   D 1 can for $0.22

6. Which does not describe the shaded part of the grid?

   A 28%

   B 0.28

   C 100 out of 28

   D $\frac{28}{100}$

7. What percent of 50 is 19?

   A 2.63%   **B** 263%

   C 3.8%   **D** 38%

8. Which is the percent for 0.092?

   A 9.2%   **B** 92%

   C 0.92%   **D** 920%

9. Which is 16% of 500?

   A 32   **B** 8

   C 80   **D** 31.25

10. What percent of 45 is 18?

   A 8.1%   **B** 2.5%

   C 25%   **D** 40%

11. 56% of what number is 28?

   A 52   **B** 56

   C 35   **D** 50

12. Evaluate.

$$\frac{2^2 (50 - 35)}{15 - (2^3 + 2)}$$

   A $\frac{2}{5}$ **B** 12

   C $\frac{60}{7}$ **D** 6

13. Artie, Bruno, Kit, and Jasper went camping. Each person took a different kind of light—a candle, matches, a flashlight, and a lantern. Bruno did not have the matches. Artie needed oil for his light. Jasper borrowed the matches to start his light. What kind of light did Bruno have?

   A lantern   **B** flashlight

   C matches   **D** candle

11

MATH AND
SOCIAL STUDIES

DATA BANK

Use the Social Studies Data
Bank on page 499 to answer
the questions.

1 How many toll center and
system codes are there that
begin with 0?

DISCRETE
MATH:
COUNTING
PROBLEMS

THEME: COMMUNICATION

2 How many area codes are there that begin with 2 or 3?

3 How many different central office codes are there that begin with 6, 7, 8, or 9?

4 **Using Critical Thinking** In the United States long distance calls usually start with a 1. This means that there can be more 10-digit phone numbers. Explain, and make up a phone number that could not be used without the 1.

Signals carrying the voices of thousands of people pass through these phone lines.

The Basic Counting Principle

LEARN ABOUT IT

EXPLORE **Study the diagram**

If you phone a friend in another town, your call may be routed along a choice of paths. First it goes to the end office for your prefix. It is then switched along one of several paths through a regional center. Think about the different paths a call from 454-6536 may take via the regional center to 555-1457.

TALK ABOUT IT

1. How many routes are there between the 454 end office and the regional center?

2. If the call gets to the regional center via route A, how many choices of routes does it have to the 555 office?

One way to count all the routes is to use a **tree diagram.**

Another way is to use the **Basic Counting Principle.**

Basic Counting Principle			
To find the total number of outcomes for an event, multiply the number of choices for completing each step of the outcome.	3 × 4 = 12
	routes to regional center	routes from regional center	routes in all

TRY IT OUT

1. Use a tree diagram to find how many complete paths are possible if a call has 3 possible routes to the first stage, 3 routes to the second stage and 2 routes to the third stage? Check your answer by using the basic counting principle.

Draw a tree diagram to answer each of these questions.

1. A model of telephone comes in red, white, black, or brown, with either push button or a dial. How many different orders could be placed for this model?

2. A certain model of car comes in either a 4-door or a 2-door, 5 speed or automatic transmission, and in either red, green, or blue. How many different orders can be placed for this model car?

Use the basic counting principle to answer these questions.

3. Doug drives from Albatross to Medusa, via Pandora. How many routes are there from Albatross to Medusa?

4. How many round trip routes are there from Albatross to Medusa and back?

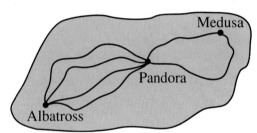

5. A type of telephone cord is available either coiled or straight. It comes in the lengths 6 ft, 15 ft and 25 ft, and in the colors black, white, brown, beige or red. How many different orders could be placed for the cord?

MATH REASONING

6. Suppose an engine serial number consists of a letter of the alphabet followed by 3 digits. Are there less than or more than 10,000 serial numbers possible?

PROBLEM SOLVING

7. Suppose that all the license plates issued in one community are either AXT followed by 3 digits or ATB followed by 2 digits and then a letter. How many license plates can be issued?

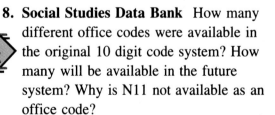

8. **Social Studies Data Bank** How many different office codes were available in the original 10 digit code system? How many will be available in the future system? Why is N11 not available as an office code?

USING CRITICAL THINKING Use Logic

9. Ada, Kwan, Monique and Alex were about to sit around a table for a game. How many different ways can they sit around the table? Two arrangements are the same if everyone has the same persons to their right and left.

Permutations

EXPLORE **Complete the diagram**

Work in groups. Jo asked Lin for her phone number. Instead of telling the number, Jo told Lin that its prefix was 555 and the last digits were 1, 6, 8, and 9. How many possible phone numbers are there?

TALK ABOUT IT

First Digit   1

Second Digit   6   8

Third Digit   8   9   6

Fourth Digit   9   8

1. The tree shows how many arrangements?

2. Draw a tree diagram showing all possible arrangements with the number 6 in the first place.

A **permutation** is an arrangement of objects in a particular order. You can use the basic counting principle to find the number of different permutations of Lin's number.

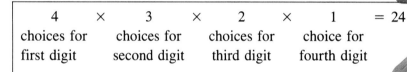

4	×	3	×	2	×	1	= 24
choices for first digit		choices for second digit		choices for third digit		choice for fourth digit	

There are 24 different permutations for Lin's number.

This product **4 × 3 × 2 × 1** is called **4-factorial** or **4!** If *n* is a whole number,
$n! = n \times (n - 1) \times (n - 2) \ldots \times 2 \times 1.$

Example

If 3 telephone books are selected from 6 telephone books and arranged on a shelf, 120 permutations are possible.

6	×	5	×	4	= 120
choices for first book		choices for second book		choices for third book	

1. How many permutations are there of the letters S, O, T, P?

2. How many permutations are there of Paul, Genaro, and Nancy?

Find the number of permutations of each set of objects.

1. D, E, N

2. a, b, c, d

3. ace, king, queen

4. math, science, history, English, and Spanish

5. 1, 4, 6, 7, 8, 9

6. Sue, Matt, Katty

Evaluate each of these factorial expressions.

7. 6!

8. 8!

9. $5 \cdot 4!$

10. 7!

11. $2! \cdot 3!$

12. $3! \cdot 4!$

13. How many 4 digit numbers are there using 3, 5, 8, and 9?

14. How many 3 digit numbers are there using 2, 5, 7, 8, and 9?

15. In how many ways can 6 swimmers finish first, second, and third?

MATH REASONING

16. Which is larger, 4^2 or 4! ?

17. Which is larger, $3! \cdot 4!$ or $(3 \cdot 4)!$?

PROBLEM SOLVING

18. The last four digits of a telephone number are 1, 2, 3, and 4. How many different numbers satisfy this condition?

19. **Social Studies Data Bank** Could the number 241-511-7219 be a United States phone number under the present system? Could it be in the future?

Write each fraction as a decimal and a percent.

20. $\frac{1}{20}$

21. $\frac{2}{5}$

22. $\frac{300}{100}$

23. $\frac{2}{7}$

24. $\frac{5}{4}$

Find the interest (I) and the total amount (A).

25. $P = \$1,000, R = 5\%, T = 3$ years

26. $P = \$200, R = 4.5\%, T = 6$ years

Problem Solving
Problems With More Than One Answer

| UNDERSTAND |
| ANALYZE DATA |
| PLAN |
| ESTIMATE |
| SOLVE |
| EXAMINE |

LEARN ABOUT IT

Some problems have more than one answer. When you find an answer to a problem, be sure to check for other answers before stopping.

Try Guess and Check.

> Try $w=5$ and $l=5$ $A=25$ $p=20$
> Try $w=4$ and $l=5$ $A=20$ $p=18$
> Try $w=4$ and $l=4$ $A=16$ $p=16$

Now check for other answers. Make an organized list to help.

The deck could be either 3 yards wide and 6 yards long or 4 yards wide and 4 yards long.

Max built a rectangular deck. When he measured the perimeter to find how many yards of railing he needed, he noticed that the area and perimeter were the same. Find the width and the length of the deck.

w	l	A	p	
1	1	1	4	
1	2	2	6	
1	3	3	8	A and p are getting
2	2	4	8	further apart
2	3	6	10	
2	4	8	12	A and p are staying the
3	3	9	12	same distance apart
3	4	12	14	
3	5	15	16	
(3	6	18	18)	
3	7	21	20	A and p are moving apart
(4	4	16	16)	
4	5	20	18	A is getting bigger than p
5	5	25	20	When the width is
5	6	30	22	greater than 4, A
6	6	36	24	is bigger than p
6	7	42	26	

TRY IT OUT

Solve. Use any problem solving strategy.

1. A rectangular patio has an area of 48 ft². Find the perimeter of the patio.

2. Dede found $1.85 in dimes and quarters in a jacket pocket. How many quarters did she find?

3. Jeanette bought some board to build a wood deck. Some of the boards were 5 ft long. She bought 92 ft altogether. How many boards of each length did Jeanette buy?

4. Kyle and Laird both work evenings. Laird has every fourth evening off and Kyle has every third evening off. They were both off March 3. When in March are they both off again?

Solve. Use any problem solving strategy.

1. The nursery sells 5 different varieties of roses. Dana wants to plant 3 different varieties in the planters on her deck. In how many different ways can she select 3 varieties?

2. Colin is building a low railing around a triangular patio. The perimeter of the patio is 54 ft. The longest side is 5 ft shorter than twice the length of the shortest side. The remaining side is 3 ft longer than the shortest side. How long is each side?

3. The city of New Orleans owns 250 parks with a total of 4,460 acres. Find the average size of each park.

4. Redwood fence posts cost $4.15 each. Niki bought 25 6-ft posts and received a 28% discount. How much did Niki save?

5. The table mat shown is made of black and white circles joined so that black circles are at the edge and white circles are in the interior. Find the length and width when the number of white circles is the same as the number of black circles.

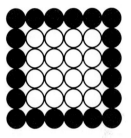

6. Kim is an apprentice carpenter. During one week he worked 36 hours and earned $369. When he completes his apprenticeship, he can earn $864 for the same number of hours. How much less does Kim make as an apprentice each week?

7. Town Builders' Supply sells brass house numbers for $3.79 each. They have all of the numbers from 0 to 9 in stock. How many different 3-digit house numbers are possible?

8. **Suppose** Juan is building a rectangular deck 15 ft wide and 18 ft long. Materials cost $3.85 per ft^2. The bid for labor is $1,150. How much will the deck cost?

   Tell which of the following information would change the solution to the problem above.

   a. The deck is 10 ft wide and 27 ft long.
   b. Materials cost $4.25 per ft^2.
   c. Juan has budgeted $2,500 for the deck.

More Practice, page 548, set B

315

Using Critical Thinking

"I created some factorial formulas!" Bob said. "Here they are."

$$\left(\frac{a}{b}\right)! = \frac{a!}{b!} \qquad (a+b)! = a! + b!$$
$$(ab)! = a! \, b! \qquad a! = a \cdot (a-1)!$$

"They look reasonable enough," Ben responded. "But you can't just make up formulas. A formula is either true or false depending on what the symbols in the formula mean."

"Now wait a minute," said Barb. "I'm not sure about that, Ben. Sometimes a formula is true for some values but not for other values. Maybe, that's what happens for these formulas."

"Maybe you're right," answered Bob. "Let's check if my formulas are correct. Suppose we substitute $a = 3$ and $b = 1$ into the first formula. Then we get $\left(\frac{3}{1}\right)! = \frac{3!}{1!}$. That's right."
"But I don't think it's always true," said Barb.

TALK ABOUT IT

1. Check the first formula for $a = 4$ and $b = 3$. Is Barb correct?

2. Do you believe that $(a + b)! = a! + b!$ for all positive number values of a and b?

3. Do you think that $(a \cdot b)!$ is ever equal to $a! \cdot b!$?

4. If a and b are both whole numbers greater than 1, are any of the above formulas true?

TRY IT OUT

Decide which of these equations are true or false.

1. $(7 - 3)! = 7! - 3!$

2. $8! = 8 \cdot 7!$

3. $\frac{4!}{2!} = 2!$

4. $\frac{5!}{4!} = 5$

5. $6! = 3! \cdot 2!$

6. $\frac{(2 + 3)!}{4!} = 5$

POWER PRACTICE/QUIZ

Draw a tree diagram or use the Basic Counting Principle to find the answers.

1. How many 2-letter words can be formed using i or a followed by n, t, or s?

2. How many 3-digit numbers use only the digits 1 and 2?

3. In how many different ways can a quiz of 5 true/false items be answered?

4. How many pizzas are possible if the choices are: small, medium, large, or jumbo size; pan style, thick, or thin crust; and 1 of 10 toppings?

5. How many 6-digit zip codes are possible if no digit is repeated?

Find the number of permutations.

6. In how many ways can 4 swimmers finish a race if there are no ties?

7. In how many ways can 3 students be arranged in a row of 5 desks?

8. In how many ways can a president, vice president, secretary, and treasurer be elected from a math club with 20 members?

9. If 6 students are finalists in a speech contest, in how many different orders can the students give their speeches? In how many ways can the students rank first, second, and third?

Evaluate each of these factorial expressions.

10. 6!   11. 5!   12. $6! \cdot 3!$

PROBLEM SOLVING

13. On a 20-item quiz, students can receive 4 points full credit, 3 points partial credit, or 1 point for trying. In how many ways can someone score exactly 15 points?

14. Each question on a 10-item multiple choice test has 4 choices. If 1 million people took the test, is it possible that none would answer exactly the same?

15. On five true/false questions, Errol is sure the fourth question is false. With these three clues, he knows all the correct answers. What are they?

#1. There are more true than false answers.
#2. No three consecutive questions have the same answer.
#3. The first and fifth questions have opposite answers.

Combinations

EXPLORE Fill in the Table

Work in groups. Tonya, Cathy, Dave, and Kuey are on the ballot for the student council. The election judge reports the first and second place winners.

- Make a list of all the possible outcomes of the election.
- Make a list of all the pairs who could be selected to the student council.

Report to Election Judge	
Highest number of votes	Second Highest number of votes

TALK ABOUT IT

1. Would (Tonya, Dave) and (Dave, Tonya) be counted as different on the report?

2. Would the listings (Tonya, Dave) and (Dave, Tonya) be considered the same in the school paper?

The election judge distinguishes between the order of the two candidates; he is concerned with **permutations.** The students, on the other hand are concerned only with which two students are selected. They are not concerned with order.

A selection of a number of objects from a set of objects, without regard to order, is called a **combination** of the objects.

List of Permutations					
C, D	C, J	C, T	D, J	D, T	J, T
D, C	J, C	T, C	J, D	T, D	T, J

Selections		
C and D	C and J	C and T
D and J	D and T	J and T

Number of Combinations of 2 selected from 4. $= \dfrac{4 \cdot 3}{2 \cdot 1}$ $\dfrac{\text{permutations of 2 students from 4 students}}{\text{permutation of 2 students from 2 students}}$

Examples Find the number of combinations.

A Choose 3 candidates from 7.

$$\frac{7 \times 6 \times 5}{3 \times 2 \times 1} = 35$$

B Choose 4 candidates from 6.

$$\frac{6 \times 5 \times 4 \times 3}{4 \times 3 \times 2 \times 1} = 15$$

Find the number of combinations.

1. 2 letters from E, L, and K

2. 3 people from a group of 6

Find the number of combinations.

1. 2 names selected from 3 names

2. 3 shirts selected from 6 shirts

3. 2 numbers selected from 10, 15, 20, and 25

4. 3 colors selected from red, green, blue, yellow

5. 4 persons selected from 5 persons

6. 4 books selected from 6 books

7. 5 finalists out of 10 contenders

8. 3 songs from the top ten

9. 4 gifts from a sack of 5 gifts

10. 1 gift from a sack of 5 gifts

11. How many pairs of doubles partners can be selected on a tennis team of 5 players?

12. How many different 3 person committees can be selected from a club with 7 members?

APPLY

MATH REASONING Which is larger, the number of combinations of:

13. a) 2 things or b) 3 things   selected from 6?

14. a) 2 things or b) 5 things   selected from 5?

PROBLEM SOLVING

15. At the first meeting of the Newcomer's Club, each of the 12 members present shook hands with each other person. How many handshakes were there?

16. Jack put five nails around a circle. If a rubberband is stretched around every three nails, how many rubberbands are needed?

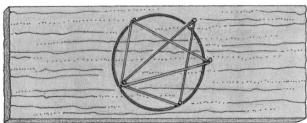

▶ **EXPLORING ALGEBRA**

The number of combinations of r objects selected from n objects, can be found by using the function $C(n, r) = \dfrac{n!}{r!\,(n - r)!}$. Use this formula to find each of these numbers.

17. $C(5, 3)$ **18.** $C(7, 3)$ **19.** $C(9, 5)$ **20.** $C(11, 8)$

Pascal's Triangle and Combinations

```
                              1 ——————————— row 0
                          1     1 ——————————— row 1
                       1     2     1 ——————————— row 2
                    1     3     3     1 ——————————— row 3
                 1    (4)    6     4     1 ——————— row 4
              1     5    10    10     5     1 ——— row 5
           1     6    15    20    (15)    6     1 — row 6
```

LEARN ABOUT IT

EXPLORE Extend Pascal's Triangle

- How are the two circled numbers related to the two numbers directly above?
- Does this relationship hold for all numbers in the triangle?
- Copy this array of numbers and add another 3 rows on your copy.

TALK ABOUT IT

1. You can add as many rows to Pascal's Triangle as you like. There is no last row. In which row does the number 84 appear? In which row does the number 210 appear?

2. How do the entries in Row 4 relate to the number of combinations of 4 objects?

Examples

A How many committees of 4 can be selected from 7 persons? The answer can be found in row 7 of Pascal's Triangle. Begin counting at zero and count across the row to number 4. The answer is 35.

Row 7	1	7	21	35	35	21	7	1
number of	zero	one	two	three	four	five	six	seven
combinations	selected from 7 objects							

B How many combinations are there of 3 names selected from 6 names?
- **20** Begin at zero and count across row 6 to entry number 3.

C How many combinations are there of 10 things taken 5 at a time?
- **252** Begin at zero and count across row 10 to entry number 5.

TRY IT OUT

Use Pascal's Triangle to find these answers.

1. How many combinations are there of 7 things taken 5 at a time?

2. How many different teams of 2 can be selected from 8 people?

Use the first ten rows of Pascal's Triangle to find the following values.

1. How many combinations of 10 things taken 4 at a time?

2. How many combinations of 10 things taken 6 at a time?

3. How many combinations of 7 things taken 4 at a time?

4. How many combinations of 8 things taken 3 at a time?

5. How many 4-person relay teams are possible from a track team with 9 runners?

6. How many ways are there for students to choose any 4 of the 5 problems on a quiz?

7. Three consecutive numbers in one row of Pascal's Triangle are shown. What are the two numbers in the next row of the triangle?

   66   220   495
      [?]   [?]

MATH REASONING Are these statements true or false? If false, give a counterexample.

8. A number does not appear in more than one row of Pascal's Triangle.

9. From row 4 on, the middle number in each row is an even number.

PROBLEM SOLVING

10. The Art Club has 12 members. How many projects committees can be formed if 6 members are to be on each?

    MIXED REVIEW

Find the answers.

11. 16% of 100

12. 22% of 200

13. 45% of 80

14. 8% of 300

15. What percent of 50 is 45?

16. 82 is what percent of 90?

17. 6 out of 20 is what percent?

18. What percent is 5 out of 250?

19. $-\frac{7}{8} + -\frac{5}{6}$

20. $-\frac{2}{7} \cdot -\frac{14}{15}$

21. $14\frac{1}{3} + -12\frac{2}{5}$

22. $2\frac{4}{5} \div 4\frac{2}{3}$

Exploring Algebra
Interpreting and Graphing Inequalities

EXPLORE Consider the Situation

Consider a pitching machine that throws balls in a target region. The machine pitches 1,000 balls and the distance (*d*) from the center of the target is recorded for each throw. The distribution of distances is shaped like a bell. The shape of the bell is determined by the values in a row of Pascal's Triangle. How do we communicate precisely about these distances?

TALK ABOUT IT

1. How is "*d* is less than 8" written mathematically?

2. How is "*d* is greater than or equal to 5" written?

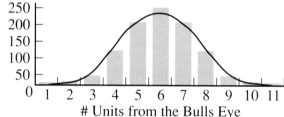

Units from the Bulls Eye

3. How do we write, "*d* is not greater than 7"?

Inequality symbols $<$, $>$, $\leq$, $\geq$ are used to describe values that a variable may have. These values can be graphed on the number line.

Examples Graph each on a number line.

A *x* is less than 10
  $x < 10$ or $10 > x$

B *k* is greater than -3 and less than or equal to 50.
  $-3 < k \leq 50$

The hole at 10 shows that *x* cannot be 10.

k cannot be -3 *k* can be 50

Write an inequality and draw a graph on a number line.

1. *y* is less than or equal to 15

2. *m* is greater than -20 and less than 2.

3. *x* is greater than 7 and less than 9

4. *d* is between 3 and 8.

Write an inequality.

1. temperature t is less than 48°F

2. their score s was at least 10 points

3. Maria's height h is more than 6 feet

4. his account a is overdrawn at least $6

Write an inequality and draw a graph.

5. x is greater than 21

6. y is greater than -8 and less than 12

7. t is less than 32 but greater than 0

8. k is greater than or equal to -7 and less than 7

Write the inequality described by each graph.

9.

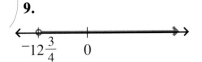

10.

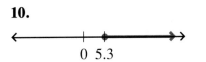

11.

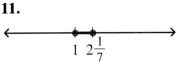

12.

13.

14.

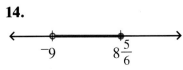

MATH REASONING

15. The graph of an inequality doesn't have to be on the number line. Trace the clock to the right. Use it to show time t is 6:00 pm or 8:30 pm, or maybe sometime in between.

PROBLEM SOLVING

16. If you travel 300 miles in less than 5 hours, what can you say about your speed?

▶ **USING CRITICAL THINKING   Justify your answer**

17. x is greater than or equal to 5 is written $x \geq 5$. Its graph is:

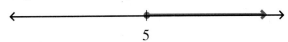

Think carefully about the numbers that would result in a true sentence if substituted for y in $|y| \geq 5$. Draw a graph to show these numbers. Explain your graph.

Problem Solving
Using the Strategies

UNDERSTAND
ANALYZE DATA
PLAN
ESTIMATE
SOLVE
EXAMINE

LEARN ABOUT IT

You have learned that using more than one strategy is often helpful when solving a problem. To solve this problem, you can use the strategies **Solve a Simpler Problem, Draw a Picture,** and **Look for a Pattern.**

> Rod lives on the corner of 1st Street and A Street. Dan lives on the corner of 5th Street and E Street. If Rod only walks east and south, how many different ways can he walk to Dan's house?

Begin with a simpler problem and Draw a Picture. The numbers show how many ways you can get to each corner.

Now Look for a Pattern in the numbers.

The number at the corners are the same as the numbers in Pascal's Triangle.

Rod can walk to Dan's house in 70 different ways.

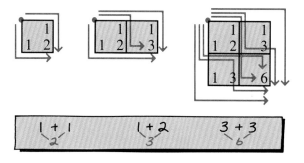

	1	1	1	1
1	2	3	4	5
1	3	+ ↓ 6	10	15
1	4	10	20	+ ↓ →35
1	5	15	35	+ ↓ →70

TRY IT OUT

1. How many different ways can you get from A to B in the figure below if you only go to the right and down?

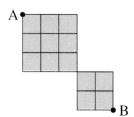

2. A patio is constructed from 100 tiles using the pattern shown. How many tiles are there in the middle row?

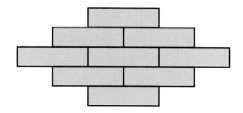

Some Strategies	
Act Out	Solve a Simpler Problem
Use Objects	Make an Organized List
Choose an Operation	Work Backward
Draw a Picture	Look for a Pattern
Guess and Check	Use Logical Reasoning
Make a Table	Write an Equation

Solve. Use any problem solving strategy.

1. The house numbers of Zu's block begin with a 3. Each number has 4 digits and ends with an even number. How many different house numbers are possible?

2. The picture below shows part of the brick border along one side of a lawn. If the border is 15 bricks long, how many different rectangles can you find?

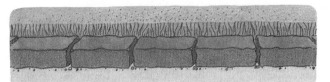

3. Three boys and 5 girls volunteered to participate in the spring festival committee. In how many ways could 3 of them be selected?

4. Leah, Perry, Jan, and Dana all walk to school 5 days a week. Perry walks twice as far as Dana. Leah walks 4 blocks less than Perry. Jan walks $\frac{1}{4}$ as far as Dana. Leah walks 12 blocks to school. How far does Jan walk?

5. Tanya lives $1\frac{1}{2}$ miles from school. Each week she spends 48 minutes more than Christy walking to school. If Christy spends 3 hours and 25 minutes, how much time does Tanya spend?

6. Dave rides the city bus to school every day. It costs $0.85 one way. If he buys a book of 16 tickets, he saves 15%. How much does the book of tickets cost?

7. Maria wants to go from Cedar Rapids to Fairfield. Use the picture to find how many different ways she can go.

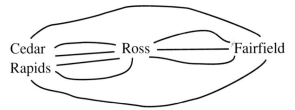

8. Aaron, Brad, Carlos, and Fred have different jobs. One is an artist, one a banker, one a contractor, and one a fireman. Only one person's name starts with the same letter as the job. Carlos is richer than either the banker or Fred. The fireman is younger than Aaron. Brad is the oldest and is a good friend of the banker. Carlos is older than Aaron. Who has which job?

More Practice, page 547, set B

Applied Problem Solving
Group Decision Making

UNDERSTAND
ANALYZE DATA
PLAN
ESTIMATE
SOLVE
EXAMINE

Group Skill:
Listen to others

You are part of a committee which will award a scholarship to an outstanding student at your school. The candidates for the scholarship have been narrowed to five students. Your group must decide which student is most qualified from the criteria available.

Facts to Consider

1. The chart summarizes the data for each candidate. The grade point average is based on a 4.0 being equivalent to an A. The number of points possible in each category is shown in parentheses.

2. You may decide that one category is worth more than another category. You can devise a way to adjust the points in that category to make them worth more.

Candidate	Essay (25)	Recommendations (25)	Community/School Activities (25)	Sports Activities (25)	Grades (4.0)
A	23	20	18	25	3.78
B	20	18	21	19	3.60
C	21	25	23	18	3.67
D	25	23	18	20	3.05
E	24	15	20	15	3.95

1. What is the total number of points possible for the first four categories? What percent of this total did each candidate score?

2. In the chart the ratios of the number of points possible in the first four categories is 25:25:25:25 or 1:1:1:1. Suppose you want to make the essay worth twice as much as the other categories. In other words, the ratios would be 50:25:25:25 or 2:1:1:1. How would you adjust the essay score for candidate A? What percent of the total points would candidate A earn for the first four categories?

3. Suppose you want the ratios of the first four categories to be 2:2:1:1. How would you adjust the scores for candidate C? What percent of the total points would candidate C earn?

4. How will you use the grade point average to help you decide who is the best candidate?

What Is Your Decision?

Which candidate did your group select? Defend your decision. What ratios did you use to adjust the scores? Give the overall percentage score for each candidate according to your scoring system.

WRAP UP

Writing in Math

Answer the following questions in your own words.

1. What is the difference between a permutation and a combination?

2. What is the Basic Counting Principle?

3. Explain the term factorial.

4. How does a tree diagram work?

5. What is the difference between an arrangement and a selection?

6. Describe Pascal's Triangle.

7. How can you use Pascal's Triangle to determine combinations?

Sometimes, Always, Never

Which of these words should go in the blank, sometimes, always, or never? Explain your choice.

8. $5!$ is _____ larger than 5^3.

9. The number of permutations for 10 people sitting in a circle is _____ less than the number of permutations of 10 people standing in line.

10. The number of combinations of objects taken three at a time is _____ greater than the number of combinations of objects taken two at a time.

11. A row of Pascal's Triangle will _____ have at least one even number.

Project

The triangular array shown below is called the Harmonic Triangle of Leibniz. Can you determine how the terms are related? Look at the terms along the diagonals that form the sides of the triangle. How do the numbers relate to Pascal's Triangle? Can you predict the next row of the Harmonic Triangle?

$$\frac{1}{1}$$
$$\frac{1}{2} \quad \frac{1}{2}$$
$$\frac{1}{3} \quad \frac{1}{6} \quad \frac{1}{3}$$
$$\frac{1}{4} \quad \frac{1}{12} \quad \frac{1}{12} \quad \frac{1}{4}$$
$$\frac{1}{5} \quad \frac{1}{20} \quad \frac{1}{30} \quad \frac{1}{20} \quad \frac{1}{5}$$
$$\frac{1}{6} \quad \frac{1}{30} \quad \frac{1}{60} \quad \frac{1}{60} \quad \frac{1}{30} \quad \frac{1}{6}$$

POWER PRACTICE/TEST

Part 1 Understanding

1. A store carries a popular shirt in all sizes and colors. What information do you need to find the minimum number of shirts that will be ordered?

Use this information for 2 and 3: Kara may select from 12 different subjects. There are 8 class periods per day.

2. Write a question based on this and permutations.

3. Write a question based on this and combinations.

4. Which is larger, 3! or 3^3?

5. Row 7 of Pascal's Triangle is: 1 7 21 35 35 21 7 1. What is row 8?

Part 2 Skills

Find the number of permutations of each.

6. q, r, s, t

7. 3 letters out of a, b, c, d, e

8. Evaluate 3! · 5!.

9. Find the number of combinations of 4 tapes selected from 7 tapes.

10. Use the formula $C(n,r) = \dfrac{n!}{r!(n-r)!}$ to find the number of combinations of 8 objects selected from 12 objects.

11. Use rows 7 and 8 of Pascal's triangle (problem 5) to find the number of combinations of 8 things taken 7 at a time.

Write an inequality and draw a graph for each.

12. *t* is less than 2

13. *v* is greater than ⁻3 and less than or equal to 4

Part 3 Applications

14. A deck has an area of 72 ft². The length of each side is a whole number of feet, and no side of the deck is less than 4 ft long. Find its perimeter.

15. Challenge Juan lives at the corner of 1st and D Street. The school is at 4th and A Street. If he only walks north and east, how many different ways can he walk from home to school?

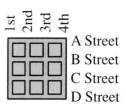

329

ENRICHMENT
The Fibonacci Sequence

Leonardo of Pisa (c. 1170–1250), nicknamed Fibonacci, discovered the number sequence below. It is called the Fibonacci sequence.

1, 1, 2, 3, 5, 8, 13 . . .

Can you guess what the next few numbers would be?

Study the pattern below:

1 + 1 = 2	1 + 2 = 3
2 + 3 = 5	3 + 5 = 8
5 + 8 = 13	8 + 13 = ?
13 + ? = ?	

Continue this pattern to find more numbers in the Fibonacci sequence.

1. List the first 25 numbers in the Fibonacci sequence.

2. Study the pattern below.

$$1 + 1 = 3 \ - 1 = 2$$
$$1 + 1 + 2 = 5 \ - 1 = 4$$
$$1 + 1 + 2 + 3 = 8 \ - 1 = 7$$
$$1 + 1 + 2 + 3 + 5 = 13 - 1 = 12$$

Write the next three rows in this pattern.

3. Use the pattern found in problem 2 to give the sum of the first ten numbers in the Fibonacci sequence.

4. Find the sum of the first 30 numbers in the Fibonacci sequence.

5. Count the number of petals in the center of the drawing of the sunflower. Then count the number of clockwise spirals circling out from the center. Finally, count the number of petals in the outermost part of the flower. How do these numbers relate to the Fibonacci sequence?

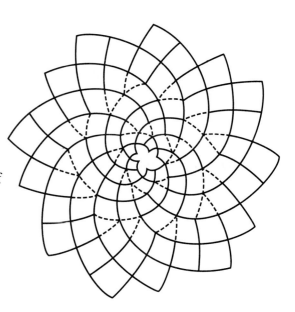

CUMULATIVE REVIEW

1. △ ABC ~ △ XYZ. Find length x.

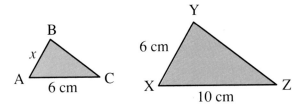

    A 10 cm   **B** 3.6 cm   **C** 3 cm   **D** 2 cm

2. Find the length of x to the nearest tenth.

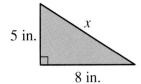

    A 3.6 in.

    B 13 in.

    C 6.2 in.

    D 9.4 in.

3. Which is the fraction for 92%?

    A $\frac{43}{50}$ **B** $\frac{23}{25}$

    C $\frac{25}{23}$ **D** $\frac{41}{50}$

4. Which is the decimal for 126%?

    A 12.6   **B** 0.126

    C 1.26   **D** 126.0

5. Which is 37% of 280?

    A 103.6   **B** $7.\overline{567}$

    C 10.36   **D** 8

6. 19 is what percent of 95?

    A 20%   **B** 5%

    C 18%   **D** 500%

7. Which is the commission on sales of $38,000 at 8.5% commission rate?

    A $323,000   **B** $32,300

    C $4,470.50   **D** $3,230

8. Which is the percent of increase from 45 to 99?

    A 97.7%   **B** 54.5%

    C 120%   **D** 45%

9. Which is the best estimate for 29% of 87?

    A 18   **B** 27

    C 16   **D** 33

10. Which is the best estimate for 75% of $24.36?

    A $15   **B** $18

    C $8   **D** $20

11. Which is the sale price?
Regular price: $19.95
Discount percent: 20%

    A $16.05   **B** $19.75

    C $3.99   **D** $15.96

12. Which is the amount (A) in a savings account after 2 years?
P = $1,250 R = 18% T = 2yr

    A $1,700   **B** $1,475

    C $450   **D** $225

13. The price of a sailboat was reduced to 80% of the original price during the first week of a sale. The next week the price was again reduced to 80% of the previous week's sale price. After the two discounts, the boat sold for $1,920. What was the original price of the sailboat?

    A $2,400   **B** $3,000

    C $2,560   **D** $2,654.21

12

PROBABILITY

MATH AND
SOCIAL STUDIES

DATA BANK

Use the Social Studies Data
Bank on page 497 to answer
the questions.

1 Of the total number of
playing pieces in the
Mesopotamian game, wh.
fraction are pyramids? What frac
tion are counters?

THEME: ANCIENT BOARD GAMES

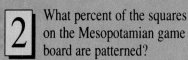 **2** What percent of the squares on the Mesopotamian game board are patterned?

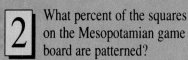 **3** Which is greater, the ratio of large dots to small dots on the Nyout board or the ratio of patterned squares to plain squares on the Mesopotamian board?

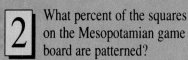 **4** **Using Critical Thinking** Do the two lines on the circular Nyout board divide it into the greatest possible spaces? What is the greatest possible number of spaces into which you can divide a circle by 3 lines? 4 lines? 5 lines?

This ancient Mesopotamian board game requires strategies based on patterns, reasoning, and probability.

333

Sample Spaces

EXPLORE **Solve to Understand**
Work in groups. The ancient Egyptian game of Bowl was
played by throwing 2 cowrie shells. You can create a similar
situation by tossing a nickel and a dime and recording your
results. Try this a total of 20 times.

TALK ABOUT IT

1. How might you describe the outcome shown?

2. What other way could there be one head and one tail?

The experiment with an element of chance is called a
probability experiment. The result of a single trial of a
probability experiment is called an **outcome**. The set of all the
outcomes is called the **sample space** of the experiment. Equally
likely outcomes have the same chance of occurring.

The experiment above has 4 equally likely outcomes. If H
represents heads and T tails, the sample space is
(H, H), (H, T), (T, H), (T, T).

Examples List the sample space for each of these probability experiments.

A Spin the spinner.   **B** Roll a number cube.   **C** Toss a coin, then roll a number cube.

Sample Space
1, 2, 3, 4, 5, 6, 7, 8

Sample Space
1, 2, 3, 4, 5, 6

Sample Space
(H, 1), (H, 2), (H, 3), (H, 4), (H, 5),
(H, 6), (T, 1), (T, 2), (T, 3), (T, 4),
(T, 5), (T, 6)

List the sample space for each of these probability experiments.

1. Toss a coin   **2.** Toss a coin, then spin a spinner numbered 1, 2, 3.

List the sample space for each of the following experiments.

1. Spin spinner 1.   2. Spin spinner 2.

3. Toss a coin, then spin spinner 2.

4. Spin spinner 1, then spin spinner 2.

5. Roll a red 6-sided number cube and then roll a green 6-sided number cube.

 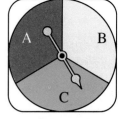

Spinner 1   **Spinner 2**

6. Toss a penny, a nickel, and a dime. Which statement describes one specific outcome in this sample space: a) two heads and a tail, or b) heads for the penny, tails for the nickel, and heads for the dime?

7. Roll a single 6-sided number cube. Which statement describes one specific outcome in this sample space: a) rolling a 5, or b) rolling a number greater than 5?

How many outcomes are there in the sample space for each experiment?

8. Toss a nickel and a dime.   9. Roll a 6-sided number cube and toss a coin.

10. Roll a number cube and spin a spinner numbered 1, 2, 3, 4.

MATH REASONING Which experiment has the most outcomes?

11. a) spin spinner 2 above   b) toss a nickel and a dime

PROBLEM SOLVING

12. One box contains 26 chips each with a different letter. A second box contains 15 chips each with a different number on it. If you select one item from each box, how many outcomes are in the sample space?

13. **Social Studies Data Bank** Suppose you were to toss 1 white pyramid and 1 blue pyramid from the game found at the Royal Tombs of Ur. How many outcomes would there be in the sample space of this experiment?

▶ **USING CRITICAL THINKING** Justify Your Answer

14. Jane had a nickel, a dime, and a quarter. She thought that when she tossed them there were only four possible outcomes: 3 heads, 2 heads and 1 tail, 1 head and 2 tails, or 3 tails. She reasoned that she should get 3 heads about 25% of the time. Do you agree? Why or why not?

More Practice, page 537, set B

Probability of Events

An **event** is an outcome or a combination of outcomes. Each event is a subset of the sample space.

EXPLORE **Analyze the Situation**

A penny, a nickel, and a dime are tossed. Each of the following is a possible event.

- Event A: Two heads and one tail
- Event B: At least one head
- Event C: All tails or all heads.

penny	nickel	dime
H	H	H
H	H	T
H	T	H
T	H	H
H	T	T
T	H	T
T	T	H
T	T	T

TALK ABOUT IT

1. How many outcomes are in event A?

2. How many outcomes are in event B? Event C?

If you roll a 6-sided number cube, you may get a 1 or a 2. This is the event "getting a number less than 3." Because there are 6 possible outcomes in all, the **probability of the event** "getting a number less than 3" is 2 out of 6. We write

$$P(\text{a number} < 3) = \frac{2}{6} = \frac{1}{3}.$$

$$P(\text{any event}) = \frac{\text{number of outcomes in the event}}{\text{number of outcomes in the sample space}}$$

- **The probability of an event is a number between 0 and 1.**
- **The probability of an impossible event is 0.**
- **The probability of an event that will always occur is 1.**

Examples Use the number cube experiment to find each probability.

A $P(3) = \frac{1}{6}$

B $P(\text{not } 3) = \frac{5}{6}$

C $P(\text{even number}) = \frac{3}{6} = \frac{1}{2}$

D $P(\text{number} < 7) = \frac{6}{6} = 1$

E $P(7) = \frac{0}{6} = 0$

Use the 6-sided number cube experiment to find each probability.

1. $P(4)$

2. $P(\text{odd number})$

3. $P(\text{number} > 4)$

4. $P(\text{number} < 1)$

Imagine spinning the spinner at the right. Find the probabilities of these events.

1. $P(3)$ **2.** $P(7)$ **3.** $P(\text{number} > 3)$

4. $P(\text{prime number})$ **5.** $P(8 \text{ or } 1)$ **6.** $P(\text{not } 8)$

7. $P(9)$ **8.** $P(\text{factor of } 24)$ **9.** $P(\text{multiple of } 3)$

10. $P(\text{number} < 3)$ **11.** $P(\text{odd number})$ **12.** $P(\text{factor of } 35)$

Consider the probability experiment of spinning the first spinner, then spinning the second spinner.

first spinner   second spinner

13. List all the ordered pairs in the sample space for this experiment.

14. Find $P(1,3)$.

15. Find $P(\text{numbers in the pairs are equal})$.

16. Find $P(\text{sum of the numbers} = 5)$.

MATH REASONING Consider the experiment of tossing a nickel and a dime. Without using paper and pencil decide if these probabilities are $\frac{1}{4}$, $\frac{1}{2}$, or $\frac{3}{4}$.

17. $P(\text{one head and one tail})$ **18.** $P(\text{both heads})$ **19.** $P(\text{at least one tail})$

PROBLEM SOLVING

20. A bicycle combination lock has a 3-digit number. Each of the digits can be either 1, 2, 3, 4, 5, or 6. If the owner forgets his combination, what is the probability that he can open his lock on the first attempt?

21. **Write Your Own Problem** Tickets for the tournament game were numbered consecutively beginning at 108192 and ending at 108746. Ben and Terri compared the numbers of their tickets.

▶ **ALGEBRA**

Let x = the number from Spinner x.
Let y = the number from Spinner y. Give the ordered pairs (x, y) for each event described.

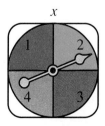
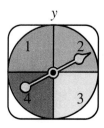

x y

22. $x + y = 5$ **23.** $x < 3$ and $y > 3$

24. $xy = 4$ **25.** $\frac{x}{y} = 1$

More Practice, page 537, set D

Experimental Probability

EXPLORE **Solve to Understand**

When a number cube is rolled 60 times, in theory each of the numbers should occur 10 times. Roll a number cube 60 times and record a table of outcomes.

face up	#1	#2	#3	#4	#5	#6
trials						

TALK ABOUT IT

1. How many numbers occurred exactly 10 times?

2. Combine your results with those of 4 other classmates. Study the combined results. How many numbers occurred exactly 50 times?

3. Did the combined data or your individual data match the theoretical probability most closely?

An **experimental probability** of an event is the number of times the event actually occurs divided by the number of trials in the experiment. If there are many trials, experimental probability is usually close to the theoretical probability.

$$\text{Experimental probability of an event} \atop \text{or Exp } P(\text{E})} = \frac{\text{number of actual outcomes of E}}{\text{number of trials in the experiment}}$$

Examples

The table at the right lists outcomes from an experiment in which a 6-sided number cube was rolled 60 times. Find the experimental probability of each.

face up	#1	#2	#3	#4	#5	#6
trials	8	10	11	12	10	9

A $\text{Exp } P(4) = \dfrac{12}{60} = \dfrac{1}{5}$

Exp $P(4)$ is close to $P(4)$.

B $\text{Exp } P(5) = \dfrac{10}{60} = \dfrac{1}{6}$

Exp $P(5)$ is equal to $P(5)$.

Use the table above to find the experimental probability of each event.

1. Event: rolling a 1
2. Event: rolling an even number
3. Event: rolling a 3 or 4

A nickel and a dime are tossed 100 times and the outcomes are recorded in the chart at the right.

outcome	number of times
(H, H)	23
(H, T)	26
(T, H)	27
(T, T)	24

1. Find Exp P(H, T).

2. Find Exp P(at least one H).

3. Find Exp P(one H and one T).

4. Find Exp P(both H or both T)

5. Toss a nickel and a dime 50 times and find the experimental probability of each of the four outcomes. Copy and complete the table below.

outcome	number of times
(H, H)	
(H, T)	
(T, H)	
(T, T)	

6. Toss a 6-sided number cube 100 times and find the experimental probability of each of the six outcomes. Copy and complete the table below.

#1	#2	#3
#4	#5	#6

MATH REASONING

7. A coin is tossed repeatedly. The results are recorded—47 heads, 43 tails. What is Exp P(H) and Exp P(T)?

PROBLEM SOLVING

8. Data Hunt. What is the experimental probability that the next student to enter your classroom will be wearing blue clothing?

 MIXED REVIEW

Find the number.

9. 50% of what number is 35?

10. 30 is 75% of what number?

Find the number of permutations.

11. of a, b, c

12. of 1, 2, 3, 4, 5

13. of Sue, Jim, Joe, Mary

Tree Diagrams and Compound Events

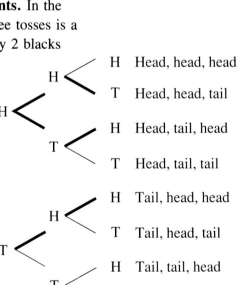

EXPLORE Study the Data

A pam-nyout is a stick used in the Korean game Nyout. When thrown, it lands either on its flat white side or on its rounded black side. The probability of each outcome is $\frac{1}{2}$. What are all the possible outcomes for three throws of a pam-nyout?

TALK ABOUT IT

1. How many outcomes have all white results?

2. How many outcomes have exactly 2 blacks and 1 white?

3. What is the probability of getting 2 blacks and 1 white in the three tosses?

A tree diagram is one way to show **compound events.** In the situation above, getting 2 blacks and 1 white in three tosses is a compound event. There are 3 outcomes with exactly 2 blacks and 1 white: BBW, BWB, and WBB.

Example

What is the probability of getting two heads and a tail when you toss three coins? What are all the possible outcomes?

There are 8 possible outcomes. There are 3 outcomes with exactly two heads and one tail. We can write $P(2$ heads and a tail$) = \frac{3}{8}$.

H < H < H Head, head, head
            T Head, head, tail
        T < H Head, tail, head
            T Head, tail, tail
T < H < H Tail, head, head
            T Tail, head, tail
        T < H Tail, tail, head
            T Tail, tail, tail

Use the tree diagram above to find each probability.

1. $P(3$ heads$)$ **2.** $P(1$ head and 2 tails$)$

3. $P(3$ tails$)$

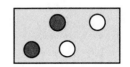

Two red chips (R) and two white chips (W) are in a box. One chip is drawn and not replaced, then a second chip is drawn. The tree diagram shows all the outcomes in the sample space for this experiment.

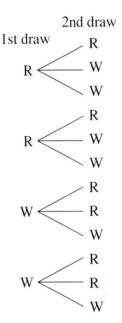

1. How many different outcomes are there in the sample space?

2. What is $P(R, W)$, the probability of drawing a red chip on the first draw and a white chip on the second?

3. What is the probability that both chips drawn will be the same color?

4. What is the probability that both chips drawn will not be the same color?

5. What is $P(R, R)$?   6. What is $P(W, W)$?

APPLY

MATH REASONING

7. If the situation above were extended to drawing a third chip, do you estimate that there will be 12, 24, or 36 different outcomes? Determine whether your estimate is correct.

PROBLEM SOLVING

8. Make a tree diagram to show the possible outcomes of 4 throws of the pam-nyout. What is the probability of throwing 4 blacks? of throwing 2 whites and 2 blacks?

DATA BANK

9. **Social Studies Data Bank** For the game of Nyout, find the probability for each outcome of throws. Compare these probabilities. Can you explain why some throws are assigned higher scores than others?

▶ ESTIMATION

Suppose that two sets of 6-sided number cubes are tossed at the same time. Find the sum of the dots that face up. For each event estimate whether the probability is closer to 0, $\frac{1}{2}$, or 1.

10. $P(\text{sum of } 25)$ 11. $P(\text{sum} < 5)$

12. $P(\text{sum} < 20)$ 13. $P(\text{sum} < 14)$

Problem Solving
Using the Strategies

| UNDERSTAND |
| ANALYZE DATA |
| PLAN |
| ESTIMATE |
| SOLVE |
| EXAMINE |

LEARN ABOUT IT

To solve this problem you could use one or more of the strategies **Solve a Simpler Problem, Draw a Picture, Make a Table,** and **Look for Patterns**.

Break this problem into simpler problems. Try out what happens with 2 players, 3 players, and so forth. By drawing a picture for each simpler problem you can see what happens as players are added.

> A group of friends are playing a card game at a large round table. There are 17 cards in the deck. The cards are passed around the table with each person taking 1 card until there are no cards left. Calvin took the first card and also ended up with the last card. He may have taken other cards as well. How many friends were playing cards?

Then, you can make a table showing the number of players and whether the number of players is a solution to the problem. By examining the table you may find a pattern.

Number of players	2	3	4	5	6	7	8	9	...	16
Does it work?	Yes	No	Yes	No	No	No	Yes	No	No	Yes

For this problem there is a pattern—any factor of 16 works. There could be either 2, 4, 8, or 16 friends playing cards.

TRY IT OUT

Solve. Use one or more of the strategies **Guess and Check, Solve a Simpler Problem, Draw a Picture, Make a Table,** and **Look for Patterns**.

1. There are 20 pennies in a row, all heads up. Tami began with the 2nd penny and turned over every other one. After replacing all the pennies heads up, the next time she began with the 3rd penny and turned over every 3rd penny. She continued in this same pattern until she had gone through the row 20 times. Which times did she turn over the 20th penny?

2. Bill made a design from square tiles as shown below. If he wants to make the same design with 20 tiles in the longest column, how many tiles will he need?

Solve. Use any problem solving strategy.

Some Strategies	
Act Out	Solve a Simpler Problem
Use Objects	Make an Organized List
Choose an Operation	Work Backward
Draw a Picture	Look for a Pattern
Guess and Check	Use Logical Reasoning
Make a Table	Write an Equation

1. In 1982, Con McCarrick played 154 games of checkers simultaneously in $4\frac{1}{2}$ hours. He won 136 of the games. What percent of the games did he win?

2. One hundred students agreed to participate in an experiment. They all sat down on the floor to begin. For step 1, every student stood up. For step 2, every 2nd student sat down. For step 3, every 3rd student who was sitting stood up and every 3rd student who was standing sat down. For step 4, every 4th student who was sitting stood up and every 4th student who was standing sat down, and so on. The students continued this experiment for 100 steps. Which students were standing after the 100th step?

3. Ben has the following coins in his pocket: 4 pennies, 3 nickels, 5 dimes, and 3 quarters. If he reaches in and takes a coin without looking, find the probability that the coin is worth more than 5¢.

4. A 15-year-old boy used 15,714 playing cards to build a 68-story house of cards. The house was 12 feet 10 inches high. About how high was each story of the house?

5. Mary, Jana, Beth, and Dee each have a different number of pennies. Dee has twice as many as Jana plus 1. Mary has half as many as Beth plus 1. Jana has 5 more than Beth. Dee has 35 pennies. How many pennies does each girl have?

6. The 3 students in Lisa's math group picked up their homework papers without looking. What is the probability that each student was matched with his or her paper?

7. Three friends bought some peanut clusters and divided them equally. After each person ate 6, the total number left was the same as each had in the beginning. How many peanut clusters did they buy?

8. One 6-sided number cube has a blank face instead of a 1-dot face. A second 6-sided number cube has a blank face instead of a 4-dot face. What is the probability of rolling a sum of 7 with these 2 number cubes?

World champion Gary Kasparov plays chess with 50 students simultaneously at the Garrett A. Morgan School in the Bronx.

More Practice, page 547, set A

Using Critical Thinking

Lisa Hamilton works in the personnel department at Consolidated Industries. She was asked to make a list of the birthdays of the 45 employees at Consolidated. The birthday of each employee will be listed in the company's monthly newsletter. She asked the company's statistician, Eva Garcia, if there were a way to predict whether two employees shared the same birthday.

Eva took a book off the shelf and showed Lisa this table.

Number of people	10	20	22	23	24	30	50
Probability that at least two of them will have the same birthday.	0.12	0.41	0.48	0.51	0.54	0.71	0.97

TALK ABOUT IT

1. What did Lisa mean by "having the same birthday"?

2. Using the table, would you predict that two employees at Consolidated Industries would have the same birthday? Explain.

3. How can Lisa find out for certain if two employees share the same birthday?

TRY IT OUT

1. What is the smallest number of people needed to have a better than even chance that at least two of them have the same birthday?

2. What is your estimate of the probability that at least two people in a group of 28 have the same birthday?

3. Suppose someone said, "The probability that at least two people in this company have the same birthday is 54%." How many people are in the company?

4. If there are 30 people in a room, would you predict that there would or would not be at least two that have the same birthday. Explain your choice.

POWER PRACTICE/QUIZ

Think about the two spinners and the coins shown.

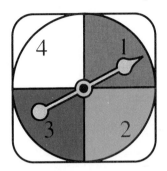 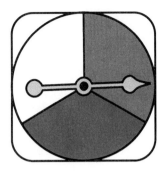 

List the sample space for each of these probability experiments.

1. Spin **A** and then spin **B**.

2. Spin **B** and then toss a dime.

Tell how many outcomes are possible for each of these probability experiments.

3. Toss a nickel and then spin **A**.

4. Toss a nickel, a dime, and a penny.

Find the probability of these outcomes.

5. P(prime) when you spin **A**.

6. P(2, red) when you spin **A** and **B**.

7. P(not blue, heads) when you spin **B** and toss a penny.

Find the experimental probabilities.

8. Exp P(red)

9. Exp P(white or green)

10. Exp P(not blue)

Results of 100 spins

red	white	blue	green
20	36	24	20

11. Are the results in the table those you would expect from a spinner with four equal parts? Why or why not?

Suppose you pick 2 marbles from a bag that has 2 red marbles and 1 blue marble. Draw a tree diagram to help you find these probabilities.

12. P(red, red)

13. P(first is red)

14. P(at least 1 red)

PROBLEM SOLVING

15. One box contains 16 chips, each with a different picture. A second box contains 20 chips, each with a different number. If you select one item from each box, how many possible outcomes are in the sample space of this experiment?

Exploring Algebra
Making Predictions

We often wish to make predictions about a large population, and we can use random samples and algebra.

EXPLORE Analyze the Situation

In the city of Sunnyglen, Brown and Cantoni are the two candidates for mayor. About 20,000 voters are expected to vote for mayor. Three random samples of voters' responses were taken in different parts of the city. Who do you think is most likely to win the election?

Sample A		Sample B		Sample C	
Brown	18	Brown	16	Brown	25
Cantoni	25	Cantoni	14	Cantoni	24
Total	43	Total	30	Total	49

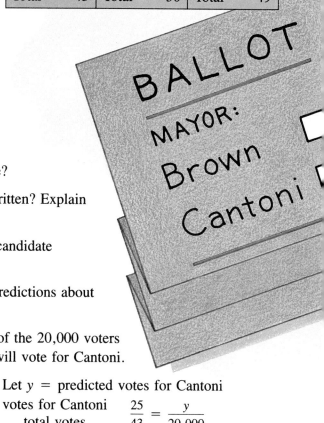

TALK ABOUT IT

1. The headline of a local newspaper read:
   "Surveys Show Brown Leading."
   What does this headline mean? Do you agree?

2. What newspaper headline would you have written? Explain your headline.

3. About how many votes do you predict each candidate will get?

You can write and solve a proportion to make predictions about the election results.

Example Use Sample A to predict how many of the 20,000 voters will vote for Brown and how many will vote for Cantoni.

Let x = predicted votes for Brown

$$\frac{\text{votes for Brown}}{\text{total votes}} \quad \frac{18}{43} = \frac{x}{20{,}000}$$
$$43x = 360{,}000$$
$$x \approx 8{,}372$$

Let y = predicted votes for Cantoni

$$\frac{\text{votes for Cantoni}}{\text{total votes}} \quad \frac{25}{43} = \frac{y}{20{,}000}$$
$$43y = 500{,}000$$
$$y \approx 11{,}628$$

Predict the number of votes for each candidate.

1. Use Sample B.   2. Use Sample C.   3. Use Samples A, B, and C combined.

Predict the number of votes each candidate will receive.

1. Total voters: 50,000

Sample	
Jamison	54
Carroll	46
Total:	100

2. Total voters: 18,000

Sample	
Maris	28
O'Leary	38
Total:	66

3. Total voters: 2,000,000

Sample	
Edwards	2,130
Mitchell	3,470
Total:	5,600

4. Total voters: 35,600

Sample	
Elkins	33
Flores	37
Garza	30
Total:	100

5. Total voters: 6,250

Sample	
Perez	15
Lin	23
Brent	12
Total:	50

6. Total voters: 25,000

Sample	
Johnson	54
Cantell	72
Morales	74
Total:	200

APPLY

MATH REASONING

7. Suppose presidential candidate A is in favor of doubling the minimum wage and candidate B wants the minimum wage unchanged. An interviewer records the responses of 500 students at Whitney High School and finds that 400 of the students would vote for candidate A. Is it reasonable to assume that 80% of the general population will vote for candidate A? Why or why not?

PROBLEM SOLVING

8. In the 1960 presidential election, John F. Kennedy received 34,226,731 votes and Richard Nixon received 34,108,157 votes. What percent of votes did Kennedy have?

MIXED REVIEW

Find the number of combinations.

9. 2 hats selected from 8 hats

10. 3 books selected from 5 books

Solve.

11. $-3x + 10 = 19$ **12.** $\frac{x}{7} + {}^-5 = 3$ **13.** $14 = 19 + 5x$ **14.** $^-6 + {}^-2x = 8$

Probability Simulations

LEARN ABOUT IT

EXPLORE **Analyze the Situation**

The Carroll family's evening newspaper is delivered at a random time between 5:30 and 6:30 p.m. The Carrolls sit down to dinner at a random time between 6:00 and 7:00 p.m. What is the probability that the newspaper will arrive before they start their dinner?

TALK ABOUT IT

1. Do you think the newspaper is more likely to arrive before or after they start eating?

2. What is your estimate of the probability that the newspaper will arrive before they start eating?

In order to **simulate** this experiment, one device is used to simulate the arrival of the newspaper and a second device is used to simulate the beginning of dinner. The spinners pictured here can be used as simulation devices.

Spin each spinner 30 times and record the results of each spin. Suppose that the results of your simulation show that the newspaper arrived before dinner 19 of the 30 times. The experimental probability you find is

Newspaper   Evening Meal

Paper 6:08   Meal 6:23

$$\text{Exp } P(\text{Newspaper before dinner}) = \frac{\text{times before dinner}}{\text{number of trials}} = \frac{19}{30}$$

TRY IT OUT

1. Using two spinners repeat the simulation described above 50 times. Record your results.

2. Find the experimental probability of "newspaper before dinner" using your simulation of 50 trials.

3. Combine the results of your entire class. What is the experimental probability of the combined simulations?

348

1. Five students each used the spinners described on the previous page 50 times. Each student recorded the number of times the newspaper arrived before dinner. The results were 41, 43, 40, 37, and 39. What is the combined probability for the 250 trials?

2. Use the results of the spins in exercise 1 to find the experimental probability that the newspaper arrives after the Carrolls begin their evening dinner.

3. Teri used the computer program at the right to simulate the newspaper-dinner problem. In 5,000 trials she found that the newspaper came before the dinner 4,384 times. Using these results, what is the probability that the newspaper will arrive before dinner begins?

```
10 RANDOMIZE: C = 0
20 FOR K = 1 TO 5000
30 P = INT(60*RND + 1):REM PAPER
40 M = INT(60*RND + 1) + 30: REM
   DINNER
50 IF P < M THEN C = C + 1
60 NEXT K
70 PRINT "PROBABILITY = "; C/5000
80 END
```

MATH REASONING

4. Suppose the newspaper arrives at a random time from 5:45 p.m. to 6:45 p.m. and the Carrolls start dinner at a random time from 6:00 p.m. to 7:00 p.m. Would the probability that the newspaper arrives before dinner be greater or less than the situation previously described? Explain your answer.

PROBLEM SOLVING

5. Use two spinners to simulate the situation described in exercise 4. Use the spinners for at least 50 trials. Using the results of your simulation what is the probability that the newspaper will arrive before dinner?

▶ **COMMUNICATION   Writing to Learn**

A fair coin is one that, when tossed, has an equal chance of coming up heads or tails. Suppose you have a coin that you believe is fair. Write a paragraph describing how you would find out if it is in fact fair. Describe a spinner you could make that would simulate the behavior of an unfair coin.

Random Numbers

In the last lesson you used spinners to generate the random numbers needed to simulate a probability experiment. **Random number** tables or random numbers generated by a computer can also be used to simulate experiments.

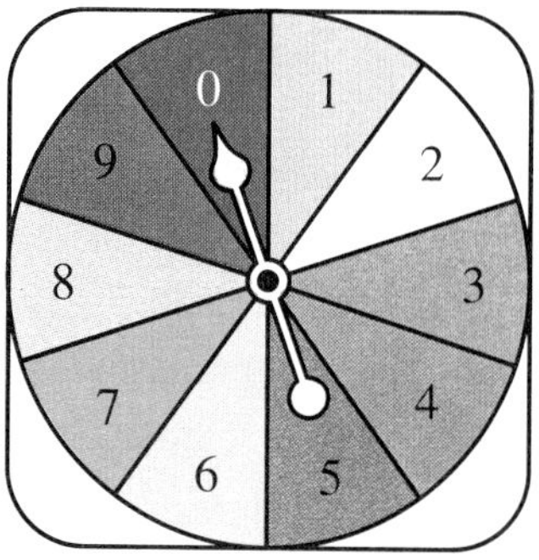

EXPLORE Study the Information

When a 10-digit spinner is spun repeatedly, its outcomes are of random numbers. The table below shows the digits obtained in 100 spins of a spinner.

TALK ABOUT IT

1. In a table of 10,000 random digits how many times would you expect the digit 8 to appear? Why?

2. Suppose you used a spinner to make yourself a table of 100 random digits. Would you expect your table to be identical to the table shown here?

100 Spinner Random Digits

```
2 5 5 6 5 7 9 3 3 9 5 5 4 2 8 1 0 1 5 4
3 9 7 8 8 2 8 2 1 2 1 2 3 1 3 2 3 5 7 9
0 9 9 0 1 5 0 4 9 3 3 2 5 2 1 0 5 3 4 5
0 8 3 6 8 6 2 4 8 1 3 1 8 3 7 5 8 2 4 5
2 9 3 8 5 7 1 6 8 6 2 7 8 1 8 4 5 6 8 8
```

A computer program will give a list of random digits to any length. The program listed below will give 100 random digits.

```
10 REM RANDOM DIGIT PROGRAM
20 RANDOMIZE
30 FOR N = 1 TO 100
40 R = INT(10*RND)
50 PRINT R
60 NEXT N
70 END
```

100 Computer Random Digits

```
3 5 6 5 2 9 7 8 6 4 3 1 4 5 5 9 0 2 7 9
9 0 2 7 9 3 0 5 1 5 3 1 6 5 4 9 3 6 8 9
6 4 0 5 0 9 5 0 0 5 7 9 6 9 0 4 2 4 8 9
6 6 5 1 4 9 0 0 6 2 8 9 8 8 5 6 8 7 4 3
3 1 6 1 0 8 6 7 8 9 7 2 2 9 4 4 3 7 7 8
```

Simulate tossing a coin 100 times by using the computer random digits. Let heads = even digit and tails = odd digit.

1. How many heads and how many tails occurred in 100 tosses?

2. How can you use this table of random digits to simulate tossing a coin three times? Find P(H, H, T).

Use the random digits tables from the previous page.

1. Let heads = even digit. Let tails = odd digit. Use the spinner random digits table to simulate tossing a nickel and a dime. How many times do each of the outcomes HH, HT, TH, TT occur?

2. Repeat exercise 1 using the computer random digits table.

3. Use the table of computer random digits to model tossing a 6-sided number cube. Since only the digits 1 to 6 are needed, ignore the digits 0, 7, 8, and 9. How many times did each of the numbers 1, 2, 3, 4, 5, and 6 occur?

4. Using your results from exercise 3 calculate the probability that each of the numbers 1, 2, 3, 4, 5, 6 will occur when you toss the number cube.

5. Copy and complete this frequency table.

Digits	0	1	2	3	4	5	6	7	8	9
Spinner Frequency	6									
Computer Frequency										

MATH REASONING

6. Which random digits table do you think gives better results for modeling a coin toss experiment? Explain.

PROBLEM SOLVING

7. **Write Your Own Problem** Write a probability problem that you can solve using a table of random numbers. Exchange problems with a classmate and solve.

▶ **CALCULATOR**

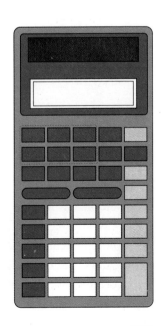

To make a table of random digits with a calculator:

1. Enter a 7-digit decimal using 7 random digits from a table.

2. Multiply it by 173.

3. Subtract the whole-number part of the result.

4. Record the digit in the tenths place. This is the first random digit.

5. Go to step 2 again, until you have enough digits.

8. Use the calculator random digits to model 60 tosses of a number cube. Ignore 0, 7, 8, and 9. Make a frequency table.

Problem Solving
Choosing a Calculation Method

| UNDERSTAND |
| ANALYZE DATA |
| PLAN |
| ESTIMATE |
| SOLVE |
| EXAMINE |

Many problems can be solved using different calculation methods. Don't always assume you need a calculator to complete a computation. Many computations are easily done using mental math.

Marcus solved the problem using mental math.

Harold went grocery shopping. He bought 3 lb of bananas, a half gallon of milk, 1 lb of ground beef, and a jar of spaghetti sauce. Below is his cash register receipt, which was torn when he put it in his pocket. What was the total cost of his groceries?

> Since the bananas are 4 lb for a dollar, the total cost of the bananas is $0.75. Milk is $1.25, ground beef 2.00, and spaghetti sauce $2.50.
> 0.75 + 1.25 = 2.00, 2.00 + 2.00 = 4.00, 4.00 + 2.50 = 6.50

Denise used a pencil and paper to solve the problem.

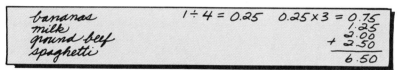

bananas
milk
ground beef
spaghetti

$$1 \div 4 = 0.25 \quad 0.25 \times 3 = 0.75$$
$$\begin{array}{r} 0.75 \\ 1.25 \\ 2.00 \\ + 2.50 \\ \hline 6.50 \end{array}$$

FAMILY FOODS

BANANAS 3 @ 4/1
            1.25
MILK   2.00
GR BEEF
SPAG SAUCE 2.50

BALANCE DUE
CASH TENDER
CHANGE DUE

Elizabeth used a calculator.

1.00 $\div$ 4 $\times$ 3 $=$ 0.75
0.75 $+$ 1.25 $+$ 2.50 $+$ 2.00 $+$ $=$ 6.5

Notice that Elizabeth's solution takes as long as the other methods. When choosing a calculation method, first try mental math. If mental math is not appropriate, choose between paper and pencil, and a calculator.

TRY IT OUT

Solve. Explain why you selected a particular calculation method.

1. Elias works after school as a grocery clerk. On Monday, he worked 4 hours. On Tuesday and Thursday he worked 3 hours each. On Saturday, he worked 5 hours. He earns $5 an hour. How much did he earn this week?

2. Elias was told to restock the frozen corn. The freezer holds 175 packages of niblets, and 125 packages of ears of corn. He found there were 20 packages of each currently on the shelf. How many packages of each type of corn did Elias need to restock the section?

Solve. Use any problem solving strategy.

1. Amos in Ames delivers apples to stores in 4 towns. The 4 towns lie on the same road. It is 50 mi from Ames to Columbus. It is 20 mi from Columbus to Baker. It is 60 mi from Dalton to Columbus. Amos has a delivery to make in Baker, and another in Dalton. How many miles does he have to travel?

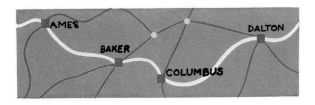

2. A farmer stores his corn in a silo that is shaped like a cylinder. The radius of the silo is 12 ft. The height of the silo is 60 ft. What is the volume of the silo?

3. Franklin was constructing a fruit stand. He was planning to sell the vegetables he was growing in his garden. He drew the plans below. What is the perimeter of the stand?

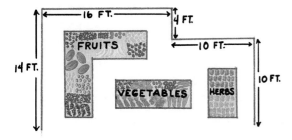

4. At Oprah's Orchard, apples are packed in cases with the type of apples printed on the outside. The orchard grows 4 different types of apples. Oprah found 3 cases of apples that had been accidentally packed without being labeled. What is the probability that all 3 cases have the same type of apples in them?

5. Brad had a bag containing 2 apples, 2 oranges, and 2 bananas. If he chooses 1 piece of fruit from the bag, what is the probability it will be an apple?

6. Sharon entered her calf in the 4-H competition at the county fair. Her calf was selected as one of the 5 finalists. The judges were going to award a first, second, and third place ribbon. How many combinations of 3 calves are possible, from the 5 finalists?

7. Andy went to the farm stand to purchase 46 ears of corn, 12 heads of lettuce, and 10 tomatoes for the class barbecue. The corn was on sale for $0.10 an ear, or 12 ears for a dollar. Is it a better deal to buy 46 ears of corn, or 48?

More Practice, page 547, set C

Data Collection and Analysis
Group Decision Making

UNDERSTAND
ANALYZE DATA
PLAN
ESTIMATE
SOLVE
EXAMINE

Doing a Survey.

Group Skill:
Explain and Summarize.

How much responsibility should teenagers have for making their own decisions? Should teenagers be solely responsible for deciding what to wear, with whom to associate, what television programs to watch, or when to be home at night? Predict who is more satisfied with the amount of responsibility they have—teenage boys or teenage girls. Conduct a survey to find out.

Collecting Data

1. Work with your group to write a survey question to find out how satisfied teenagers in your school are with the amount of responsibility they have. The question should have three or four choices from which to select.

2. Conduct a survey with at least 30 teenagers. Discuss how to select your sample in order to have appropriate representation of the teenagers at your school. Remember that you want to compare boys' responses versus girls' responses.

3. Make a table like the one below to record the responses to your survey.

Number of girls in the survey = 15

Girls	Number of Responses	Percent of Total Responses
Choice A	7	$\frac{7}{15}$ or 47%
Choice B	2	$\frac{2}{15}$ or 13%
Choice C	—	—

Number of boys in the survey = ____

Boys	Number of Responses	Percent of Total Responses
Choice A	—	—
Choice B	—	—
Choice C	—	—

Organizing Data

4. Count how many people choose each answer to your survey question or questions.

5. Make two circle graphs using the data in the chart. What will each circle graph represent?

6. How many parts will each circle graph have? What measuring instruments will you need? How can you use the number of degrees in a circle to help you construct the graph?

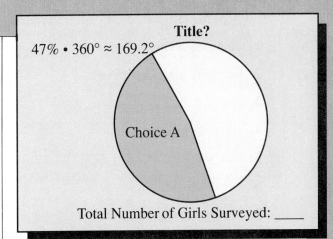

Title?

$47\% \cdot 360° \approx 169.2°$

Choice A

Total Number of Girls Surveyed: ____

7. Make sure to label what the choices A, B, and C are on your graphs.

Presenting Your Analysis

8. Tell how you selected your sample. Was your sample selected randomly? Did your sample include a fair representation of all teenagers in your school? Explain.

9. Who thinks they should have more responsibility, boys or girls? Do you think your results would be similar if you surveyed teenagers from all over the United States? Justify your answer.

10. What can you conclude from your survey results? Write a short report summarizing your findings.

WRAP UP

Probability Pairs

Tell how the terms in each pair are related.

1. outcome/event

2. tree diagram/sample space

3. event/mutually exclusive

4. simulate/random numbers

5. outcome/experiment

6. event/sample space

7. chance/equally likely

8. experiment/event

9. experimental probability/number of trials

Sometimes, Always, Never

Which of these words should go in the blank, *sometimes, always, never*? Explain your choice.

10. Tossing a coin and rolling a number cube _____ have more outcomes than flipping three coins.

11. Spinning a spinner _____ has more outcomes than flipping a coin.

12. When tossing a quarter and a dime, the probability of getting at least one head is _____ the same as the probability of getting at least one tail

Project

The diagram at right shows the sample space for rolling two number cubes. Copy the diagram. Then use colored pencils or crayons to show the ways that the following events can occur.
a. obtaining a double
b. obtaining a sum of 4
c. obtaining at least one six
d. obtaining a sum of 11
e. obtaining a sum greater than 5 but less than 10
f. obtaining a sum of 8

356

POWER PRACTICE/TEST

Part 1 Understanding

1. The probability of an event is a number between __?__ and __?__. Why?

2. Jeff performs an experiment 10 times and finds the experimental probability of each event. Melanie performs the same experiment 100 times. Who would be likely to find values closer to the mathematical probabilities? Why?

3. Name two methods for making predictions about a large population without surveying the entire population.

Part 2 Skills

List the sample space for each experiment.

4. Draw one marble from a bag of 5 marbles numbered 1 through 5.

5. Toss a quarter and roll a 6-sided number cube.

A   B

6. Imagine spinning Spinner B. Find P (odd number).

7. Imagine spinning both spinners. Find P(2,4).

8. Let a = number from Spinner A. Let b = number from Spinner B. Name the event described by $a + b > 7$.

Four chips labeled A, A, B, and C are placed in a bag and 3 are drawn separately and not replaced.

9. Make a tree diagram to show the possible outcomes.

10. What is the probability that both A chips are drawn?

Part 3 Applications

11. During one hour, 20 small pins, 25 medium pins, and 16 large pins were sold. What is the probability that the next pin sold will be small?

12. In a sample of 15,000 voters, 35 said they would vote for Kelley and 25 said they would vote for Ortez. Predict the number of votes by which Kelley will win.

13. **Challenge** People coming to a mall randomly use 1 of 3 entrances. Describe a way to simulate a person's choice of entrance.

ENRICHMENT
Bias and Inference

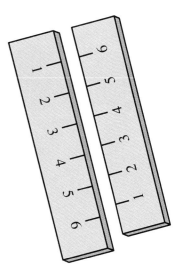

When a researcher gets data unfairly, whether on purpose, by accident, or oversight, the data may be biased, and conclusions from the data cannot be trusted.

Measuring involves some random error, which is expected, but bias is systematic error in data, and researchers work hard to avoid it. There are many ways things can go wrong. Here are a few examples.

A stretchable ruler. You measure the heights of 25 students to find their average height, but the yardstick stretches a lot, and everyone seems to be 3 ft tall.

The oversized ruler. Your friend does the same experiment with a tape measure that doesn't stretch. Unfortunately, it is 1% longer than it is supposed to be: 1 ft is actually 1.01 ft, 2 ft is actually 2.02 ft, and so on. Try this: Make up five "true" measurements and calculate the "true" mean. Now add 1% to each "true" measurement to get the "biased" measurements, and calculate the "biased" mean. How do the "true" and "biased" means compare?

The wrong sample. Another friend has a good tape measure, but only measures students on the basketball teams. A group of randomly chosen subjects is less biased.

Describe why the data these researchers get may be biased, what false inferences might be made, and what might be done to avoid bias.

1. To find the average length of words in English, a researcher uses names from a page of a phone book.

2. A researcher with slow reflexes uses a stopwatch to determine the average time a runner can run 100 meters.

3. A researcher studying voting habits asks the question, "Did you vote for Smith because she's the underdog?"

CUMULATIVE REVIEW

1. Express 0.15% as a decimal.

   A 0.15   **B** 0.0015
   C 15.0   **D** 0.015

2. 60% of what number is 30?

   A 50   **B** 18   **C** 5   **D** 20

3. Find the percent of change from 95 to 42 to the nearest tenth.

   A 126.2% decrease

   B 55.8% increase

   C 126.2% increase

   D 55.8% decrease

4. Select the best estimate of 78% of 395.

   A 50   **B** 100   **C** 300   **D** 270

5. When making a circle graph, how many degrees are needed in an angle to show 40%?

   A 144°   **B** 40°
   C 60°   **D** 180°

6. Evaluate $\dfrac{3(4^2 - 2)}{(8 + 4) + 2}$.

   A $3\frac{5}{6}$ **B** 7

   C $4\frac{3}{5}$ **D** 3

7. Find the number of permutations of 1, 3, 7, and 9.

   A 189   **B** 10
   C 24   **D** 16

8. Find the number of combinations of 4 things selected from 7.

   A 840   **B** 35   **C** 28   **D** 210

9. What is the 4th row of Pascal's Triangle?

   A 1 3 3 1

   B 1 5 10 10 5 1

   C 1 4 4 1

   D 1 4 6 4 1

10. In $1.15 of change, there are only nickels and quarters. In how many possible ways could this occur?

    A 10   **B** 7
    C 4   **D** 6

11. Write mathematically that t is greater than or equal to 5 and less than 10.

    A $5 \le t < 10$ **B** $5 \ge t < 10$
    C $5 \le t \le 10$ **D** $5 < t < 10$

12. What inequality is described by this graph?

    A $r > 0$ **B** $r \ge 4$
    C $0 < r < 4$ **D** $r > 4$

13. A $495 stereo is on sale for 15% off. Find the discount.

    A $480   **B** $74.25
    C $420.75   **D** $15.00

14. There are 3 entrances to the parking lot, 2 entrances to the stadium, and 4 entrances to the stadium seats. In how many ways could a person enter the parking lot and get to the stadium seats?

    A 24   **B** 9
    C 10   **D** 12

13

GEOMETRY

MATH AND
FINE ARTS

DATA BANK

Use the Fine Arts Data Bank
on page 501 to answer the
questions.

THEME: GEOMETRY IN ART

1 In diagram 1 from Leonard
da Vinci's notebooks, name
two triangles, each of which
has one segment that is part of the
central line of gravity.

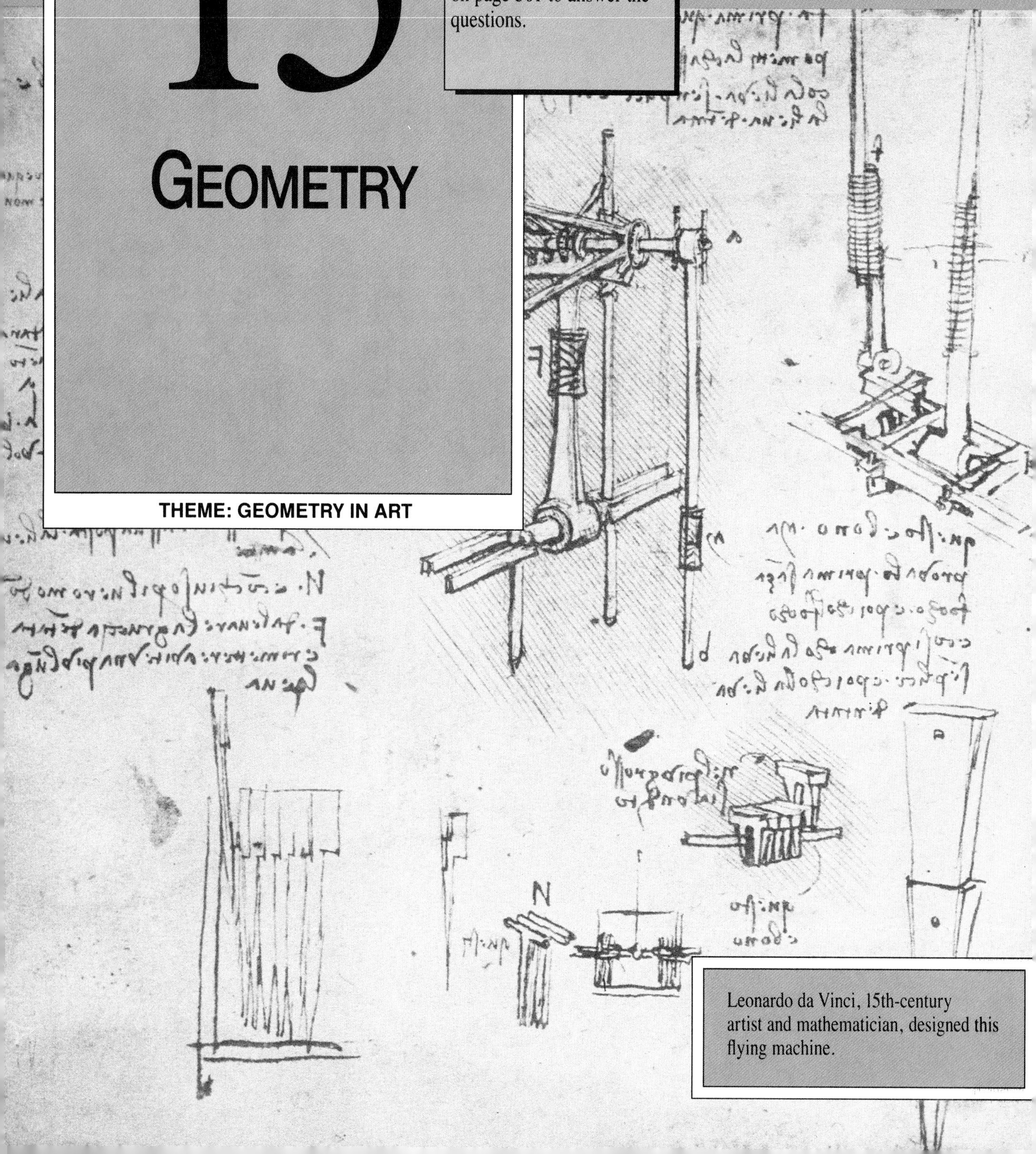

Leonardo da Vinci, 15th-century
artist and mathematician, designed this
flying machine.

2 In the same diagram, name an angle measuring less than 90°, a 90° angle and an angle measuring more than 90°.

3 In the same diagram if ∠ *EBH* measures 73° and ∠ *HEB* measures 35°, what is the measure of ∠ *BHE*?

4 **Using Critical Thinking** Is there any way to divide the architectural layout (diagram 2) into square rooms?

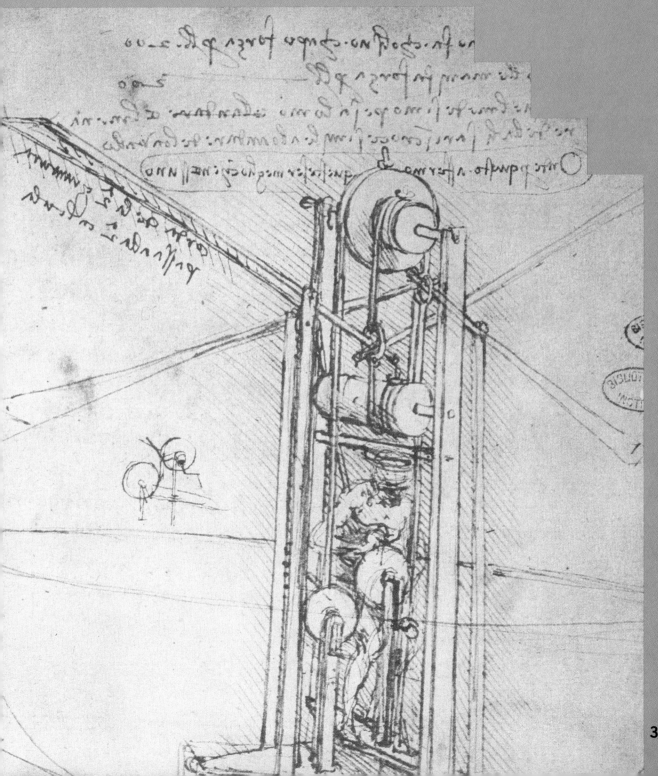

Basic Geometric Concepts

Recall that an angle is formed by two rays joined at their end points.
A protractor is used to find the degree measure of the angle.

EXPLORE

Estimate the measures of each of these
angles. Check your estimate by measuring
the angles to the nearest degree.

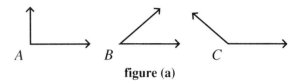

figure (a)

TALK ABOUT IT

1. An **acute** angle has measure less than
   90°. Which angle is an acute angle?

2. An **obtuse** angle has measure greater than 90°. Which angle
   is an obtuse angle?

Two angles are **complementary** if their measures have a sum of
90°. Two angles are **supplementary** if their measures have a
sum of 180°.

Two lines are **parallel** if they do not
intersect. A line that intersects two parallel
lines is called a **transversal**. When a pair of
parallel lines is cut by a transversal as
shown in this figure, $\angle 3$ and $\angle 5$ are
supplementary and all angles have a
measure equal to either $\angle 1$ or $\angle 2$.

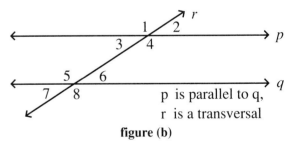

p is parallel to q,
r is a transversal

figure (b)

Example Name three angles whose measures are equal to
$m\angle 3$ and two angles that are supplementary to $\angle 3$.

Solution $m\angle 3 = m\angle 2 = m\angle 6 = m\angle 7$
$\angle 3$ is supplementary to each of $\angle 4$ and $\angle 5$.

Use figure (b) to answer the questions.

1. Name three angles whose measures are equal to $m\angle 8$.

2. Name two angles supplementary to $\angle 5$.

Use the diagram at the right to answer the questions.

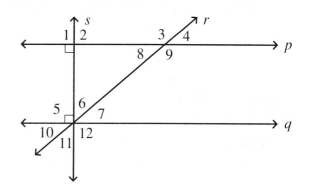

1. Name a right angle.

2. Name two angles supplementary to ∠9.

3. Name an angle complementary to ∠6.

4. Name a pair of parallel lines.

5. Name two transversals.

6. If $m\angle 9 = 140°$ find $m\angle 8$.

7. Name an acute angle.

8. Name an obtuse angle.

9. If $m\angle 10 = 35°$, find $m\angle 11$.

10. If $m\angle 8 = 27°$, find $m\angle 7$.

MATH REASONING

11. Fold a piece of paper once, and fold it again as shown. Open the folded paper. What do you discover about the four angles formed by the folds? Make additional folds to obtain a pair of folds that you know are parallel.

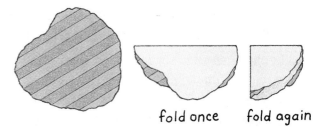

fold once   fold again

PROBLEM SOLVING

12. A carpenter is to make the side for a set of stairs. The ceiling is parallel to the floor. Sides $\overline{AC}$ and $\overline{BD}$ are parallel since they are the sides of a board. If $m\angle BDC = 38°$ what is $m\angle DBA$?

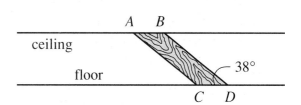

▶ **EXPLORING ALGEBRA**

In this figure lines p and q are parallel. One angle in this figure has measure $x°$ as shown. Complete each of the following with $x°$, $180° - x°$, or $90° - x°$.

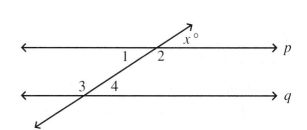

13. $m\angle 1 = \square$ 14. $m\angle 2 = \square$

15. $m\angle 3 = \square$ 16. $m\angle 4 = \square$

More Practice, page 538, set B

Pentomino Polygons

A **polygon** is a closed geometric figure whose sides are segments. A **pentomino** is a polygon that is the boundary of 5 squares.

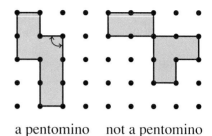

a pentomino   not a pentomino

EXPLORE Solve to Understand

Work in groups. There are 12 different pentomino shapes. Draw as many of them as you can find.

TALK ABOUT IT

1. How many of the pentominoes include 4 squares in a row?

2. How many of the pentominoes are 6 sided? 8 sided?

Pentominoes have **vertex angles** and turn angles. Vertex angles measure either 270° or 90°. Turn angles measure either +90° or −90°.

The measure of a vertex angle is determined by the size of the shaded arc on the inside of the pentomino. This pentomino has two 270° and six 90° vertex angles. If you were to walk around the pentomino in the direction of the arrows, a clockwise turn is a +90° turn angle, and a counterclockwise turn is a −90° turn angle.

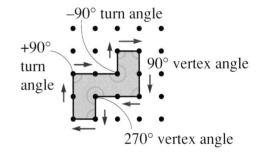

−90° turn angle

+90° turn angle

90° vertex angle

270° vertex angle

Sum of vertex angles
= 2 · 270° + 6 · 90° = 1,080°

Sum of turn angles
= (+90) + (⁻90) + (+90) + (+90) + (+90) + (⁻90) + (+90) + (+90) = 360°

For each of these polygons, find the sum of the vertex angles and the sum of the turn angles.

1.

2.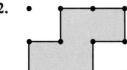

3.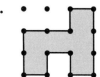

Find the sum of the vertex angles for each of these polygons.

1. 2. 3.  4.

5. 6. 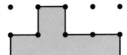 7. 8.

Find the sum of the turn angles when you go around each polygon in the direction of the arrow.

9. 10. 11. 12.

13. Draw a polygon the sum of whose vertex angles is 1,800°.

APPLY

MATH REASONING

14. What is the sum of the turn angles if you go around the polygons in problems 9–12 in the opposite direction?

PROBLEM SOLVING

15. What is the maximum number of different shaped pentominoes that can be placed on a 5 × 5 grid of squares with no overlapping? Draw such an arrangement.

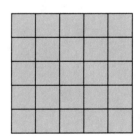

▶ USING CRITICAL THINKING Justify Your Answer

16. Complete this table.

Number of sides	4	6	8	10	12
Sum of vertex angles					
Sum of turn angles					

17. What generalization can you make about the sum of the turn angles?

18. Find a pattern for the sum of the vertex angles. Then find the sum of the vertex angles for a 20-sided polygon.

More Practice, page 538, set C

Polygons

Polygons are named according to the number of sides. A polygon is a **regular polygon** if all its sides are the same length and all its vertex angles are the same measure.

Polygon	Number of sides
Triangle	3
Quadrilateral	4
Pentagon	5
Hexagon	6
Octagon	8
n-gon	n

EXPLORE Use the Table

Draw each of these types of polygons:

- a pentagon that has a right angle.
- a hexagon that has an obtuse angle.
- a octagon that has an acute, an obtuse, and a right angle.
- a polygon for which the maximum number of **diagonals** that can be drawn from a single vertex is four.

TALK ABOUT IT

1. What is the maximum number of diagonals that can be drawn from one vertex of a pentagon? a hexagon?

2. When you draw all diagonals from one vertex of a polygon with n sides how many triangles are formed?

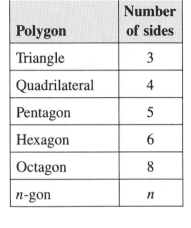

vertex

diagonals

vertex angle

To find the sum (S) of the measures of the vertex angles of a polygon, divide the polygon into triangles using all diagonals from one vertex.

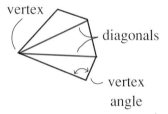

$S = 2 \cdot 180°$ $S = 3 \cdot 180°$ $S = 4 \cdot 180°$

We can find the sum of the measures of the vertex angles of a polygon with n sides by using the formula. $S = 180° (n - 2)$.

TRY IT OUT

Find the sum of the measures of the vertex angles.

1.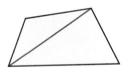

2.

3.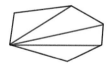

Name each polygon. Find the sum of the measures of the vertex angles.

1.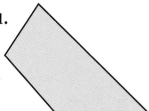

2.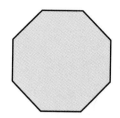

3.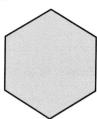

4.

5.

6.

Find the measure of each vertex angle of these regular polygons.

7. pentagon   **8.** hexagon   **9.** octagon   **10.** decagon

APPLY

MATH REASONING

11. This figure shows that the sum of the vertex angle measures of two equilateral triangles and two regular hexagons is 360°. Find two other combinations of regular polygons that surround a vertex with no gaps or overlapping.

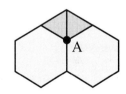

PROBLEM SOLVING

12. In quadrilateral *ABCD*, *m∠A* = 123°, *m∠C* = 75°, and *∠A* and *∠B* are supplementary. Find *m∠D*.

13. Suppose that two angles of a triangle are complementary. What is the measure of the third angle?

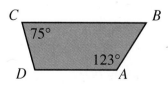

▶ **EXPLORING ALGEBRA**

14. In pentagon *ABCDE*, *m∠A* = *x*, *m∠B* = 2*x*, *m∠C* = *y*, *m∠D* = 120°, and *m∠E* = 90°. What is the sum of the vertex angles of this polygon? Write an equation about the sum of the angles of this polygon.

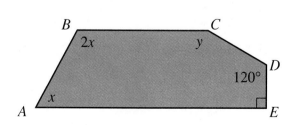

More Practice, page 538, set D

Tessellations

LEARN ABOUT IT

A collection of polygons form a **tessellation** if they cover the entire plane with no overlapping. The tessellation at right is based on a sketch from one of Leonardo da Vinci's notebooks. It shows ways in which both squares and triangles can tessellate the plane. Would any quadrilateral or triangle tessellate the plane?

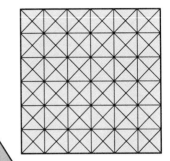

EXPLORE Use Dot Paper

Work in groups. Arrange about 12 of each polygon on dot paper to form a tessellation of that polygon.

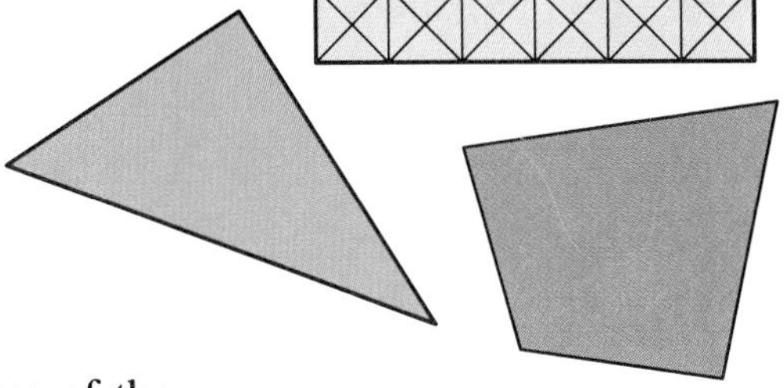

TALK ABOUT IT

1. In your tessellation of triangles do your vertices of the triangles touch other triangles only at vertices? How many triangles surround each vertex?

2. In your tessellation of quadrilaterals how many of them surround each vertex?

Did your tessellations look something like these? How are we using the relationships about the sum of the measures of a polygon?

$m\angle 1 + m\angle 2 + m\angle 3 = 180°$

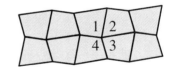

$m\angle 1 + m\angle 2 + m\angle 3 + m\angle 4 = 360°$

All triangles tessellate the plane. All quadrilaterals tessellate the plane.

TRY IT OUT

Draw tessellations of these shapes on square dot paper.

1.

2.

3.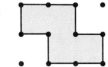

368

Draw a tessellation of these shapes on square dot paper.

1.    **2.**    **3.**    **4.**

5.   **6.** 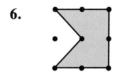   **7.**   **8.**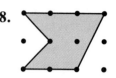

Draw a tessellation of these shapes on isometric dot paper.

9.   **10.**    **11.**    **12.**

APPLY

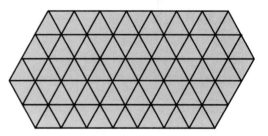

MATH REASONING Copy and color this tessellation of equilateral triangles to create the following:

13. A tessellation of diamonds.

14. A tessellation of regular hexagons and trapezoids.

15. A tessellation of regular hexagons and equilateral triangles.

PROBLEM SOLVING

16. Fine Arts Data Bank Add to the drawing of the architectural layout from da Vinci's notebook to make it a tessellation of 2 polygons. Could you make tessellations from each of the problems taken separately?

MIXED REVIEW

Find the probability of the event, based on the spinner at the right.

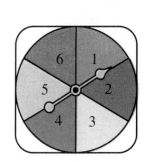

17. $P(4)$ **18.** $P(\text{multiple of 2})$ **19.** $P(\text{prime number})$

Evaluate each expression for $a = \frac{1}{4}$, $b = -\frac{2}{5}$, $c = -\frac{5}{7}$

20. $ab + c$ **21.** $a + bc$ **22.** $(a + b)c$

More Practice, page 539, set A

Using Critical Thinking

Mr. Garcia wanted to build a factory on an equilateral triangular piece of land that was bounded by three intersecting highways. "Our factory must be built where the sum of the distances a, b, and c to the three roads is smallest," he said as he looked at the map. "That will allow us to ship our product out for the lowest cost." Then he called Mr. Jackson, his assistant, and requested, "Please have a report for me on Monday that shows the best place for us to build."

Mr. Jackson thought for a moment and said, "I think I know the answer already. But I'm going to need a ruler and protractor to try out a few things. You'll be surprised, Mr. Garcia."

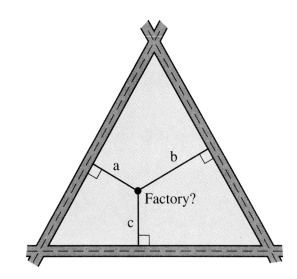

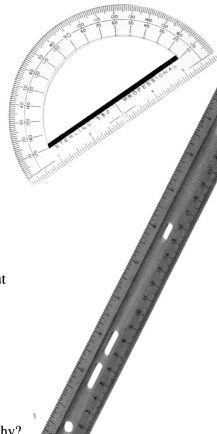

TALK ABOUT IT

1. What was Mr. Garcia planning to do? What was Mr. Jackson's first task?

2. If you were Mr. Jackson, how would you go about finding the best place for the factory? Try your method.

3. What is your conclusion? Give reasons to support your conclusion.

TRY IT OUT

1. Copy and complete this statement to form a conjecture about the situation above:
   For any point inside an equilateral triangle, the sum of its distances . . .
   Why is this conjecture true?

2. Do you think you have proved that your conjecture is true? Explain.

3. Where do you think Mr. Garcia would build the factory? Why?

POWER PRACTICE/QUIZ

Name the following.

1. a pair of parallel lines

2. a pair of perpendicular lines

3. two transversals

4. two complementary angles

5. an obtuse angle

6. two supplementary angles

7. If $m\angle 1 = 35°$, then $m\angle 2 = $ ▨.

8. If $m\angle 7 = 55°$, then $m\angle 8 = $ ▨.

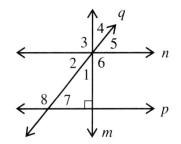

For each pentomino, find the sum of the:

9. vertex angle measures

10. turn angle measures

11. Draw a tessellation using pentomino C.

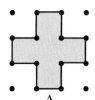

A

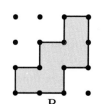

B

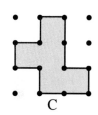

C

Name each polygon. Give the sum of the measures of the angles.

12.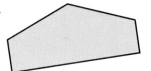

13.

14.

15.

16.

17.

PROBLEM SOLVING

18. How much larger is the vertex angle of a regular decagon than the vertex angle of a regular octagon?

19. In a tessellation of equilateral triangles and squares, how many of each shape surround one vertex? Draw such a tessellation, showing at least four vertices.

20. To cut this board to make a triangle with a right angle as shown, and so that angles 1 and 2 are equal, what should the measures of angles 1 and 2 be?

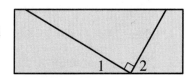

Circles

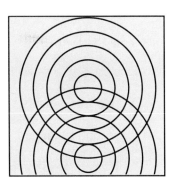

A **circle** is all the points in a plane that are the same distance from one point called the **center**. If two circles have the same center they are called **concentric circles**. Leonardo da Vinci drew a diagram like this one to show that concentric circles made by dropping stones in water will retain their shape even when they intersect.

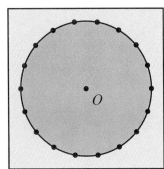

EXPLORE Use Circle Dot Paper

Draw a circle through 18 dots on the paper. Then draw the following:

- a segment $\overline{AB}$ between two dots and through the center.
- a line $\overleftrightarrow{CD}$ that passes through two other points, C and D.
- a segment $\overline{AE}$ that does not pass through the center.
- an angle $\angle EOF$ whose vertex is the center.
- a segment $\overline{OH}$.

TALK ABOUT IT

1. Read the six definitions below. Then name in your drawing:
   a) a diameter   b) a chord that is not a diameter
   c) a radius   d) a central angle

A **chord** is a segment with its end points on the circle. $\overline{CD}$ is a chord.

A **diameter** is a chord that passes through the center of the circle. $\overline{AB}$ is a diameter.

A **radius** is a segment from the center of the circle to a point on the circle. $\overline{OA}$ is a radius.

A **central angle** has its vertex at the center of a circle. $\angle EOF$ is a central angle.

An **inscribed angle** has its vertex on the circle. $\angle BAE$ is an inscribed angle.

A **tangent** line intersects the circle in just one point. Line t is a tangent line.

A **secant** is a line that intersects the circle in two points $\overleftrightarrow{CD}$ is a secant line.

TRY IT OUT

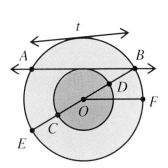

The two circles in the figure are concentric circles with center O.

1. Name three radii of the large circle.

2. Name a diameter of the small circle.

3. Name a secant line of the large circle.

372

1. Name three radii of the circle.

2. Name a diameter of the circle.

3. Name a secant line of the circle.

4. Name a chord of the circle.

5. Name a tangent line of the circle.

6. Name a central angle of the circle.

7. Name an angle that is not a central angle.

8. Name an inscribed angle.

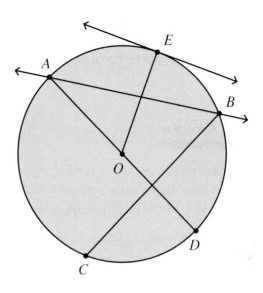

APPLY

MATH REASONING Use a compass to copy each of these figures which appear in da Vinci's notebooks.

9.

10.

PROBLEM SOLVING

11. How many lines are tangent to both of these circles at the same time? Construct two circles like these and draw all of these tangent lines.

12. **Fine Arts Data Bank** Show how the geometrical drawing in da Vinci's study for The Last Supper would be used to construct an octagon.

▶ **USING CRITICAL THINKING**   Justify Your Answer

13. Da Vinci was fascinated by the relationships of area in geometrical drawings that combined circles or arcs with triangles of squares. He thought the shaded parts of this diagram, taken together, would be comparable in area to the area of the triangle. Do you think the two areas could be exactly equal or approximately equal? Why?

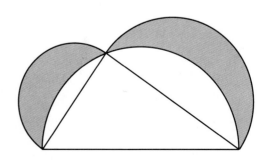

Problem Solving
Using the Strategies

UNDERSTAND
ANALYZE DATA
PLAN
ESTIMATE
SOLVE
EXAMINE

LEARN ABOUT IT

For some problems, using several strategies may be helpful. To solve this problem, you can **Draw a Picture**, and **Make a Table**.

Begin by Drawing a Picture of a corral.

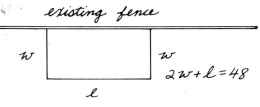

existing fence

w w

l

$2w + l = 48$

Josh works at Greenhorn Ranch during vacations. They are building a rectangular corral using an existing fence for one side and 48 m of new fencing for the remaining sides. How wide and how long should they make the corral to get the largest possible area?

Then Make a Table, try some different widths and lengths, and watch what happens to the area.

w	l	area
1	46	46
2	44	88
3	42	126
6	36	216
8	32	256
10	28	280
11	26	286
12	24	288
13	22	286
14	20	280

It looks like the area is largest when the width is 12. Check 11 and 13 to be certain.

They should make the corral 12 m wide and 24 m long to get the largest possible area.

TRY IT OUT

Solve. Use any problem solving strategy.

1. Rosa has 60 m of fencing to build a rectangular corral that has the largest area possible. She has to fence all 4 sides. How wide and how long should she make the corral?

2. The Ranch wants to make a pasture with an area of 800 m². There is a river along one side so they only need to fence 3 sides. Find the least amount of fencing they can use.

Solve. Use any problem solving strategy.

1. A camp offers 4 different water sports. Three times as many people signed up for swimming as for water-skiing. Half as many signed up for sailing as for canoeing. Nine more people signed up for swimming than canoeing. If 15 people signed up for sailing, how many signed up for water-skiing?

2. Each day, Greenhorn Ranch offers a choice of 8 different activities. You can participate in 3. How many different combinations of 3 activities can you choose?

3. Kate is making a water container for the new corral. She bought a sheet of metal 30 in. wide and 48 in. long for $12.49. She plans to cut a square out of each corner and then fold up the sides. What size square should she cut out to get the largest possible volume?

4. Mr. Fernandez is a riding instructor at the Ranch for 12 weeks each summer. He receives room and board and $\frac{1}{3}$ of the total amount paid for riding lessons. During 1 week, he taught 23 lessons at $15 each. How much did he receive?

Some Strategies	
Act Out	Solve a Simpler Problem
Use Objects	Make an Organized List
Choose an Operation	Work Backward
Draw a Picture	Look for a Pattern
Guess and Check	Use Logical Reasoning
Make a Table	Write an Equation

5. A survey asked 1,317 households to name their most popular snack fruits. Use the graph to find how many households named apples.

6. Use the graph to find about how many more households named bananas than oranges and strawberries.

Most popular fruit snacks

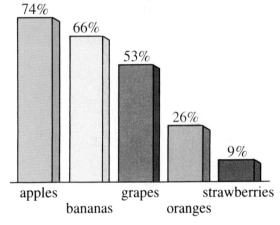

7. A riding ring is in the shape of an octagon. Each side is 42 ft long. There is a fence post at each corner and every 6 ft in between. How many fence posts are there?

8. Jen, Deanna, and Terri put their shorts and tops in the laundry. When they came back, each girl had another girl's shorts, and yet another girl's top. Jen got Terri's top. Whose shorts and whose top did each girl get?

More Practice, page 545, set E

Parallel and Perpendicular Lines

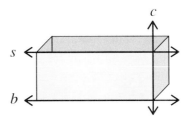

lines *s* and *b*
are parallel

lines *s* and *c*
are perpendicular

EXPLORE **Think About the Process**

A. Construct a line perpendicular to a given line.

Given   Step 1   Step 2   Step 3

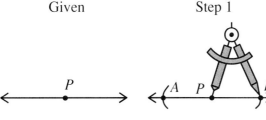 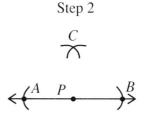 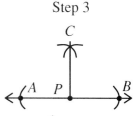

Draw arcs with center at *P*. Label points *A* and *B*.

Open the compass wider and draw arcs with centers *A* and *B*. Label the point of intersection *C*.

Draw $\overleftrightarrow{CP}$.
$\overleftrightarrow{CP} \perp \overleftrightarrow{AB}$ at point *P*.

B. Construct a line parallel to a given line.

Given   Step 1   Step 2

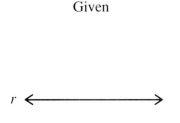 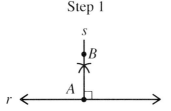 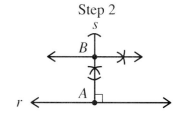

Mark a point *A* on line *r*. Construct a line *s* through *A* perpendicular to *r*. Mark a point *B* on line *s*.

Construct line *t* through point *B* so that *t* $\perp AB$. *t* ∥ *r*.

TALK ABOUT IT

1. Explain why the steps in **A** give perpendicular lines.

2. Explain why the steps in **B** give parallel lines.

1. Draw a line *l* and mark a point *P* on the line. Construct a line *m* through *P* perpendicular to *l*.

2. Draw any line *n*. Construct a line *q* parallel to *n*.

1. Name a line perpendicular to $\overleftrightarrow{AB}$.

2. Name a pair of parallel lines.

3. What is the measure of $\angle BDE$?

4. What is the measure of $\angle ABD$?

5. Name a pair of perpendicular lines intersecting at C.

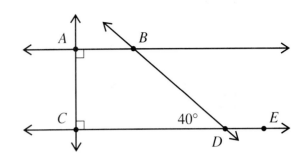

Use a compass and straight edge to complete exercises 6 to 8.

6. Draw point P on line p. Construct a line perpendicular to p through point P.

7. Draw a line q and points x and y on q. Construct a line through x and one through y that are parallel to each other.

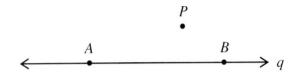

8. Draw a line q and points A and B on q as shown. Draw point P off line q. Then construct a rectangle $ABCD$ where point P is on line $\overleftrightarrow{CD}$.

APPLY

MATH REASONING

9. Construct a square in which all sides have length $2s$.

10. Construct a hexagon which has one pair of parallel sides.

PROBLEM SOLVING

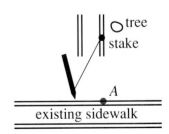

11. **Talk About Your Solution** A contractor is building a new sidewalk against a stake located next to a tree. How can he locate a point A so that the edge of the new sidewalk through A is perpendicular to the existing sidewalk? (He has a string with a pencil tied to its end that can be used as a compass. He can use taut string as a straight edge.)

▶ COMMUNICATION Writing to Learn

12. Look up the phrase "plumb line" in a reference and write a paragraph that describes how it is used in construction to find a perpendicular.

Constructing Angle and Segment Bisectors

EXPLORE Think About the Process

A geometric figure is bisected if it is divided into two equal measures.

A. Construct the perpendicular bisector of a segment.

Given	Step 1	Step 2	Step 3

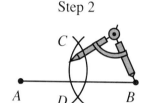
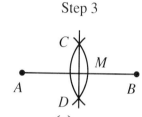

Open the compass to more than one half the length of *AB* and draw an arc with center at *A*.

With the same opening, draw an arc with center *B*. Label the intersections of the arcs *C* and *D*.

Draw $\overleftrightarrow{CD}$. Label point *M*. *M* bisects $\overline{AB}$. $\overleftrightarrow{CD}$ ⊥ bis $\overline{AB}$.

B. Construct the bisector of an angle.

Given	Step 1	Step 2	Step 3

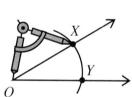
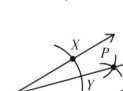

Draw any arc with center *O*. Label points *X* and *Y*.

Draw arcs from points *X* and *Y*. Label the intersection *P*.

Draw $\overrightarrow{OP}$. $\overrightarrow{OP}$ bisects ∠ *XOY*.

TALK ABOUT IT

1. How do you know $\overline{CD}$ in part **A** is a perpendicular of $\overline{AB}$?

2. How do you know that $\overline{OP}$ in part **B** bisects ∠*ABC*?

1. Draw a line and construct its perpendicular bisector.

2. Draw an angle and construct its bisector.

1. Draw an obtuse angle and construct three rays that divide the angle into four angles of equal measure.

2. Construct an equilateral triangle and bisect an angle to construct a 30° angle.

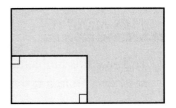

3. Construct a 45° angle.   4. Construct a $22\frac{1}{2}$° angle.

5. Construct two rectangles, the smaller in the corner of the larger with an area $\frac{1}{4}$ the area of the larger one.

6. Construct a regular hexagon inscribed in a circle. Bisect a central angle of the circle to construct a regular 12 sided polygon.

7. Draw a segment that is about 4 cm long. Then construct a segment that is $1\frac{1}{2}$ times as long.

APPLY

MATH REASONING

8. Construct a trapezoid whose long base is twice as long as its short base.

9. Construct a rhombus with a 45° vertex angle.

PROBLEM SOLVING

10. The three angle bisectors of a triangle intersect at a point C and the three perpendicular bisectors of the sides intersect at a point O. Experiment and discover for what kind of triangle, points O and C are the same point.

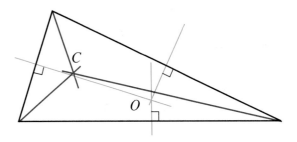

 ## MIXED REVIEW

A drawer contains 3 red socks (R), 4 blue socks (B), and 2 white socks (W). One sock is drawn and not replaced, then a second sock is drawn. Find the probabilities.

11. $P(R, R)$ **12.** $P(B, B)$ **13.** $P(W, W)$

Find the answers.

14. 15% of 50   **15.** 2% of 50   **16.** 300% of 50

Problem Solving
Data from a Menu

UNDERSTAND
ANALYZE DATA
PLAN
ESTIMATE
SOLVE
EXAMINE

To solve this problem, you need data from a restaurant menu.

Chuck went to Eduardo's for dinner. He had a spinach salad and vegetarian lasagna. How much was his bill including tax?

Menu

Soups
Cup $1.60   Bowl $2.25
Clam Chowder
Black Bean
Broccoli Cheese

Salads
Mixed Greens $1.65
Spinach $2.75
Caesar for 2 $7.50

Entrees
Add $2.50 for complete dinners.
Snapper Veracruz $7.95
Chicken Toscano $8.25
Vegetarian Lasagna $5.75
New York Steak $11.50

Desserts
Ice Cream $1.75
Cheese Cake $2.50
Fruit Tart $2.35

Beverages
Coffee $0.85
Tea $0.75
Mineral Water $0.60

prices do not include 6% sales tax

Look under salad for the price of the spinach salad and under entree for the price of the lasagna. Then add the 2 prices.

spinach salad $2.75 lasagna $5.75
$2.75 + $5.75 = $8.50

Multiply by 0.06 to find the tax.

$8.50 × 0.06 = $0.51

Add to find the total bill including tax.

Chuck's bill including tax was $9.01.

$8.50 + $0.51 = $9.01

Solve. Use data from the menu above when necessary.

1. Erika ordered Snapper Veracruz as a complete dinner. How much was her bill, including tax?

2. Hans wants a cup of soup, a mixed greens salad, and coffee with Chicken Toscano. How much does he save if he orders a dinner rather than à la carte?

Solve. Use any problem solving strategy.

1. Six people each ordered vegetarian lasagna as a complete dinner. How much was their bill before tax?

2. Kai wants to order a cup of soup, salad, an entree, and dessert. How many different meals can she choose?

3. The owner of Eduardo's kept a record for 3 weeks of how many people ordered each entree. Use the table to find how many fewer people ordered New York Steak than chicken.

Entree	Number Ordered
Snapper Veracruz	271
Chicken Toscano	305
Vegetarian Lasagna	283
New York Steak	124

4. Will ordered a bowl of black bean soup, a spinach salad, ice cream, and tea. How much did he spend including tax and a 15% tip?

5. Paul has been a waiter at Eduardo's for $3\frac{1}{2}$ years. He earns $7.35 an hour. Last week he worked 38 hours. How much did he earn?

6. A diagonal of a polygon is a line segment that connects any 2 nonadjacent vertices. How many diagonals does a 12-sided polygon have?

7. Dan and Jason ordered Caesar salad for 2. Each one also ordered a bowl of clam chowder. Their total bill including tax was $12.72. How much was the tax?

8. **Suppose** Robin has a coupon for Eduardo's. Robin ordered Chicken Toscano and her friend ordered Snapper Veracruz. How much was the bill including tax?

Tell which of the following information would change the solution to the problem above.

a. Robin's friend ordered Vegetarian Lasagna.
b. Robin ordered New York Steak.
c. Robin left a 15% tip.

Eduardo's
Buy 1 complete dinner, get the 2nd dinner (same price or less) free.
Does not include tax & tip.

Exploring Algebra
More on Graphing Functions

EXPLORE Make a Graph

Rita's science fair project related the size of bubbles to different combinations of soap and water. She graphed the surface area of a sphere as a function of the diameter using $A = \pi d^2$. Then when she blew a bubble and caught it on paper, she could measure the wet spot and read the diameter directly. Make a graph like Rita's.

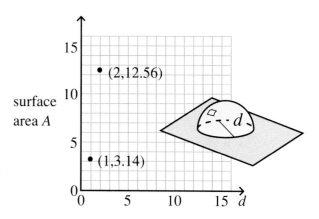

TALK ABOUT IT

1. What is the surface area if the diameter is 1 inch? Graph this ordered pair (1, ?).

2. What is the surface area if the diameter is 2 inches? Graph this ordered pair (2, ?).

3. Graph ordered pairs for diameters: 0, 3, 4, 5, 6

Functions with variables that have an exponent greater than 1 have graphs that are curves rather than lines.

Example Graph $y = 0.5x^2$

Let $x = {}^-6, {}^-4, {}^-2, 0, 2, 4, 6$ and complete a table of values for (x, y).

x	$^-6$	$^-4$	$^-2$	0	2	4	6
y	18	8	2	0	2	8	18

Graph these points. Complete the graph by connecting these points.

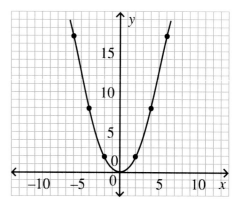

1. Complete a table of (x, y) values for the given values of x and graph of the function $y = x^2 - 3$ for $x = {}^-4, {}^-3, {}^-1, 0, 1, 4$.

PRACTICE

Complete a table of (x, y) values for the given values of x and graph the function.

1. $y = x^2 + 3$ for $x = -5, -3, -1, 0, 1, 3, 5$

2. $y = 2x^2 - 20$ for $x = -6, -4, -2, 0, 2, 4, 6$

3. $y = 10 - x^2$ for $x = -5, -4, -3, -2, -1, 0, 1, 2, 3, 4, 5$

4. $y = x^3 - 10$ for $x = -3, -2, -1, 0, 1, 2, 3$

5. Match the graph to the correct function.

    A. $y = x^2$ **B.** $y = 15 - x^2$ **C.** $y = x^2 - 15$ **D.** $y = 15x^2$

APPLY

MATH REASONING

6. Use a calculator to see what happens "in between" the integers for $y = x^2$. Evaluate and graph this function for $x = -3, -2.5, -2, -1.5, -1, -0.5, 0, 0.5, 1, 1.5, 2, 2.5, 3$

PROBLEM SOLVING

7. Rita's bubble was 4.1 inches in diameter. Find the surface area of this winner.

8. A small pizza has a radius of 4 inches. A large pizza has a radius of 8 inches. How many times larger is the large pizza?

9. The distance you can see across the ocean depends on your height. The two are related by $h = \frac{2}{3}d^2$, where h is the height in feet and d is the distance in miles. How high would the crow's nest on a ship need to be for the sailor to see a boat 5 miles away?

CALCULATOR

10. The distance a car travels, once the brakes are applied, is given by $d = 0.026s^2$, where d is the distance in ft and s is the speed in mph. Use a calculator and determine the distance it takes to stop for these speeds: 10 mph, 20 mph, 30 mph, 40 mph, 55 mph, 65 mph, 75 mph.

Applied Problem Solving
Group Decision Making

UNDERSTAND
ANALYZE DATA
PLAN
ESTIMATE
SOLVE
EXAMINE

Group Skill:
Encourage and Respect Others

The Pizza Palace is opening soon. Your group's job is to figure out a floor plan showing the location, size, and shape of all the tables and of the salad bar in the restaurant. Your group needs to make a scale drawing of your plan.

Facts to Consider

- You want to seat the maximum number of people.
- There should be seating for at least:

  two parties of 2
  three parties of 4
  two parties of 6
  one party of 8–10

- The floor space available is 20 ft by 40 ft.
- There must be at least 2 ft between tables.
- Tables can be square, rectangular, circular, or any other geometric shape.
- The salad bar is shaped like a trapezoid. It is 3 ft wide and its parallel sides are 4 ft and 5 ft long.
- Each person should have a space about 3 ft long and 2 ft wide at the table.
- Suggested scale is $\frac{1}{2}$ in. = 1 ft.

1. How many people can be seated around a rectangular table 3 ft by 4 ft?

2. About how many people can be seated around a circular table with a radius of 3 ft?

3. How large a circular table will accommodate 10 people? how large a rectangular table?

Compare your floor plan with other groups' plans. How many people does your floor plan seat?

WRAP UP

Identifying Prefixes

Use a dictionary to find the meaning of each prefix. Then find a word from the chapter that contains the prefix.

Prefix	Prefix Meaning	Word From Chapter 13
1. hepta		
2. poly		
3. nona		
4. tri		
5. hexa		
6. quad		
7. dia		
8. deca		
9. penta		
10. octa		

Sometimes, Always, Never

Which of these words should go in the blank, *sometimes, always, never?* Explain your choice.

11. A pentomino _____ has eight turn angles.

12. The diameter of a circle is _____ longer than a chord.

13. A regular pentagon _____ tessellates the plane.

Project

A polymino is a polygon that is the boundary of adjacent squares. A hexamino is a polymino made up of six unit squares. The drawings at right show three different hexaminoes. See how many more hexaminoes you can create. Then use graph paper to create at least five different octaminoes.

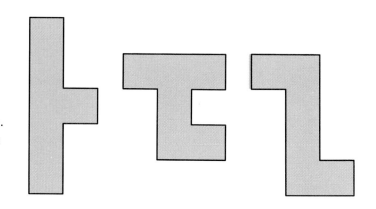

POWER PRACTICE/TEST

Part 1   Understanding

Use the diagram at the right to answer questions 1–4.

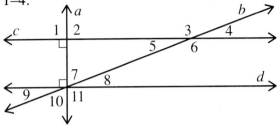

1. Name a right angle.

2. Name a transversal.

3. Name three angles supplementary to $\angle 6$.

4. Name three angles complementary to $\angle 7$.

5. True or false: Polygons in a tesselation can be different shapes.

6. True or false: two lines in a plane must be parallel or perpendicular.

Use the diagram at the right to answer questions 7–10.

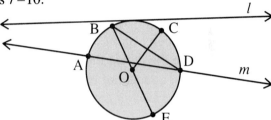

7. Name a tangent line.

8. Name a secant line.

9. Name a central angle.

10. Name a chord that is not a diameter.

11. Describe the graph of a function with a variable whose exponent is greater than 1.

Part 2   Skills

12. Find the sum of the vertex angles and the sum of the turn angles if you go in the direction of the arrow.

13. Find the sum of the measures of the vertex angles of a hexagon.

Use a compass and straightedge for problems 15–17.

14. Construct two parallel lines.

15. Draw an angle and construct its bisector.

16. Complete a table of (x,y) values for $y = x^2 - 2$ and graph the function. Let $x = {}^-2, {}^-1, 0, 1, 2$.

Part 3   Applications

17. An old menu lists steak and eggs for $2.15, ham and eggs for $1.85, and ham for $1.15. What would the steaks cost?

18. **Challenge** A rectangular corral is twice as wide as it is long. It has an area of 450 ft^2. Find its length and width.

387

ENRICHMENT
The Five Platonic Solids

Tetrahedron

Cube

Octahedron

Dodecahedron

Icosahedron

The five **regular polyhedrons** above are called the Platonic Solids. They are named after the Greek philosopher Plato. The faces of each polyhedron are composed of regular congruent polygons. It can be proven that there are only 5 possible regular polyhedrons. This is because the sum of the angles of the polygons meeting at each vertex must be less than 360°.

A pattern for each polyhedron is given below. Make larger patterns of each polyhedron on light posterboard. Cut out the patterns, fold on the dotted line segments and tape the edges together to make a model of each Platonic solid.

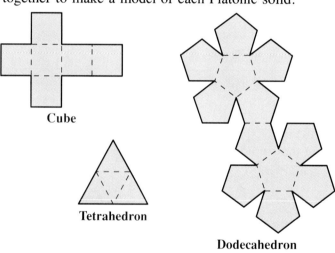
Cube

Tetrahedron

Dodecahedron

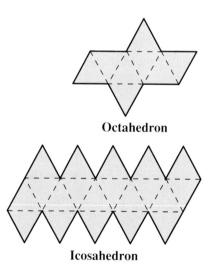
Octahedron

Icosahedron

Use the models to complete this table.

Name	Faces (F)	Vertices (V)	Edges (E)	F + V − E
Tetrahedron				
Cube				
Octahedron				
Dodecahedron				
Icosahedron				

388

CUMULATIVE REVIEW

1. Find the commission.
total sales: $936
commission rate: 8%

   A $748.80   **B** $80.00

   C $861.12   **D** $74.88

2. Find the sale price.
regular price: $27.50
discount percent: 20%

   A $7.50   **B** $22.00

   C $5.50   **D** $20.00

3. Find the interest.
$P = \$700; R = 6\%; T = 2$ yr

   A $42   **B** $12

   C $84   **D** $840

4. Evaluate $2! \cdot 4!$.

   A 48   **B** 8

   C 40,320   **D** 20

5. Which is the graph of the inequality
$12 > s \geqslant 5$?

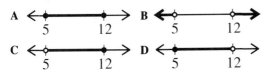

6. How many different pairs can be selected
from 6 objects?

   A 30   **B** 360

   C 12   **D** 15

7. A cube with sides numbered 1 through 6
is rolled. Find P(even number).

   A $\frac{6}{3}$ **B** $\frac{3}{3}$ **C** $\frac{1}{2}$ **D** $\frac{1}{3}$

8. A six-sided number cube is rolled 20
times. A 4 is rolled three times. Find
Exp P(4).

   A $\frac{4}{20}$ **B** $\frac{3}{20}$ **C** $\frac{1}{6}$ **D** $\frac{12}{20}$

9. A bag contains 3 red marbles and 2
white marbles. One is drawn and not
replaced. A second is drawn and not
replaced. Find the probability that both
marbles drawn will be the same color.

   A $\frac{5}{12}$ **B** $\frac{3}{8}$ **C** $\frac{2}{5}$ **D** $\frac{5}{24}$

10. Use this table of
random digits to
find P(prime
number) when a
cube with sides
numbered 1
through 6 is
rolled.

3 5	6 5	2 9 7			

  3 5 6 5 2 9 7
  8 6 4 3 1 4 5
  5 9 0 2 7 6 9
  0 2 7 9 3 0 5
  1 5 3 1 6 5 4

   A $\frac{2}{5}$ **B** $\frac{7}{12}$ **C** $\frac{17}{35}$ **D** $\frac{17}{24}$

11. A serial number consists of 1 letter and
3 digits. How many possible serial
numbers are there?

   A 18,720   **B** 18,954

   C 13,104   **D** 26,000

12. Find the cost of mailing a $3\frac{1}{2}$ ounce
letter.

Weight	Rate
1st oz.	$0.25
Each additional oz. or fraction of an oz. up to 12 oz.	$0.20

   A $0.65 **B** $0.85 **C** $0.80 **D** $0.45

14

MATH AND
SOCIAL STUDIES

DATA BANK

Use the Social Studies
Data Bank on page 495 to
answer the questions.

1 If Thales found that a
pyramid's shadow extended
200 ft from the center of its
base, while his own shadow had the
same length as his own height, how
tall would the pyramid be?

SQUARE ROOTS AND SPECIAL TRIANGLES

THEME: ANCIENT PYRAMIDS

2 If Thales found that a 4 ft stick had a 3 ft shadow, while a temple had a 42 ft shadow, how tall would the temple be?

3 If Egyptian surveyors were creating a right angle with a rope that had one knot 18 ft from the end, where would the other knot be?

4 **Using Critical Thinking**
If the Pythagorean Theorem was formulated about 800 years after the Egypt's rope stretchers are known to have worked, why do you think the theorem might have been considered a breakthrough?

Scribes, priests, and workmen used mathematics to build the Egyptian pyramids.

Squares and Square Roots

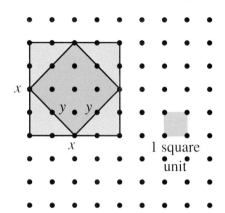

LEARN ABOUT IT

EXPLORE **Compare the Squares**

Draw this pattern of two squares on dot paper. Divide the two squares into triangles. What is the relationship of the areas of the 2 squares?

TALK ABOUT IT

1. What is the length of x?

2. Since the area of the large square is 16, $x^2 = $ ▦.

3. From the area of the small square we see that $y^2 = $ ▦.

Each positive number has two square roots.
The **positive square root** of 16 is 4 because $4 \cdot 4 = 16$. $\sqrt{16} = 4$
The **negative square root** of 16 is -4 because $-4 \cdot {}^-4 = 16$. ${}^-\sqrt{16} = {}^-4$

The symbol $\sqrt{}$ is called a **radical sign** and is used to indicate the positive square root of a number.

$\sqrt{16}$ is read "the square root of 16."

The numbers 1, 4, 9, 16, 25, 36, . . . are called **perfect squares** because their square roots are integers. In this lesson you will be finding square roots of perfect squares.

Examples   Find each square root.

A $\sqrt{49} = 7$ **B** ${}^-\sqrt{100} = {}^-10$ **C** ${}^-\sqrt{36} = {}^-6$ **D** $\sqrt{121} = 11$

Square roots can be solutions to equations.

Both $\sqrt{2}$ and ${}^-\sqrt{2}$ are solutions to $x^2 = 2$
since $\sqrt{2} \cdot \sqrt{2} = 2$ and $({}^-\sqrt{2}) \cdot ({}^-\sqrt{2}) = 2$

TRY IT OUT

Find each square root.

1. $\sqrt{64}$ 2. ${}^-\sqrt{25}$ 3. $\sqrt{81}$ 4. ${}^-\sqrt{9}$

5. $\sqrt{36}$ 6. ${}^-\sqrt{121}$ 7. ${}^-\sqrt{64}$ 8. $\sqrt{9}$

Find the length of a side of each square.

1.   Area
4 ft²

2.   Area
81 mi²

3.   Area
25 in²

Find each square root.

4. $\sqrt{4}$

5. $^-\sqrt{36}$

6. $^-\sqrt{64}$

7. $\sqrt{100}$

8. $^-\sqrt{9}$

9. $^-\sqrt{81}$

10. $\sqrt{144}$

11. $^-\sqrt{1}$

12. $\sqrt{8100}$

13. $^-\sqrt{169}$

14. $^-\sqrt{196}$

15. $\sqrt{225}$

16. The square root of 256

17. The negative square root of 361

Write two solutions to each of these equations.

18. $x^2 = 25$

19. $x^2 = 36$

20. $x^2 = 16$

21. $x^2 = 9$

APPLY

MATH REASONING Solve each equation.

22. $x = \sqrt{81} + \sqrt{9}$

23. $x = \sqrt{16 + 9}$

24. $x = \sqrt{169 - 25}$

PROBLEM SOLVING

25. A large square tarpaulin covers a baseball diamond. If each side is about 30 m, how much area is covered?

26. A square tarpaulin covering a softball field has an area of 441 m². What is the length of one side of the tarpaulin?

27. The Great Pyramid of Cheops has a square base that covers about 53,000 m². Estimate how far it is around the base.

28. Data Hunt The Zimmermanns paid $1,600 for the carpet in their 4 m by 4 m family room. Was this a good value?

▶ **USING CRITICAL THINKING Find the Pattern**

29. Copy this pyramid onto another piece of paper and fill in the blanks. Do the patterns continue?

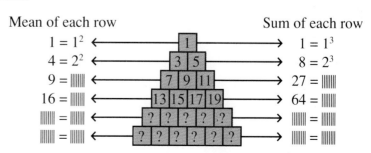

Mean of each row

$1 = 1^2$

$4 = 2^2$

$9 = \text{▥}$

$16 = \text{▥}$

$\text{▥} = \text{▥}$

$\text{▥} = \text{▥}$

Sum of each row

$1 = 1^3$

$8 = 2^3$

$27 = \text{▥}$

$64 = \text{▥}$

$\text{▥} = \text{▥}$

$\text{▥} = \text{▥}$

More Practice, page 540, set B

Approximate Square Roots

The square root of any whole number which is not a perfect square can only be approximated as a decimal. For example, $\sqrt{18} \approx 4.243$. Since $(4.243)^2 = 18.003$, you can see that the decimal 4.243 only approximates $\sqrt{18}$.

EXPLORE Use a Calculator

Use the $\boxed{\sqrt{\ }}$ key on your calculator to find an approximate square root rounded to the nearest thousandth. Show it is an approximation by squaring the result.

$\sqrt{15} \approx$ ▦ $\sqrt{40} =$ ▦ $^{-}\sqrt{75} \approx$ ▦

CALCULATOR SQUARE ROOTS
Input Press Display
15   $\boxed{\sqrt{\ }}$ 3.8729833
$\sqrt{15} \approx 3.873$

TALK ABOUT IT

1. $\sqrt{13}$ rounded to the nearest thousandth is ▦.

2. $(3.606)^2 =$ ▦. This shows that $\sqrt{13}$ (is, is not) exactly 3.606.

3. Do you estimate that $\sqrt{47}$ is closer to 6 or to 7? Why?

You have used the $\boxed{\sqrt{\ }}$ key on your calculator to find approximations to square roots. You can also use a table.

Examples

A Use this table to find an approximation for $\sqrt{40}$. $\sqrt{40} \approx 6.324$.

B Solve $x^2 = 40$. Find an exact value and an approximation for x.
$x = \sqrt{40}$ $x \approx 6.324$

Number	Square Root	Number	Square Root
2	1.414	20	4.472
3	1.732	30	5.477
4	2	40	6.324
5	2.236	50	7.071
6	2.449	60	7.746
7	2.646	70	8.367
8	2.828	80	8.944
9	3	90	9.487
10	3.162	100	10

Use the table or a calculator to find each square root. Round answers to the nearest thousandth.

1. $\sqrt{7}$ 2. $\sqrt{3}$ 3. $\sqrt{50}$ 4. $\sqrt{60}$ 5. $\sqrt{30}$

Use the table of square roots on page 551 to find each square root.

1. $\sqrt{6}$ **2.** $^-\sqrt{60}$ **3.** $^-\sqrt{9}$ **4.** $\sqrt{90}$ **5.** $\sqrt{3}$

6. $\sqrt{10}$ **7.** $\sqrt{100}$ **8.** $\sqrt{36}$ **9.** $\sqrt{30}$ **10.** $\sqrt{2}$

Use a calculator to find these square roots to the nearest thousandth.

11. $^-\sqrt{23}$ **12.** $\sqrt{69}$ **13.** $\sqrt{317}$ **14.** $\sqrt{97}$ **15.** $\sqrt{129}$

16. $\sqrt{72}$ **17.** $\sqrt{24}$ **18.** $\sqrt{225}$ **19.** $^-\sqrt{335}$ **20.** $\sqrt{7744}$

Use the table values to find an integer m.

21. $\sqrt{m} \approx 1.732$ **22.** $\sqrt{m} \approx 2.236$ **23.** $\sqrt{m} = 9$

24. $\sqrt{m} \approx 4.472$ **25.** $\sqrt{m} \approx 9.487$ **26.** $\sqrt{m} = 4$

APPLY

MATH REASONING For each equation write a positive number that is an exact solution. Then find an approximate solution.

27. $x^2 = 45$ **28.** $x^2 = 74$ **29.** $x^2 = 120$

PROBLEM SOLVING

30. What is the area of a square game board measuring 50 cm on each side?

31. A square has an area of 10 cm². What is the length of a side to the nearest mm?

32. Maria has trim for the edge of a square tablecloth. How much material does she need? Will you first find the area or the perimeter of the material?

33. Randy ran 10 laps around a square field with an area of 8,100 m². How many km did he run?

▶ **ALGEBRA**

Find the square roots. Then add or multiply as indicated.

34. Compare $\sqrt{8}$ and $\sqrt{2} \cdot \sqrt{4}$ **35.** Compare $\sqrt{20}$ and $\sqrt{4} \cdot \sqrt{5}$

36. Compare $\sqrt{50}$ and $\sqrt{2} \cdot \sqrt{25}$ **37.** Compare $\sqrt{7}$ and $\sqrt{3} + \sqrt{4}$

Use your results from above to decide if either of these equations is true for all positive values of x and y.

38. $\sqrt{x \cdot y} = \sqrt{x} \cdot \sqrt{y}$ **39.** $\sqrt{x + y} = \sqrt{x} + \sqrt{y}$

More Practice, page 540, set C

Square Roots and Irrational Numbers

When a square root is a **repeating** or a **terminating** decimal, it is a **rational** number. Numbers represented by **nonrepeating and nonterminating** decimals are called **irrational** numbers.

EXPLORE Use Your Calculator

Decide which of these square roots are terminating or repeating decimals, and hence rational numbers.

$\sqrt{2.25}$ $\sqrt{2.9}$

$\sqrt{1.5625}$ $\sqrt{3.0625}$

TALK ABOUT IT

1. Using a calculator, can you tell when a decimal is terminating?

2. How many of the above square roots are terminating?

3. Experiment. Find a whole number whose square root does not appear to be terminating.

If a number is a perfect square or a quotient of perfect squares, then its square root is a rational number. All other square roots are irrational numbers.

Examples Express each square root as a decimal. Tell if it is rational or irrational.

A $\sqrt{\dfrac{16}{9}} = \dfrac{4}{3} = 1.333\ldots$ rational

$16 \boxed{\div} 9 \boxed{=} \boxed{\sqrt{}} \boxed{1.3333333}$

B $\sqrt{3} = 1.7320508\ldots$ irrational

$3 \boxed{\sqrt{}} \boxed{1.7320508}$

Express each square root as a decimal rounded to the nearest thousandth. State if it is rational or irrational.

1. $\sqrt{441}$ 2. $\sqrt{23}$ 3. $\sqrt{\dfrac{81}{16}}$ 4. $\sqrt{42}$ 5. $\sqrt{18}$

State if the decimal represents a rational number or an irrational number.

6. $0.\overline{78}$ 7. 0.1298930 8. $0.12112111211112\ldots$ 9. 0.333

State if the decimal represents a rational or an irrational number.

1. $0.14\overline{27}$ **2.** $0.123849230\ldots$ **3.** $0.10110111\ldots$ **4.** $0.\overline{23}$

5. $7.5555\ldots$ **6.** 1.2345459 **7.** $3.41423798\ldots$ **8.** 0.8572

Express each square root as a decimal rounded to the nearest thousandth.

9. $\sqrt{121}$ **10.** $\sqrt{125}$ **11.** $\sqrt{7}$ **12.** $\sqrt{12}$ **13.** $\sqrt{841}$

14. $\sqrt{9}$ **15.** $\sqrt{\frac{22}{7}}$ **16.** $\sqrt{1.6}$ **17.** $\sqrt{\frac{81}{64}}$ **18.** $\sqrt{35}$

19. $\sqrt{\frac{16}{25}}$ **20.** $\sqrt{\frac{4}{5}}$ **21.** $\sqrt{0.8}$ **22.** $\sqrt{\frac{144}{225}}$ **23.** $\sqrt{\frac{81}{196}}$

MATH REASONING Each decimal has a pattern. Find the next three digits in the pattern. State whether the number is rational or irrational.

24. $0.123123\ldots$ **25.** $0.1287128\ldots$ **26.** $0.121121112\ldots$ **27.** $0.12131415\ldots$

PROBLEM SOLVING

28. A survey team wants to mark the boundary of a square 40 m² in area. Let x be the length of one side. What equation would you solve to find the length of a side of the square?

29. The area of a square is 65 m². What is the length of one side of the square? Why can't the sides of this square be measured exactly?

Find the area of each polygon.

30.
7 in.
7 in.

31.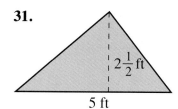
$2\frac{1}{2}$ ft
5 ft

32.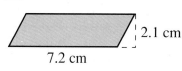
2.1 cm
7.2 cm

Solve.

33. $5x + {}^-2 = 8$ **34.** $7 + 9x = {}^-2$ **35.** $\frac{x}{10} + {}^-14 = {}^-24$

More Practice, page 540, set D

Exploring Algebra
Solving Inequalities by the Addition Property

LEARN ABOUT IT

You have graphed inequalities such as $x < 5$.
Here is the graph of $x \geq \sqrt{2}$.

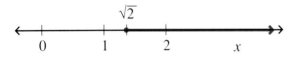

EXPLORE Draw a Conclusion

A man and his son tried to weigh
themselves on a pay scale using only
one quarter. When the boy got on, the
scale read 119 pounds. His father joined
him and the scale went past its 300 pound
limit. What conclusions can you draw?

TALK ABOUT IT

1. If w stands for the man's weight, is $w > 300$?

2. How do you know that $w + 119 > 300$?

3. If the boy steps off the scale, what inequality represents
   the situation?

You can solve an inequality like $w + 119 > 300$ by adding the
same number to each side. Use one of these properties of
inequalities which are true for all numbers a, b, and c.

If $a \leq b$, then $a + c \leq b + c$.   **If $a \leq b$, then $a - c \leq b - c$.**

Examples Solve and graph these inequalities.

A
$$y - 2 \leq 17.1$$
$$y - 2 + 2 \leq 17.1 + 2$$
$$y \leq 19.1$$

B
$$^-60 < w + ^-8$$
$$^-60 + 8 < w + ^-8 + 8$$
$$^-52 < w$$

TRY IT OUT

Solve and graph these inequalities.

1. $t + 30 < 153$ 2. $^-7 \geq y - 4$ 3. $x - 3 < ^-2$

Solve and graph these inequalities.

1. $v + 7 < 20$

2. $x - 10 > 15$

3. $^-6 \leq y + 4$

4. $t - 14 > {}^-5$

5. $m + {}^-3 \leq {}^-4$

6. $x - 7 \geq {}^-0.7$

7. $t - 2 < {}^-3$

8. $k + 2 > \sqrt{4}$

9. $n + 6 > -\frac{1}{2}$

10. $4.8 > 3.5 + y$

11. $3 \leq 5 + x$

12. $t - 1\frac{3}{4} \geq 2\frac{1}{2}$

13. $x - 0.1 < 1.3$

14. $^-4.25 + m \leq 4.5$

15. $^-5 \leq y - 2\frac{1}{2}$

16. $\sqrt{9} < t + 8$

17. $3\frac{3}{4} + n \geq 1\frac{1}{2}$

18. $0.75 - b < {}^-1.39$

APPLY

MATH REASONING Write and solve inequalities represented by the pictures.

19.

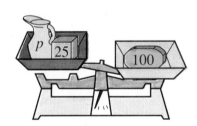

20.

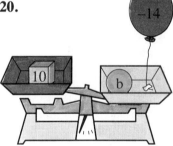

21.

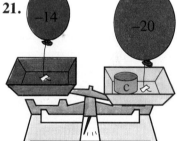

PROBLEM SOLVING

22. A woman and her identical twins have a total weight of 153.2 pounds. The woman weighs 131 pounds by herself. How much does each baby weigh?

23. Normal body temperature is 98.6° F. You should call a doctor when you have a prolonged fever of more than 3° above normal. What thermometer reading, if maintained, means you need to see a doctor?

▶ **ESTIMATION**

Estimate solutions to the nearest whole number.

24. $x + 99.89 \leq 231.78$

25. $x - 14\frac{8}{9} > 83.001$

26. $-1,000 < x + 381.12$

Using Critical Thinking

LEARN ABOUT IT

Reyna's track coach asked her to measure and mark the track where the low hurdles should be placed for the race in which the hurdles were to be set 20 meters apart. Reyna asked Kelly to help her.

Kelly said, "Two normal steps of mine measures about 1 meter, so I'll just pace 40 steps between each hurdle."

Reyna disagreed, "That's not measuring, that's just guessing at the correct distance. I think that we should use this plastic tape measure and measure 2,000 cm between each hurdle."

Kelly responded, "But that plastic tape stretches a bit. Let's use this steel tape, marked off in meters."

TALK ABOUT IT

1. To what extent is using 40 of Kelly's steps measuring?

2. Can you be as accurate with a meter tape as with a centimeter tape in making this measurement?

3. Would you use the steel meter tape or the plastic centimeter tape to complete the most accurate measurement?

4. Is a measurement to the nearest centimeter more precise or less precise than measuring to the nearest meter?

5. What is the difference between measuring **accurately** and choosing a unit of measure that will result in a **precise** measurement?

TRY IT OUT

1. Why would it be more accurate to set the hurdles using a 25 meter tape than a meter stick?

2. To measure a distance in a road atlas would you use a meter stick, a centimeter ruler, or a 100 meter measuring tape?

POWER PRACTICE/QUIZ

Find the length of a side of each square.

1.

64 in²

2.

36 mi²

3.

441 ft²

Find each square root.

4. $\sqrt{400}$ **5.** $\sqrt{144}$ **6.** $^-\sqrt{81}$ **7.** $^-\sqrt{225}$

Use a table or a calculator to find each square root to the nearest thousandth.

8. $\sqrt{8}$ **9.** $\sqrt{125}$ **10.** $^-\sqrt{54}$

11. $^-\sqrt{64}$ **12.** $\sqrt{17}$ **13.** $\sqrt{21}$

14. $\sqrt{82}$ **15.** $\sqrt{35}$ **16.** $^-\sqrt{29}$

Express each square root as a decimal rounded to the nearest thousandth. State if it is rational or irrational.

17. $\sqrt{133}$ **18.** $\sqrt{\frac{64}{81}}$ **19.** $^-\sqrt{8.1}$ **20.** $\sqrt{\frac{5}{13}}$

Solve.

21. $x^2 = 36$ **22.** $x^2 = 100$ **23.** $\sqrt{m} = 4$ **24.** $\sqrt{m} = 2$

Solve and graph these inequalities.

25. $x + 5 \geq 4$ **26.** $x - 5 < 2$ **27.** $^-6 + x \leq 0$

PROBLEM SOLVING

28. Ray planted a square garden that covers an area 200 ft². How many feet of fencing does he need to surround the garden?

29. Claire and Juanita each ran 7 mi. Claire ran 3 mi west and then 4 mi north. Juanita ran 2 mi east and 5 mi south. Who was farther from her starting point?

Using the Pythagorean Relationship

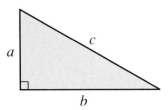

If a and b are the lengths of the legs of a right triangle and if c is the length of the hypotenuse, then $c^2 = a^2 + b^2$.

EXPLORE **Study the Drawing**

Surveyors often have to calculate distances they can't measure directly. One of their tools is the Pythagorean Relationship. For example, suppose they have to find the distance d from A to B in this figure.

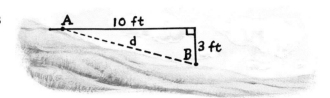

TALK ABOUT IT

1. Write an equation that results from the Pythagorean Relationship applied to the right triangle shown in the figure.

2. Since $d^2 = 109$, then $d = $ ___?___.

3. Length d is between which two whole numbers?

The Pythagorean Relationship allows us to find the length of a side of a right triangle if the other two side lengths are known.

Examples

A Find the length of hypotenuse c.

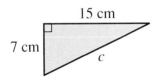

$$c^2 = 7^2 + 15^2$$
$$c^2 = 49 + 225 = 274$$
$$c = \sqrt{274} \text{ or } c \approx 16.553 \text{ cm}$$

B Find the length of leg a.

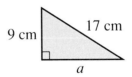

$$17^2 = a^2 + 9^2$$
$$289 = a^2 + 81$$
$$a^2 = 289 - 81 = 208$$
$$a = \sqrt{208} \text{ or } a \approx 14.422 \text{ cm}$$

Find the length of the unknown side of each right triangle to the nearest hundredth. Use a table of square roots or a calculator.

1. $a = 3$, $b = 4$, find c 2. $a = 20$, $c = 25$, find b 3. $b = 6$, $c = 12$, find a

PRACTICE

Use a table of square roots or a calculator to find the length of each hypotenuse to the nearest thousandth.

1.
7 cm, c, 18 cm

2.
8 cm, c, 5 cm

3.
13 cm, c, 9 cm

Find the missing length of each right triangle to the nearest thousandth.

4.
a, 24 cm, 11 cm

5.
a, 15 cm, 6 cm

6.
a, 9 cm, 31 cm

7. $a = 8$ cm
$b = 35$ cm
find c

8. $a = 12$ mm
$b = 19$ mm
find c

9. $a = 3$ m
$c = 25$ m
find b

10. $b = 8$ cm
$c = 16$ cm
find a

APPLY

MATH REASONING

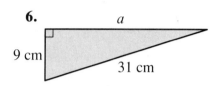

11. Explain how you can determine whether length c is greater than or less than 11 using mental math.

PROBLEM SOLVING

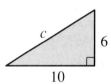

12. A surveyor measures lengths $\overline{AB}$ and $\overline{BC}$ to be 2 mi and 3 mi. $\angle ABC$ is a right angle. How far, to the nearest mi, is it from dock A to dock C across the lake?

13. Social Studies Data Bank A team of Egyptian surveyors has a rope for making right angles. The rope has a knot 45 ft from one end. What is a possible total length for the rope?

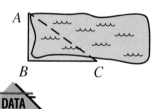

DATA BANK

▶ **CALCULATOR**

The key sequence $3\,\boxed{x^2}\,\boxed{+}\,4\,\boxed{x^2}\,\boxed{=}\,\boxed{\sqrt{}}$ will find the length of the hypotenuse (c) of the right triangle with legs $a = 3$ and $b = 4$.

Find the length of the hypotenuse c for right triangles with these legs.

14. $a = 7, b = 8$

15. $a = 12, b = 17$

16. $a = 9, b = 19$

More Practice, page 540, set E

403

Problem Solving
Using the Strategies

| UNDERSTAND |
| ANALYZE DATA |
| PLAN |
| ESTIMATE |
| SOLVE |
| EXAMINE |

LEARN ABOUT IT

For some problems you may find it helpful to combine two or more strategies. For this problem you can **Make a Table,** and then **Work Backwards** and **Use Logical Reasoning.**

Two boys, José and Dave, were playing a game. They decided to play two more rounds. At the end of each of the last two rounds the loser had to double the winner's points by giving away some of his own. José lost round 1 and Dave lost round 2. The game ended in a tie with each boy having 8 points. How many points did each boy have before the last two rounds?

Make a Table to show players, rounds, and ending points.

Because Dave lost round 2, he had to double José's points. This means José had 8 ÷ 2 = 4 points at the beginning of round 2 and Dave had to give him 4 points. Therefore Dave had 8 + 4 = 12 points at the beginning of round 2.

José lost round 1 and had to double Dave's points. So Dave had 12 ÷ 2 = 6 points at the beginning of round 1. Since José had to give him 6 points, José had 4 ÷ 6 = 10 points at the beginning of round 1.

José had 10 points and Dave had 6 points before they played the last two rounds.

	José	Dave
1		
2		
end	8	8

	José	Dave
1		
2	4	12
end	8	8

	José	Dave
1	10	6
2	4	12
end	8	8

TRY IT OUT

Solve. Use any problem solving strategy.

1. In the game above suppose each boy had 40 points at the end and the loser had to give one third of his points to the winner. How many points did each boy have before the last two rounds?

2. Three girls played three more rounds. In each round there were 2 winners. The loser had to double the points of each winner. Each girl lost one round. In the end, each had 24 points. How many points did each girl have before the three rounds?

Solve. Use any problem solving strategy.

Some Strategies	
Act Out	Solve a Simpler Problem
Use Objects	Make an Organized List
Choose an Operation	Work Backward
Draw a Picture	Look for a Pattern
Guess and Check	Use Logical Reasoning
Make a Table	Write an Equation

1. Lee and her friends are writing a report about African board games. They worked together three afternoons. The first afternoon they worked for 55 minutes. The third afternoon they worked twice as long as the first and half as long as the second. How long did they work altogether?

2. Luke and his group are playing a game of Zulu Marble Golf. Players try to roll marbles into a series of six holes with as few rolls as possible. Luke's scores for five games are 13, 11, 15, 14, and 12. What does he need to score next to have an average of 13?

3. Angie took $15 out of her savings account to buy a game. She paid $4.39 for a dart board and $6.25 for a box of 12 darts. How much did Angie spend?

4. Yvonne and Amelia are playing a game. They have 16 markers in a bag. The markers are numbered 1 to 16. The even numbered markers are red and the odd numbered markers are blue. They take turns picking a marker out of the bag until all the markers are gone. They then add up the amount on their markers. The girl with the highest total wins. Is it possible for the girls to get the same total?

5. Milly counted out 45 marbles and put a different number in each of 4 bags. Then she put 2 more in the first bag, took 2 out of the second bag, doubled the number in the third bag, and took half of the marbles out of the fourth bag. Now each bag contains the same number of marbles. How many did Milly first put in each bag?

6. Art was tossing a beanbag into a box. Each time he hit the box he got 2 points. Each time he missed he lost 5 points. Art tossed the beanbag 15 times. How many times did he have to hit the box to get more points than he lost?

7. Boyd and two friends are playing a game. Each round has one loser and two winners. The loser has to take half of his points and divide them equally between the two winners. Each boy loses one round. After three rounds each had 16 points. How many points did each boy have before the last three rounds?

Go, a board game of strategy and logic, originated in Asia over 4,000 years ago.

More Practice, page 546, set D

45°–45° Right Triangles

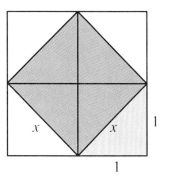

LEARN ABOUT IT

An isosceles right triangle has two 45° angles. Any such triangle is called a **45°–45° right triangle.** Drawing the diagonal of a square forms two of these triangles.

EXPLORE Study the Design

The design at the right consists of eight 45°–45° right triangles.

TALK ABOUT IT

1. Each edge of the shaded square is a hypotenuse of a 45°–45° right triangles. What is the area of the shaded square?

2. Which equation is true? a)$x^2 = \sqrt{2}$ b) $x^2 = 2$ c) $x^2 = 4$

3. What is the length of x?

The above design gives one way to reason that $x = \sqrt{2}$. Another way is to use the Pythagorean Relationship.

$$x^2 = 1^2 + 1^2$$
$$x^2 = 2$$
$$x = \sqrt{2}$$

Suppose $\triangle DEF$ is a 45°–45° right triangle with legs of length 3. Since all 45°–45° right triangles are similar, $\triangle DEF$ is similar to $\triangle ABC$. Therefore, a proportion can be used to find the hypotenuse of $\triangle DEF$.

$$\frac{3}{1} = \frac{y}{\sqrt{2}}$$
$$y = 3 \cdot \sqrt{2}$$

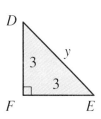

If a 45°–45° right triangle has legs x units long, the hypotenuse is $x \cdot \sqrt{2}$ units long.

Example

A surveyor must find the distance across the diagonal of a square field that is 30 meters on a side. Find this length.

Solution: $d = 30\sqrt{2} \approx 30 \cdot 1.414 = 42.42$ m

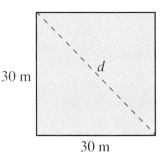

TRY IT OUT

Find the hypotenuse of each 45°–45° right triangle given the length of its legs.

1. 2 dm   **2.** 4 cm   **3.** 15 m   **4.** 25 km

406

Find the hypotenuse for each 45°–45° right triangle. Express your answer both in radical form and as a decimal approximation to the nearest thousandth. Use $\sqrt{2} \approx 1.414$.

1.
12
12

2.
8
8

3.
3.2 3.2

4.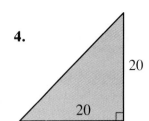
20
20

5. Find the length of the hypotenuse of a 45°–45° right triangle if the length of each leg is 5 centimeters.

APPLY

MATH REASONING

6. Use a calculator to decide which of these numbers represents the length x.

A $\dfrac{4}{\sqrt{2}}$ **B** $2\sqrt{2}$ **C** $\dfrac{2}{\sqrt{2}}$

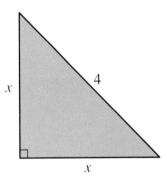
x
4
x

PROBLEM SOLVING

7. In baseball the distance between bases is 90 feet. Approximately how far is it from home plate to second base?

8. A survey team is locating corners A, B, C, and D of the foundation for a square building that is to be 120 feet on a *side*. After marking the four corners they measure distance AC and find it to be 165 feet. They conclude that they have incorrectly located A, B, C, and D. Explain why.

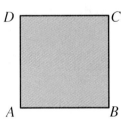
D C
A B

MIXED REVIEW

Find the area of each circle with the given radius. Use 3.14 for π.

9. $r = 7$ cm   **10.** $r = 60$ ft   **11.** $r = 1.3$ m

Find the unit price to the nearest cent.

12. 12 oz for $0.69   **13.** 30 cans for $24.50   **14.** 1.6 L for $4.20

30°–60° Right Triangles

EXPLORE **Copy the Triangle**

Work in groups. Copy and cut out equilateral triangle *ABD*. Fold the triangle along its line of symmetry. $\overline{BC}$.

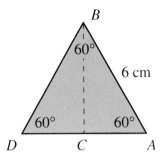
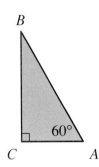

TALK ABOUT IT

1. How long is $\overline{AC}$ if the length of each side of $\triangle ABD$ is 6 cm?

2. How does m $\angle ABC$ compare to m $\angle ABD$? Why is $\triangle ABC$ called a 30°–60° right triangle?

In any **30°–60° right triangle,** the length of the leg opposite the 30° angle is half the length of the hypotenuse.

Using this fact and applying the Pythagorean Relationship to the triangles below, we can make the following conclusion.

$$z^2 + 1^2 = 2^2$$
$$z^2 = 2^2 - 1^2 = 4 - 1 = 3$$
$$z = \sqrt{3}$$

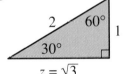

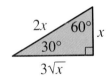

In any 30°–60° right triangle, the length of the leg opposite the 60° angle is $\sqrt{3}$ times the length of the leg opposite the 30° angle.

Example Find the lengths *x* and *y* of the legs of this triangle.

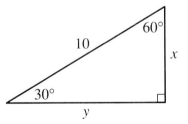

x is half the length of the hypotenuse, so $x = \frac{10}{2} = 5$.

y is $\sqrt{3}$ times *x*, so $y = 5 \cdot \sqrt{3}$.

Given one length, find the lengths of the other two sides.

1.

2.

3.

Find x and y for each triangle. Express answers in radical form.

1.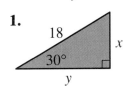

2.

3.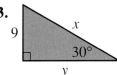

4.

Find the missing lengths in each problem.

5. If $z = 4$, find x and y.　　**6.** If $z = 20$, find x and y.

7. If $z = 15$, find x and y.　　**8.** If $z = 8.6$, find x and y.

9. If $x = 20$, find y and z.　　**10.** If $x = 4$, find y and z.

11. If $x = 15$, find y and z.　　**12.** If $y = 6\sqrt{3}$, find x and z.

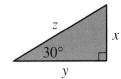

APPLY

13. Find the area of this 30°–60° right triangle.

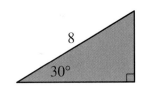

PROBLEM SOLVING

14. To find the length of a pond, a surveyor made the measurements shown in this diagram. What is the length of the pond?

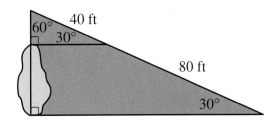

15. Social Studies Data Bank If you were on a team of rope stretchers and wanted to make a rope especially for creating 30°–60° right triangles, what length rope might you use, and where would you put the knots? How would you make the triangle?

▶ **USING CRITICAL THINKING** **Justify Your Answer**

16. Quarter-circles are constructed on each side of 30°–60° right triangle with side lengths 2, 1, and $\sqrt{3}$. How does the area of region C compare to the areas of regions A and B? Is the relationship you discovered true for all 30°–60° right triangles?

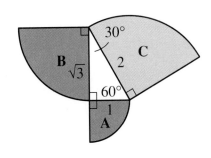

More Practice, page 541, set A

409

Problem Solving
Using a Calculator

UNDERSTAND
ANALYZE DATA
PLAN
ESTIMATE
SOLVE
EXAMINE

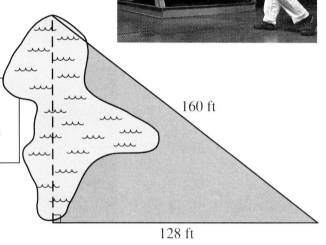

LEARN ABOUT IT

When a problem has several steps it is
important to analyze and understand the
sequence of the steps before using a
calculator. Then you can use a calculator
to carry out the steps.

A telephone company wants to lay a
cable from one end of a small lake to
the opposite end. They have made these
measurements. How long is the lake?

160 ft

128 ft

Use the Pythagorean Relationship to solve
this problem. First square 160, then subtract
128^2.

$$160^2 - 128^2$$

Find the square root of the result to get the
answer.

$$\sqrt{160^2 - 128^2}$$

To solve this problem on a calculator, use the following key
sequence.

160 $\boxed{x^2}$ $\boxed{-}$ 128 $\boxed{x^2}$ $\boxed{=}$ $\boxed{\sqrt{}}$ $\boxed{96}$

The lake is 96 feet long.

TRY IT OUT

Solve using your calculator. Use any problem solving strategy.
Round answers to the nearest hundredth.

1. A 36 ft ladder is leaning against the wall
   of a building. The bottom of the ladder
   is 5 ft from the bottom of the wall. How
   far up the wall is the top of the ladder?

2. An airplane took off from an airport.
   When it was directly above a park
   13.5 mi from the airport, its altitude was
   3.7 mi. How far had the plane flown?

Solve. Use any problem solving strategy. Round answers to the nearest hundredth.

1. A 14 ft diagonal brace on a garage door makes an angle of 30° with the top of the door. The door is 12.1 ft wide. How high is the door?

2. Jeremy lives on Acacia Drive, 257 yd from the intersection of Acacia and Elm Street. Penny lives on Elm, 113 yd from its intersection with Acacia. Use the picture to find how many yards Penny can save by walking directly to Jeremy's house instead of walking along the streets.

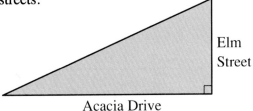

Elm Street

Acacia Drive

3. A class set of 36 calculators cost $190.04 including $10.76 tax. How much did each calculator cost before the tax?

4. A CB radio station is located 1.9 mi off a main highway. It has a range of 4.3 mi. Use the picture to find how many miles of the highway are within its range.

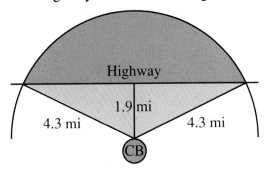

Highway

1.9 mi

4.3 mi   4.3 mi

CB

5. Jake saved $45 to buy a programmable calculator. He found one on sale for 30% off. The regular price was $44.95. About how much did Jake save?

6. Some people are standing in a circle for a game. They are evenly spaced and numbered in order. The 9th person is directly opposite the 23rd person. How many people are in the circle?

7. An equilateral triangle can be divided into many smaller equilateral triangles. How many point-up triangles of all sizes are there in this triangle?

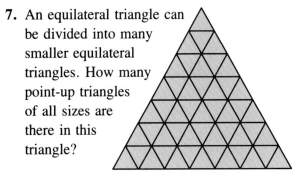

8. The telephone operator asked Tory to deposit $0.50 in a phone that takes quarters, dimes and nickels. She deposited less than 5 coins. What coins were they?

Rob started to make an organized list to help solve this problem. Copy and finish Rob's list to determine what coins Tory deposited.

Quarters	Dimes	Nickles
2	0	0
1	2	1
1	1	?

Data Collection and Analysis
Group Decision Making

Doing An Investigation

Group Skill:
Check for Understanding

How do you think the price of a used car is related to its age? You can use the classified ads section of a newspaper to investigate this relationship.

Collecting Data

1. Work with your group to decide how to get a representative sample of cars from the classified section of your newspaper. It is possible to choose your sample randomly? Try to have a minimum of 30 cars in your sample.

2. Make a list of every car in your sample showing the kind of car, the year it was made, and its price.

Car	Year	Price
1. Centurion	1985	$3,850
2.	1983	$2,500
3.	1988	. . . .

Organizing Data

3. Make a scattergraph using the data from your investigation. Plot a point for each car. Each point represents an ordered pair giving the year and the price of a particular car. Label the point so that you will know what car that point represents. Adjust the scales on your graph to fit the data you collected.

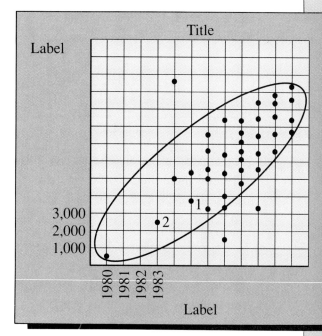

4. Discuss why the scattergraph is a better choice for organizing this data than a line graph.

5. Draw an ellipse on your graph so that most of the points are inside the ellipse. Make it as narrow as you can. Does the ellipse go up or down from left to right, or is it flat? What does this mean?

6. Can you find a point that lies far away from the main cluster of points? If so which car is this? Why do you think it is away from the main cluster?

413

WRAP UP

Rational and Irrational Numbers

Choose the term or terms that complete each sentence correctly.

repeating decimals	integer	Pythagorean Relationship
terminating decimals	addition property	45°–45° right triangle
non-terminating decimals		non-repeating decimals

1. To solve an inequality you can use the _____.

2. The square root of a perfect square is a(n) _____.

3. You can use the _____ to find missing sides of a right triangle.

4. A rational number has square roots that are _____ or _____.

5. The hypotenuse of a _____ with legs x units long is $x \cdot \sqrt{2}$.

6. An irrational number has square roots that are _____ and _____.

Sometimes, Always, Never

Which of these words should go in the blank, *sometimes, always,* or *never*? Explain your choice.

7. The square root of a perfect square is _____ an integer.

8. A whole number raised to the fourth power _____ results in a perfect square.

Project

Imagine a pyramid made of balls piled so that each layer is a square, beginning with one ball at the top, 4 in the next layer and so on. The numbers that result when you add the number in successive layers are pyramidal numbers. The first is 1. The next layer has 4 balls, so the next pyramidal number is 1 + 4 = 5. Write the first ten pyramidal numbers. Then find a formula for pyramidal numbers. Use the formula to find the eighteenth pyramidal number.

POWER PRACTICE/TEST

Part 1   Understanding

1. Name two numbers whose square is 25.

2. Which of the following statements is false for positive values
   of x and y? Give a counterexample for the false statement.

   a. $\sqrt{x} - \sqrt{y} = \sqrt{x - y}$ b. $\sqrt{x} \cdot \sqrt{y} = \sqrt{x \cdot y}$

State if the decimal represents a rational or irrational number.

3. $0.121231234\ldots$ 4. $0.123123123\ldots$ 5. 0.1234

6. Let a and b equal the lengths of the legs and c equal the
   hypotenuse of a right triangle. Which of the following are true?

   a. $(a + b)^2 = c^2$ b. $a \cdot \sqrt{2} = c^2$ c. $c = 2a$ if side a is opposite a $30°$ angle.

Part 2   Skills

Use the table of square roots on page 551 to find the value of x.

7. $x = \sqrt{27}$ 8. $x = -\sqrt{90}$ 9. $x^2 = 84$

10. Express $\sqrt{\dfrac{121}{81}}$ as a decimal rounded to the nearest thousandth.

    State if it is rational or irrational.

Solve and graph these inequalities.

11. $x + 2 < \sqrt{9}$ 12. $5 \geqslant y - 4$

Find the length of the unknown side of each right triangle to the
nearest hundredth. Use the table of square roots on page 551, as needed.

13. $a = 5$, $b = 7$, find c.   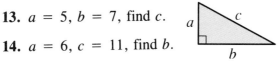   15. Find a and b.

14. $a = 6$, $c = 11$, find b.

Part 3   Applications

16. A 220-pound man got on a scale
    holding a package. The scale's needle
    went past the 250-pound limit. What
    could he determine about the weight of
    the package?

17. **Challenge** Red Hill is 4 km east of
    Croton. Riverton is 7 km south of
    Croton. Write the calculator sequence
    you could use to find the distance from
    Red Hill to Riverton. Then solve.
    Round your answer to the nearest km.

415

ENRICHMENT
Sine and Cosine Ratios

You have studied the tangent ratio in right triangles earlier. The **sine (sin)** and **cosine (cos)** ratios are also important and useful ratios.

$$\sin A = \frac{\text{opposite side}}{\text{hypotenuse}}$$

$$\cos A = \frac{\text{adjacent side}}{\text{hypotenuse}}$$

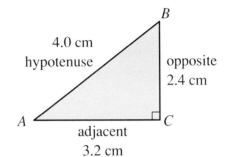

In $\triangle ABC$ these ratios are approximately

$$\sin 37° = \frac{2.4}{4.0} = 0.6 \qquad \cos 37° = \frac{3.2}{4.0} = 0.8$$

Calculators can give more exact values for sines and cosines of angles. Use this key code.

37 $\boxed{\sin}$ $\boxed{0.601815}$

37 $\boxed{\cos}$ $\boxed{0.7986355}$

Find sin A and cos A to the nearest thousandth.

1.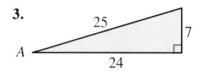

2.

3.

Use a protractor to draw a right triangle with m∠A as given. Measure the lengths of the legs and the hypotenuse. Find sin A and cos A.

4. 60°

5. 30°

6. 50°

7. 40°

8. Draw any right triangle. Choose one acute angle as ∠A. Measure the lengths of all 3 sides. Then compute the sine and cosine ratios for m∠A.

9. (Pythagoras) Choose any angle measure A and compute $(\sin A)^2 + (\cos A)^2$. Try other values for A. Why do you always get 1?

416

CUMULATIVE REVIEW

1. How many 4-digit numbers are possible using the digits 2, 4, 6, 8, 9?

   A 15   B 120

   C 24   D 20

2. Use this 6th row of Pascal's Triangle to find how many combinations of 6 things there are taken 3 at a time.

   1   6   15   20   15   6   1

   A 20   B 15   C 6   D 64

3. Which of the following outcomes is possible when a penny is tossed and then a cube with sides numbered 1 through 6 is rolled?

   A (T,7)   B (2,2)

   C (4,T)   D (H,3)

4. Which statement is false?

   A The probability of an impossible event is 0.

   B The probability of a certain event is 1.

   C The probability of an event may be less than 1.

   D The probability of an event may be greater than 1.

5. Angle A is supplementary to an angle whose measure is 60°. What is $m\angle A$?

   A 120°   B 30°

   C 60°   D 90°

6. Find the sum of the vertex angles in this figure.

   A 1,440°   B 1,080°

   C 540°   D 720°

7. In quadrilateral $ABCD$, $m\angle A = 75°$, $m\angle B = 115°$, and $m\angle C = 70°$. What is the $m\angle D$?

   A 90°   B 100°

   C 105°   D 120°

8. A 90° angle is drawn. When its bisector is constructed, what will be the measure of each angle formed?

   A 30°   B 180°

   C 45°   D 90°

9. Name a pair of parallel lines in this figure.

   A $\overleftrightarrow{AB}$ and $\overleftrightarrow{BA}$ B $\overleftrightarrow{AB}$ and $\overleftrightarrow{BD}$

   C $\overleftrightarrow{AB}$ and $\overleftrightarrow{AC}$ D $\overleftrightarrow{AB}$ and $\overleftrightarrow{CD}$

10. Which of these lines would have only one point in common with a circle?

    A chord   B tangent line

    C diameter   D secant line

11. Find the cost of salad, quiche, and tea plus 6% tax.

    A $5.83   B $5.50

    C $8.80   D $5.56

MENU	
Soup	$1.50
Salad	1.25
Quiche	3.50
Tea	0.75

12. Dustin has half as many pennies as Joe. Brett has a third as many as Joe. Tom's and Brett's pennies together are as many as Dustin has. Joe has 48 pennies. How many pennies does Tom have?

    A 16   B 12   C 24   D 8

15

MOTION GEOMETRY

MATH AND
FINE ARTS

DATA BANK

Use the Fine Arts Data Bank
on page 503 to answer the
questions.

1 In the computer image
Sharps, by Mike Newman
which figures are the same
size and the same shape? Which
figures are the same shape but not
the same size?

THEME: COMPUTER GRAPHICS

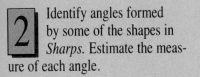

2 Identify angles formed by some of the shapes in *Sharps*. Estimate the measure of each angle.

3 To create a 1-minute television commercial using computer animation, how many individual frames are needed?

4 **Using Critical Thinking**
A computer artist often makes an image, then repeats it in different sizes, positions, and colors. What repeated images do you find in *Sharps?* How are the repetitions alike? How do they differ?

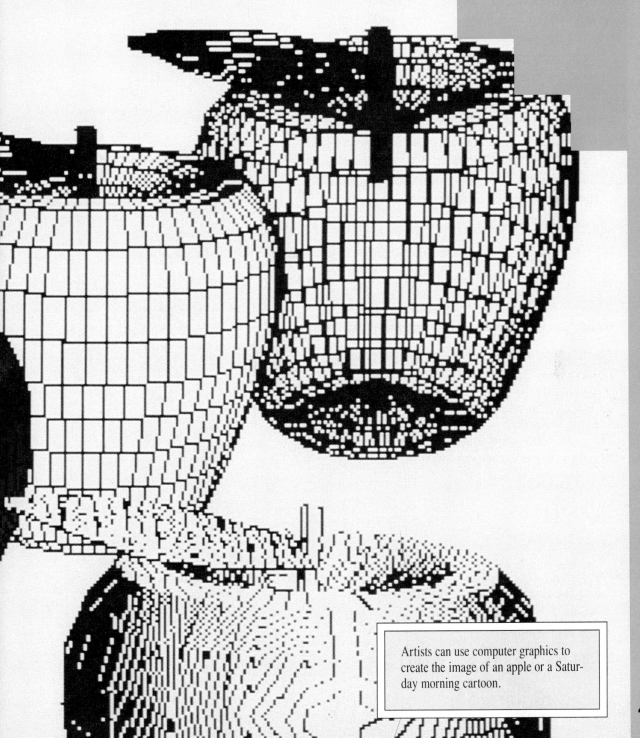

Artists can use computer graphics to create the image of an apple or a Saturday morning cartoon.

419

Translations

From ancient through modern times, artists have used repeated images in their work. Do you see any similarities between this detail from an Assyrian mural and the computer graphic on pages 418–419?

EXPLORE **Solve to Understand**

- Use dot paper to draw the quadrilateral shown.
- Draw the quadrilateral after you slide every point 5 units right and 2 units up. The quadrilateral in the new position is called the **slide image** or **translation image** of the original quadrilateral.

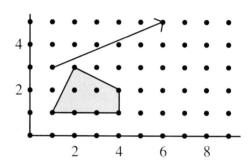

TALK ABOUT IT

1. What are the coordinates of each vertex of the original quadrilateral?

2. What are the coordinates of the translation image?

Suppose each point of the coordinate plane is translated in the direction of the arrow $\overrightarrow{AB}$.

The translation image of $P(2, 1)$ is the point $P'(2 + 4, 1 + 3)$. The translation image of $Q(1, 3)$ is the point $Q'(1 + 4, 3 + 3)$. (P' is read "P prime.")

Thus, the translation image of general point. $R(x, y)$ is the point $R'(x + 4, y + 3)$.

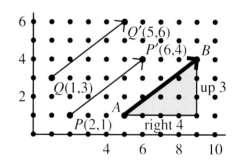

TRY IT OUT

1. Draw $\triangle ABC$ on dot paper and then draw its translation image for the translation $\overrightarrow{DE}$.

Using the translation $\overrightarrow{DE}$, find the coordinates for the translation image of each of the following.

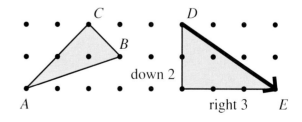

2. $P(4, 1)$ **3.** $Q(1, 6)$ **4.** $R(-2, 4)$ **5.** $S(3, -2)$

420

Use dot paper to draw the polygon and its translation image for
the translation shown.

1. 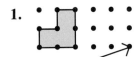   2.   3.

Use the translation described by the arrow at the right to find
the coordinates of the translation image of each point.

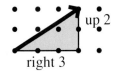

up 2

right 3

4. $P(2, 1)$ **5.** $Q(4, 5)$ **6.** $R(-1, 3)$ **7.** $S(4, -3)$

Use the art depicting polygons A, B, and C to answer 8–11.

8. To translate polygon A to polygon B you would take
point (x, y) to a) $(x + 2, y + 2)$,   b) $(x + 2, y + 3)$,
c) $(x + 2, y + 1)$

9. To translate polygon C to polygon A you would take
point (x, y) to a) $(x + 5, y + 1)$,   b) $(x - 5, y + 1)$,
c) $(x - 5, y - 1)$

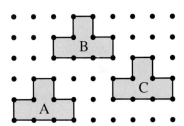

MATH REASONING

10. Translate point (x, y) to _____ to move
polygon B to polygon C.

11. Translate point (x, y) to _____ to move
polygon B to polygon A.

PROBLEM SOLVING

12. An artist is using a computer to create a
graphic image of a flag. She slides the same
curve she used for the bottom edge to create
the top edge. Does this process represent a
translation that moves 6, 4, or 2 centimeters?

13. Fine Arts Data Bank In the computer image
Sharps, identify where translations were used.

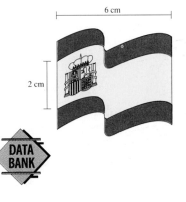

6 cm

2 cm

DATA
BANK

▶ **MENTAL MATH**

Solve this problem without using paper and pencil.

14. What single translation accomplishes the same as the
following combination: (right 5, up 3) followed by (right 2,
down 1) followed by (left 3, down 4)?

Reflections

LEARN ABOUT IT

EXPLORE Examine the Graph

Reflections are mirror images. Quadrilateral *ABCD* and quadrilateral *EFGH* are **reflection images** of each other.

These Turkish gloves are an example of a reflection.

TALK ABOUT IT

1. What are the coordinates of the vertices of quadrilateral *ABCD*? Of *EFGH*?

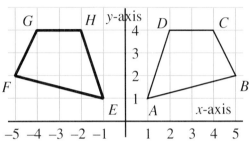

2. What are the coordinates of the reflection image over the *y*-axis of the point (1, 1)? The point (2, 4)?

3. Is the reflection image over the *y*-axis of the point P(*x, y*) the point Q(−*x, y*), Q(*x*, −*y*) or Q(−*x*, −*y*)?

4. What are the coordinates of the reflection image over the *x*-axis of the point (1, 1)? The point (2, 4)?

Draw any line *l* and any point *P* in the plane. The **reflection image** of *P* over line *l* is the point *P'* where *l* is the perpendicular bisector for $\overline{PP'}$.

This definition suggests a way to draw the reflection image of a point over a line.

Given a point *P* and a line *m*.

Draw a line *q* through *P* that is perpendicular to *m*.

Find *P'* on *q* so that *m* bisects $\overline{PP'}$.

TRY IT OUT

1. Trace this triangle and line *l*. Then draw the reflection image of the triangle over *l*.

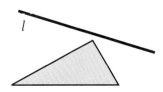

2. Graph quadrilateral *JKLM* with vertices (1, 1), (1, 2), (2, 3), and (3, 1). Draw its reflection image over the *x*-axis and label the coordinates of its vertices.

Trace the figure and line *l*. Then, draw the reflection image of the figure over *l*.

1.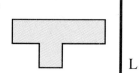

2.

3.

Use graph paper to draw each polygon positioned as shown. Then, draw the reflection image over line *l* of each polygon. Label the vertex coordinates of both the original polygon and its reflection image.

4.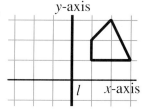

5.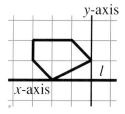

6.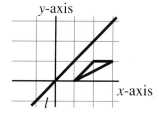

7. Graph quadrilateral RSTQ with vertices (1, 1), (2, 3), (4, 2) and (3, 1). Draw its reflection image over the *y*-axis and label the coordinates of its vertices.

MATH REASONING

8. Copy the figure at the right on graph paper. First, reflect the L-shaped polygon over the *y*-axis. Then translate it right 2 and up 3. Find the coordinates of the vertices of the polygon's final position.

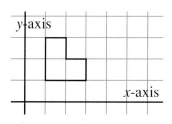

PROBLEM SOLVING

9. Extra Data Suppose you are sitting 8 feet from a mirrored wall in a sidewalk cafe. The cafe is 80 feet long and 30 feet wide. How far away from you will your reflection image appear to be? Which data is not needed to solve this problem?

▶ **USING CRITICAL THINKING**

10. Discover a Pattern Find the coordinates of the reflection image over line *l* for each of these points. What is the reflection image over line *l* for a general point (*x*, *y*)?

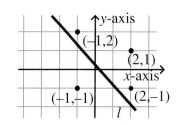

Rotations

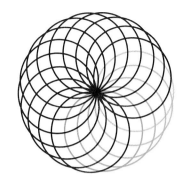

Rotation is often used in computer animation to create the impression of movement.

EXPLORE **Examine the Diagram**

Imagine that the figure at the right has been given a $\frac{1}{4}$ turn. The resulting figure is called a $\frac{1}{4}$ **turn image** or **rotation image** of the original figure.

TALK ABOUT IT

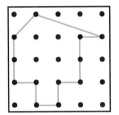

1. Complete the drawing of the $\frac{1}{4}$ turn image at the far right. Describe the procedure you used.

2. If you trace your right hand on a sheet of paper and rotate your tracing, will the rotation image be a right or left hand?

3. Discuss whether the arrows at the right are $\frac{1}{2}$ turn images of each other.

_____

Example Draw the $\frac{1}{4}$ turn image of the pentagon below. Then take that rotation image and turn it $\frac{1}{2}$ turn to create a second rotation image.

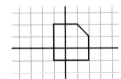 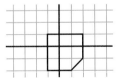 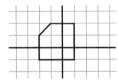

The pentagon *ABCDE* has vertices $(-1, 2)$, $(1, 2)$, $(2, 1)$, $(2, -1)$ and $(-1, -1)$.

Trace pentagon *ABCDE* and turn the tracing paper $\frac{1}{4}$ turn keeping the **turn center** $(0, 0)$ fixed. The $\frac{1}{4}$ turn image is shown.

Keeping the turn center at $(0, 0)$ turn the rotation image another $\frac{1}{2}$ turn. The second rotation image is shown here.

1. Draw the $\frac{3}{4}$ turn image of the original pentagon *ABCDE* above. Compare it to the example shown on this page. What do you notice?

2. Graph triangle ABC with vertices $(-3, -5)$, $(-5, 3)$, and $(6, 2)$. Keeping the turn center at $(0, 0)$, draw the $\frac{1}{2}$ turn rotation image of triangle *ABC*.

For each figure use graph paper to draw the $\frac{1}{4}$ turn image with turn center at (0, 0).

1.

2.

3.

For each point, find the coordinates of the $\frac{1}{4}$ turn image with turn center (0, 0). Use the L-shaped line to visualize the rotation image. Repeat for a $\frac{3}{4}$ rotation.

4. (1,2)

5. (−2,2)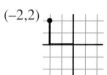

6. (−2,−1)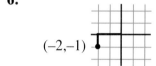

MATH REASONING

7. Use graph paper to draw the $\frac{1}{4}$, $\frac{1}{2}$, and $\frac{3}{4}$ turn images of the figure at the right. Use the turn center (0, 0).

PROBLEM SOLVING

8. Discover a Pattern Draw these points and their $\frac{1}{4}$ turn images on graph paper. Complete the following table and find the $\frac{1}{4}$ turn image for a general point (x, y).

point	(1, 3)	(3, −1)	(2, −3)	(−1, −1)	(−2, 1)	•••	(x, y)
$\frac{1}{4}$ turn image	(3, 1)	?	?	?	?		?

9. Fine Arts Data Bank If the arm of an animated figure rotates $\frac{1}{4}$ turn in 2 seconds, what is the change in rotation from one frame to the next?

DATA BANK

Write each ratio as a percent.

10. $\frac{2}{50}$

11. $\frac{20}{50}$

12. $\frac{50}{50}$

13. $\frac{100}{50}$

14. $\frac{1}{500}$

More Practice, page 541, set C

Symmetry

EXPLORE Study the Patterns

Since translations, reflections, and rotations are ways that a geometric figure can be changed or transformed, they are called **transformations.** Each transformation describes a type of **symmetry.**

This beaded bag from Saudi Arabia was handwoven from hand-dyed yarns.

TALK ABOUT IT

1. Suppose you traced the patterns at the right on tracing paper. Which patterns could be folded so one half exactly coincides with the other half?

2. Which pattern will look identical to the original when it is rotated using $\frac{1}{4}$, $\frac{1}{2}$, and $\frac{3}{4}$ turns?

If a figure or pattern can be folded so one half exactly coincides with the other, then that figure or pattern has **reflectional symmetry.** The fold line is called a **line of symmetry.**

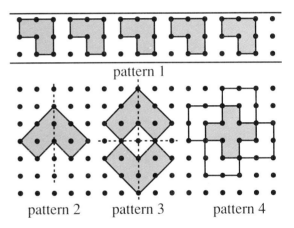

pattern 1

pattern 2   pattern 3   pattern 4

If a figure or pattern must be turned a full turn (360°) around a fixed center point before it coincides with the original, it does **not** have **rotational symmetry.**

If you slide a figure a fixed distance repeatedly in opposite directions, the resulting pattern has **translational symmetry.**

Identify the type or types of symmetry for each figure or pattern. If a figure or pattern has reflectional symmetry identify at least one line of symmetry.

1.   **2.**   **3.**   **4.**    **5.**

Identify the type or types of symmetry for each figure or pattern. If a figure or pattern has reflectional symmetry identify at least one line of symmetry. If it has rotational symmetry identify whether it has $\frac{1}{4}$, $\frac{1}{2}$, or $\frac{3}{4}$ rotational symmetry.

1. 　　**2.** 　　**3.** 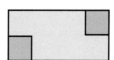　　**4.**

5. 　　**6.** 　　**7.** 　　**8.**

APPLY

MATH REASONING

9. Analyze the lines of symmetry of these regular polygons. Complete this table and discover a pattern.

equilateral triangle　　square　　regular hexagon　　regular octagon

number of sides	3	4	5	6	7	8 ●●● n
number of lines of symmetry	3	?	?	?	?	

PROBLEM SOLVING

10. Which of the lines shown are lines of symmetry of the parallelogram? Trace the parallelogram and draw its reflection image to check your work.

　　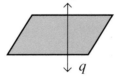　　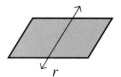

USING CRITICAL THINKING

11. Can you draw a figure or pattern that has reflectional, rotational, and translational symmetry? If your answer is yes, supply an example. If your answer is no, explain why no such figure exists.

12. Which capital letters of the alphabet have reflectional symmetry? Which have rotational symmetry?

More Practice, page 541, set D

Congruent Figures

LEARN ABOUT IT

When two figures are the same size and shape they are called
congruent figures.

EXPLORE Examine the Pictures

Study each set of three figures. In each case
select the figure that is not congruent to the
other two.

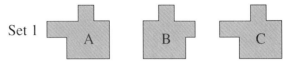

TALK ABOUT IT

1. Which polygons are translational images
   of each other?

2. Which polygons are the rotation images
   of each other?

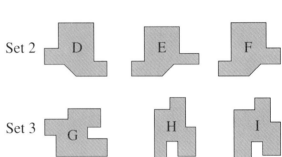

3. Which polygons are the reflection images
   of each other?

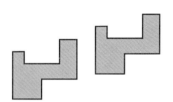

**When one figure is the
translation image of the
other, the figures are
congruent.**

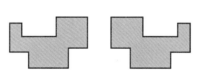

**When one figure is the
reflection image of the
other, the figures are
congruent.**

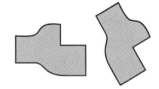

**When one figure is the
rotation image of the
other, the figures are
congruent.**

Given two congruent figures there, is some sequence of translations,
rotations, and reflections that moves one figure to the other.

TRY IT OUT

Is the given pair of figures congruent? If so, what transformation
moves one to the other?

Find the figure congruent to each figure listed.

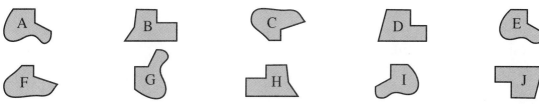

1. Figure C   **2.** Figure A   **3.** Figure J   **4.** Figure E

5. Is Figure H the translational image of Figure B or the result of a translation followed by a reflection?

APPLY

MATH REASONING

Explain why each pair of figures is *not* congruent.

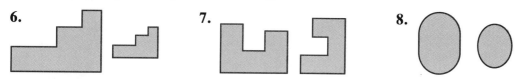

6.   **7.**   **8.**

PROBLEM SOLVING

9. Rectangles *ABCD* and *EFGH* are congruent. Find the coordinates of the vertices *F*, *G*, and *H*.

10. Draw the rectangles at the right on graph paper. Then, draw the translation image of *ABCD* for the translation that moves (x, y) to $(x + 3, y - 3)$.

C(−2,5)

D

E(1,2)

F

A(−7,1)   *B*(−2,1)

H   *G*

11. The translation image you found in exercise 10 can be rotated onto *EFGH*. What point is the center of that rotation?

▶ **ESTIMATION**

Which figure appears closest to being congruent to the first figure of the set?

12.

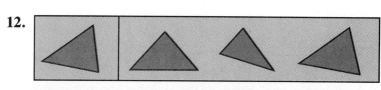

13.

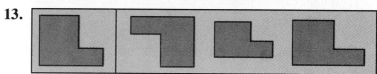

Using Critical Thinking

You can use your knowledge of motion geometry to answer each question.

A sign appeared beside a public swimming pool. The top nail had fallen out and the sign had changed position. What do you notice?

A slice is missing from this picture of a cake. What must you do to the picture to find the slice?

What must you do to this card to hatch a duck?

Why did Oliver Lee want this number to appear on his license plate?

Put a mirror or Mira on the dashed line. How do you explain what you see?

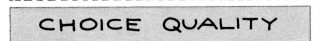

Put a mirror along the dashed line. Why is the name Rebecca reversed but the name Timothy is not?

TALK ABOUT IT

1. Which situations involve a reflection?

2. Which involve a rotation?

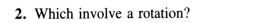

TRY IT OUT

1. Which capital letters of the alphabet are mirror images of themselves?

2. Write some words that are mirror images of themselves.

POWER PRACTICE/QUIZ

Draw the polygon and its translation image.

1. What are the coordinates of each vertex of quadrilateral *PQRS*?

2. What are the coordinates of each vertex of the translation image?

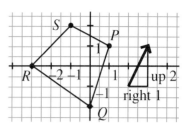

Draw the figure and its reflection image over the *x*-axis.

3. What are the coordinates of the vertices of pentagon *ABCDE*?

4. What are the coordinates of the vertices of the reflection image of pentagon *ABCDE*?

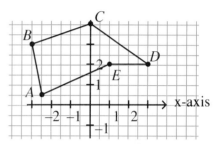

5. Draw a $\frac{1}{4}$ turn image of the figure below using (0, 0) as the turn center.

6. Which of these figures is congruent? How do you know?

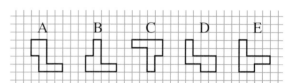

Identify the type or types of symmetry for each figure. If a figure has reflectional symmetry identify at least one line of symmetry.

7.

8.

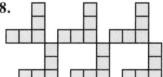

9.

PROBLEM SOLVING

Copy the quadrilateral on graph paper. Use exercises 10–12 to complete the chart.

10. Reflect the figure over the *x*-axis.

11. Reflect the figure over the *y*-axis.

12. Draw a $\frac{1}{4}$ turn image with center (0, 0).

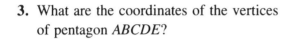

	A	B	C	D
coordinates of original				
coordinates of reflection over x-axis				
coordinates of reflection over y-axis				
coordinates of $\frac{1}{4}$ turn image				

Exploring Algebra
Graphing Two Linear Equations

EXPLORE Study the Graph

Jack graphed the equation $y = x$, but was out of paper and had to use the same axis for $C = \frac{5}{9}(F - 32)$. Examine the outcome shown here. How many ordered pairs (x, y) will satisfy both equations?

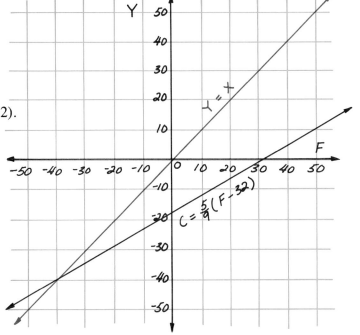

TALK ABOUT IT

1. What is true about each ordered pair (x, y) on the line $y = x$?

2. Is the pair $(-40, -40)$ on the line $C = \frac{5}{9}(F - 32)$?

3. What is true for the Celsius and Fahrenheit readings at the point $(-40, -40)$?

If two linear equations cross each other when graphed, that point is a solution to both equations. The two lines to the right appear to intersect at the point $(-1, 1)$. To check, substitute $(^-1, 1)$ in each equation.

$$y = x + 2 \qquad y = -2x - 1$$
$$1 = -1 + 2 \qquad 1 = -2 \cdot -1 - 1$$
$$1 = 1 \qquad 1 = 2 - 1$$
True.   True.

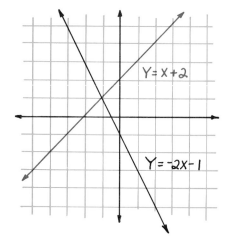

Graph each of these equations. If the lines intersect, give the coordinates of the point of intersection.

1. $y = x + 6$
   $y = 3x + 2$

2. $y = 6 - x$
   $y = x + 6$

3. $y = 2x + 3$
   $y = x + 1$

4. $y = x - 1$
   $y = 3 - x$

Graph each of these equations. If the lines intersect, give the coordinates of the point of intersection.

1. $y = x + 1$
  $y = -x + 3$

2. $y = x$
  $y = -x + 2$

3. $y = 3 - x$
  $y = 2x$

4. $y = 2x - 1$
  $y = x + 2$

5. $y = 3x + 1$
  $y = x - 1$

6. $y = -2x - 3$
  $y = -x + 3$

7. Two linear equations, when graphed, don't always intersect. Graph the two equations to the right. How can you tell from the graph that there is no ordered pair that solves both equations?

  $y = x + 4$
  $y = x - 2$

MATH REASONING

8. The shaded region represents all points in the coordinate plane whose ordered pairs satisfy one of the two linear inequalities listed below. Select several points in the shaded region. Which one of these inequalities do they satisfy?

  a) $y \leq 2x - 10$ b) $y \geq 2x - 10$.

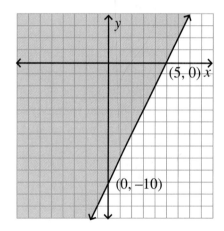

9. The shaded region at the right is called the **graph of the inequality** $y \geq 2x - 10$. Draw the graph of the inequality $y \leq x + 5$.

PROBLEM SOLVING

10. Mr. Sanchez agrees to pay his student employees either $5 per hour or $3 per hour plus $12 to cover the cost of the uniforms they must buy. If Jim works x hours and earns y dollars the two payment options are described by $y = 5x$ and $y = 3x + 12$. How many hours of work will give the same pay for the two payment options?

▶ **CALCULATOR**

Use your calculator to determine which of these ordered pairs names points of the graph of $y \leq 14x + 326.8$.

11. (36, 118)   **12.** (−19, 81)   **13.** (13.2, 723)   **14.** (−18.3, 29)

Problem Solving
Using the Strategies

UNDERSTAND
ANALYZE DATA
PLAN
ESTIMATE
SOLVE
EXAMINE

LEARN ABOUT IT

Some problems can be solved if you use the strategies **Use Logical Reasoning** or **Draw a Picture.** Study the problem at the right.

To use logical reasoning, remember that there are 3 persons. That means the last person has to wait 2 minutes before starting to get food, and the same person would take 1 minute at each type of food. So in 5 minutes that last person would be done.

A picture can also be used to solve the problem.

Each column represents a food type, or station, and each row represents one minute. A, B, and C represent the 3 persons. Only 5 rows are needed to make sure the last person (C) has gotten to all three foods.

It took 5 minutes for 3 people to go through the line.

> The art club had a special lunch. They had salads, main dishes, and desserts on the buffet table. The guests went through the line one person at a time. If each person spent 1 minute at each of the types of food, how long did it take 3 people to go through the line?

	Salad	Main Dish	Dessert	(done)
1 minute	A			
2 minutes	B	A		
3 minutes	C	B	A	
4 minutes		C	B	A
5 minutes			C	B	A

TRY IT OUT

Solve. Use the strategies **Use Logical Reasoning** or **Draw a Picture.**

1. Jon and Lauren made fried wontons for appetizers. Jon filled each wonton and Lauren fried it. Each step took 10 seconds. How long did it take them to make 6 fricd wontons?

2. The students in Ms. Monaghan's class set up 3 science displays. Guests of the school's open house line up to see the displays. Guest 1 observes display 1, then moves to display 2. Then, guest 2 moves to display 1 and so on. How long will it take 4 guests to see the displays if each guest spends about 5 minutes looking at a display?

Solve. Use any problem solving strategy.

Some Strategies	
Act Out	Solve a Simpler Problem
Use Objects	Make an Organized List
Choose an Operation	Work Backward
Draw a Picture	Look for a Pattern
Guess and Check	Use Logical Reasoning
Make a Table	Write an Equation

1. Twenty-seven people came to the club lunch. Eight were parents, 13 were friends, and the rest were club members. How many were club members?

2. Zane and 2 friends were setting tables for a buffet. The first friend set placemats on the first table, then went on to the second table. Then, the second friend placed silverware on the first table and went on to the second table. Next, Zane folded and placed napkins on the first table and went on to the second table. Each step took about 2 minutes per table. How long did it take them to set 4 tables?

3. Carla bought 8 packages of plates, 3 packages of plastic glasses, and a package of napkins for the buffet. Use the price list below to find out how much she spent.

Paper plates	Pkg. of 12	$1.20
Napkins	Pkg. of 100	$1.40
Plastic glasses	Pkg. of 20	$2.00
Place Mats	Pkg. of 8	$3.00

4. Jeff had three $10 bills. He spent $27 on placemats. Use the price list above to find out how many packages of placemats Jeff bought.

5. Some of the club members are studying a foreign language. One-fourth of them take French and $\frac{1}{2}$ of the rest take Spanish. One third as many students take Japanese as Spanish. There are 8 students taking Japanese. How many students are taking French?

6. For open house, Ms. Monaghan planned special activities in 3 different rooms. Group 1 went to activity 1, then to activity 2. Then, group 2 went to activity 1, then to activity 2 and so on. Each activity took 10 minutes. How long did it take 5 groups of people to see all 3 activities?

7. There were 18 dishes at the lunch. Five were dessert. What percent were not desserts?

8. Rita has 7 souvenirs from Spain, Japan, Egypt, Brazil, India, Greece, and New Zealand. She arranged them in a row on the table behind the buffet table with New Zealand in the middle. How many different ways can Rita arrange the 7 objects?

Constructing Congruent Segments and Angles

EXPLORE Examine the Pictures

Congruent segments have the same length. **Congruent angles** have the same measure.

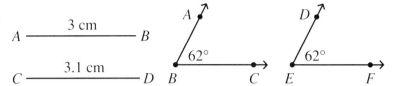

A —— 3 cm —— B

C —— 3.1 cm —— D

TALK ABOUT IT

1. Are these two segments congruent?

2. Are these two angles congruent?

Construct a segment congruent to _PQ_.

P   Q   R

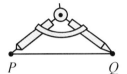

P   Q

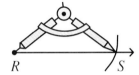

R   S

1. Draw a ray from R longer than the given segment $\overline{PQ}$.

2. Open your compass to the length _PQ_.

3. Use the opening from _P_ to _Q_ to mark _S_. $\overline{PQ} \cong \overline{RS}$

Construct an angle congruent to ∠_A_.

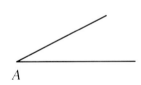

A

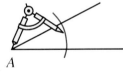

A

C   D

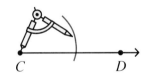

C   D

1. Draw an arc that intersects both rays of the ∠_A_.

2. Draw a ray to be one side of the new angle.

3. Use the compass setting from (1) to draw an arc crossing the ray.

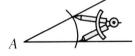

A

C   D

C   D

4. Measure the opening of ∠_A_ as shown.

5. Use the setting from (4) to draw an arc as shown.

6. Draw the second side to complete the second angle.

TRY IT OUT

1. Use a straightedge to draw a segment. Construct a segment.

2. Use a straightedge to draw an angle. Construct a congruent angle.

Construct a congruent copy of each figure.

1.

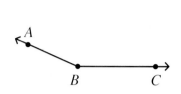

2.

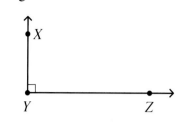

3.

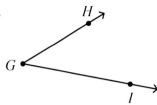

4.

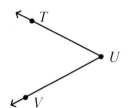

5.

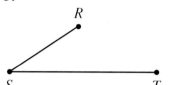

6.

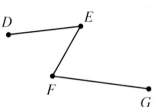

MATH REASONING

7. Use a straightedge to draw an acute $\angle A$. Then, construct an isosceles triangle that includes two angles congruent to $\angle A$.

PROBLEM SOLVING

8. **Develop a Plan** Which plan would you follow to construct a congruent copy of this right triangle?

   a) Construct a congruent copy of $\angle C$. On one side construct a segment congruent to $\overline{CB}$ and on the other side construct a segment congruent to $\overline{CA}$.

   b) Construct a segment congruent to $\overline{AC}$. Construct a segment with endpoint A congruent to $\overline{AB}$ and a segment with endpoint C congruent to $\overline{BC}$.

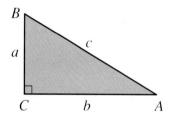

▶ **ALGEBRA**

Use the angles with measures x and y shown below to construct angles with each of the following measures.

9. $x + y$ **10.** $x - y$ **11.** $2x$ **12.** $3y$ **13.** $2x - 3y$

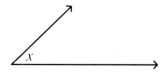

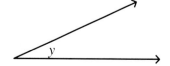

Congruent Triangles

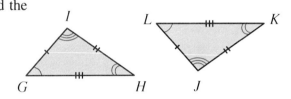

EXPLORE Solve to Understand

Trace △ *ABC* and cut out the tracing. Position the
cutout on △ *DEF* to show that the two triangles are congruent.

TALK ABOUT IT

1. ∠*A* is congruent to which other angle?
   ∠*B*? ∠*C*?

2. Side $\overline{AB}$ is congruent to which side? $\overline{AC}$?
   $\overline{BC}$?

When two triangles are congruent the angles and the
sides of one triangle can be matched with the
corresponding parts of the other triangle. Slash
and arc marks indicate congruent parts.

∠*G* ≅ ∠*L*	$\overline{GI}$ ≅ $\overline{LJ}$
∠*H* ≅ ∠*K*	$\overline{GH}$ ≅ $\overline{LK}$
∠*I* ≅ ∠*J*	$\overline{HI}$ ≅ $\overline{KJ}$

△ GHI is congruent to △ LKJ.
△ GHI ≅ △ LKJ

It is not necessary to show that all six of these congruence
relations are satisfied in order to show that two triangles
are congruent. If three sides of one triangle are congruent to
three sides of another triangle, then the triangles are congruent.
This property is called **side-side-side (SSS) congruence.**

You can construct a triangle congruent to △ *GHI* by using SSS congruence.

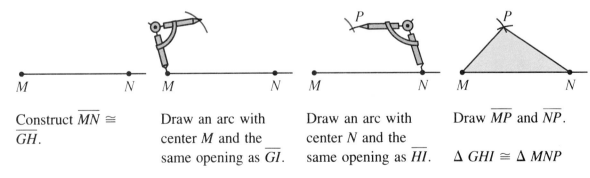

Construct $\overline{MN}$ ≅
$\overline{GH}$.

Draw an arc with
center *M* and the
same opening as $\overline{GI}$.

Draw an arc with
center *N* and the
same opening as $\overline{HI}$.

Draw $\overline{MP}$ and $\overline{NP}$.

△ *GHI* ≅ △ *MNP*

1. Use a straightedge to draw a triangle. Then construct a
   congruent copy of it.

List the pairs of congruent sides and angles for each pair of
congruent triangles. Use ≅ to show congruence.

1.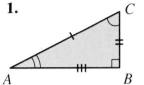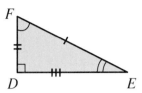

2.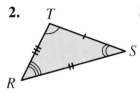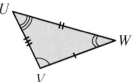

Write a statement of congruence for each pair of congruent triangles.

3.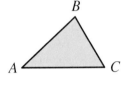

4.

5.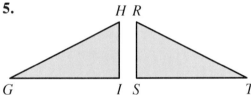

6.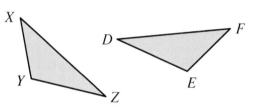

7. Trace △ JKL. Then construct a triangle
congruent to it.

MATH REASONING Suppose that △ ABC is an isosceles
· triangle with AB = AC and △ DBF congruent
to △ DCE.

8. Find x. Explain your reasoning.

9. Find y. Explain your reasoning.

PROBLEM SOLVING

10. Trace WXYZ. Then construct a
quadrilateral identical in size and shape.

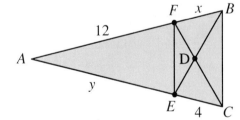

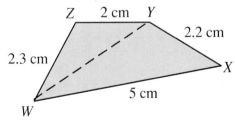

▶ **USING CRITICAL THINKING   Give a Counterexample**

11. Rob said, "Any quadrilateral whose sides have lengths 2,
2.2, 2.4, and 5 cm is congruent to WXYZ in exercise 10."
Draw a quadrilateral that is a counterexample.

More Practice, page 542, set B

SAS and ASA Congruence

EXPLORE Solve to Understand

Two segments and an angle
are given. Construct two sides
and the included angle as shown.

Two angles and a segment are
given. Construct two angles
and the included side as shown.

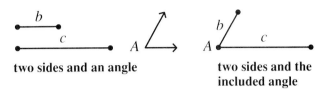

two sides and an angle

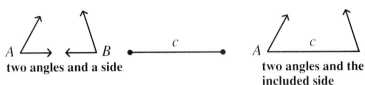

two sides and the
included angle

two angles and a side

two angles and the
included side

TALK ABOUT IT

1. How many different triangles can be
constructed by joining the two endpoints
on the "two sides and the included
angle" figure you constructed?

2. How many different triangles can be
constructed by extending the sides of the
angles on the "two angles and the
included side" figure that you
constructed?

If two sides and the included angle of one
triangle are congruent to two sides and the
included angle of another triangle, the two
triangles are congruent by **side-angle-side
(SAS) congruence.**

If two angles and the included side of one
triangle are congruent to two angles and the
included side of another triangle, the two
triangles are congruent by **angle-side-angle
(ASA) congruence.**

SAS Congruence

ASA Congruence

State whether these triangles are congruent by SAS, ASA, or
SSS, or if they are not congruent.

1.

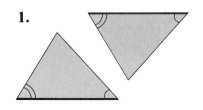

2.

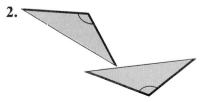

3.

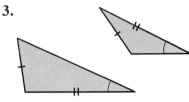

State whether these triangles are congruent by SAS, ASA, or SSS congruence, or if they are not congruent.

1.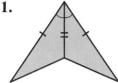

2.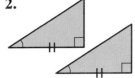

3.

4.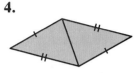

5. Trace Δ *KLM*. Use SAS congruence to construct a triangle congruent to Δ *KLM*.

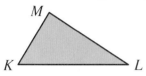

6. Trace Δ *RST*. Use ASA congruence to construct a triangle congruent to Δ *RST*.

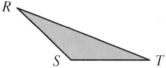

7. Construct a triangle with two sides and the included angle congruent to the sides and angle below.

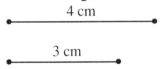

8. Construct a triangle with two angles and the included side congruent to the angles and side below.

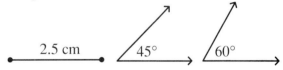

MATH REASONING

9. Dan said, "If three angles of one triangle are equal to three angles of a second triangle, then the triangles are congruent to each other." Was Dan correct?

PROBLEM SOLVING

10. Draw two triangles that are *not* congruent but that have two sides and an angle congruent to each other.

 MIXED REVIEW

Evaluate $5x^2 - 8$ for each value of x.

11. 2   **12.** 1   **13.** 0   **14.** −2

More Practice, page 542, set C

Problem Solving
Developing a Plan

UNDERSTAND
ANALYZE DATA
PLAN
ESTIMATE
SOLVE
EXAMINE

LEARN ABOUT IT

Many problems can be solved by more than one strategy. It is helpful to develop a plan before you start to solve the problem.

You could solve this problem by **Guess and Check** or you could try **Making a Table.**

By constructing the table at the right you can show the cost for different numbers of tickets.

By using the completed table you can find the correct combination of number of tickets and cost.

The drama club bought nine $5 tickets and seven $8 tickets.

The Repertory Theater is presenting 6 performances of "The Mousetrap." The drama club bought 16 tickets and spent $101. They bought less than 12 of each kind of ticket. How many tickets of each kind did they buy?

Center Section $8
Side Sections $5

$5 tickets	Number	1	2	3	4	5	6	7	8	9	10	11
	Cost	5	10	15	20	25	30	35	40	45	50	55
$8 tickets	Number	1	2	3	4	5	6	7	8	9	10	11
	Cost	8	16	24	32	40	48	56	64	72	80	88

TRY IT OUT

Before solving each problem, list at least 2 strategies you think might help you solve the problem. Then, solve the problem.

1. The side section of a theater has 90 seats. There are 2 seats in the first row, 3 in the second row, 4 in the third row, and so on. How many seats are there in the last row?

2. During intermission, Judi bought some juice for $0.85. She had the exact change in 5 coins. What coins did Judi have?

3. 42% of the tickets for one play were bought for Friday night. The other 174 tickets were bought for Saturday night. How many tickets were bought in all?

4. The last 4 people to arrive at a theater find that there are 6 seats left. How many different ways can they choose seats?

Solve. Use any problem solving strategy.

1. The graph shows the average price of movie tickets in 5 countries. Eric has enough money to buy a movie ticket in the U.S. How much more does he need to buy a movie ticket in Sweden?

Countries with the most expensive movie tickets

Average cost of a ticket in the USA: $5.25.
Average ticket prices

Japan	$11.34
Finland	$7.99
Switzerland	$7.80
Sweden	$6.45
Denmark	$6.29

NOW PLAYING

2. Use the graph to find out how much more a family of 4 would have to pay to see a movie in Japan than in the U.S.

3. Mexico has the least expensive movie tickets. A ticket in Mexico costs 5% of a ticket in Switzerland. How much does a movie ticket in Mexico cost?

4. The cafe next door to the theater has 2-person tables and 4-person tables. There are fewer than 20 of each type of table. After the play, 80 people came into the cafe and completely filled all 29 tables. How many tables of each size does the cafe have?

Some Strategies

Act Out	Solve a Simpler Problem
Use Objects	Make an Organized List
Choose an Operation	Work Backward
Draw a Picture	Look for a Pattern
Guess and Check	Use Logical Reasoning
Make a Table	Write an Equation

5. The play *"Fiddler on the Roof"* ran on Broadway for about 8 years. During that time there were 3,242 performances. About how many performances were there in a week?

6. Hamlet is the longest of Shakespeare's plays. It has 4,042 lines and 29,551 words—11,610 of the words are spoken by the character Hamlet. About what percent of the words are spoken by the other characters in the play?

7. After a play, the 5 members of the cast stood in a reception line. Eighty-five people came to meet them. Each person who went through the line talked to each member of the cast for about 20 seconds. About how long did it take for 7 people to go through the reception line?

8. **Write Your Own Problem**
Write a problem that the table below would help you solve. Then, solve your problem.

2	4	6	8	· · ·	?
7	14	21	28	· · ·	84

More Practice, page 548, set C

Applied Problem Solving
Group Decision Making

UNDERSTAND
ANALYZE DATA
PLAN
ESTIMATE
SOLVE
EXAMINE

Group Skill:
Explain and Summarize

Your group is entering an Indian artwork design contest. If the group's geometric design is chosen, it will be used on the cover of a journal featuring articles about the life and history of American Indians.

Facts to Consider

1. The design must have reflectional, rotational, or translational symmetry.

2. You must use these four pattern blocks in the design: equilateral triangle, rhombus, isosceles trapezoid, and regular hexagon.

3. You will use the triangle as a measure of one square unit of area.

4. Your design must have an area of at least 300 square units.

1. Given that the area of the triangle is one square unit, what is the area of the other pattern blocks?

2. If your geometric design has 25 hexagons, 16 trapezoids, 8 rhombuses, and 24 triangles will it meet the area requirement of 300 square units.

3. What kinds of symmetry does your design have?

What Is Your Decision?

Discuss the features of your group's design that you think are unique and would make it a winner.

WRAP UP

Define the Terms

Give definitions for each of the following terms.

1. translational image
2. reflectional image
3. rotational image

4. transformation
5. line of symmetry
6. regular polygon

7. congruent figures
8. SAS congruence
9. ASA congruence

Sometimes, Always, Never

Which of these words should go in the blank, *sometimes, always, never*? Explain your choice.

10. When the reflection image of a quadrilateral is drawn over the y-axis, the y-coordinates of each vertex _____ remain the same.

11. When the reflection image of a triangle is drawn over the x-axis, the y-coordinates of each vertex _____ remain the same.

12. A $\frac{1}{4}$ turn of a triangle will _____ produce the same image as a $\frac{3}{4}$ turn of the same triangle.

13. When a point (x, y) is rotated $\frac{1}{2}$ turn in the coordinate plane, the resulting point is _____ $(-x, -y)$.

Project

Use a pencil and paper or eight toothpicks and a button to form the fish shown on the right. Now see if you can move the button and three toothpicks to make the same fish, facing in the opposite direction.

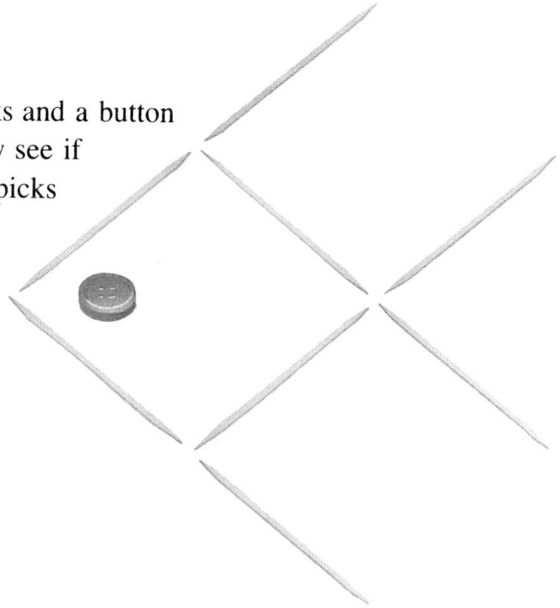

POWER PRACTICE/TEST

Part 1   Understanding

1. The translation image of P(4,7) is P′(1,9). What is the translation image of the point R(0,0) where the same translation is used?

2. Name the reflection image of the point (2,3) over the *x*-axis.

3. What symmetry is represented by a pair of shoes?

State whether each pair of figures is congruent. If so, tell what transformation moves one to the other.

4.

5.

6. Which is *not* a congruence property for triangles?

   A SSS   B AAA   C SAS   D ASA

Part 2   Skills

For problems 7 and 8, draw a polygon with vertices at (1,1), (5,1), (5,4), and (2,3). Use graph paper.

7. Draw the polygon's translation by taking each point (*x*,*y*) to (*x* + 3, *y* − 5).

8. Draw the original polygon's reflection over the *y*-axis.

Use a compass and straightedge for problems 9 and 10.

9. Construct a triangle with two sides and the included angle congruent to the sides and angle below.

10. Construct a triangle with two angles and the included side congruent to the angles and side below.

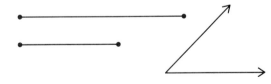

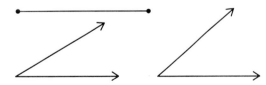

Part 3   Applications

11. A nursery sells roses for $1 each and other garden plants for $0.75 each. Marlo spent $8.25 and bought at least 2 roses and more than 3 other garden plants. How many of each type plant did he buy?

12. **Challenge** This is a diagram of $\frac{1}{4}$ of a garden area. Complete the diagram by drawing the $\frac{1}{4}, \frac{1}{2},$ and $\frac{3}{4}$ turn images of the part shown using A as the turn center.

A

447

ENRICHMENT
The Moebius Strip

A branch of geometry known as **topology** began about the middle of the nineteenth century. A. F. Moebius, a German mathematician and astronomer, founded topology discovering a surface known now as a **Moebius Strip.** The Moebius strip has only one side and one edge!

Make a Moebius Strip by following these steps.

- Cut a strip of paper about 30 cm long and 4 cm wide.

A [   ] B

- Give the strip a half-twist and tape ends A and B together.

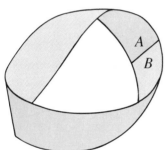

This is a Moebius Strip.

You can discover some interesting properties of the Moebius strip by trying these experiments with the model you have made.

1. Mark a small point at the edge of the strip. Start at that point and trace around the edge of the strip with your finger. Stop when you get back to your starting point. How many edges does the strip have?

2. Draw a line down the middle of the strip continuing around the loop without lifting your pencil from the paper. You will get back to your starting point. What does this show about the number of sides that the strip has?

3. Use scissors to cut around the loop following the line you have drawn. Describe what you have found.

4. Guess what will happen if you cut through the middle of the new strip you now have all the way around. Then try it.

5. Make a new Moebius strip. Start cutting the strip one-third of the distance from the edge. Continue cutting until you get back to your starting point. Describe the result.

CUMULATIVE REVIEW

1. Three spinners are spun in an experiment. One has 5 sections, one has 4, and the other has 2. How many branches will the tree diagram for this experiment have?

   A 40   B 22   C 20   D 11

Use this figure for problems 2 and 3.

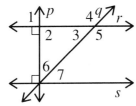

2. Name two complementary angles.

   A <2 and <6   B <6 and <7
   C <3 and <4   D <1 and <2

3. Name two perpendicular lines.

   A p and r B r and s
   C p and q D q and r

4. A collection of polygons forms a tessellation. Which statement is true about these polygons?

   A They are different sizes.
   B They must be triangles and quadrilaterals.
   C They cover part of a surface.
   D They do not overlap.

5. Which is an ordered pair for the function $y = 2x^2 + 1$?

   A $(-2, -7)$ B $(-2, -3)$
   C $(-2, 9)$ D $(-2, 5)$

6. Find an exact solution to the equation $x^2 = 72$.

   A 8.4852813   B $\sqrt{72}$
   C 8   D 8.485

7. Find a possible solution for $-3.2 < j \le 5$.

   A 6   B -4 C 0   D -3.2

8. Identify the irrational number.

   A 3.232323 . . .   B 3.232232223 . . .
   C $3.\overline{23}$ D 3.232232223

9. $a = 9$ m, $b = 12$ m, find c.

   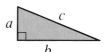

   A $\sqrt{21}$ m   B 225 m
   C 21 m   D 15 m

10. Find the hypotenuse of a 45°–45° right triangle with legs 6 in. long.

    A 12 in.   B $6\sqrt{2}$ in.
    C $\sqrt{36}$ in.   D $6\sqrt{3}$ in.

11. The hypotenuse of a 30°–60° right triangle is 12 cm. Find the length of the leg opposite the 30° angle.

    A $2\sqrt{3}$ cm   B $6\sqrt{2}$ cm
    C $6\sqrt{3}$ cm   D 6 cm

12. A garage door opener has a 4-digit combination. Each digit may be from 0 through 9. If the owner forgets the combination, what is the probability that he can open the door on his first attempt?

    A $\dfrac{1}{6{,}561}$ B $\dfrac{1}{10{,}000}$ C $\dfrac{1}{40}$ D $\dfrac{1}{36}$

13. One side of a square room is 16 ft. What is the area of this room?

    A 256 ft²   B 4 ft²
    C 64 ft²   D 128 ft²

16

EXTENDING LOGICAL REASONING

THEME: ANIMAL POPULATIONS

MATH AND SCIENCE

DATA BANK

Use the Science Data Bank on pages 492 and 493 to answer the questions.

1 Records of furs bought from trappers by the Hudson Bay Company in Canada are used to study cycles in some animal populations. In what year did the number of snowshoe hare furs bought by the Hudson Bay Company reach its peak?

2 Estimate the numbers of lynx and snowshoe hare furs bought by the Hudson Bay Company in 1875. Use variables to express the relationship between numbers of each type of fur bought that year.

3 Describe the pattern in the populations of lynx and snowshoe hare that can be seen in the records of furs bought by the Hudson Bay Company.

4 **Using Critical Thinking** What types of trees have branch patterns similar to the one shown? Can you estimate how many branches will be connected by the next growth contour?

The Arctic hare must survive predators, extreme cold, and periodic epidemics.

451

Inductive Reasoning
Discovering Number Patterns

EXPLORE **Look for a Pattern**

The students wanted to build a domino pyramid, and use the whole classroom. They calculated the room would hold 120 rows. How many dominoes would they need? Make a chart like the one shown and discover what they learned.

Dominoes in Row #	Sum so far . . .
1	1
2	3
3	6
4	10

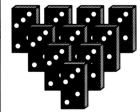

TALK ABOUT IT

1. How many dominoes are needed for 5 rows?

2. How many are needed for 6 rows of dominoes?

3. Look for a pattern. Try your pattern on the next row.

4. How many dominoes would be needed for 120 rows? n rows?

When you use **inductive reasoning,** you make a generalization about a situation after looking at simple cases. You never know for sure if you are right until your generalization is proved.

Example Find the sum of the 100 numbers in
$$1 + -2 + 3 + -4 + 5 + -6 + \ldots + 99 + -100.$$

Number	Sum to that number
1	1
-2	$1 + -2 = -1$
3	$1 + -2 + 3 = 2$
-4	$1 + -2 + 3 + -4 = -2$
5	$1 + -2 + 3 + -4 + 5 = 3$
-6	$1 + -2 + 3 + -4 + 5 + -6 = -3$

It appears that the even numbers give sums half their value.

The sum to -100 is -50.

1. Find the sum of the first 30 numbers of the sequence
$$-1 + -3 + -5 + -7 + -9 + \ldots + -57 + -59$$

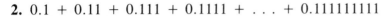

Copy and complete each table to find each sum.

1. $-2 + -4 + -6 + \ldots + -98 + -100$

number	-2 -4 -6 -8 -10 $\ldots$ -100
sum to that number	-2 -6 -12 $?$ $?$ $?$

2. $0.1 + 0.11 + 0.111 + 0.1111 + \ldots + 0.111111111$

number	0.1 0.11 0.111 $\ldots$ 0.111111111
sum to that number	0.1 0.21 $?$ $?$

Make a table and find each sum.

3. $10 + 20 + 30 + 40 + \ldots + 1{,}990 + 2{,}000$

4. $5 + 10 + 15 + 20 + \ldots + 100$

5. $1\frac{1}{2} - 2\frac{1}{2} + 3\frac{1}{2} - 4\frac{1}{2} + \ldots + 99\frac{1}{2} - 100\frac{1}{2}$

APPLY

MATH REASONING Use a calculator to help you discover a pattern.

6. What is the ones digit in the standard form of 9^{10}?

7. What is the ones digit in the standard form of 3^{17}?

PROBLEM SOLVING

8. If a classroom could hold only 100 rows of dominoes, how many dominoes would the class need?

9. How many posts would be required for 150 feet of fencing if there were a post every ten feet?

▶ **USING CRITICAL THINKING Visualize**

10. For which of these top views of dominoes would they all fall, when the one in front is pushed over?

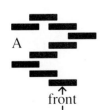
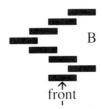
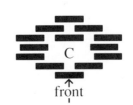
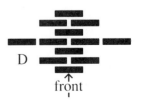

A
front

B
front

C
front

D
front

More Practice, page 542, set D

Inductive Reasoning
Discovering Geometric Patterns

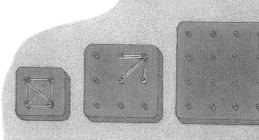

LEARN ABOUT IT

Biologists find it helpful to explore and generalize from
geometric patterns to understand similar patterns in nature.
Generalizing from simple cases is useful in geometry.

EXPLORE Use Dot Paper

Work in groups. How many rubber bands would
you need to put 1 from each peg to all its adjacent
pegs on a geoboard? Use dot paper to illustrate this.

TALK ABOUT IT

1. How many rubber bands do you need for a 2 × 2 geoboard?
   a 3 × 3 geoboard?

2. Do you see a pattern? Keep working until you discover one.

3. How many rubber bands are needed for a 10 × 10 geoboard?

Inductive reasoning means reasoning from individual cases to
a general case. Here is another example.

Example How many nests are in a honeycomb that consists of
a queen nest surrounded by 100 rings of nests?

Ring number	nests per ring	total so far
1	6	6 (6·1)
2	12	18 (6·3)
3	18	36 (6·6)
4	24	60 (6·10)

The familiar pattern 1, 3, 6, 10, . . . from
the last lesson emerges. Try the formula $6 \cdot \frac{(n)(n+1)}{2}$
to find the number of nests. The formula checks for the
first 5 rings. A hive with 100 rings of nests has 30,300 nests,
not counting the very center nest.

TRY IT OUT

1. How many rubber bands are needed for just the horizontal
   and vertical neighbors for each peg, on a 10 × 10 geoboard?

Draw the 100th figure for each pattern below.

1.

1st   2nd   3rd   4th   5th   6th   7th   8th   9th

2.

1st   2nd   3rd   4th   5th   6th   7th   8th   9th

APPLY

MATH REASONING

3. To the right is a rectangle. The picture below it shows that 1 vertical line produces 3 rectangles, the original plus 2 smaller ones. How many rectangles would be formed by 100 such vertical lines?

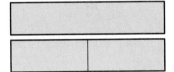

PROBLEM SOLVING

4. It takes 8 corner pieces to build a cube that is 1 stick high. It takes 27 corner pieces to build a cube 2 sticks high. How many corner pieces would it take to build a cube 20 sticks high?

1   2

5. The little bug to the right imitated the queen bee. But, she built square nests instead of hexagonal nests. How many nests would be in the comb within a radius of 100 nests from the center?

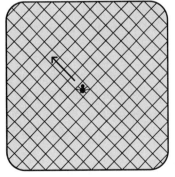

6. Science Data Bank Look at the pattern of tree branching. What would be the total number of branches from the first to the tenth growth contour?

DATA BANK

► CALCULATOR

7. Use a calculator to find the number of blocks used to build a pyramid like the one shown, but with 10 blocks along the bottom row.

side view   top view

Discovering Relationships

EXPLORE Study the Information

What do you notice about the numbers on the chalkboard? Can you make the same discovery that Arthur Hamann, a 7th grader, is credited with?

$2 = 5 - 3 \quad 4 = 7 - 3 \quad 6 = 11 - 5 \quad 8 = 11 - 3$

$10 = 13 - 3 \quad 12 = 19 - 7 \quad 14 = 19 - 5$

$50 = 53 - 3 \quad 52 = 59 - 7 \quad \text{- - -}$

TALK ABOUT IT

1. What type of numbers are to the left in each equation?

2. What type of odd numbers are to the right in each equation?

3. What is Arthur's discovery? Can you be sure it is true?

Until a discovery is proved or disproved, it remains simply a curiosity.

Examples

A For years people wondered about map coloring. The conjecture was that any map could be colored in 4 colors or less, with no regions that touch each other (in more than a point) being the same color. No one could prove the conjecture false and no one could prove it was true either. Finally in 1976 the conjecture was proven to be true.

B Try folding a sheet of paper over onto itself. An obscure discovery is that it can't be done more than 8 times, no matter the size of the sheet of paper.

1. Open a book to any page. Is the left- or right-hand page an odd number?

2. Is the product of the two pages always going to be an odd number, or an even number?

456

1. Write the even numbers from 16 to 50 as the difference of two primes.

2. Trace over this map and color it with 4 colors. Don't forget the outside.

3. Draw a line segment, then construct its perpendicular bisector by folding the paper.

APPLY

MATH REASONING

4. Is there a prime between 2 and 4? between 3 and 6? between 4 and 8? between 5 and 10? between 50 and 100? Can you think of a conjecture to make?

PROBLEM SOLVING

5. Marcy opened her math book and found the sum of the facing pages. Was it an even number, or an odd number?

6. A dozen balls are packed tightly in a box of 3 rows, with 4 balls in each row. Each ball has a radius of 2 in. What are the inside dimensions of the box?

 MIXED REVIEW

Find the number of permutations.

7. of x, y, z

8. of 5, 4, 3, 2, 1

9. of Al, Ben, Sam

Use the Pythagorean Theorem to find the missing lengths.

10. $a = 4, b = 3, c = ?$

11. $a = ?, b = 12, c = 13$

12. $a = 6, b = ?, c = 10$

13. $a = 6, b = 8, c = ?$

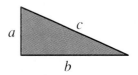

More Practice, page 543, set B

Problem Solving
Using the Strategies

UNDERSTAND
ANALYZE DATA
PLAN
ESTIMATE
SOLVE
EXAMINE

LEARN ABOUT IT

In some problems it may be difficult to understand the relationships among the data given. You may find it helpful to draw a Venn diagram to show the relationships and then Use Logical Reasoning.

You can begin by drawing a Venn diagram to show the relationships among dogs, fish, and cats.

Since 9 students have all 3 pets, you can put 9 where the 3 circles overlap.

12 students have both dogs and fish, so $12 - 9 = 3$ students have dogs and fish, but not cats. You can do the same for the other combinations.

35 have dogs so $35 - (3 + 9 + 4) = 19$ have dogs only. Repeat for fish only and cats only.

Now, you can add the numbers to find how many were surveyed.

There were 51 8th graders surveyed.

A survey of 8th graders at Oakmont Junior High found that 35 have dogs, 24 have fish, and 27 have cats. Of this group, 12 have both dogs and fish, 19 have both fish and cats, and 13 have both dogs and cats. There are 9 students who have all 3 pets. How many 8th graders were surveyed?

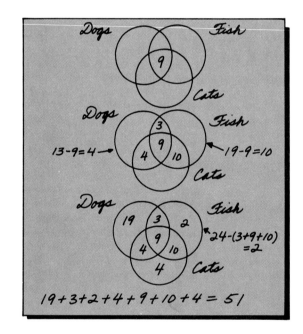

TRY IT OUT

Solve. Use any problem solving strategy.

1. There are 47 students who play soccer, 31 who play softball, and 39 who play basketball. Of these, 12 play soccer and softball, 17 play softball and basketball, and 15 play basketball and soccer. Five students play all 3. How many play only 1 sport?

2. There are 286 8th graders at Roosevelt Junior High. Before lunch, 158 of them have science and 135 have math. There are 71 students who take math and science in the afternoon. How many have both math and science before lunch?

Solve. Use any problem solving strategy.

1. In 1988, a record 1.2 million dogs were registered with the American Kennel Club. The table shows the 5 most popular breeds. Use the table to find what percent of the dogs were spaniels.

5 Most Popular Breeds of Dog	
Breed	*Number registered*
Cocker Spaniel	108,720
Labrador Retriever	86,446
Poodle	82,600
Golden Retriever	62,950
German Shepherd	57,139

2. Use the table to find how many more labrador retrievers than golden retrievers were registered.

3. In 1988, there were 1.2 million dogs registered with the American Kennel Club. How many of these dogs were not one of the 5 most popular breeds?

4. The Chess Club, Student Council, and Pep Club meet at lunchtime on the same day. Not every member can attend because some belong to more than one club. 12 are students in the Chess Club, 14 in Student Council, and 18 in the Pep Club. Half of the Student Council is in the Pep Club, 7 students are in both the Chess Club and Student Council, and $\frac{1}{3}$ of the Pep Club is in the Chess Club. Two students belong to all 3. How many are in more than 1 club?

5. Use the advertisement to find how much you can save per pound if you buy the 50-lb bag of dog food instead of the 10-lb bag.

Dog Food		Cat Food	
5 lb	$3.72	*Kibble*	
10 lb	$6.69	4 lb	$4.29
25 lb	$12.69	10 lb	$9.69
50 lb	$20.99	*Canned*	
		13 oz	2 for $1.30
		6 oz	3 for $1.15

6. Jerry bought 27 cans of cat food for $11.95. Use the ad to find how many of each kind of cat food he bought.

7. There are cats in 29.4% of United States households, and dogs in 38.7% of United States households. In 1987, there were 89,479,000 households. How many of them had cats?

8. The 29 students in Ms. Cline's English class have been reading novels for homework. Fourteen have read *Animal Farm,* and 21 have read *Wind in the Door.* There are 8 students who read both. How many did not read either *Animal Farm* or *Wind in the Door*?

Using Critical Thinking

LEARN ABOUT IT

"This question of the week really has me puzzled," Fred told Jeri. "I think I know the answer, but I can't prove it."

"It's easy!" Jeri said as she showed Fred her paper below. "Just by looking at twos that are factors you can convince someone that the answer is no."

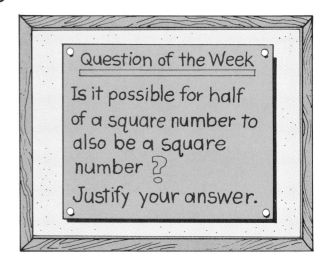

Question of the Week

Is it possible for half of a square number to also be a square number? Justify your answer.

MY PROOF by Jeri

A square number *always* has an *even* number of 2-factors. Here are examples.	Half a square number would *always* have an *odd* number of 2-factors and couldn't be a square number.
$4 = 2 \times 2$ $9 = 3 \times 3$	$\frac{1}{2}$ of 4 is 2
$16 = 2 \times 2 \times 2 \times 2$ $36 = 2 \times 2 \times 3 \times 3$	$\frac{1}{2}$ of 16 is 8, or $2 \times 2 \times 2$
$64 = 2 \times 2 \times 2 \times 2 \times 2 \times 2$ $100 = 2 \times 2 \times 5 \times 5$	$\frac{1}{2}$ of 36 is 18, or $2 \times 3 \times 3$

TALK ABOUT IT

1. What does the question ask? What is a square number?

2. Do you agree with Jeri's first statement? Explain your thinking.

3. Do you think Jeri has proved that the answer to the question of the week is no? Why or why not?

TRY IT OUT

1. Explain why the square of an odd number is an odd number.

2. Explain why the square of an even number has two 2-factors.

3. Explain why half of a number has one less 2-factor than the number.

POWER PRACTICE/QUIZ

Use tables and inductive reasoning to find the following.

1. The sum of the first 10 odd whole numbers:
   $1 + 3 + 5 + 7 + \ldots + 19$.

2. The sum of the first 500 odd whole numbers:
   $1 + 3 + 5 + 7 + \ldots + 999$.

3. Calculate: $0 - 1 + 2 - 3 + 4 \ldots + 50$.

4. Calculate: $0 - 1 + 2 - 3 + 4 \ldots - 77$.

number	1	3	5	7
sum to that number	1	4		

number	0	1	2	3
up to that number	0	−1	1	−2

Consider this geometric pattern.

5. What are the next three figures in the pattern?

6. What is the 100th figure in the pattern?

Use the figures and the table to answer the questions below.

Number in a row	1	2	3	4	...
Area	1	3	...	...	...
Perimeter	4	...	...	...	...

7. What is the area of the tenth "L"?

8. What is the relationship between the number of squares in a row and the area?

9. What is the perimeter of the 100th "L"?

10. What is the relationship between the number of squares in a row and the perimeter?

11. What do you notice about the sum when the areas are added together?

PROBLEM SOLVING

12. Copy and color the map using as few colors as possible.

13. The sum $1 + 2 + 3 + 4 + \ldots + n$ can be found by using the formula $\frac{n \cdot (n + 1)}{2}$.

    Find the sum $\frac{1}{2} + 1 + 1\frac{1}{2} + 2 + 2\frac{1}{2} + \ldots + 5$ for the first 10 addends. For the first 100 addends. For the first n addends.

461

Verifying Conjectures by Reasoning

Proof is an essential part of mathematics.

n	$n^2 + n + 41$	prime
1	43	yes
2		
3		

LEARN ABOUT IT

EXPLORE Make a Table

Work in groups. Complete the table to evaluate the expression

$$n^2 + n + 41$$

for the first 12 counting numbers n. Do you get a prime number each time?

TALK ABOUT IT

1. Does $n^2 + n + 41$ give a prime number for any counting number n?

2. Have you proved that $n^2 + n + 41$ gives a prime for any counting number n?

Inductive reasoning can lead to incorrect generalizations. Evaluating the formula for $n = 41$ results in $41^2 + 41 + 41 = 41(41 + 1 + 1)$. The formula does not always give a prime number.

Example

How many segments are determined by 100 points on a circle?

By counting and filling in the chart, a pattern appears. n points appear to give $n \cdot (n - 1) \div 2$ segments. Counting shows the formula works for 6 and 7 points too. But is it always true?

Each of the n points is connected to $n - 1$ other points by a segment. This gives $n \cdot (n - 1)$ segments, except each has been counted twice (once at each of its two end points). Dividing by 2 corrects the count, proving that $n \cdot (n - 1) \div 2$ is the number of segments for n points. Therefore, 100 points would give $100 \cdot 99 \div 2$ segments.

points	segments
2	1
3	3
4	6
5	10

TRY IT OUT

1. Verify whether it is true that $n^2 + n + 1$ is a prime number for all counting numbers n.

462

1. Complete the table to evaluate the expression $n^2 - n + 41$ for $n = 1$ to 10. Do you always get a prime number?

n	$n^2 - n + 41$	prime
1	41	yes
2	43	
3		

2. Evaluate $n^2 - n + 41$ for $n = 41$. Do you get a prime number? How can you tell?

3. Draw two points on a circle and the segment determined by these two points. How many regions is the circle divided into? Repeat this process for 3 points, 4 points, and 5 points. Use the pattern you notice to predict for 6 points.

number of:	
points	*regions*
2	2
3	.
4	.
5	.
6	.

MATH REASONING

4. Draw a large circle with 6 points on the edge, connect all the points, and count the regions formed. Does your answer agree with the prediction you made in problem 3?

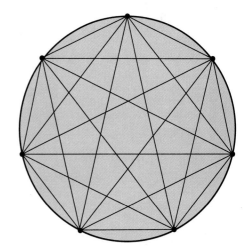

5. The circle to the right has 7 points. Count the regions. Does the pattern you used above hold true?

PROBLEM SOLVING

6. Jerome's string art project is started to the right. If he has to connect each hole with every other hole, how many lines of thread will someone see when they look at it?

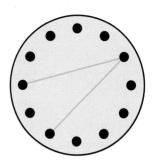

▶ **ESTIMATION**

How can you estimate the number of segments determined by points on a circle?

Use your method of estimation to estimate the number of segments determined by each of the following:

7. 100 points   **8.** 500 points   **9.** 1,000 points

Reasoning in Algebra

You have experienced the exploratory nature of mathematics. Now you will see an equally important aspect—verifying ideas with logical thought.

EXPLORE **Solve to Understand**

Try the number trick to the right with several different numbers. Try a negative number. Are you convinced that it always works?

Choose a number
Triple it
Add the number 1 more than the result
Add 5
Divide by 6
Subtract the original number
Do you get 1

TALK ABOUT IT

1. Use *n* as a variable for the number. How do you write the triple of *n*?

2. What algebraic expression results at the conclusion of step 3?

Examples

A *The number trick*

Choose any number.
Add the next larger number.

Add 5, then take half the result.

Subtract your number.
Is the answer 3?

Explanation

Let *n* represent the number.
$n + (n+1) = 2n+1$.

$(2n+1) + 5 = 2n+6$. $\frac{1}{2}(2n+6) = n+3$.

$(n+3) - n = 3$.
Yes, no matter what *n* represents.

B Explain why pulse rates are always recorded as an even number.

Explanation: When a pulse is taken, the heartbeat is counted for 15 seconds and multiplied by 4 to get beats per minute.

Let x be the number of heart beats counted.
Then $4x$ is the number recorded.
2 is a factor of $4x$, since $4x \div 2 = 2x$.
By definition then, $4x$ is an even number.

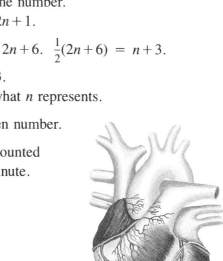

1. Use Example A as a model. Write an algebraic explanation for the number trick at the top of the page.

Write an algebraic explanation for these number tricks.

1. Choose any number.
Subtract 2.
Multiply by 3.
Add 6. Divide by 3.
Is the answer the original number?

2. Start with 9. Multiply by any number.
Subtract 10. Add 1.
Divide by 9. Subtract what you
multiplied by.
Is the answer -1?

3. If your heartbeat were counted for 10
seconds and multiplied by 6, would your
pulse always be an even number? Prove
it or give a counterexample.

4. If your heartbeat were counted for 20
seconds and multiplied by 3, would your
pulse always be an even number? Prove
it or give a counterexample.

MATH REASONING

5. Give reasoning that shows that the product of the facing
pages of an open book is an even number. Justify each step
by choosing from the terms: odd, even, prime, commutative,
associative, distributive, substitution.

Let l be the left page number, r the right page number.
$l = 2n$ for some number n because l is an _____ number.
The product $lr = 2nr$ by _____.
$2nr = 2(nr)$ because of the _____ property of multiplication.
Then by definition, the product is an _____ number.

PROBLEM SOLVING

6. Sam has 3 cups and 11 coins. How can
he put an odd number of coins in each
cup?

7. Prove that if Sam has 10 coins, he can't
put an odd number in each of 3 cups.

▶ **CRITICAL THINKING   Justify Your Answer**

8. Show how Sam could place an odd number of coins in each
of 3 cups with 10 coins overall, with an unusual
interpretation of the problem.

Reasoning in Geometry

[diagram of room outline with measurements: 4.5m, 2.0m, 5.9m, 1.5m, 4.3m, 6.5m]

LEARN ABOUT IT

EXPLORE Consider the Situation

Jorge planned to stencil a pattern around the walls of a room and was adding the 6 lengths to find the perimeter. Natalie suggested an easier way. She remarked that one corner looked as if it had been "cut away" from the rectangle.

TALK ABOUT IT

1. How would you find the perimeter of the room if this corner had not been "cut away"?

2. What is the total length of the 2 "cut away" edges? Is this the same as the distance if they had not been "cut away?"

3. Does adding the six individual lengths give the same perimeter as 2·(5.8 + 6.5)?

Give a reason that the perimeter (*P*) of a rectangle with rectangular corners removed is given by the formula *P* = 2(*l* + *w*).

Solution Consider the figure shown. Start by adding the lengths just as if you were walking around the figure.

$P = l + (w - y) + x + y + (l - w) + w$	Add all individual lengths.
$= l + w - y + x + y + l - w + w$	Remove parentheses.
$= l + w + l + w$	$^-y + y$ and $x - x$ are zero.
$= 2(l + w)$	Collect like terms and factor.

Natalie has good intuition.

TRY IT OUT

Find the perimeters of these figures using Natalie's reasoning.

1.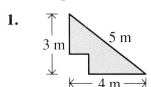

2.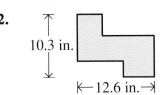

3.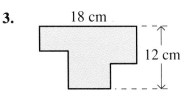

466

Find the perimeters. Assume all "cut aways" are rectangles.

1.

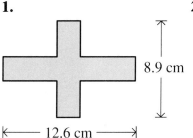

8.9 cm

12.6 cm

2.

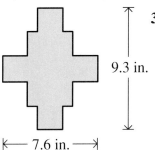

9.3 in.

7.6 in.

3.

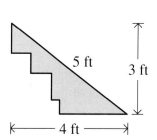

5 ft

3 ft

4 ft

4. The figure to the right is made from five identical circles. If the diameter of each circle is 10 inches, how far is it around the shaded, inner region?

APPLY

MATH REASONING

5. Find the area of the figure at right.

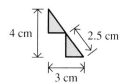

4 cm

2.5 cm

3 cm

PROBLEM SOLVING

6. Most people have one stride, right or left, slightly longer than the other. This means that if you lose your bearings and think you're walking a straight line, you'll actually be walking in a large circle. The distance one walks before returning to the starting point is approximated by $\frac{144}{d}$, where d is the difference in inches between stride lengths. If one stride is $\frac{1}{32}$ of an inch longer, how far will you walk?

MIXED REVIEW

A nickel is tossed and then a dime is tossed. Use a tree diagram to find the probabilities.

7. $P(H,H)$　　**8.** $P(H,T)$　　**9.** $P(T,T)$　　**10.** $P(T,H)$

11. Find the mean for the scores.

12. Find the median for the scores.

13. Find the mode for the scores.

Quiz Score	Frequency
10	4
9	2
8	7
7	5
5	4

More Practice, page 543, set D

Reasoning from Graphs

EXPLORE Study the Graph

The singing of blackbirds varies during the year. The number of blackbirds singing in early morning is greatest in nesting season.

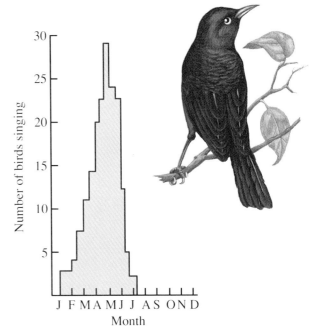

TALK ABOUT IT

1. What does it mean for the graph to slope down? slope up? stay at the same level?

2. For how many months of the year does the blackbird sing?

3. When does the number of blackbirds singing reach its peak? When is nesting season?

In the graph above, time (*t*) on the horizontal axis is called the **independent variable.** The number of blackbirds (*n*) is the **dependent variable.** We say *n* is a function of *t*, or $n = f(t)$.

Example

The graph shows Mary's heart rate for a recent 24-hour period. The heart rate depends on the time. *b* is the dependent variable and *t* the independent variable. We say *b* is a function of *t* and write: **$b = f(t)$.**

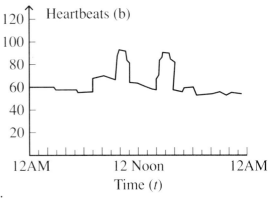

Story behind the graph Mary awoke at 7 a.m. and went to school. She had PE from 11 a.m.–12 p.m., then returned to class. Soccer practice was from 3 p.m.–5 p.m. She ate, did her homework, and went to bed at 8 p.m.

A level part of the graph shows Mary's heartbeat at a constant rate. The rate increases when she is active.

1. Draw a set of axes like the one above. Change the graph to show Mary having a nightmare from 2 a.m.–3 a.m. that made her heart rate rise to 80, and her PE class was from 9–10 a.m.

468

1. Draw a set of axes. Make a graph for this new story.

   A bird flew directly from the nest to a limb. She flew down at $t = 4$ minutes and got a worm and took it to the nest. From the nest she spotted another worm and flew down and brought it back at $t = 6$ minutes. She went directly to the bird feeder at $t = 8$ minutes, stayed for 5 minutes, and returned.

2. Make up a story that would explain Mary's heart rate graph for a Saturday during the school year.

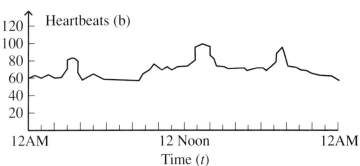

APPLY

MATH REASONING The graph above shows $f(t) = 80$ when $t = 4$ a.m. Give the correct value for ▥.

3. $f(t) =$ ▥ when $t = 1$ a.m.

4. $f(t) =$ ▥ when $t = 10$ a.m.

5. $f(t) =$ ▥ when $t = 2$ p.m.

6. $f(t) =$ ▥ when $t = 6$ p.m.

PROBLEM SOLVING

7. **Science Data Bank** Do the population of the lynx and the snowshoe hare peak at the same time? The hare cycle seems to depend on climate and availability of plant food. What do you think the lynx population depends on? Explain.

▶ CRITICAL THINKING **Create a puzzle**

8. Make a graph of the relative amount of something you do every day, such as talk, watch TV, or eat. Use time of day as the independent variable, but don't label the other axis. Can a friend decide what your dependent variable is?

More Reasoning with Graphs

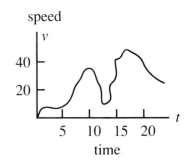

speed

LEARN ABOUT IT

EXPLORE Study the Graph

This graph shows a roller coaster ride. Time is the
independent variable and speed the dependent variable. The
slope of the graph is positive when the graph goes up, negative
when it goes down, and zero when it is horizontal.

TALK ABOUT IT

1. Is the slope positive or negative when you are gaining
   speed? slowing down?

2. Is the slope positive or negative when you are going uphill?
   going downhill?

3. How many places on the graph show the slope as zero? Is
   the roller coaster moving?

Studying the **slope** of a graph can tell the story of a graph like
the one above.

Example

This graph shows the total
trip of another roller
coaster. In it t is the
independent variable and v
is the dependent variable.
Write $v = f(t)$.

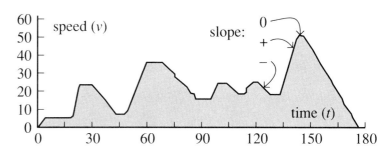

The speed **increases** during the 6 time periods the slope is
positive. It **decreases** during the 5 time periods the slope is
negative. It is **constant** when the slope is **zero.**

TRY IT OUT

Trace the axes and the graph above. Change the graph to show
each situation below.

1. The first hill was made steeper so the
   ride would reach a velocity of 30 mph at
   $t = 25$.

2. The ride was smoothed out so the slope
   was 0 from $t = 100$ through $t = 120$.

Use the graph to find who was ahead in the football game at each of the following times.

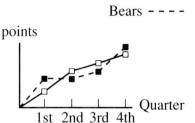

Lions ——
Bears - - - -

points

1. end of the 1st quarter?   2. end of the 2nd quarter?

3. end of the 3rd quarter?   4. end of the game?

5. Why does the graph show a slope of zero for the Bears during the 2nd quarter?

This graph shows another roller coaster.

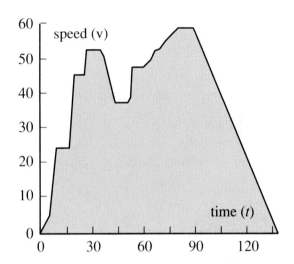

6. Is the ride going uphill or downhill when $5 < t < 10$?

7. Is the speed increasing at $t = 45$?

8. Is the slope positive or negative when $95 < t < 130$?

9. Give 3 values of t when the roller coaster is travelling at a constant speed.

10. What is the highest speed attained?

11. How long is the ride, in minutes and seconds?

MATH REASONING Match each situation with one of the graphs.

12. A strike is caught by the catcher in a baseball game.

13. A pitch hit sharply, but caught by a fielder.

PROBLEM SOLVING

14. The tallest roller coaster, in Japan, is 246 ft high. If each story on a building is about 14 ft high, how many stories tall is the roller coaster?

15. The fastest roller coaster in the world has been clocked at 66.31 mph. How much faster is this than the legal highway speed limit of 55 mph?

▶ **ESTIMATION**

16. Use estimation to draw a time vs. speed graph for this roller coaster. Its maximum speed is 55 mph.

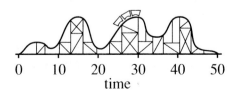

Problem Solving
Estimating the Answer

UNDERSTAND
ANALYZE DATA
PLAN
ESTIMATE
SOLVE
EXAMINE

LEARN ABOUT IT

Before you solve a problem, it is important to decide what would be a reasonable answer. You can begin by estimating the answer.

Mr. Abram's 8th grade science class went to Marine World. There were 28 students and 3 adults in the group. How much did they spend for tickets?

Adults	$8.75
Children under 12	$4.50
Students	$5.25

Before solving the problem, estimate the answer.

Round $5.25 down to $5.00 and round 28 up to 30. Then multiply to estimate the cost of the student tickets.

Round $8.75 up to $9.00 and multiply by 3 to estimate the cost of the adult tickets.

Add the estimates to estimate the total.

$$\$5.25 \rightarrow \$5.00$$
$$28 \qquad 30$$
$$\$5.00 \times 30 = \$150$$

$$\$8.75 \rightarrow \$9.00$$
$$\$9.00 \times 3 = \$27$$

$$\$150 + \$27 = \$177$$

The answer to the problem should be about $177.

Solve the problem.

$$\$5.25 \times 28 = \$147.00$$
$$\$8.75 \times 3 = \$26.25 \qquad \$147.00 + \$26.25 = \$173.25$$

$173.25 is a reasonable answer since it is close to $177.

TRY IT OUT

Before solving each problem, estimate the answer. Then solve the problem and decide if the answer is reasonable.

1. Students can buy an annual pass to Marine World for $21. Last year, Ray went to Marine World 6 times. How much did he save by using a pass?

2. The largest known giant squid was found in New Zealand in 1887. It was 57 ft long. Its tentacles were 86% of its total length. How long were its tentacles?

Solve. Estimate your answer first. Use any problem solving strategy.

Some Strategies	
Act Out	Solve a Simpler Problem
Use Objects	Make an Organized List
Choose an Operation	Work Backward
Draw a Picture	Look for a Pattern
Guess and Check	Use Logical Reasoning
Make a Table	Write an Equation

1. The brain of an adult human being weighs about 3 lb. A sperm whale has the largest brain of any living animal. It can weigh 6.5 times as much as a human brain. How much can the brain of a sperm whale weigh?

2. An African elephant is about $10\frac{1}{2}$ ft tall at the shoulder. The average American woman is $5\frac{1}{3}$ ft tall. How much taller is an African elephant?

3. A survey of marine mammal centers found that only one has elephant seals, sea otters, and porpoises. Seven have porpoises, 9 have sea otters, and 5 have elephant seals. Two have porpoises only. Five have sea otters only and 1 has elephant seals only. How many of the centers do not have elephant seals or porpoises?

4. The average American boy is about 85% of his adult height at age 12 and almost 60% of his adult weight. Steve is 12 years old, 5 ft tall, and weighs 92 lb. Predict his adult height and weight.

5. Marine World has a seal, a porpoise, and a pilot whale in one tank. Use the table to find the combined weight of the three animals.

Animal Weights	
Guinea Pig	1.54 lb
Otter	13 lb
Beaver	58.5 lb
Porpoise	103 lb
Man	162 lb
Seal	197.5 lb
Polar Bear	715 lb
Pilot Whale	1,500 lb

6. The average horse weighs 5.9 times as much as the average man. An African elephant weighs about 15 times as much as a horse. Use the table to find about how much an African elephant weighs.

7. The life expectancy of an elephant is 5 times that of a rabbit. A horse lives about half as long as an elephant. The average American woman lives to be 76 years old. The average American woman outlives an elephant by 16 years. What is the life expectancy of a rabbit?

8. A newborn blue whale may be 23 ft long and weigh 3 tons. An adult blue whale may be 95 ft long and weigh 150 tons. What percent of the adult whale's weight is the newborn's weight?

More Practice, page 548, set D

473

Data Collection and Analysis
Group Decision Making

UNDERSTAND
ANALYZE DATA
PLAN
ESTIMATE
SOLVE
EXAMINE

Doing a Simulation

Group Skill:
Encourage and Respect Others

A clothing store is giving away tickets which can win special prizes. Each ticket has two areas to scratch off with a coin. If you find a star in one of the areas, you get 10% off your next purchase. If you find a star under both areas you get a $100 gift certificate. The tickets are made so that the chances of getting a star in one area are about 1 out of 6. Do a simulation to find out about how often someone will win each prize.

Collecting Data

1. You will use a pair of number cubes to simulate the outcome on the tickets. Talk with your group about why number cubes are a better choice than flipping coins.

2. Decide which number on the number cubes will represent finding a star. If you roll that number on one cube you get 10% off on your next purchase. If you roll that number on both cubes, you win a $100 gift certificate. Take turns rolling both number cubes. Keep track of the total number of rolls with 0 stars, the number of 1-star rolls, and the number of 2-star rolls. Roll a total of 200 times and record the data in a chart.

SCRATCH and WIN!

Organizing Data

3. Count the number of rolls in each category of your table. Find what percent this number is of the total number of rolls.

	Number of rolls	Percent of the Total
0 stars	125	$\frac{125}{200} = 62.5\%$
1 star	....	....
2 stars	....	....

4. Talk with your group about why the data above would make a good circle graph.

5. Make a circle graph using the data. Remember to compute the number of degrees in the central angles of a circle graph, multiply the number of degrees in a circle by the percent of the total represented by each part of the circle graph.

	Percent of the Total	Central Angle Degrees
0 stars	$\frac{125}{200} = 62.5\%$	$360° \times 62.5\% = 225°$
1 star	....	....
2 stars	....	....

Presenting Your Analysis

6. What can you tell by looking at the circle graph?

7. About what percent of the time does someone win a 10% discount? a $100 gift certificate? Were you surprised by the outcomes? Explain why or why not.

WRAP UP

Word Scavenger Hunt

Each of the math words described below appears in this chapter. Name the words.

1. A 5-letter word that describes a number that has only itself and one as factors

2. A 9-letter word for the kind of reasoning that draws conclusions from general cases

3. A 3-letter word that describes a number that cannot be divided evenly by 2

4. A 6-letter word that means to divide something into equal parts

5. A 13-letter word that describes the relationship between lines that meet at right angles

6. A 3-letter word that is the result of adding

7. A 6-letter word that means to multiply a number by 3

8. A 4-letter word that describes a number divisible by 2

9. An 8-letter word that describes two lines in the same plane that never meet

10. A 7-letter word that means a part of a line

Sometimes, Always, Never

Which of these words should go in the blank, *sometimes, always, never*? Explain your choice.

11. The formula $2n^2 - 1$ _____ gives a perfect square.

12. A generalization made from specific cases will _____ be accurate.

13. A map can _____ be colored in four colors without areas of the same color ever touching, except at one point.

Project

The chart below shows the first six perfect squares. Find the difference between successive squares. What do you notice about the numbers? Now find the difference between these numbers, or the second difference. What happens when you do this?

Make a similar chart for the first six perfect cubes. Find the first, second, and third differences. What do you notice about the numbers in each row?

1		4		9		16		25		36
	3		5		___		___		___	
		2		___		___		___		

476

POWER PRACTICE/TEST

Part 1   Understanding

1. What is inductive reasoning?

2. Name a possible drawback of using inductive reasoning.

3. Will the product of any three consecutively numbered pages in a book be an odd or even number?

The graph shows average temperature during part of the year.

4. Identify the independent and dependent variables.

5. What does it mean for the graph to slope up? For it to stay the same level?

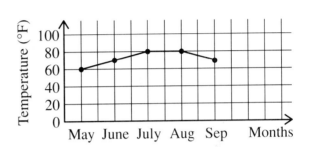

Part 2   Skills

6. Find the sum of $0.01 + 0.02 + 0.03 + \ldots + 0.99$.

7. Draw the 100th figure for this pattern.

| | | | | | | | | |
| 1st | 2nd | 3rd | 4th | 5th | 6th | 7th | 8th | 9th |

8. Make a table to see whether it is true that $n^0 = n^1 \cdot n^{-1} = 1$ for all integers n. Use integers from $^-2$ to 2 in your table.

Part 3   Applications

9. How many cuts are needed to cut a 30-ft board into 1-ft pieces?

10. How many handshakes will it take for each of eight people to shake hands with everyone else?

11. The rectangular tile in this pattern is 1 in. $\times$ 3 in. How many of each size tile is needed to complete this pattern for 3 ft?

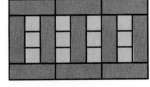

12. **Challenge** Mr. Williams will buy railing to go around all sides of his deck that do not touch the house. It costs $2.39 per foot. Find the cost of the railing.

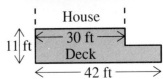

ENRICHMENT
Experiments with Ellipses

An ellipse is an oval-shaped geometric figure. The picture at the right shows one way to draw an ellipse.

Place a loop of string around two map pins on cardboard or soft wooden board. Place the point of your pencil in the loops and, keeping the loop taut against the pins, draw the ellipse.

Now try these experiments.

1. Keep the loop of string the same size but change the distance between the two map pins. How does this change the shapes of the ellipses?

2. Keep the two pins in the same location but use longer loops of string. How does this change the shapes of the ellipses?

3. Look at the ellipse below. Using one of the small squares of the grid as a unit square, estimate the area of the ellipse.

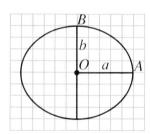

4. The area of an ellipse can be found by the formula:

$$A = \pi \times \text{length } (\overline{OA}) \times \text{length } (\overline{OB}) \text{ or } A = \pi \cdot ab$$

Use the formula to find the area of the ellipse above. How does it compare with your estimate?

5. Draw an ellipse on graph paper. Estimate the area. Then use the formula to find the area.

CUMULATIVE REVIEW

1. Which statement is true?

   A A chord is a diameter.

   B A diameter is a chord.

   C A chord is a secant.

   D A radius is part of a tangent.

2. Triangle *ABC* is reflected over the *y*-axis. Point *A* is $(-1, -4)$. What is *A*'s reflection image?

   A (1,4) B $(-1,4)$ C $(-1,-4)$ D $(1,-4)$

3. Find the coordinates of Point *B* after a $\frac{1}{4}$ turn using (0,0) as the turn center.

   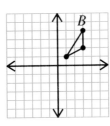

   A $(4,-3)$ B $(-1,4)$

   C $(-3,-4)$ D $(-2,3)$

4. Which letter has rotational and reflectional symmetry?

   A E   B S   C T   D O

5. Which figure is congruent to this figure?

   A    B

   C   D

6. Which pair of triangles might not be congruent?

   A two triangles with all sides equal

   B two triangles, each having two angles and the included side equal

   C two triangles with all angles equal

   D two triangles, each having two sides and the included angle equal

7. Which pattern has translational symmetry?

   A    B

   C    D

8. Which square root is irrational?

   A $\sqrt{49}$ B $\sqrt{169}$ C $\sqrt{\frac{144}{25}}$ D $\sqrt{27}$

9. The sum of the page numbers on three consecutive pages is odd. What could those page numbers be?

   A 3 even numbers   B 1 odd and 2 even numbers

   C 3 odd numbers   D 1 even and 2 odd numbers

10. Use the measurements the surveyor has already made to find the width of this lake.

    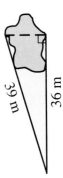

    39 m   36 m

    A 18 m   B 53 m

    C 38 m   D 15 m

RESOURCE BANK
AND
APPENDIX

APPENDIX

Rounding Numbers

In the 1984 presidential election, Ronald Reagan received 54,455,075 votes, and Walter Mondale received 37,577,185 votes.

We can remember these numbers more easily if we round them to the nearest million votes.

54,455,075 is between 54 million and 55 million, but is closer to 54 million. We say that 54,455,075 is 54,000,000 rounded to the nearest million.

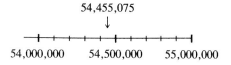

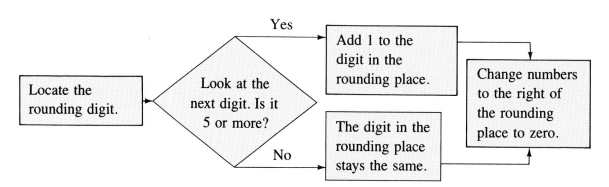

Round 37,577,185 to the nearest million.

37,577,185   37,577,185   38,000,000

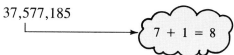

Round 82.1347 to the nearest hundredth.

82.1347   82.1347   82.1300 = 82.13

TRY IT OUT

Round each to the a) nearest whole number, and b) nearest tenth.

1. 54.18   **2.** 1.718   **3.** 449.882   **4.** 12.6718   **5.** 1.457   **6.** 81.110

Multiplying Decimals

Gas is advertised as $1.19 per gallon with a credit card, and $1.12 per gallon if paid with cash. Michelle purchases 15.3 gallons of gas. The amount shown on the pump is the price to be paid with a credit card. Michelle pays with cash, and she wants to know how much her gas costs.

To find her cost, Michelle can multiply the price of the gas, $1.12 times the amount of gas, 15.3 gallons.

$$1.12 \times 15.3$$

Multiply as with whole numbers.	Write the product so it has the same number of decimal places as the sum of the decimal places in the factors.

Estimate to determine if your answer is reasonable.

```
        1.12                  1.12   ← 2 decimal places
     ×  15.3               ×  15.3   ← 1 decimal place
        336                  336
       5600                 5600
      11200                11200
      17136               17.136     ← 3 decimal places
```

$1.12 \approx 1$
$15.3 \approx 15$

$15 \times 1 = 15$

The gas costs $17.136, or rounded to the nearest cent, $17.14.
This is reasonable as the estimate is $15

TRY IT OUT

1.	1.37	2.	0.015	3.	42.8	4.	2.09	5.	8.26
	×2.13		× 6.1		×3.67		×3.08		×0.09

Dividing by Whole Numbers

The total cost for costumes and scenery for the school musical is $852.50. The auditorium holds 275 persons, and the show is sure to sell out. What is the least that the tickets must cost for the drama club to break even?

We can divide, $852.50 ÷ 275$.

Decide where to start and where the decimal point goes.
↓

$$\begin{array}{r} 3. \\ 275\overline{)852.50} \\ \underline{825} \\ 27 \end{array}$$
← Divide.
← Multiply.
← Subtract and compare.

Estimate: $\dfrac{900}{300} = \dfrac{9}{3} = 3$

$$\begin{array}{r} 3.10 \\ 275\overline{)852.50} \\ \underline{825} \\ 27\ 50 \\ \underline{27\ 50} \end{array}$$
← Divide.
← Multiply.
← Subtract and compare.

Estimate: $\dfrac{2750}{275} = \dfrac{10}{1} = 10$

$852.50 ÷ 275 = 3.10. Tickets should cost at least $3.10.

TRY IT OUT

1. 40.4 2. $14\overline{)70.84}$ 3. $320\overline{)655.36}$ 4. $48\overline{)2.64}$ 5. $3\overline{)16.25}$

Dividing by Decimals

Nicole's family wants to know the number of miles per gallon the family car gets so they can budget for gasoline. Nicole notes that after traveling 342 miles, it takes 17.2 gallons of gas to fill the gas tank. How many miles per gallon to the nearest tenth did the car get on this trip?

Nicole can find the answer by dividing, $342 \div 17.2$. To find the answer to the nearest tenth, she divides to the hundredth place and rounds to the nearest tenth.

Multiply the divisor and dividend by a power of 10 that will make the divisor a whole number.	Decide to what place to end the division. Place zeros if needed.	Divide as for whole numbers. Place the decimal point.	Round to the place desired.

$17.2\overline{)342.0}$

$17\;2\overline{)3420.00}$

We divide to the hundredths place to round to the tenths place.

$$19.88 \approx 19.9$$

$$
\begin{array}{r}
19.88 \\
172\overline{)3420.00} \\
\underline{172} \\
1700 \\
\underline{1548} \\
1520 \\
\underline{1376} \\
1440 \\
\underline{1376} \\
64
\end{array}
$$

On this trip, the car got 19.9 miles per gallon. This answer is reasonable as the estimate is 20.

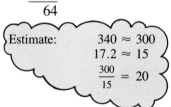

Estimate: $\quad 340 \approx 300$
$\quad\quad\quad 17.2 \approx 15$
$\quad\quad\quad \frac{300}{15} = 20$

TRY IT OUT

Divide. Round to the nearest hundredth if necessary.

1. $0.54\overline{)0.3888}$ **2.** $7.5\overline{)105}$ **3.** $13.2\overline{)54.37}$ **4.** $3.2\overline{)86.52}$ **5.** $2.08\overline{)51.2}$

Adding Fractions

Michael wants to reupholster the seats in his car. He needs $5\frac{3}{4}$ yards of material for each front seat and $8\frac{1}{8}$ yards of material for the back seat. How much material does he need altogether?

He adds $5\frac{3}{4} + 5\frac{3}{4} + 8\frac{1}{8}$.

Look at the denominators.	Write equivalent fractions with a common denominator	Add the whole numbers and the fractions.	Trade if needed. Simplify if needed.

$5\frac{3}{4}$ 　　　　$5\frac{3}{4} = 5\frac{6}{8}$ 　　　　$5\frac{6}{8}$

$5\frac{3}{4}$ 　　　　$5\frac{3}{4} = 5\frac{6}{8}$ 　　$\left(\dfrac{3}{4} \times \dfrac{2}{2} = \dfrac{6}{8}\right)$ 　　$5\frac{6}{8}$

$+8\frac{1}{8}$ 　　$+8\frac{1}{8} = 8\frac{1}{8}$ 　　　　$+8\frac{1}{8}$

$$= 18 + 1 + \frac{5}{8} =$$

Michael needs $19\frac{5}{8}$ yards of material. This is reasonable as the estimate is 20 yards.

Estimate to determine if your answer is reasonable.

$5\frac{3}{4} \approx 6$

$8\frac{1}{8} \approx 8$

$6 + 6 + 8 = 20$

Other Examples

Add $7\frac{5}{8} + 6\frac{1}{3}$

$7\frac{5}{8} = 7\frac{15}{24}$

$+6\frac{1}{3} = 6\frac{8}{24}$

$\rule{3cm}{0.4pt}$

$13\frac{23}{24}$

The LCM for 8 and 3 is 24.

Add $12\frac{2}{3} + \frac{1}{4} + 8\frac{5}{12}$

$12\frac{2}{3} = 12\frac{8}{12}$

$\frac{1}{4} = \frac{3}{12}$

$+ \ 8\frac{5}{12} = 8\frac{5}{12}$

$\rule{4cm}{0.4pt}$

$20\frac{16}{12} = 21\frac{4}{12} = 21\frac{1}{3}$

TRY IT OUT

1. $4\frac{1}{6} + 2\frac{3}{8}$ 　　　2. $16\frac{1}{2} + 32\frac{4}{5}$ 　　　3. $14\frac{2}{3} + 8\frac{5}{6} + 5\frac{1}{2}$ 　　4. $18 + \frac{7}{11} + 22\frac{19}{22}$

Subtracting Fractions

Students in the Home Economics class at Los Amigos Middle School are baking bread and biscuits. Dirk's group is making bread, and the recipe calls for $5\frac{2}{3}$ cups of flour. The flour canister has $8\frac{1}{4}$ cups of flour left in it. After Dirk's group takes the flour for their bread, will there be enough left over for Marta's group? They need $2\frac{1}{2}$ cups of flour to make biscuits.

Subtracting $8\frac{1}{4} - 5\frac{2}{3}$ will tell how much flour will be left.

Determine a common denominator for all of the fractions.	Write equivalent fractions with a common denominator.	Trade if necessary.	Subtract the whole numbers and the fractions. Simplify if needed.

$$8\frac{1}{4}$$
$$-5\frac{2}{3}$$

$$8\frac{1}{4} = 8\frac{3}{12}$$
$$-5\frac{2}{3} = 5\frac{8}{12}$$

$$8\overset{7\ \ \overset{3}{\cancel{3}\frac{3}{12}}}{\cancel{\frac{1}{12}}} = 7\frac{15}{12}$$
$$-5\frac{8}{12} = 5\frac{8}{12}$$

$$7\frac{15}{12}$$
$$-5\frac{8}{12}$$
$$\overline{2\frac{7}{12}}$$

There will be $2\frac{7}{12}$ cups of flour left. Marta's group needs $2\frac{1}{2} = 2\frac{6}{12}$ cups of flour. There will be enough flour left if both groups are careful.

> Estimate to determine if your answer is reasonable.
>
> $8\frac{1}{4} \approx 8$
> $5\frac{2}{3} \approx 6$
> $8 - 6 = 2$

Other Examples

$$6\frac{3}{4} = 6\overset{1\ \overset{15}{\cancel{\frac{15}{20}}}}{\cancel{\frac{15}{20}}} = 5\frac{35}{20}$$
$$-5\frac{4}{5} = 5\frac{16}{20} = 5\frac{16}{20}$$
$$\overline{\phantom{-5\frac{4}{5} = 5\frac{16}{20} =\ }\frac{19}{20}}$$

$$\overset{15\ \ 1}{\cancel{16}} = 15\frac{7}{7}$$
$$-\ \ \frac{3}{7} = \frac{3}{7}$$
$$\overline{\phantom{-\frac{3}{7} =\ }15\frac{4}{7}}$$

$$10\frac{2}{3}$$
$$-\ 8$$
$$\overline{2\frac{2}{3}}$$

TRY IT OUT

1. $6\frac{1}{5} - 1\frac{5}{6}$ **2.** $8\frac{9}{10} - 3\frac{1}{4}$ **3.** $16 - 5\frac{9}{15}$ **4.** $25\frac{1}{2} - 10$

Multiplying Fractions

The scenery committee is building a platform for the school play. They find 15 pieces of wood, each $4\frac{3}{4}$ inches wide. They plan to lay each piece of wood side-by-side on a frame. How wide must they build the frame?

They can multiply $15 \times 4\frac{3}{4}$ to find the width of the frame.

Write mixed numbers or whole numbers as improper fractions.	Multiply the numerators, and multiply the denominators.	Write as a mixed fraction, and simplify if necessary.

$$15 \times 4\frac{3}{4} = \frac{15}{1} \times \frac{19}{4} = \frac{285}{4} = 71\frac{1}{4}$$

$$4\frac{3}{4} = 4 \; \frac{3}{4} = \frac{19}{4}$$

The platform must be $71\frac{1}{4}$ inches wide. This is reasonable as the estimate of the width is 75 inches.

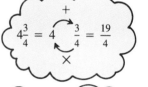

Estimate to determine if your answer is reasonable.

$$4\frac{3}{4} \approx 5$$
$$15 \times 5 = 75$$

Other Examples

$$1\frac{1}{6} \times 3\frac{3}{5} = \frac{7}{6} \times \frac{18}{5} = \frac{21}{5} = 4\frac{1}{5}$$

Use the multiplication short cut. $\frac{18}{6} = \frac{3}{1}$

$$2\frac{2}{5} \times 3\frac{5}{6} = \frac{12}{5} \times \frac{23}{6} = \frac{46}{5} = 9\frac{1}{5}$$

$$\frac{12}{6} = \frac{2}{1}$$

TRY IT OUT

$3\frac{5}{12} \times 4$

2. $5\frac{3}{7} \times 3\frac{1}{2}$

3. $8\frac{2}{3} \times 2\frac{1}{6}$

4. $\frac{5}{7} \times 2\frac{5}{8}$

Dividing Fractions

Members of the eighth grade class at Irving Junior High School have volunteered to paint the $5\frac{1}{2}$ mile school fence during spring vacation. The first day they paint $1\frac{3}{8}$ miles of the fence. If they continue at this rate, how many days of their spring vacation will they have to work?

We can divide $5\frac{1}{2}$ by $1\frac{3}{8}$ to find how many days it will take them.

Write mixed numbers or whole numbers as improper fractions.	Multiply the dividend by the reciprocal of the divisor.	Simplify if necessary.

$$5\frac{1}{2} \div 1\frac{3}{8} = \frac{11}{2} \div \frac{11}{8} = \frac{\overset{1}{\cancel{11}}}{\underset{1}{\cancel{2}}} \times \frac{\overset{4}{\cancel{8}}}{\underset{1}{\cancel{11}}} = \frac{4}{1} = 4$$

It will take the class 4 days to paint the fence. This is reasonable as the estimate is 5 days.

Estimate to determine if your answer is reasonable.

$$5\frac{1}{2} \approx 5$$
$$1\frac{3}{8} \approx 1$$
$$5 \div 1 = 5$$

Other Examples

$$8\frac{1}{3} \div 5 = \frac{25}{3} \div \frac{5}{1} = \frac{\overset{5}{\cancel{25}}}{3} \times \frac{1}{\underset{1}{\cancel{5}}} = \frac{5}{3} = 1\frac{2}{3}$$

$$6 \div 7\frac{1}{2} = \frac{6}{1} \div \frac{15}{2} = \frac{\overset{2}{\cancel{6}}}{1} \times \frac{2}{\underset{5}{\cancel{15}}} = \frac{4}{5}$$

TRY IT OUT

1. $18 \div 1\frac{4}{5}$

2. $3\frac{5}{12} \div 1\frac{7}{10}$

3. $\frac{3}{4} \div 7\frac{4}{5}$

4. $6\frac{2}{3} \div 3$

Math and Health and Fitness Data Bank

"No Decompression" Limits

Depth in feet	Bottom time limit in minutes	Depth in feet	Bottom time limit in minutes
Less than 33	No limit	110	20
35	310	120	15
40	200	130	10
50	100	140	10
60	60	150	5
70	50	160	5
80	40	170	5
90	30	180	5
100	25	190	5

Standard Air Decompression Table

	Bottom time (min)	Time to first stop (min:sec)	90	80	70	60	50	40	30	20	10	Total ascent (min:sec)
140	10										0	2:2C
	15	2:10									2	4:20
	20	2:10									6	8:20
	25	2:00								2	14	18:20
	30	2:00								5	21	28:20
	40	1:50							2	16	26	46:20
150	5										0	2:30
	10	2:20									1	3:30
	15	2:20									3	5:30
	20	2:10								2	7	11:30
	25	2:10								4	17	23:30
	30	2:10								8	24	34:30
	40	2:00							5	19	33	59:30
160	5										0	2:40
	10	2:30									1	3:40
	15	2:20							1	4	7:40
	20	2:20							3	11	16:40
	25	2:20							7	20	29:40
	30	2:10						2	11	25	40:40
	40	2:10						7	23	39	71:40

⁻ive to a maximum depth of 140 ft for a bottom time of 25 min, the diver would
‚ to the following schedule.

at 60 fpm · remain at 20 ft for 2 min · ascend to 10 ft at 60 fpm · remain at 10 ft
.scend to surface.

489

Math and Health and Fitness Data Bank

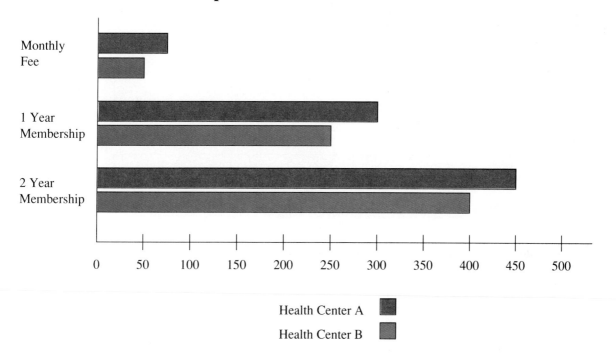

Comparison of Health Center Fees

Health Center A
Health Center B

Average Body Fat for Male and Female Athletes in Various Sports

Sport	Males (% fat)	Females (% fat)
Baseball or softball	12–14	16–26
Basketball	7–10	16–27
Gymnastics	4–6	9–14
Skiing	7–14	18–20
Swimming	5–10	14–26
Track and Field		
Sprinters	6–9	8–20
Middle distance runners	6–12	8–16
Distance runners	4–8	6–12
Discus	14–18	16–24
Shot put	14–18	20–30
Jumpers and hurdlers	6–9	8–16
Tennis	14–16	18–22
Volleyball	8–14	16–26

Math and Science Data Bank

Electron Volt Measurements

Unit of Measure	Number of electron volts (eV)
kiloelectron volt (KeV)	1,000 eV
megaelectron volt (MeV)	1,000,000 eV
gigaelectron volt (GeV)	1,000,000,000 eV
tetraelectron volt (TeV)	1,000,000,000,000 eV

Electric Charges of Quarks and Leptons

Quarks	Electric charge	Leptons	Electric charge
up	$\frac{2}{3}$	electron	-1
down	$-\frac{1}{3}$	electron neutrino	0
charm	$\frac{2}{3}$	muon	-1
strange	$-\frac{1}{3}$	muon neutrino	0
top	$\frac{2}{3}$	tau	-1
bottom	$-\frac{1}{3}$	tau neutrino	0

The lines in red,
called growth contours,
connect centers of branches
of equal length.
The number of branches
connected by the contour
is written above it.

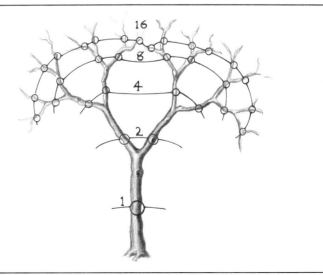

Math and Science Data Bank

Record of the Lynx and Snowshoe Hare Furs
Bought by the Hudson Bay Company

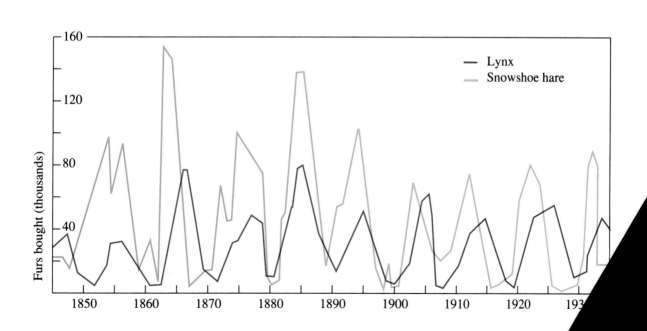

Math and Science Data Bank

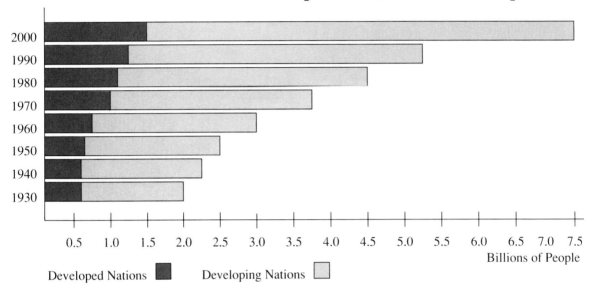

Estimated Growth of World Population (in Billions of People)

Developed Nations ■   Developing Nations □

World Distribution of Species

There are more than 1.5 million identified species of plants and animals on Earth. Between 60% and 80% of all species live in the tropics. About 40% of all species live in tropical rain forest areas.

			Plants	
	Species	Extinct	Endangered	Threatened
Europe	11,500	20	120	2,300
South Africa	23,000	40	110	2,100
Australia	25,000	120	200	1,700
USA	20,000	90	840	1,200
USSR	21,000	20	160	70

Extinct Species of Vertebrate Animals

Century	Number of species that became extinct
1600s	21
s	36
0s	84
00s (projected)	270

Math and Social Studies Data Bank

Egypt's Rope Stretchers

The Egyptians needed surveyors to plan
complex engineering projects such as
pyramids. Surveyors also had to redraw
property lines because the Nile River flooded
every year, washing away boundary markers
and changing the shape of the land. Egyptian
surveyors were called rope-stretchers. A rope
trick they are known to have used in about
1400 BC shows that they understood properties
of triangles with side length ratios of 3:4:5.
Teams of rope-stretchers had ropes with knots
that divided them into sections having the
ratios 3:4:5, such as 6 ft, 8 ft, 10 ft. They
created right triangles with these ropes by
holding the two middle knots steady to create a
line, then bringing the two ends together to
make a triangle. They knew that with these
side length ratios, the triangle had to have a
right angle. Modern surveyors create right
angles by using their measuring tapes in a
similar manner.

Thales Measures the Pyramids

Several ancient texts include accounts of the
Greek surveyor and mathematician Thales
(624–547 BC) using similar triangles to
measure heights. Thales succeeded in
measuring the pyramids by observing the
length of their shadow when his shadow was
equal to his height. Thales set up a stick at the
end of the shadow cast by the pyramid, and
showed that the ratio of the pyramid to the
stick was the same as the ratio of the two
shadows.

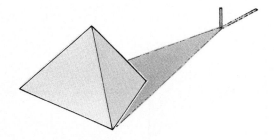

Math and Social Studies Data Bank

The Pyramid of the Sun at Teotihuacán, Mexico

The Pyramid of the Sun, the largest pyramid in North and South America, is part of a huge complex that includes wide avenues and many structures, including other pyramids. It was probably built around 100 AD. It is 742.5 ft long, 732.6 ft wide, and 207.9 ft high.

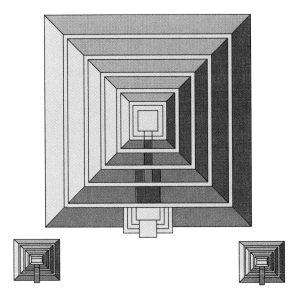

The Great Ball Court at Chichén Itzá, Mexico

The ceremonial ball courts of the Mayans were shaped like the one shown here and had sloping stone sides. The ball game was played with a hard rubber ball, and it resembled volleyball.

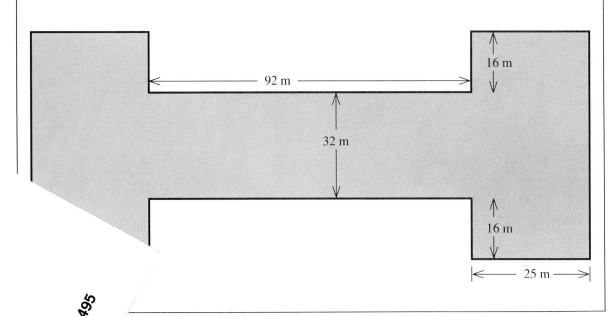

Math and Social Studies Data Bank

The Game of Nyout

The game of Nyout originated in the Kingdom of Korea about 1120 BC. It is an example of a Cross and Circle game that has survived unchanged through centuries.

The playing pieces of the game are called Mal and are moved according to the throw of 4 sticks called pam-nyout. A pam-nyout is about 7 in. long. It has a rounded black side and a flat white side. The outcome of the throw determines the order of play and the movement of the Mal. The object of the game is to be the first player or team to move 4 Mal from Start to Home.

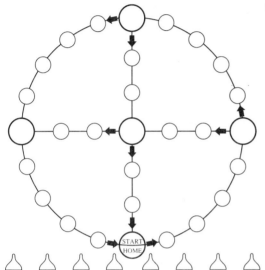

Outcome of throw	score	
4 black sides up	5	(player also gets
4 white sides up	4	another turn)
exactly 3 white sides up	3	
exactly 2 white sides up	2	
exactly 1 white side up	1	

Gaming Board for the Royal Tombs of Ur in Mesopotamia, about 3000 BC.

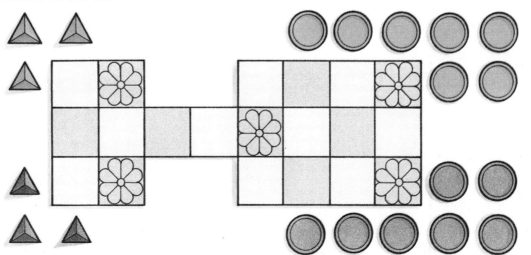

Inside the gaming board, which was hollow, were found 7 black counters, 7 white counters, and 6 small pyramids.

Math and Social Studies Data Bank

Brick Sizes

Bricks come in many shapes and sizes. A standard U.S. brick has a nominal size of 4 in. $\times$ 8 in. $\times$ $2\frac{2}{3}$ in. The actual size of the brick is about $\frac{3}{8}$ in. to $\frac{1}{2}$ in. less than the nominal size for each dimension. The total length of the brick plus the mortar joint make up the nominal size. A standard English brick has an actual size of 4 in. $\times$ 8 in. $\times$ $2\frac{5}{8}$ in. and is used with a $\frac{3}{8}$ in. mortar joint.

Formulas for ordering bricks for paving and walls.

Paving such as patios and paths:
Find the area to be paved in square feet. Order 5 bricks per square foot and add 5%.

Walls (8 in. thick):
Multiply the length by the height of the wall. Order 15 bricks per square foot.

Pattern A

Pattern B

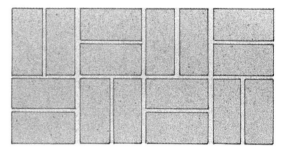

Pattern C

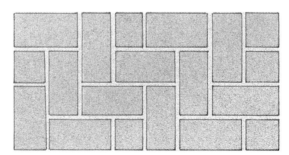

Pattern D

Math and Social Studies Data Bank

Telephone Code Partitioning
Toll Center and System Codes
000–099, 100–199
Service Codes
211, 311, 411, 511, 611, 711, 811, 911
Area Codes

200–210	212–219	600–610	612–619
300–310	312–319	700–710	712–719
400–410	412–419	800–810	812–819
500–510	512–519	900–910	912–919

Central Office Codes (prefixes)

220–299	620–699
320–399	720–799
420–499	820–899
520–599	920–999

Evolution of the 10-digit Telephone Number

Period of use	Area code	Office code	Line number
Original	N0/1X	NNX	XXXX
Current	N0/1X	NXX	XXXX
Future	NXX	NXX	XXXX

N = 2 through 9
X = 0 through 9
0/1 = either 0 or 1

Areas in which customers do not dial 1 before an area code still use the original system.
N11 is used for service codes.

Math and Fine Arts Data Bank

Motion Picture Camera Exposure Times

Shutter angle	2 fps	4 fps	6 fps	8 fps	10 fps	12 fps	14 fps
235°	$\frac{1}{3}$	$\frac{1}{6}$	$\frac{1}{9}$	$\frac{1}{12}$	$\frac{1}{15}$	$\frac{1}{18}$	$\frac{1}{21}$
180°	$\frac{1}{4}$	$\frac{1}{8}$	$\frac{1}{12}$	$\frac{1}{16}$	$\frac{1}{20}$	$\frac{1}{24}$	$\frac{1}{28}$
90°	$\frac{1}{8}$	$\frac{1}{16}$	$\frac{1}{24}$	$\frac{1}{32}$	$\frac{1}{40}$	$\frac{1}{48}$	$\frac{1}{56}$

Shutter angle	16 fps	18 fps	20 fps	22 fps	24 fps	32 fps	40 fps
235°	$\frac{1}{25}$	$\frac{1}{27}$	$\frac{1}{31}$	$\frac{1}{34}$	$\frac{1}{37}$	$\frac{1}{49}$	$\frac{1}{62}$
180°	$\frac{1}{32}$	$\frac{1}{36}$	$\frac{1}{40}$	$\frac{1}{44}$	$\frac{1}{48}$	$\frac{1}{64}$	$\frac{1}{80}$
90°	$\frac{1}{64}$	$\frac{1}{72}$	$\frac{1}{80}$	$\frac{1}{88}$	$\frac{1}{96}$	$\frac{1}{128}$	$\frac{1}{160}$

Shutter angle	48 fps	64 fps	72 fps	96 fps	120 fps	128 fps
235°	$\frac{1}{77}$	$\frac{1}{98}$	$\frac{1}{110}$	$\frac{1}{147}$	$\frac{1}{184}$	$\frac{1}{196}$
180°	$\frac{1}{96}$	$\frac{1}{128}$	$\frac{1}{144}$	$\frac{1}{192}$	$\frac{1}{240}$	$\frac{1}{256}$
90°	$\frac{1}{192}$	$\frac{1}{256}$	$\frac{1}{288}$	$\frac{1}{384}$	$\frac{1}{480}$	$\frac{1}{512}$

Scale drawings of film formats.

Math and Fine Arts Data Bank

Diagram 1

A = head joint
B = hip joint
C = knee joint
D = heel joint
EF = central line of gravity

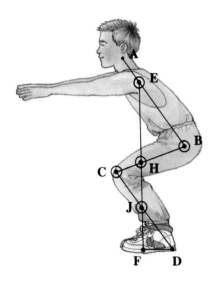

Diagram 2

This is an architectural layout and side view of a house Leonardo da Vinci designed.

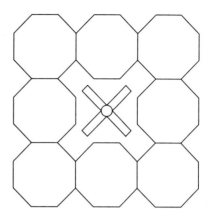

Study for *The Last Supper*

This is a copy of a page from da Vinci's notebook which includes a study for his mural *The Last Supper*, geometrical drawings, and text in mirror-image writing on constructing an octagon inside a circle.

Math and Fine Arts Data Bank

Music Royalties and Packaging Deductions

A musician is paid for his or her recordings in royalties. Royalties are a percentage of the list price of the record, tape, or CD. The first royalties are used to pay off the recording costs. Then the musician starts receiving royalty checks. Recording companies pay royalties on the list price minus a packaging deduction.

Type of Package   Packaging Deduction

Record   10% or $\frac{1}{10}$ the suggested list price

Cassette Tape   20% or $\frac{1}{5}$ the suggested list price

CD   25% or $\frac{1}{4}$ the suggested list price. The royalty is also 80% or $\frac{4}{5}$ of the record or tape royalty.

Who pays for the video?

Videos rarely earn much money. Therefore, the record companies prefer to split the cost of making the video with the musicians. In a 50–50 split, half the cost of the video comes out of the musicians' record royalties and the other half comes out of the video income. Once the cost of the video is paid off, the net income (the income after costs are paid off) is split 50–50 between the artist and the record company.

Math and Fine Arts Data Bank

Artists use the computer as a tool to assist them in creating graphics and animation. *Sharps* by Mike Newman was created through the use of a computer. By using the computer, the artist can repeat, relocate, or resize images to create patterns of new images.

In the past, animated images were created by hand drawing each frame and then using photography to create the finished film. Computers have assisted animators by providing ways to simulate images. To create a 1-minute television commercial, animators must produce images for 30 frames per second.

Early American Almanac Authors

During the 1700s and 1800s almanacs were indispensable books of information published each year. They had calendars, weather predictions, interesting facts, proverbs, and even whimsical poetry. Benjamin Franklin and Benjamin Banneker both published almanacs in the early days of the colonies.

Benjamin Franklin (1706–1790) was a wise, hardworking, yet fun-loving man. He organized the first police force and fire company in the colonies. He was also postmaster of Philadelphia and ran a printing business. He invented the Franklin stove and the lightning rod. In 1752, he offered proof that lightning was electricity.

Franklin first published *Poor Richard's Almanac* in 1732 when he was 26 and continued it for 25 years. Franklin's proverbs have been quoted for over two centuries.

No gains without pains.

Good sense is a thing all need, few have, and none think they want.

Old young and old long.

Fish and visitors stink after three days.

Early to bed and early to rise, makes a man healthy, wealthy, and wise.

Proverbs from Benjamin Franklin

Benjamin Banneker (1731–1806) was one of few free black American men in the early eighteenth century. He was an astronomer, mathematician, and writer. He was a member of the team that surveyed the District of Columbia in 1791 and helped lay out the plan for our nation's capital city. In 1791, Banneker corresponded with Secretary of State Thomas Jefferson to gain support for the abolition of slavery.

Benjamin Banneker's first almanac was published in 1751 and the last in 1797.

M D	W D	Remarkable days, aspects, weather, &c.	☉ rises	☉ sets
1	6	△ ♂ ♀ Sultry	4 43	7 17
2	7	and	4 42	7 18
3	G	Trinity Sund. *dry,*	4 42	7 18
4	2	*close*	4 41	7 19
5	3	Spica ♍ sets 1, 47.	4 41	7 19
6	4	*weather,*	4 41	7 19
7	5	*followed by*	4 40	7 20
8	6	△ ♂ ☿ *thunder*	4 40	7 20
9	7	*and rain.*	4 40	7 20
10	G	1ſt. Sun. aft. Trin.	4 39	7 21
11	2	St. Barnabas. *Cool*	4 39	7 21
12	3	△ ☉ ♃ *breezes,*	4 39	7 21

Page from *Benjamin Banneker's Almanac*

Math and Language Arts Data Bank

Excerpts from Lewis Carroll's Symbolic Logic

1. No birds, except ostriches, are 9 feet high.
2. There are no birds in this aviary that belong to anyone but me.
3. No ostrich lives on mince pies.
4. I have no birds less than 9 feet high.

variables used in statements

a = in this aviary
b = living on mince pies
c = my (or mine)
d = 9 feet high
e = ostriches

Lewis Carroll's Alphabet Game

Take 4 or 5 complete alphabets. Put the vowels into one bag, the consonants into another. Shake the bags. Draw 9 vowels and 21 consonants. With these you must make 6 real words, no proper names, to use up as many of the letters as possible. If two people want to try this, after drawing a set of letters, pick out a set of duplicates for the other player. You can make the game shorter by drawing 6 vowels and 14 consonants, and making 4 words.

Lewis Carroll's Letter Registers

Lewis Carroll kept a register of the letters he wrote from January 1, 1861 until his death on January 14, 1898. The register ended at letter number 98,721. Carroll had a separate 10-year register for letters he wrote as part of his job as Curator of the Senior Common Room at Oxford College. The number of letters in that register is unknown. He kept no record of the letters he wrote up to age 29.

Solving Equations

Enter the largest number you can on your calculator. Now clear your calculator. Pressing $\boxed{\text{CE/C}}$ clears the last entry and error conditions. Pressing $\boxed{\text{CE/C}}$ $\boxed{\text{CE/C}}$ clears the display and the operation. Pressing $\boxed{\text{ON/AC}}$ clears the memory, display, and operation.

To instruct your calculator to solve problems involving the basic operations ($+$, $-$, $\times$, and $\div$), enter the key code just the way you say the problem. Below are some examples. Try them on your calculator.

Problem	Key Code	Display
1464 + 34 =	1464 $\boxed{+}$ 34 $\boxed{=}$	1498
165.87 − 32.4 =	165.87 $\boxed{-}$ 32.4 $\boxed{=}$	133.47
1.009 × 1.54 =	1.009 $\boxed{\times}$ 1.54 $\boxed{=}$	1.55386
46 ÷ 2.5 =	46 $\boxed{\div}$ 2.5 $\boxed{=}$	18.4
99999999 + 1 =	99999999 $\boxed{+}$ 1 $\boxed{=}$	Error
0.0001 ÷ 10000 =	.0001 $\boxed{\div}$ 10000 $\boxed{=}$	Error
96 ÷ 0	96 $\boxed{\div}$ 0 $\boxed{=}$	Error

The last three problems create Error conditions. When a number is too large, many calculators display an Overflow Error. When a number is too small for the calculator, there is an Underflow Error. Attempting to divide by zero creates a Logic or Arithmetic Error.

With most calculators, if you divide 93 by 4, your result is 23.25. The $\boxed{\text{Int} \div}$ key on the Math Explorer compares the quotient and remainder.

$$93 \ \boxed{\text{INT} \div} \ 4 \ \boxed{=} \qquad 23 \quad 1$$
$$\text{-Q-} \quad \text{-R-}$$

Activity

Find a digit for each letter.

1. $yyy + yy + y + y + y = 1{,}000$

2. $c \times cc \times c \times cc \times c = 3{,}872$

3. $stop - tops = pots$

4. $abba \ \boxed{\text{Int} \div} \ aa = aa \text{ R } bb$

Order of Operations

To solve a multiple-step problem, do operations inside parentheses first. Next multiply and divide from left to right. Then add and subtract from left to right.

Enter the problem $6 + 9 \times 5$ on your calculator. If your calculator displays the correct total, 51, it follows order of operations. If your calculator displays 75, it performs operations as they are entered. You can find the correct total by entering the problem as $9 \times 5 + 6$.

Enter $(7 + 5) \times 12$. Your display should show 144.

You can use the memory keys on your calculator to remember the result of one calculation while you do another calculation.

M+	Adds the display to the calculator's memory
M−	Subtracts the display from the calculator's memory
MR	Recalls the total in memory

Example: Find $7 \times 12 - 104 \div 8$.

	Enter	Display
ON/AC	7 × 12 = M+	84
	104 ÷ 8 = M−	13
	MR	71

Example: Find y if $y = 15 - (91 - 84)$. Then evaluate $(5 + y) \times (y - 3)$.

ON/AC 15 − (91 − 84) = M+	8
((5 + MR)) × ((MR − 3)) =	65

If $(6 + 12) \div (34 - 28) = c$, what is the value of $96 \div c + 15$? (47)

Activity

Place parentheses where necessary to make the two expressions equal. (Hint: each side of the equation equals 9.)

$$\frac{18 + 9 \div 3 \times 8}{49 \div 7 + 9 - 8} = \frac{12 \times 6 \div 16 \div 4}{16 - 4 + 3 \times 2}$$

Fractions and Decimals

To find the decimal equivalent of a fraction, divide the numerator by the denominator. Find the decimal for 15/44.

Enter ON/AC 15 ÷ 44 = .The display shows 0.3409091. Find decimals for 3/8, 17/6, 24/25, and 7/5. Your display should show 0.375, 2.8333333, 0.96, and 1.4

To add, subtract, multiply, or divide fractions, use their decimal equivalents. First change mixed numbers to improper fractions.

Subtract 3 1/2 − 4/5. First change the problem to 7/2 − 4/5.

ON/AC 7 ÷ 2 − 4 ÷ 5 =   2.7

Multiply 7/8 × 3/4.

ON/AC 7 ÷ 8 × 3 ÷ 4 =   0.65625

To divide by a fraction, you can multiply by its reciprocal. Use the reciprocal key 1/ x to find the reciprocal of 2/3.

Enter 2 ÷ 3 = 1/ x . The display will show 1.5.

Below are three ways to divide 3/10 ÷ 2/3. Try them.

ON/AC 3 ÷ 10 = M+ 2 ÷ 3 = 1/× × MR =   0.45

ON/AC 3 ÷ 10 × 3 ÷ 2 =   0.45

ON/AC 3 ÷ 10 ÷ ((2 ÷ 3)) =   0.45

Activity

Match a numbered expression with a lettered expression. Figure out the message below.

1. 3/4 + 5/16   **2.** 5/12 × 4/5   **3.** 5/16 − 3/16
4. 1/12 + 2/3   **5.** 3/10 × 5/6   **6.** 5/12 ÷ 5/6
7. 3/4 − 3/16   **8.** 5/6 + 2/3   **9.** 1/2 × 5/8
E. 3/4 × 1/6   **O.** 1/4 ÷ 3/4   **C.** 9/16 ÷ 3/8
Y. 1/8 + 3/16   **A.** 1 1/2 − 7/16   **L.** 3/8 ÷ 2/3
U. 3/5 × 5/6   **T.** 5/6 × 9/10   **N.** 5/12 − 1/6

9̄ 2̄ 6̄   8̄ 1̄ 5̄   8̄ 1̄ 7̄ 8̄ 6̄ 7̄ 1̄ 4̄ 3̄

Computing with Fractions

The $\boxed{F\circlearrowleft D}$ key on your Math Explorer calculator changes a fraction to a decimal or a decimal to a fraction (if the decimal has 3 or fewer places). Find the decimal for 7/8. Use the $\boxed{/}$ key to enter the fraction.

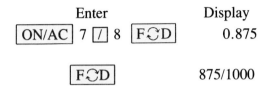

Enter	Display
$\boxed{ON/AC}$ 7 $\boxed{/}$ 8 $\boxed{F\circlearrowleft D}$	0.875
$\boxed{F\circlearrowleft D}$	875/1000

N/D → n/d in the display means that the fraction is not in simplest form. To simplify the fraction, press $\boxed{Simp}$ $\boxed{=}$ until N/D → n/d disappears from the display. You may also simplify the fraction by a factor you choose.

$\boxed{ON/AC}$ .875 $\boxed{F\circlearrowleft D}$ $\boxed{Simp}$ 125 $\boxed{=}$ 7/8

Use the Math Explorer's $\boxed{Unit}$ key to enter the whole number part of a mixed number. Find the decimal for 3 3/4.

$\boxed{ON/AC}$ 3 $\boxed{Unit}$ 3 $\boxed{/}$ 4 $\boxed{F\circlearrowleft D}$ 3.75

The $\boxed{Ab/c}$ key on the Math Explorer changes improper fractions to mixed numbers. For example, 23 $\boxed{/}$ 7 $\boxed{Ab/c}$ gives a display of 3 u 2/7.

To solve problems involving fractions on the Math Explorer, enter the key code just the way you write the problem.

Problem	Key Code	Display
1/2 − 1/8 + 5/6	1 $\boxed{/}$ 2 $\boxed{-}$ 1 $\boxed{/}$ 8 $\boxed{+}$ 5 $\boxed{/}$ 6 $\boxed{=}$ $\boxed{Ab/c}$	1 u 5/24
2 5/12 − 2/3	2 $\boxed{Unit}$ 5 $\boxed{/}$ 12 $\boxed{-}$ 2 $\boxed{/}$ 3 $\boxed{=}$ $\boxed{Simp}$ $\boxed{=}$	1 u 3/4
(1/5 + 1/2) × 3/4	$\boxed{(}$ 1 $\boxed{/}$ 5 $\boxed{+}$ 1 $\boxed{/}$ 2 $\boxed{)}$ 3 $\boxed{/}$ 4 $\boxed{=}$	21/40

Activity

Put these fractions in the squares so that the sum of the three numbers along each line is 1. 1/8, 1/5, 7/16, 9/16, 1/2, 1/16, 3/16, 17/40, 3/8

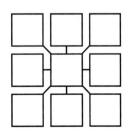

Using Constants to Evaluate Expressions

Here is a fast way to do the same calculation on a group of numbers. Use the constant key $\boxed{\text{Cons}}$ to store an operation and a number. Then, when you press the constant key, the calculation will be performed on the number in the display.

Evaluate $m + 4$ for $m = 12, 23, 96,$ and 100.

$\boxed{\text{ON/AC}}$ $\boxed{+}$ 4 $\boxed{\text{Cons}}$ 12 $\boxed{\text{Cons}}$ 23 $\boxed{\text{Cons}}$ 96 $\boxed{\text{Cons}}$ $\boxed{\text{Cons}}$.

The display should show 16, 27, 100, 104.

With some calculators, the $\boxed{=}$ key acts as a constant key. Entering $\boxed{+}$ 4 $\boxed{=}$ sets $+ 4$ as the constant. Try the key code above, but enter $\boxed{=}$ in place of $\boxed{\text{Cons}}$.

Evaluate the expressions $m + 4$, $m - 4$, $m \div 4$, and $m \times 4$ for $m = 4, 12, 36,$ and 400. Check mentally.

Calculations often require the number π. Entering $\boxed{\times}$ $\boxed{\pi}$ $\boxed{\text{Cons}}$ sets the constant key to multiply by 3.1415927. Evaluate $r \times \pi$ for $r = 3, 5,$ and 10.

$\boxed{\text{ON/AC}}$ $\boxed{\times}$ $\boxed{\pi}$ $\boxed{\text{Cons}}$ 3 $\boxed{\text{Cons}}$ 5 $\boxed{\text{Cons}}$ 10 $\boxed{\text{Cons}}$

Estimate to decide if your calculator is multiplying by π.

Most calculators allow the number of decimal places in the display to vary. The $\boxed{\text{Fix}}$ key on the Math Explorer lets you choose from 0 to 7 decimal places. $\boxed{\text{ON/AC}}$ $\boxed{\pi}$ $\boxed{\text{Fix}}$ 2 gives a display of 3.14 and $\boxed{\text{ON/AC}}$ $\boxed{\pi}$ $\boxed{\text{Fix}}$ 6 gives a display of 3.141593.

Use the $\boxed{\text{Fix}}$ key to find values for π with 3, 4, and 5 decimal places.

Activity

The formula for finding the lateral area of a cylinder is $A = 2\pi rh$. Find the area of the label on each side of these cans.

Can	Radius	Height	Area
Soup	4 cm	10.5 cm	
Sauce	32 mm	70 mm	
Tuna	1.6 in.	1.75 in.	
Olives	1 1/4 in.	1 1/2 in.	

Computing with Integers

The $\boxed{+C-}$ key changes the sign of the number in the display. Enter $\boxed{\text{ON/AC}}$ 4 $\boxed{+C-}$. Then press $\boxed{+C-}$ again. The display will first show -4 and then 4.

Use the $\boxed{+C-}$ key to do these problems involving integers.

$5 + -5$	5 $\boxed{+}$ 5 $\boxed{+C-}$ $\boxed{=}$	0
$-5 + -5$	5 $\boxed{+C-}$ $\boxed{+}$ 5 $\boxed{+C-}$ $\boxed{=}$	-10
$-13 - 8$	13 $\boxed{+C-}$ $\boxed{-}$ 8 $\boxed{=}$	-21
$-13 - -8$	13 $\boxed{+C-}$ $\boxed{-}$ 8 $\boxed{+C-}$ $\boxed{=}$	-5
-7×9	7 $\boxed{+C-}$ $\boxed{\times}$ 9 $\boxed{=}$	-63
-7×-9	7 $\boxed{+C-}$ $\boxed{\times}$ 9 $\boxed{+C-}$ $\boxed{=}$	63
$-45 \div 5$	45 $\boxed{+C-}$ $\boxed{\div}$ 5 $\boxed{=}$	-9
$-45 \div -5$	45 $\boxed{+C-}$ $\boxed{\div}$ 5 $\boxed{+C-}$ $\boxed{=}$	9
$-32 \div -4 - 5$	32 $\boxed{+C-}$ $\boxed{\div}$ 4 $\boxed{+C-}$ $\boxed{-}$ 5 $\boxed{=}$	3
$-(9 - 3) \div 2$	$\boxed{(}$ 9 $\boxed{-}$ 3 $\boxed{)}$ $\boxed{+C-}$ $\boxed{\div}$ 2 $\boxed{=}$	-3
$-9 + 7 \times -3$	9 $\boxed{+C-}$ $\boxed{+}$ 7 $\boxed{\times}$ 3 $\boxed{+C-}$ $\boxed{=}$	-30
$64 \div -8 \div -2$	64 $\boxed{\div}$ 8 $\boxed{+C-}$ $\boxed{\div}$ 2 $\boxed{+C-}$ $\boxed{=}$	4

Activity

Write a positive $(+)$ or negative $(-)$ sign in front of each integer to make a true equation.

1. $9 + 6 = -3$ **2.** $14 - 11 = -3$ **3.** $105 \div 15 = +7$

4. $17 \times 7 = -119$ **5.** $(3 + 4) + 14 = +7$ **6.** $63 \div (15 + 6) = +7$

Exponents, Powers, and Roots

The $\boxed{x^2}$ key multiples a number by itself, or **squares** a number.

To find 14^2, use this key code: Display
$\boxed{\text{ON/AC}}$ 14 $\boxed{x^2}$ 196

The $\boxed{\sqrt{}}$ key finds the **square root** of the number in the display. It finds a number that can be multiplied by itself to equal the display number.

$\boxed{\text{ON/AC}}$ 196 $\boxed{\sqrt{}}$ 14
$\boxed{\text{ON/AC}}$ 196 $\boxed{+\mathcal{C}-}$ $\boxed{\sqrt{}}$ Error

You cannot take the square root of a negative number. The calculator will display a **Sign Error**. To calculate powers of 10 use the $\boxed{10^n}$ key.

10^4 $\boxed{\text{ON/AC}}$ $\boxed{10^n}$ 4   10000
7.2×10^{-4} $\boxed{\text{ON/AC}}$ 7.2 $\boxed{\times}$ $\boxed{10^n}$ $\boxed{+\mathcal{C}-}$ 4 $\boxed{=}$ 0.00072

To find 14^5 you can use several different key codes. Using the $\boxed{y^x}$ key is the most efficient way to raise a number to a power.

$\boxed{\text{ON/AC}}$ 14 $\boxed{\times}$ 14 $\boxed{\times}$ 14 $\boxed{\times}$ 14 $\boxed{\times}$ 14 $\boxed{=}$ 537824
$\boxed{\text{ON/AC}}$ 14 $\boxed{y^x}$ 5 $\boxed{=}$ 537824

Finding the 5th root of 537824, or $\sqrt[5]{537824}$, is the inverse of finding 14 raised to the 5th power.

$\boxed{\text{ON/AC}}$ 537824 $\boxed{y^x}$ 5 $\boxed{1/x}$ $\boxed{=}$ 14

Use the $\boxed{+\mathcal{C}-}$ key to raise a number to a negative power. To find 5^{-2} enter $\boxed{\text{ON/AC}}$ 5 $\boxed{y^x}$ 2 $\boxed{+\mathcal{C}-}$ $\boxed{=}$. The display will show 0.04.

Activity

Find a digit, 1–9, for each letter. Make a true equation.

1. $a^4 = b^2$ **2.** $a^3 = b^2$ **3.** $\sqrt[3]{a} = \sqrt{b}$

4. $a^3 + b^3 = c^2$ **5.** $\sqrt[3]{a} + \sqrt[3]{b} = \sqrt{c}$ **6.** $a^2 + b^2 = 10^c$

Percent

The percent key $\boxed{\%}$ converts the number in the display to a decimal by dividing it by 100. Try this.

Enter $\boxed{\text{ON/AC}}$ 35 $\boxed{\%}$. The display will show 0.35.

Here is how to use the calculator to solve some common percent problems.

Percent of a Number. If sales tax rate is 6%, what is the tax on $57.80?

Enter $\boxed{\text{ON/AC}}$ 57.80 $\boxed{\times}$ 6 $\boxed{\%}$ $\boxed{=}$. The display will be 3.468.

Pressing $\boxed{\text{Fix}}$ 2 sets 2 decimal places, and rounds the display to 3.47.

Mary moved 30% of the plants in her shop to larger pots. She moved 36 plants. How many plants are in Mary's shop?

$\boxed{\text{ON/AC}}$ 36 $\boxed{\div}$ 30 $\boxed{\%}$ $\boxed{=}$ 120

Percent of Increase. There is 15% more snow this year than last year. Last year's snowfall was 42 inches. How many inches are there this year?

$\boxed{\text{ON/AC}}$ 42 $\boxed{+}$ 15 $\boxed{\%}$ $\boxed{=}$ 48.3

or   42 $\boxed{\text{M}+}$ $\boxed{\times}$ 15 $\boxed{\%}$ $\boxed{=}$ $\boxed{\text{M}+}$ $\boxed{\text{MR}}$ 48.3

or   42 $\boxed{\times}$ 115 $\boxed{\%}$ $\boxed{=}$ 48.3

Percent Discount. At 35% off, what is the sale price of a lamp that originally sells for $89.80?

$\boxed{\text{ON/AC}}$ 89.80 $\boxed{-}$ 35 $\boxed{\%}$ $\boxed{=}$ 58.37

or   89.80 $\boxed{\times}$ 65 $\boxed{\%}$ $\boxed{=}$ 58.37

Activity

The wholesale price Delia pays for stereo equipment is shown in the chart. The retail price in her store is 65% above the wholesale price. For her yearly inventory sale, Delia discounts the retail price by 25%. Find the retail price and sale price for each item. Round to the nearest cent.

Item	Wholesale Price	Retail Price (W + 65%)	Sale Price (R − 25%)
Receiver	$315		
Speakers	364		
Turntable	180		
Tape Deck	145		
CD Player	280		

Repeating Decimals

Maria used her calculator to find a repeating decimal for a fraction. When she divided the numerator by the denominator her calculator showed 0.3076923. Maria thought this was probably a repeating decimal and would bc 0.307692307692 if more digits could be shown on the calculator.

Maria could not remember the fraction she used to get the decimal. Can you find it by using your calculator?

The program below can be used to help you find the lowest-terms fraction for any decimal.

```
10 PRINT: PRINT: PRINT "REPEATING DECIMALS": PRINT "THE COMPUTER WILL
        CALCULATE THE LOWEST": PRINT "TERMS FRACTION FOR ANY DECIMAL.
        USE"
20 PRINT "ONLY REPEATING DECIMALS BETWEEN 0 AND 1"
30 PRINT "SUCH AS 0.2454545 . . .
40 PRINT: INPUT "ENTER THE REPEATING DECIMAL";D$
50 PRINT: PRINT "HOW MANY DIGITS AFTER THE DECIMAL"
55 PRINT "ARE NOT PART OF THE REPEATING"
60 PRINT "PERIOD OF THE DECIMAL? TYPE A 0"
70 INPUT "IF THERE ARE NONE.";A
80 IF A = 0 THEN 100
90 INPUT "TYPE THOSE DIGITS WITHOUT A DECIMAL";K
100 PRINT: PRINT "HOW MANY DIGITS ARE IN ONE PERIOD OF": INPUT "THE
        REPEATING PART?";P
110 PRINT "TYPE THE DIGITS IN ONE PERIOD OF THE": INPUT "REPEATING PART.";B
120 N = K * (10 ^ P − 1) + B:D = (10 ^ A) * (10 ^ p − 1)
130 N1 = N:D1 = D
140 Q = INT (D/N):A = INT(D − Q * N + .5)
150 IF R = 0 THEN 170
160 D = N:N = R: GOTO 140
170 PRINT: PRINT "THE FRACTION FOR "D$
180 PRINT "IS" N1/N "/" D1/N
190 END
```

Solving Equations

What is the solution to the equation $15x + 37 = 322$? How long did it take you to solve it?

Suppose you were given 50 equations to solve. Even though you may be excellent at solving equations, it would take time and you might make some mistakes.

The computer program below will solve equations like the one above. It will let you choose the three numbers you want for the equation. You can use both positive and negative numbers in the equation.

```
10 PRINT: PRINT: PRINT "SOLVING EQUATIONS"
20 PRINT "THIS PROGRAM WILL SOLVE EQUATIONS LIKE"
30 PRINT "AX + B = C, WHERE A, B, AND C ARE"
40 PRINT "INTEGERS."
50 PRINT: PRINT "ENTER A, B, AND C"
60 INPUT "A ="; A: INPUT "B ="; B: INPUT "C =";C
70 X = (C − B)/A
80 PRINT: PRINT "EQUATION:";A;"X + ";B"=";C
90 PRINT: PRINT "X = ";X
100 PRINT: INPUT "DO YOU WANT ANOTHER EQUATION?";Y$
110 IF LEFT$(Y$,1) = "Y" THEN 50
120 END
```

Guess and Check

A friend secretly adds 3 consecutive whole numbers and then tells you that their sum is 426. Find the three numbers that were added. Can you use the Guess and Check Strategy or other problem solving strategies to find the three numbers?

The computer program below can be used to help you find the three numbers using the strategy of Guess and Check. Try working some problems using it with one of your classmates.

```
10 S = INT(999 * RND (1) + 1)
20 IF S/3 <> INT(S/3) THEN GOTO 10
30 PRINT: PRINT: PRINT "GUESS AND CHECK": PRINT "USE THE GUESS AND CHECK
       STRATEGY TO": PRINT "FIND THE THREE CONSECUTIVE WHOLE": PRINT
       "NUMBERS THAT ADD UP TO "S"."
40 PRINT: PRINT "GUESS THE SMALLEST WHOLE NUMBER OF THE": INPUT
       "THREE.";N:K = 3 * N + 3
50 PRINT: PRINT "CHECKING THE GUESS."
60 PRINT N," + ";N + 1;" + ";N + 2;" = ";K
70 IF K = S THEN PRINT "YOU HAVE GUESSED THE NUMBERS.": GOTO 90
80 PRINT "NOT CORRECT! GUESS AGAIN.": GOTO 40
90 PRINT: INPUT "DO YOU WANT TO TRY AGAIN?";Y$
100 IF LEFT$(Y$,1) = "Y" THEN PRINT: GOTO 10
110 END
```

Estimating Length

Suppose the small segment shown below is 1 unit in length.
What is your estimate of the length of the longer segment, AB?

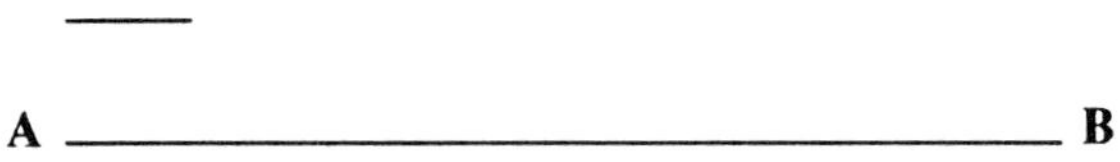

_____

A ——————————————————————— B

Is your estimate of the segment length within 1 unit of the
actual length? Find a way to check your estimate.

```
10 U = INT(6 * RND(1) + 3)
20 S = INT(78 * RND(1) + 1)
30 IF S < U THEN 10
40 L = INT(S/U * 10)/10
50 PRINT: PRINT: FOR N = 1 TO U: PRINT"-";: NEXT N: PRINT "1 UNIT": PRINT: PRINT:
        FOR N = 1 TO S: PRINT"-";: NEXT N
60 PRINT: PRINT: GOSUB 150: PRINT: INPUT "WHAT IS YOUR ESTIMATE?";E
70 PRINT: PRINT "LENGTH", "EST.","DIFF."
80 PRINT L, E, ABS (L − E)
90 PRINT: INPUT "TRY AGAIN? (Y/N)";Y$
100 IF LEFT$(Y$,1) = "Y" THEN 10
130 END
150 PRINT: PRINT "ESTIMATING LENGTH"
160 PRINT "USE THE UNIT SEGMENT TO ESTIMATE THE"
170 PRINT "LENGTH OF THE UNMARKED SEGMENT TO THE"
180 PRINT "NEAREST TENTH OF A UNIT."
190 RETURN
```

Expected Outcomes

Casey and Kim were tossing a 6-sided die in a probability experiment. They decided to toss the die 60 times. Kim thought a 3 would come up about 10 times. Casey said that he thought a 6 would come up about 12 times. The table shows the frequency of each of the numbers on the die for 60 tosses.

Number	Frequency
1	11
2	10
3	8
4	8
5	9
6	14

Which of the six numbers came up exactly as many times as its expected outcome?

The computer program below can be used to simulate tossing a die. You also can choose the number of sides you want on a die. For example, choosing a 10-sided die is equivalent to choosing a spinner divided into 10 sectors numbered 1 to 10.

```
10 GOSUB 140: PRINT
20 PRINT: PRINT "HOW MANY FACES DO YOU WANT ON THE": INPUT "DIE?";X
30 FOR N = 1 TO X:D(N) = 0: NEXT N
40 INPUT "HOW MANY DIE TOSSES?";Y
50 INPUT "WHAT NUMBER DO YOU WANT?";Z
60 IF Z > X THEN 50
70 INPUT "PREDICT THE NUMBER OF TIMES YOUR NUMBER WILL COME UP?";G
80 FOR N = 1 TO Y:R = INT(X * RND(1)) + 1
90 LET D(R) = D(R) + 1: NEXT N
100 PRINT: PRINT "NUMBER", "FREQUENCY"
110 FOR N = 1 TO X: PRINT N, D(N): NEXT N
115 PRINT
120 PRINT: PRINT "YOU MISSED YOUR GUESS BY";ABS(G - D(Z))
130 END
140 PRINT: PRINT: PRINT "EXPECTED OUTCOMES"
150 PRINT "CHOOSE THE NUMBER OF SIDES YOU WANT ON": PRINT "THE DIE AND
        HOW MANY TIMES THE DIE WILL"
160 PRINT "BE TOSSED. PREDICT HOW MANY TIMES A": PRINT "PARTICULAR NUMBER
        WILL COME UP."
170 RETURN
```

The 21 NIM Game

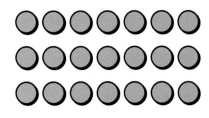

NIM is an ancient game that may have been invented by the Chinese. It is a game for two players and has many different forms. In this version there are 21 counters. Each player in turn must pick up 1, 2, or 3 counters. The person who must pick up the last counter loses the game.

Suppose it is your turn to pick up counters and you see that 6 counters are left. How many counters would you pick up? What strategy would win the game?

The computer program below simulates the 21 NIM Game. Think about strategies that may help you win.

```
10 GOSUB 150
20 S = 21
30 GOSUB 110
40 FOR K = 1 TO 2: PRINT: GOSUB 70: NEXT K
50 IF S > 0 THEN 40
60 END
70 PRINT "PLAYER" K: INPUT "CHOOSE 1, 2, OR 3 STARS.";C
80 IF C < 1 OR C > 3 THEN 70
90 S = S − C
100 IF S < 1 THEN PRINT "PLAYER "K" LOSES.": GOTO 60
110 PRINT: FOR N = 1 TO S: PRINT "*";
120 NEXT N: PRINT""S" STARS LEFT"
130 RETURN
150 PRINT: PRINT: PRINT "THE NIM GAME"
160 PRINT "THERE ARE 21 COUNTERS, EACH REPRESENTED"
170 PRINT "BY A STAR. EACH PLAYER TAKES TURNS AND"
180 PRINT "PICKS UP 1, 2, OR 3 STARS. THE PLAYER"
190 PRINT "WHO MUST TAKE THE LAST STAR LOSES THE": PRINT "GAME."
200 PRINT: PRINT: INPUT "PRESS <RETURN>";Y$
210 RETURN
```

Estimating Means

Ms. Janesco is a computer consultant and often travels to different cities for conferences. The table shows the distance she has traveled on recent trips from her home office in Dallas to 5 other cities.

Round Trip Distances (mi.)	
St. Louis	1,074
Chicago	1,618
Atlanta	1,442
New Orleans	886
Boston	3,102

Ms. Janesco estimates that she travels an average of about 2,000 miles each trip. Do you think this is a good estimate? What is your estimate of the mean or average distance of the 5 trips?

Estimating the mean before computing it is a good skill to develop. Try the computer program below for practice in estimating means. You can choose the amount and size of numbers that you wish to use.

```
10 GOSUB 130
20 PRINT "HOW MANY NUMBERS DO YOU WANT IN THE": INPUT "LIST?";N
30 PRINT "WHAT IS THE RANGE OF THE NUMBERS?"
40 INPUT "SMALLEST NUMBER = ";A
50 INPUT "LARGEST NUMBER = ";B
60 PRINT: FOR I = 1 TO N
70 K = INT((B - A) * RND(1) + A + 1)
80 PRINT, K:T = T + K: NEXT I
90 PRINT: INPUT "ESTIMATE THE MEAN";E
100 PRINT "MEAN", "EST", "DIFF."
110 PRINT T/N, E, ABS(T/N - E)
120 END
130 PRINT: PRINT: PRINT "ESTIMATING MEANS"
140 PRINT "ENTER HOW MANY NUMBERS YOU WANT IN THE"
150 PRINT "LIST AND THE RANGE OF THE NUMBERS. THE"
160 PRINT "COMPUTER WILL GENERATE A LIST WITHIN"
170 PRINT "THAT RANGE. ESTIMATE THE MEAN."
180 PRINT: RETURN
```

Pythagorean Relationship

A 12-foot ladder is placed against a vertical wall. The foot of the ladder is 2.5 feet from the base of the wall. How far up the wall will the top of the ladder reach?

Can you estimate the answer to this problem? What would you do to find a more exact answer?

You can use the Pythagorean Relationship about right triangles to solve the problem. You must decide which side lengths are given for the problem.

The computer program below allows you to make decisions to find a solution for the problem.

```
10 GOSUB 130: PRINT "DO YOU WANT TO FIND:": PRINT
20 PRINT "(1) THE HYPOTENUSE": PRINT "(2) A LEG": PRINT
30 INPUT "TYPE THE NUMBER OF YOUR CHOICE.";N
40 IF N = 2 THEN GOTO 80
50 INPUT "LEG A = ";A: INPUT "LEG B = ";B
60 C = SQR(A * A + B * B): PRINT
70 PRINT "HYPOTENUSE = ";C: GOTO 120
80 PRINT: INPUT "HYPOTENUSE = ";C
90 INPUT "LEG = ";A: IF A > C THEN PRINT "HYPOTENUSE MUST BE LARGER THAN
        THE LEG.": GOTO 80
100 B = SQR(C * C - A * A)
110 PRINT "OTHER LEG = ";B
120 END
130 PRINT: PRINT: PRINT "PYTHAGOREAN RELATIONSHIP"
140 PRINT "GIVE TWO SIDES OF A RIGHT TRIANGLE AND"
150 PRINT "THE COMPUTER WILL CALCULATE EITHER THE"
160 PRINT "HYPOTENUSE OR A LEG."
170 PRINT: RETURN
```

MORE PRACTICE BANK

Set A   For use after page 5

Write each number in standard notation.

1. 2.5 million

2. 57.5 billion

3. 2.01 thousand

4. 1.32 billion

5. 21.5 thousand

6. 9.24 million

Write each number in terms of its largest place value period.

7. 2,340,000

8. 79,060,000,000

9. 555,000,000

Set B   For use after page 7

Evaluate each expression. Name the property you used.

1. $28 + 0 = $ ▦

2. $219 \times 1 = $ ▦

3. $219 \times $ ▦ $= 0$

4. $13 \times 46 = 46 \times $ ▦

5. $39 + 25 = 25 + $ ▦

6. $2,391 \times $ ▦ $= 2,391$

7. $(9 + 72) + $ ▦ $= 9 + (72 + 8)$

8. $5 ($▦$ + 2) = (5 \cdot 20) + (5 \cdot 2)$

Set C   For use after page 9

Solve using mental math. Tell which technique you used.

1. $82 - 3$

2. $4 \times 68 \times 10$

3. $84 + 99 + 87$

4. 9×92

5. $76 + 30$

6. 62×9

7. 49×5

8. $78 + 30$

9. 98×89

10. 29×3

11. $4 \times 7 \times 5$

12. 299×7

Set D   For use after page 11

Estimate. Name the technique you used.

1. 318×597

2. 27×513

3. $377 + 406 + 410 + 394$

4. $6,412 + 6,387 + 6,291$

5. $819 \div 39$

6. $276 + 615 + 425 + 585$

7. $2,871 \div 29$

8. $837 - 62$

9. $91 \times 87 \times 98$

Set E   For use after page 17

Find the value of each expression. Use the order of operations.

1. $16 - 9 + 2$

2. $16 - (9 + 2)$

3. $12 + 2 \times 3$

4. $(12 + 2) \times 3$

5. $7 \cdot 3 + 8 \cdot 9$

6. $25 - (3 \cdot 8)$

7. $17 + 3 \times 11$

8. $(23 + 2) \div 5$

9. $38 - (6 + 7) \cdot 2$

10. $(21 \div 7) + (8 \cdot 2) - 3$

11. $(40 + 10) - (35 - 20)$

Set A   For use after page 19

Solve.

1. Write two subtraction problems you can solve if you know
   86 + 14 = 100.

2. Write a multiplication problem that would help you solve
   63 ÷ 9.

3. Write two division problems you can solve if you know 24
   × 66 = 1,584.

Set B   For use after page 33

Use the graph to answer the questions.

1. How many days of smog alerts did
   Oldport have?

2. How many days of mild smog alerts did
   Rim City have?

3. How many more days of serious smog
   alerts did Oldport have than Willard?

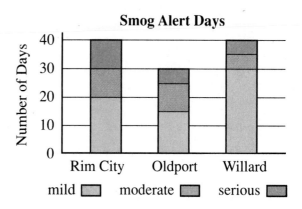

Smog Alert Days

Set C   For use after page 37

Which types of graphs are appropriate for each set of data?

1. Types of Trees	
Oak	29%
Cedar	15%
Fir	47%
Maple	9%

2. Bulb Prices	
Tulip	$6.95
Daffodil	$3.89
Iris	$4.77
Gladiola	$2.99

3. Money Raised	
1990	$78.75
1989	$529.50
1988	$467.65
1987	$423.25

Set D   For use after page 41

Use the stem and leaf plot to answer each question.

1. How many leaves does the stem 7 have?

2. How many times does the temperature 72° appear?

3. How many times does the temperature 70° appear?

4. Which temperature occurs more frequently, 67° or 59°?

5. Which temperature occurs less frequently, 72° or 75°?

6. What is the lowest temperature? the highest?

Temperatures (in °F)

Stem	Leaf
5	1, 9, 3, 9, 4, 9, 6
6	5, 2, 6, 7, 8, 7, 9, 9
7	4, 2, 1, 2, 5, 8, 7, 8, 2, 5
8	3, 2, 1, 0, 3

Set A   For use after page 43

1. Make a frequency table for the data shown.

2. Use the frequency table you made to make a histogram.

3. Make a frequency table for the data shown.

4. Use the frequency table you made to make a histogram.

Bank Customer Transaction Times

3:20	6:30	3:52	6:06
4:35	5:48	3:46	3:18
5:15	3:10	2:45	3:47
2:58	4:49	3:22	4:08

Amount of Sales

$2.50	$3.15	$2.10	$6.35
$5.65	$5.10	$4.90	$8.75
$7.40	$2.45	$3.95	$1.90
$5.25	$3.25	$7.90	$2.95

Set B   For use after page 49

Draw a box and whisker graph for each set of data.

1. 2, 3, 7, 11, 16, 17, 19, 20, 23

2. 24, 27, 30, 35, 37, 40, 46, 51, 58

3. 25, 32, 46, 63, 81, 77

4. 126, 132, 168, 95, 87, 66, 124, 75

Set C   For use after page 51

Use a calculator to find the mean of each set of data. Round each mean to the correct number of significant digits.

1. 2.5, 3.6, 1.9, 5.4, 4.8, 6.2

2. 9.2, 8.5, 6.7, 10.6, 7.8, 5.3

3. 13.4, 12.2, 21.6, 23, 14.91, 17, 21

4. 0.3, 0.56, 0.7, 0.71, 0.083, 0.02

Set D   For use after page 65

Draw each region on dot paper. Find the area of each region.

1.

2.

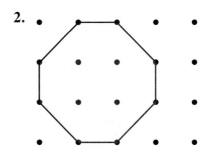

Set A   For use after page 67

Find the area of each polygon.

1.

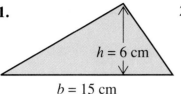

$h = 6$ cm

$b = 15$ cm

2.

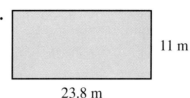

11 m

23.8 m

3.

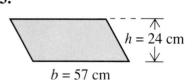

$h = 24$ cm

$b = 57$ cm

Set B   For use after page 69

Find the area of each circle to the nearest tenth. Use 3.14 for π.

1. $r = 5$ cm   **2.** $r = 3.8$ in.   **3.** $d = 16$ ft   **4.** $d = 40.6$ m   **5.** $r = 19$ cm

Set C   For use after page 77

Find the surface area of each space figure.

1.

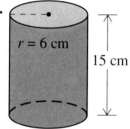

$r = 6$ cm

15 cm

2.

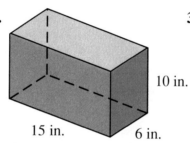

10 in.

15 in.

6 in.

3.

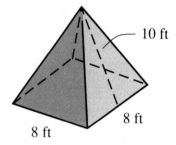

10 ft

8 ft

8 ft

Set D   For use after page 79

Find the volume and surface area of each figure.

1.

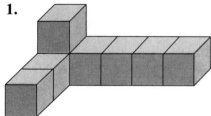

2.

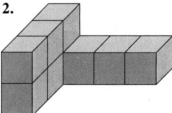

3. Draw a figure that has a surface area of 20 units^2 and a volume of 6 units^3.

4. Draw a figure that has a surface area of 26 units^2 and a volume of 6 units^3.

5. Draw a figure that has a surface area of 22 units^2 and a volume of 6 units^3.

6. What is the smallest surface area that a figure with a volume of 6 units^3 can have?

MORE PRACTICE BANK

Set A   For use after page 81

Find the volume of each rectangular prism.

1. $l = 14$ cm
$w = 5$ cm
$h = 8.3$ cm

2. $l = 20$ cm
$w = 4$ cm
$h = 6$ cm

3. $l = 13.3$ in.
$w = 5.2$ in.
$h = 4$ in.

4. $l = 10$ ft
$w = 6.1$ ft
$h = 11$ ft

Find the volume of each cylinder to the nearest hundredth. Use 3.14 for π.

5. $r = 5$ ft
$h = 10$ ft

6. $r = 13.3$ mm
$h = 5$ mm

7. $r = 8$ cm
$h = 12$ cm

8. $r = 1.1$ in.
$h = 5$ in.

Set B   For use after page 83

Find the volume of each pyramid.

1. $B = 550$ m^2
$h = 9$ m

2. $B = 452$ ft^2
$h = 1.2$ ft

3. $B = 1{,}250$ cm^2
$h = 48$ cm

4. $B = 300$ ft^2
$h = 2.4$ ft

Find the volume of each cone. Round your answer to the nearest hundredth. Use 3.14 for π.

5. $r = 5$ cm
$h = 6$ cm

6. $r = 3.8$ m
$h = 9.3$ m

7. $r = 0.8$ in.
$h = 1.2$ in.

8. $r = 15$ m
$h = 10.3$ m

Set C   For use after page 95

These scales are balanced.

1. Draw another scale that is balanced.

2. Draw a scale that is not balanced.

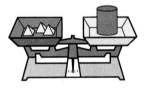
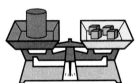

Set D   For use after page 97

Solve each equation using mental math.

1. $b - 15 = 8$

2. $n + 18 = 24$

3. $r + 35 = 72$

4. $y - 56 = 7$

5. $r + 35 = 75$

6. $k - 17 = 15$

7. $y - 56 = 7$

8. $x + 29 = 36$

9. $z + 64 = 100$

10. $20 + s = 42$

11. $j - 33 = 2$

12. $t + 30 = 48$

13. $a - 24 = 9$

14. $h + 17 = 17$

15. $46 + p = 60$

16. $x - 8 = 14$

Set A   For use after page 101

Show the inverse operation needed to simplify each expression so the variable is the result.

1. $x - 35$

2. $12a$

3. $y + 72$

4. $\dfrac{n}{13}$

5. $\dfrac{t}{23}$

6. $b - 67$

7. $51s$

8. $21 + x$

Set B   For use after page 103

Solve each equation.

1. $30 + x = 55$

2. $b - 16 = 100$

3. $p + \dfrac{5}{8} = \dfrac{15}{16}$

4. $w - 2.8 = 5.3$

5. $16h = 48$

6. $\dfrac{p}{17} = 6$

7. $3d = 99$

8. $45 = \dfrac{2}{3}k$

Set C   For use after page 109

Write the steps that show how you build and undo these expressions.

1. $3y - 3$

2. $\dfrac{d}{12} + 4$

3. $7n - 19$

4. $\dfrac{k}{5} - 1$

Set D   For use after page 111

Solve each equation.

1. $\dfrac{m}{5} + 3 = 9$

2. $4b - 16 = 4$

3. $\dfrac{y}{7} - 11 = 2$

4. $12w + 20 = 80$

5. $2x - 16 = 10$

6. $3c + 11 = 83$

7. $5 + 11s = 71$

8. $6x - 99 = 63$

Set E   For use after page 113

Fill in each ⦀ with $\geq$ or $\leq$ to make the statement true.

1. $12 \ ⦀ \ 9$

2. $\dfrac{3}{5} \ ⦀ \ \dfrac{2}{7}$

3. $12 \ ⦀ \ 5 + 8$

4. $3 \cdot 3 \ ⦀ \ 2 \cdot 7$

Find all the solutions to each inequality selected from the set. 1, 2, 3, 4, 5, 6, 7.

5. $x > 2$

6. $t < 7$

7. $k \leq 4$

8. $s \geq 1$

9. $d \leq 3$

10. $y > 5$

11. $h \geq 7$

12. $z < 6$

Set A   For use after page 117

Construct tables of input-output pairs $(n, f(n))$ for these function rules. Include input values $n = 1, 2, 3, 4, 5$.

1. $15n - 1$ **2.** $(n + 7) - 3$ **3.** $5 - n$ **4.** $10 - 2n$

5. $7 - n$ **6.** $4n + 2$ **7.** $2 + n$ **8.** $n + 3$

Set B   For use after page 119

Make a coordinate plane like the one shown here. Graph each function on the plane.

1. $y = \dfrac{x}{4}$

2. $y = x + 3$

3. $y = 3 - x$

4. $y = 2x$

Set C   For use after page 121

Write each number in standard form.

1. 12^2 **2.** 6^6 **3.** 127^0 **4.** 1^{22} **5.** 17^2 **6.** $(1.4)^3$

Write each expression in exponential form.

7. 3 **8.** $4 \cdot 4 \cdot 4 \cdot 4 \cdot 4$ **9.** $7 \cdot 7 \cdot 7 \cdot 7 \cdot 7$ **10.** $9 \cdot 9 \cdot 9 \cdot 9 \cdot 9$

Write the exponent for each.

11. $4^3 \cdot 4^7 = 4^?$ **12.** $2^5 \cdot 2^8 = 2^?$ **13.** $\dfrac{9^6}{9^3} = 9^?$ **14.** $\dfrac{5^6}{5^1} = 5^?$

Set D   For use after page 131

Find the absolute value.

1. $|6|$ **2.** $|{}^-5|$ **3.** $|{}^-10|$ **4.** $|1|$ **5.** $|{}^-6|$ **6.** $|-1|$

Set E   For use after page 133

Find the sum.

1. ${}^-2 + {}^-2$ **2.** ${}^-2 + 3$ **3.** ${}^-10 + 8$ **4.** ${}^-1 + 7$

5. $9 + ({}^-5 + {}^-4)$ **6.** $({}^-11 + 5) + 4$ **7.** ${}^-8 + 5 + {}^-1$ **8.** ${}^-5 + 12 + {}^-17$

Set A   For use after page 135

Subtract. Remember the order of operations.

1. $5 - {}^-4$　　**2.** ${}^-8 - 3$　　**3.** $11 - {}^-5$　　**4.** ${}^-5 - 6$　　**5.** ${}^-9 - {}^-9$

6. ${}^-13 - 21$　**7.** $12 - {}^-25$　**8.** $67 - 85$　**9.** ${}^-53 - {}^-76$　**10.** ${}^-81 - 76$

11. ${}^-8 - (7 - {}^-4)$　**12.** $(8 - {}^-7) - 5$　**13.** $(9 - 17) - 8$　**14.** $(15 - 29) - 12$

Set B   For use after page 137

Compute. Remember the order of operations.

1. $5 \cdot {}^-3$　　**2.** ${}^-4 \cdot 9$　　**3.** $7 \cdot 3$　　**4.** $12 \div {}^-3$　　**5.** ${}^-15 \cdot {}^-5$

6. ${}^-84 \div 12$　**7.** $99 \cdot {}^-10$　**8.** ${}^-13 \cdot {}^-12$　**9.** $-165 \div 15$　**10.** ${}^-81 \div {}^-9$

11. $6 \cdot ({}^-7 + 9)$　　**12.** $12 \div {}^-4 \cdot 3$　　**13.** $6 \cdot {}^-9 + 7$　　**14.** $-17 \cdot ({}^-19 + 19)$

Set C   For use after page 141

Solve each equation using mental math.

1. $n + 5 = 4$　**2.** $x - 6 = {}^-2$　**3.** $10y = 80$　　**4.** ${}^-12y = {}^-36$　**5.** ${}^-6x = 180$

6. $6 + k = 13$　**7.** $m + {}^-5 = 2$　**8.** $7 \cdot t = {}^-63$　**9.** $\frac{r}{{}^-6} = {}^-12$　**10.** ${}^-9x = {}^-9$

Set D   For use after page 143

Solve each equation.

1. $c + 11 = 3$　　**2.** $r - {}^-5 = {}^-12$　　**3.** $x + {}^-3 = 10$　　**4.** $w - 18 = {}^-17$

5. $b + 1 = 22$　　**6.** $\frac{n}{7} = {}^-7$　　　**7.** $16x = 48$　　**8.** $\frac{r}{{}^-8} = 7$

Set E   For use after page 145

Solve.

1. $8a - 5 = 27$　　**2.** $\frac{h}{5} + {}^-10 = {}^-12$　**3.** $\frac{y}{{}^-5} - {}^-11 = {}^-8$　**4.** $12p + {}^-3 = {}^-39$

5. $3x - 7 = {}^-22$　　**6.** $25 - 3x = 19$　　**7.** $15d + 9 = {}^-36$　**8.** ${}^-8k + {}^-13 = {}^-61$

Set F   For use after page 149

Use grid paper and make a coordinate plane. Plot these points.

1. $H\,(4, 6)$　　**2.** $I\,({}^-2, 8)$　　**3.** $J\,(2, {}^-3)$　　**4.** $K\,(9, {}^-3)$　　**5.** $L\,(5, 3)$

MORE PRACTICE BANK

Set A   **For use after page 151**

Complete each table of input-output values.

1. $y = x - 2$

x	4	2	0	$^-2$	$^-4$
y	▥	▥	▥	▥	▥

2. $y = 4 - x$

x	4	2	0	$^-2$	$^-4$
y	▥	▥	▥	▥	▥

3. $y = 3x$

x	4	2	0	$^-2$	$^-4$
y	▥	▥	▥	▥	▥

4. $y = 2x + 1$

x	4	2	0	$^-2$	$^-4$
y	▥	▥	▥	▥	▥

Set B   **For use after page 153**

Make a table of input-output values for each function. Graph each function.

1. $y = x - 2$ **2.** $y = 4 - x$ **3.** $y = x + 5$ **4.** $y = 2x$

5. $y = 5x - 3$ **6.** $y = \frac{1}{2}x$ **7.** $y = {}^-2x$ **8.** $y = 3x - 1$

Set C   **For use after page 165**

List the first four nonzero multiples of each number. You may want to use a calculator.

1. 9   **2.** 20   **3.** 100   **4.** 7   **5.** 11

6. 14   **7.** 23   **8.** 12   **9.** 13   **10.** 15

Find all the factors of each number.

11. 20   **12.** 40   **13.** 60   **14.** 34   **15.** 84

16. 105   **17.** 24   **18.** 21   **19.** 18   **20.** 75

Set D   **For use after page 167**

State whether each number is divisible by 2, 3, 5, 9, or 10.

1. 213   **2.** 513   **3.** 624   **4.** 115   **5.** 810

State whether each number is divisible by 11.

6. 143   **7.** 275   **8.** 391   **9.** 41,151   **10.** 10,989

Set A   For use after page 169

List all the factors of each number. Then state whether each number is prime or composite.

1. 18   **2.** 40   **3.** 33   **4.** 29   **5.** 42   **6.** 32

7. 38   **8.** 95   **9.** 15   **10.** 83   **11.** 22   **12.** 119

13. 67   **14.** 81   **15.** 99   **16.** 27   **17.** 24   **18.** 36

19. 35   **20.** 37   **21.** 34   **22.** 28   **23.** 100   **24.** 150

Set B   For use after page 173

Find the prime factorization of each number.

1. 30   **2.** 48   **3.** 36   **4.** 90   **5.** 160   **6.** 17

7. 18   **8.** 16   **9.** 50   **10.** 181   **11.** 72   **12.** 24

13. 25   **14.** 32   **15.** 105   **16.** 20   **17.** 75   **18.** 12

Set C   For use after page 177

Find the GCF of each pair of numbers.

1. 63, 42   **2.** 12, 30   **3.** 17, 34   **4.** 18, 35   **5.** 64, 80

6. 12, 14   **7.** 23, 92   **8.** 12, 18   **9.** 13, 78   **10.** 15, 25

11. 6, 31   **12.** 10, 12   **13.** 24, 36   **14.** 18, 28   **15.** 32, 12

Set D   For use after page 179

Find the LCM of each pair of numbers.

1. 10, 15   **2.** 28, 40   **3.** 6, 15   **4.** 9, 15   **5.** 81, 18

6. 4, 5   **7.** 4, 12   **8.** 7, 84   **9.** 26, 7   **10.** 3, 18

Set E   For use after page 193

Write $=$ or $\neq$ for each ▥.

1. $\frac{4}{32}$ ▥ $\frac{5}{40}$ **2.** $\frac{10}{15}$ ▥ $\frac{25}{40}$ **3.** $\frac{10}{15}$ ▥ $\frac{12}{18}$ **4.** $\frac{12}{15}$ ▥ $\frac{16}{20}$ **5.** $\frac{12}{18}$ ▥ $\frac{14}{20}$

Set A   For use after page 195

Write a fraction or mixed number and a decimal that corresponds to the given point.

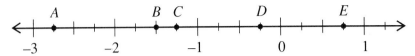

1. Point A **2.** Point B **3.** Point C **4.** Point D **5.** Point E

Set B   For use after page 197

Compare.

1. $^-5$ ||| $^-4$ **2.** $^-1$ ||| 3 **3.** 11 ||| 9 **4.** $^-3$ ||| $^-5$ **5.** $^-8$ ||| $^-12$

6. $^-10$ ||| 4 **7.** 9 ||| $^-10$ **8.** $^-13$ ||| $^-12$ **9.** $^-17$ ||| $^-15$ **10.** $^-8$ ||| $^-9$

Set C   For use after page 199

Find a decimal for each fraction.

1. $\dfrac{5}{9}$ **2.** $\dfrac{1}{11}$ **3.** $\dfrac{3}{75}$ **4.** $\dfrac{7}{20}$ **5.** $\dfrac{8}{66}$ **6.** $\dfrac{7}{55}$

7. $\dfrac{^-5}{8}$ **8.** $\dfrac{3}{8}$ **9.** $\dfrac{^-4}{9}$ **10.** $\dfrac{5}{7}$ **11.** $\dfrac{^-13}{21}$ **12.** $\dfrac{3}{10}$

Set D   For use after page 201

Find each sum or difference.

1. $\dfrac{5}{8} + \dfrac{^-3}{8}$ **2.** $\dfrac{^-7}{10} + \dfrac{3}{10}$ **3.** $\dfrac{^-1}{6} + \dfrac{^-5}{6}$ **4.** $\dfrac{7}{10} - \dfrac{9}{10}$ **5.** $\dfrac{^-2}{5} - \dfrac{3}{5}$

6. $\dfrac{4}{9} - \dfrac{^-3}{9}$ **7.** $\dfrac{^-3}{8} + \dfrac{^-1}{2}$ **8.** $\dfrac{^-5}{8} - \dfrac{^-3}{4}$ **9.** $\dfrac{^-3}{5} + \dfrac{^-1}{2}$ **10.** $\dfrac{^-1}{7} + \dfrac{^-8}{21}$

11. $\dfrac{5}{8} + \dfrac{^-3}{4} + \dfrac{^-3}{8}$ **12.** $\left(\dfrac{2}{3} - \dfrac{^-3}{8}\right) + \dfrac{5}{6}$ **13.** $\dfrac{3}{8} + \dfrac{^-3}{8} - \dfrac{^-3}{8}$ **14.** $\left(\dfrac{^-1}{3} - \dfrac{1}{2}\right) + \dfrac{3}{4}$

Set E   For use after page 203

Find each sum or difference.

1. $2\dfrac{1}{2} + \dfrac{^-1}{2}$ **2.** $\dfrac{^-7}{8} + 1$ **3.** $\dfrac{^-5}{3} + \dfrac{2}{3}$ **4.** $2\dfrac{7}{8} - \dfrac{^-1}{8}$ **5.** $4\dfrac{3}{4} - 5$

Set A   **For use after page 207**

Find each product. Express as a mixed number or fraction in lowest terms.

1. $\frac{2}{5} \cdot \frac{^-5}{8}$ **2.** $\frac{^-3}{8} \cdot \frac{4}{3}$ **3.** $\frac{5}{6} \cdot \frac{3}{10}$ **4.** $\frac{1}{2} \cdot {}^-12$ **5.** $\frac{^-1}{4} \cdot \frac{^-1}{2}$ **6.** $4\frac{2}{3} \cdot {}^-5\frac{3}{8}$

7. $\frac{3}{5} \cdot 2\frac{2}{3}$ **8.** ${}^-3\frac{3}{7} \cdot {}^-1\frac{11}{18}$ **9.** $2\frac{8}{9} \cdot \frac{4}{7}$ **10.** $2\frac{1}{3} \cdot {}^-3\frac{3}{4}$ **11.** $3\frac{2}{5} \cdot 7\frac{1}{10}$ **12.** $\frac{5}{9} \cdot {}^-10$

Set B   **For use after page 211**

Find each quotient. Express as a mixed number or fraction in lowest terms.

1. $\frac{4}{5} \div \frac{2}{3}$ **2.** $\frac{5}{6} \div \frac{^-1}{2}$ **3.** $\frac{^-2}{3} \div \frac{^-3}{4}$ **4.** $\frac{^-3}{5} \div \frac{3}{5}$ **5.** $2 \div \frac{^-3}{4}$

Set C   **For use after page 215**

Write each in scientific notation.

1. 0.0038   **2.** 15,000,000   **3.** 279,000,000,000   **4.** 0.0000137

Write each in standard notation.

5. 8.5×10^{-4} **6.** 6.22×10^3 **7.** 4×10^{-6} **8.** 1.11×10^7 **9.** 4.12×10^{-8}

10. 5.7×10^5 **11.** 6.9×10^{-1} **12.** 9.48×10^0 **13.** 2.03×10^5 **14.** 7.009×10^{-1}

Set D   **For use after page 227**

Write each ratio in two other ways.

1. $\frac{3}{5}$ **2.** 6 to 7   **3.** 5:9   **4.** $\frac{7}{33}$ **5.** 13 to 20   **6.** 3:4

Write the next three ratios in each pattern.

7. $\frac{2}{3} = \frac{4}{6} = \frac{\blacksquare}{\blacksquare} = \frac{\blacksquare}{\blacksquare} = \frac{\blacksquare}{\blacksquare}$ **8.** 3:1, 6:2, $\blacksquare$, $\blacksquare$, $\blacksquare$ **9.** 2 to 5, 4 to 10, $\blacksquare$, $\blacksquare$, $\blacksquare$

Set E   **For use after page 229**

Simplify each rate.

1. $\frac{25 \text{ m}}{5 \text{ s}}$ **2.** $\frac{\$7.50}{5 \text{ h}}$ **3.** $\frac{72 \text{ km}}{6 \text{ min}}$ **4.** $\frac{72 \text{ revs}}{3 \text{ h}}$ **5.** $\frac{100 \text{ ft}}{20 \text{ s}}$ **6.** $\frac{540 \text{ mi}}{12 \text{ gal}}$

Set A   For use after page 231

Find the unit price. Round the answers to the nearest cent.

1. Bread: 1.5 lb for $2.49

2. Raisins: 6 oz for $1.09

3. Cottage cheese: 8 oz for $1.29

4. Grapefruit: 3 for $0.89

Set B   For use after page 235

Give the actual distance between the two points.

1.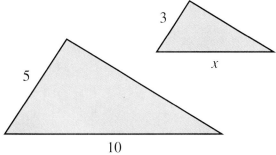

Scale: 3 cm : 50 m

2.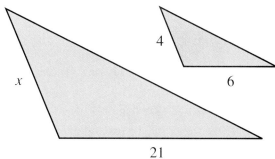

Scale: 5 cm : 360 m

Set C   For use after page 239

Each pair of triangles is similar. Find length x for each pair.

1.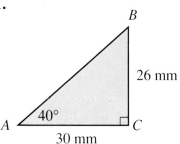

2.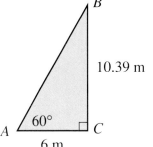

Set D   For use after page 243

Find tan A to the nearest thousandth.

1.

2.

3.

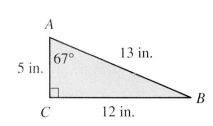

Set A   For use after page 259

Write a percent for each fraction.

1. $\frac{3}{5}$ 2. $\frac{1}{12}$ 3. $\frac{5}{6}$ 4. $\frac{3}{10}$ 5. $\frac{6}{25}$ 6. $\frac{2}{3}$ 7. $\frac{4}{11}$ 8. $\frac{2}{9}$

9. $\frac{8}{9}$ 10. $\frac{3}{8}$ 11. $\frac{4}{25}$ 12. $\frac{5}{9}$ 13. $\frac{7}{10}$ 14. $\frac{5}{8}$ 15. $\frac{22}{50}$ 16. $\frac{23}{25}$

Set B   For use after page 263

Find the percent of each number.

1. 75% of 100   2. 3% of 20   3. 40% of 300   4. 17% of 650   5. 10% of 600

6. 12.5% of 50   7. 300% of 10   8. 37.5% of 12   9. 125% of 50   10. 7.5% of 30

11. 1.5% of 20   12. 6% of 20   13. 0.5% of 25   14. 5% of 380   15. 125% of 300

Set C   For use after page 265

1. What percent of 36 is 9?   2. 5 is what percent of 80?

3. 12 out of 72 is what percent?   4. What percent of 150 is 15?

5. What percent of 60 is 25?   6. 250 is what percent of 50?

7. 13 is what percent of 65?   8. 15 out of 65 is what percent?

Set D   For use after page 271

1. 25% of what number is 6?   2. 21 is $33\frac{1}{3}$% of what number?

3. 52 is 104% of what number?   4. 35% of what number is 70?

5. 80% of what number is 12   6. 75 is 15% of what number?

7. 120 is $66\frac{2}{3}$% of what number?   8. 2% of what number is 13?

Set E   For use after page 285

Find the commission using a calculator. Round to the nearest cent.

1. total sales: $85.95
   commission rate: 2.5%

2. total sales: $1,300.00
   commission rate: 11.33%

3. total sales: $139.95
   commission rate: 7.5%

4. total sales: $1,750.00
   commission rate: 10.5%

5. total sales: $898.00
   commission rate: 13.5%

6. total sales: $4,500.00
   commission rate: 2.5%

Set A   For use after page 287

Find the percent increase or decrease. Round to the nearest tenth.

1. 225 to 135   **2.** 56 to 75   **3.** 590 to 425   **4.** 25 to 150   **5.** 16 to 12

6. 24 to 60   **7.** 80 to 60   **8.** 140 to 100   **9.** 13 to 39   **10.** 240 to 300

Set B   For use after page 289

Estimate the percent for each ratio.

1. 14 out of 21   **2.** 16 to 29   **3.** 61 out of 79   **4.** 59 out of 121   **5.** 38 to 118

6. 24 to 97   **7.** 27 to 88   **8.** 77 out of 60   **9.** 99 to 19   **10.** 150 to 25

Set C   For use after page 295

Find the discount and the sale price. Round to the nearest cent.

1. Regular Price: $66.80
Discount Percent: 5%

2. Regular Price: $7.80
Discount Percent: 15%

3. Regular Price: $59.95
Discount Percent: 20%

4. Regular Price: $79.95
Discount Percent: 35%

5. Regular Price: $45.89
Discount Percent: 25%

6. Regular Price: $450.00
Discount Percent: 10%

Set D   For use after page 299

Draw a circle graph for the information below.

Income from Crops			
Crop	Corn	Wheat	Soybeans	Oats
Income	$16,000	$12,000	$10,000	$2,000

Set E   For use after page 311

Draw a tree diagram to solve each problem.

1. Tony has 4 shirts, 4 pairs of pants, and 3 ties. How many different outfits can he wear to work?

2. A certain car comes in 4-door, 2-door, or hatchback, in red, blue, or gray, and with or without stereo. How many different ways can the car be ordered?

3. Regency 5 Cinema shows five different movies at three different times. How many different ways could you choose to watch three movies?

4. At lunch students may choose a turkey, cheese, or tuna sandwich, an apple or pear, and milk or juice. How many different lunches are available?

Set A   For use after page 313

Find the number of permutations of each.

1. 1, 3, 5, 7, 9

2. red, yellow, blue, green

3. T, O, P, R

4. English, French, German

5. sand, gravel, tar

6. 10, 9, 8, 7, 6, 5, 4

Set B   For use after page 319

Find the number of combinations.

1. 3 names selected from 5 names

2. 2 books selected from 7 books

3. 2 winners selected from 6 runners

4. 5 cars selected from 8 cars

5. 4 candidates from 6 candidates

6. 3 toppings from 12 toppings

Set C   For use after page 335

List the sample space for each experiment.

1. Shuffle cards numbered 1–12 and draw a card.

2. Toss a coin, then spin a spinner numbered 1, 2, 3, 4, 5.

3. Spin a spinner numbered 1, 2, 3, 4, then spin a spinner numbered 1, 2, 3.

4. Spin a spinner numbered 1, 2, 3, then toss a number cube.

5. Spin a spinner colored red, blue, and green then toss a number cube.

Set D   For use after page 337

Imagine spinning the spinner shown. Find the probability of each event.

1. $P(9)$

2. $P(6)$

3. $P(\text{number} < 4)$

4. $P(6 \text{ or } 9)$

5. $P(\text{not } 7)$

6. $P(\text{even number})$

7. $P(\text{number} > 5)$

8. $P(10)$

9. $P(\text{multiple of } 3)$

Consider the probability tossing a coin, then tossing a number cube.

10. List all the ordered pairs in the sample space.

11. Find $P(H, 3)$.

12. Find $P(T, 2)$

13. Find $P(H, T)$

Set A   For use after page 339

The table lists the outcomes from an experiment in which a nickel and a dime were tossed 75 times.

1. Find Exp P(T,H)

2. Find Exp P(one H and one T)

3. Find Exp P(H,H)

4. Find Exp P(at least one T)

Outcome	Number of times
(H,H)	21
(H,T)	18
(T,H)	19
(T,T)	17

Set B   For use after page 363

Use the diagram to answer the questions.

1. Name a pair of parallel lines.

2. Name a transversal.

3. Name a right angle.

4. Name an acute angle.

5. Name two angles that are supplementary.

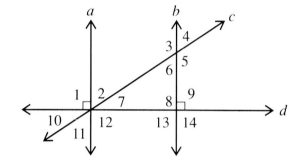

Set C   For use after page 365

Find the sum of the vertex angle measures for each polygon.

1. 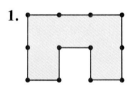   **2.** 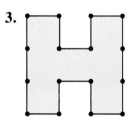   **3.** **4.**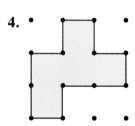

Set D   For use after page 367

Name each polygon. Find the sum of the measures of the vertex angles.

1.    **2.**    **3.**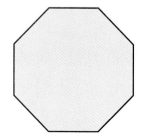

Set A   For use after page 369

Draw a tessellation of these shapes on dot paper.

1.

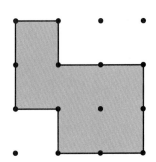

2.

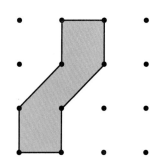

Set B   For use after page 373

Use the circle shown for exercises 1–6.

1. Name a diameter of the circle.

2. Name three radii of the circle.

3. Name two chords of the circle.

4. Name two central angles of the circle.

5. Name a tangent line.

6. Name a secant line.

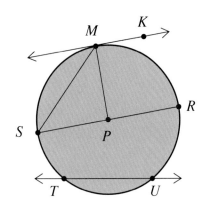

Set C   For use after page 377

Use the figure at the right for exercises 1–7.

$r \| s$, $q \perp r$, and $q \perp s$

1. Name three right angles.

2. Name two transversals of lines r and s.

3. Name two transversals of lines t and q.

4. What is the measure of $\angle 1$?

5. Name a pair of parallel lines.

6. Name a pair of perpendicular lines.

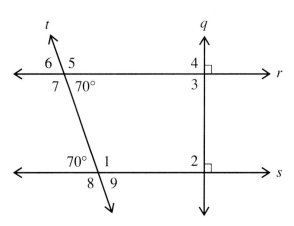

Set A   For use after page 379

1. Draw a segment about 6 cm long and construct its perpendicular bisector.

2. Draw an angle with measure greater than 90° and construct its bisector.

3. Draw a triangle. Construct the perpendicular bisector of each side.

4. Draw a triangle. Construct the bisector of each angle.

Set B   For use after page 393

Find each square root.

1. $\sqrt{81}$ 2. $\sqrt{196}$ 3. $^-\sqrt{4,900}$ 4. $^-\sqrt{1,600}$ 5. $^-\sqrt{1}$

6. $^-\sqrt{225}$ 7. $\sqrt{225}$ 8. $\sqrt{625}$ 9. $\sqrt{100}$ 10. $^-\sqrt{900}$

Set C   For use after page 395

Use the table of square roots or a calculator to find each square root to the nearest thousandth.

1. $\sqrt{14}$ 2. $\sqrt{26}$ 3. $^-\sqrt{13}$ 4. $^-\sqrt{49}$ 5. $\sqrt{1,000}$

6. $\sqrt{28}$ 7. $^-\sqrt{50}$ 8. $\sqrt{12}$ 9. $^-\sqrt{70}$ 10. $\sqrt{86}$

11. $\sqrt{71}$ 12. $^-\sqrt{63}$ 13. $\sqrt{45}$ 14. $^-\sqrt{51}$ 15. $\sqrt{21}$

Set D   For use after page 397

Decide if each represents a rational number or an irrational number.

1. $\sqrt{64}$ 2. $\sqrt{5}$ 3. 1.44   4. 2.787787778   5. 1.6

6. $\sqrt{225}$ 7. $\sqrt{8}$ 8. $\sqrt{1.2}$ 9. $\sqrt{2.4}$ 10. $\sqrt{86}$

11. $\sqrt{29}$ 12. $^-\sqrt{6.3}$ 13. $\sqrt{45}$ 14. $\sqrt{0.51}$ 15. $0.31\overline{31}$

Set E   For use after page 403

Find the missing length of each right triangle, with hypotenuse c, to the nearest thousandth.

1. $a = 5$ cm
   $b = 14$ cm
   find c

2. $b = 7$ ft
   $c = 15$ ft
   find a

3. $a = 12$ m
   $c = 18$ m
   find b

Set A   For use after page 409

Find the missing lengths in each problem.

1. $z = 14$, find x and y **2.** $x = 3$, find y and z

3. $z = 6$, find x and y

Set B   For use after page 423

Trace the figure and the line l. Then draw the reflection image of the figure over l.

1.

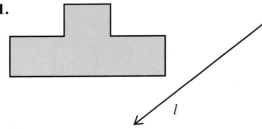

2.

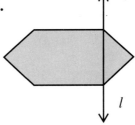

Set C   For use after page 425

For each figure, use graph paper to draw the $\frac{1}{2}$ turn image with turn center at $(0, 0)$.

1.

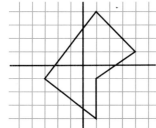

2.

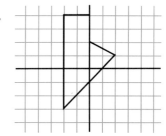

Set D   For use after page 427

Identify the type or types of symmetry for each figure. If a figure has reflectional symmetry identify at least one line of symmetry.

1.

2.

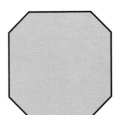

3.

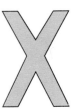

Set A **For use after page 437**

Trace each figure. Then construct a congruent copy of each figure.

1.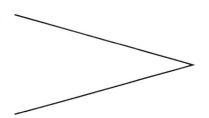

2.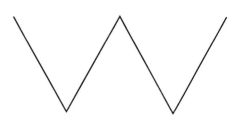

Set B **For use after page 439**

List the pairs of congruent sides and angles for each pair of congruent triangles. Use ≅ to show congruence.

1.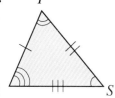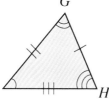

2.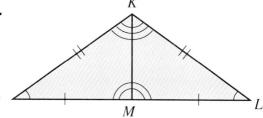

Set C **For use after page 441**

Solve.

1. Trace $\triangle MNO$. Use SAS congruence to construct a triangle congruent to $\triangle MNO$.

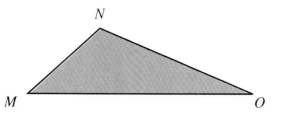

2. Trace $\triangle JKL$. Use ASA congruence to construct a triangle congruent to $\triangle JKL$.

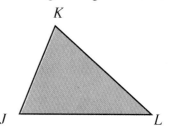

Set D **For use after page 453**

Copy and complete the table to find each sum.

1. $18\frac{3}{4} + 18\frac{3}{4} - \frac{1}{4} + 18\frac{1}{2} - \frac{1}{4} + 18\frac{1}{4} - \frac{1}{4} \ldots$

number	$18\frac{3}{4}$	$18\frac{1}{2}$	$18\frac{1}{4}$	. . .	$\frac{1}{4}$	0
sum to that number	$18\frac{3}{4}$	$37\frac{1}{4}$	$36\frac{3}{4}$	. . .		0

Set A   For use after page 455

Draw the 100th figure for this pattern.

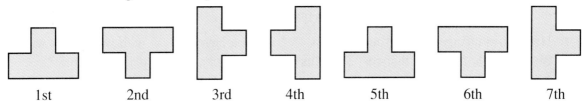

1st   2nd   3rd   4th   5th   6th   7th

Set B   For use after page 457

Discover a quick way to determine the sum of all the
consecutive whole numbers $1 + 2 + 3 + 4 + \ldots 100$.
Consider the sums below.

$1 + 99 = 100, 2 + 98 = 100, 3 + 97 = 100, \ldots$

Set C   For use after page 465

Write an algebraic explanation for the number trick.

Start with any number. Subtract 4.

Multiply by 2. Add 8. Divide by 2.

Set D   For use after page 467

Find the perimeters. Assume all "cut aways" are rectangles.

1.

2.

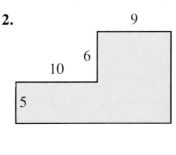

3.

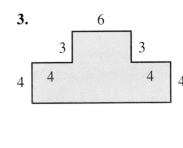

4-6. Find the areas of the yellow figures in problems 1-3
above.

7. Write a brief paragraph describing how you did exercises
1-6 in this set.

Set A   For use after page 21

Decide if you need an exact answer or an estimate, determine
the best calculation method, and solve the problem.

1. How much change should you get from
two $20 bills for shoes that cost $32 plus
4% tax?

2. You have $16.00 with which you want
to purchase three plants for $6.89,
$4.55, and $3.88. Do you have enough
money?

Set B   For use after page 53

Write a question to complete each problem.

1. One year California farms produced
31,484 tons (T) of fresh asparagus and
7,484 T of asparagus to be processed.

2. The total value of strawberries grown in
California in 1980 was $203,812,000.
This was $33,120,000 more than the
value of the strawberry crop in 1979.

Set C   For use after page 85

Before solving each problem, estimate the answer. Then solve
the problem and decide if your answer is reasonable. Use 3.14 for π.

1. The Wangs want to tile the three 8-ft
high walls and the floor of a shower.
One wall is 4 ft long and the other two
walls are each 3 ft long. What is the area
of the shower that will be tiled?

2. Tess drained oil from her car into 8-in.
high cylindrical jars with a 4-in. radius
base. She filled 4 jars. How much oil did
she drain?

Set D   For use after page 147

Solve. Use the strategy Write an Equation.

1. Sally collects baseball cards. She has 5
more than twice the number she had last
year at this time. She has a total of 155
cards. How many baseball cards has she
collected in the past year?

2. Juan bought 8 packages of baseball
cards. The total for his purchase was
$4.24. Tax on the cards was 6%. How
much did each package of cards cost?

3. Gloria and her brother have a total of
171 baseball cards. Before she sold a set
of 12 cards, Gloria had twice as many
cards as her brother. How many cards
does Gloria's brother have?

4. Two of Gloria's cards have a combined
value of $17. One of the cards is worth
three times as much as the other. How
much is each card worth?

MORE PRACTICE BANK

Set A   For use after page 155

Solve. Estimate by rounding to the nearest whole number. Then find the exact answer.

1. The school record for the standing broad jump was $20\frac{1}{2}$ ft. Bonnie made a jump of $18\frac{5}{6}$ ft. How much shorter than the school record was her jump?

2. Franklin ran in a 2-mile race. He ran the first mile in $5\frac{1}{2}$ min. He ran the second mile in $6\frac{1}{10}$ min. What was his total time for the race?

Set B   For use after page 175

Solve.

1. A $6\frac{1}{2}$ oz can of water-packed tuna provides 45 grams of protein. If a family of 4 shares equally a hot dish made from 13 oz of tuna, how much protein will each family member consume?

2. The average American consumes 5 grams of sodium a day. This is ten times the daily amount the average person needs. What is the daily requirement for the average person?

Set C   For use after page 247

Write each phrase as an algebraic expression.

1. the sum of x and 9

2. 5 less than 12

3. 3 more than n

4. a number divided by 4

5. the product of t and 8

6. a number increased by 7

Set D   For use after page 269

Solve.

1. A season's pass for 5 Act Two theatre productions is $69.95. Tickets for a single production are $15.99 each. How much would you save with a season pass?

2. Grandma's Attic costumes rent for $21.50 a day or $120 a week. If you need the costumes for 12 days, is it cheaper to rent by the day or by the week?

Set E   For use after page 375

Solve.

1. Jed mixed 2 partly used cans of paint. He poured as much red paint into the blue as was left in the blue can, then poured into the red can as much of this mixture as the red paint left in the can. This left 8 pints in each can. How much of each color did he use?

2. An interior decorator mixed 4 parts of white paint to 1 part of yellow paint to make the shade she wanted. How much of each color paint will she need to mix to paint a 500 sq ft area if 1 quart covers 100 sq ft?

545

Set A   **For use after page 275**

Solve.

1. Applicants for law enforcement positions in one city must miss no more than 50 questions on a written exam of 200 questions to qualify. What percent of the questions must be answered correctly?

2. One question on the law enforcement exam was missed by 38 out of 51 applicants. Estimate the percentage of applicants who missed the question.

Set B   **For use after page 293**

Estimate a percent for each problem.

1. At Oakridge School, 25 out of 300 students joined the chess club. Estimate what percent this was.

2. At another school, 37 out of 150 students said they wanted to join the army after their schooling had ended. Estimate this percent.

Set C   **For use after page 213**

Solve.

1. At an awards dinner two school coaches went around to greet guests. One coach spent 2 minutes at each table she visited. The other spent 4 minutes per table. How long did it take for all 30 tables to be greeted if no table was greeted by both coaches?

2. The awards dinner was attended by 208 people in all. There were 4 more female students than male students and twice as many adults as male students. How many students and how many adults attended the dinner?

Set D   **For use after page 405**

Solve. If there is no solution, tell why.

1. Raisa used $1 to buy a $0.60 bag of peanuts. She received 4 coins in change. None of the coins was a dime. What coins did she receive?

2. Loren gave 5 coins to pay for a $0.78 drink. He received a nickel in change. What coins did Loren use to buy the drink?

Set E   **For use after page 105**

Solve.

1. Althea sold $2, $4, and $8 raffle tickets. She sold 5 tickets for a total of $24. How many tickets of each price did she sell?

2. Juan said he had 17 coins totaling $1.15. How many coins of each type did he have?

MORE PRACTICE BANK

Set A   For use after page 343   Solve.

1. Kara has a salad with avocado, melon, pineapple, and a strawberry. She won't eat pineapple right after a strawberry. In how many different orders can she eat each fruit?

2. Leif made a list to see how many different ways the letters in his name could be arranged. How many of the arrangements of the letters of his name form words?

Set B   For use after page 325   Solve.

1. The first four triangular numbers are given. Find the tenth triangular number.

2. How many different equilateral triangles are there in the figure below?

Set C   For use after page 183   Solve.

1. A large size cube-shaped gift box has a volume that is 8 times the volume of a medium size box in the same shape. The medium size box is 6 in. high. What is the height of the large size box?

2. A frozen yogurt cone and a cylindrical dish have the same base. The cone's height is 6 times the cylinder's height. How much greater than the volume of the cylinder is the volume of the cone?

Set D   For use after page 241   Solve. Estimate your answer first.

1. A compact disc holds 70 min of music. A record album holds 50 min of music. How many more minutes of music does the compact disc give?

2. A compact disc sale advertised 35% off the regular price of $12.99 per disc. A competing store advertised 2 discs for $18.99. Which sale offers the better price per disc?

Set E   For use after page 217   Write conclusions from chaining these statements.

1. If I read the novel, then I will be entertained. If I am entertained, then I will be happy.

2. If Tom is taller than Bill, then he is taller than 6 feet. If Bill is taller than Fred, then Bill is taller than 6 feet 3 inches.

Set F   For use after page 473   Solve.

1. A factory inspector found defects in 3 out of every 25 rafts she inspected. At this rate, how many defective rafts might she expect to find in 375 rafts?

2. A boat would cover 35 miles a day, then drift back 10 miles each night. At this rate, how many days will it take to go 150 miles?

Set A   For use after page 301

Solve. If the problem has no solution, show why.

1. Adrian said he had 5 coins totaling $1.15. How many coins of each type did he have?

2. Lena said she had $0.72. She said she had 5 coins, the largest of which was a quarter. What 5 coins did Lena have?

Set B   For use after page 315

Solve. Use any problem solving strategy.

1. Juanita spent $36 on tickets for a play. She bought 2 student tickets at $6 each and at least one child's ticket at $3. How many tickets did she buy?

2. Lawrence is 13 years old. His father is 35 years old. How old will Lawrence be when he is half as old as his father?

Set C   For use after page 443

Before solving the problem, list at least 2 strategies you think might help you solve the problem. Then solve the problem.

1. Roberto started a drama club. He was the only one at the first meeting. Each week that followed one more person came than the week before. How many people came the 9th week?

2. A drama club with 9 members set up a schedule so that each member worked on a presentation paired with every other member one time. How many presentations would be given?

Set D   For use after page 473

Before solving each problem, estimate the answer. Then solve the problem and decide if the answer is reasonable.

1. The average weight of a woman is equal to the weight of 9.6 cats. The average woman weighs 135 lb. What is the average weight of a cat?

2. The average weight of a chicken is half as much as the average weight of a fox. The average weight of a raccoon is equal to that of the chicken and fox combined. Altogether they weigh 42 lbs. How much does each weigh?

3. By the time they are 12 years old, most boys have reached about 85% of their adult height and 60% of their adult weight. Zack is 12 years old, 5 ft 2 in. tall, and weighs 104 lb. Predict Zack's adult height and weight.

4. The average adult blue whale weighs about 150 tons. This is about the same as the combined weight of 23 adult African elephants. About how much does the average adult African elephant weigh?

Metric system	**Customary Units**

Length

Metric system	Customary Units
1 meter (m) $\begin{cases}$ 1,000 millimeters (mm) 100 centimeters (cm) 10 decimeters (dm) $\end{cases}$	1 foot (ft) 12 inches (in.)
1 kilometer (km) 1,000 meters (m)	1 yard (yd) $\begin{cases}$ 36 inches (in.) 3 feet (ft) $\end{cases}$
1 hectometer (hm) 100 meters, (m)	1 mile (mi) $\begin{cases}$ 5,280 feet (ft) 1,760 yards (yd) $\end{cases}$
1 dekameter (dam) 10 meters (m)	
1 decimeter (dm) 0.1 meter (m)	1 nautical mile 6,076 feet (ft)
1 centimeter (cm) 0.01 meter (m)	
1 millimeter (mm) 0.001 meter (m)	

Area

Metric system	Customary Units
1 square meter (m^2) $\begin{cases}$ 100 square decimeters (dm^2) 10,000 square centimeters (cm^2) $\end{cases}$	1 square foot (ft^2) 144 square inches $(in.^2)$
1 hectare (ha) $\begin{cases}$ 0.01 square kilometer (km^2) 10,000 square meters (m^2) $\end{cases}$	1 square yard (yd^2) $\begin{cases}$ 9 square feet (ft^2) 1,296 square inches $(in.^2)$ $\end{cases}$
1 square kilometer (km^2) $\begin{cases}$ 1,000,000 square meters (m^2) 100 hectares (ha) $\end{cases}$	1 acre (a.) $\begin{cases}$ 43,560 square feet (ft^2) 4,840 square yards (yd^2) $\end{cases}$
	1 square mile (mi^2) 640 acres (a.)

Volume

Metric system	Customary Units
1 cubic decimeter (dm^3) $\begin{cases}$ 0.001 cubic meter (m^3) 1,000 cubic centimeters (cm^3) 1 liter (L) $\end{cases}$	1 cubic foot (ft^3) 1,728 cubic inches $(in.^3)$
1 cubic meter (m^3) $\begin{cases}$ 1,000,000 cubic centimeters (cm^3) 1,000 cubic decimeters (dm^3) $\end{cases}$	1 cubic yard (yd^3) $\begin{cases}$ 27 cubic feet (ft^3) 46,656 cubic inches $(in.^3)$ $\end{cases}$

Capacity

Metric system	Customary Units
1 teaspoon 5 milliliters (mL)	1 cup (c) 8 fluid ounces (fl oz)
1 tablespoon 12.5 milliliters (mL)	1 pint (pt) $\begin{cases}$ 16 fluid ounces (fl oz) 2 cups (c) $\end{cases}$
1 liter (L) $\begin{cases}$ 1,000 milliliters (mL) 1,000 cubic centimeters (cm^3) 1 cubic decimeter (dm^3) 4 metric cups $\end{cases}$	1 quart (qt) $\begin{cases}$ 32 fluid ounces (fl oz) 4 cups (c) 2 pints (pt) $\end{cases}$
1 kiloliter (kL) 1,000 liters (L)	1 gallon (gal) $\begin{cases}$ 128 fluid ounces (fl oz) 16 cups (c) 8 pints (pt) 4 quarts (qt) $\end{cases}$

Mass	**Weight**
1 gram (g) 1,000 milligrams (mg)	1 pound (lb) 16 ounces (oz)
1 kilogram (kg) 1,000 grams (g)	1 ton (T) 2,000 pounds (lb)
1 metric ton (t) 1,000 kilograms (kg)	

MATHEMATICAL SYMBOLS

$\lvert 6 \rvert$	Absolute value of	$\overleftrightarrow{AB}$	Line through points A and B
$=$	Is equal to	$\overrightarrow{AB}$	Ray AB
$\neq$	Is not equal to	$\overline{AB}$	Segment with endpoints A and B
$>$	Is greater than	$\angle ABC$	Angle ABC
$<$	Is less than	m $\angle ABC$	Measure of angle ABC
$\geq$	Is greater than or equal to	$\triangle ABC$	Triangle ABC
$\leq$	Is less than or equal to	RS	Arc with endpoints R and S
$\approx$	Is approximately equal to	$AB \perp CD$	Line AB perpendicular to line CD
$\cong$	Is congruent to	$AB \parallel CD$	Line AB is parallel to line CD
$\sim$	Is similar to	$35°$	Thirty-five *degrees*
$\%$	Percent		
π	Pi		
$0.\overline{6}$	Repeating decimal		
$\sqrt{}$	Square root		

METRIC SYSTEM PREFIXES

tera-	T	one trillion		deci-	d	one tenth
giga-	G	one billion		centi-	c	one hundredth
mega-	M	one million		milli-	m	one thousandth
kilo-	k	one thousand		micro-	μ	one millionth
hecto-	h	one hundred		nano-	n	one billionth
deka-	da	ten		pico-	p	one trillionth

FORMULAS

$P = a + b + c$	Perimeter of triangle	$a^2 + b^2 = c^2$	Pythagorean Theorem
$P = 2(l + w)$	Perimeter of rectangle	$C = \pi d$	Circumference of circle
$A = lw$	Area of rectangle	$A = \pi r^2$	Area of circle
$A = bh$	Area of parallelogram	$A = 2\pi rh$	Lateral area of cylinder
$A = \frac{1}{2}(b_1 + b_2)h$	Area of trapezoid	$A = 2\pi r^2 + 2\pi rh$	Surface area of cylinder
$A = \frac{1}{2}bh$	Area of triangle	$A = 2(lh + lw + wh)$	Surface area of rectangular prism
$V = lwh$	Volume of rectangular solid	$A = 4\pi r^2$	Surface area of sphere
$V = Bh$	Volume of prism		
$V = \pi r^2 h$	Volume of cylinder		
$V = \frac{1}{3}Bh$	Volume of pyramid		
$V = \frac{1}{3}\pi r^2 h$	Volume of cone		

TABLE OF TANGENT RATIOS

Angle	tan A	Angle	tan A	N	$\sqrt{N}$	N	$\sqrt{N}$	N	$\sqrt{N}$
1	.0175	46	1.036	1	1	36	6	71	8.426
2	.0349	47	1.072	2	1.414	37	6.083	72	8.485
3	.0524	48	1.111	3	1.732	38	6.164	73	8.544
4	.0699	49	1.150	4	2	39	6.245	74	8.602
5	.0875	50	1.192	5	2.236	40	6.325	75	8.660
6	.1051	51	1.235	6	2.449	41	6.403	76	8.718
7	.1228	52	1.280	7	2.646	42	6.481	77	8.775
8	.1405	53	1.327	8	2.828	43	6.557	78	8.832
9	.1584	54	1.376	9	3	44	6.633	79	8.888
10	.1763	55	1.428	10	3.162	45	6.708	80	8.944
11	.1944	56	1.483	11	3.317	46	6.782	81	9
12	.2126	57	1.540	12	3.464	47	6.856	82	9.055
13	.2309	58	1.600	13	3.606	48	6.928	83	9.110
14	.2493	59	1.664	14	3.742	49	7	84	9.165
15	.2679	60	1.732	15	3.873	50	7.071	85	9.220
16	.2867	61	1.804	16	4	51	7.141	86	9.274
17	.3057	62	1.881	17	4.123	52	7.211	87	9.327
18	.3249	63	1.963	18	4.243	53	7.280	88	9.381
19	.3443	64	2.050	19	4.359	54	7.348	89	9.434
20	.3640	65	2.145	20	4.472	55	7.416	90	9.487
21	.3839	66	2.246	21	4.583	56	7.483	91	9.539
22	.4040	67	2.356	22	4.690	57	7.550	92	9.592
23	.4245	68	2.475	23	4.796	58	7.616	93	9.644
24	.4452	69	2.605	24	4.899	59	7.681	94	9.695
25	.4663	70	2.747	25	5	60	7.746	95	9.747
26	.4877	71	2.904	26	5.099	61	7.810	96	9.798
27	.5095	72	3.078	27	5.196	62	7.874	97	9.849
28	.5317	73	3.271	28	5.292	63	7.937	98	9.899
29	.5543	74	3.487	29	5.385	64	8	99	9.950
30	.5774	75	3.732	30	5.477	65	8.062	100	10
31	.6009	76	4.011	31	5.568	66	8.124		
32	.6249	77	4.331	32	5.657	67	8.185		
33	.6494	78	4.705	33	5.745	68	8.246		
34	.6745	79	5.145	34	5.831	69	8.307		
35	.7002	80	5.671	35	5.916	70	8.367		
36	.7265	81	6.314						
37	.7536	82	7.115						
38	.7813	83	8.144						
39	.8098	84	9.514						
40	.8391	85	11.430						
41	.8693	86	14.301						
42	.9004	87	19.081						
43	.9325	88	28.636						
44	.9657	89	57.290						
45	1.0000	90	NONE						

absolute value (|a|) The absolute value of a number, written with a double bar, is its distance from 0. Thus |3| = 3; |−3| = 3

acute angle An angle less than 90° in measure.

acute triangle A triangle in which every angle is acute.

addend A number that is added.

angle Two rays with the same endpoint.

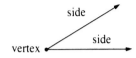

arc A part of a circle.

area The measure of a plane region in square units.

associative property The sum (product) of three or more numbers is the same regardless of grouping: $(a + b) + c = a + (b + c)$ and $(ab)c = a(bc)$

average See *mean*.

axis See *coordinate axes*.

base (in exponential notation) See *exponent*.

base (in numeration systems) The type of grouping used in a system. The decimal system is base ten.

base (of a polygon) Any side may be called the base of a polygon.

Base (of a solid) See examples below.

Bases of   Base of   Base of
a cylinder   a cone   a pyramid

basic counting principle If one thing can be done m ways, and a second thing done n ways, then the two things can be done in $m \cdot n$ ways.

bias Systematic error in gathering data.

bis See *bisect*.

bisect To divide a geometric figure into two congruent parts.

box and whiskers graph A graph which shows how a collection of data are grouped and spread.

capacity The volume of a solid in terms of liquid measure.

central angle (of a circle) An angle with its vertex at the center of a circle.

chord (of a circle) A line segment with endpoints on the circle.

circle A set of points which are all the same distance from a given point, called the center of the circle.

circumference (of a circle) The distance around the circle.

combination A selection of a number of objects from a set, without regard to order.

commission Pay based on a percent of sales.

commutative property The sum (product) of two numbers is the same regardless of order: $a + b = b + a$ and $ab = ba$

complementary angles Pair of angles whose measures have a sum of 90°.

composite number A whole number with at least two different factors.

concentric circles Circles with the same center.

cone A solid with a circular base and one vertex.

congruent Having the same size and shape.

construction A drawing of a geometrical figure made only with compass and straightedge, and without measuring tools.

coordinate axes Two intersecting lines (number lines) used for graphing ordered number pairs.

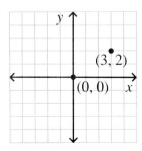

GLOSSARY

coordinates An ordered pair of numbers that is matched with a point in the coordinate plane.

cross products In the equation $\frac{a}{b} = \frac{c}{d}$, the products ad and bc are called cross products. The two ratios are equal if and only if $ad = bc$.

cube (number) A number raised to the third power.

cube (solid) A solid whose faces are congruent squares.

cylinder A solid with parallel circular bases.

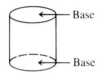

data A collection of facts, usually measures or frequency counts.

decagon A polygon with ten sides.

degree (°) A unit of measure for angles, $\frac{1}{90}$ of a right angle.

denominator In the fraction $\frac{a}{b}$, b is the denominator.

diagonal A segment connecting two nonadjacent vertices of a polygon.

diameter (of a circle) A chord that contains the center of the circle.

difference The number resulting from subtraction.

digit One of the basic symbols used in a place-value system. The base ten numerals are 0, 1, 2, 3, 4, 5, 6, 7, 8, and 9.

distributive property Relates multiplication and addition as follows:
$a(b + c) = ab + ac$

dividend The number to be divided in a division problem.

$$\begin{array}{r} 3 \leftarrow \text{Quotient} \\ \text{Divisor} \rightarrow 5\overline{)17} \leftarrow \text{Dividend} \\ \underline{15} \\ 2 \leftarrow \text{Remainder} \end{array}$$

divisible One number is divisible by another if the remainder is zero.

divisor See *dividend*.

dodecahedron A solid with twelve faces.

edge A segment that is the side of a face on a polyhedron.

ellipse A plane curve generated by a point P moving in such a way that the sum of the distances from P to two fixed points F and G never changes.

equally likely outcomes Outcomes that have the same chance of occurring.

equation A mathematical sentence using the equality symbol (=). $x + 3 = 1$ is an equation.

equilateral triangle A triangle with all three sides the same length.

equivalent fractions Fractions that represent the same number.

estimate An approximation for a given number. Often used in the sense of a rough calculation.

event A set of one or more outcomes in a sample space.

expanded form A number represented as a sum of products, such as:
$435 = 400 + 30 + 5$ or
$483.5 = 4 \cdot 10^2 + 8 \cdot 10 + 3 \cdot 1 + 5 \cdot 10^{-1}$

exponent A number that tells how many times another number (the base) is to be used as a factor.

$$125 = 5 \cdot 5 \cdot 5 = 5^2 \quad \begin{array}{l} \leftarrow \text{exponent} \\ \leftarrow \text{base} \end{array}$$

experimental probability An estimate of the probability of an event found by repeated trials, such as tossing a coin repeatedly to determine the probability of getting a head.

$$\text{Exp } P(\text{an event}) = \frac{\text{number of successful trials}}{\text{number of trials in all}}$$

expression (algebraic) Any combination of variables, numbers, operations, and parentheses that represents a number or range of numbers.

face Any polygonal region that is part of the surface of a polyhedron.

factor A number or expression to be multiplied.

factorial The product $1 \cdot 2 \cdot 3 \cdot \ldots \cdot (n - 1) \cdot n$ is n factorial. It is written $n!$. $0!$ is defined to be 1.

flowchart A diagram that organizes steps or instructions in a logical sequence.

fraction The quotient of two numbers in the form $\frac{a}{b}$.

frequency table A table that gives the number of times each outcome or group of outcomes occurs in a set of data.

function A rule, often given as an equation, table, or graph that relates each member (usually a number) from one set of numbers to a specific member of another set. The equation $y = 2x$ is a function that doubles each number x.

x	1	0.2	-9	10	0
y	2	0.4	-18	20	0

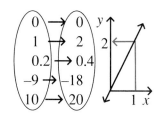

greatest common factor (GCF) The GCF of two or more numbers is the greatest number that is a factor of each of them.

greatest possible error (GPE) Half of the basic unit in which a measurement is given. Example: the GPE of a measurement of 13 ft is 0.5 ft.

heptagon A seven-sided polygon.

hexagon A six-sided polygon.

hypotenuse The side of a right triangle opposite the right angle.

improper fraction A fraction whose numerator is greater than its denominator.

inductive reasoning Making a conclusion based on patterns; generalizing from examples.

integer A whole number or the opposite of a whole number.

inverse operations Operations that undo each other. Adding 5 is the inverse of subtracting 5.

interest A percent of money borrowed or loaned, as payment for the use of that money by the borrower.

irrational number A number that cannot be represented exactly as a quotient of two integers, such as $\sqrt{5}$ or $-\pi$. Irrational numbers have nonrepeating, nonterminating decimal representations.

isosceles triangle A triangle with at least two congruent sides.

least common denominator (LCD) The LCM of the denominators of two or more fractions. The LCD of $\frac{5}{6}$ and $\frac{3}{4}$ is 12.

least common multiple (LCM) The smallest nonzero number that is a multiple of two or more whole numbers is their LCM. The LCM of 6 and 4 is 12.

linear function A function whose graph forms a straight line. The equation for a linear function can always be written as $y = ax + b$, where a and b are any numbers.

lowest-terms fraction A fraction for which the GCF of the numerator and denominator is 1.

mean The quotient obtained when the sum of two or more numbers is divided by the number of addends. An average.

median The middle number of a set of numerical data arranged from least to greatest. If there is no single middle number, it is the mean of the two middle numbers.

midpoint That point halfway between the endpoints of a line segment.

mixed number A number that has both a whole number part and a fractional part.

mode The most common value in a set of data. There may be no mode or several modes.

multiple (of a number) Any product of that number and a whole number.

negative integer Number that is less than 0 and the opposite of a whole number.

nonagon A nine-sided polygon.

GLOSSARY

numeral A symbol for a number.

numerator For a fraction $\frac{x}{y}$ the numerator is x.

obtuse angle An angle whose measure is greater than 90° and less than 180°.

obtuse triangle A triangle with one obtuse angle.

octagon An eight-sided polygon.

ones property See *property of one*.

opposites property The sum of any number and its opposite is zero.

ordered pair Two numbers in a particular order, often associated with points on the coordinate plane.

origin The ordered pair (0, 0) at which coordinate axes intersect.

outcome See *sample space* and *event*.

parallel lines Lines in the same plane, that do not intersect.

parallelogram A quadrilateral with opposite sides parallel (and equal in length).

pentagon A five-sided polygon.

percent Literally, "per hundred." 6% means the ratio 6 per hundred.

perimeter The sum of the length of the sides of a polygon.

period In a decimal numeral, each group of three digits, starting with the unit digit, is a period.

permutation A selection of a number of objects from a set, and in a particular order.

perpendicular Two flat figures (lines, planes, polygons, segments) are perpendicular if they meet at right angles.

perpendicular bisector A line that is perpendicular to a segment and bisects it.

pi The ratio the circumference of a circle to its diameter; an irrational number approximated by 3.141592654.

place value The value given to a place a digit may occupy in a numeral. In the decimal system, the value of each place it 10 times the value of the place to its right.

polygon A plane figure formed by line segments that is closed (which means it has one inside and one outside).

polyhedron A solid whose surface is made up of polygonal regions. It is closed.

positive number A number greater than zero.

precision One measurement is more precise than another if the first measurement uses a smaller unit and has a smaller GPE.

prime factorization The expression of a composite number as a product of prime factors.

prime number A whole number greater than 1 that has only the factors of 1 and itself.

principal Money loaned, usually at a given interest rate and for a specified time.

prism A solid whose bases are congruent parallel polygons, and whose sides are parallelograms.

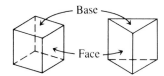

probability (of an event) The ratio of the number of ways an event can occur to the total number of possible outcomes.

product The result of multiplication.

properties of equality Properties that allow one to change each side of an equation in the same way (such as adding the same value to each side), so that the result is also an equation.

property of one The product of any number x and 1 is x.

property of zero The sum of any number x and 0 is x.

proportion An equation stating that two ratios are equal.

protractor An instrument for measuring the number of degrees (°) in an angle.

pyramid A solid with a polygonal base and triangular faces with a common vertex.

Pythagorean Property (Theorem) In a right triangle, the sum of the areas on the squares of the legs equals the area on the square of the hypotenuse. The formulas is $a^2 + b^2 = c^2$.

quadrilateral A four-sided polygon.

quotient The result of division. See also *dividend*.

radius A segment whose endpoints are the center of a circle and any point on the circle. Also the length of such a segment. Half the diameter.

random An object (number) is selected randomly if it is selected in a way that gives all possible objects an equal chance.

rate A ratio of two quantities with different units of measure.

ratio A comparison of two numbers, usually expressed as a fraction: 3 to 4 may be written $\frac{3}{4}$.

rational number The quotient of two integers.

ray A part of a line with one endpoint; a ray continues without end in one direction.

real number A rational or irrational number; any number on a number line.

reciprocals Two numbers whose product is 1. The reciprocal of x is $\frac{1}{x}$.

rectangle A parallelogram with four right angles.

reflection A transformation (motion) of a geometric figure as by a mirror. $\triangle ABC$ and $\triangle A'B'C'$ are reflections of each other.

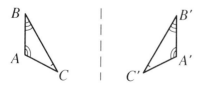

regular polygon A polygon with congruent sides and congruent angles.

regular polyhedron A solid, such as a cube, all of whose faces are congruent regular polygons. There are only five different regular polyhedra (also called Platonic solids).

relatively prime Two numbers are relatively prime if their GCF is 1.

repeating decimal A decimal whose digits after a given place repeat endlessly. $25 \div 99 = 0.252525 \ldots = 0.\overline{25}$.

rhombus A parallelogram with congruent sides.

right angle An angle that measures 90°.

right triangle A triangle with one right angle.

rotation A transformation (motion) of a geometric figure resulting from a turn about any given point. $\triangle ABC$ and $\triangle A'B'C'$ are rotations of each other.

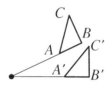

sample space The set of all possible outcomes of an experiment. The sample space of a coin toss consists of the two outcomes *heads*, *tails*.

scale drawing A drawing of an object in which the lengths in the drawing are proportional to the actual lengths of the object.

scalene triangle A triangle all of whose angles have different measures.

scientific notation A system of writing numbers using exponents and powers of ten. Thus, 2,300,000 would be written 2.3×10^6.

secant A line that intersects a circle at two points.

segment Two points and all the points in between them.

similar figures Figures that are the same shape, but not necessarily the same size.

skew lines Lines in space that are not parallel and do not intersect.

solid A continuous three-dimensional geometric figure whose points do not all lie in the same plane.

space figure See *solid*.

sphere A solid composed of all points that are the same distance from a given point (the center).

square (geometry) A quadrilateral with four congruent sides and four congruent angles.

square (numeration) The square of a number p is $q = p \cdot p$, also written p^2.

square root The square root $\sqrt{x}$ of a number x is a number y such that $y \cdot y = x$. If y is positive, then $-y$ is the negative square root.

stem and leaf plot A system for organizing and presenting numerical data so that frequencies can be compared.

stem	leaf
3	2, 6
4	1, 5
5	4
	2

straight angle An angle with a measure of 180°; a straight line.

supplementary angles Two angles with measures that add to 180°.

surface area The sum of the areas of all the surfaces of a solid.

tangent (to a circle) A line that intersects the circle in one point.

tangent ratio In a right triangle, the tangent ratio of a lesser angle is the quotient of the length of the leg opposite the angle and the length of the leg that makes up part of the angle.

terminating decimal A decimal that represents the quotient of an integer and a power of ten.

tetrahedron A polyhedron with four faces, all triangles.

tesselation An infinite set of congruent figures that can be fitted together without overlap to fill a plane completely, like floor tiles.

translation A transformation (motion) of a geometric figure by a slide, and without rotation. $\triangle ABC$ and $\triangle A'B'C'$ are translations of each other.

transversal Given two lines, any line that intersects them is a transversal of the two lines.

trapezoid A quadrilateral with exactly one pair of parallel sides.

tree diagram A way to diagram sequences of possible options or divisions.

triangle A three-sided polygon.

unit An amount or quantity used as a standard of measure.

unit price The cost per unit (such as pound, liter, ounce) of a given item, used to simplify comparing prices of similar goods.

variable A letter or other symbol that stands for a number (or numbers) in an expression or mathematical sentence.

vertex The common point of the two rays of an angle. Also the common point of two sides of a polygon, or the common point of three or more faces of a polyhedron.

volume The measure of a solid, in terms of a unit cube.

whole number Any of the numbers 0, 1, 2, 3, 4, . . .

zero property See *property of zero.*

1 Operations, Properties, and Problem Solving

Page 5
1. 326,000 **6.** 947,600 **9.** 62 billion
12. 34.1 billion

Page 7
2. 238 **5.** 154, associative **8.** 804,
distributive **15.** ×; × **19.** $26.50
22. $n = 73$ **25.** $n = 53$

Page 9
2. 77 **6.** 65 **9.** 14 **12.** 124 **20.**
$440,000 **23.** 7,100,000 **26.** 1; Identity for
Mult. **31.** 40.96

Page 11
1. 3,900 **6.** 10 **9.** 2,700 **21.** $3,000

Page 13
1. $4.50 **4.** 30 pages **7.** 24 pictures

Page 17
1. 12 **6.** 4 **10.** 88 **13.** 10 **16.** $54

Page 19
12. 1,024 ancestors

Page 21
2. Exact; mental math (compensation); $7.05

Page 23
2. 147 **5.** 7 **10.** 23
14. 240 **18.** $21

2 Data Analysis and Statistics

Page 33
1. Comedy **4.** 23,000; 2,000; 3,000

Page 35
1. 85% **4.** 40 teenagers **7.** 1,200 drivers

Page 37
8. 15 yr

Page 39
1. $10.95 **6.** 48 min

Page 41
2. 28 and 41 **9.** 8,300,000 **13.** 7;
Distributive property

Page 43
7. 30 **12.** 5.5

Page 47
2. teachers **3.** higher **13.** 80

Page 49
5. C **9.** C

Page 51
1. $103.7 thousand **3.** $106.1 thousand
7. 33 points

Page 53
1. 5.8 h **6.** about 42.5 ft.

Page 55
2. 26 **5.** 49.2 **8.** 21 **10.** 86°F
13. 98.6°F **16.** Female: 147.6°;
Male: 212.4° **19.** 8.711 million **25.** 400

3 Area and Volume

Page 65
2. $6\frac{1}{2}$ units^2 **7.** 11 units^2

Page 67
2. 24.85 ft^2 **7.** 106.5 ft^2 **10.** 115 m^2
13. 1; Identity for mult. **16.** 64.8

Page 69
1. 28.26 cm^2 **4.** 907.46 in^2 **7.** 10.046 ft^2
10. 429.83 ft^2 **13.** 572.26 ft^2 **20.** 15.2 km^2
26. 536.25π ft^2 or $\approx$ 1,683.83 ft^2

Page 71
3. 17.14 m **8.** 9 in^2 **14.** 9 m^2

Page 73
2. 28 adults **6.** 42 m × 50 m **8.** 2,270 mi

Page 77
2. 240 cm^2 **5.** 178 cm^2 **8.** 113.04 cm^2

Page 79
2. $V = 5$ units^3; $S = 22$ units^2 **5.** 11 units^3
9. 12 units^3

Page 81
2. 270 mm³   **5.** 180 cm³   **9.** 339.12 in.³
12. 4.5 m³ of concrete   **15.** 11   **19.** 8

Page 83
2. 26.67 in.³   **5.** 50.59 ft³   **8.** 55.73 cm³
11. 175 ft³

Page 85
1. 15.75 ft³   **4.** 900.3 in.²   **8.** $73.75

4 Equations in Algebra

Page 95
1. Yes, $4d = 2t$ **5.** Yes, $p + b = 6d$
9. Yes, $p + b = 3t$ **11.** 52 oz

Page 97
1. $t = 19$ **4.** $w = 30$ **8.** $n = 200$
12. $m = 75$ **15.** $x = 160$ **21.** $t = 7$ h
24. $y \approx 12$

Page 99
2. 18, 19, 20   **5.** 3 groups

Page 101
2. $n + 20 - 20 = n$ **7.** $\frac{75p}{75} = p$

12. $\frac{y}{10} \cdot \frac{10}{1} = y$ **16.** $\frac{32.4c}{32.4} = c$
18. $b + \$24.50$; subtraction

Page 103
1. $x + 22 - 22 = 49 - 22; x = 27$

5. $\frac{c}{20} \cdot \frac{20}{1} = 8 \cdot \frac{20}{1}; c = 160$

11. $\frac{6y}{6} = \frac{36.6}{6}; y = 6.1$

14. $a - 2\frac{2}{3} + 2\frac{2}{3} = 5\frac{1}{3} + 2\frac{2}{3}; a = 8$

22. 120 lb

Page 105
1. $29.85   **4.** $3.27   **7.** $4.11

Page 109
3.

	Build	Undo	
Start	*x*	$9x - 4$	*Start*
Multiply by 9	$9x$	$9x$	Add 4
Subtract 4	$9x - 4$	x	Divide by 9

17. $x = 3$

Page 111
2. Solve: $3y - 18 + 18 = 54 + 18$;
    $3y = 72; \frac{3y}{3} = \frac{72}{3}; y = 24$
  Check: $3(24) - 18 = 54; 72 - 18 = 54; 54 =$
      54
18. $7.20   **21.** 200.96 cm²   **24.** ≈ 34.67 cm³

Page 113
2. $>, \geq$ **6.** $\geq, \leq$ **10.** $y = 5, 6, 7$
15. $x = 2, 3, 4, 5, 6, 7$ **20.** $\geq$

Page 115
1. 70, 105, 140, 175   **8.** 1,750 mi

Page 117
2. 12, 17, 22   **8.** $n + 3$ **10.** 300 g

Page 121
1. 81   **4.** 64   **7.** 16   **10.** 2^5 **15.** 7^2
18. 4; 256   **21.** 0; 1   **31.** 2^{63}

5 Integers and Integer Equations

Page 131
1. $^-35$ **4.** $^+129$ **7.** $<$ **10.** $<$ **14.** 86
19. 0   **22.** $^+7$ **27.** $^-86$ **30.** $^-282$ ft

Page 133
1. 3   **4.** $^-4$ **7.** $^-13$ **10.** $^-1$ **14.** $^-6$
19. 4   **24.** $^-5$ **26.** 12   **28.** $1.00
32. 23

Page 135
1. $^-7$ **6.** 1   **9.** $^-4$ **14.** 0   **19.** 5
23. 35   **26.** 5   **30.** 8,687 m   **33.** 175

Page 137
1. $^-39$ **3.** 2   **7.** 162   **12.** 0   **16.** $^-4$
18. 504   **21.** $^-10$ **24.** $^-8$
27. 9   **31.** $11.55   **34.** $p = 5$
37. 62.8 cm

Page 141
1. $x = {}^-30$ **3.** $n = {}^-2$ **8.** $x = 40$
12. $m = 126$ **15.** $n = {}^-10$ **20.** $x = {}^-1$
24. $^-56°F$

Page 143
2. $x = {}^-4$ **5.** $n = {}^-85$ **10.** $j = 3$
14. $x = 15$ **18.** $b = {}^-5$ **25.** $^-3$ ft

Page 145
1. $x = 11$ **4.** $y = 7$ **8.** $b = 3$
11. $x = {}^-11$ **14.** $t = 300$ **18.** 13 days
22. $^-352$

Page 147
1. $71°$ **4.** 130 ft   **8.** 15 pairs

Page 149
1. (4, 1)   **4.** $(^-4, ^-3)$ **9.** (2, 3)   **13.** (0, 2)

Page 151
3. $(^-2, ^-13), (^-1, ^-9), (0, ^-5), (1, ^-1), (2, 3)$
12. 3,350 psi   **15.** 7^3 **19.** 5

Page 153
18. 95°C; 85°C

Page 155
1. 13,215 ft   **8.** about 37,596

6 Number Theory

Page 165
2. No; the only factors of 14 are 1, 2, 7, and 14
11. 1, 2, 3, 6, 9, 18   **22.** 8, 16, 24, 32, 40

Page 167
2. 5   **5.** neither   **10.** 2 and 5   **15.** Yes
19. Yes   **24.** Yes   **28.** No   **31.** 12 h

Page 169
3. 1,31; prime   **10.** 1, 3, 17, 51; composite

Page 173
3. $2^2 \cdot 3^2$ **11.** 2^6 **18.** $3 \cdot 11^2$ **23.** 81
31. 4 blocks high   **35.** $^-3$ **42.** 4.3

Page 175
1. 256 people   **8.** 11 ways

Page 177
1. 8; 1, 2, 4, 8; 24: 1, 2, 3, 4, 6, 8, 12, 24; 8
12. $28 = 2^2 \cdot 7$; $44 = 2^2 \cdot 11$; 2^2 or 4

Page 179
1. 6: 6, 12, 18, 24, 30, 36, . . .
    10: 10, 20, 30, 40, . . .
    LCM = 30
10. $20 = 2^2 \cdot 5$; $25 = 5^2$; LCM $= 2^2 \cdot 5^2 = 100$
22. 80   **34.** 60 m   **37.** 7   **40.** 1,256 mm²

Page 181
1. 25, 12.2, 5, 59.45, 106.25   **10.** 33 lb

Page 183
1. 1,791.4 mi   **5.** 426 ft

7 Rational Numbers

Page 193
2. $\neq$ **7.** $4\frac{2}{3}$ **12.** $4\frac{3}{4}$ **21.** 5 pizzas

Page 195
2. $-\frac{1}{2}$; -0.5 **6.** $-\frac{5}{6}$; $\frac{^-5}{6}$; $\frac{5}{^-6}$ **15.** $\frac{6}{7}$
23. $\frac{^-4}{5}$
26. fallen

Page 197
2. $<$ **7.** $<$ **13.** $<$ **18.** $-8 < -4 < -1$

Page 199
1. 0.6 **8.** -0.35 **11.** $0.\overline{2}$ **33.** 0.327

Page 201
2. $1\frac{7}{20}$ **5.** $-\frac{3}{10}$ **10.** $1\frac{7}{15}$ **15.** $-\frac{3}{8}$
19. $x = \frac{3}{8}$ **31.** 2   **36.** -2

Page 203
2. $15\frac{7}{12}$ **6.** $\frac{17}{20}$ **9.** $24\frac{1}{8}$ **14.** $6\frac{7}{12}$
21. $12\frac{17}{24}$ **25.** $11\frac{7}{8}$ **27.** $3\frac{7}{8}$ **30.** 8

Page 207
1. $\frac{7}{16}$ **6.** $-1\frac{9}{16}$ **11.** 10   **16.** $22\frac{1}{2}$
19. -1 **25.** $7\frac{1}{2}$ days   **30.** $9\frac{1}{2}$

Page 209
2. $\frac{3}{2}$ or $1\frac{1}{2}$ **7.** $\frac{1}{6^3}$ **10.** 10^3 **15.** 2^4
20. y^9 **23.** $n = -1$ **26.** $x = 25$

Page 211
2. $\frac{2}{3}$ **7.** $1\frac{5}{13}$ **12.** $1\frac{31}{32}$ **15.** $\frac{1}{35}$ **19.** 2

25. $2 \cdot 23$ **30.** 24   **35.** $x = 1$

Page 213

1. $3\frac{5}{12}$h   **5.** 30,760 computers

Page 215
1. 37,000   **7.** 0.0045   **14.** 8×10^8
19. 9.08×10^{-4} **24.** 9.3779×10^8

Page 217
1. 10 servings   **5.** 6.48 g

8 Ratio and Proportion

Page 227

1. $3{:}5, \frac{3}{5}$ **8.** $8{:}3, \frac{8}{3}$ **17.** $\frac{3}{5} > \frac{4}{7}$ **19.** 16 oz

23. $\frac{15}{3} = \frac{5}{1} = 5$

Page 229
1. 10 km/h   **8.** 50 people/mi^2
14. 35.8 mi/gal   **17.** 21,600 frames

Page 231
1. \$0.63/lb   **6.** \$0.24/grapefruit   **11.** 1 gal
14. 2.2 lb   **18.** $2\frac{1}{8}$ **23.** $-\frac{9}{16}$ **26.** $x = 9$

Page 233

2. $33x = 33$ **7.** $a = 78$ **12.** $s = 22\frac{1}{2}$
15. $n = 7$ **22.** 7.5 L

Page 235
1. 1 m   **4.** 0.0025 mm   **7.** 36 m $\times$ 31.2 m $\times$ 24 m

Page 239
2. $x = 24$ **8.** 28.8 m

Page 241
2. 154 new lockers   **5.** 38.4 m

Page 243
3. $\tan 50° = 1.20$ **6.** $\tan 4° = 0.07$
12. $\tan A = 0.333$ **15.** $-2\frac{6}{7}$ **19.** 0.625

Page 245
3. 0.364   **8.** 1.327   **17.** 66.5 m   **20.** true

Page 247
1. \$39 a day   **7.** 67 km/h

9 Percent

Page 257
2. $\frac{36}{100}$; 0.36; 36%   **8.** $\frac{44}{50}$; 0.88; 88%

11. $\frac{23}{100}$ **18.** $\frac{5}{100} = \frac{1}{20}$ **24.** 60%

Page 259
2. 75%   **7.** 22%   **10.** $83\frac{1}{3}$%   **15.** $\frac{1}{9}$

19. 3.5%, 0.07, $\frac{5}{20}$ **23.** 20

Page 261
1. 2.25   **7.** 0.025   **10.** 1,400%   **15.** $\frac{37}{200}$
21. 3.125%   **26.** \$300   **29.** \$0.06/oz
32. $x = -5$ **36.** 1, 2, 23, 46

Page 263
2. 112   **7.** 11.7   **12.** 121.5   **17.** 27
26. 36   **30.** 2.5   **34.** \$0.84

Page 265
1. 18.75%   **6.** 16%   **11.** 7.5%   **18.** 0.5%
23. 200%   **28.** $16\frac{2}{3}$%

Page 269
2. 12   **7.** 21 pennies

Page 271
1. 150   **6.** 50   **11.** 165   **17.** \$51,700
23. $13\frac{1}{3}$ **27.** prime; 1, 31   **29.** $y = 3$

Page 273
2. 4   **7.** 32   **13.** 16   **19.** 17   **27.** 2,150

Page 275
2. 53.2%   **6.** 28 homes

10 Applications of Percent

Page 285
2. \$31.50   **8.** \$2,860.15   **14.** \$14.36

Page 287
1. 28% increase **6.** 75% increase
11. 22% decrease **18.** 1.7% increase
25. 75%

Page 289
3. 16 **9.** 30% **15.** 75% **24.** $x = 1.25$ cm

Page 293
2. 204 squares **7.** 194%

Page 295
1. discount: $24; sale price: $8
8. discount: $21; sale price: $119
14. 15% off of $80

Page 297
1. $I = \$57$; $A = \$147$ **6.** $I = \$2.40$;
  $A = \$3.40$ **9.** 4 years **13.** $52.50

Page 299
6. 120 **9.** $0.72/L

Page 301
1. $0.09 **6.** $98.16

11 Discrete Math: Counting Problems

Page 311
1. 8 orders **5.** 30 orders **7.** 3,600

Page 313
2. 24 **7.** 720 **13.** $4! = 24$ **18.** 24
20. 0.05; 5% **25.** $I = \$150$; $A = \$1,150$

Page 315
2. 14 ft, 17 ft, 23 ft **6.** $495

Page 319
3. 6 **7.** 252 **11.** 10 **15.** 66 handshakes

Page 321
2. 210 **6.** 5 **12.** 44 **19.** $-1\frac{17}{24}$

Page 323
2. $s \geq 10$ **16.** $s > 60$ mph

Page 325
1. 500 **6.** 2 blocks

12 Probability

Page 335
8. 4 **12.** 390

Page 337
1. $\frac{1}{8}$ **8.** $\frac{3}{4}$ **14.** $\frac{1}{12}$ **18.** $\frac{1}{4}$ **20.** $\frac{1}{6^3}$ or $\frac{1}{216}$

Page 339
1. $\frac{13}{50}$ **4.** $\frac{47}{100}$ **9.** 70

Page 341
1. 12 **4.** $\frac{2}{3}$ **6.** $\frac{1}{6}$

Page 343
1. About 88.3% **5.** Mary: 7; Jana: 17; Beth: 12; Dee: 35

Page 347
2. Maris: 7,636; O'Leary: 10,364 **6.** Johnson: 6,750; Cantell: 9,000; Morales: 9,250
8. 50.01% **10.** 10 **12.** $x = 56$

Page 349
3. 0.8768

Page 353
2. 27,129.6 ft³ **5.** $\frac{1}{3}$
7. 48 ears

13. Geometry

Page 363
1. $\angle 5$, $\angle 2$, $\angle 12$ **4.** p and q **9.** 55°

Page 365
1. 720° **4.** 1,080° **7.** 1,440° **10.** 360°

Page 367
1. quadrilateral; 360° **5.** pentagon; 540°
9. 135° **12.** 105°

Page 369
17. $\frac{1}{6}$ **20.** $-\frac{57}{70}$

Page 375
1. 13 people   5. 975 households
8. 56 fence posts

Page 377
3. 140°

Page 379
11. $\frac{1}{12}$ 16. 150

Page 381
1. $49.50   4. $9.08

Page 383
7. 16.81 π in.^{2} ≈ 52.78 in.^{2}

14 Square Roots and Special Triangles

Page 393
1. 2 ft   4. 2   7. 10   9. −9   14. −14
18. $x = 5, -5$ 24. $x = 12$ 27. 920 m

Page 395
1. 2.499   5. 1.732   11. −4.796
14. 9.849   21. 3   24. 20
28. $x = \sqrt{74} \approx 8.602$ 30. 2,500 cm^2
35. $\sqrt{20} = \sqrt{4} \cdot \sqrt{5} \approx 4.472$ 38. true

Page 397
1. rational   3. irrational   8. rational
11. 2.646   16. 1.265   20. 0.894
25. 712; rational   28. $x^2 = 40$
33. $x = 2$

Page 399
19. $p + 25 < 100; p < 75$ 22. 11.1 lb
24. $x \leq 132$

Page 403
2. $c = 9.434$ cm   6. $a = 29.665$ cm
9. $b = 24.819$ m   12. 4 mi

Page 405
1. 385 min or 6 h 25 min   5. 8; 12; 5; 20

Page 407
1. $12\sqrt{2}$; 16.968   5. $5\sqrt{2}$ cm   7. 127.3 ft
9. 153.86 cm^2 12. $0.06/oz

Page 409
2. $x = 3; y = 3\sqrt{3}$ 5. $x = 2; y = 2\sqrt{3}$
10. $y = 4\sqrt{3}; z = 8$ 14. 40 ft

Page 411
2. 89.25 yd   4. 7.71 ml

15 Motion Geometry

Page 421
4. (5, 3)   8. b   10. $(x + 3, y - 2)$
12. 4 cm

Page 423
9. 16 feet; Dimensions of room are not needed.

Page 425
9. $\frac{1}{240}$ 12. 100%

Page 427
10. None of the lines shown are lines of symmetry.

Page 429
1. Figure F   5. Figure H is the result of a
translation followed by a reflection.   11. (1, 2)

Page 433
7. The lines are parallel.   10. 6 h   14. yes

Page 435
1. 6 club members   6. 70 min

Page 439
3. $\triangle ABC \cong \triangle RSQ$ 6. $\triangle XYZ \cong \triangle DEF$

Page 441
1. SAS   4. SSS   11. 12   14. 12
16. −3

Page 443
1. $1.20   4. Eighteen 2-person tables; eleven
4-person tables

16 Extending Logical Reasoning

Page 453
2. 0.321; 0.987654321   4. 1,050   8. 5,050

Page 455
4. 9,261 pieces   6. 1,023 branches

Page 457
6. 12 in. × 16 in.   8. 120   12. 8

Page 459
2. 23,496 more   6. 6 13-oz cans, 21 6-oz cans
8. 2 students

Page 463
3. 32   6. 66 lines   9. 500,000

Page 465
1. *The number trick*   *Algebraic explanation*
Choose any number. Let *n* represent the number.
Subtract 2. $n - 2$

Multiply by 3. $3(n - 2)$ or $3n - 6$
Add 6. $3n - 6 + 6$ or $3n$
Divide by 3. $3n \div 3$ or n
6. 3, 3, 5 or 1, 3, 7 or 1, 5, 5 or 1, 1, 9

Page 467
2. 33.8 in.   7. $\frac{1}{4}$ 11. 7.68

Page 471
1. Bears   5. They didn't score that quarter.
8. negative   11. 2 min 20 sec   14. about 18
18 stories

Page 473
2. $5\frac{1}{6}$ ft   5. 1,800.5 lb   7. 12 yr

Illustration Acknowledgments

Doron Ben-Ami p. 188, 290, 398

Alex Bloch p. 12, 13, 234, 235

Tom Bowker p. 246

Fred Carlson p. 71

Linda Cook p. 493, 505

Kenneth P. Crippen p. 180, 231, 233, 236, 243

David Cunningham p. 68, 85, 280

Simon Galkin p. 9, 76, 148, 211, 262, 464, 468

Betty Gee p. 491, 496, 497, 500, 501

Bill Gerhold p. 428

Jeff Hukill p. 495, 497, 498, 501

Robert Lawson p. 478

Rich Lo p. 14, 16, 23, 40, 41, 48, 56, 72, 83, 84, 96, 98, 106, 109, 138, 146, 151, 154, 156, 168, 174, 175, 182, 185, 204, 208, 212, 218, 240, 268, 274, 280, 288, 292, 296, 300, 314, 316, 318, 324, 352, 374, 380, 381, 399, 404, 410, 411, 434, 442, 458, 460, 464, 467, 472, 474

Tim McWilliams p. 88, 220, 414, 446

Debbie Morse p. 340

Tim O'Toole p. 402, 453, 459

Alison Perreault p. 222, 252

Linda Reilly p. 184

Rick Sams p. 504

Nancy Spier p. 492

Carol Stutz p. 244, 245, 266, 460

Dave Taylor p. 467

Sam Thiewes p. 130, 155, 206, 213

Nancy Lee Walters p. 8, 26, 140, 141, 207, 210, 230, 232, 247, 260, 272, 319, 325, 342, 346, 363, 380, 404, 430, 435, 454, 456, 462, 466, 474

Peter Wells p. 192, 336, 338, 339, 341, 345

Jim Williams p. 443

Photo Acknowledgments

Table of Contents: iii Lawrence Migdale*; iv Andree Abecassis/Photo 20-20; v Lawrence Migdale*; vi Lawrence Migdale*; vii Lawrence Migdale*; viii Lawrence Migdale*; ix Lawrence Migdale*; x Lawrence Migdale*; xi Lawrence Migdale*; xii Lawrence Migdale*.

Chapter 1: 2-3 Tony Stone Worldwide; 4 Andree Abecassis/Photo 20-20; 7 (c) David R. Frazier Photolibrary; 11 (c) William Warren/West Light; 17 Lawrence Migdale*; 18 Ken Karp*; 19A Ken Karp*; 19B The Bettmann Archive; 20 (c) Jeffry W. Myers/West Stock; 21 (c) Larry Lee/West Light; 25 Diane Graham-Henry*.

Chapter 2: 30-31 Claus Meyer/Black Star; 34 David Stoecklein/The Stock Market; 38 (c) Bill Melton/New England Stock Photo; 39 Lawrence Migdale*; 40 Kathleen Culbert-Aguilar*; 46 Kathleen Culbert-Aguilar*; 51 Peter Russell Clemens/International Stock Photo; 52 NASA; 53 NASA; 57 Diane Graham-Henry*; 58 Lawrence Migdale*.

Chapter 3: 62-63 Victor Englebert/Black Star; 70 Lawrence Migdale*; 73B Brian Vikander/West Light; 73T Diana Rasche/West Light; 74 Lawrence Migdale*; 82 Lawrence Migdale*; 83 NASA; 85L Kathleen Culbert-Aguilar*; 85R (c) 1983 Arthur Meyerson; 86-87 Lawrence Migdale*.

Chapter 4: 92-93 Gary Milburn/Tom Stack & Associates; 94 Kathleen Culbert-Aguilar*; 95 Kathleen Culbert-Aguilar*; 96 Kathleen Culbert-Aguilar*; 98 (c) Don & Pat Valenti 1989; 99 Lawrence Migdale*; 100 Wide World Photos; 104 Lawrence Migdale*; 105 Ken Karp*; 108 Diane Graham-Henry*; 110 (c) Don & Pat Valenti 1989; 114 Diane Graham-Henry*; 115 (c) Don Wilson/West Stock; 116 Lawrence Migdale*; 119 (c) Brooks Dodge/New England Stock Photo; 123 Diane Graham-Henry*.

Chapter 5: 128-129 Stephen Frink/The Stock Market; 131 (c) David Muench 1989; 135 (c) William Thompson; 136 Diane Graham-Henry*; 137 Kathleen Culbert-Aguilar*; 142 (c) McConnell McNamara & Company 1989; 143 (c) 1989 by Cameramann International, Ltd.; 144 Kathleen Culbert-Aguilar*; 147 Carl Roessler/Bruce Coleman Inc.; 150 Robert Abrams/Bruce Coleman Inc.; 154 Kathleen Culbert-Aguilar*; 155 (c) Brian Drake/Sportschrome East-West; 157 Lawrence Migdale*.

Chapter 6: 162-163 Stephen Frisch*; 167 Kathleen Culbert-Aguilar*; 170 Kathleen Culbert-Aguilar*; 172 Kathleen Culbert-Aguilar*; 175 W. Metzen/H. Armstrong Roberts; 177 (c) Bob Daemmrich; 178 Diane Graham-Henry*; 183 R. Ian Lloyd/The Stock Market; 184 Diane Graham-Henry*.

Chapter 7: 190-191 James Sugar/Black Star; 196 Lawrence Migdale*; 199 Focus on Sports; 200 Kathleen Culbert-Aguilar*; 201 (c) Bob Daemmrich; 202 Kathleen Culbert-Aguilar*; 209 (c) Chuck O'Rear/West Light; 212B (c) Bob Daemmrich; 212T Kathleen Culbert-Aguilar*; 213 (c) Bob Daemmrich; 214B Jet Propulsion Lab/NASA; 214T (c) Bill Longcore/Science Source, Photo Researchers; 216 Lawrence Migdale*; 217 Lawrence Migdale*; 218-219 Lawrence Migdale*.

Chapter 8: 224-225 Stephen Frisch*; 226 (c) Don & Pat Valenti 1989; 228 (c) Robert Landau/West Light; 229 Gene Stein/West Light; 234 Magicam; 235 Runk-Schoenberger/Grant Heilman Photography; 239 Kathleen Culbert-Aguilar*; 240 Kathleen Culbert-Aguilar*; 241 Lawrence Migdale*; 247 Lawrence Migdale*; 248 Diane Graham-Henry*.

Chapter 9: 254-255 Stephen Frisch*; 256 H. Abernathy/H. Armstrong Roberts; 264 (c) Gant W. Eichrodt; 269 (c) 1989 Jack Vartoogian. All rights reserved; 270 Stephen Frisch*; 275 (c) 1987 Russ Kinne/Comstock; 276 Lawrence Migdale*; 277 Lawrence Migdale*; 280 The Bettmann Archive.

ACKNOWLEDGMENTS

Chapter 10: 282-283 Janice Sheldon*; 284 (c) Don & Pat Valenti 1989; 292 John Hollis*; 293L Kathleen Culbert-Aguilar*; 293R (c) 1988 Russ Kinne/Comstock; 294 (c) Don & Pat Valenti 1989; 298 (c) Jim Markham; 300 John Hollis*; 301 (c) Cameron Davidson 1989; 302 Diane Graham-Henry*; 304 Lawrence Migdale*.

Chapter 11: 308-309 Ellis Herwig/Stock, Boston; 310 John Hollis*; 311 John Hollis*; 312 Lawrence Migdale*; 314 John Hollis*; 315 (c) 1988 Mark E. Gibson/Marilyn Gartman Agency; 319 John Hollis*; 322 Focus on Sports; 325 (c) Sepp Seitz/Woodfin Camp & Associates; 327 Diane Graham-Henry*; 330 (c) D.L. Wedking/West Stock.

Chapter 12: 332-333 Robert Harding Picture Library Ltd.; 334 Lawrence Migdale*; 339 John Hollis*; 342 John Hollis*; 343 Wilbur Funches/Wide World Photos; 348 (c) Brent Jones; 349 John Hollis*; 353 Larry Lefever/Grant Heilman Photography; 354 Diane Graham-Henry*.

Chapter 13: 360-361 Giraudon/Art Resource; 370 John Hollis*; 374 Phil Savoie/Bruce Coleman Inc.; 375 (c) David Lissy/Sportschrome East-West; 381 (c) Tom Campbell/West Light; 383 Lawrence Migdale*; 384-385 Lawrence Migdale*.

Chapter 14: 390-391 Larry Lee/West Light; 394 Kathleen Culbert-Aguilar*; 400 Focus on Sports; 405 Lawrence Migdale*; 410 Tom Tracy/FPG International; 412 Diane Graham-Henry*.

Chapter 15: 418-419 Regina Tolbert/Paracomp Inc.; 420 Aleppo Museum/Hirmer Verlag; 422 Ken Karp*; 426 Stephen Frisch*; 435 Nimatal Lah/Art Resource, New York; 441 (c) Scott Berner/Nawrocki Stock Photo; 442 Joe McDonald/Bruce Coleman Inc.; 443 John Hollis*; 444-445 Lawrence Migdale*; 448 John Hollis*.

Chapter 16: 450-451 L.L. Rue III/Bruce Coleman Inc.; 452 John Hollis*; 458 Norman Owen Tomalin/Bruce Coleman Inc.; 464 (c) David R. Frazier Photolibrary; 465 John Hollis*; 469 (c) Rod Planck; 472 Kenneth W. Fink/Bruce Coleman Inc.; 473 Wendell Metzen/Bruce Coleman Inc.; 474-475 Lawrence Migdale*.

Skills Review Bank: 482 (c) Michael Sullivan/TexaStock; 483 Comstock; 484 (c) Cheryl Walsh Bellville; 485 M. Stuckey/Comstock; 486 Walter Hodges/West Light; 487 M & C Werner/Comstock; 488 (c) Cheryl Walsh Bellville; 489 Thomas Lindley/FPG International.

Data Bank: 501 Windsor Castle, Royal Library, (c) Her Majesty, The Queen; 503 Mike Newman/Crossfield-Dicomed Corp.

*Photographed expressly for Addison-Wesley Publishing Company, Inc.

Special thanks to The Music Annex, San Francisco, CA